Lecture Notes in Computer Science 15902

Founding Editors

Gerhard Goos
Juris Hartmanis

Editorial Board Members

Elisa Bertino, USA
Wen Gao, China
Bernhard Steffen, Germany
Moti Yung, USA

Advanced Research in Computing and Software Science
Subline of Lecture Notes in Computer Science

Subline Series Editors

Giorgio Ausiello, *University of Rome 'La Sapienza', Italy*
Vladimiro Sassone, *University of Southampton, UK*

Subline Advisory Board

Susanne Albers, *TU Munich, Germany*
Benjamin C. Pierce, *University of Pennsylvania, USA*
Bernhard Steffen, *University of Dortmund, Germany*
Deng Xiaotie, *Peking University, Beijing, China*
Jeannette M. Wing, *Microsoft Research, Redmond, WA, USA*

More information about this series at https://link.springer.com/bookseries/558

Wolfgang E. Nagel · Diana Goehringer ·
Pedro C. Diniz
Editors

Euro-Par 2025: Parallel Processing

31st European Conference on Parallel and Distributed Processing
Dresden, Germany, August 25–29, 2025
Proceedings, Part III

Editors
Wolfgang E. Nagel
Technische Universität Dresden
Dresden, Germany

Diana Goehringer
Technische Universität Dresden
Dresden, Germany

Pedro C. Diniz
University of Porto
Porto, Portugal

ISSN 0302-9743　　　　　　ISSN 1611-3349　(electronic)
Lecture Notes in Computer Science
ISBN 978-3-031-99871-3　　　ISBN 978-3-031-99872-0　(eBook)
https://doi.org/10.1007/978-3-031-99872-0

© The Editor(s) (if applicable) and The Author(s), under exclusive license to Springer Nature Switzerland AG 2026

This work is subject to copyright. All rights are solely and exclusively licensed by the Publisher, whether the whole or part of the material is concerned, specifically the rights of translation, reprinting, reuse of illustrations, recitation, broadcasting, reproduction on microfilms or in any other physical way, and transmission or information storage and retrieval, electronic adaptation, computer software, or by similar or dissimilar methodology now known or hereafter developed.
The use of general descriptive names, registered names, trademarks, service marks, etc. in this publication does not imply, even in the absence of a specific statement, that such names are exempt from the relevant protective laws and regulations and therefore free for general use.
The publisher, the authors and the editors are safe to assume that the advice and information in this book are believed to be true and accurate at the date of publication. Neither the publisher nor the authors or the editors give a warranty, expressed or implied, with respect to the material contained herein or for any errors or omissions that may have been made. The publisher remains neutral with regard to jurisdictional claims in published maps and institutional affiliations.

This Springer imprint is published by the registered company Springer Nature Switzerland AG
The registered company address is: Gewerbestrasse 11, 6330 Cham, Switzerland

If disposing of this product, please recycle the paper.

Preface

This book is one of the three volumes comprising the proceedings of the 31st International Conference on Parallel and Distributed Computing (Euro-Par 2025), which took place in Dresden, Germany, from 25 to 29 August 2025. Euro-Par 2025 was jointly organized by the Center for Information Services and High Performance Computing (ZIH) and the Faculty of Computer Science at Technische Universität Dresden.

Euro-Par is the prime European conference covering all aspects of parallel and distributed processing, ranging from theory to practice, from small to the largest parallel and distributed systems and infrastructures, from fundamental computational problems to applications, from architecture, compiler, language and interface design and implementation, to tools, support infrastructures, as well as application performance aspects.

Euro-Par participants include researchers from academic institutions, government laboratories, and industrial organizations. Euro-Par aims to be the primary choice of such professionals for presenting new results in their specific areas. Euro-Par provides an excellent forum for focused technical discussion, as well as interaction with a large, broad, and diverse audience. In addition, Euro-Par provides a platform for a number of technical workshops aimed at smaller and emerging communities.

Previous conference editions were held in Stockholm, Lyon, Passau, Southampton, Toulouse, Munich, Manchester, Paderborn, Klagenfurt, Pisa, Lisbon, Dresden, Rennes, Las Palmas, Delft, Ischia, Bordeaux, Rhodes, Aachen, Porto, Vienna, Grenoble, Santiago de Compostela, Turin, Göttingen, Warsaw, Lisbon, Glasgow, Limassol, and Madrid.

This year's Euro-Par 2025 accepted papers were organized in the following 6 tracks:

- Programming, Compilers and Performance
- Scheduling, Resource Management, Cloud, Edge Computing and Workflows
- Architectures and Accelerators
- Data Analytics, AI and Computational Science
- Theory and Algorithms
- Multidisciplinary, Domain-Specific and Applied Parallel and Distributed Computing

A total of 264 full papers were submitted by authors from 41 different countries representing all populated continents. The selection process was very competitive with each submission having an average number of 3.77 double-blind reviews. No paper had fewer than 3 reviews and several papers had 5 reviews. After intensive online discussions between the reviewers, each track proposed sets of papers for acceptance, further discussion, or rejection. The papers from all tracks were reviewed and discussed in an online selection meeting in April 2025. As a result, 78 papers were selected to be presented at the conference and published in these proceedings, resulting in a 29.5% acceptance rate.

In addition, the following 6 accepted papers were invited to be presented in a plenary session and compete for the Euro-Par 2025 *Best Paper* award:

- A. Delval, P. de Oliveira Castro, W. Jalby, E. Renault, "Noise Injection for Performance Bottleneck Analysis".
- L.-C. Canon, A. Dugois, I. Jecker, P.-C. Héam, "Approximation Bounds for SLACK on Identical Parallel Machines".
- J. Xue, T. Xiong, L. Chao, R. Xue, "SimPoint+: More Stable, Accurate and Efficient Program Analysis".
- X. Wang, S. Miao, Z. Zhu, P. Qu, Y. Zhang, "AlphaSparseTensor: Discovering Faster Sparse Matrix Multiplication Algorithms on GPUs for LLM Inference".
- J. Spaan, K.-H. Chen, D. A. Bader, A.-L. Varbanescu, "Wedge-Parallel Triangle Counting for GPUs".
- A. Sahu, A. S. P. V. M. Aditya, G. Ramakrishna, M. S. Nikhil, K. Kothapalli, D. S. Banerjee, "External GPU Biconnected Components".

To enhance the reproducibility of research publications in Euro-Par, the conference encourages authors to submit artifacts, such as source code, data sets, and reproducibility instructions. Following the notification of acceptance, the authors were encouraged to submit artifacts for evaluation. A total of 28 artifacts were submitted in support of accepted papers and evaluated by the Artifact Evaluation Committee (AEC) coordinated by Massimo Torquati and Olaf Krzikalla, who successfully reproduced results for 16 artifacts. These papers are marked in the proceedings by a special stamp and the artifacts are available online in the Zenodo repository.

In addition to the technical program, we had the pleasure of hosting three distinguished *Keynote* talks by:

- Florina Ciorba, University of Basel, Switzerland.
- Martin Schulz, Technical University of Munich, Germany.
- Domenico Talia, University of Calabria, Italy.

Euro-Par 2025 began with two days of workshops coordinated by Jeronimo Castrillón and Demetris Zeinalipour, which was followed by three full conference days dedicated to the main sessions. A poster and demo session, a PhD symposium organized by Michael Färber and Leonel Sousa, and a special session for female scientists were held alongside the main conference. Ahmed Kamaleldin and Lester Kalms were responsible for managing the poster and demo session. The invited session for female scientists was organized by Ayesha Afzal and Marta Garcia-Gasulla. A selection of the papers presented at the workshops are published in separate Springer LNCS volumes. Contributions presented at the PhD symposium, the poster session, and the invited session for female scientists are also published in the same volume.

We would like to thank all the Authors, Chairs, Program Committee Members, and Reviewers who contributed to the success of Euro-Par 2025. We would also like to thank all our industrial and institutional sponsors for their support. Our gratitude goes out to the Euro-Par Steering Committee and the organizers of Euro-Par 2024 for their invaluable support throughout the preparation of this year's event. Finally, we would like to thank Diana Häsener, Jacqueline Papperitz, and the local organizing team at the Center for Information Services and High Performance Computing (ZIH) and the Faculty of Computer Science at Technische Universität Dresden, whose dedication and hard work made this event possible. It was a great pleasure and honor to host Euro-Par 2025 at Technische Universität Dresden. We hope that all participants enjoyed the event.

August 2025

Wolfgang E. Nagel
Diana Goehringer
Pedro C. Diniz

Organization

General Chair

Wolfgang E. Nagel　　　　　TU Dresden, Germany

Program Committee Chair

Diana Goehringer　　　　　TU Dresden, Germany

Workshop Chairs

Jerónimo Castrillón　　　　　TU Dresden, Germany
Demetris Zeinalipour　　　　University of Cyprus, Cyprus

Proceedings Chair

Pedro C. Diniz　　　　　　　Universidade do Porto, Portugal

PhD Symposium Chairs

Michael Färber　　　　　　　TU Dresden, Germany
Leonel Sousa　　　　　　　　Universidade de Lisboa, Portugal

Posters and Demos Chairs

Ahmed Kamaleldin　　　　　TU Dresden, Germany
Lester Kalms　　　　　　　　TU Dresden, Germany

Women in HPC Chairs

Marta Garcia-Gasulla   Barcelona Supercomputing Center, Spain
Ayesha Afzal   University of Erlangen-Nürnberg, Germany

Local Organization Chair

Diana Häsener   TU Dresden, Germany

Web Chairs

Jacqueline Papperitz   TU Dresden, Germany
Ahmed Kamaleldin   TU Dresden, Germany

Steering Committee

Fernando Silva (SC Chair)   University of Porto, Portugal
Dora Blanco Heras (Vice-chair) University of Santiago de Compostela, Spain
Christos Kaklamanis   Computer Technology Institute and Press
                                "Diophantus", Greece
Demetris Zeinalipour   University of Cyprus, Cyprus
Ewa Deelman   University of Southern California, USA
Felix Wolf   Technical University of Darmstadt, Germany
George Papadopoulos   University of Cyprus, Cyprus
Henk Sips   Delft University of Technology, The Netherlands
Ivona Brandić   Technical University of Wien, Austria
Jesus Carretero   University Carlos III of Madrid, Spain
Krzysztof Rzadca   University of Warsaw, Poland
Leonel Sousa   University of Lisbon, Portugal
Maciej Malawski   AGH University of Science and Technology,
                                Poland
Marco Aldinucci   University of Turin, Italy
Massimo Torquati   University of Pisa, Italy
Phil Trinder   University of Glasgow, UK
Ramin Yahyapour   GWDG, Göttingen, Germany
Rosa M. Badia   Barcelona Supercomputing Center, Spain
Tomàs Margalef   Autonomous University of Barcelona, Spain
Wolfgang E. Nagel   TU Dresden, Germany

Honorary Members

Christian Lengauer　　　　　University of Passau, Germany
Luc Bougé　　　　　　　　　ENS Rennes, France
Ron Perrott　　　　　　　　　University of Oxford, UK
Karl Dieter Reinartz　　　　　University of Erlangen-Nürnberg, Germany

Scientific Organization

Track 1: Programming, Compilers and Performance

Chairs

Ana-Lucia Varbanescu　　　University of Amsterdam, The Netherlands
João M. P. Cardoso　　　　　Universidade do Porto, Portugal

Program Committee

Lucas Mello Schnorr　　　　Universidade Federal de Rio Grande do Sul, Brazil
Walter Binder　　　　　　　University of Lugano, Italy
Peter Thoman　　　　　　　University of Innsbruck, Austria
Johannes Doerfert　　　　　Lawrence Livermore National Laboratory, USA
Cristina Silvano　　　　　　Politecnico di Milano, Italy
Georg Hager　　　　　　　　Erlangen Regional Computing Center, Germany
Carlo Bertolli　　　　　　　AMD, Inc., USA
Guoliang Jin　　　　　　　　North Carolina State University, USA
Bruno Bodin　　　　　　　　Yale-NUS College, Singapore
Ivy Peng　　　　　　　　　　KTH Royal Institute of Technology, Sweden
Tobias Kenter　　　　　　　University of Paderborn, Germany
Nick Brown　　　　　　　　　University of Edinburgh, UK
Veronica Vergara Larrea　　　Oak Ridge National Laboratory, USA
Sotirios Xydis　　　　　　　National Technical University of Athens, Greece
Ivan Ivanov　　　　　　　　Tokyo Institute of Technology, Japan
Orlando Moreira　　　　　　Snap, Inc., The Netherlands
R. Govindarajan　　　　　　Indian Institute of Science, India
Artur Podobas　　　　　　　KTH Royal Institute of Technology, Sweden
Stéphane Genaud　　　　　　Icube - University of Strasbourg, France
Stefano Markidis　　　　　　KTH Royal Institute of Technology, Sweden
Siegfried Benkner　　　　　　University of Vienna, Austria
Miwako Tsuji　　　　　　　　RIKEN, Japan

Bernhard Egger — Seoul National University, South Korea
Hans Vandierendonck — Queen's University Belfast, UK
Jean-Baptiste Besnard — Data Direct Networks, USA
Tom Deakin — University of Bristol, UK
Paul Carpenter — Barcelona Supercomputing Center, Spain
Serena Curzel — Politecnico di Milano, Italy
Giuseppe Tagliavini — University of Bologna, Italy
Seyong Lee — Oak Ridge National Laboratory, USA
Pedro Valero-Lara — Oak Ridge National Laboratory, USA
Diego R. Llanos — University of Valladolid, Spain

Track 2: Scheduling, Resource Management, Cloud, Edge Computing and Workflows

Chairs
Sascha Hunold — TU Wien, Austria
Daniel Cordeiro — Universidade de São Paulo, Brazil

Program Committee
Anirban Mandal — Renaissance Computing Institute, USA
Dante Sánchez-Gallegos — Universidad Carlos III de Madrid, Spain
Radu Prodan — University of Klagenfurt, Austria
Luciana Arantes — Sorbonne University, France
Luiz F. Bittencourt — University of Campinas, Brazil
Valeria Cardellini — University of Roma "Tor Vergata", Italy
Loris Marchal — Centre National de la Recherche Scientifique, France
Jacopo Soldani — University of Pisa, Italy
Marco Lapegna — University of Naples Federico II, Italy
Joanna Berlińska — Adam Mickiewicz University, Poland
Francesc Lordan — Barcelona Supercomputing Center, Spain
Guillaume Pallez — Inria, France
Anne Benoit — École normale supérieure de Lyon, France
Maciej Malawski — AGH University of Science and Technology, Poland
Nectarios Koziris — National Technical University of Athens, Greece
Nikela Papadopoulou — University of Glasgow, UK
Jason Riedy — Advanced Micro Devices, Inc., USA
Minming Li — City University of Hong Kong, China
Oliver Sinnen — University of Auckland, New Zealand
Pierre-Francois Dutot — Université Grenoble Alpes, France

Silvio Rizzi	Argonne National Laboratory, USA
Javid Taheri	Karlstad University, Sweden
Alok Tripathy	UC Berkeley, USA
Massimo Villari	University of Messina, Italy
Veronika Rehn-Sonigo	FEMTO-ST, France
Alfredo Goldman	University of São Paulo, Brazil
Carla Osthoff Barros	National Laboratory for Scientific Computing LNCC, USA
Muhammad Ajmal Azad	Birmingham City University, UK
Anthony Danalis	University of Tennessee, USA
Carlos Guerrero	Universitat de les Illes Balears, Spain
Krzysztof Rzadca	University of Warsaw, Poland
Vladimir Vlassov	KTH Royal Institute of Technology, Sweden
Katzalin Olcoz	Universidad Complutense de Madrid, Spain
Maxime Gonthier	University of Chicago, USA
Fanny Pascual	Sorbonne Université, France
Anderson Andrei da Silva	Hewlett Packard Labs, USA
Marios Dikaiakos	University of Cyprus, Cyprus
Carlos A. Varela	Rensselaer Polytechnic Institute, USA
Atakan Aral	University of Vienna, Austria
Francisco Brasileiro	Universidade Federal de Campina Grande, Brazil
Ramin Yahyapour	University of Göttingen, Germany
Rodrigo N. Calheiros	Western Sydney University, Australia
Ciprian Dobre	University Politehnica of Bucharest, Romania

Track 3: Architectures and Accelerators

Chairs

Kentaro Sano	RIKEN, Japan
Holger Fröning	Heidelberg University, Germany

Program Committee

Xing Cai	Simula Research Laboratory, Norway
Teresa Cervero	Barcelona Supercomputing Center, Spain
Manuel F. Dolz	Universitat Jaume I, Spain
Jorge G. Barbosa	University of Porto, Portugal
Hatem Ltaief	King Abdullah University of Science and Technology, Saudi Arabia
Carlos Reaño	Universitat de València, Spain
Ryohei Kobayashi	Institute of Science Tokyo, Japan
Julio Sahuquillo	Universitat Politècnica de València, Spain

Vladimir Getov	University of Westminster, UK
Pedro Javier Garcia	Universidad de Castilla-La Mancha, Spain
Tanja Harbaum	Karlsruhe Institute of Technology, Germany
Jesus Escudero-Sahuquillo	University of Castilla-La Mancha, Spain
Antonio J. Peña	Barcelona Supercomputing Center, Spain
Marcus Paradies	LMU Munich, Germany
Dirk Pleiter	University of Groningen, The Netherlands
Kazem Shekofteh	Heidelberg University, Germany
Esteban Mocskos	University of Buenos Aires, Argentina
Rohit Prasad	CEA, France
George Michelogiannakis	Lawrence Berkeley National Laboratory, USA
Yoshiki Yamaguchi	University of Tsukuba, Japan
Boma Anantasatya Adhi	Universitas Indonesia, Indonesia
Christian Plessl	Paderborn University, Germany
Christoph Kessler	Linköping University, Sweden
Antonino Tumeo	Pacific Northwest National Laboratory, USA
Davide Bertozzi	University of Manchester, UK
Keita Teranishi	Oak Ridge National Laboratory, USA
Samuel Thibault	Université Bordeaux 1, France
Tomohiro Ueno	RIKEN, Japan
Toshihiro Hanawa	University of Tokyo, Japan
Jason Bakos	University of South Carolina, USA
Mattias O'Nils	Mid Sweden University, Sweden
Giovanni Agosta	Politecnico di Milano, Italy
Shinji Sumimoto	University of Tokyo, Japan
Dhabaleswar Panda	Ohio State University, USA
Heiner Litz	Stanford University, USA
Ryusuke Egawa	Tokyo Denki University, Japan
Kazuhiko Komatsu	Tohoku University, Japan
Li Zhang	TU Darmstadt, Germany
Benjamin Klenk	NVIDIA Inc., USA
Francesca Palumbo	University of Cagliari, Italy
Christian Terboven	RWTH Aachen University, Germany
Alex Delis	University of Athens, Greece
Oscar Plata	University of Málaga, Spain

Track 4: Data Analytics, AI and Computational Science

Chairs

Erhard Rahm	Leipzig University, Germany
Jeyan Thiyagalingam	Rutherford Appleton Laboratory, UK

Program Committee

Shadi Ibrahim	Inria, Rennes Bretagne Atlantique Research Center, France
Rizos Sakellariou	University of Manchester, UK
Massimo Torquati	University of Pisa, Italy
Jorji Nonaka	RIKEN, Japan
Hao Dai	Shenzhen Institutes of Advanced Technology, China
Rafael Tolosana-Calasanz	Universidad de Zaragoza, Spain
Yang Wang	Shenzhen Institutes of Advanced Technology, China
Michael Kuhn	Otto von Guericke University Magdeburg, Germany
Achim Basermann	German Aerospace Center, Germany
Ashiq Anjum	University of Leicester, UK
Ramon Nou	Universitat Politécnica de Catalunya, Spain
Jože M. Rožanec	Jožef Stefan Institute, Slovenia
Dana Petcu	West University of Timisoara, Romania
Douglas Thain	University of Notre Dame, USA
Dalibor Klusacek	CESNET, Czech Republic
Hideyuki Kawashima	Keio University, Japan
José M. Cecilia	Universitat Politècnica de València, Spain
Manolis Marazakis	Institute of Computer Science, FORTH, Greece
Feiyi Wang	Oak Ridge National Laboratory, USA
Rafael Ferreira da Silva	Oak Ridge National Laboratory, USA
Matthias Boehm	TU Berlin, Germany
Alexandru Costan	Inria, France
Youngjae Kim	Sogang University, South Korea
M. Mustafa Rafique	Rochester Institute of Technology, USA
Ligang He	University of Warwick, UK
Osamu Tatebe	University of Tsukuba, Japan
Odej Kao	TU Berlin, Germany
Josef Spillner	Zurich University of Applied Sciences, Switzerland
Sukhpal Singh Gill	Queen Mary University of London, UK
Reza Farahani	University of Klagenfurt, Austria

Track 5: Theory and Algorithms

Chairs

Francesco Silvestri	University of Padova, Italy
Erik Saule	University of North Carolina Charlotte, USA

Program Committee

Othon Michail	University of Liverpool, UK
Pierre Fraigniaud	Université Paris Cité and CNRS, France
Jee Choi	Georgia Institute of Technology, USA
Samuel McCauley	Williams College, USA
Rezaul Chowdhury	State University of New York at Stony Brook, USA
Achour Mostéfaoui	Université Nantes, France
Manuel Penschuck	Goethe University Frankfurt, Germany
Vaishali Surianarayanan	University of California, Santa Barbara, USA
Lionel Eyraud-Dubois	Inria Bordeaux Sud-Ouest, France
Lata Narayanan	Concordia University, Canada
Helen Xu	Georgia Tech, USA
Yusuke Nagasaka	Fujitsu Limited, Japan
Albert-Jan Yzelman	Huawei Technologies France, France
Shikha Singh	Williams College, USA
Quanquan Liu	Northwestern University, USA
Fabien Dufoulon	Lancaster University, UK
Sanjukta Bhowmick	University of North Texas, USA
Flavio Vella	University of Trento, Italy
Kirk Pruhs	University of Pittsburgh, USA
Cynthia Phillips	Sandia National Laboratories, USA

Track 6: Multidisciplinary, Domain-Specific and Applied Parallel and Distributed Computing

Chairs

Alba C. Melo	University of Brasília, Brazil
Gihan Mudalige	University of Warwick, UK

Program Committee

Stefka Fidanova	Institute of Information and Communication Technologies, Bulgaria
Yiannis Papadopoulos	Advanced Micro Devices, Inc., USA
Dragi Kimovski	University of Klagenfurt, Austria
Tobias Flynn	Imperial College London, UK
Alvaro Coutinho	Universidade Federal do Rio de Janeiro, Brazil
Pasqua D'Ambra	Institute of Applied Mathematics-CNR, Italy
Maria Fazio	University of Messina, Italy
Davor Davidovic	Rudjer Bošković Institute, Croatia
Juan F. R. Herrera	University of Edinburgh, UK

Steven Wright	University of York, UK
Jonas Thies	Delft University of Technology, The Netherlands
Salvador Abreu	University of Évora, Portugal
Paolo Trunfio	University of Calabria, Italy
Amir Raoofy	Technical University of Munich, Germany
Ramon Bertran	IBM, Inc., USA
Mario Dantas	Universidade Federal de Juiz de Fora, Brazil
Claude Tadonki	Mines ParisTech/CRI, France
George Bisbas	Imperial College London, UK
Tze Meng Low	Carnegie Mellon University, USA
Cristina Boeres	Universidade Federal Fluminense, Brazil
Istvan Reguly	Pázmány Péter Catholic University, Hungary
Santiago Marco-Sola	Centro Nacional de Análisis Genómico, Spain
Pedro Ribeiro	University of Porto, Portugal
Balazs Gerofi	University of Tokyo, Japan
Rocío Carratalá-Sáez	Universitat de València, Spain
Emilo Luque	Autonomous University of Barcelona, Spain
Rajkumar Kettimuthu	Argonne National Laboratory, USA
Vladislav Kashansky	South Ural State University, Russia
Maria Pantoja	California Polytechnic State University San Luis Obispo, USA
Philippe Navaux	Universidade Federal de Rio Grande do Sul, Brazil
George Teodoro	Universidade Federal de Minas Gerais, Brazil
Philipp Gschwandtner	University of Innsbruck, Austria
Kamalavasan Kamalakkannan	Los Alamos National Laboratory, USA
Schahram Dustdar	Vienna University of Technology, Austria
Benjamin Brock	University of California, Berkeley, USA
Paul Bartholomew	EPCC, University of Edinburgh, UK
Juan Lorenzo Del Castillo	École Nationale Supérieure de L'Électronique et de ses Applications, France
Juan R. Gallego	Foundation for Computing and Advanced Technology of Extremadura, Spain
Lena Mashayekhy	University of Delaware, USA
Fabrizio Marozzo	University of Calabria, Italy
Lu Liu	University of Leicester, UK

Artifact Evaluation

Chairs

Massimo Torquati — University of Pisa, Italy
Olaf Krzikalla — German Aerospace Center, Germany

Artifact Evaluation Committee

Valerio Besozzi — Università di Pisa, Italy
Johannes Wendler — German Aerospace Center, Germany
Javier Garcia Blas — Universidad Carlos III de Madrid, Spain
Julian Braun — German Aerospace Center, Germany
Jasmin Mohnke — German Aerospace Center, Germany
Maximilian Höchel — German Aerospace Center, Germany
Marco Edoardo Santimaria — University of Turin, Italy
Nicolò Tonci — University of Pisa, Italy
Gabriele Mencagli — University of Pisa, Italy
Giulio Malenza — University of Turin, Italy
Dominik Vietinghoff — German Aerospace Center, Germany

Contents – Part III

Theory and Algorithms

Wedge-Parallel Triangle Counting for GPUs 3
    *Jeffrey Spaan, Kuan-Hsun Chen, David A. Bader,
and Ana-Lucia Varbanescu*

Cache Management for Mixture-of-Experts LLMs 18
    *Spyros Angelopoulos, Loris Marchal, Adrien Obrecht,
and Bertrand Simon*

Byzantine-Tolerant Consensus in GPU-Inspired Shared Memory 33
    Chryssis Georgiou, Manaswini Piduguralla, and Sathya Peri

Supervised Distributed Computing 48
    John Augustine, Christian Scheideler, and Julian Werthmann

Near-Optimal Contraction Strategies for the Scalar Product
in the Tensor-Train Format 63
    *Atte Torri, Przemysław Dominikowski, Brice Pointal, Oguz Kaya,
Laércio Lima Pilla, and Olivier Coulaud*

Partial Detectors Versus Replication to Cope with Silent Errors 78
    Anne Benoit, Thomas Herault, Yves Robert, and Alix Tremodeux

Partitioning In-Place on Massively Parallel Architectures 93
    Thomas Koopman, Sven-Bodo Scholz, and Bernard van Gastel

**Multidisciplinary, Domain-Specific and Applied Parallel and
Distributed Computing**

Quantum Delta Encoding: Optimizing Data Storage on Quantum
Computers with Resource Efficiency 109
    Jiale Zhang, Xilong Che, Yuzhe Fan, and Juncheng Hu

ScaleRunner: A Fast MPI-Based Random Walk Engine for Multi-CPU
Systems 124
    Florian Willich and Henning Meyerhenke

External GPU Biconnected Components 139
    Abhijeet Sahu, Andaluri S. P. V. M. Aditya, G. Ramakrishna, Malleti Sai Nikhil, Kishore Kothapalli, and Dip Sankar Banerjee

Disaggregated Design for GPU-Based Volumetric Data Structures 154
    Massimiliano Meneghin and Ahmed H. Mahmoud

SQ-DeAR: Sparsified and Quantized Gradient Compression for Distributed Training 169
    Xinrui Yang and Shaohuai Shi

SWBWA: A Highly Efficient NGS Aligner on the New Sunway Architecture 183
    Lifeng Yan, Zekun Yin, Qixin Chang, Tong Zhang, Zhisong Wang, Xiaohui Duan, Bertil Schmidt, and Weiguo Liu

SimPart: A Simple Yet Effective Replication-Aided Partitioning Algorithm for Logic Simulation on GPU 197
    Yi-Hua Chung, Shui Jiang, Wan-Luan Lee, Yanqing Zhang, Haoxing Ren, Tsung-Yi Ho, and Tsung-Wei Huang

Efficient Task Graph Scheduling for Parallel QR Factorization in SLSQP 211
    Soumyajit Chatterjee, Rahul Utkoor, Uppu Eshwar, Sathya Peri, and V. Krishna Nandivada

Breaking the I/O Barrier: 1.2 Tb/s Ethernet Packet Processing on a GPU 225
    John W. Romein

GECKO: A Write-Optimized Adaptive Radix Tree for Disaggregated Memory 239
    Tianyu Wan, Shijia Gong, Yangyang Hu, and Jianxi Chen

Scalable OpenMP Remote Offloading via Asynchronous MPI and Coroutine-Driven Communication 254
    Jhonatan Cléto, Guilherme Valarini, Marcio M. Pereira, Guido Araujo, and Hervé Yviquel

SProBench: Stream Processing Benchmark for High Performance Computing Infrastructure 268
    Apurv Deepak Kulkarni and Siavash Ghiasvand

NetSenseML: Network-Adaptive Compression for Efficient Distributed Machine Learning 283
    Yisu Wang, Xinjiao Li, Ruilong Wu, Huangxun Chen, and Dirk Kutscher

Efficient Pyramidal Analysis of Gigapixel Images on a Decentralized
Modest Computer Cluster 298
   Marie Reinbigler, Rishi Sharma, Rafael Pires, Elisabeth Brunet,
   Anne-Marie Kermarrec, and Catalin Fetita

Accelerating Independent Multi-Agent Reinforcement Learning
on Multi-GPU Platforms 313
   Samuel Wiggins, Nikunj Gupta, Grace Zgheib, Mahesh A. Iyer,
   and Viktor Prasanna

ScheInfer: Efficient Inference of Large Language Models with Task
Scheduling on Moderate GPUs 327
   Wenxiang Lin, Xinglin Pan, Shaohuai Shi, Xuan Wang, and Xiaowen Chu

Uniform Dense Blocking for Efficient Sparse LU Factorization
in First-Principles Materials Simulation 341
   Chao Wang, Junshi Chen, Longsheng Song, Haijie Hou, Dongdong Tan,
   Yueqiang He, Wentiao Wu, Sihan Lu, and Hong An

Author Index 355

Theory and Algorithms

Wedge-Parallel Triangle Counting for GPUs

Jeffrey Spaan[1]($\boxtimes$), Kuan-Hsun Chen[1], David A. Bader[2], and Ana-Lucia Varbanescu[1]

[1] University of Twente, Enschede, The Netherlands
{j.p.spaan,k.h.chen, a.l.varbanescu}@utwente.nl
[2] New Jersey Institute of Technology, Newark, USA
david.bader@njit.edu

Abstract. For fast processing of increasingly large graphs, triangle counting – a common building block of graph processing algorithms, is often performed on GPUs. However, applying massive parallelism to triangle counting is challenging due to the algorithm's inherent irregular access patterns and workload imbalance. In this work, we propose WeTriC, a novel _wedge_-parallel triangle counting algorithm for GPUs, which, using fine(r)-grained parallelism through a lightweight static mapping of wedges to threads, improves load balancing and efficiency. Our theoretical analysis compares different parallelization granularities, while optimizations enhance caching, reduce work-per-intersection, and minimize overhead. Performance experiments indicate that WeTriC yields 5.63× and 4.69× speedup over optimized vertex-parallel and edge-parallel binary search triangle counting algorithms, respectively. Furthermore, we show that WeTriC consistently outperforms the state-of-the-art (i.e., on avg. 2.86× faster than TRUST and 2.32× faster than GroupTC).

Keywords: Triangle Counting · Graph Processing · Parallel Computing on GPUs · Wedge-Parallel Approaches

1 Introduction

Graphs are flexible data structures that can efficiently capture entities (vertices) and their relations (edges). Graph processing algorithms – like shortest path, page rank, or betweenness centrality – are built to analyze such interconnected data to extract non-trivial (often statistical) information.

Graph processing algorithms vary in complexity, and become challenging to solve in reasonable time for very large input graphs. In fact, graph processing performance is dependent on the graph properties, the selected algorithm(s) and their implementation, and the hardware platform of choice. Especially when using parallel systems - like multi-core CPUs and GPUs - choosing an incorrect mix of (algorithm, implementation, platform) for the given graph workload can lead to significant performance loss (i.e., 2–3 orders of magnitude) [22].

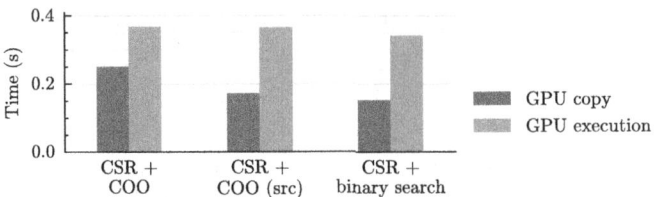

Fig. 1. Performance for different edge-retrieval strategies for the Wikipedia graph (see Table 3). Each thread finds their edge (v, w) and performs BINARYSEARCH$(N(w), v)$.

This work focuses on a specific graph processing problem – triangle counting – and a specific target platform – a GPU. Triangle counting is a common building block for algorithms such as k-truss [23], clustering coefficient [20], and link recommendation [7]. While many algorithms [1,3,6,11,14,17,18,24] have been proposed, we observe that the task size of these algorithms is often imbalanced. Commonly, a vertex or an edge is assigned for processing to every thread, warp or block. However, the work per vertex or edge is graph-dependent, and can vary wildly. Their remedies, such as dynamic scheduling (like work-stealing) and oversubscribing, not only create an overhead in managing and synchronizing the workload – they can also lead to underutilization due to many idling threads.

Our algorithm, WETRIC, reduces this waste by introducing a new, finer, *wedge-parallel* granularity, which, through a static lightweight array of indices (equal in size to the number of vertices), minimizes load imbalance. Its performance stems from two key insights: (1) allocating more threads or blocks is inexpensive, meaning that we can process one wedge per thread even for a very large number of wedges, and (2) inferring the vertices of a wedge is a relatively cheap operation. Figure 1 shows the execution time for a kernel that retrieves an edge (v, w) and computes BINARYSEARCH$(N(w), v)$. From left to right, the source vertex v is retrieved from an edge list (COO), a source-only edge list, and by binary searching the CSR's row pointer. We observe that binary searching is always favored over storing an edge list, meaning that this approach can save both time and space. Thus, in the same vein, we apply a similar strategy for wedges to overcome the space restrictions of fully materializing a *wedge list*. This paper makes the following contributions:

- We present a novel GPU algorithm WETRIC for counting triangles in static undirected sparse graphs (Sect. 3), together with an in-depth complexity analysis (Sect. 4).
- We apply and evaluate a series of algorithm optimizations, on top of our wedge-based approach, to further balance the workload, decrease overhead, improve caching, and reduce the work per intersection (Sect. 5).
- We provide a C+CUDA implementation[1] of the algorithm, and show its scalability and performance across a diverse pool of graphs. The evaluation shows that WETRIC consistently outperforms the state-of-the-art (Sect. 6).

---

[1] https://github.com/jeffreyspaan/wedge-parallel-triangle-counting.

Table 1. Graph terminology.

$G(V,E)$	A *graph* with vertices V and edges E.	$N(v)$	*Neighborhood* of v (i.e., $w \in N(v)$ for every edge (v,w).
v	A *vertex* or *node* with ID v.	$d(v)$	The *degree* of v (i.e., $|N(v)|$).
(v,w)	An *edge* from v to w (we say w neighbors v).	$N(v)_{w+}$	Neighborhood of v where $u > w$ for all $u \in N(v)$.
(v,w,u)	A *wedge* where v is a *base* vertex and w and u are *leaf* vertices.	$d(v)_{w+}$	$|N(v)_{w+}|$.
n	Number of vertices (i.e, $|V|$).	d_{avg}	Average degree (i.e., $\frac{m}{n}$).
m	Number of edges (i.e, $|E|$).	d_{max}	Maximum degree.

2 Background and Related Work

2.1 Graphs and Data Structures

Graphs are collection of vertices connected by edges. Graph topology – that is, intuitively, the 'shape' of the graph – is characterized by a graph's (statistical) properties, like average degree or diameter. We summarize all graph properties used in this work, and their notations, in Table 1.

Dense graphs can be captured in an $n \times n$ *adjacency matrix*, where every possible edge, whether present in the graph or not, is stored on disk. For large sparse graphs (i.e., $m \ll n^2$), this structure is far too wasteful since most entries are zero. Instead, sparse graphs (and matrices) are commonly stored in compressed formats, like Compressed Sparse Row (CSR) or Coordinate (COO). The COO format consists of two arrays: one for the source vertices v and one for the destination vertices w. The CSR format compresses the former into indices (the *row pointer*) which point into a destination vertices array (the *column index*).

2.2 Triangle Counting

A *clique* is a subgraph in which each vertex is directly connected to all the other vertices in the clique. Triangle counting is the operation of determining how many triangles (3-cliques) are in a graph. The main strategy for triangle counting is *intersecting*: for every vertex v, determine how much v's neighborhood overlaps with the neighborhood of each of v's neighbors w. In other words: we want to find (the size of) the intersection $N(v) \cap N(w)$ for all $w \in N(v)$.

Binary search is the most common strategy for triangle counting on GPUs. It intersects by binary searching each u from $N(v)_{w+}$ in $N(w)$ for each w in $N(v)$. Binary-search-based triangle counting is attractive for many-core architectures because each wedge is independently evaluated. Furthermore, since the worst case-complexity per-wedge is logarithmic, i.e., $\mathcal{O}(\log(d(w)))$, it can reduce the workload difference between w's with diverse degrees. Examples include HTC [24], GroupTC [14], TriCore [11], and HyKernel [1].

Merge-path intersects by merging $N(v)$ and $N(w)$ at the same time. The obvious benefit of this technique is that $N(w)$ is only searched once. In turn, this means the per-edge worst-case complexity of this algorithm is $\mathcal{O}(d(v) + d(w))$, which is lower than the alternatives. Although predominantly used for sequential triangle counting algorithms, parallelized versions have been proposed by, among others, Mailthody et al. [15] and Pearson et al. [19].

Hashing replaces the binary search with a hash-table lookup. The main benefit of hashing-based triangle counting is the $\mathcal{O}(1)$ complexity for evaluating a wedge. The drawbacks are the construction and synchronization overhead, collisions – multiple vertices sharing the same hash, and increased workload imbalance. Hashing is implemented in the GraphChallenge[2] champion H-INDEX [17] and its successor TRUST [18]. On a coarser scale, Bisson et al. [6] use a bitmap (i.e., a full adjacency matrix row) while HTC [24] uses a *segmented* bitmap approach, where empty parts of the bitmap are omitted.

2.3 Parallelization Granularity

The granularity denotes the level at which the workload is divided between processors. Choosing a different granularity can change the amount of work per processor, the context, and the overlap between processors. For GPUs, the workload is often parallelized by the vertices, by the edges, or by a combination of the two. Figure 2 contrasts the processing of a vertex v with $d(v) = 5$ in vertex-parallel (1 thread), edge-parallel (4 threads) and wedge-parallel (10 threads).

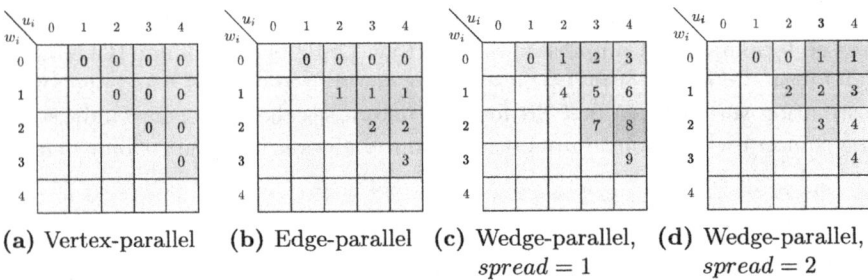

(a) Vertex-parallel (b) Edge-parallel (c) Wedge-parallel, $spread = 1$ (d) Wedge-parallel, $spread = 2$

Fig. 2. Assignment of threads to the wedges of v, depicted as a triangular $N(v) \times N(v)$ matrix. Each cell is a wedge (v, w, u) comprised of v plus the neighbor shown in the horizontal ($u = N(v)[u_i]$) and vertical ($w = N(v)[w_i]$) axis. Cell numbers indicate the ID of the executing thread.

Vertex-parallel. Parallelizing by the vertices, where each thread calculates the triangles for a fixed number of vertices, allows for flexibility in the way that $N(v)$ and $N(w)$ are iterated because each thread has exclusive access to all wedges of v. Unfortunately, this is also a drawback: because the overlap between adjacent threads is low, there are few opportunities for reusing and/or coalescing data. HTC [24] uses this granularity for low-degree vertices.

---

[2] https://graphchallenge.mit.edu/.

Edge-parallel. Alternatively, one can assign a fixed number of edges to each thread. As shown in Fig. 2b, the maximum difference in the number of wedges per thread is now $d(v) - 1$, compared to d_{max}. HTC [24] uses this granularity for high-degree vertices. HyKernel [1] and H-INDEX [17] exclusively parallelize by the edges. Bader et al. [4] parallelize by the *edge cover*, a subset of the edges.
Vectorized. Some algorithms do not map vertices or edges to *threads* but rather to blocks, warps, or subwarps. Here, each collection of (a fixed number of) threads iterates over the wedges of one vertex or edge until all wedges are exhausted. Examples include GroupTC [14], Hu's algorithm [10], Bisson's [6], and TRUST [18]. A drawback is that this approach can under- or overshoot the number of threads required (a.k.a. oversubscribing). For instance, a warp-based approach (32 threads) has 31 idling threads for a 1- or 63-wedge vertex.

3 WeTriC

The input of our algorithm is an undirected graph, which we scan for duplicates, reorder (see Sect. 5.1), and turn into a directed graph (in CSR format). This procedure is identical to the state-of-the-art. Next, instead of storing the wedges, which would not be scalable (e.g., the Wikipedia graph in CSR format requires ~1 GiB, while storing all wedges would take up ~75 GiB), we construct the wedges dynamically. Our approach, as presented in Fig. 3, allows each thread to dynamically construct its wedge tuple (v, w, u) with only n additional memory. On the GPU, each thread follows the following three steps:
(a) Finding the Base Vertex v. First, each thread (with index i) searches an array named wedgeSums containing the cumulative number of wedges per vertex to find the index v where $a = \text{wedgeSums}[v] \leq i < b = \text{wedgeSums}[v+1]$ is true. In other words, if we consider all wedges stored in an array (like the virtual array in Fig. 3b), a and b define the boundaries of the wedges of vertex v in that

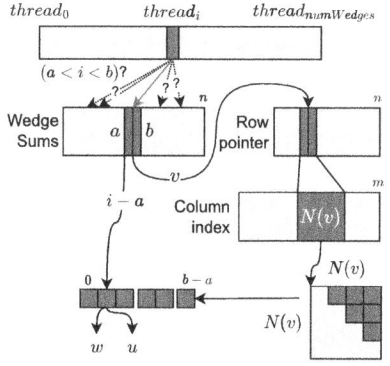

(a) Wedge i (v, w, u) is highlighted.

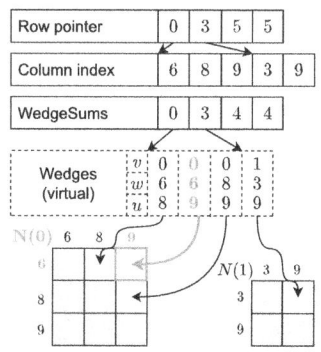

(b) Wedge 1 $(0, 6, 9)$ is highlighted.

Fig. 3. An overview of the algorithm, focusing on the process of retrieving a wedge: (a) the mechanism and (b) an example.

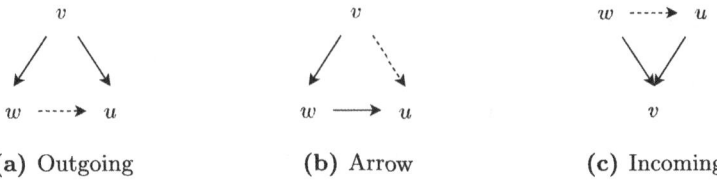

Fig. 4. Wedge styles. Closing edges are dotted.

array, in the same way that $\texttt{rowPointer}[v] \leq e < \texttt{rowPointer}[v+1]$ define the boundaries of all edges e in the column index for vertex v.

In practice, we calculate $\texttt{wedgeSums}$ a priori using a prefix sum of the per-vertex wedge counts: $\binom{d(v)}{2}$. Furthermore, on the GPU, each thread performs a *binary* search to find v (and thereby a and b). This operation is relatively inexpensive because adjacent threads will share all but one level of the binary search tree, which allows for coalescing and/or caching of the lower levels.

(b) Finding the Leaf Vertices w and u. Knowing both v and a, we can find the relative index of this wedge within the wedges of v: $i - a$. If we consider all neighbor pairs w and u (i.e., the wedges) of v laid out in a $N(v) \times N(v)$ grid (like in Fig. 2), the cell with linear index $i-a$ will give us the x and y coordinates[3] (i.e., the w and u) of this wedge. In fact, this grid is an upper triangular matrix as we only consider wedges where $v < w < u$ to only count each triangle once.

(c) Intersecting. When the thread has calculated the base and leaf vertices, it binary searches $N(w)$ for u to determine whether the wedge (v, w, u) is a triangle. This operation has a worst-case complexity of $\mathcal{O}(\log(d(w)))$.

4 Theoretical Analysis

4.1 Wedge Styles

Along with the granularity, the wedge *style* is a key component of the workload distribution. Besides *outgoing* wedges, there are two other types of wedges (as depicted in Fig. 4): *arrow* wedges, and *incoming* wedges . The latter is, for our purposes, identical to the outgoing variant. Arrow wedges, however, are substantially different. Specifically, the number of consecutive closing edges (v, u) with the same target neighborhood is $d(v) \cdot d(w)$ compared to $d(v)_{w+}$ for outgoing wedges (on average, $(d_{\text{avg}})^2$ versus $\frac{d_{\text{avg}}-1}{2}$). TRUST [18] leverages this property to make hashing the neighbors of v more efficient in terms of lookups per table and total number of tables (n versus m). The arrow style does come with an important drawback: the total number of wedges increases to $\sum_{v=0}^{n} \sum_{w \in N(v)} d(w)$ (assuming every degree is d_{avg}, $\sim 2\times$ more). For this reason, and because inferring an arrow wedge is costlier, this style was found to perform worse.

---

[3] The conversion of linear to Cartesian coordinates for a triangular matrix of a fixed size $(d(v))$, which was not discovered by us, finds its origin in triangular numbers [2].

In contrast, for the edge-parallel algorithm, we found that using arrow wedges was faster than using outgoing wedges, likely because the number of adjacent threads searching the same neighborhood is $d(v)$, compared to 0.

Lastly, we can also alternate the outgoing and arrow style dynamically depending on the current workload. We refer to this style as *mixed*. Interestingly, the vertex-parallel algorithm prefers the mixed wedge style. We believe this is because it has the lowest total amount of work and (like the outgoing style) the smallest maximum imbalance between threads (see Table 2). Furthermore, in contrast to the edge-parallel algorithm, it does not matter whether we binary search in $N(v)$ or $N(w)$ as neither is accessed by adjacent threads.

4.2 Wedge-Parallel

Compared to the vertex- and edge-parallel algorithms, the wedge-parallel algorithm excels at workload balance. As shown in Fig. 2, for the outgoing style, the number of wedges per thread ranges from 0 to $\binom{d_{\max}}{2}$ when parallelizing by vertex (Fig. 2a), 0 to $d_{\max} - 1$ when parallelizing by edge (Fig. 2b), and 1 when parallelizing per wedge (Fig. 2c). Moreover, among the outgoing variants, the wedge-parallel algorithm has the best spatial locality. Adjacent threads in the vertex- and edge-parallel algorithms binary search in different neighborhoods, and thus access unrelated (and therefore likely uncached) data. Instead, in the outgoing wedge-parallel algorithm, a thread shares its search neighborhood with, on average, $\frac{d_{\mathrm{avg}} - 1}{2}$ adjacent threads.

5 Optimizations

5.1 Graph Reordering

Like other triangle counting works [14,18,24], we first perform a *reordering* of the vertices by their (undirected) degree. This optimization benefits triangle counting because it (1) increases the median degree, improving locality, (2) flattens the degree curve, improving load-balancing, and (3) reduces outliers, reducing the number of wedges. We clearly observe (2) and (3) in Fig. 5. For our algorithm, removing high-degree outliers is the most important aspect because the number

Table 2. Theoretical properties of parallelization strategies.

	Vertex-parallel			Edge-parallel			Wedge-Parallel	
	Outgoing	Arrow	Mixed	Outgoing	Arrow	Mixed	Outgoing	Arrow
Total work	Medium[a]	High[b]	Low[c]	Medium[a]	High[b]	Low[c]	Medium[a]	High[b]
Extra data	×	×	×	×	×	×	n	$m + n$
Extra work to retrieve the vertex/edge/wedge	×	×	×	$\log(n)$	$\log(n)$	$\log(n)$	$\log(n)$	$\log(n) + \log(d(v))$
Maximum imbalance[d]	$\binom{d_{\max}}{2}$	$d_{\max}^2$	$\binom{d_{\max}}{2}$	$d_{\max}$	$d_{\max}$	$d_{\max}$	0	0
Num. of adjacent threads searching in the same neighborhood	0	0	0	0	$d(v)$	0 or $d(v)$	$d(v)^e_{w+}$	$d(v) \cdot d(w)^e$
Num. of adjacent threads iterating over the same neighborhood	0	0	0	$d(v)$	0	$d(v)$ or 0	$\binom{d(v)}{2}$/spread	$\frac{d(w)}{\mathrm{spread}}$

[a] $\sum_{v \in V} \sum_{w \in N(v)} d(v)_{w+}$
[b] $\sum_{v \in V} \sum_{w \in N(v)} d(w)$
[c] $\sum_{v \in V} \sum_{w \in N(v)} \min(d(v)_{w+}, d(w))$
[d] In the number of binary searches (i.e., wedges) between adjacent threads.
[e] If spread = 1, or spread > 1 (see Sect. 5.2) and threads cooperate (see Sect. 5.3).

of wedges per vertex is quadratic in its degree. For instance, for the Wikipedia graph (WKL), reordering reduces the maximum degree from approximately 10^6 to 10^3, resulting in 94% fewer wedges (overall).

Although degree-based reordering is the most popular strategy (e.g. [14]), other orderings prioritizing different metrics have been proposed. For example, TRUST [18] uses a degree-based ordering combined with heuristics to minimize the number of hash-table collisions, while HTC [24] reorders using the integration of density and degree (following Han et al. [9]), aiming to improve locality.

5.2 Spreading

To amortize the extra work introduced by the binary search to find the base vertex v, we can increase the work (i.e., number of wedges) per thread. We name this amount the *spread*. Increasing the spread is beneficial because finding the next wedge $(v_{i+1}, w_{i+1}, u_{i+1})$ from a known wedge (v_i, w_i, u_i) is (compared to two binary searches) relatively cheap. We either increment u_i (in $N(v)$), increment w_i (in $N(v)$), or increment v and reset the w_i and u_i indices to 0 and 1. Figure 2d shows the iteration pattern for a spread of 2. Note that this optimization increases the workload per thread, but does not alter the workload balance; each thread still evaluates a constant number of wedges.

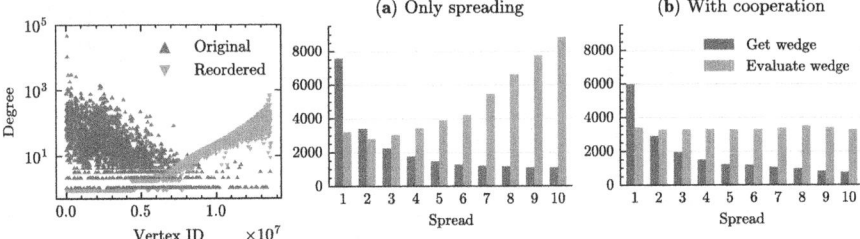

Fig. 5. (Out)degree distribution of the WKL graph.

Fig. 6. Average number of cycles (y-axis) required to retrieve and evaluate a wedge for WKL.

5.3 Cooperation

An unfortunate consequence of spreading is that a thread with starting wedge (v, w, u) will share fewer vertices with adjacent threads, i.e., we trade spatial locality for temporal locality, which means we have conflicting goals when it comes to the spread: we both want to increase it (for fewer memory loads) and decrease it (for more cached and/or coalesced memory loads). Our solution is to store the wedges in shared memory and, when all wedges are stored, iterate over them as if the spread were 1, e.g., thread 0 stores its wedges at index $0, 1, ..., (spread - 1)$ but reads at $0, blockSize, ..., blockSize \cdot (spread - 1)$. This ensures that, in the same timestep, the wedges to be evaluated are in the original order $(0, 1, 2, ...)$. We refer to this optimization as *cooperation*. The benefit of cooperation can be seen in Fig. 6a versus Fig. 6b.

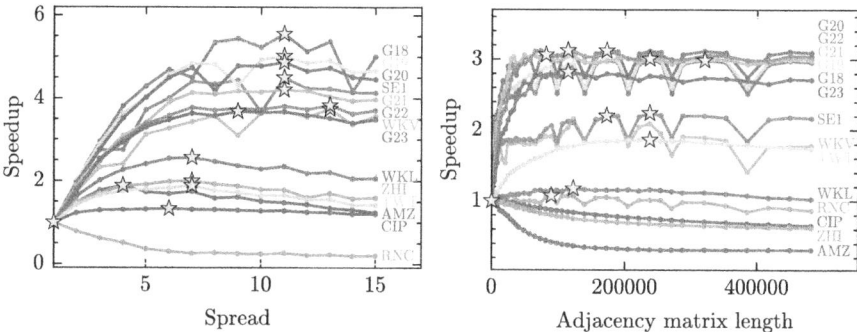

Fig. 7. Speedup for increasing spreads (with cooperation). The best speedup for each graph is marked with a golden star.

Fig. 8. Speedup for increasing adjacency matrix lengths. The best speedup for each graph is marked with a golden star.

Figure 7 shows the speedup when increasing the spread for all graphs listed in Table 3. For most graphs, we observe a steep rise in performance with the spread until ~7, after which the impact stagnates.

5.4 Adjacency Matrix

To improve the intersection performance, we store some neighborhoods in an *adjacency matrix* (bitmap). Although this is practically unfeasible for the full graph, fortunately, because we store undirected edges as directed edges, i.e., $v < w$ is true for every edge (v, w), we can exclusively store the neighborhoods of the last x vertices, i.e., the vertices from ID $n - x$ to $n - 1$. This is possible because $d(v) < x$ is guaranteed if $v \geq n - x$. Conceptually, we only store a (bottom-right) submatrix of the (triangular) adjacency matrix. Coincidentally, this is also the region where the densest vertices are. Since we sort the vertices by their ascending degree and we work on undirected graphs, $d(v)_{in} = d(v)_{out}$ holds, meaning that the first vertex to be included in the adjacency matrix (vertex $n - 1$) is by definition the most popular destination vertex.

Figure 8 shows the speedup when increasing adjacency matrix length x. The data indicates that an adjacency length between 25000 and 300000 is preferable for most graphs, although the optimal length – and its impact – depends on the degree distribution of the graph. As expected, we observe the highest speedups for graphs with power-law degree distributions, e.g., the Graph500 graphs.

Not all graphs benefit from the adjacency matrix optimization, which could be due to data duplication (of the CSR graph and A), a too balanced distribution, a low maximum degree, or a combination thereof.

6 Evaluation

In this section, we compare WETRIC against the state-of-the-art, examine the impacts of our optimizations, and investigate the end-to-end performance.

Table 3. Graphs statistics (after preprocessing).

Graph	Abbr.	n	m	#wedges	d_{avg}	d_{med}	d_{max}	#triangles
roadNet-CA	RNC	1,965,206	2,766,607	$1.2 \cdot 10^6$	1.4	2	4	$1.2 \cdot 10^5$
Amazon0302	AMZ	262,111	899,792	$1.4 \cdot 10^6$	3.4	4	11	$7.2 \cdot 10^5$
wiki-vote	WKV	7,115	100,762	$1.7 \cdot 10^6$	14.2	4	74	$6.1 \cdot 10^5$
soc-epinions1	SE1	75,879	405,740	$5.7 \cdot 10^6$	5.3	1	121	$1.6 \cdot 10^6$
cit-patents	CIP	3,774,768	16,518,947	$5.0 \cdot 10^7$	4.4	4	77	$7.5 \cdot 10^6$
graph500_scale18[a]	G18	174,147	3,800,348	$2.0 \cdot 10^8$	21.8	5	432	$8.2 \cdot 10^7$
graph500_scale19[a]	G19	335,318	7,729,675	$5.0 \cdot 10^8$	23.0	5	560	$1.9 \cdot 10^8$
zhishi	ZHI	7,825,669	62,246,014	$7.2 \cdot 10^8$	8.0	4	377	$1.1 \cdot 10^8$
graph500_scale20[a]	G20	645,820	15,680,861	$1.2 \cdot 10^9$	24.3	5	715	$4.2 \cdot 10^8$
graph500_scale21[a]	G21	1,243,072	31,731,650	$3.0 \cdot 10^9$	25.5	5	885	$9.4 \cdot 10^8$
graph500_scale22[a]	G22	2,393,285	64,097,004	$7.2 \cdot 10^9$	26.8	5	1,107	$2.1 \cdot 10^9$
graph500_scale23[a]	G23	4,606,314	129,250,705	$1.8 \cdot 10^{10}$	28.1	4	1,439	$4.5 \cdot 10^9$
wikipedia_link_en	WKL	13,593,032	334,591,525	$2.0 \cdot 10^{10}$	24.6	4	1,156	$1.4 \cdot 10^{10}$
twitter (WWW)[b]	TWT	41,652,230	1,202,513,046	$1.5 \cdot 10^{11}$	28.9	10	4,102	$3.5 \cdot 10^{10}$

[a] $a=0.57, b=0.19, c=0.19, d=0.05$, edge factor=16. [b] a.k.a. twitter7 in SNAP [13].

6.1 Evaluation Setup

We evaluate WETRIC on 14 graphs, ranging from 10^6 to 10^{11} wedges, as listed in Table 3. We selected 8 real graphs (RNC, AMZ, WKV, SE1, CIP from SNAP [13] and ZHI, WKL, and TWT from KONECT [12]), and 6 synthetic sparse graphs (G18-G23 are generated by the Graph500 [8] generator).

We compiled our implementation (~1000 LOC) with CUDA 12.3. We performed most experiments on NVIDIA's RTX A4000 on the DAS-6 [5]. Because this GPU does not have enough device memory to contain TWT, all experiments for this graph were instead performed using Nvidia's RTX A6000.[4] For performance comparisons, we only consider the GPU execution time. All reported results are averaged over 10 runs. Standard deviation was consistently less than 1%. We calculate average speedups using the geometric mean. Occupancy data is collected using Nvidia Nsight Compute [16].

---

[4] Using a modified implementation with 64-bit row pointers and multiple kernel launches to handle large number of (w)edges.

For TRUST, we executed 48 blocks with 1024 threads per block, using the best-performing chunk size per graph (determined empirically). For GroupTC, we follow the default parameters: 48 blocks with 256 threads per block. Unfortunately, we were unable to compare WeTriC to HTC [24], which claims an average speedup of 1.4× over TRUST, since their implementation is proprietary.

6.2 Comparison with Vertex and Edge-Parallel

Table 4 shows the speedup of our wedge-parallel algorithm over the vertex-parallel and edge-parallel binary search triangle counting algorithms[5]. We achieve an average speedup of 5.63× over the vertex-parallel algorithm and 4.69× over the edge-parallel algorithm. The highest speedups for the latter come from the Graph500 graphs. For most other graphs, the edge-parallel algorithm outperforms the vertex-parallel algorithm. When increasing the Graph500 scale – and thereby the workload imbalance, WeTriC increasingly outperforms both. We also observe similar performance for all pre-balanced graphs. RNC for instance has a maximum degree of 4, meaning that the maximum workload imbalance is $\binom{4}{2} = 6$, and, as a result, all granularities perform similarly.

Table 4. WeTriC versus the state-of-the-art. Execution times are in milliseconds. Speedups (in parentheses) are relative to WeTriC.

	WeTriC	Vertex-parallel	Edge-parallel	TRUST [18]	GroupTC [14]
RNC	0.19	0.17 (0.86×)	0.22 (1.15×)	1.33 (6.81×)	0.55 (2.81×)
AMZ	0.10	0.10 (1.01×)	0.11 (1.05×)	0.51 (5.06×)	0.33 (3.24×)
WKV	0.04	0.47 (10.67×)	0.05 (1.07×)	0.30 (6.77×)	0.23 (5.34×)
SE1	0.11	1.08 (9.40×)	0.46 (4.01×)	0.51 (4.41×)	0.4 (3.45×)
CIP	5.63	10.62 (1.89×)	12.52 (2.22×)	8.18 (1.45×)	7.05 (1.25×)
G18	3.19	31.08 (9.73×)	20.24 (6.34×)	10.32 (3.23×)	7.34 (2.30×)
G19	8.76	77.34 (8.83×)	90.55 (10.34×)	27.95 (3.19×)	21.34 (2.44×)
ZHI	40.79	204.67 (5.02×)	81.34 (1.99×)	48.03 (1.18×)	44.33 (1.09×)
G20	23.14	194.32 (8.40×)	323.90 (14.00×)	74.23 (3.21×)	62.76 (2.71×)
G21	67.36	453.86 (6.74×)	934.26 (13.87×)	193.87 (2.88×)	179.10 (2.66×)
G22	173.88	1556.38 (8.95×)	2875.25 (16.54×)	513.43 (2.95×)	489.25 (2.81×)
G23	446.20	5145.86 (11.53×)	8074.26 (18.10×)	1279.12 (2.87×)	1294.06 (2.9×)
WKL	809.71	8084.13 (9.98×)	2299.04 (2.84×)	612.76 (0.76×)	834.08 (1.03×)
TWT	2611.38	20108.23 (7.70×)	25921.28 (9.93×)	5819.69 (2.23×)	4388.28 (1.68×)

---

[5] With: the same preprocessing, all applicable optimizations from Sect. 5, and the best-performing wedge style from Sect. 4.

Table 5. Indicators of workload balance for different granularities (average ± std).

Granularity	Vertex-parallel			Edge-parallel		Wedge-Parallel	
Style	Outgoing	Arrow	Mixed	Outgoing	Arrow Mixed	Outgoing	Arrow
Active warps (average, %)	43 ± 18	48 ± 16	41 ± 19	80 ± 7	86 ± 3 77 ± 8	81 ± 15	83 ± 14
Active threads per warp (average)	18 ± 6	14 ± 4	13 ± 5	21 ± 3	17 ± 3 15 ± 3	29 ± 3	29 ± 2

Table 5 shows the measured average number of active *threads* in a warp (max 32) and the average number of active *warps* compared to the theoretical maximum (a.k.a. *achieved occupancy*). We observe a clear increasing trend in the average active threads with finer granularity. Thus, the amount of (absolute time- and instruction-wise) thread divergence and early termination decreases with the workload imbalance. The number of active warps also increases with the granularity, but remains the same for the edge- and wedge-parallel algorithms. Although inter-warp balance is not as important as intra-warp balance (as warps are not executed in lockstep), WeTriC is not able to consistently improve it.

6.3 Comparison with State-of-the-Art

The performance of WeTriC compared to Trust and GroupTC can be seen in Table 4. In comparison to Trust, we achieve a minimum speedup of 0.76×, a maximum speedup of 6.81×, and an average speedup of 2.86×.

Although WeTriC generally outperforms Trust, it is hard to determine why, simply because Trust, a vectorized hashing-based algorithm, is different on a fundamental level. Besides this, the performance is also highly dependent on the graph distribution. For instance, G23 and WKL have similar graph properties (Table 3) but yield wildly different speedups (2.87 vs. 0.76). This is likely because WKL's distribution is flatter, thereby lowering the potential of the adjacency matrix optimization (see Fig. 9), and of the finer granularity (observe the relatively lower speedups in Table 4 versus the edge- and vertex-parallel algorithms compared to G23). In the interest of fairness, we repeated the experiments on Nvidia's A5000, A6000, A100, and A2 GPU, yielding average speedups (excluding TWT) of 4.15×, 4.95×, 10.27×, and 3.24×, respectively.

Compared to GroupTC, WeTriC achieves a minimum speedup of 1.03×, a maximum speedup of 5.34×, and an average speedup of 2.32×. Unlike Trust, the average speedups on different GPUs remain consistent: 2.66×, 2.67×, 2.80×, 1.98×, likely because both algorithms, unlike Trust, are binary-search-based.

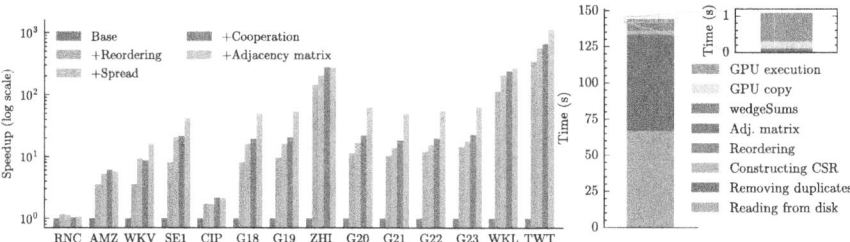

Fig. 9. Performance impact of optimizations (cumulative). Higher is better.

Fig. 10. End-to-end performance for WKL.

6.4 Optimizations Impact

Figure 9 shows the cumulative performance impact of our optimizations. Reordering, spreading, cooperation, and adjacency matrix yield an average speedup of 12.3×, 1.5×, 1.2×, and 1.8× over the previous version, respectively. Although all graphs massively benefit from reordering, ZHI, WKL, and TWT benefit the most with a speedup of 144×, 114×, and 346×, respectively, most likely due to the high reduction in the number of wedges (99.4%, 94%, and 99.7%).

SE1 and WKV highly benefit from the spread, but are hampered by cooperation. Most other graphs benefit from both. Overall, we observe very similar speedups for the Graph500 graphs. In addition, note that the optimal spread (see Fig. 7) and adjacency matrix length (see Fig. 8) do not increase with the scale. Thus, the speedup of our optimizations likely persists at larger scales.

6.5 End-To-End Performance

Figure 10 shows the execution time for all steps of our algorithm. Although the preprocessing time overshadows the execution time, note that this part is not our focus, and thus largely unparallized and unoptimized. Furthermore, an important observation is that some of the preprocessing time is compensated with algorithmic speedups. For example, although reordering WKL takes 7 seconds, counting the triangles of an *unordered* WKL takes 228.7 (instead of ~2) seconds.

7 Conclusion

GPU-based triangle counting algorithms are promising for processing massive sparse graphs with high performance. However, state-of-the-art algorithms suffer from large workload imbalance. To alleviate this problem, we propose WET-RIC, a novel wedge-parallel triangle counting algorithm for GPUs, that uses a lightweight data structure to resolve workload imbalance. We analyze the theoretical properties and advantages of WeTriC compared to state-of-the-art solutions, and apply several optimizations to further improve its efficiency. Our extensive empirical analysis shows WeTriC consistently outperforms the state-of-the-art – by, on average, 2.86× (Trust [18]) and 2.32× (GroupTC [14]).

Disclosure of Interests. The authors have no competing interests to declare.

Acknowledgments and Artifact Availability. David Bader is supported in part by U.S. National Science Foundation grants CCF-2109988 and OAC-2402560. The artifact is available in the Zenodo repository [21].

References

1. Almasri, M., Vasudeva, N., Nagi, R., Xiong, J., Hwu, W.M.: HyKernel: a hybrid selection of one/two-phase kernels for triangle counting on GPUs. In: IEEE HPEC (2021)
2. Angeletti, M., Bonny, J.M., Koko, J.: Parallel euclidean distance matrix computation on big datasets (2019), hal-02047514
3. Bader, D.A.: Fast triangle counting. In: IEEE HPEC (2023)
4. Bader, D.A., et al.: Triangle counting through cover-edges. In: IEEE HPEC (2023)
5. Bal, H., et al.: A medium-scale distributed system for computer science research: Infrastructure for the long term. Computer **49**(5), 54–63 (2016)
6. Bisson, M., Fatica, M.: High performance exact triangle counting on GPUs. IEEE Trans. Parallel Distrib. Syst. **28**(12), 3501–3510 (2017)
7. Dong, Y., et al.: Link prediction and recommendation across heterogeneous social networks. In: IEEE ICDM (2012)
8. Graph 500 Steering Committee: The Graph500 Benchmark. https://www.graph500.org (2010)
9. Han, S., Zou, L., Yu, J.X.: Speeding up set intersections in graph algorithms using SIMD instructions. In: ACM SIGMOD (2018)
10. Hu, L., Guan, N., Zou, L.: Triangle counting on gpu using fine-grained task distribution. In: IEEE ICDEW (2019)
11. Hu, Y., Liu, H., Huang, H.H.: TriCore: parallel triangle counting on GPUs. In: ACM SC (2018)
12. Kunegis, J.: Konect: the koblenz network collection. In: ACM WWW (2013)
13. Leskovec, J., Krevl, A.: SNAP datasets: stanford large network dataset collection. http://snap.stanford.edu/data (2014)
14. Li, J., Xu, Z., Pham, M., Tu, Y., Zhou, Q.: A comparative study of intersection-based triangle counting algorithms on GPUs. In: IEEE IPDPS (2024)
15. Mailthody, V.S., et al.: Collaborative (CPU + GPU) algorithms for triangle counting and truss decomposition. In: IEEE HPEC (2018)
16. Nvidia: Nsight Compute (2025), https://docs.nvidia.com/nsight-compute/
17. Pandey, S., Li, X.S., Buluc, A., Xu, J., Liu, H.: H-INDEX: hash-indexing for parallel triangle counting on GPUs. In: IEEE HPEC (2019)
18. Pandey, S., et al.: Trust: Triangle counting reloaded on gpus. IEEE Trans. Parallel Distrib. Syst. **32**(11), 2646–2660 (2021)
19. Pearson, C., et al.: Update on triangle counting on GPU. In: IEEE HPEC (2019)

20. Schank, T.: Algorithmic aspects of triangle-based network analysis. Ph.D. thesis, University of Karlsruhe (2007)
21. Spaan, J., Chen, K.H., Bader, D.A., Varbanescu, A.L.: Artifact of the paper: wedge-parallel triangle counting for GPUs (2025). https://doi.org/10.5281/zenodo.15611508
22. Verstraaten, M.: Analysis and prediction of GPU graph algorithm performance. Ph.D. thesis, University of Amsterdam (2022)
23. Wang, J., Cheng, J.: Truss decomposition in massive networks. Proc. VLDB Endow. **5**(9), 812–823 (2012)
24. Zeng, L., Yang, K., Cai, H., Zhou, J., Zhao, R., Chen, X.: HTC: hybrid vertex-parallel and edge-parallel triangle counting. In: IEEE HPEC (2022)

Cache Management for Mixture-of-Experts LLMs

Spyros Angelopoulos[1], Loris Marchal[1(✉)], Adrien Obrecht[2], and Bertrand Simon[3]

[1] CNRS, International Laboratory on Learning Systems, Montreal, Canada
{spyros.angelopoulos, loris.marchal}@cnrs.fr
[2] École Normale Supérieure de Lyon, Lyon, France
adrien.obrecht@ens-lyon.fr
[3] CNRS IN2P3 Computing Center, Lyon, France
bertrand.simon@cnrs.fr

Abstract. Large language models (LLMs) have demonstrated remarkable capabilities across a variety of tasks. One of the main challenges towards the successful deployment of LLMs is memory management, since they typically involve billions of parameters. To this end, architectures based on Mixture-of-Experts have been proposed, which aim to reduce the size of the parameters that are activated when producing a token. This raises the equally critical issue of efficiently managing the limited *cache* of the system, in that frequently used experts should be stored in the fast cache rather than in the slower secondary memory.

In this work, we introduce and study a new *paging* problem that models expert management optimization. Our formulation captures both the layered architecture of LLMs and the requirement that experts are cached efficiently. We first present lower bounds on the *competitive ratio* of both deterministic and randomized algorithms, which show that under mild assumptions, LRU-like policies have good theoretical competitive performance. We then propose a layer-based extension of LRU that is tailored to the problem at hand. Extensive simulations on both synthetic datasets and actual traces of MoE usage show that our algorithm outperforms policies for the classic paging problem, such as the standard LRU.

Keywords: Caching/Paging · Large Language Models · online algorithms · competitive analysis

1 Introduction

Large Language Models (LLMs) have revolutionized the application of AI in fields as diverse as text generation, machine translation, and natural language understanding. LLMs such as GPT-4, PaLM and LLaMA are at the core of applications ranging from conversational agents to code generation tools, bringing unprecedented fluency and accuracy to text production. The performance of

LLMs is closely tied to their *size*, with modern models consisting of billions or even trillions of parameters [16]. While this scale greatly enhances performance, it also poses a major challenge: the management of the immense computational resources required for their training and usage.

Once trained, LLMs are deployed for *inference*, the process of generating text or predictions, which typically needs to be rapid for real-time applications. However, inference is computationally intensive, and thus particularly demanding in resource-constrained environments such as mobile devices or systems with limited memory and processing power. This challenge has led to extensive research into optimization methods that enhance efficiency without significantly compromising model accuracy. Notable approaches include model compression techniques such as quantization [18], which reduces the precision of model parameters (commonly known as *weights*), and sparsification [12], which prunes less important parameters.

One well-established strategy for model sparsification is the Mixture of Experts (MoE) architecture. We provide a high-level overview of this model, and we refer to [7,21] for a more detailed technical definition. A MoE model consists of a sequence of *transformer layers* (or layers, for simplicity). Each layer is composed of an *attention* mechanism, which selectively focuses on the most relevant parts of the input, and a MoE block, as depicted in Fig. 1. A *gating* function uses the attention output to determine which experts in the MoE block are activated, while the others remain inactive. This approach offers two key advantages: first, it achieves high accuracy in text generation tasks because the model can leverage a large pool of weights across all the experts. Second, since only a small proportion of experts are active during each inference, it significantly reduces storage and computational costs.

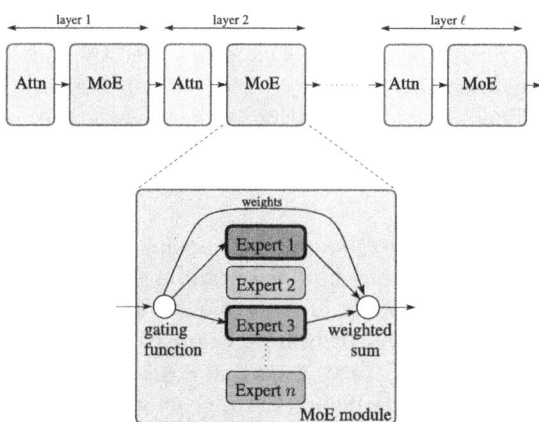

Fig. 1. High-level illustration of the Mixture-of-Experts architecture

While MoE models allow for a selective, and parsimonious activation of experts, their management remains challenging. First, in order to maintain high accuracy, the combined size of all the experts' weights is generally larger than the total size of weights in non-MoE models [16], leading to storage complications. LLMs are autoregressive models, meaning that the entire pipeline of *all* layers has to be processed for the production of each token–a word or a portion of a word in the generated text. Hence, even though only a limited number of experts are activated per layer for each token, loading their weights into memory incurs a significant cost that adds to the overall computational cost. Such issues were observed in [8], which showed that caching certain experts weights in the memory, instead of reloading them for each layer, improved the inference time. This was achieved using a simple Least-Recently-Used (LRU) replacement policy. However, the following question arises naturally:

What are the power and limitations of caching policies for MoE models of LLMs? What theoretical and experimental improvements can one obtain, especially relative to standard caching approaches suitable for much simpler environments, such as LRU?

1.1 Contribution

In this work, we answer the above question by introducing and studying a new model of *online caching* that is tailored to the characteristics of MoE-based LLMs. The model allows us to provide rigorous theoretical bounds on the performance of both deterministic and randomized caching policies, using the framework of *competitive* analysis [5]. This framework has been infuential in the study of many other variants of caching (see Sect. 1.2 for related works) and we likewise demonstrate, for the first time, that it can be equally useful in the context of LLMs.

In Sect. 2 we describe in detail a *layered* model of caching, which defines the interactions between the experts across the layers, and involves parameters such as the number of layers ℓ, the number of experts n, and the cache size k. In Sect. 3 we give lower bounds on the competitive ratio of deterministic and randomized caching policies. These bounds show that as long as the parameters n or ℓ are constant (which is typically the case in all current models), the best-possible competitive ratios cannot improve, asymptotically, upon standard policies such as LRU.

While the theoretical lower bounds may seem, at first sight, quite restrictive, they provide insights about how to obtain algorithms that perform better in practice. In Sect. 4 we propose an extension of LRU that is adapted to the problem at hand. In Sect. 5 we perform an extensive experimental evaluation of our algorithm on a variety of traces from real data of MoE usage, as well as on synthetic datasets. The results demonstrate that our algorithm clearly outperforms standard LRU, and showcases the benefits of a layered-based approach in the deployment of efficient cache policies.

1.2 Related Work

Online caching, also known as *paging*, is one of the fundamental online optimization problems, and has served as proving grounds for the introduction and the development of competitive analysis. In their seminal work, Sleator and Tarjan [20] considered the standard model with a cache size k, and showed that an optimal deterministic competitive ratio equal to k can be achieved by a variety of *marking* policies, to which LRU belongs. Randomization can help improve the competitive ratio to a tight bound $H_k = \Theta(\log k)$, where H_n is the n-th harmonic number [11].

2 Layered Paging: a Model for MoE Caching in LLMs

In this section, we formulate the problem we will study, and which serves as a model of LLM caching. We first discuss, in Sect. 2.1, the pertinent structure and properties of MoE architectures, then in Sect. 2.2 we define the problem of layered paging.

2.1 Caching in MoE Architectures

Text generation with LLMs involves producing a sequence of *tokens*, which are units of text that can represent words, subwords, or punctuation marks. To generate a single token, the model processes information through ℓ layers sequentially. Once the last layer is processed, the token is produced and then fed back into the first layer to begin the computation for the next token. This cycle repeats until an "End of Text" token is generated or the maximum number of tokens is reached. In modern LLMs, the number of layers ℓ typically ranges from 10 to 100, depending on the model's size and complexity. In the MoE paradigm, in particular, each layer involves n experts, which are specialized neural network modules that enhance model efficiency and performance. In current models, n generally varies between 8 and 256. We denote by $E_i^{(j)}$ the ith expert in layer j, where $i \in [1, n]$ and $j \in [1, \ell]$.

In a MoE module, only a few experts, among the n total, are typically required. For simplicity, we consider here that a single expert per layer is requested. That is, in order to produce a single token, the required (ordered) series of experts is of the form $E_{i_1}^{(1)}, E_{i_2}^{(2)}, \ldots, E_{i_\ell}^{(\ell)}$, for some $i_1, \ldots, i_\ell$. Hence, the total series of experts that we have to process to produce all tokens is of the form

$$E_{i_1^1}^{(1)}, E_{i_2^1}^{(2)}, \ldots, E_{i_\ell^1}^{(\ell)}, E_{i_1^2}^{(1)}, E_{i_2^2}^{(2)}, \ldots, E_{i_\ell^2}^{(\ell)}, \ldots$$

Computing an expert requires its data (i.e., the weights of the neural network) to be loaded in the memory. Thus, to speed up computation, it is important to ensure that frequently reused expert data are kept in the fast cache memory which is of limited size k (we assume that all experts produce data of the same size). Figure 2 provides an illustration.

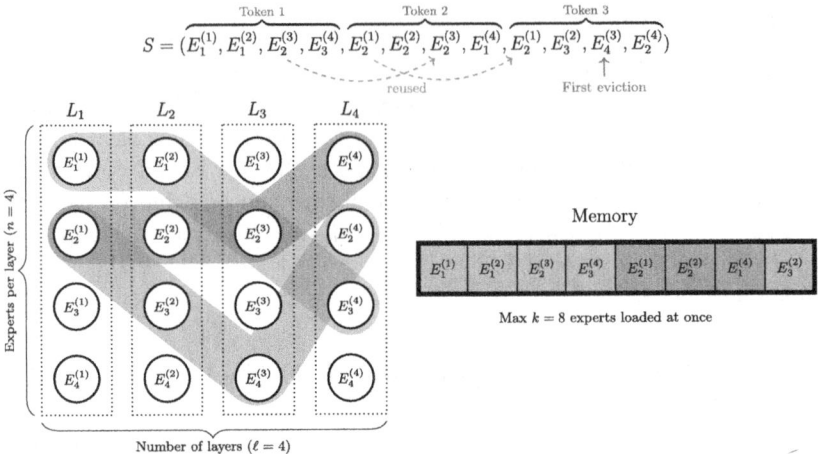

Fig. 2. Example of experts used in the production of three tokens. The models has $\ell = 4$ layers, each with $n = 4$ experts. The experts used for each token are represented by a different color. Expert $E_2^{(3)}$ is used for token 1 and reused for 2, hence resulting in a cache hit. The figure on the right depicts the state of the cache when processing the third layer for token 3: Expert $E_4^{(3)}$ is requested, but the memory is already full, hence some other expert needs to be evicted.

2.2 Layered Paging

We now proceed with the formal definition of our problem, which captures the setting discussed in the previous section. We say that the data produced by each expert corresponds to a *page*, and recall that the cache has a capacity k, in that it can store k pages. There are $n\ell$ possible pages in total, given that each of the n experts may produce a page in each of the ℓ layers. The set of pages P can be thus decomposed in ℓ disjoint sets $L_1, \ldots L_\ell$, each of cardinality n. We denote the pages inside each set L_i as $\{p_1^{(i)}, p_2^{(i)}, \ldots, p_n^{(i)}\}$. The input σ to our problem is a sequence of pages $\sigma = p_1, p_2, \ldots$, with the constraint that $p_i \in L_{(i-1 \bmod \ell)+1}$, modeling the layered structure of experts in the MoE architecture. For the purpose of analysis, a *round* in σ is defined as a consecutive block of pages of the form $p_j, \ldots, p_{j+\ell-1}$ where p_i with $i \in [j, j+\ell-1]$ belongs to layer L_{i-j+1}, so ℓ divides $j-1$. For an illustration, each round is depicted in Fig. 2 by its proper color.

Having defined the set of pages and the structure of an input sequence, the optimization objective is as in the standard online paging. Namely, if a requested page is present in the cache, which corresponds to a cache *hit*, then the page is served at zero cost. In contrast, if a requested page is not in the cache, which corresponds to a cache *miss*, then the algorithm must determine which page to evict from the cache, in order to bring in the requested page. In this case, the page is served at cost equal to 1. Note that any paging algorithm can be fully described as a cache eviction policy, which determines the page to be evicted in the event of a cache miss.

We will refer to the above problem as the ℓ-*layer paging* problem, or *layered paging*, for simplicity. Note that this problem is a generalization of standard online paging, since the latter is equivalent to 1-layered paging. To analyze the performance of algorithms for the problem, we will rely on the canonical framework of competitive analysis. Let A denote an online paging algorithm, and $A(\sigma)$ its *cost* on input σ, i.e., the total number of cache misses it incurs on σ. Let also OPT denote an optimal *offline* algorithm that has foreknowledge of σ. It is known that an optimal offline algorithm is the one that, upon each request that results in a cache miss, evicts a page that will be requested the furthest in the future [3].

Definition 1 (Competitive Ratio). *A deterministic algorithm A is r-competitive if there is a constant $c \in \mathbb{R}$ such that for any request sequence σ, it holds that*
$$A(\sigma) \leqslant r \cdot \mathrm{OPT}(\sigma) + c.$$
Similarly, a randomized algorithm A is r-competitive if for every request σ
$$\mathbb{E}(A(\sigma)) \leqslant r \cdot \mathrm{OPT}(\sigma) + c,$$
where the expectation is over the random choices of A.

We will denote by $\mathrm{Cr}(A)$ the competitive ratio of an algorithm A.

3 Competitive Analysis of Layered Paging

In this section, we present theoretical results on the competitive ratio of deterministic and randomized algorithms for layered paging. Due to space limitations, we omit or only sketch certain technical proofs. We refer to the complete version of this work [2] for all technical details and proofs.

3.1 Deterministic Algorithms

A first approach is to consider an online algorithm that devotes a predetermined portion of the cache to requests of each layer; e.g., a portion of size approximately equal to k/ℓ to each layer. While such simple approaches are used in practical implementations [8], we show that they result in poor theoretical performance. Fixed cache partitions lead to inefficiencies, aligning with prior results on parallel paging [1].

Theorem 1. *Any deterministic algorithm that allocates a fixed portion of the cache to a requests of a given layer has unbounded competitive ratio, as long as $n \geqslant 2$ and $\ell \geqslant 2$.*

The following theorem provides a lower bound on the competitive ratio of any deterministic algorithm. The result shows that the best competitive ratio cannot be much smaller than that of standard online paging, namely k.

Theorem 2. *For every value of ℓ, every deterministic layered paging algorithm has a competitive ratio at least $k - \ell + 1$.*

LRU is k-competitive for layered paging, since it is k-competitive in standard paging, but does it achieve a better competitive ratio for ℓ-layered paging? The following theorem answers in the negative, for any ℓ.

Theorem 3. *For any ℓ and k such that ℓ divides $k+1$, $Cr(\text{LRU}) \geq k$.*

3.2 Randomized Algorithms

In this section we turn our attention to randomized algorithms. Recall that in standard online paging, randomization can help improving the competitive ratio to $H_k = \Theta(\log k)$, which is tight, as discussed in Sect. 1.2. The following theorem is the main result of this section, which establishes a lower bound on the competitive ratio for the layered paging problem.

Theorem 4. *Every randomized algorithm for ℓ-layered paging with n experts has competitive ratio at least $\max(H_n, \frac{\log(\ell)}{6n})$.*

Before we present the proof of Theorem 4, let us discuss its significance. First, note that layered paging becomes trivial from the point of view of competitive analysis if $k \geq n\ell$: this is because the algorithm can store all pages in the cache, and thus achieve a competitive ratio equal to 1. We can thus assume that $k \leq n\ell$. Hence, if $n \in O(1)$, then Theorem 4 shows a lower bound $\Omega(\log \ell) = \Omega(\log k)$. Similarly, if $\ell \in O(1)$, then the theorem shows a lower bound of $\Omega(\log n) = \Omega(\log k)$. Therefore, the result shows that if either n or ℓ is constant (as typically in practice), then any randomized algorithm has competitive ratio at least $\Omega(\log k)$, which is tight.

To prove Theorem 4, we will rely on a variant of the coupon collector problem known as the *parallel* coupon collector problem [10]. In this problem, there are N different types of coupons, and C agents (collectors). In each round, each of the C agents selects one of the N coupon types uniformly at random. Agents are not allowed to exchange or share their coupons. Define $T(N, C)$ as the number of rounds after which each agent has collected all N coupons. Note that this problem is a generalization of the well-known vanilla coupon collector problem in which $C = 1$ [4], which is a key part in the analysis of the standard online paging problem [17]. We are interested in bounding from below the *cover time*, namely the quantity $\mathbb{E}(T(N, C))$. We accomplish this in the following theorem, as previous work did not establish usable bounds [10].

Theorem 5. *For the parallel coupon collector with $N \geq 2$ coupons and C agents, its cover time is such that*

$$\mathbb{E}(T(N, C)) \geq \max\{N \cdot H_N, \frac{\log C}{6}\}.$$

Proof. We prove the lower bounds separately, starting by $\mathbb{E}(T(N,C)) \geqslant N \cdot H_N$.

We focus of the first collector, corresponding to the first layer. We know from the traditional coupon collector problem that it will finish on average after NH_N rounds. By definition, all the collectors finish collecting their coupons after the first collector finishes its collection, hence the first bound: $\mathbb{E}(T(N,C)) \geqslant \mathbb{E}(T(N,1)) = NH_N$.

We now show that $\mathbb{E}(T(N,C)) \geqslant \frac{\log(C)}{6}$ for $N \geqslant 2$.

We first compute the probability of the expected time to complete all collections to be larger than t. By definition:

$$\mathbb{P}(T(N,C) \geqslant t) = 1 - \mathbb{P}(T(N,C) < t) = 1 - \prod_{i=1}^{\ell} \mathbb{P}(T(N,1) < t).$$

Considering only the probability of not getting the first coupon, we get:

$$\mathbb{P}(T(N,C) \geqslant t) \geqslant 1 - (1 - (\frac{N-1}{N})^t)^C \geqslant 1 - \exp(-C(\frac{N-1}{N})^t).$$

For $t = \log(\frac{C}{\log(2)}) / \log(\frac{N}{N-1})$, we have $\mathbb{P}(T(N,C) \geqslant t) \geqslant \frac{1}{2}$.

Thus $\mathbb{E}(T(N,C)) \geqslant \log(\frac{C}{\log(2)}) / 2\log(\frac{N}{N-1}) \geqslant \frac{\log(C)}{6}$.

□

We can now proceed with the proof of Theorem 4. It relies on showing that every randomized paging algorithm has a competitive ratio at least $\frac{\ell}{k} \cdot \mathbb{E}(T(n,\ell))$.

Proof. (Theorem 4).

We consider an instance of the layered paging problem such that $n\ell = k+1$. Let A be a randomized algorithm. Using Yao's principle, we consider a random sequence σ as input, such that the i-th requested page σ_i is drawn uniformly at random among the n pages of layer $i \mod \ell$, while A is considered deterministic.

At the start of a round, the deterministic algorithm has all pages but one in cache. There is at least a $\frac{1}{n}$ chance of having a cache miss per round, the probability of drawing the missing page. There are $\frac{|\sigma|}{\ell}$ rounds, thus we have:

$$\mathbb{E}(A(\sigma)) \geqslant \frac{|\sigma|}{\ell n}.$$

For the analysis of the optimal algorithm OPT, we partition the random sequence σ into blocks such that each block is a minimal contiguous sub-sequence containing $k+1$ distinct elements. OPT must suffer at least one cache miss per block, as its cache is missing one requested page at the start of each block. It remains to estimate the size of the blocks. There is an equivalence with the parallel coupon collector problem, with n coupons and ℓ collectors, associating a round of ℓ requests to one parallel step of all collectors. The average length of a block is then $\mathbb{E}(T(n,\ell))$ rounds of ℓ requests. For a sequence σ long enough compared to n and ℓ, we can estimate the number of blocks in the sequence to the inverse of the average length of a block times the length of the sequence. We therefore obtain $\mathbb{E}(\text{OPT}(\sigma)) \leqslant \frac{|\sigma|}{\ell \mathbb{E}(T(n,\ell))}$. We conclude:

$$\mathbb{E}(A(\sigma)) \geqslant \frac{|\sigma|}{\ell n} \geqslant \mathbb{E}(\text{OPT}(\sigma)) \frac{\ell \mathbb{E}(T(n,\ell))}{\ell n}.$$

Thus $\text{Cr}(A) \geqslant \frac{\mathbb{E}(T(n,\ell))}{n}$, for a long enough σ.

Theorem 4 then follows from Theorem 5 :

$$\text{Cr}(A) \geqslant \frac{\mathbb{E}(T(n,\ell))}{n} \geqslant \max\left(H_n, \frac{\log(\ell)}{6n}\right).$$

□

Contrarily to the classical paging problem, it is still an open question whether there exist randomized algorithms reaching this ratio, or simply with a better competitive ratio that H_k.

4 A Layered Extension of the LRU Algorithm

In this section, we propose an extension of the LRU algorithm adapted to the problem at hand. The algorithm handles better some pathological scenarios specific to this problem. More specifically, note that the standard LRU policy evicts the oldest page in the cache, regardless of which layer it belongs to. This is intuitively inefficient: if a page of layer i is currently served, then it is generally unsafe to evict a page belonging to layer $i + 1$, since it may be requested in the immediately following step. Instead, a more reasonable choice is to evict a page of layer $i - 1$ or even i. We thus seek a *layer-specific* variant of LRU, and to this end we define two quantities, specific to a page p in cache and a time t.

Definition 2. *Given a page p in the cache at the current time t, let $\tau(p,t)$ denote the last time that p was requested. We define the* last-round index *of p, denoted by $R(p,t) = \lfloor \frac{t-\tau(p,t)}{\ell} \rfloor$, as the number of rounds between $\tau(p,t)$ and t. We also define the* relative layer distance *of p, noted $D(p,t) = \tau(p,t) - t \mod \ell$, as the number of requests needed before reaching the layer in which p belongs.*

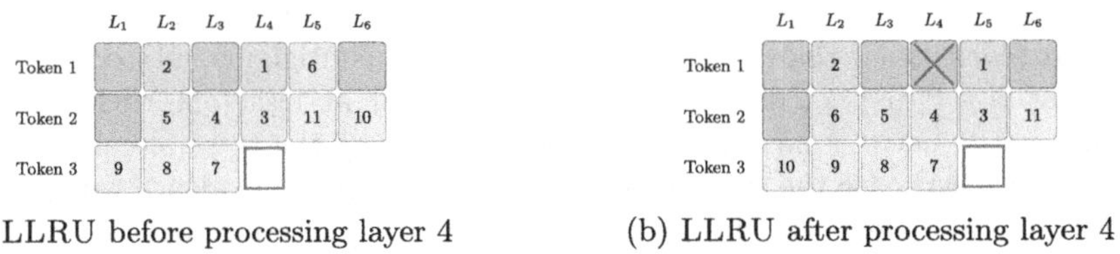

(a) LLRU before processing layer 4

(b) LLRU after processing layer 4

Fig. 3. One step of the LLRU algorithm. The colored pages are the ones still in the cache. All pages that have the same last-round index are of the same color, with the number indicating the eviction priority given by the LLRU algorithm.

Using the above definitions, we define the *Layered Last Recently Used* caching algorithm (LLRU), as the policy which, on a cache miss at time t, evicts the page p with largest index $R(p,t)$, and in the event of ties evicts the page with largest index $D(p,t)$. This allows, intuitively, to evict pages which have not been requested since a large number of rounds, and whose layer will be requested the latest. Figure 3 illustrates an execution of LLRU.

5 Performance Evaluation Through Simulations

5.1 Datasets and Paging Strategies

Datasets. We use two different datasets in this section: traces coming from real MoE usage, and synthetic datasets to study the sensitivity of caching strategies to specific parameters.

The synthetic dataset is created by associating to each page a frequency of usage, sampled using a Zipf distribution. Such distributions have been proven to accurately model real-life cache systems [6,14]. In a nutshell, a few pages will be frequently requested, while the other pages will rarely be requested. In practice, with two law parameters a and b, the j-th page of a layer will have a probability of being sampled $p_j \sim \frac{1}{(j+b)^a}$.

Regarding MoE traces, we use two MoE LLMs: (a) the Mixtral 7B model [13] (with $\ell = 32$ layers and $n = 8$ experts per layer) on 1000 prompts from the VMWare Open Instruct dataset[1] and (b) the Llama-MoE model [22] (with $n = 16$ and $\ell = 32$) on 100 prompts from the "helpful instructions" dataset [9]. For each model, we record the experts used for each token, for each layer. Since both models use several experts for each layer (2 among 8 for Mixtral, 4 among 16 for Llama-MoE), while our model assumes a single expert used for each layer, we create several rounds for the processing of a single token: one round for the first expert, a second round for the second expert, etc. For instance, for the Mixtral model, if the experts used to produce one token are $(E_1^{(1)}, E_2^{(1)})$ for the first layer, $(E_1^{(2)}, E_2^{(2)})$ for the second layer, up to $(E_1^{(32)}, E_2^{(32)})$, we replace this sequence by the following two rounds: $E_1^{(1)}, \ldots, E_1^{(32)}$ then $E_2^{(1)}, \ldots, E_2^{(32)}$.

Strategies. In addition to the LLRU strategy described above, we use strategies from the classical paging problem: LRU as well as the MARKING randomized algorithm [11]. These strategies can be applied either on the whole problem with the whole cache, without being aware of the layers, or on each layer with a specific cache of size k/ℓ per layer. We denote this last variant by DIST: LRU-DIST, MARKER-DIST, etc., to show that the cache is distributed among layers. We also consider an optimal offline strategy OPT (that knows the whole sequence of requests) that follow Belady's rule [3] for comparison.

---

[1] https://huggingface.co/datasets/VMware/open-instruct.

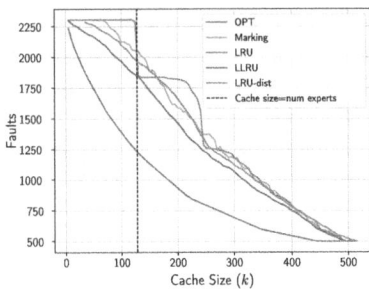 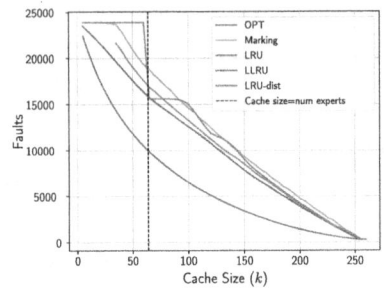

(a) Cache performance on one Llama trace

(b) Cache performance on one Mixtral trace

Fig. 4. Comparison of LRU, LLRU, MARKING and OPT caching policies while varying cache size k

5.2 Results on MoE Traces

Our first experiments are direct comparisons of the previously described caching strategies on real MoE traces. In Fig. 4, we plot the number of cache misses of each algorithm on a single MoE trace with a cache size k varying from 1 (no cache hit) to $n\ell$ (no cache miss). As expected in both extreme cases, all the strategies fault equally as much as OPT and the scheduling strategies are irrelevant. The intermediate values exhibit differences between strategies, and a sizable gap to OPT that can go up to ×2.5. The first observation from this figure is the great fluctuation in performance of LRU depending on k. This well-known phenomenon is inherent to the cyclic behavior of LRU which can evict pages right before they get requested again, similarly to its worst case against OPT described in Sect. 3.1. This is the reason why real life applications use the LRU-DIST strategy instead which limits the fluctuations of performance, but we observe that this decision comes with an increased number of faults which we will further evaluate in the next section. In comparison, we observe that LLRU gets the best of both worlds, achieving the lowest number of faults across online strategies, while keeping a very smooth progression with respect to the cache size. These observations are confirmed by Fig. 5, which represents the distribution of the normalized number of cache faults of each previously mentioned algorithm for ten MoE traces. Here, we take a cache of fixed size 200 for both models to display two different "modes": Mixtral almost fits entirely (256 total experts) while LLama can't even store half (512 experts). The relative performance of algorithms is consistent with other cache sizes and in particular LLRU significantly outperforms other policies. In this particular setting, LLRU makes $\sim 15\%$ less faults than LRU and $\sim 7\%$ less than LLRU-DIST for the LLama model, and is still ~ 4–5% faster than LRU-DIST on the Mixtral traces, though the choice of k makes the instances very constrained. Furthermore, this figures demonstrates that these performance gains are pretty consistent, with a rather small interquartile spread.

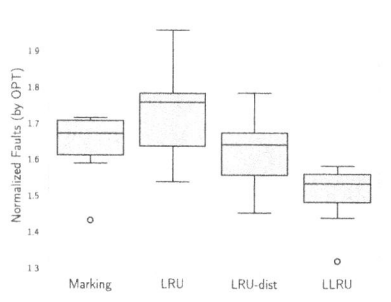
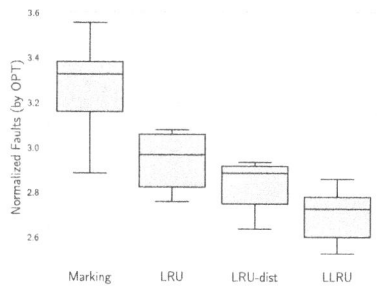

(a) Cache performance on 10 Llama traces

(b) Cache performance on 10 Mixtral traces

Fig. 5. Comparison of normalized faults (by OPT) for the LRU, LRU-DIST, LLRU and MARKING caching policies with $k = 200$

5.3 Shared Vs. Distributed Cache

This second set of experiments aims at exploring the performance gap between shared and unified cache systems. We saw in Sect. 3 that an algorithm that splits the cache can have an arbitrarily big competitive ratio, which we want to test in practice. In Fig. 6a, we compare the number of faults of OPT and OPT-DIST using a synthetic trace generated with a Zipf distribution, for a range of values of n and ℓ and a fixed cache of size k. We observe that for the values for which everything fits in the cache, the ratio is 1, but whenever this is not possible anymore, OPT-DIST makes significantly more cache faults, up to 3× more than OPT. Using some reasonable values for an MoE system (32 layers, 8 experts per layer and 64 experts fitting in the cache), we show in Figrue 6b how the a parameter of the underlying Zipf law affects the performances. We observe two effects: when a is very big, the data disparity is such that almost always the

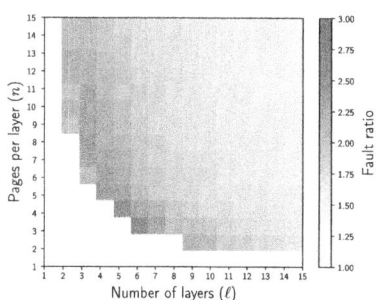
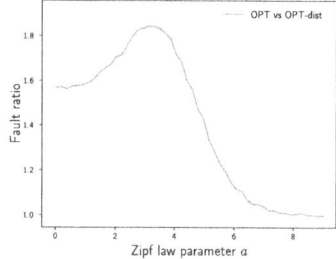

(a) Comparison of OPT and OPT-DIST on a Zipf distribution of parameter 2 with $k = 16$ and several values of n and ℓ

(b) Fault ratio between OPT and OPT-DIST on a Zipf distribution with $k = 64$, $\ell = 32$ and $n = 8$ with a varying law parameter a

Fig. 6. Comparison of OPT and OPT-DIST

same one expert will be chosen at each layer, hence both OPT and OPT-DIST achieve similar results. Whenever a gets smaller, page disparity between layers is still present, and OPT-DIST starts underperforming, with up to 1.8× more page faults. More importantly, whenever a gets close to 0, i.e. there is no rank imbalance, OPT-DIST still performs poorly. This further solidifies the theoretical findings of Sect. 3 and real life experiments of Sect. 5.2 which states that split caching is sub-optimal and should not be used in practice.

6 Conclusion

We introduced and studied a new online paging problem, namely *layered paging*, as a formulation of cache management in the widely-used Mixture-of-Experts architecture of Large Language Systems. To our knowledge, this is the first study of competitive analysis in the context of LLM caching. We established several lower bounds on the competitive ratio that characterize the limitations of both deterministic and randomized algorithms, and which are near-tight if either the number of layers or the number of experts is a small constant, as typical in practice. We also proposed a simple, yet efficient adaptation of the Least-Recently-Used paging strategy that is tailored to LLMs/MoEs, while retaining the worst-case guarantees of the standard LRU. We experimentally demonstrated, using both real and synthetic data, that this new strategy yields significant improvements over the standard LRU.

This work paves the way for future studies of this challenging problem. Notably, we would like to close the theoretical gap between the lower and the upper bounds which exists if n and ℓ are allowed to have arbitrary and unrestricted growth. In addition, while our formulation assumes, for simplicity, that a single expert is used at each layer, it would be interesting to consider the more general model in which several experts are involved in each layer. Last, an interesting direction for future work is to consider *learning-augmented* variants, in which the algorithm can leverage a machine-learned prediction about future input items. Such prediction models have been extremely influential in the standard online paging [15], and some simple predictors have already been proposed in the context of MoE/LLMs [8].

Artifact Availability. The artifact is available in the Zenodo repository [19].

Acknowledgments. This work was partially funded by the project PREDICTIONS, grant ANR-23-CE48-0010 from the French National Research Agency (ANR).

Disclosure of Interests. The authors have no competing interests to declare that are relevant to the content of this article.

References

1. Agrawal, K., Bender, M.A., Das, R., Kuszmaul, W., Peserico, E., Scquizzato, M.: Green paging and parallel paging. In: ACM Symposium on Parallelism in Algorithms and Architectures (SPAA), pp. 493–495 (2020)
2. Angelopoulos, S., Marchal, L., Obrecht, A., Simon, B.: Cache management for mixture-of-experts LLMs – extended version (2025), https://hal.science/hal-04961621
3. Belady, L.A.: A study of replacement algorithms for virtual-storage computer. IBM Syst. J. **5**(2), 78–101 (1966)
4. Blom, G., Holst, L., Sandell, D.: Problems and Snapshots from the World of Probability. Springer Science & Business Media (1993)
5. Borodin, A., El-Yaniv, R.: Online Computation and Competitive Analysis. Cambridge University Press, New York, NY, USA (1998)
6. Canon, L.C., Dugois, A., Marchal, L., Rivière, E.: Hector: a framework to design and evaluate scheduling strategies in persistent key-value stores. In: International Conference on Parallel Processing, ICPP 2023, pp. 535–545 (2023)
7. Du, N., et al.: Glam: efficient scaling of language models with mixture-of-experts. In: International Conference on Machine Learning, pp. 5547–5569 (2022)
8. Eliseev, A., Mazur, D.: Fast inference of mixture-of-experts language models with offloading (2023), https://arxiv.org/abs/2312.17238
9. Face, H.: Helpful instructions dataset, https://huggingface.co/datasets/HuggingFaceH4/helpful-instructions
10. Ferrante, M., Tagliavini, A.: On the coupon-collector's problem with several parallel collections (2016), https://arxiv.org/abs/1609.04174
11. Fiat, A., Karp, R.M., Luby, M., McGeoch, L.A., Sleator, D.D., Young, N.E.: Competitive paging algorithms. J. Algorithms **12**(4), 685–699 (1991)
12. Hoefler, T., Alistarh, D., Ben-Nun, T., Dryden, N., Peste, A.: Sparsity in deep learning: pruning and growth for efficient inference and training in neural networks. J. Mach. Learn. Res. **22**(241), 1–124 (2021)
13. Jiang, A.Q., et al.: Mixtral of experts (2024), https://doi.org/10.48550/arXiv.2401.04088
14. Kotera, I., Egawa, R., Takizawa, H., Kobayashi, H.: Modeling of cache access behavior based on Zipf's law. In: 9th Workshop on MEmory Performance: DEaling with Applications, Systems and Architecture, MEDEA 2008, pp. 9–15 (2008)
15. Lykouris, T., Vassilvitskii, S.: Competitive caching with machine learned advice. In: Dy, J.G., Krause, A. (eds.) International Conference on Machine Learning, (ICML), vol. 80, pp. 3302–3311 (2018)
16. Minaee, S., et al.: Large language models: a survey (2024), https://arxiv.org/abs/2402.06196
17. Motwani, R., Raghavan, P.: Randomized Algorithms. Cambridge University Press (1995)
18. Nagel, M., Fournarakis, M., Amjad, R.A., Bondarenko, Y., van Baalen, M., Blankevoort, T.: A white paper on neural network quantization (2021), https://arxiv.org/abs/2106.08295
19. Simon, B., Marchal, L., Angelopoulos, S., Obrecht, A.: Artifact of the paper: cache management for mixture-of-experts LLMs, June 2025, https://doi.org/10.5281/zenodo.15576758
20. Sleator, D.D., Tarjan, R.E.: Amortized efficiency of list update and paging rules. Commun. ACM **28**(2), 202–208 (1985)

21. Vaswani, A., et al.: Attention is all you need. In: Neural Information Processing Systems conference (NeurIPS), pp. 5998–6008 (2017)
22. Zhu, T., et al.: Llama-moe: building mixture-of-experts from llama with continual pre-training (2024), https://arxiv.org/abs/2406.16554

Byzantine-Tolerant Consensus in GPU-Inspired Shared Memory

Chryssis Georgiou[1], Manaswini Piduguralla[2(✉)], and Sathya Peri[2]

[1] University of Cyprus, Nicosia, Cyprus
chryssis@ucy.ac.cy
[2] Indian Institute of Technology Hyderabad, Hyderabad, India
cs20resch11007@iith.ac.in, sathya_p@cse.iith.ac.in

Abstract. In this work, we formalize a novel shared memory model inspired by the popular GPU architecture. Within this model, we develop algorithmic solutions to the Byzantine Consensus problem and analyze their fault-resilience.

Keywords: GPU · Byzantine failures · Consensus · Shared memory · CAS

1 Introduction

In modern computing, Graphics Processing Units (GPUs) have transcended their traditional role in graphics rendering, emerging as powerful platforms for parallel computation. Unlike conventional CPUs, which have been widely studied, GPUs offer a fundamentally different architectural approach. We believe that leveraging GPU-based models can provide innovative solutions to critical distributed computing challenges, including consensus, leader election, and atomic broadcast. In this paper, we introduce a GPU-inspired computational model and demonstrate its effectiveness in addressing the Byzantine consensus problem. To establish a foundational understanding of GPU architecture, we first present key concepts.

The GPU Architecture. GPU is a specialized processor originally developed to meet the demands of the rapidly expanding video game industry. Designed to execute a large number of floating point calculations and memory operations per video frame in advanced games, GPUs have since found widespread applications in scientific computing, artificial intelligence (AI), and high performance computing (HPC) [13]. Unlike traditional Central Processing Units (CPUs), which excel at managing complex control logic, GPUs are optimized for efficiently handling thousands of simple parallel tasks.

Figure 1 presents a high-level overview of a typical GPU architecture. The architecture is built around *Streaming Multiprocessors (SMs)*, which are the fundamental computational units. Each SM comprises multiple processing units, known as *streaming processors* or *cores*. However, these cores lack individual

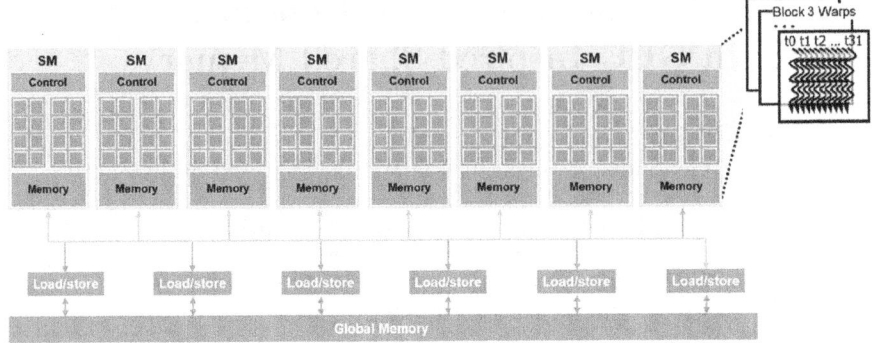

Fig. 1. Illustration of CUDA-capable GPU Architecture [13]

program counters, unlike CPU cores. Within an SM, the computation is further organized into **thread blocks**, where each block consists of a group of threads that collaborate and share local resources, such as registers and shared memory. Execution within an SM occurs in groups of (currently) 32 threads, referred to as *warps*, which operate under the **Single Instruction, Multiple Threads (SIMT)** execution model. In this model, all threads within a warp execute the same instructions simultaneously but possibly on different data. Additionally, suppose that the total number of active threads in a warp is fewer than the number of available cores. In that case, the unused cores will remain idle, underutilizing the GPU's processing power. Thus, *threads within a warp execute synchronously* in a lock-step fashion, whereas *warps within a block execute asynchronously* and may proceed in any order relative to one another. The hierarchy of GPU components and the execution model is illustrated in Fig. 2.

Registers and shared memory are on-chip memories, and registers are allocated to individual threads; each thread can access only its own registers [13]. Shared memory is allocated to thread blocks; all threads in a block can access shared memory variables declared for the block. Some GPU implementations (example: NVIDIA) come with their own hardware internal scheduler, called **warp scheduler**, which allocates the warps to whatever GPU hardware is present [22]. Each warp executes instructions in cycles, with the warp scheduler selecting which warps to execute based on resource availability. In each cycle, a warp executes a constant (e.g., one or two) number of instructions [6,19]. This scheduling approach is

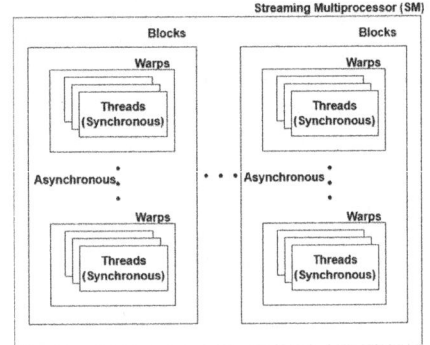

Fig. 2. Illustration of GPU Hierarchy

designed to mask the latency that warps experience while preparing the next instruction for execution.

GPUs and CPUs have fundamentally different architectures which are optimized for distinct workloads. CPUs are designed to minimize instruction execution latency, whereas GPUs are built to maximize throughput [13]. As discussed earlier, threads within a warp execute synchronously, while execution across warps is asynchronous. The warp scheduler also ensures progress for the threads, which otherwise can be a major challenge in designing solutions for asynchronous processes. Additionally, constructing shared memory with varying read-write access across multiple threads is not as straightforward as in CPUs.

Byzantine Faults in GPU Systems. In modern computing environments, GPUs are increasingly shared across multiple processes, such as in NVIDIA's Multi-Process Service (MPS), requiring a mechanism for fair, efficient and fault-tolerant resource allocation [25]. Furthermore, in HPC clusters, where multiple GPUs collaborate on complex computations, failures in individual nodes can jeopardize the integrity of the entire task. Another key motivation stems from the well-documented observation that GPUs exhibit a higher susceptibility to hardware errors compared to CPUs [4].

These hardware faults can manifest as arbitrary or erroneous software behavior, which can be particularly challenging to predict and mitigate. Transient faults, such as bit flips caused by cosmic rays or voltage fluctuations, are notoriously difficult to model. We argue that a Byzantine fault-tolerant (BFT) approach is well-suited for handling such unpredictable failures, as it can provide correctness guarantees even in the presence of arbitrary faults.

Motivation for Byzantine Consensus in GPUs. Agreement among multiple parties is a fundamental problem in distributed computing for a wide range of applications [16]. Considerable research efforts have been directed toward delving into consensus mechanisms within shared memory systems. Currently, there is an increased emphasis on Byzantine fault-tolerant shared objects [5, 15]. This interest is further motivated by the universality of consensus [9], as solving consensus enables the wait-free implementation of all shared objects in asynchronous systems.

A robust consensus protocol can ensure priority-aware scheduling, prevent resource starvation, and optimize performance in multi-tenant GPU systems [14]. Thus, considering the popularity of GPU systems and the Byzantine errors that can possibly be exhibited by these systems (as argued above), in this work we explore Byzantine Fault-tolerant Consensus algorithms in GPU Shared memory systems.

Contributions. The main contributions of this paper are the following:

(a) We formalize a novel GPU-inspired Shared Memory Model that abstracts the unique features of the GPU architecture detailed above (Sect. 2).
(b) We detail the Byzantine Consensus problems we consider in this work (Sect. 3) and develop a Byzantine-tolerant consensus solution tailored for this memory model, thus demonstrating its utility (Sect. 4). Our solution

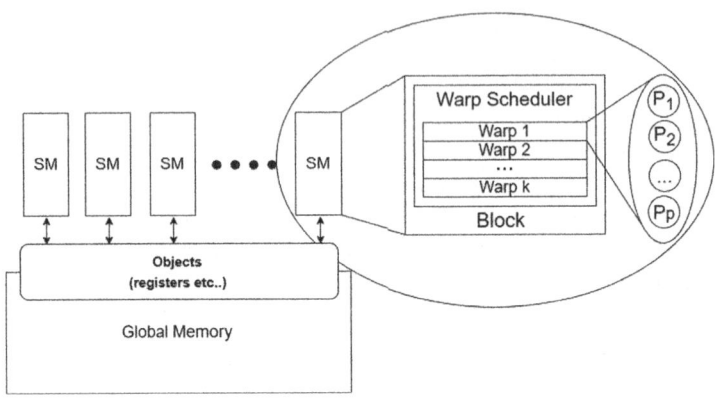

Fig. 3. Illustration of the system model

utilizes the StickyCAS object, a novel shared object we introduce and specify. (In [7], we provide a StickyCAS implementation which is built using CAS.)
(c) We prove the solution's correctness and fault-resilience (Sect. 5).

2 The GPU-Inspired Shared Memory Model

In this section, we formalize a shared memory model inspired by the GPU framework detailed in Sect. 1. We consider a shared memory system where processes communicate only by accessing shared memory objects. Following Cohen and Keidar [5], we assume that the shared memory is reliable (e.g., it cannot become inaccessible or corrupted), which is also commonly assumed in HPC Applications [11]. The proposed model is depicted in Fig. 3 and the various components are detailed here.

Processes. The system consists of a known static set of n processes, $P_1, P_2, ... P_n$. These processes correspond to *threads* of a block of a Streaming Multiprocessor in a GPU. As discussed, these threads are distributed in *warps* (recall Fig. 2). We denote by p the size (number of processes) of a warp. Thus, the system consists of $\lceil n/p \rceil$ warps. In this paper, we focus on a single block of a single SM as our system (the circled components in Fig. 3).

Phase-Based Computation. The computation proceeds in *synchronized phases*. In a given phase, only one warp is scheduled by the *warp scheduler* (recall Sect. 1; also see below). Since there is one warp per phase in our model, the terms "warp" and "phase" inherently mean the same in this document. Within a phase, each process can perform a constant number of instructions, which include access to the shared objects along with some local computation. Recall from Sect. 1 that processes (threads) in the same warp operate synchronously in a lock-step fashion, whereas processes across different warps operate asynchronously. Thus, processes in the same phase are synchronous and perform the same instructions (except Byzantine ones – see below), but phase duration might be different. However, due to the small warp cycle approach of GPUs (cf. Section 1), the latency of the phases is bounded to a specific number of instructions. In other words, the scheduler enables processes in a warp to perform the same (small) number of instructions (even for the Byzantine ones).

Shared Memory System. Shared memory systems are characterized by a unified address space that is accessible to all components within the system [16]. As typically assumed in the shared memory model, cf. [5], the shared memory is non-corruptible and can only be accesses through objects like registers. Specifically, the communication between processes is through the APIs exposed by the objects in the system; processes invoke operations that in turn, return some response back to the process.

Failure Model. We consider *Byzantine failures* [17]. In particular, we consider an adversary that may adaptively corrupt up to $f < n$ processes in the course of the computation. A corrupted process, called *Byzantine* or *faulty*, may deviate arbitrarily from the specified protocol (for example, instead of performing a read, it might choose to perform a write) [5]. More specific to our model, a faulty process within a warp in a given phase might perform a different set of instructions than the one indicated by the protocol. However, it cannot exceed the latency of the given phase or impersonate another process (and thus gain access to a phase in place of another process). A process that is not corrupted, called *correct*, follows the protocol and takes infinitely many steps. We will be referring to a protocol that can tolerate up to f Byzantine processes as f-*resilient*.

Warp Scheduler. As mentioned, GPU architectures typically include a hardware scheduler to schedule the warps [19]. The scheduler maps each thread in the warp to an individual core, and then the threads start executing. Threads (e.g., Byzantine) cannot masquerade as others to deceive the scheduler nor can they bypass the scheduler, as by design, processes/threads can only be activated for computation by the scheduler. Motivated by existing hardware available to multi-core systems, in this work we consider *fair scheduling* [23, 26], which gives every process a chance to execute. Further, we assume that the warp scheduler does not exhibit Byzantine behavior, as otherwise it would not be fair anymore.

As one might conclude, our proposed model abstracts the components and the operation of modern GPUs, as extensively analyzed in Sect. 1. By establishing this model, we aim to explore its potential for solving fundamental problems in the field. To our knowledge, this is the first work that leverages a shared memory system model inspired by GPU architectures to address the Byzantine consensus problem, which we present next.

3 Byzantine Consensus

Generally speaking, in the consensus problem, a collection of n processes propose values, and they need to agree on a value. Depending on the requirements imposed on the value agreed (validity property), we have different variations of the (Byzantine) consensus problem. In this work, we consider two variations of Byzantine consensus:

(a) *Common-value Byzantine Consensus*, where if all correct processes propose the same value, then this should be the one decided [2].
(b) *Strong Byzantine Consensus*, where correct processes must agree on a value proposed by at least one correct process [3,20].

For completeness, we also briefly discuss Weak Byzantine Consensus [20], although this is not the focus of this work.

Definition 1 (Common-value Byzantine Consensus). *Given a set of n processes out of which $f < n$ might be faulty, and a set of values V_c proposed by correct processes, the following must hold:*

- **Termination:** *Every correct process must eventually decide.*
- **Agreement:** *The value decided by correct process must be identical.*
- **Common Validity:** *If $V_c = \{v\}$, then v must be the consensus value.*

Definition 2 (Strong Byzantine Consensus). *Given a set of n processes out of which $f < n$ might be faulty, and a set of values V_c proposed by correct processes, the following must hold:*

- **Termination:** *Every correct process must eventually decide.*
- **Agreement:** *The value decided by every correct process must be identical.*
- **Strong Validity:** *The consensus value must be proposed by at least one correct process, i.e., final decision $\in V_c$.*

A few remarks on this definition: (a) The set $V_c \subseteq V$, where V is the set of all the values proposed, including those proposed by Byzantine processes. (b) Correct processes do not know the subset V_c in advance. (c) Malkhi et al. [20] originally introduced Strong Byzantine Consensus in the context of binary consensus (decided value is either 0 or 1). Our definition generalizes it to support multi-valued consensus.

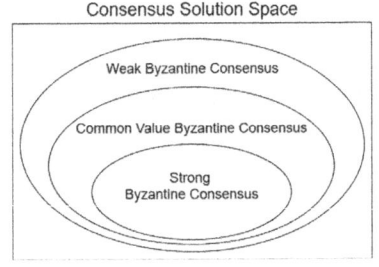

Fig. 4. Illustration of Consensus Solution Space

Malkhi et al. [20] also considered *weak consensus* in the context of binary proposal values, that is, the decided value is not necessarily one proposed by a correct process. This represents the most lenient approach, where, even if all correct processes propose the same value (e.g., 0), the consensus might still settle on a different value (e.g., 1) due to potential influence from faulty processes. This flexibility allows for the final decision to possibly be an input from a faulty process as well.

Definition 3 (Weak Byzantine Consensus). *Given a set of n processes out of which $f < n$ might be faulty, and a set of values V_c proposed by correct processes, the following must hold:*

- **Termination:** *Every correct process must eventually decide.*
- **Agreement:** *The value decided by every correct process must be identical.*

Figure 4 visually depicts the consensus solution space of the three types of Byzantine consensus mechanisms explored in this work. Observe that Strong Byzantine Consensus enforces strict criteria, ensuring that only values proposed by correct processes are eligible for the final decision. This makes Strong Byzantine Consensus the most reliable consensus method, as it guarantees that no erroneous values from faulty processes can influence the outcome. In contrast, Common-value Byzantine Consensus relaxes the validity requirement. When only a single unique value is proposed by correct processes, that value is chosen as the consensus value. However, if multiple values are proposed, the protocol does not mandate a specific choice (it could even be a non-proposed value), as long as the decision is consistent across correct processes.

4 Byzantine Consensus Solution

In this section, we present our solution for addressing both the Strong Byzantine Consensus and Common-value Byzantine Consensus. We first describe the design a novel object, called StickyCAS object (inspired from sticky bits), which is leveraged by the consensus algorithm.

StickyCAS Shared Object. As we discussed in Sect. 2, the processes can access the shared memory via shared objects. In addition, the warp scheduler is scheduling the processes, in a fair manner, to execute their protocol, including accessing the memory. As argued by Malkhi *et al.* [20], in shared memory, and in the presence of Byzantine processes, a form of *persistent non-corruptible* object, like sticky bits, is needed to solve consensus. Otherwise, a value written by a correct process could later be overwritten by a Byzantine one, and hence leading to inconsistent states, which in turn can prevent reaching agreement. (Thus, simple registers or similar objects cannot be used.)

Sticky bits [20] are restricted to binary values (and hence useful for binary consensus). Since we consider multi-valued consensus, we needed to utilize a different object. In particular, we assume that the processes have access to a non-corruptible shared object, which we call *Sticky Compare&Swap*, or StickyCAS for short (combination of sticky bits and CAS object); through this object the processes can access the shared global memory.

Specification. StickyCAS maintains a *totally ordered list* of n values, initially empty. It supports two operations StickyCAS-append(*val*) and StickyCAS-read(*len*).

Algorithm 1: Consensus Algorithm

1 DECIDE :
   /* On receiving first access to the *StickyCAS* by the Scheduler   */
2 StickyCAS-append(*proposedValue*) ;
   /* On receiving further accesses to the *StickyCAS* by the Scheduler */
3 ProposedList ← StickyCAS-read($\lceil n/p \rceil$);
4 **return** *mode*(ProposedList);

1. StickyCAS-append(*val*):
   (a) It attempts to append *val* to the list of values maintained if the maximum limit has not been reached.
   (b) It returns *write successful* if *val* is appended successfully; *write failed* if append failed, and *limit reached* if n values have been already appended.

2. StickyCAS-read(*len*): Returns the first *len* values added to the list.

Properties. Recall that in our model, processes are grouped into warps, and in any given phase, only one warp is executing. Furthermore, (correct) processes within the same warp execute the same instructions. So, when multiple processes in the same phase invoke StickyCAS-append(), and provided the limit has not been reached, *only one* can succeed; all other processes should receive *failed*. In other words, in any given phase, at most one process can change (append) the state of the list (and once a value is written, it cannot be overwritten or be deleted, as no such operations are available). StickyCAS-read, on the other hand is a concurrent read-only method. We elaborate more on these issues in Sect. 5.

Consensus Algorithm. We proceed with the description of the consensus algorithm, Algorithm 1. The key issues that lead to its correctness are detailed in Sect. 5.

Recall that the systems consists of $\lceil n/p \rceil$ warps (p = warp size), and each warp execution is a phase in the model. Specifically, in every phase, the warp scheduler grants access to a different warp of p processes to execute a fixed number of instructions from their protocol. As we discussed later, the warp scheduler ensures that once a process is given access to execute, it will again be given access after $\lceil n/p \rceil$ phases (*i.e.*, after all other warps were granted access).

The consensus algorithm is designed to ensure agreement among processes using StickyCAS as a fundamental building block. Initially, each (correct) process, upon its first access to StickyCAS, attempts to write its proposed value using StickyCAS-append (Line 2). This ensures that all participating processes compete to contribute their values to the shared memory structure. Subsequently, when a process gains further access to StickyCAS (regardless of the outcome of its StickyCAS-append operation), it retrieves a subset of previously written values using StickyCAS-read, which returns the first $\lceil n/p \rceil$ values appended in the list. The process then determines the consensus decision by computing the *mode*[1] of the retrieved values, selecting the most frequently occurring value. The use of StickyCAS ensures that all processes have access to the same sequence of written values, and by taking the mode, the system converges to a single consensus value.

Conceptually the idea seems simple, but there are a few subtle issues that need to be examined carefully in order to show that this indeed solves Byzantine Consensus. We do so in the next section.

5 Correctness and Fault-Resilience of the Solution

In order to show that Algorithm 1 solves both versions of Byzantine consensus we consider in this work (cf. Section 3), we impose specific assumptions on top of the model presented in Sect. 2. We justify these assumptions based on existing GPU architectures. The reason we have not imposed these assumptions in the model is because we want to keep the model more general (to be used in other fundamental problems); these assumptions are needed for the specific solution we provide. (We do not claim that these specific assumptions are necessary to solve consensus, they are however, sufficient for the consensus solution we provide.)

Specific Assumptions. To solve Byzantine consensus we further assume:

(a) Round Robin (RR) Warp Scheduler. GPUs are designed with an internal warp scheduler to efficiently manage core utilization and prevent idling or resource wastage. This scheduler ensures that computational resources are allocated effectively, maintaining high throughput. Recall that in our proposed model (Sect. 2), we assume that the scheduler functions as a fair scheduler, meaning it treats all warps equitably and is not influenced by external disruptions. Furthermore, we assume that Byzantine processes cannot affect the scheduler's behavior. In this section, additionally, we assume that the scheduler follows a *round-robin* scheduling strategy, distributing phases evenly among all available warps where each warp is scheduled again, only after all other warps have been scheduled. We believe this is a reasonable and realistic assumption, as Round-robin in GPUs is a baseline scheduling approach that chooses warps according to their warp ID in either increasing or decreasing order [12]. Multiple improvements have been proposed and implemented over the baseline scheduling approach for efficient utilization of the GPU cores.

(b) StickyCAS Operations within a Warp Phase. As detailed in Sect. 2, modern GPUs schedule a constant number of instructions before switching warps [6]. Here, we make the latency of a phase more specific with respect to the StickyCAS operations. Since StickyCAS-append(val) appends to the end of the list, it requires a constant number of instructions regardless of the list's length. Thus, we assume that this operation fits within a single phase, and for simplicity, no more

---

[1] The *mode* of a set S is defined as the element $x \in S$ that occurs most frequently. In case of a tie, the smallest such element is chosen.

than one StickyCAS-append can occur per phase (otherwise, the termination bounds shown in the forthcoming analysis could be adjusted accordingly). However, StickyCAS-read(*len*) may span multiple phases due to the list's variable size. Specifically, we set $r \leq n$ to be the number of values that StickyCAS-read can reads within a phase. This means that reading *len* values takes $\lceil n/p \rceil \cdot \lceil len/r \rceil$ phases. Given current warp scheduling behavior," this assumption aligns with the working of modern hardware architectures.

(c) Global Memory Access. In our solution, we assume that the global memory isn't directly accessible to processes. Instead, it can only be reached through specific objects, like the sticky bits [20] or the StickyCAS object we've designed. These objects serve as controlled gateways to the global memory, ensuring that all interactions go through well-defined methods. The APIs of these objects cannot be changed, meaning processes have to work within the constraints of the existing methods to read or modify the state. This approach helps maintain consistency and control over how the global memory is used.

With these assumptions in place, we are now ready to prove the correctness and resilience of our consensus solution.

Table 1. System Parameters

Parameter	Description
n	The total number of processes in the system.
V	The set of proposed values from all processes including the faulty ones.
V_c	The set of proposed values by correct processes.
f	The maximum Byzantine processes that the system can tolerate.
p	The number of processes assigned per warp or phase.
r	The number of memory elements that can be read in a given phase.

Correctness Proofs. For convenience, we provide Table 1 that summarizes the main system parameters. In Theorem 1 we prove that Strong Byzantine Consensus is solved within $\Theta(n^2/p^2 r)$ phases, provided that $f < \frac{n}{(|V_c|+1)p}$. It follows that the same algorithm solves Common-value Byzantine Consensus within the same number of phases, with $f < \lceil \frac{n}{2p} \rceil$, since $|V_c| = 1$.

Theorem 1. *Algorithm 1 solves the Strong Byzantine Consensus problem within $\Theta(n^2/p^2 r)$ phases, for $f < \frac{n}{(|V_c|+1)p}$.*

Proof. For Strong Byzantine Consensus, we want the decided consensus value to be proposed by at least one correct process. We show that Agreement, Strong Validity, and Termination properties follow essentially from the properties of the StickyCAS object and the RR Warp Scheduler.

Properties of StickyCAS and RR Scheduler: StickyCAS ensures that in a given phase, if p processes attempt to invoke StickyCAS-append simultaneously, then only one will succeed, while the others will fail (see StickyCAS-append.4). Therefore, if a Byzantine process executes StickyCAS-append in a phase, it can potentially succeed, *i.e.*, *win* the StickyCAS-append, and append a value v. The RR scheduler ensures that a second access to a process is only allowed after all processes have completed their first access. Thus, if process P_i executes an StickyCAS-append request in phase ℓ, it will be able to invoke StickyCAS-read($\lceil n/p \rceil$) in phase $\ell + \lceil n/p \rceil$.

Agreement: All the StickyCAS-append calls in a single phase try to append to the list in a single position as they execute in lock step manner. This is the position in the array next to the last appended proposed value in the StickyCAS object. Once appended, the value can not be modified and access to the memory is allowed only through the StickyCAS object. Therefore StickyCAS guarantees that *ProposedList* is consistent across all processes. So all correct processes will read the same list, compute the same mode value, agree on the same value and thus, fulfilling the agreement property.

Strong Validity: Given that there are f Byzantine processes, in the worst-case scenario, all Byzantine processes can win the StickyCAS-append() in f phases. Consequently, the maximum number of phases with Byzantine presence is f out of the $\lceil n/p \rceil$. The remaining $\lceil n/p \rceil - f$ values are proposed by correct processes. We consider the following cases. A more detailed breakdown of these cases is given in the extended version [7].

Case (a): The Byzantine processes propose NULL or an empty value. The $mode(ProposedList)$ results in a value proposed only by correct processes.

Case (b): All Byzantine processes propose a different value. In this case the values proposed by byzantine processes will never gain majority. In a scenario where correct processes also propose different values, a solution is only possible if at least two correct processes propose the same value.

Case (c): The Byzantine processes collude on appending the same value $v' \notin V_c$. The value proposed by the Byzantine processes can only be chosen if one or more correct processes also propose v', making it the result of $mode(ProposedList)$.

Case (d): Byzantine processes proposing values from V_c. In this case, Byzantine processes do not introduce any new values but instead propose values already present in V_c, the set of values proposed by correct processes. However, because there are at most f Byzantine processes and at least $(\lceil n/p \rceil) - f$ correct values, their ability to shift the mode is limited.

Case (e): A Mix of Strategies by Byzantine Processes. In this case, Byzantine processes do not follow a single strategy but instead use a combination of the previous approaches.

Termination: In our system model, during any given phase, each process performs a fixed number of instructions. An StickyCAS-append operation requires a constant number of instructions and will complete within the phase. With a RR scheduler, each process's StickyCAS-append invocation will occur once within the first $\lceil n/p \rceil$ phases. The StickyCAS-read(len) operation might span multiple phases to complete and will take $\lceil n/p \rceil \cdot \lceil len/r \rceil$ phases for each process. Combining StickyCAS-append and StickyCAS-read, and given that $len = \lceil n/p \rceil$ (as per Algorithm 1), all correct processes will decide on the same value within $\Theta(n^2/(p^2 r))$ phases, provided that $f < \frac{n}{(|V_c|+1)p}$. This completes the proof. □

From Theorem 1 we get the following result for Common-value Byzantine Consensus. (In [7], we illustrate that in the Byzantine consensus solution space Fig. 4, any algorithm solving Strong Byzantine Consensus will solve Common-value Byzantine Consensus.)

Corollary 1. *Algorithm 1 solves the Common-value Byzantine Consensus problem within $\Theta(n^2/p^2 r)$ phases, for $f < \lceil \frac{n}{2p} \rceil$.*

Remarks on Resilience. Observe that for Strong Byzantine Consensus the resilience depends on $|V_c|$: as the size of V_c increases, the resilience decreases, and when $|V_c|+1 \geq \lceil n/p \rceil$, the algorithm is no longer resilient. It would be interesting to investigate whether this is not only a sufficient, but also a necessary condition within the system model we consider.

Also observe that the resilience depends on p, the number of processes that the scheduler permits access to StickyCAS in a given phase. The lower p is, the higher resilience we get. In the case that $p = 1$ and $|V_c| = 1$, f can be as large as $\lceil n/2 \rceil$ for Strong Byzantine Consensus and Common-value Byzantine Consensus.

It is essential to highlight that the current analysis adopts a deliberately pessimistic perspective. This work is an initial step toward understanding the model's resilience under worst-case adversarial conditions. We assume that a single Byzantine thread in a phase always succeeds in writing its own value, while honest threads fail, which is an unrealistic scenario that likely underestimates practical resilience. A more optimistic probabilistic fault model, where, e.g., all threads have equal chances of success, could reveal significantly higher resilience.

6 Related Work

In this work, we aim to formalize the model of GPUs with Byzantine faults and explore the problems that can be solved within this framework. Consensus is one of the problems that is being extensively studied in message passing [8, 18, 21] and shared memory [1, 2, 20]. Diverse researchers have approached the Byzantine consensus problem in shared memory systems in various ways. Malkhi et al. [20] demonstrated that Byzantine-tolerant objects in shared memory can be constructed with $f < n/3$ tolerance, using access control lists, persistent objects with defined fault tolerance limits, and redundancy. Sticky bits were utilized by Alon et al. [1] to solve Strong Byzantine Consensus among n processes where $n \geq 3f + 1$, f being the number of faulty processes. Attie [2] showed that weak

Byzantine consensus can be achieved, but only by using non-resettable or sticky shared objects even in a reliable shared memory setting. Attie [2] has also detailed an impossibility proof that shows that even with limited-access restriction to Byzantine processes, it is impossible to achieve Byzantine consensus. However, we have not been able to find any implementation of sticky bits in hardware. The closest available technology, Write-Once-Read-Many (WORM) [24], lacks concurrency support.

Construction of shared memory objects like Byzantine tolerant single writer multi reader (SWMR) registers have been extensively explored over the years [5, 10,20]. Hu and Toueg have recently proposed implementation of SWMR registers from SWSR registers [10] using signatures. A new computing paradigm where shared memory objects are protected by fine-grained access policies was introduced by Bessani et al. [3]. Their research highlights the need for byzantine tolerant protocols and objects for shared memory specifically as such solutions have been long prevalent in message passing systems. Construction of a shared memory object called Policy-Enforced Augmented Tuple Space (PEATS) is also detailed in their work. Their proposed model has a resistance of $n \geq 3f + 1$.

These studies underscore the necessity for Byzantine-tolerant protocols and objects in shared memory systems. Note that most research assumes security premises such as Public Key Infrastructure (PKI) or controlled access, which are complex to implement and design. We build on these works to design a system framework that leverages existing hardware to tolerate Byzantine faults.

7 Discussion and Conclusion

Our research aims to leverage existing hardware and software capabilities to address the challenges posed by Byzantine faults. In this paper, we formalize a model of shared memory systems inspired by GPU architectures, which can handle processes exhibiting Byzantine faults.

Our contributions include demonstrating the feasibility of achieving Strong Byzantine Consensus and Common-value Byzantine Consensus within this model by utilizing a concurrent object, called StickyCAS. In Georgiou et al. [7], the interested reader can find a crash-tolerant implementation of StickyCAS in a non-corruptible shared memory setting; the implementation builds on Compare&Swap (CAS) objects, which are known to be implemented in hardware.

One might wonder why we cannot use a CAS object in place of StickyCAS. CAS is used for accessing a specific memory location. For the needs of our consensus algorithms, we want to ensure that once a value is successfully written in a memory location, it cannot be modified. In the presence of a Byzantine process, it seems that CAS cannot "protect" a memory location from not being updated again. This requirement of memory protection is facilitated by StickyCAS.

We believe our work opens new opportunities for the Distributed and Parallel Computing community to explore. Our abstraction focused on a single block of a single SM, as multiple schedulers may operate across different blocks. Future work could investigate synergies between warp schedulers for interblock computations. Additionally, we aim to enhance the understanding and modeling of

GPU behavior under Byzantine faults, by considering other fundamental problems of distributed computing within the GPU-inspired model we have devised. An interesting question is whether the resilience achieved in this work is optimal.

Acknowledgements. We would like to thank Gadi Taubenfeld and reviewers for their insightful comments.

Disclosure of Interests. The authors have no competing interests to declare that are relevant to the content of this article.

References

1. Alon, N., Merritt, M., Reingold, O., Taubenfeld, G., Wright, R.N.: Tight bounds for shared memory systems accessed by Byzantine processes. Distrib. Comput
2. Attie, P.: Wait-free Byzantine consensus. Inf. Process. Lett. **83**(4), 221–227 (2002)
3. Bessani, A.N., Correia, M., da Silva Fraga, J., Cheuk Lung, L.: Sharing memory between byzantine processes using policy-enforced tuple spaces. IEEE Trans. Parallel Distrib. Syst. **20**(3), 419–432 (2009)
4. Cini, N., Yalcin, G.: A methodology for comparing the reliability of GPU-based and CPU-based HPCs. ACM Comput. Surv. **53**(1) (2020)
5. Cohen, S., Keidar, I.: Tame the wild with byzantine linearizability: reliable broadcast, snapshots, and asset transfer. In: DISC 2021, pp. 18:1–18:18 (2021)
6. Corporation, N.: CUDA C++ programming guide (2024), https://docs.nvidia.com/cuda/cuda-c-programming-guide/, Accessed 12 Mar 2025
7. Georgiou, C., Piduguralla, M., Peri, S.: Byzantine-tolerant consensus in GPU-inspired shared memory (2025), https://arxiv.org/abs/2503.12788
8. Gilad, Y., Hemo, R., Micali, S., Vlachos, G., Zeldovich, N.: Algorand: scaling byzantine agreements for cryptocurrencies. In: 26th SOSP, pp. 51–68 (2017)
9. Herlihy, M.: Wait-free synchronization. ACM Trans. Program. Lang. Syst. **13**(1), 124–149 (1991). https://doi.org/10.1145/114005.102808
10. Hu, X., Toueg, S.: On implementing SWMR registers from SWSR registers in systems with byzantine failures. CoRR **abs/2207.01470** (2022)
11. Huang, Y., Guo, S., Di, S., Li, G., Cappello, F.: Mitigating silent data corruptions in HPC applications across multiple program inputs. In: SC22, pp. 1–14 (2022)
12. Jeon, H.: GPU Architecture, pp. 531–559. Springer Nature Singapore (2025)
13. Kirk, D.B., mei W. Hwu, W.: Chapter 4 - memory and data locality. In: Programming Massively Parallel Processors (Third Edition), pp. 71–101 (2017)
14. Kolesnichenko, A., Poskitt, C.M., Nanz, S.: SafeGPU: contract- and library-based GPGPU for object-oriented languages. Comput. Lang. Syst. Struct. **48** (2017), special Issue on the 14th International Conference on GPCE
15. Kowalski, V., Mostéfaoui, A., Perrin, M.: Atomic register abstractions for byzantine-prone distributed systems. In: OPODIS 2023 (2023)
16. Kshemkalyani, A.D., Singhal, M.: Distributed Computing: Principles, Algorithms, and Systems. 1st edn. Cambridge University Press (2011)
17. Lamport, L., Shostak, R., Pease, M.: The byzantine generals problem. ACM Trans. Program. Lang. Syst. **4**(3), 382–401 (1982)
18. Liu, J., Li, W., Karame, G.O., Asokan, N.: Scalable byzantine consensus via hardware-assisted secret sharing. IEEE Trans. Comput. **68**(1) (2019)

19. Maitre, O.: Understanding nvidia gpgpu hardware. In: Massively Parallel Evolutionary Computation on GPGPUs, pp. 15–34 (2013)
20. Malkhi, D., Merritt, M., Reiter, M.K., Taubenfeld, G.: Objects shared by byzantine processes. Distrib. Comput. **16**(1), 37–48 (2003)
21. Miller, A., Xia, Y., Croman, K., Shi, E., Song, D.: The honey badger of BFT protocols. In: Proceedings of the 2016 ACM SIGSAC Conference on Computer and Communications Security. pp. 31–42 (2016)
22. Olmedo, I.S., Capodieci, N., Martinez, J.L., Marongiu, A., Bertogna, M.: Dissecting the cuda scheduling hierarchy: a performance and predictability perspective. In: IEEE RTAS 2020, pp. 213–225 (2020)
23. Pabla, C.S.: Completely fair scheduler. Linux J. **2009**(184), 4 (2009)
24. Sheldon, R.: Worm (write once, read many) (2022), https://www.techtarget.com/searchstorage/definition/WORM-write-once-read-many
25. Weaver, A., et al.: Granularity- and interference-aware gpu sharing with mps. In: SC24-W: Workshops of SC24, pp. 1630–1637 (2024)
26. Wong, C.S., Tan, I., Kumari, R.D., Wey, F.: Towards achieving fairness in the Linux scheduler. ACM SIGOPS Operat. Syst. Rev. **42**(5), 34–43 (2008)

Supervised Distributed Computing

John Augustine[1], Christian Scheideler[2], and Julian Werthmann[2](✉)

[1] IIT Madras, Chennai, India
augustine@iitm.ac.in
[2] Paderborn University, Paderborn, Germany
scheideler@upb.de, jwerth@mail.upb.de

Abstract. We introduce a new framework for distributed computing that extends and refines the standard master-worker approach of scheduling multi-threaded computations. In this framework, there are different roles: a supervisor, a source, a target, and a collection of workers. Initially, the source stores some instance I of a computational problem, and at the end, the target is supposed to store a correct solution $S(I)$ for that instance. We assume that the computation required for $S(I)$ can be modeled as a directed acyclic graph $G = (V, E)$, where V is a set of tasks and $(v, w) \in E$ if and only if task w needs information from task v in order to be executed. Given G, the role of the supervisor is to schedule the execution of the tasks in G by assigning them to the workers. If all workers are honest, information can be exchanged between the workers, and the workers have access to the source and target, the supervisor only needs to know G to successfully schedule the computations. I.e., the supervisor does not have to handle any data itself like in standard master-worker approaches, which has the tremendous benefit that tasks can be run massively in parallel in large distributed environments without the supervisor becoming a bottleneck. But what if a constant fraction of the workers is adversarial? Interestingly, we show that under certain assumptions a data-agnostic scheduling approach would even work in an adversarial setting without (asymptotically) increasing the work required for communication and computations. We demonstrate the validity of these assumptions by presenting concrete solutions for supervised matrix multiplication and sorting.

Keywords: Distributed Computing · Fault Tolerance · Peer-to-peer Networks

1 Introduction

There is a long line of work in the literature on scheduling multithreaded computations (see, e.g., [20] for a survey). Many approaches follow the master-worker paradigm, where a master delivers tasks among workers and collects their outcomes. In the most simple setting, there is a single master that delivers all work, but this limits scalability. However, with approaches such as MapReduce, where every worker can become a master allowing work to be delivered recursively, the scalability can be significantly increased. In massive computations that use a large number of workers, it cannot be assumed that all workers work reliably all the time. Therefore, suitable mechanisms are needed to obtain the desired degree of reliability. In the Hadoop MapReduce framework, for example, a worker is expected to report back periodically to its master with completed work and status updates. If a worker falls silent for longer than a given interval, the master records the worker as dead and reassigns its work to another worker [29].

In a closed or trusted environment, it is reasonable to assume that the worst case worker behavior is crash failures. In situations where work leaves a trusted environment, one also has to worry about adversarial behavior. A popular example for such a situation is volunteer-based computing. An early example of this approach is SETI@home (1998–2020), where tasks were given to volunteers to analyze astronomical data for extraterrestrial life. To prevent cheating, SETI@home gave each task to two volunteers. If their results disagree, additional volunteers would be contacted for that task until enough results agree. Its follow-up service, BOINC [3], is nowadays used for a wide range of scientific computations. In both SETI@home and BOINC all tasks are delivered by a trusted server since it appears to be challenging to apply the MapReduce paradigm in a setting with untrusted volunteers. This server has to receive all input data from some source, which can be problematic for applications with massive amounts of data, like in data science and natural sciences, since that creates a bottleneck. If, instead, the server could just focus on scheduling computations without handling input and output data, it would be easy for a single server to schedule even millions of tasks. In fact, a recent study has shown that such an approach would indeed be beneficial [24]. Thus, we will address the following central question:

Can the handling of data be decoupled from the problem of scheduling the execution of tasks, even under adversarial behavior of some of the workers?

At first glance, that looks like a bad idea because it is unclear how a server can know that tasks were executed correctly without seeing the input or output. Alternatively, the source could do the checking, but it might not have or be willing to provide the resources for output verifications. Thus, we are left with the workers. If there is an output verification mechanism for the tasks whose runtime is much lower than executing a task, an obvious strategy for the server would to ask a single worker to execute a task (based on input provided by the source) and send its output to a quorum of workers for verification. Suppose that the fraction of adversarial workers is sufficiently small and the quorum consists of a logarithmic number of randomly chosen workers. Then one can easily prove that if a majority of workers in that quorum tells the server that the output is correct, at least one honest worker in that quorum received the correct output, with high probability[1], irrespective of whether the executing worker is adversarial or not. However, for any constant fraction β of adversarial workers with $\beta > 0$, this approach has an inherent logarithmic factor communication overhead (unless the

---

[1] *With high probability* or *w.h.p.* denotes a probability of at least $1 - 1/n^c$ for some constant $c > 1$ that can be chosen arbitrarily high.

verification mechanism can be turned into a robust distributed version) because a logarithmic number of quorum members is necessary to be able to trust the quorum vote with high probability, and in general the quorum members need to know the entire input to verify the output. Thus, the following question arises:

Is there a data-agnostic scheduling approach with a constant factor overhead for the computation and the communication?

Interestingly, for computations that are given as task graphs, we present a general framework achieving a constant factor overhead given that a lightweight verification mechanism is available for the tasks. Moreover, we demonstrate the validity of that assumption by presenting solutions for two standard problems: sorting and matrix multiplication. Our tailored verification mechanisms have the following approach in common, which might be of independent interest:

Standard verification mechanisms assume the verifier knows the correct input and receives the output together with a certificate that allows it to check its correctness. An exception are probabilistically checkable proofs, where a verifier can be convinced about the correctness of an output with a digest of the certificate. We are following a related approach in a sense that the server obtains digests of the tasks' outputs allowing it to help workers assigned to a task to determine the correctness of the inputs received from preceding tasks. While the server does not know the instance stored in the source, it can fetch a digest of the instance from the always honest source, yielding a trusted base for local verifications.

Of course, it is not yet clear to which extent this approach can also be used for other problems, but in recent years, enormous progress has been made on lightweight verification, as discussed in the related works section below. Thus, we believe that our approach can also be applied to a wide range of other problems.

1.1 Supervised Distributed Computing Framework

In our supervised framework, we have a *supervisor*, a *source*, a *target*, and a collection of *workers*. We use the word 'supervisor' instead of 'server' to emphasize our light-weight scheduling approach. The source represents a storage environment with read-only access, while the supervisor and the target can execute algorithms. All three are assumed to be reliable in a sense that they operate on time and do not experience crashes or adversarial behavior. Given an instance I of a computational problem initially stored in the source, the goal of the supervisor is to use the workers to compute a solution $S(I)$ for I that is ultimately stored in the target. Depending on the application, some of these roles might be associated with the same entity. For example, if $S(I)$ is small ('yes' or 'no'), it might be convenient that supervisor and target are the same entity. On the other hand, the source might be distributed among multiple entities (e.g., webpages).

We will focus on approaches where the computation of I can be represented as a directed acyclic graph (DAG) $G = (V, E)$. Each node $v \in V$ represents a task and $(v, w) \in E$ if and only if task w needs information from task v to be executed. We call this graph a *task graph*. The *initial tasks* of G, i.e., tasks without incoming edges, need information from the source about I, while the *final tasks* of G, i.e., tasks without outgoing edges, send information to the target so that it can assemble $S(I)$. G and its tasks are assumed to be known to the supervisor and the workers. For most problems in this paper, we use $n = |V|$ to denote the size of G and D to denote the *span* of G, i.e., is the length of a longest directed path in G. G, n, and D might depend on I.

In this paper, we assume that the supervisor has access to a black-box worker-sampling mechanism that returns a worker that is adversarial with probability at most β for some fixed $\beta \geq 0$ not known to the supervisor. Other ways of selecting workers can certainly be considered and are subject to future research. The number of workers might change over time. However, when an honest worker is selected for some task, we assume that it remains available and honest as long as the supervisor needs it for the computation. We allow all adversarial workers to be controlled by a single adversarial entity that can make decisions based on any information currently available in the system, but it does not know future random choices of supervisor, target, or honest workers. Thus, the adversary is omniscient w.r.t. the past and present but oblivious to the sampling process since it cannot convert an honest worker into an adversarial one *after* being picked by the sampling process. Furthermore, the adversary cannot change, drop, delay, or reroute messages between supervisor, source, target, and honest workers.

For simplicity, we assume that time proceeds in synchronous *rounds*. A round is long enough for the supervisor to select workers for all currently executable tasks and introduce them to all workers they need information from (i.e., for a worker assigned to task w, all workers v with $(v, w) \in E$). Additionally, the selected workers can receive all required information (as long as both sides are honest) and perform the necessary verifications and computations for the tasks. This is reasonable if all tasks require approximately the same computational effort so that the overall computation can progress in an efficient way.

To find an efficient and robust supervised solution for a problem P, several issues must be addressed: First, instance I might have to be stored in the source in a preprocessed way, and the time needed to preprocess I should be bounded by $O(|I|)$. Second, a family of task graphs with low span, low total work, and low maximum work per task is needed for P to ensure low runtime, and high work efficiency, and parallelism for the workers. Third, a robust scheduling strategy is needed for the supervisor to assign workers to the tasks ensuring that a correct solution can be assembled at the target. The primary challenge here is to design lightweight verification mechanisms for the supervisor and the workers allowing them to identify malicious behavior. The goal is to match the following bounds:

- Total preprocessing time and communication work of the source: $O(|I|)$.
- Total work of supervisor: $\tilde{O}(|V| + |E|)^2$.
- Total work of workers, including verifications: $O(W)$. W is the total work over all tasks in G, excluding verfications.
- Runtime of the computation: $O(D)$.
- Total work of target: $O(S)$. S is the worst-case size of a solution for I.

---

[2] $\tilde{O}$ hides polylogarithmic factors.

Here, *work* includes communication as well as computational work ruling out trivial scheduling strategies like giving the entire computation to a single worker. Since a worker can only finish one task per round, the runtime would be $O(|V|)$, which can be significantly larger than D. It also rules out getting the supervisor involved in inputs and outputs because its work would be in the same order as the source's or target's work, which can be significantly larger than G.

1.2 Use Cases

With our approach, services like SETI@home and BOINC can be realized in a much more lightweight fashion for the server (w.r.t. storage and communication) since data handling would be decoupled from scheduling, without putting a much higher burden on the source. The superviser could also be implemented in a standard cloud because with a small overhead and small cloud fees.

Another use case would be *pure* P2P computing. A standard approach for robust and scalable computations in P2P systems without mutual trust is to partition the peers into random quorums of logarithmic size so that, w.h.p., the fraction of adversarial peers within a quorum is roughly equal to the total fraction of adversarial peers. If this fraction is sufficiently low, quorums can assume the role of the supervisor. More precisely, whenever a quorum is supposed to execute some task, it selects one of its members at random to be the worker for that task, introduces that worker to the workers of the preceding tasks in the task graph by contacting their respective quorums, and runs a standard consensus algorithm to arrive at an agreement on the answer of the worker. Since the supervisor is data-agnostic, *the quorum does not have to replicate any input or output data for this approach to work* so that the overhead of using a quorum is negligible given that the amount of data that needs to be handled is sufficiently high. As a by-product, this significantly improves the computational overhead of all *provably* robust distributed computing solutions that have been proposed for P2P systems in the literature before, where the data handling and/or the computations have at least a logarithmic overhead. See the related work for further details.

Another interesting use case would be blockchain-based volunteer computing. In blockchains, space is a particularly delicate resource since blocks have limited size and placing information in them is not free. Thus, it is important to save as much space as possible to coordinate distributed computations via a blockchain. If the blockchain is used to emulate the supervisor, it just needs to store all information that a supervisor would have to handle, which only depends on the size of the task graph. Workers may then be assigned to tasks by announcing their interest in an executable task in the blockchain, so that the source or the predecessors in the task graph know which worker to send the information to. Working out the details might open up interesting new research directions.

1.3 Related Work

Several works proposed models that are related to our approach. A highly influential one is due to Blum et al. [7], who consider a setting where a data structure is under an adversary's control and operations on that data structure are initiated by a reliable checker. The goal is to come up with a strategy for the checker to verify the execution of the operations on that data structure using as little memory as possible so that any error in the execution of an operation will be detected by the checker with high probability. Their work inspired a large collection of works on authenticated data structures (see [28] for a survey). A standard assumption for that approach is that there is a trusted source, an untrusted server, and a client. The source provides the data for the server and a digest on the current state of the data to the clients. The server is supposed to organize the data received from the source in a data structure. Whenever the client asks the server to execute a request on that data structure, it expects an answer together with a certificate that allows it to verify together with the digest from the source that the answer from the server is correct. Thus, the source role is similar to our source role, the untrusted server can be seen as the untrusted computation by the workers, and the client might be identified with the target. While research in this area has focused on data structures, some of the techniques, like using digests of the input, are also useful in our context.

Goodrich [15] adapted parallel fault diagnosis results to prevent cheating in grid computing. However, the supervisor is still an I/O bottleneck.

Closer to our approach are *certifying algorithms* [2], which compute, in addition to an output, a witness certifying that the output is correct. A checker for such a witness, which is usually much faster than the original algorithm, then checks the output's correctness. Certifying algorithms have been found for various problems in the sequential domain (e.g. [21]), which we expect to be useful for our approach as well, but so far no generic approach has been proposed.

The problem of finding generic approaches for delegating work to potentially untrusted computational entities has been heavily studied in the cryptographic community (see, e.g., [9] for a survey). In delegation of computation, a computationally weak client provides one (or more) computationally powerful servers with a program and an input. The server returns the output and some proof that the output is actually correct. This setting is formalized with interactive proof systems (see, e.g., [10] for an overview), where a prover aims to convince a verifier that some statement is true. For the delegation to be useful, it is typically required that generating the proof takes no longer than executing the program, and verifying the proof takes time linear in the size of the input (both up to polylogarithmic factors). Especially but not only in the context of blockchains, non-interactive arguments have been considered, where the prover and the verifier do not need to exchange information over multiple rounds. Rather, the prover just provides one message (say, by posting it on the blockchain) that is sufficient to convince the verifier. An *argument* is a relaxation of a proof. While the generation of proofs for false statements is required to be impossible, it suffices to be computationally infeasible for arguments. Notable classes of non-interactive arguments are SNARGs and SNARKs (see, e.g., [8,23] for introductions to them).

Robust leader-based computations have been heavily pursued in the BFT (Byzantine fault tolerance), and blockchain communities (see, e.g., [30] for a recent survey on BFT consensus protocols and blockchains) since they scale much better in practice than decentralized approaches. There, leaders are either elected (e.g. in PAXOS [25]) or assumed to be trusted dealers so that, e.g., a BFT algorithm can be initialized appropriately (see, e.g., [18]) or reliable broadcasting can be performed. The solutions proposed in these communities can certainly be used to perform robust distributed computations, but we are not aware of any works on how to use a trusted dealer to just *supervise* (in our sense) executions of tasks for computational problems instead of getting directly involved. A significant amount of work has also been invested in decentralized approaches, such as secure multi-party computations (see, e.g., [31] for a survey). However, their overhead under adversarial behavior (compared to the naive approach) is at least linear in the group size for all solutions presented so far. Thus they are not helpful for reducing the overhead to a constant in our context.

Other directions assume the existence of a reliable cloud. Friedman et al. [14] propose a model where processes exchange information with messages or by accessing a reliable and highly-available register hosted in the cloud. They show a lower bound on the number of register accesses in deterministic consensus protocols and provide a simple deterministic consensus protocol meeting this bound for compare-and-swap (CAS) registers. Other results on distributed computing with the cloud are considered in [1,4]. In [1], no adversarial behavior is considered, while in [4], a certain fraction of the peers can be adversarial. The latter paper provides robust solutions for the Download problem, where the cloud stores a collection of bits and these bits must be downloaded to all (honest) peers, and the problem of computing the Disjunction and Parity of the bits in the cloud.

In algorithmic research on peer-to-peer systems, a common strategy to address adversarial behavior is to employ quorums of logarithmically many peers. Various strategies have been proposed to form random quorums (e.g., [6]), and various protocols have been presented that use quorums to ensure reliable operations in a peer-to-peer system (e.g., [12,16,22]). Other techniques do not rely on quorums (e.g., [11,27]), but these still incur at least a logarithmic overhead compared to the setting where all peers are honest. Jaiyeola et al. [17] investigate the case that quorums are only of $O(\log \log n)$ size and show that when combining this with a suitably chosen overlay network, all but a $O(1/\text{poly}(\log n))$ fraction of peers can successfully route messages to all but a $O(1/\text{poly}(\log n))$-fraction of peers. They show that this can then be used to solve various important problems like routing or broadcasting with just $O(\text{poly}(\log \log n))$ overhead per peer. However, they did not address the issue of reliable distributed computation.

1.4 Our Contributions

In this paper, we consider a new approach for robust distributed computing, called supervised distributed computing. We first present a general framework that assumes, for simplicity, that the workers can locally and without the help of the supervisor verify the correctness of information received from other workers. For the case that the task graph is a path of length n and the black-box sampling mechanism selects an adversarial worker with probability at most β for some sufficiently small constant $\beta > 0$, we obtain the following results (see Theorem 1):

- The computation completes in $(1 + O(\beta))n$ rounds, w.h.p.;
- on expectation, the source sends the input (to the initial task) $1 + O(\beta)$ times and the target receives the solution (from the final task) $1 + O(\beta)$ times;
- the expected total (computational and communication) work of the honest workers is within a $1 + O(\beta)$ factor of optimal (i.e., when $\beta = 0$).

All of these bounds are asymptotically optimal if the workers have to be selected via the black-box sampling mechanism, due to a simple observation: The expected number of samples for some task until some honest worker is chosen is

$$\sum_{i \geq 1} i \cdot \beta^{i-1}(1 - \beta) = \frac{1}{1 - \beta} = 1 + \frac{\beta}{1 - \beta}.$$

Note that the bounds are not obvious since we are dealing with a mixed adversarial-stochastic process, where adversarial workers are allowed to show *any* behavior based on the supervisor strategy and the current state of the system. Consequently, the trivial solution of using the same worker for all tasks is not a good idea since an adversarial worker would simply behave honest until the last task, which would force the supervisor to redo the entire computation since it has no records of the task outputs. Thus, the best runtime guarantee that can be given in this case, w.h.p., would just be $O(n \log n)$ instead of $O(n)$.

For arbitrary DAGs of size n with degree d and span $D \geq \log n$ and a sufficiently small $\beta = O(1/d^{2+\epsilon})$ (for any constant $\epsilon > 0$), we show that the number of rounds to complete the computation is $O(D)$, w.h.p. Furthermore, any such DAG can be extended without increasing the runtime bound so that the expected communication work of the source and target are asymptotically optimal, as formally stated in Theorem 2. The bound on β is close to the optimal bound of $1/d$ for our approach, as stated in Sect. 3 of the paper's full version [5]. For the analysis, we adapt a technique for non-adversarial settings, the delay sequence argument (see, e.g., [19,26]), to a mixed adversarial-stochastic setting, which might be of independent interest. Note that we did not try to optimize the bounds on β since our primary focus is on showing our approach's feasibility.

Afterwards, we present solutions for two concrete problems. For the matrix multiplication problem, we combine a well-known divide-and-conquer approach with Freivalds' algorithm for cross-checking matrix multiplications in order to obtain a task graph of span $O(\log n)$ for the multiplication of two $n \times n$-matrices. As long as $\beta > 0$ is a sufficiently small constant, the number of rounds to complete the computation is $O(\log n)$, w.h.p., the expected overhead of the source and the target is a constant, and the expected computational work for the honest workers is $O(n^3)$ (see Theorem 3), which matches the sequential work for the standard matrix multiplication. Using more efficient approaches like Strassen's algorithm would result in better work bounds, but we did not explore these here.

We provide a new way of performing parallel mergesort by designing a task graph that is a leveled network with $O(\log n)$ levels and n nodes per level, which might be of independent interest. As summarized formally in Theorem 4, for any instance of m numbers with $m \geq n \log n$ and a sufficiently low constant $\beta > 0$, the number of rounds to complete the computation is $O(\log n)$, w.h.p., the expected overhead for the source and target is constant, the expected total amount of computational work for the honest workers is $O(m \log m)$, and their expected total amount of communication work is $O(m \log n)$. Thus, our solution only incurs a constant overhead compared to the sequential mergesort algorithm.

The path case is considered in Sect. 2 and the DAG case in Sect. 3. A brief overview of the solutions for matrix multiplication and sorting is presented in Sect. 4. The proofs have been moved to the full version of the paper [5].

2 The Case of Path Graphs

Our starting point will be to solve the supervised distributed computing problem for task graphs that form a directed path of n nodes $v_1, \ldots, v_n$, i.e., each node v_i represents a task whose input is the output of v_{i-1} (resp. the input stored at the source if $i = 1$) and the output of v_n is the solution to the problem.

We will exclusively focus on scheduling and therefore assume that an honest worker assigned to some task v_i, $1 \leq i \leq n$ can verify the output of task v_{i-1} without the help of the supervisor, and that the target can verify the output of task v_n. Recall that we assume a round to be long enough to cover the time for receiving v_i's input from v_{i-1} (or the source if $i = 1$), verifying it, executing v_i and sending a short feedback to the supervisor, if the workers assigned to v_{i-1} and v_i are honest. Also, recall that the supervisor has access to a black-box sampling mechanism choosing an adversarial worker with probability at most β.

Consider the following scheduling approach. Initially, the supervisor s picks a random worker p_1 for task v_1 and introduces it to the source so that it can obtain the given instance. Similar to the Hadoop MapReduce framework, s expects p_1 to reply to it by the end of that round with a DONE, meaning that p_1 finished the execution of task v_1. If s does not receive that message by the end of the round, s picks a new random worker p_1 for task v_1 for the next round and introduces it to the source until it receives a DONE. Once this is the case, it will pick a random worker p_2 for v_2 and introduce p_1 and p_2 to each other (so that p_1 knows whom to send its output to and p_2 knows whom to expect the output from).

In general, for any worker p_i assigned to task v_i at the beginning of some round, for $i > 1$, the supervisor introduces p_{i-1} and p_i to each other and expects p_i to reply to it by the end of that round with one of the following messages:

- DONE: This means that p_i is ready to forward its output to the worker assigned to v_{i+1}, resp. the target if $i = n$.
- REJECT: This means that p_i rejects the input sent to it from p_{i-1}, or p_i has not received anything from p_{i-1} at the beginning of that round.

Note that for specific problems, more complex replies (like digests of outputs) might be expected by the supervisor, but we just use DONE as a placeholder here. The supervisor s will react to the reply of p_i as follows. If it receives

- a DONE from p_i, $i < n$, it picks a random worker p_{i+1} to continue the execution at v_{i+1}. After a DONE from p_n, it asks p_n to send its output to the target. A DONE from the target terminates the computation;
- no reply from p_i, s picks a new random worker p'_i to execute v_i;
- a REJECT from p_i with $i > 1$ or the target, it picks a new random worker p_{i-1} to execute v_{i-1}. We call this a *rollback*. For $i = 1$ it replaces p_1.

If the computation is currently at v_i, s will remember the last worker p_j assigned to v_j for all $j < i$. In case of a rollback to v_{i-1} due to a REJECT from p_i, it asks the worker last assigned to v_{i-2} to deliver its output to the new worker assigned to v_{i-1}. If a rollback happens at v_1, the supervisor assigns a new worker to v_1.

We prove the following theorem in the full version of the paper.

Theorem 1. *For a path graph of size n it holds: If $\beta \leq 1/12$ then under any adversarial strategy, the supervised computation correctly terminates in $(1+O(\beta))n$ rounds, w.h.p. Furthermore, the source just needs to send the input $1 + O(\beta)$ times and the target just needs to receive the solution $1 + O(\beta)$ times, on expectation. Moreover, the total computational and communication work of the workers is within a $1 + O(\beta)$ factor of optimal (i.e., when $\beta = 0$).*

3 The Case of Arbitrary DAGs

Next, we consider an arbitrary DAG $G = (V, E)$ with span D. It is well-known that the nodes $v \in V$ can be labeled with numbers $\ell(v) \in \{0, \ldots, D\}$ so that the nodes are topologically sorted, i.e., for all $(v, w) \in E$, $\ell(v) < \ell(w)$. Suppose on the contrary that there is a node v that requires a label larger than D for the nodes to be topologically sorted. Start with the node v of highest label. Certainly, v must have a predecessor u with $\ell(u) = \ell(v) - 1$ since otherwise the label of v can be reduced. Continuing with this argument would result in a directed path of length more than D, contradicting the assumption that G has a span of D. If a labeling with labels in $\{0, \ldots, D\}$ can be found so that for all $(v, w) \in E$, $\ell(w) = \ell(v) + 1$, then G is called a *leveled network*. If this is not the case for some $(v, w) \in E$, then we may simply replace (v, w) with a path of $\ell(w) - \ell(v)$ edges, where the only purpose of the inner nodes is to verify the output of the predecessor and, if found correct, to forward it to the successor. This creates more work, but if the verification work is insignificant compared to the work of executing the tasks, this is justified for the following reason:

The path replacement strategy is necessary if we want to reach a runtime of $O(D + \log n)$ w.h.p. To see that, consider a task graph consisting of a path of tasks $v_0, \ldots, v_D$ and an edge from v_0 to v_D. Whenever an adversarial worker is selected for v_0, its optimal strategy is to play honest till the computation has reached v_D and then to send a wrong input to v_D, which causes the entire computation to roll back to v_0. Certainly, in this case the best possible runtime bound that can be shown to hold w.h.p. for a constant $\beta > 0$ is $O(D \log n)$.

For the rest of this section, we assume w.l.o.g. that G is a leveled network. We again exclusively focus on the scheduling and assume for simplicity that an honest worker assigned to some task $v \in V$ is able to verify without the supervisor whether the outputs of the preceding tasks (i.e., the tasks $u \in V$ with $(u, v) \in E$) are correct. Furthermore, we again assume a round to be long enough for an honest worker to handle all tasks assigned to it, i.e., for every such v, the worker can receive the outputs from all predecessors of v (if these are honest) and verify these, execute v and then send a feedback on that to the supervisor.

To schedule the computation in a leveled network, the supervisor maintains a set $F \subseteq V$ of *finished* tasks whose executions it already considers to be done, and for each task $v \in F$ it also remembers the worker p_v last assigned to it. Our scheduling strategy for path graphs can easily be generalized to a leveled graph. In particular, given that worker p_v has been assigned to executable task v, it can reply DONE signaling readiness to forward its output to all successors or REJECT(R) rejecting a subset R of its predecessors. If the supervisor receives DONE from p_v, it adds v to F. If it receives REJECT(R) it removes the nodes in R and all tasks reachable from a task in R from F. If it receives no reply, it does not change F. Once we reach a round where $F = V$, i.e., all final nodes sent their outputs to the target and the target accepted them, the execution terminates. If the target rejects an output of a final node v, v is not added to F. Let d be an upper bound on the indegree and outdegree of a node in G and $n = |V|$. We prove the following theorem in the full version of the paper.

Theorem 2. *For any DAG G of degree d and span D, G can be extended to a graph G' so that it holds: If $\beta \leq (1/2(2d+1))^{2+\epsilon}$ for any constant $\epsilon > 0$ then under any adversarial strategy, the supervised computation correctly terminates in $O((D + \log n)/\epsilon)$ rounds, w.h.p. Furthermore, the source and the target just need to send the input and receive the output $O(1)$ times, on expectation.*

4 Applications

We start by giving an overview of the supervised algorithm for multiplying two $m \times m$ matrices. The complete version can be found in the full paper [5]. In the following, n denotes the number tasks that actually compute submatrices rather than just forwarding or duplicating data. The task graph consists of $\Theta(n \log n)$ tasks in total ensuring that our probability bounds still hold w.r.t. its size. We divide the input matrices into $k = \sqrt{n}$ many stripes of width m/k (i.e., $m \times (m/k)$ or $(m/k) \times m$ submatrices). There are k^2 tasks performing the multiplications of the stripes. Since each stripe is required as an input by k of these tasks, there are also $2k$ complete binary trees with k leaves where each task forwards its input to its child tasks. Finally, we add initial lists and final lists of length $c \cdot \log n$ before every binary tree's root task and after every multiplication task.

To verify the subresults, we employ *Freivald's algorithm*, which uses Lemma 1 (directly follows from [13]). We amplify the success probability by repeating the verification τ times. Any failing node is considered malicious.

Lemma 1. *Consider any three matrices $A_i \in \mathcal{M}_{m/k,m}$, $B_j \in \mathcal{M}_{m,m/k}$ and $C_{i,j} \in \mathcal{M}_{m/k,m/k}$ with $A_i \cdot B_j \neq C_{i,j}$ and let $r \in \mathbb{R}^{m/k}$ be a vector chosen uniformly and independently at random. Then $\Pr[A_i \cdot B_j \cdot r = C_{i,j} \cdot r] \leq 1/2$.*

We prove the following theorem in the full version of the paper.

Theorem 3. *If $\beta + 1/2^\tau \leq 1/200$ and $m \geq \sqrt{n} \log n$ then for any adversarial strategy, the supervised matrix multiplication terminates correctly in $O(\log n)$ rounds, w.h.p. Furthermore, the total computational work of the workers is at most $O(m^3)$ on expectation, the maximum computational work for an individual task is $O(m^3/n)$, the total work by the source and the target is at most $O(m^2)$ on expectation and the total work of the supervisor is at most $O(n \log^3 n)$.*

Next, we consider the problem that the source has m data items it wants to sort. Each layer of the task graph has the same number of nodes, which we denote as n. We assume $m = \Omega(n \log n)$. We present the task graph in the full version of the paper. Here, we describe a simplified version. Each of its layers corresponds to one merging step of a mergesort execution. In layer 0, each task sorts the data items it received from the source. In layer i ($1 \leq i \leq \log n$), blocks of data items from layer $i-1$ are merged to a larger block. To accommodate the growing blocks, we distribute the blocks in layer i among 2^i nodes. After layer $\log n$ is executed, the items are sorted and forwarded to the target.

To ensure that each task only has out-dergee 2, we pick n cutoff points called *quantiles* and sort them as part of the preprocessing. We distribute them among the tasks of layer 0 according to the bit reversal permutation. When merging two adjacent blocks of layer $i-1$, each task responsible for the resulting block in layer i receives the data items in the interval between two adjacent quantiles. We show in the full version of the paper that the bit reversal permutation ensures that the origins of the quantiles alternate, i.e., each task has one quantile from each of the two blocks. Thus, each task has at most two successors.

The initial data items are signed to prevent the injection new data items. Additionally, the workers inform the supervisor how many items they send to each successor to track whether workers actually forward the items they received.

We prove the following theorem in the full version of the paper.

Theorem 4. *If $\beta \leq 1/200$ then for any adversarial strategy, the supervised mergesort algorithm terminates within $O(\log n)$ rounds, w.h.p. Furthermore, the source and the target just need $O(m)$ computational and communication work on expectation, the supervisor needs $O(n \log n)$ work, w.h.p, the total computational work performed by the workers is $O(m \log m)$ and the total communication work is $O(m \log n)$ on expectation, and the maximum work of a task is $O((m/n)(\log m / \log n + \log n))$, w.h.p.*

5 Conclusion

We presented a new framework in distributed computing that employs a reliable supervisor, source, and target to orchestrate potentially unreliable workers to solve problems decomposable into a task graph. We demonstrated the power of this framework by applying it to matrix multiplication and sorting.

We believe that our framework can be applied to many other problems that can be parallelized well. The challenge is that lightweight verification mechanisms have to be found, which might open up an interesting new direction of distributed verifiability. Additionally, it should be possible to apply our framework to the case where a majority of peers is adversarial (e.g., by using different scheduling approaches), which would further underline the power of our approach.

Acknowledgements:. John Augustine is supported by the Centre for Cybersecurity, Trust and Reliability (CyStar), IIT Madras. Christian Scheideler and Julian Werthmann are funded by the Deutsche Forschungsgemeinschaft (DFG, German Research Foundation) – 549499840.

Disclosure of Interests. The authors have no competing interests to declare that are relevant to the content of this article.

References

1. Afek, Y., Giladi, G., Patt-Shamir, B.: Distributed computing with the cloud. In: Proceedings of SSS 2021, pp. 1–20 (2021). https://doi.org/10.1007/978-3-030-91081-5_1
2. Alkassar, E., Böhme, S., Mehlhorn, K., Rizkallah, C.: A framework for the verification of certifying computations. J. Autom. Reason. **52**(3), 241–273 (2014). https://doi.org/10.1007/S10817-013-9289-2
3. Anderson, D.P.: https://boinc.berkeley.edu/anderson/, March 2025
4. Augustine, J., Biju, J., Meir, S., Peleg, D., Ramachandran, S., Thiruvengadam, A.: Byzantine resilient computing with the cloud. CoRR **abs/2309.16359** (2023), https://doi.org/10.48550/arXiv.2309.16359
5. Augustine, J., Scheideler, C., Werthmann, J.: Supervised distributed computing (2025), arxiv:2503.11600
6. Awerbuch, B., Scheideler, C.: Towards a scalable and robust DHT. Theor. Comput. Syst. **45**(2), 234–260 (2009)
7. Blum, M., Evans, W.S., Gemmell, P., Kannan, S., Naor, M.: Checking the correctness of memories. In: 32nd Annual Symposium on Foundations of Computer Science, San Juan, Puerto Rico, 1–4 October 1991, pp. 90–99. IEEE Computer Society (1991). https://doi.org/10.1109/SFCS.1991.185352,
8. Chiesa, A.: Succinct non-Interactive arguments. Ph.D. thesis, Massachusetts Institute of Technology (2014)
9. Crescenzo, G.D., Khodjaeva, M., Kahrobaei, D., Shpilrain, V.: A survey on delegated computation. In: Diekert, V., Volkov, M.V. (eds.) Developments in Language Theory - 26th International Conference, DLT 2022, Tampa, FL, USA, 9–13 May 2022, Proceedings. Lecture Notes in Computer Science, vol. 13257, pp. 33–53. Springer (2022). https://doi.org/10.1007/978-3-031-05578-2_3,

10. Feigenbaum, J.: Overview of interactive proof systems and zero-knowledge. Contemp. Cryptology Sci. Inf. Integrity 423–439 (1992)
11. Fiat, A., Saia, J.: Censorship resistant peer-to-peer networks. Theor. Comput. **3**(1), 1–23 (2007)
12. Fiat, A., Saia, J., Young, M.: Making chord robust to byzantine attacks. In: Brodal, G.S., Leonardi, S. (eds.) ESA 2005. LNCS, vol. 3669, pp. 803–814. Springer, Heidelberg (2005). https://doi.org/10.1007/11561071_71
13. Freivalds, R.M.: Probabilistic machines can use less running time. In: Proceedings of IFIP Congress 1977, pp. 839–842 (1977)
14. Friedman, R., Kliot, G., Kogan, A.: Hybrid distributed consensus. In: Baldoni, R., Nisse, N., van Steen, M. (eds.) OPODIS 2013. LNCS, vol. 8304, pp. 145–159. Springer, Cham (2013). https://doi.org/10.1007/978-3-319-03850-6_11
15. Goodrich, M.T.: Pipelined algorithms to detect cheating in long-term grid computations. Theor. Comput. Sci. **408**(2–3), 199–207 (2008). https://doi.org/10.1016/J.TCS.2008.08.008
16. Hildrum, K., Kubiatowicz, J.: Asymptotically efficient approaches to fault-tolerance in peer-to-peer networks. In: Fich, F.E. (ed.) DISC 2003. LNCS, vol. 2848, pp. 321–336. Springer, Heidelberg (2003). https://doi.org/10.1007/978-3-540-39989-6_23
17. Jaiyeola, M.O., Patron, K., Saia, J., Young, M., Zhou, Q.M.: Tiny groups tackle Byzantine adversaries. In: Proceedings of IPDPS 2018, pp. 1030–1039 (2018)
18. Kokoris-Kogias, E., Malkhi, D., Spiegelman, A.: Asynchronous distributed key generation for computationally-secure randomness, consensus, and threshold signatures. In: CCS 2020, pp. 1751–1767. ACM (2020)
19. Leighton, F.T., Maggs, B.M., Ranade, A.G., Rao, S.: Randomized routing and sorting on fixed-connection networks. J. Algorithms **17**(1), 157–205 (1994)
20. Leung, J.Y. (ed.): Handbook of Scheduling - Algorithms, Models, and Performance Analysis. Chapman and Hall/CRC (2004)
21. McConnell, R.M., Mehlhorn, K., Näher, S., Schweitzer, P.: Certifying algorithms. Comput. Sci. Rev. **5**(2), 119–161 (2011). https://doi.org/10.1016/J.COSREV.2010.09.009
22. Naor, M., Wieder, U.: A simple fault tolerant distributed hash table. In: Kaashoek, M.F., Stoica, I. (eds.) IPTPS 2003. LNCS, vol. 2735, pp. 88–97. Springer, Heidelberg (2003). https://doi.org/10.1007/978-3-540-45172-3_8
23. Nitulescu, A.: zk-snarks: a gentle introduction. Ecole Normale Superieure (2020)
24. Pastrana-Cruz, A., Lafond, M.: A lightweight semi-centralized strategy for the massive parallelization of branching algorithms. Parallel Comput. **116**, 103024 (2023). https://doi.org/10.1016/J.PARCO.2023.103024
25. Pease, M.C., Shostak, R.E., Lamport, L.: Reaching agreement in the presence of faults. J. ACM **27**(2), 228–234 (1980). https://doi.org/10.1145/322186.322188
26. Ranade, A.G.: How to emulate shared memory. J. Comput. Syst. Sci. **42**(3), 307–326 (1991)
27. Saia, J., Fiat, A., Gribble, S., Karlin, A.R., Saroiu, S.: Dynamically fault-tolerant content addressable networks. In: Druschel, P., Kaashoek, F., Rowstron, A. (eds.) IPTPS 2002. LNCS, vol. 2429, pp. 270–279. Springer, Heidelberg (2002). https://doi.org/10.1007/3-540-45748-8_26
28. Tamassia, R.: Authenticated data structures. In: Proceedings of 11th European Symposium on Algorithms (ESA 2003), pp. 2–5 (2003). https://doi.org/10.1007/978-3-540-39658-1_2
29. Tutorial, H.M.: https://hadoop.apache.org/docs/r1.2.1/mapred_tutorial.html, March 2025

30. Zhang, G., et al.: Reaching consensus in the byzantine empire: a comprehensive review of BFT consensus algorithms. ACM Comput. Surv. **56**(5), 134:1–134:41 (2024)
31. Zhao, C., et al.: Secure multi-party computation: theory, practice and applications. Inf. Sci. **476**, 357–372 (2019). https://doi.org/10.1016/j.ins.2018.10.024

Near-Optimal Contraction Strategies for the Scalar Product in the Tensor-Train Format

Atte Torri[1,2,3]({{mail}})[iD], Przemysław Dominikowski[1,4][iD], Brice Pointal[1,2,3][iD], Oguz Kaya[1,2,3][iD], Laércio Lima Pilla[6][iD], and Olivier Coulaud[5][iD]

[1] Université Paris-Saclay, Gif-sur-Yvette, France
atte.torri@universite-paris-saclay.fr
[2] LISN, Gif-sur-Yvette, France
[3] CNRS, Gif-sur-Yvette, France
[4] Inria, Palaiseau, France
[5] Inria, Bordeaux, France
[6] Univ. Bordeaux, CNRS, Bordeaux INP, Inria, LaBRI, Talence, France

Abstract. Tensor-train (TT) decomposition has garnered tremendous popularity for its efficiency in handling high-dimensional data arising in scientific and quantum computing as well as machine learning applications. It provides a compact representation for matrices and vectors with a Kronecker product-like low-rank structure and enables efficient matrix-vector operations in this compressed form. The vector scalar product is among such key operations, comprising a series of tensor contractions in a specific tensor network topology whose order significantly impacts the computational cost. In this work, we propose efficient algorithms for finding near-optimal contraction orderings for tensor networks representing scalar products in the TT format. We show that our algorithms outperform all existing contraction ordering methods for general tensor networks where the best existing method incurs up to 15% higher cost for $x^T y$, twice the cost for $x^T A y$, and ten times higher cost for $x^T A B y$ scalar products where x, y and A, B are vectors and matrices expressed in the TT format, respectively.

Keywords: Numerical linear algebra · Multilinear algebra · Tensor decomposition · Tensor-train decomposition · Scalar product · Tensor contraction ordering · Dynamic programming

1 Introduction

In multilinear algebra, a tensor is an element of the tensor product of multiple vector spaces and is capable of representing multidimensional data. Specifically, an N-dimensional tensor $\mathcal{X} \in \mathbb{R}^{I_1 \times \cdots \times I_N}$ has $\prod_{n=1}^{N} I_n$ elements $\mathcal{X}(i_1, \ldots, i_N)$ for $1 \leq i_n \leq I_n$ and $1 \leq n \leq N$. Tensor methods have gained tremendous popularity in numerous domains, including quantum computing, machine learning, scientific computing, signal processing, and many others [7], due to their aptitude in naturally representing high-dimensional data as well as manipulating it efficiently through tensor operations. Among such key operations is the contraction of two tensors, which is reminiscent of the multiplication of two matrices $C = AB$ where $A \in \mathbb{R}^{M \times K}$, $B \in \mathbb{R}^{K \times N}$, and $C \in \mathbb{R}^{M \times N}$ with elements $C(i,j) = \sum_{k=1}^{K} A(i,k) B(k,j)$, which requires $\mathcal{O}(MNK)$ operations. In the tensor case, the contraction of two tensors $\mathcal{A} \in \mathbb{R}^{M_1 \times \cdots \times M_m \times K_1 \times \cdots \times K_k}$ and $\mathcal{B} \in \mathbb{R}^{K_1 \times \cdots \times K_k \times N_1 \times \cdots \times N_n}$ along dimensions $K_1, \ldots, K_k$ yields a tensor $\mathcal{C}$ such that $\mathcal{C}(i_1, \ldots, i_n, j_1, \ldots, j_m) = \sum_{l_1, \ldots, l_k}^{K_1, \ldots, K_k} \mathcal{A}(i_1, \ldots, i_n, l_1, \ldots, l_k) \mathcal{B}(l_1, \ldots, l_k j_1, \ldots, j_m)$. Here, the resulting tensor $\mathcal{C}$ can be computed with $\mathcal{O}(\prod_{i=1}^{m} M_i \prod_{j=1}^{n} N_j \prod_{l=1}^{k} K_l)$ operations, where $\mathcal{C} \in \mathbb{R}^{M_1 \times \cdots \times M_m \times N_1 \times \cdots \times N_n}$.

A fundamental limitation of tensor computations is the exponential growth of the computational and memory cost with the number of tensor dimensions, a phenomenon known as *the curse of dimensionality* [7]. Specifically, a tensor $\mathcal{X} \in \mathbb{R}^{I_1 \times \cdots \times I_N}$ requires $\mathcal{O}(I_1 \ldots I_N)$ space, which grows exponentially with N. Fortunately, a high-dimensional tensor can often be represented as or approximated by a network of small-dimensional tensors, called a *tensor decomposition* [7]. The contraction of these tensors over their shared dimensions reconstructs the original tensor. Among various tensor decomposition network topologies, tensor-train (TT) decomposition [12] has garnered great interest from numerous applications. Formally, it represents a tensor $\mathcal{X}$ using N three-dimensional tensors $\mathcal{G}_1, \ldots, \mathcal{G}_N$ in a decomposed form $\mathcal{X} = \mathcal{G}_1 \times_{r_1} \mathcal{G}_2 \times_{r_2} \cdots \times_{r_{N-1}} \mathcal{G}_N$ with $\mathcal{G}_n \in \mathbb{R}^{r_{n-1} \times I_n \times r_n}$ and $r_0 = r_N = 1$. Here, the contraction of $\mathcal{G}_n$ along common/inner network dimensions $r_1, \ldots, r_{N-1}$ yields $\mathcal{X}$ with elements $\mathcal{X}(i_1, i_2, \ldots, i_N) = \sum \mathcal{G}_1(i_1, \alpha_1) \mathcal{G}_2(\alpha_1, i_2, \alpha_2) \ldots \mathcal{G}_N(\alpha_{N-1}, i_N)$ for all $1 \leq \alpha_n \leq r_n$ and $1 \leq n \leq N$. This representation effectively reduces the storage complexity from $\mathcal{O}(I^N)$ to $\mathcal{O}(NIR^2)$ where $R = \max_{1 \leq n \leq N} r_n$ and r_n is called the *rank* of the decomposition. To effectively compress the data, R should remain low, in which case the tensor $\mathcal{X}$ is said to be of *low rank*. This applies in many quantum computing applications where vectors representing a quantum state inherently exhibit a Kronecker product structure, e.g., $x = \sum_{j=1}^{R} \bigotimes_{i=1}^{N} x_i$ for $x_i \in \mathbb{R}^{I_i}$, which can be effectively represented using a low-rank N-dimensional TT decomposition [14]. Similarly, in many scientific computing applications, such Kronecker-like structures exist naturally or can be imposed on a vector $x \in \mathbb{R}^M$ to obtain an $N = \log_2 M$-dimensional tensor representation $\mathcal{X} \in \mathbb{R}^{2 \times \cdots \times 2}$ of vector elements via a process called *quantization* [6]. When done correctly, this preserves a low TT decomposition rank and thereby allows effective compression. We refer to this as the *TT-vector* representation of a vector x. Similarly to vectors, matrices/operators can also have an inherent low-rank structure, e.g., $A = \sum_{j=1}^{R} \bigotimes_{i=1}^{N} A_i$ where $A_i \in \mathbb{R}^{I_i \times J_i}$, or can be likewise *quantized* into such a structure. An N-dimensional TT decomposition can then be used to compactly represent these matrices, which we refer to as the *TT-matrix* representation where each tensor in the decomposition has two free dimensions instead of one. The first and second free dimensions of all tensors in a TT-matrix represent the rows and columns of the full matrix A, respectively.

Once matrices and vectors are represented in this way, the TT framework provides efficient algorithms to carry out all matrix-vector operations, including basic matrix/vector arithmetic and matrix-vector multiplication, within the TT-matrix and TT-vector formats [12]. This capability enables the development of high-dimensional numerical algorithms that leverage the efficiency of compact TT representations. Among these operations is the *scalar product* of two TT-vectors, which is an essential step in many applications. In numerical solvers, the vector scalar product is a key operation used to compute the vector norm ($\sqrt{x^T x}$) or Rayleigh coefficient ($x^T A x / x^T x$), to name a few examples. In quantum chemistry applications, CholeskyQR algorithm is used to orthogonalize a basis $B = [b_1, \ldots, b_s]$ of s TT-vectors, necessitating the formation of the Gram matrix $G = B^T B$. This requires $\mathcal{O}(s^2)$ scalar products involving TT-vectors in B, which constitutes one of the most computationally expensive steps in the application [14]. In machine learning, kernel methods have recently been extended to use TT-vectors where kernel functions leverage scalar products $x^T y$ or $x^T A y$ of TT-vectors x and y where A is a TT-matrix [1].

The main focus of this work is to perform such TT scalar product computations near-optimally in order to accelerate the applications whose performance heavily depends on this fundamental operation. In Figs. 1a and b, we provide the tensor network diagrams corresponding to the scalar products $x^T y$ and $x^T A y$ where x and y are TT-vectors and A is a TT-matrix with corresponding dimensions. In this diagram, each node represents a tensor in the network, and each outgoing edge from a node represents a dimension of the tensor. A common dimension connecting two tensors indicates a contraction to be performed between them along this dimension. In Fig. 1a, p_n and q_n respectively represent the ranks of TT-vectors x and y, while c_n represent common vector dimensions. Similarly, in Fig. 1b, the TT-matrix A comprises N four-dimensional tensors with row dimensions c_n, column dimensions d_n, and rank dimensions q_n. In both cases, the scalar product is obtained by the pairwise contraction of all tensors in the network in any order, yielding a 0-dimensional tensor, i.e., a scalar, as no free edge would remain in the network after contractions. However, the order in which these contractions are performed has a significant impact on the total contraction cost. For a general tensor network, finding an optimal contraction order is an NP-hard problem [8]. Our goal in this work is to design efficient algorithms tailored specifically for TT scalar product networks to find a near-optimal contraction ordering in a reasonable time.

2 Related Work

Optimal Algorithms: There are three main approaches to finding an optimal contraction order in a general tensor network: depth-first approaches [8,13], breadth-first strategies [5,13], and a dynamic programming formulation with memoization [13]. Cost capping and outer product restrictions can be leveraged to make optimal algorithms more efficient by pruning unwanted subtrees that are deemed too expensive or involve contractions of unconnected tensors [13].

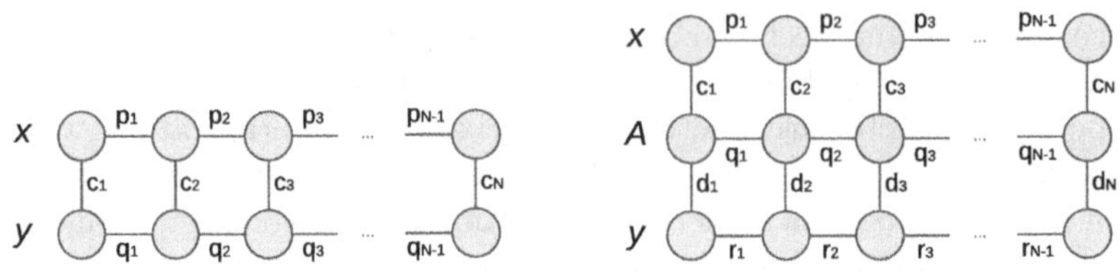

Fig. 1. Tensor network diagram for a TT scalar product

The cotengra library [4] provides an optimized implementation based on the depth-first strategy, which we refer to as *Optimal* in the rest of the paper.

Greedy Algorithms: A simple greedy heuristic consists of sorting all possible contractions in the network by their costs at each step and then carrying out the least expensive one. Since this approach ignores the impact of this choice on the cost of remaining contractions, it is susceptible to causing a high total contraction cost in the end. To address this limitation, another metric for the greedy approach is proposed in [4], which sorts all possible immediate contractions with a heuristic cost function involving the size difference between the contracted tensors $\mathcal{A}$ and $\mathcal{B}$ and the resulting tensor $\mathcal{C}$ of the contraction. This method also includes a weighting parameter α that multiplies the size of the input tensors, resulting in the heuristic cost function $cost(\mathcal{A}, \mathcal{B}) = size(\mathcal{C}) - \alpha(size(\mathcal{A}) + size(\mathcal{B}))$. Furthermore, to allow the algorithm to sample multiple greedy paths, a probabilistic *Boltzmann factor* τ is introduced. The algorithm that tunes the parameter α and performs Boltzmann sampling on the factor τ to return one of the best contraction paths is part of the cotengra library [4], which we refer to as *Hyper-Greedy*. Recent work [11] extends this approach by using multiple cost functions where each function provides a different contraction order, and the best one is kept. We denote this strategy as *Cgreedy*.

Recursive Tensor Network Partitioning: Another strategy introduced in [4] involves building the contraction tree with a top-down approach by recursively partitioning the network into multiple subnetworks, contracting tensors within each subnetwork among themselves, and finally combining the resulting tensors with another set of contractions. Specifically, the algorithm starts with the root vertex corresponding to the set V containing all tensors in the network. Then, it partitions V into k vertex sets ($V = V_1 \cup V_2 \cup \cdots \cup V_k$) each forming a subnetwork, which are then contracted within themselves with the same partitioning algorithm used recursively. When the size of a subnetwork $|V_k|$ falls below a threshold, another algorithm such as *Optimal* or *Hyper-Greedy* can be used instead. Once each subnetwork is contracted into a single tensor, the resulting tensors are contracted among themselves to obtain the final contraction, for which the order can be determined using one of these two algorithms. One such state-of-the-art partitioner is provided by the KaHyPar library [15].

The cotengra library [4] uses this partitioner by repeatedly sampling contraction paths and tuning the parameters k and ϵ to keep the path with the minimum cost. We denote this approach as *Hyper-Kahypar*.

Tree Decomposition Approaches: Some strategies perform a *tree decomposition* on the line graph of the tensor network [9]. A tree decomposition maps a graph into a tree structure where each node (bag) represents a subset of vertices from the original graph, capturing its connectivity structure. An optimal tree decomposition has minimal *width* [9] (i.e. equal to *treewidth*). Given an optimal tree decomposition for the line graph of the tensor network, one can use a polynomial-time deterministic algorithm to find an optimal contraction ordering [9]. However, finding an optimal tree decomposition is an NP-hard problem [9] for which there exist heuristics such as *QuickBB* [3] and *FlowCutter* [2,17]. *QuickBB* employs a branch-and-bound strategy to find a tree decomposition, with the aim of effectively pruning the search space. *FlowCutter* uses a graph partitioning approach, leveraging the equivalence between multilevel partitionings and tree decompositions [17]. It performs recursive bisections on the line graph to find a partitioning and compares it with previous results until the treewidth can no longer be notably improved.

Learning Strategies: Reinforcement learning (RL) has emerged as a promising approach for addressing combinatorial optimization problems. In the context of graph-based problems, Graph Neural Networks (GNNs) demonstrate a significant potential. This approach has been applied to the tensor network contraction ordering problem [10], where the problem is modeled as a Markov decision process. In this formulation, the state space comprises all possible graphs, the action space consists of potential edge contractions, the transition function maps the current graph to the subsequent graph with the selected edge contracted, and the reward function quantifies the cost of the chosen contraction. The RL agent is initialized with a graph representing a tensor network and, at each step, selects an edge to contract based on a probability distribution. The agent is trained to minimize contraction costs using proximal policy optimization (PPO) [10,16]. The authors introduce additional techniques to enhance performance, such as path pruning to handle the extensive search space and incorporating existing algorithms to solve part of the problem. We trained and evaluated this method on TT scalar product networks, which we refer to as *RL-TNCO*.

Standard Approach for TT Scalar Product Networks: The standard approach for the TT scalar product performs all contractions involving tensors in the leftmost dimension in a fixed order, which effectively reduces the network's width by one, then repeats the same process on the remaining network. Such an ordering prevents the formation of high-dimensional intermediate tensors, indirectly bounding the contraction cost. In Fig. 1a, this approach corresponds to contracting the edge c_1 first and p_1 next. This would eliminate tensors in the first two dimensions yet add an edge q_1 parallel to c_2 in the second dimension. The algorithm similarly proceeds to eliminate the following dimensions (contracting the edge $q_1 c_2$ first, p_2 next, etc.) until the entire network is contracted. We extend this strategy to the scalar product $x^T A y$ with respect to a TT-matrix A. In Fig. 1b, this corresponds to the contraction of edges c_1, d_1, and q_1 in order, which eliminates the first dimension while similarly adding parallel edges p_1 to c_2 and r_1 to d_2. The algorithm then proceeds to contract the tensors in the remaining dimensions in the same order (by contracting edges p_1c_2, r_1d_2, and q_2, etc.). In both cases, the algorithm runs on both sides of the network and picks the best of two orderings. We denote this approach as the *Sweep* method, which is widely used in tensor libraries such as TT-Toolbox [12].

3 Effective Contraction Ordering Strategies for TT Scalar Product Networks

In this section, we propose two new algorithms, namely *Sweep-opt* and Δ-*opt*, which take advantage of the special structure of TT scalar product networks to find near-optimal contraction orderings using efficient dynamic programming.

3.1 Optimal Sweep Algorithm

For computing $x^T y$, the *Sweep* method eliminates each dimension i by contracting the edge c_i followed by p_i, resulting in the addition of an edge q_i parallel to c_{i+1} in the network. However, this dimension can also be eliminated by contracting c_i and q_i or p_i and q_i, which adds edge p_i or c_i parallel to c_{i+1}, respectively. In all cases, parallel edges are equivalent to having one edge whose size is the product of the sizes of parallel edges. The goal of the *Sweep-opt* algorithm is to eliminate one dimension at a time similarly while making optimal decisions.

Since the choice of two contractions (p_i/c_i, q_i/c_i, or p_i/q_i) to eliminate a dimension modifies the remaining network, a straightforward approach would consider all $\mathcal{O}(3^N)$ possibilities and keep the best, which is infeasible for large N. Fortunately, we observe that the number of possible modifications to the remaining network is limited, restricting the search space and creating a small number of overlapping subproblems. Performing a contraction on p_i/c_i or q_i/c_i eliminates all existing parallel edges on c_i, adding solely the edge q_i or p_i parallel to c_{i+1}, respectively. However, a p_i/q_i contraction propagates all current parallel edges of c_i as well as c_i itself onto c_{i+1}. Therefore, for any dimension i, the set of edges parallel to c_i can only be of the form $\{p_k, c_{k+1}, \ldots, c_{i-1}\}$ or $\{q_k, c_{k+1}, \ldots, c_{i-1}\}$ for $0 \leq k < i$ (Fig. 2). We define $\mathcal{F}_p(i, k)$ as the optimal contraction cost of the *Sweep-opt* strategy for the subnetwork involving dimensions $[i, N]$, given that c_i has parallel edges $\{p_k, c_{k+1}, \ldots, c_{i-1}\}$. We define $\mathcal{F}_q$ in an analogous manner. This creates $\mathcal{O}(N^2)$ subproblems with an overlapping structure depending on the choice of two contractions per dimension as follows:

$$\mathcal{F}_p(i,k) \begin{array}{c} \xrightarrow{p_i/c_i} \mathcal{F}_q(i+1,i) \\ \xrightarrow{q_i/c_i} \mathcal{F}_p(i+1,i) \\ \xrightarrow{p_i/q_i} \mathcal{F}_p(i+1,k) \end{array} \qquad \mathcal{F}_q(i,k) \begin{array}{c} \xrightarrow{p_i/c_i} \mathcal{F}_q(i+1,i) \\ \xrightarrow{q_i/c_i} \mathcal{F}_p(i+1,i) \\ \xrightarrow{p_i/q_i} \mathcal{F}_q(i+1,k) \end{array} \qquad (1)$$

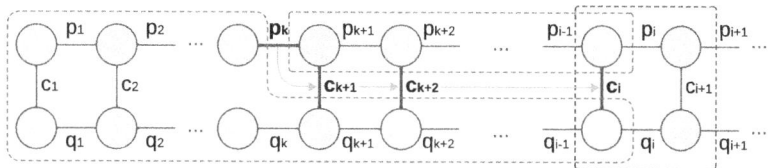

Fig. 2. Formation of the edge set $\{p_k, c_{k+1}, \ldots, c_{i-1}\}$ parallel to c_i

Let $\mathcal{C}_{pc}(i,k)$ be the minimum of the cost of contracting p_i first and c_i next or vice versa on a subnetwork $[i, N]$ having edges $\{p_k, c_{k+1}, \ldots, c_{i-1}\}$ parallel to c_i. We define $\mathcal{C}_{qc}$ and $\mathcal{C}_{pq}$ similarly. Following Eq. (1), we can then define the optimal sweeping contraction cost for this subnetwork as

$$\mathcal{F}_p(i,k) = \min\{\mathcal{F}_q(i+1,i) + \mathcal{C}_{pc}(i,k), \mathcal{F}_p(i+1,i) + \mathcal{C}_{qc}(i,k), \mathcal{F}_p(i+1,k) + \mathcal{C}_{pq}(i,k)\}$$

and express $\mathcal{F}_q(i,k)$ analogously.

Complexity: If the values $p_k c_{k+1} \ldots c_i$ and $q_k c_{k+1} \ldots c_i$ are precomputed for all $0 \leq k < i \leq N$ in $\mathcal{O}(N^2)$ time, each evaluation of $\mathcal{C}$ can be performed in constant time. The same holds then for the computation of $\mathcal{F}_p(i,k)$ and $\mathcal{F}_q(i,k)$, yielding $\mathcal{O}(N^2)$ time and space complexity for the *Sweep-opt* algorithm. We run the algorithm from both ends of the tensor network and keep the best solution.

3.2 Optimal Δ-Window Algorithm

Despite being very efficient, *Sweep-opt* has two potential drawbacks. First, for networks with very irregular ranks or dimension sizes, eliminating a single dimension at a time, albeit optimally, might still diverge from the optimal contraction order. Second, it cannot be generalized to scalar products involving matrices (e.g., $x^T A y$) with the same quadratic complexity. To remedy these, we propose another algorithm, Δ-*opt*, which aims to optimally eliminate multiple dimensions at a time within a small window of Δ dimensions.

Consider the tensor network for $x^T y$ whose tensors in the first $i-1$ dimensions are already contracted. Regardless of the order of these contractions, we note that this creates an intermediate tensor of size $p_{i-1} \times q_{i-1}$ connected to the rest of the network that involves tensors in dimensions $[i, N]$ and remains unmodified. The aim of Δ-*opt* is to find a near-optimal contraction cost from this starting configuration to contract all tensors up to dimension $j \geq i$, which we represent as $\mathcal{G}_{LR}(i,j)$. A key observation is that performing these contractions creates the same initial configuration for the dimension $j+1$ this time, with an intermediate tensor of size $p_j \times q_j$ connected to the rest of the network for dimensions $[j+1, N]$ which remain unmodified. If the window size is deemed small (i.e., $j - i < \Delta$), we resort to an optimal solver. Otherwise, we consider all possible splits and take the minimum, that is, $\mathcal{G}_{LR}(i,j) = \min_{k=i \ldots j-1} (\mathcal{G}_{LR}(i,k) + \mathcal{G}_{LR}(k+1,j))$. However, since $\mathcal{G}_{LR}(i,k)$ itself may be composed of splits, these splits eventually produce a series of windows smaller than Δ, which are solved optimally. Therefore, it is unnecessary to consider $k \geq i + \Delta$, which simplifies the formulation to

$$\mathcal{G}_{LR}(i,j) = \begin{cases} \mathcal{G}_{LR}^{(opt)}(i,j), & j - i < \Delta \\ \min_{k=i\ldots\min(i+\Delta-1,N)} (\mathcal{G}_{LR}(i,k) + \mathcal{G}_{LR}(k+1,j)) & \text{otherwise} \end{cases} \quad (2)$$

where $\mathcal{G}_{LR}^{(opt)}(i,j)$ is the contraction cost obtained from an optimal solver. We similarly compute all $\mathcal{G}_{RL}(i,j)$ from the other end of the network.

Finally, we consider all one-sided or meet-in-the-middle contraction scenarios for the final solution as

$$\min \begin{pmatrix} \mathcal{G}_{LR}(1,N), \\ \mathcal{G}_{RL}(1,N), \\ \min_{i=1\ldots N-1} (\mathcal{G}_{LR}(1,i) + \mathcal{G}_{RL}(i+1,N) + p_i q_i) \end{pmatrix} \quad (3)$$

where $p_i q_i$ represents the cost of the final contraction when both subnetworks $[1,i)$ and $(i+1,N]$ are contracted beforehand.

Complexity: In the Δ-opt implementation, we first precompute the optimal solutions $\mathcal{G}_{LR}^{(opt)}(i,j)$ for all windows $1 \leq i \leq j \leq \min(i + \Delta - 1, N)$ and set the base cases for the dynamic programming formulation. Then, we compute each $\mathcal{G}_{LR}(i,j)$ using $O(\Delta)$ table lookups, which gives $\mathcal{O}(N^2 \Delta + N \sum_{d=1}^{\Delta} opt_{2d+1})$ time and $\mathcal{O}(N^2)$ space complexity where opt_k is the cost of running an optimal solver on a network with k tensors. The final step in Eq. (3) only takes $\mathcal{O}(N)$ time. The algorithm generalizes to products such as $x^T A y$ or $x^T A B y$; we skip the details.

Choice of Δ: If Δ is chosen to be a very small constant, the algorithm has $\mathcal{O}(N^2)$ time and space complexity; however, the cost can escalate with increasing Δ due to the optimal solver. Therefore, we suggest iterative discovery of Δ in practice, starting with a small window ($\Delta = 2$) and increasing it until either the solution no longer improves or the optimal solver becomes too expensive.

4 Experiments

In this section, we compare the contraction cost and execution time of our algorithms against those of *Optimal*, *Hyper-Greedy*, *Cgreedy*, *Hyper-Kahypar*, *Flow-Cutter*, *QuickBB*, *RL-TNCO*, and *Sweep* approaches. The implementation of our algorithms, along with scripts to generate our results, is available on GitHub.[1]

4.1 Setup

For all algorithms except *RL-TNCO*, we used the implementations provided in the `cotengra` library (version 0.6.2). Additionally, Δ-opt incorporates the *Optimal* implementation from `cotengra` as a subroutine.

---

[1] https://github.com/Blixodus/TT-ScalProdOpt.

Our benchmarks consist of TT scalar products of the form $x^T y$, $x^T A y$, and $x^T A B y$, using TTs with a number of dimensions ranging from 2 to 100, as well as varying rank and dimension size characteristics as follows:

- *rand-rand* (random-random): Dimensions and ranks follow a uniform random distribution, with dimension sizes between 2 and 50, and ranks ranging from 1 to 200.
- *quant-rand* (quantized-random): All dimensions are set to 2 as in the quantized TT formats [6], and the ranks follow a uniform random distribution between 1 and 200.
- *quant-incr* (quantized-increasing): All dimensions are equal to 2, and ranks progressively increase towards the center of TT with some random variation. The peak rank is achieved around the middle of the network for matrices A and B, and around the first and third quartile of dimensions for vectors x and y, respectively. Such patterns are commonly observed in many applications that use TTs to represent low-rank high-dimensional data [6].

In all cases, TTs are ensured to meet the rank feasibility conditions, i.e., $p_i \leq p_{i+1} c_{i+1}$ and $p_i \leq p_{i-1} c_i$, which are enforced in practice by TT-SVD and rank reduction algorithms [12]. We also tested the cases $x^T x$ and $x^T A x$, which correspond to vector norm and A-norm computations, respectively, and using lower (up to 50) and higher (up to 1000) maximum ranks. The results were comparable to $x^T y$ and $x^T A y$ experiments with ranks up to 200; therefore, for brevity, we do not report them here.

For each test case and number of TT dimensions, we evaluated 50 instances. For each instance and algorithm, the contraction cost was normalized with respect to the minimum cost obtained for that instance across all algorithms. In our visualizations, the dark lines represent the geometric mean of these 50 normalized results, while the lighter-shaded regions represent the geometric standard deviation from this mean. A solid vertical black line marks the point beyond which the optimal algorithm is no longer executed due to exceeding a computational time threshold of 60 min. Beyond this cutoff, cost normalization is performed using the lowest cost achieved among the remaining algorithms.

For *RL-TNCO*, we trained the model on a diverse set of TT scalar product networks. Specifically, for each TT type (*rand-rand*, *quant-rand*, *quant-incr*), we generated 100 training instances, each with 100 dimensions. During training, all reinforcement learning parameters were kept at their default values. Due to machine availability constraints, we evaluated *RL-TNCO* with a subset of the dataset used for other methods, considering only 25 instances per configuration and only networks of type $x^T y$ and $x^T A y$. For some instances, *RL-TNCO* failed to produce a valid ordering; these cases were excluded from the statistical analysis.

In addition to synthetic benchmarks, we evaluate the algorithms on a quantum chemistry application that aims to compute the vibrational spectra of molecules [14]. This application employs a TT-based iterative eigensolver, where both $x^T y$ and $x^T A y$ serve as key steps within each iteration. We evaluated using

TTs with 60 dimensions generated during the first iteration, using an error tolerance of $\epsilon = 10^{-6}$ for rank truncation.

We performed our experiments, excluding *RL-TNCO*, on machines equipped with two 20-core *Intel ® Xeon ® Gold 6230* processors operating at a fixed frequency of 2.1 GHz, along with 192 GB of RAM. For *RL-TNCO*, which requires a GPU, we used machines with the same processors but with 768 GB of RAM, and an *Nvidia ® Tesla ® V100* GPU featuring 32 GB of VRAM. All algorithms, except *RL-TNCO*, were run on a single core using a unified C++ wrapper to mitigate overhead effects associated with parsing the TT descriptor and invoking the respective libraries. The reported execution times exclusively correspond to the function responsible for computing and returning the contraction cost for each algorithm.

4.2 Results

Vector-Vector Product $(\boldsymbol{x^T y})$: In Figs. 3a, b, c, we report the total contraction cost for computing $x^T y$ for all algorithms. We first note that in all three cases of *rand-rand*, *quant-rand*, and *quant-incr*, *Sweep-opt* gives results that are indistinguishable from the optimal and provides a dramatic improvement over *Sweep*. This not only suggests that contracting tensors site-by-site is preferable for such TT scalar products, but also demonstrates that choosing the optimal contraction ordering among $p_i q_i$, $p_i c_i$, or $q_i c_i$ is crucial for minimizing the total contraction cost, thus advocating the use of *Sweep-opt* for such networks. Δ-*opt* similarly gives near-optimal results in all three cases using a window size Δ as small as 2, as it can similarly identify the ideal contraction order owing to the use of an optimal algorithm in a small window. Among other methods, *Hyper-Greedy* performs the best, starting close to the optimal for small networks, yet slowly diverging from it as the number of dimensions increases, yielding up to 15% higher contraction cost for 100 dimensions. Next, *Cgreedy* performs significantly worse than *Hyper-Greedy* overall, while *FlowCutter* and *QuickBB* converge to a non-optimal plateau in all three cases. *Hyper-Kahypar* incurs a notably high contraction cost overall, while displaying erratic contraction costs beyond 35 dimensions. This suggests that although hypergraph partitioning can be very useful for general tensor networks, it is not an effective strategy for structured networks exhibiting a 1D-like structure, such as our case. Finally, *RL-TNCO* performs poorly, particularly in the *quant-incr* case, which disqualifies it as an effective strategy for such scenarios, especially considering its high training and inference costs for RL, when near-optimal solutions can be computed using *Sweep-opt*.

In Fig. 3h, we provide the results using TTs from the quantum chemistry application. We observe that *Hyper-Kahypar* performs very poorly, causing more than eight times higher contraction cost than *Optimal*. Next, similar to Figs. 3a, b, c, both *Sweep-opt* and Δ-*opt* using $\Delta \geq 2$ perform identical to *Optimal*. Among the remaining methods, *RL-TNCO* has the worst performance with 11% higher contraction cost than *Optimal*, and surprisingly, *Sweep* is the best with

7% higher cost than *Optimal*. This is mostly due to this network having fixed dimension sizes ($c_i = 15$) and low-rank variation, making the problem "easier".

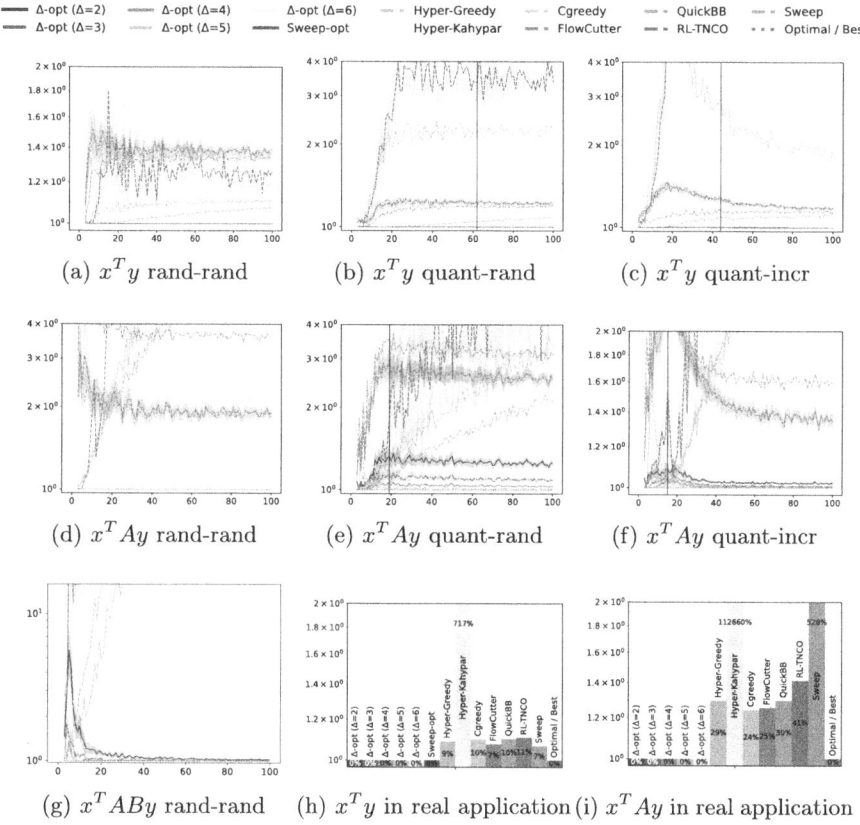

Fig. 3. Contraction cost for different types of TT scalar products. The y-axis represents the contraction cost relative to the optimal/best method. For Figs. 3a, b, c, d, e, f, and g, the x-axis is the number of TT dimensions. For Figs. 3h and i, each bar represents a method.

Vector-Matrix-Vector Product ($x^T Ay$): 3d to f, we provide the contraction costs for all algorithms except *Sweep-opt* for the $x^T Ay$ computation. In the *rand-rand* case in Fig. 3d, we first note that Δ-*opt* provides near-optimal results for Δ as small as 2 across all tensor network sizes. Next, we observe that *QuickBB* and *FlowCutter* significantly outperform other methods, while incurring up to twice the contraction cost of Δ-*opt*. Finally, *Sweep* converges to approximately four times the contraction cost of Δ-*opt* for larger tensor networks, whereas the remaining methods (*Hyper-Greedy*, *Cgreedy*, *Hyper-Kahypar*, *RL-TNCO*) incur more than ten times the optimal cost for such networks.

Next, in the *quant-rand* case in Fig. 3e, we first observe that Δ-*opt* no longer finds near-optimal orderings for $\Delta = 2$, but it converges to a plateau of around 26% higher cost than the optimal. Increasing the window size to 3 reduces this to around 9%, and for $\Delta > 4$, the results become near-optimal for all instances. The best contender in this case is *Hyper-Greedy*, which incurs a higher contraction cost as the number of dimensions increases, requiring more than twice the optimal cost for large networks. *Cgreedy* performs worse than *Hyper-Greedy* similarly, *QuickBB* and *FlowCutter* converge to a non-optimal plateau, and *Hyper-Kahypar* and *RL-TNCO* diverge from the optimal.

In Fig. 3f, *quant-incr* shows similar tendencies, except that even for $\Delta = 3$, Δ-*opt* manages to find near-optimal solutions in most instances. Finally, Fig. 3i provides the results of $x^T A y$ contraction from the quantum chemistry application, where *Hyper-Kahypar* performs the worst, and *Sweep* incurs more than six times the cost of *Optimal* this time. Δ-*opt* stays indistinguishable from *Optimal* even for $\Delta = 2$, proving to be the method of choice for such networks. *Cgreedy* is the best among the remaining methods with 24% higher cost than *Optimal*.

Vector-Matrix-Matrix-Vector Product ($x^T ABy$): In Fig. 3g, we provide the contraction cost for all algorithms except *Sweep-opt* for the $x^T ABy$ *rand-rand* case, to test how adding another layer into the network would affect their performance. We observe that Δ-*opt* provides near-optimal results for large networks even for $\Delta = 2$, whereas we need to have $\Delta > 4$ to guarantee such results for all network sizes. In contrast, all other algorithms rapidly diverge from the optimal, incurring a higher contraction cost of more than 10× as the number of dimensions goes beyond 25. Comparing this result with those in Figs. 4a and c for $x^T y$ and $x^T Ay$, the advantage of Δ-*opt* seems to increase as the tensor network involves more layers.

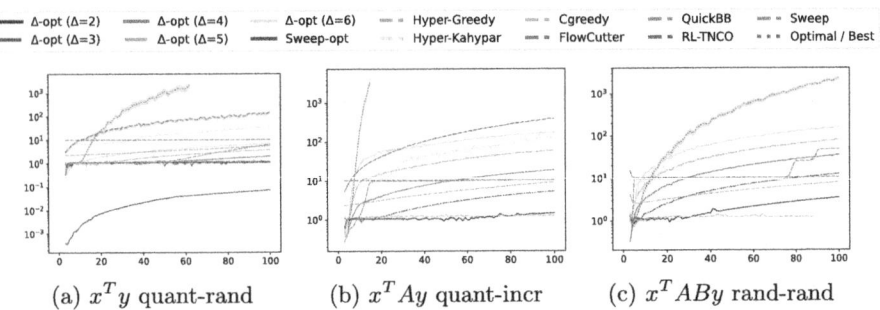

Fig. 4. Execution time of algorithms for specific instances. The y-axis is the algorithm's execution time in seconds. The x-axis is the number of TT dimensions.

Execution Time: In Fig. 4a, we provide the execution time of all algorithms. Figure 4a shows the execution time for the $x^T y$ computation in the *quant-rand* setting. We first observe that *Sweep-opt* significantly outperforms all other methods, requiring only a fraction of their execution time, which makes it the method of choice for $x^T y$ scalar products given that it also provides near-optimal results as provided in Figs. 3a to c. Next, we observe that Δ-*opt* remains among the fastest algorithms for $\Delta = 2$ or 3, and the cost progressively increases as Δ grows. The execution cost of *Optimal* grows rapidly, and the algorithm becomes infeasible for medium to large networks. *Cgreedy* is the fastest among our benchmarks and remains competitive with Δ-*opt* using small window sizes. Δ-*opt* stays very competitive for $\Delta \leq 4$ and its cost progressively rises as Δ grows larger. *RL-TNCO* is the slowest among all algorithms except *Optimal*, despite the fact that it uses a GPU for inference, showing that it is not a viable option for this type of structured tensor network.

Next, in Fig. 4b, we provide the execution time for the $x^T A y$ computation in the *quant-incr* setting. Here, we first observe that the optimal algorithm quickly becomes infeasible, even for small networks. *Cgreedy* and Δ-*opt* with $\Delta = 2$ are the fastest in this case, and *Hyper-Greedy* follows suit. Δ-*opt* for $\Delta = 6$ remains comparable to *Hyper-Kahypar* in this case. Δ-*opt* stays very efficient up to $\Delta = 4$, which is sufficient to ensure near-optimal results as shown in Fig.3e, and gets progressively more expensive for larger window sizes. *QuickBB* and *FlowCutter* converge to a plateau and become comparable to *Hyper-Greedy* for large tensor networks. In light of these results, we conclude that Δ-*opt* with a small window size is indeed the method of choice for this type of network.

Finally, in Fig. 4c, we provide the timings for the $x^T A B y$ case in the *rand-rand* setting, which trends similar to Fig. 4b, with Δ-*opt* getting slightly more expensive due to the added layer in the network. Another interesting observation is that *Optimal*, although very expensive, manages to find a solution for larger networks this time. This is mostly due to the randomization in both tensor dimensions and ranks, which provides aggressive pruning possibilities in the branch-and-bound search. Nonetheless, these results again suggest the use of Δ-*opt* with a small Δ to find a near-optimal ordering for such tensor networks.

5 Conclusion

In this work, we introduced two new algorithms, namely *Sweep-opt* and Δ-*opt*, to find a near-optimal contraction ordering for the scalar product of vectors in TT form. These algorithms provide a significant improvement compared to existing algorithms for finding an efficient contraction ordering for a general tensor network, reducing the contraction cost by more than tenfold in some instances. Experiments show that our algorithms provide solutions close to the optimal algorithm in most test cases while necessitating only a fraction of the time the optimal solver requires, thus offering an efficient mechanism for finding a near-optimal contraction ordering for the scalar product of TTs. Owing to this, we aim to accelerate a critical step in numerical solvers that leverage the TT format to represent high-dimensional operators and vectors, as well as kernel methods whose performance heavily relies on such scalar products.

Acknowledgments. This work was supported by the NumPEx Exa-SofT(ANR-22-EXNU-0003) and SELESTE (ANR-20-CE46-0008-01) projects of the French National Research Agency (ANR), and Paris Ile-de-France Region (DIM RFSI RC-TENSOR No. 2021-05). The experiments are carried out using computational resources from the "Mésocentre" computing center of Université Paris-Saclay, CentraleSupélec, and École Normale Supérieure Paris-Saclay supported by CNRS and Région Île-de-France (https://mesocentre.universite-paris-saclay.fr/).

Disclosure of Interests. The authors have no competing interests to declare that are relevant to the content of this article.

References

1. Chen, C., Batselier, K., Yu, W., Wong, N.: Kernelized support tensor train machines. Pattern Recogn. **122**, 108337 (2022)
2. Dudek, J.M., Dueñas-Osorio, L., Vardi, M.Y.: Efficient contraction of large tensor networks for weighted model counting through graph decompositions. arXiv (2019)
3. Gogate, V., Dechter, R.: A complete anytime algorithm for treewidth. In: Proceedings of the 20th Conference on Uncertainty in Artificial Intelligence, UAI 2004, pp. 201–208. AUAI Press, Arlington, Virginia, USA (2004)
4. Gray, J., Kourtis, S.: Hyper-optimized tensor network contraction. Quantum **5**, 410 (2021)
5. Hartono, A., et al.: Automated operation minimization of tensor contraction expressions in electronic structure calculations. In: Sunderam, V.S., van Albada, G.D., Sloot, P.M.A., Dongarra, J.J. (eds.) ICCS 2005. LNCS, vol. 3514, pp. 155–164. Springer, Heidelberg (2005). https://doi.org/10.1007/11428831_20
6. Khoromskij, B.N.: O(dlogN)-quantics approximation of N-d tensors in high-dimensional numerical modeling. Constr. Approx. **34**(2), 257–280 (2011)
7. Kolda, T.G., Bader, B.W.: Tensor decompositions and applications. SIAM Rev. **51**(3), 455–500 (2009)
8. Lam, C.C., Sadayappan, P., Wenger, R.: On optimizing a class of multi-dimensional loops with reduction for parallel execution. Parall. Process. Lett. **07**(02), 157–168 (1997)
9. Markov, I.L., Shi, Y.: Simulating quantum computation by contracting tensor networks. SIAM J. Comput. **38**(3), 963–981 (2008)
10. Merom, E., Maron, H., Mannor, S., Chechick, G.: Optimizing tensor network contraction using reinforcement learning. In: Proceedings of the 39th International Conference on Machine Learning, vol. 162, pp. 15278–15292. PMLR (2022)
11. Orgler, S., Blacher, M.: Optimizing tensor contraction paths: a greedy algorithm approach with improved cost functions. arXiv (2024)
12. Oseledets, I.V.: Tensor-train decomposition. SIAM J. Sci. Comput. **33**(5), 2295–2317 (2011)
13. Pfeifer, R.N.C., Haegeman, J., Verstraete, F.: Faster identification of optimal contraction sequences for tensor networks. Phys. Rev. E **90**(3), 033315 (2014)
14. Rakhuba, M., Oseledets, I.V.: Calculating vibrational spectra of molecules using TT decomposition. J. Chem. Phys. **145**(12), 124101 (2016)

15. Schlag, S., Heuer, T., Gottesbüren, L., Akhremtsev, Y., Schulz, C., Sanders, P.: High-quality hypergraph partitioning. ACM J. Exp. Algorithmics **27**, 1.9:1–1.9:39 (2023)
16. Schulman, J., Wolski, F., Dhariwal, P., Radford, A., Klimov, O.: Proximal policy optimization algorithms. arXiv (2017)
17. Strasser, B.: Computing tree decompositions with FlowCutter: PACE 2017 submission. arXiv (2017)

Partial Detectors Versus Replication to Cope with Silent Errors

Anne Benoit[1,2], Thomas Herault[3], Yves Robert[1(✉)], and Alix Tremodeux[1]

[1] Laboratoire LIP, ENS Lyon & Inria,
Lyon, France
{anne.benoit,yves.robert,
alix.tremodeux}@inria.fr
[2] Institut Universitaire de France and IDEaS,
Georgia Tech, Atlanta, USA
[3] Inria, Bordeaux, France
thomas.herault@inria.fr

Abstract. This work studies an iterative algorithm running on an error-prone platform, where silent errors strike each iteration with some probability. A detector verifies correctness before taking a checkpoint but may fail to detect errors. Specifically, an error at iteration I is detected only after iteration $(I-1)+X$, where X follows a bounded probability distribution like a truncated geometric distribution. Intuitively, the error silently amplifies during some iterations before it can be detected at distance X or higher, and there is the risk of missing an error that has struck recently but cannot be detected yet. X is bounded by D, the maximum detection latency. To mitigate undetected errors during verification, a simple strategy keeps two checkpoints and divides the execution into $D-1$ iteration segments, each followed by verification and checkpoint. In steady state: (i) if verification succeeds, the oldest checkpoint is erased and replaced; (ii) if it fails, rollback occurs to the oldest verified checkpoint. This work explores whether this scheme outperforms replication and determines the optimal number of checkpoints and segment lengths, both theoretically and via Monte Carlo simulations.

1 Introduction

Let us consider an iterative algorithm whose execution is struck by silent errors. The only application-independent approach to mitigate the impact of such errors is *replication*, which works as follows:

- The execution is partitioned into *segments* of M iterations, each followed by a checkpoint. Assume that the initial data can also be recovered if necessary;
- The execution of a new segment (after a checkpoint C) consists of at least two attempts, and possibly more:
  - First attempt: execute the segment and checkpoint the result res_1;
  - While the results after $t \geq 1$ attempts are all different, execute new attempt $t+1$, i.e., recover from the checkpoint C, redo the M iterations and checkpoint the result res_{t+1};

- Keep the outcome of the two identical checkpoints and proceed to the next segment.

Here, the classical hypothesis is that two errors will never lead to the same (incorrect) result; more precisely, one neglects this event whose probability is extremely low. Hence, the rationale is to make attempts until the same result is obtained twice, because that result will necessarily be correct. Interestingly, the optimal value of M (the segment length) can be obtained numerically as a function of the resilience parameters, namely the fault-rate and checkpoint cost. The optimal value is defined as minimizing the expected time per iteration. We provide such a derivation in Sect. 4. Note that, to the best of our knowledge, this derivation is new, despite the many related studies on replication.

While replication is the only general-purpose approach to cope with silent errors, several application-specific methods have been introduced. We survey several examples of such detectors in Sect. 2, which is devoted to related work. In a nutshell, one uses a detector (typically an application-specific routine) to verify that the current state of the computation is correct. The main problem with silent errors is their detection latency: when a silent error strikes, it does not manifest immediately to the application, but only after some non-deterministic number of iterations. A detector is required to verify the application's correctness. Without one (and without replication), any detected error forces a full re-execution, as the exact moment of failure is unknown, making intermediate checkpoints unreliable. With a detector, errors can be identified before taking a checkpoint, ensuring a safe restart point. Crucially, the detector must be *perfect*, meaning it can detect all silent errors as soon as it strikes. With a perfect detector, The optimal strategy to place checkpoints is well-known [3], as well as a first-order approximation that is the counterpart for silent errors of the Young & Daly formula for fail-stop errors [10,19].

Unfortunately, it is very difficult, if at all possible, to design perfect detectors. More likely, one can design *partial* detectors that will detect many errors, but not all. One can envision several trade-offs where the recall[1] of the detector can be adjusted as a function of the cost of the verification mechanism. The more comprehensive the verification, the higher the recall of the detector, but also the higher its cost [1,11].

Using partial detectors instead of replication seems a promising cost-effective alternative to replication. To ensure correctness, one must assume that detection latency is bounded. If a silent error occurs during an iteration and remains undetected for all subsequent iterations, the final result will be invalid – and there will be no way to determine whether this has happened. Henceforth, we study partial detectors whose detection latency is bounded. More precisely, we envision the following scenario: when a silent error strikes during iteration I, one will be able to detect it by applying the partial detector at iteration $(I-1)+X$ or after, where X is a random variable obeying a probability distribution with bounded support $[1, D]$. For instance say a silent error strikes at iteration $I = 10$, and draw $X = 3$. Applying the detector at the end of iterations $I = 10$ or $I = 11$ will

---

[1] The recall of a detector is defined as the fraction of errors that it can detect. If it is lower than 1, some errors, the *false negatives*, are missed by the detector.

not detect this error, but it will be detected for any iteration $I \geq 12$. Regardless of the value of X, the partial detector will systematically detect the error D iterations later, where D is the maximum detection latency, The rationale for this model if that we expect the impact of the silent error on the application data to grow and become more and more *detectable*. For computation errors, this corresponds to a numerical amplification of the error as the execution progresses.

The main focus of this work is to provide a comprehensive assessment of the above scenario. Given a partial detector of bounded latency, what is the best (less costly) execution scheme to ensure correctness? How does it compare to replication? The simplest scheme is to have segments of $M = D - 1$ iterations and to keep two checkpoints in memory, as illustrated below:

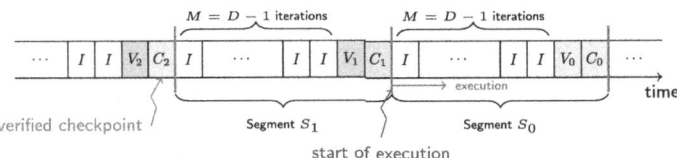

When executing segment S_0, checkpoints C_1 and C_2 are stored in memory. By induction, the oldest checkpoint C_2 is certified to be verified, but this is not yet the case for checkpoint C_1. When we complete the execution of the current segment S_0, we apply the detector through verification V_0. There are two cases:

- No error is detected. Then checkpoint C_1 is verified, because all errors that might have struck during segment S_1 did so at least D iterations before and would have been detected by V_0. For instance, if an error struck during the last iteration of S_1, then its distance to the last iteration of segment S_0 is the maximum detection latency D (remember that we include the original struck iteration in the distance count). We can safely take checkpoint C_0 and overwrite the older checkpoint C_2.
- An error is detected. We must roll back. But there is no way of knowing whether the error struck during segment S_0 or earlier on during S_1; in the latter case, the error went through undetected when verification V_1 was applied. Hence, we need to roll back to checkpoint C_2, which is known to be verified, and to re-execute S_1 followed by S_0. But now, if an error is detected by V_1, we can roll back to C_2 again, because C_2 is verified.

Despite simple to understand, this scheme is not easy to evaluate and compare with replication. Our main contribution is to assess the efficiency of this scheme and more complicated ones, involving many segments. In fact, we solve the main optimization problem: how many segments, or equivalently how many checkpoints to keep in memory? And how many iterations to execute within each segment? These results lay the theoretical foundations for the problem of comparing partial detectors and replication.

The rest of the paper is organized as follows. Section 2 surveys related work. In Sect. 3, we detail the framework. Section 4 is devoted to analyzing replication and its optimization. Section 5 is the heart of the paper, where we assess partial detectors: we compute the expected time per iteration for a general scheme, and we provide the optimal values of its parameters. This theoretical analysis is complemented by Monte Carlo simulations in Sect. 6. Finally, we give concluding remarks and hints for future work in Sect. 7.

2 Related Work

Due to lack of space, an extensive discussion of related work can be found in the companion research report [5], with some background on silent errors, a review of partial detectors, and a discussion on recall and precision.

In a nutshell, considerable efforts have been directed at designing detectors to reveal silent errors, because the only general-purpose method, replication, is very costly. Application-specific information can be very useful to enable ad-hoc solutions, which dramatically decreases the cost of detection. Many techniques have been advocated [2,7–9,12–17]. None of them is perfect, but these techniques cover a substantial number of silent errors, and more importantly, they incur very low overheads. These properties make them attractive candidates for designing efficient protocols based upon partial detection.

Perfect detectors would be very appealing because they can be applied before taking a checkpoint, which by definition will be verified since all potential errors would have been detected. With a perfect detector, the approach is to use a single segment of execution, and a single checkpoint is kept in memory. Partial detectors can be added in the middle of that segment to speed-up detection. However, perfect detectors are more a perspective than an actual proposal. Without a perfect detector, replication was the only known approach before this work. Introducing a partial detector with bounded detection latency, and assessing its performance, is the key contribution of this work.

3 Framework

This section details the framework and the objective function. We focus on a generic iterative application, because it is easier to express every quantity in terms of numbers of iterations. In particular, we account for the cost of every resilience mechanism (detector, checkpoint, recovery) as a number of iterations. This makes the approach agnostic of the granularity of the application, which can range from sequential to massively parallel, and of the nature of errors, either silent or transient.

The application is subject to the occurrence of errors, which can be mitigated either by replication or by applying a partial detector. We consider two main probability distribution laws to model error rates and latency detections:

- Occurrence: A silent error may strike each iteration independently and with a fixed probability f. In other words, error inter-arrival times obey a Geometric distribution law of parameter f.
- Detection: When an error strikes during iteration I, it can be detected (by applying the partial detector) only at iteration $(I-1)+X$ or after, where X is the detection distance, or latency. X obeys a truncated Geometric distribution

law: we have $X = \min(Y, D)$, where Y is a random Geometric variable of parameter θ, and D is the maximum detection latency. This leads to $P(X = d) = P(Y = d) = (1-\theta)^{d-1}\theta$ if $1 \leq d < D$, and $P(X = D) = P(Y \geq D) = (1-\theta)^{D-1}$. The support of X is the interval $[1, D]$, and $X = 0$ elsewhere.

Again, once an error manifests, it never autocorrects and keeps manifesting during the following iterations until it can be detected. This is like tossing a biased coin (with probability θ for heads and $1 - \theta$ for tails) every iteration during which or after the error struck, until the first head is drawn, but we bound the maximum number of tosses to ensure correctness in the worst case. Table 1 helps get an insight on typical values for the maximum detection distance D. For an efficient partial detector ($\theta = 0.9$), distance detection never exceeds 10 in practice. For a poor partial detector ($\theta = 0.2$, capturing only 20% of errors), distance detection never exceeds 100 in practice.

Table 1. Bound for D as a function of θ

θ	$\min\{d|P(X \geq d) \leq 10^{-6}\}$	$\min\{d|P(X \geq d) \leq 10^{-9}\}$
0.2	62	93
0.4	28	41
0.9	6	9

All the random variables for occurrence and detection are assumed to be independent. For error detection, one needs to restrict to a Poisson process (memoryless probability distribution for error inter-arrival times). Because time is discretized into iterations, we need to use a Geometric law instead of an Exponential law. While independence and memorylessness are restrictive assumptions, they represent the state-of-the art of all studies in resilience for HPC, as explained in [6,11]. However, this study can be directly extended to any bounded-support probability distribution law for error detection.

We further assume that the partial detector has precision 1 (no false alarm). This is only a simplification rather than an intrinsic limitation of partial detectors. Indeed, we can extend the complicated derivation provided in Sect. 5 to account for the extra rollbacks, recoveries and re-executions that would be caused by false alarms. Such an extended derivation is set for future work.

The execution scheme partitions the application into segments of M iterations followed by a checkpoint. We always apply the partial detector, whose cost is V iterations, before taking a checkpoint, whose cost is C iterations. Note that: (i) we take that checkpoint only if no error is detected; and (ii) the checkpoint may still not be verified because some error has struck and remained undetected. However, some checkpoints are guaranteed to include no error; we call such checkpoint a *verified checkpoint*. If an error is detected by the verification, the application rolls back to the last verified checkpoint and pays a recovery, whose cost is R iterations, before resuming the execution from that point on.

The existence of a verified checkpoint is an invariant of the execution scheme and is proven by induction (see details in Sect. 5). There are no errors during verifications, checkpoints and recoveries.

Finally, the objective function is to minimize the expected slowdown $\mathcal{S}$ per iteration, which characterizes the diminution of the application progress due to error mitigation. If the cost to execute a segment of M iterations is $cost(M)$, then the slowdown is $\mathcal{S} = \frac{cost(M)}{M}$.

4 Replication

As discussed in Sect. 1, replication uses segments of M iterations followed by a checkpoint. Each segment is executed several times, until the results of two execution attempts are identical. The cost of the first attempt is $M + C$, while the cost of the following attempts is $R + M + C$ because each of them starts with a recovery. While we need to perform further attempts, we have to keep the checkpoints of all previous attempts in memory so that we can check whether the results of two attempts are identical. The number of attempts (which corresponds to the number of checkpoints that have to be stored) until one is successful obeys a geometric distribution law of parameter p_S, the probability of executing a segment of M iterations without any error. We have $p_S = (1-f)^M$, and the expected number of attempts until one is successful is $\frac{1}{p_S}$. The expected number of attempts until two are successful is $\frac{2}{p_S}$. Since the first attempt has cost $M + C$ and the following ones have cost $R + M + C$, the expected cost to execute a segment is

$$cost(M) = (M + C) + \left(\frac{2}{p_S} - 1\right)(R + M + C) = \frac{2(R + M + C)}{p_S} - R,$$

and the expected slowdown is $\mathcal{S} = \frac{cost(M)}{M} = \frac{2(R+C)}{Mp_S} + \frac{2}{p_S} - \frac{R}{M}$. With $p_S = (1-f)^M$, we let $g(M) = \frac{2(R+C)}{M(1-f)^M} + \frac{2}{(1-f)^M} - \frac{R}{M}$ and aim at minimizing $g(M)$. We get $g'(M) = \frac{(1-f)^{-M}}{M^2}\left(R((1-f)^M - 2) - 2M\ln(1-f)(C + R + M) - 2C\right)$. The optimal value M_{opt}^{rep} of M is such that $g'(M_{opt}^{rep}) = 0$. Unfortunately, this equation does not have a closed-form solution when f, C and R are unknown parameters, even when $R = C$. We need to resort to numerical methods to find the optimal value M_{opt}^{rep} when the values of the parameters are given.

Note that the replication strategy has significant advantages: it is application-independent, and its performance depends only on the statistical properties of the risk of errors. However, as we will see in Sect. 6, it comes with a high cost, which may be prohibitive in practice.

5 Partial Detectors

In this section, we assess the use of the partial detector. We consider an execution scheme with k segments and k checkpoints stored in memory. Each segment consists of M iterations, followed by a verification and a checkpoint. Segment S_i, $0 \leq i \leq k-1$, is followed by verification V_i and checkpoint C_i. Figure 1 provides an illustration with $k = 3$ and $M = 5$.

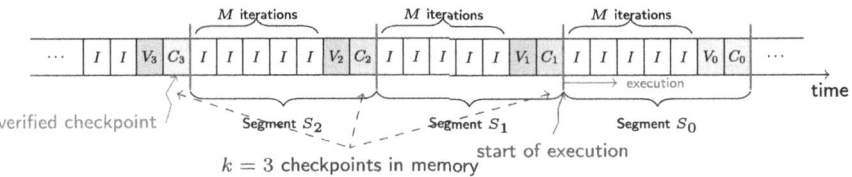

Fig. 1. Example with $k = 3$ and $M = 5$

First, there is some relation to enforce between M, k and the maximum detection latency D for the execution scheme to be valid. We are currently executing segment S_0 and aiming to ensure that checkpoint C_{k-1} (C_2 in the example) is verified, so that we can overwrite C_3 by C_0 if verification V_0 is successful. This requires that any error that may have struck within segment S_{k-1} (S_2 in the example) is detected by V_0 eventually, if it has not been detected by previous verifications $V_{k-1}, V_{k-2}, \ldots, V_1$ earlier on. This requirement is fulfilled if we enforce that $(k-1)M \geq D - 1$, because an error that struck at the last iteration of segment S_{k-1} is at distance $(k-1)M + 1 \geq D$ from the last iteration of segment S_0, and it will be detected by V_0 if it has not been detected before. Given a value for M, we will use

$$k = \left\lceil \frac{D-1}{M} \right\rceil + 1 \qquad (1)$$

as the minimum number of checkpoints that must be kept in memory; this is also the minimum number of segments for the execution scheme. Note that $k \geq 2$ unless $D = 1$, which corresponds to a perfect detector. In the example, $M = 5$ and $k = 3$, hence we must have $D \leq 11$.

When executing the current segment S_0, checkpoints C_1 to C_k are in memory, and checkpoint C_k is known to be verified, since all errors previous to C_k would have been detected by V_1 at the latest. However, errors having struck segments S_{k-1} to S_1 may have remained undetected up to verification V_1 included.

Our objective is to determine the expected time needed to complete the M iterations of segment S_0 and to replace the oldest checkpoint C_k by a new one at the end of S_0. Once V_0 is successful, we know for sure that C_{k-1} is a verified checkpoint; but if V_0 detects an error, we have to roll back to C_k, the last verified checkpoint, and to re-execute all the k segments.

We start by computing the probability that an error is detected during a given verification. Let $P_{i,j}$ be the probability that an error that struck at the i-th iteration of the ℓ-th segment (for $1 \leq i \leq M$ and $0 \leq \ell \leq k-1$) is detected at $V_{\ell-j}$ (for $0 \leq j \leq \ell$). Hence, for $j = 0$, this is the probability that the error is detected immediately at the end of the segment where it struck; otherwise, it is the probability of detection after j other segments have been executed. We have

$$P_{i,j} = P(X \leq jM + (M - i + 1)) \quad - \quad P(X \leq (j-1)M + (M - i + 1)). \quad (2)$$

The probability to detect an error striking at iteration i in segment ℓ to be detected after $V_{\ell-j}$ is denoted as $P_{i,>j} = P(X > jM + (M - i + 1))$.

Let E_0 be the expected time required to process segment S_0 entirely, and then to take a new checkpoint C_0 after a successful verification, hence deleting C_k from memory and moving on to the next segment. By induction, C_k is a verified checkpoint when we start executing S_0, but the more recent $k-1$ checkpoints are not yet verified. The objective is to compute E_0.

Because different rollbacks may be needed to complete the process of segment S_0, we introduce E_j for $1 \leq j \leq k-1$ as the expected time required to go all the way up to taking C_0 starting at the first iteration of segment S_j, and knowing that no error has been detected by the previous verifications $V_{j'}$, where $j' \geq j + 1$: hence, no error has been detected in the first segments before C_{j+1} and the start of segment S_j. The execution goes as follows: we execute S_0 and V_0. If V_0 is successful, we take checkpoint C_0, and we are done. Otherwise, we roll back to C_k and re-execute all the last k segments, recovering from C_k which is the only verified checkpoint. Now, during this re-execution, some errors may strike, among which some may be detected. The execution progresses until an error is detected, in which case we roll back to C_k.

First Segment S_{k-1}. We start by considering the first segment S_{k-1}, just after the verified checkpoint C_k. Let Q_0 be the probability that either there is no error during the M iterations of S_{k-1}, or that none of the errors that struck during these iterations are detected by V_{k-1}. In other words, Q_0 is the probability to go through V_{k-1} (so to speak), checkpoint and proceed to segment S_{k-2}:

$$\begin{aligned} E_{k-1} = {} & R + M + V & & \text{recovery, computation and verification done in all cases} \\ & + Q_0(C + E_{k-2}) & & \text{no error in} S_{k-1} \text{that is detected by} V_{k-1} \\ & + (1 - Q_0)E_{k-1} & & \text{roll back and start over: detected error} \end{aligned}$$

Since C_k is correct by induction hypothesis, an error detected by V_{k-1} can only have occurred in S_{k-1}, not before. Hence: $Q_0 = \prod_{i=1}^{M}(1 - fP_{i,0})$. Indeed, an error occurs at iteration i of S_{k-1} with probability f, it is detected at V_{k-1} with probability $P_{i,0}$ (current segment), hence there is a probability $1 - fP_{i,0}$ that there were no error nor any detected error from iteration i. Note that Q_0 can actually be used for any segment, since it only considers errors occurring during the segment and detected at the end of that segment.

Next Segments S_j, $1 \leq j \leq k-2$. We extend the formula to any E_j as follows, for $j \geq 1$ (the case E_0 is slightly different):

$$E_j = M + V \qquad \text{computation and verification done in all cases}$$
$$+ \left(\prod_{\ell=0}^{k-1-j} Q_\ell\right)(C + E_{j-1}) \quad \text{no error that is detected by } V_j, \text{ move to } S_{j-1}$$
$$+ \left(1 - \prod_{\ell=0}^{k-1-j} Q_\ell\right) E_{k-1} \quad \text{roll back and start over from } S_{k-1}: \text{detected error}$$

Here is how we compute the different probabilities. In order to be able to move to the next segment S_{j-1}, we now need to consider several cases:

- No error in S_j has been detected by V_j at the end of the segment: this happens with probability Q_0 as defined above.
- We must however also look for errors that may come from previous segments, and hence generalize the formula. Q_ℓ is the probability that there is no error coming from the ℓ-th previous segment that is detected by V_j, for $0 \leq \ell \leq k-2$. Hence, for $\ell = 1$, we are looking at errors coming from the segment just before S_j (hence in S_{j+1}). For each previous segment, there are three possibilities for any of the M potential error locations:
  - There is no error, with a probability $(1-f)$.
  - There is an error that is not detected by V_j, but that will be detected later. By conditional definition of E_j, the error was not detected before either (with $V_{j'}$, where $j' > j$), and hence this is the probability $fP_{i,>\ell}$ (there is an error, it is detected later).
  - Finally, there might have been an error that is detected by the current verification V_j, and this comes with a probability $fP_{i,\ell}$.

  All probabilities must therefore be normalized by the sum of the probabilities of the three cases, which is $(1-f) + f(P_{i,>\ell} + P_{i,\ell})$. For $\ell = 0$, this sums to 1 since the error is either detected at the end of the current segment ($P_{i,0}$) or later ($P_{i,>0}$), and therefore we obtain the previous formula of Q_0 again. We finally obtain $Q_\ell = \prod_{i=1}^{M} \left(1 - \frac{fP_{i,\ell}}{(1-f)+f(P_{i,>\ell}+P_{i,\ell})}\right)$.
- By combining all possible locations of errors that remain undetected at V_j, coming from the current segment S_j or previous ones (up to $k-1-j$ previous segments), we obtain the probability that no error is detected at V_j and that we can move forward to S_{j-1}, expressed as $\prod_{\ell=0}^{k-1-j} Q_\ell$.

Last Segment E_0. Finally, for E_0, when we consider faults from segment S_{k-1}, they are necessarily detected by V_0, which slightly changes the computation of probabilities to complete. Indeed, the expression of Q_{k-1} further considers that any error at S_{k-1} will necessarily be detected at most at V_0, because the distance of detection D is exceeded. Again, because of the conditional expression of E_0, we know that no error in S_{k-1} has been detected before, and therefore, either there was no error (probability $(1-f)$), or the error is detected at V_0

(probability $P_{i,k-1}$). Hence, we write: $Q_{k-1} = \prod_{i=1}^{M}\left(1 - \frac{fP_{i,k-1}}{(1-f)+f(P_{i,k-1})}\right)$. We point out that this is the same formula as above because $P_{i,>k-1} = 0$ (remember that the distance detection is upper bounded by D).

We can finally write E_0, which is the quantity that we aim at minimizing, i.e., the time to progress to the next segment, add a new checkpoint and delete checkpoint C_k:

$$E_0 = M + V \qquad \text{computation and verification done in all cases}$$

$$+ \left(\prod_{\ell=0}^{k-1} Q_\ell\right) C \qquad \text{no error that is detected at } V_0, \text{take a checkpoint}$$

$$+ \left(1 - \prod_{\ell=0}^{k-1} Q_\ell\right) E_{k-1} \quad \text{roll back and start over from } S_{k-1} : \text{detected error}$$

We check that this is indeed the same expression as for E_j with $1 \leq j \leq k-2$ if we let $E_{-1} = 0$, which is comforting.

In [5], we show by induction how these models can be used to derive the value for E_0, defining values a_k, b_k and c_k. We then aim at minimizing the expected slowdown $\mathcal{S} = \frac{E_0}{M}$, for all possible values of M. For each value of M, the value of k is given by Eq. (1) and is large enough to guarantee correctness. We do this with a simple exhaustive loop, where the upper bound UB is chosen to be large experimentally:

$$M_{opt}^{par} = 0; k_{opt} = 0; \mathcal{S} = \infty$$
$$\textbf{for } M = 1 \textbf{ to } UB$$
$$\quad k = \lceil\tfrac{D-1}{M}\rceil + 1; E^{iter} = \tfrac{E_0}{M} = a_k\tfrac{C}{M} + b_k(1+\tfrac{V}{M}) + c_k\tfrac{R}{M}$$
$$\quad \textbf{if } E^{iter} < \mathcal{S} \textbf{ then } M_{opt}^{par} = M; k_{opt} = k; \mathcal{S} = E^{iter}$$

6 Evaluation

In order to evaluate the different models, we have implemented a set of discrete events simulations that follow the protocols described above. The simulations are written in C, and are publicly available for reproducibility purposes in [4]. Each execution that we simulate is 100,000 iterations long, and as per our models above, C, V, R are all measured in terms of iterations. For each set of parameters, we simulate 10,000 executions and measure for each the total time of execution (*wall time*, in number of iterations), the number of errors, rollbacks, and the number of checkpoints taken. We then compute the mean and the variance of these values. Errors are injected following the model described in Sect. 3.

We have set the following parameters for the simulations: C and R are both equal and set to 3 iterations to account for the overheads in communications and I/O; V is set to 1 iteration, as verification is usually a fast operation (see [18] and the references therein). The other parameters of the simulations are varied to evaluate their respective impacts on the performance. The probability of occurrence of an error during an iteration, f, ranges between 10^{-4} (producing only a handful of errors during the 100,000 iterations of an execution) and $8.6 \cdot 10^{-3}$ (leading up to 4,500 errors during the execution); we consider all values for θ between 10% and 90%; as suggested by Table 1, we consider values of D ranging from 10 to 100. In order to validate the model, we evaluate the protocols for all values of M, and set k using Eq. (1). We compare the optimal value for (k, M_{opt}^{par}) predicted by the model with the experimental value.

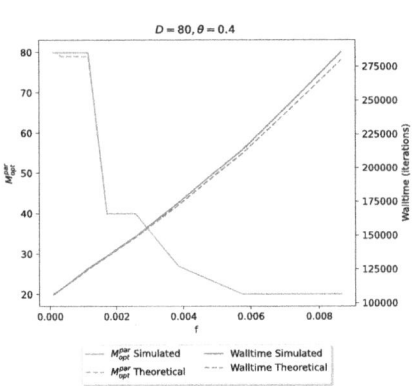

Fig. 2. Comparison between the model and the simulations

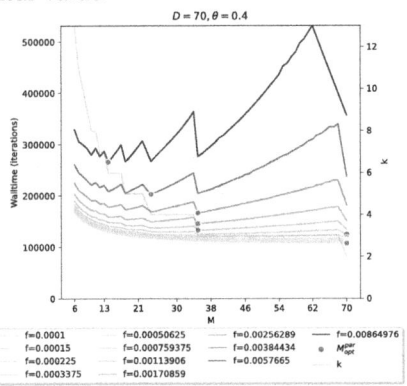

Fig. 3. Simulated mean wall time function of risk of error (f) and number of iterations (M)

Validation. Figure 2 shows, for a specific configuration ($D = 80, \theta = 0.4$), the optimal interval between checkpoints for the Partial Detector strategy (on the left axis), and the wall time of a run of 100,000 iterations (on the right axis), as calculated by the theoretical model and as measured by the simulations. The goal of this figure is to validate that both the mathematical model and the simulation reach the same measurement on the key metrics. The wall time predicted by the model is slightly smaller than the wall time measured during simulations for very high f (when the frequency of errors is high), but the difference remains under 5%. Conjointly, M_{opt}^{par} according to the theoretical model is different by one iteration from the value extracted from the simulations, on a small range of low f values. These small differences are due to rounding errors in the simulation framework.

Parameter Exploration. Figure 3 shows the simulated mean wall time for $\theta = 0.4$ and $D = 70$, varying the risk of error (f) and the number of iterations between two checkpoints (M). For each value of f, we consider all possible values of M between C (number of iterations to take a single checkpoint) and D (maximum latency to detect an error). For each M, we set k, the number of checkpoints to keep, according to Eq. (1). First, we observe that simulations with a low f ($f \leq 0.00113906$), taking more checkpoints than the minimal two or using an interval between checkpoints lower than D is detrimental to performance. Errors are so rare in this situation (low f), and the chance that they are detected right away is so high ($\theta = 0.4, D = 70$), that the most efficient strategy consists in waiting as long as possible before introducing a verification and a checkpoint.

When the risk of error increases, however, we see that the optimal strategy changes. The wall time figure then looks like a step-wise function, with steps happening every time M divides D into equal intervals. The low points of this step-wise function define a parabolic curve that accepts a minimal value of the wall time for various couples (k, M_{opt}^{par}) that are identified in the figure. For instance, when $f = 0.00864976$, the couple $(k = 6, M = 14)$ defines a low point, where the wall time is at 266,027 (so 2.66 times slower than the execution without faults nor fault tolerance enabled).

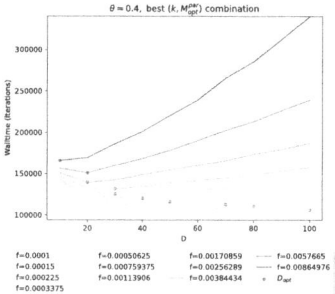

Fig. 4. Impact of the detection bound (D) on the wall time for $\theta = 0.4$, varying the risk of error (f)

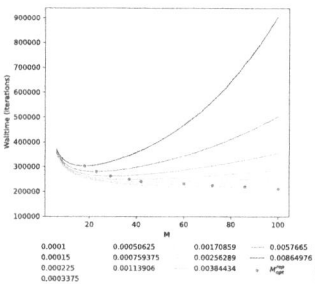

Fig. 5. Wall time for replication, as a function of M and the risk of error (f)

Figure 4 shows the impact of the detection bound (D) on the wall time for $\theta = 0.4$, varying the risk of error (f). All curves show a parabolic behavior, with an optimal that depends on D. For experiments where the risk of error is low, a high D value turns out more efficient than a lower D value, which is to be expected as errors being rare, longer working periods allow us to reduce the overheads due to forced (and useless) checkpoints. Three of the curves shown in this figure are limited to values of D that are suboptimal ($D = 100$), and even higher values of D could be explored. These curves represent the runs in which errors are the most unlikely to occur. For more volatile experiments, when f has a high value and many errors impact the system, a lower D value is optimal. However, D is not a parameter that the user can choose for performance reasons, but is strongly constrained by the properties of the partial detector. It is possible, depending on the detector properties, that D becomes higher than the optimal value. If this is the case, this figure also shows that performance can be significantly impacted, for highly volatile systems.

Comparison with Replication. Figure 5 shows the wall time for the replication strategy, as a function of the interval between two checkpoints (M) and the risk of error (f). As for the partial detector strategy, the wall time exhibits a parabolic behavior, with an optimal value M_{opt}^{rep} that depends on f. The figure shows the location of this optimal value for each different value of f. As f decreases, M_{opt}^{rep} increases, and more importantly, the wall time decreases to asymptotically reach a factor two when f is low enough and almost no errors hit the system. By construction, the replication strategy cannot be more efficient than this limit, as each segment must be executed at least twice to validate the result. This is the cost to pay to have a generic and perfect error mitigation mechanism.

Figure 6 shows the best interval between two checkpoints in the case of the replication strategy (M_{opt}^{rep}), compared between the simulation results and the theoretical model. Additionally, the second axis shows how many checkpoints need to be kept in the worst cases. The figure shows that the theoretical model is very close to the simulation results, for values of f bigger than 0.00050625. For $f < 0.00050625$, the simulation artificially bounded the maximum value of M_{opt}^{rep} to D (as it was done in the case of the partial detector strategy), and the minimum value is observed in simulations for that bound, while the model predicts much higher values of M_{opt}^{rep}. The figure also shows that the maximum number of checkpoints required in the simulations is relatively small, with a maximum of 10 checkpoints required in the worst case that we have considered.

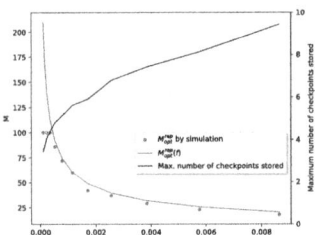

Fig. 6. Comparison between the simulation results and the theoretical model for replication

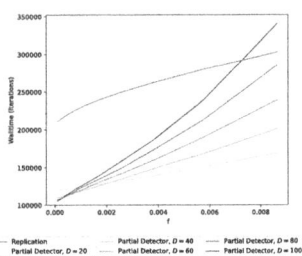

Fig. 7. Comparison of the wall time of replication with partial detection for various values of D

Figure 7 compares the performance of the replication strategy with the partial detector strategy for a few values of D and θ. As we have observed that θ does not have a significant impact on the performance (see the companion research report [5] for details), we have chosen to show only the results for $\theta = 0.4$. The figure shows that the replication strategy is less efficient than the partial detector strategy in a large range of D and f values. Only when errors are very frequent (for $f = 0.008$, executions typically experience more than 4,000 errors to execute the 100,000 iterations), and the error detector is so unreliable that the bound for the maximum number of iterations to detect an error is 100, the replication strategy becomes more efficient.

7 Conclusion

This work is the first study devoted to comparing replication with the use of partial detectors with bounded latency. We have formalized the problem, and provided a detailed analysis of the optimal schemes for both approaches. Given the application and platform parameters, we derived the optimal number of iterations that should be executed between two checkpoints, as well as the number of checkpoints to keep in memory in the case of partial detectors.

Next, we have assessed and compared the performance of both strategies through a comprehensive set of Monte-Carlo simulations. Simulated results perfectly match the theoretical predictions, and illustrate the gain that results from using non-trivial patterns in terms of number of segments and number of iterations. More importantly, the simulations demonstrate that the use of partial detectors can massively outperform replication, allowing the application to complete within a significantly smaller time (typically, twice faster in the presence of few errors). Furthermore, the number of checkpoints that need to be stored to guarantee that we can always recover from a verified checkpoint is fixed with partial detectors, while it is unclear how many checkpoints will have to remain in memory when using replication.

We plan to extend this work by considering more complex patterns for rollbacks, trying to rollback to intermediate unverified checkpoints and combining replication with partial detectors to verify some of them. An experimental validation with some iterative numerical application (the Preconditioned Conjugate Gradient method would be an ideal candidate) would also further demonstrate the usefulness of partial detectors.

Acknowledgements and Artifact Availability. As part of the "France 2030" initiative, this work has benefited from a national grant managed by the French National Research Agency (Agence Nationale de la Recherche) attributed to the Exa-MA project of the NumPEx PEPR program, under the reference ANR-22-EXNU-0002. The software used to produce the results of this paper is available in [4].

References

1. Bautista-Gomez, L., Benoit, A., Cavelan, A., Raina, S., Robert, Y., Sun, H.: Coping with recall and precision of soft error detectors. JPDC **98**, 8–24 (2016)
2. Bautista Gomez, L., Cappello, F.: Detecting silent data corruption through data dynamic monitoring for scientific applications. SIGPLAN **49**(8), 381–382 (2014)
3. Benoit, A., Cavelan, A., Robert, Y., Sun, H.: Assessing general-purpose algorithms to cope with fail-stop and silent errors. ACM TOPC **3**(2), 1–36 (2016)
4. Benoit, A., Herault, T., Robert, Y., Tremodeux, A.: Artifact of the paper: partial detectors versus replication to cope with silent errors (2025). https://doi.org/10.5281/zenodo.15591615
5. Benoit, A., Herault, T., Robert, Y., Trémodeux, A.: Partial detectors versus replication to cope with silent errors. Research report 9581, INRIA (2025). https://inria.hal.science/hal-04996292v1

6. Benoit, A., Perotin, L., Robert, Y., Vivien, F.: Checkpointing strategies to tolerate non-memoryless failures on HPC platforms. ACM Trans. Parallel Comput. **11**(1), 1–26 (2024)
7. Benson, A.R., Schmit, S., Schreiber, R.: Silent error detection in numerical time-stepping schemes. Int. J. High Perform. Comput. Appl. **29**(4), 403–421 (2014)
8. Berrocal, E., Bautista-Gomez, L., Di, S., Lan, Z., Cappello, F.: Lightweight silent data corruption detection based on runtime data analysis for HPC applications. In: HPDC. ACM (2015)
9. Chen, Z.: Online-ABFT: an online algorithm based fault tolerance scheme for soft error detection in iterative methods. In: Proceedings of PPoPP, pp. 167–176 (2013)
10. Daly, J.T.: A higher order estimate of the optimum checkpoint interval for restart dumps. FGCS **22**(3), 303–312 (2006)
11. Herault, T., Robert, Y. (eds.) Fault-Tolerance Techniques for High-Performance Computing. Springer (2015)
12. Heroux, M., Hoemmen, M.: Fault-tolerant iterative methods via selective reliability. Research report SAND2011-3915 C, Sandia National Laboratories (2011)
13. Huang, K.-H., Abraham, J.A.: Algorithm-based fault tolerance for matrix operations. IEEE Trans. Comput. **33**(6), 518–528 (1984)
14. Hwang, A.A., Stefanovici, I.A., Schroeder, B.: Cosmic rays don't strike twice: understanding the nature of DRAM errors and the implications for system design. SIGARCH Comput. Archit. News **40**(1), 111–122 (2012)
15. Li, S., Di, S., Zhao, K., Liang, X., Chen, Z., Cappello, F.: Resilient error-bounded lossy compressor for data transfer. In: SC 1994, SC 2021. ACM (2021)
16. Sao, P., Vuduc, R.: Self-stabilizing iterative solvers. In: ScalA 2013 (2013)
17. Shantharam, M., Srinivasmurthy, S., Raghavan, P.: Fault tolerant preconditioned conjugate gradient for sparse linear system solution. In: CS. ACM (2012)
18. Tremodeux, A., Agullo, E., Benoit, A., Giraud, L., Herault, T., Robert, Y.: Fault-tolerant numerical iterative algorithms at scale. Technical Report RR-9567, Inria Lyon (2025)
19. Young, J.W.: A first order approximation to the optimum checkpoint interval. Comm. ACM **17**(9), 530–531 (1974)

Partitioning In-Place on Massively Parallel Architectures

Thomas Koopman, Sven-Bodo Scholz(✉), and Bernard van Gastel

Radboud University, NJ 08544 Nijmegen,
The Netherlands
{thomas.koopman,svenbodo.scholz,
bernard.vangastel}@ru.nl

Abstract. Data partitioning, i.e. rearranging data according to a Boolean predicate, is needed for many operations on large data. This includes algorithms such as sorting, convex hull computations, in load balancing across a cluster, or in graph algorithms.

Several efficient implementations for data partitioning have been proposed in the literature. Some of these focus on the ability to compute the result with only a constant amount of additional memory, known as in-place implementations. Others focus on efficient parallel executions. Our described strategy of implementing an in-place algorithm on GPUs includes keeping the memory requirements and movements as low as possible while maintaining enough parallelism and coalesced access patterns. We present an in-place partitioning algorithm that can be executed on massively parallel systems. Our implementation maps well to GPU architectures while moving only a negligible amount of data more than necessary, for non-adversarial input. We quantify 'negligible' by providing a probabilistic bound for random input and derive a worst-case bound.

Our performance evaluation demonstrates that our algorithm achieves between 94% and 100% of peak performance on large random arrays for two different GPU architectures. Even in the worst-case scenario of small, adversarially ordered arrays, our algorithm attains 60% of peak performance.

Keywords: Partitioning · Parallel algorithms · GPUs

1 Introduction

Partitioning is a fundamental algorithm for rearranging data. It takes an array of elements and a condition, permuting this array so all elements satisfying the condition are on the left of the array, and all elements that do not satisfy this criterion are on the right. More formally, for an array X and a predicate pred, we compute a permutation Y of X and an index m such that $\text{pred}(Y[i])$ for $i < m$ and $\neg \text{pred}(Y[i])$ for $i \geq m$. It can be used on its own in programs that classify data, but also as a subroutine in sorting [6] and computational geometry algorithms [14].

As this algorithm mainly moves data, it benefits from hardware that has high bandwidth. Graphics Processing Unit (*GPU*) are widely available processors and have much higher bandwidth than a CPU in the same price and power category, making them suitable candidates for partition algorithms.

These processors have such high bandwidth in part because the memory is physically attached to the processor. As a consequence, GPUs have less overall memory than comparable CPUs. This makes it important to use as little additional memory as possible, preferably a constant amount. In other words, GPU algorithms are ideally in-place, i.e., using $O(1)$ auxillary memory.

This paper proposes an in-place partition algorithm for GPUs that is almost as fast as state-of-the-art out-of-place algorithms. Overall, we make the following contributions.

- We describe an in-place parallel algorithm for partitioning that maps well on GPUs.
- We prove our algorithm has at most $3n + O(1)$ data movements for any input of size n, and approximately $2n$ for random input.
- We evaluate our implementation on two GPUs for a range of inputs.

2 Background

2.1 Graphics Processing Units

A GPU is a specialized processor that emphasizes execution units at the cost of control logic. To decrease demand on the control logic, the programmer needs to have groups of threads do the same instruction (*SIMT*) for optimal performance. For similar reasons, the threads must access memory in specific patterns to make full use of the bandwidth. This is called *coalesced* access.

A GPU has different levels of parallelism that allow for different levels of flexibility. On the lowest and least flexible level are groups of usually 32 threads (*warps*) that must be programmed SIMT style. These warps are grouped in *thread blocks* that are mapped on hardware units called *streaming multiprocessors (SMs)*, sharing some fast memory. We map multiple of these groups on one SM so the SM can hide latency by switching between thread blocks.

2.2 Distributed Computing

If a data structure is too large to fit on one physical machine, it has to be distributed over a network of processors, each with their own memory. Coordinating such a network to collaboratively compute some task is called *distributed computing*. This is relevant to this paper as we will look at a GPU as a distributed system.

Following the notational convention of [3], we write p for the total number of processors and $P(s)$ for the processor with index $0 \leq s < p$. A division of a large data structure X into a collection of smaller data structures $\{X^{(s)} : 0 \leq s < p\}$ and a correspondence between them is called a *distribution*. The subset $X^{(s)}$ is local to processor $P(s)$. Figure 1 illustrates some examples of distributions. If X has index set $I = \{0, \cdots, n-1\}$, we define the block-cyclic distribution with block-size b over p processors as

$$I^{(s)} = \{(k \cdot p + s) \cdot b + j : 0 \leq j < b,\ 0 \leq (k \cdot p + s) \cdot b + j < n\},$$

where $X^{(s)} := \{X[i] : i \in I^{(s)}\}$. The block distribution is one extreme of this, with $b = \left\lceil \frac{n}{p} \right\rceil$, and the cyclic distribution the other extreme with $b = 1$. It will be convenient to use interval notation with global indices: $X^{(s)}[a, b) := \{X[i] : i \in I^{(s)},\ a \leq i < b\}$.

Using a distributed data structure requires data movement between machines for accessing non-local data. This is an expensive operation, so designing a fast distributed algorithm often boils down to choosing the distribution in a way that minimizes data movement.

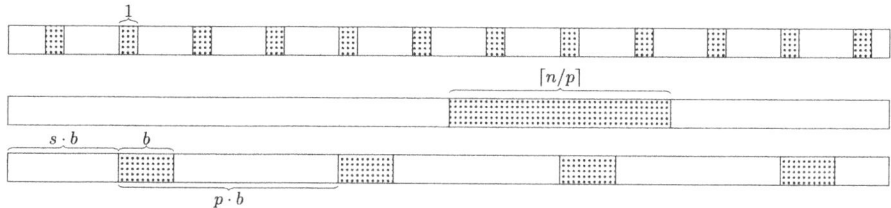

Fig. 1. Three distributions of n elements over p processors. The dotted region is the subarray $X^{(s)}$ that belongs to $P(s)$. From top to bottom: cyclic, block, block-cyclic (with block size b)

2.3 Computational Model

We use the following mental model: we consider the GPU a distributed computer, where the processors are GPU thread blocks. Within that model, each processor is itself a parallel computer that uses the SIMT paradigm.

We model the cost of an algorithm by data movement, more specifically reads and writes to global memory. The cost of computation and the cost of data movement in local memory is not significant for algorithms with low algorithmic complexity.

In contrast to clusters, most GPUs are not partially allocated. For this reason, we consider the number of processors constant, and aim to expose sufficient concurrency to fully saturate the hardware, rather than maximizing scalability of the algorithm.

3 Partition Algorithm

The main idea behind the algorithm is to minimise overall data movement by choosing a suitable distribution. The algorithm consists of two phases: a *local partition* where each processor $P(s)$ partitions its local data $X^{(s)}$ without coordinating with the other processors, and then a *cleanup phase* where we correct any mistakes. Figure 2 illustrates the result of the local partition using a block-cyclic distribution. Each processor permutes its $X^{(s)}$ and computes a local split m_s such that $X^{(s)}[0, m_s)$ satisfies pred and $X^{(s)}[m_s, n)$ does not. The global split m is equal to $\sum_{s=0}^{p-1} |X^{(s)}[0, m_s)|$. This divides the incorrect points into two sets: a set L that should be moved to the left, and a set R that should be moved to the right, or more precisely

$$L := \bigcup_{s \in J} X^{(s)}[m, m_s), \quad R := \bigcup_{s \notin J} X^{(s)}[m_s, m), \quad J := \{s : m_s > m\}.$$

The cleanup phase swaps L and R.

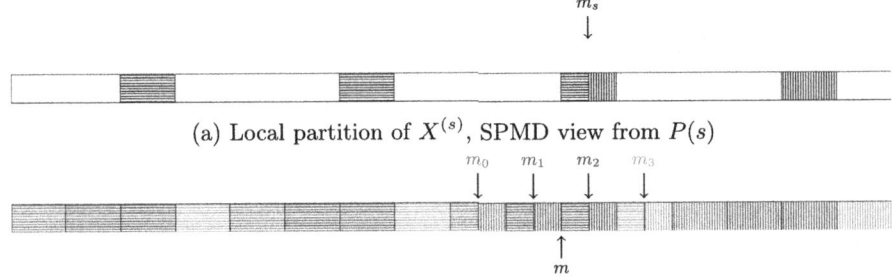

(a) Local partition of $X^{(s)}$, SPMD view from $P(s)$

(b) Local partition for four processors, depicted in different colours.

Fig. 2. Local partition of each subarray $X^{(s)}$. The horizontal lines satisfy pred, while the vertical do not

Note here that all processors, i.e., all GPU thread blocks can be executed independently during the local partition phase, and that a block-cyclic distribution of input on reasonably distributed input will lead to a reasonably small sets L and R relative to the overall size of the input. The two remaining challenges are to use individual GPU thread blocks to partition their corresponding local array $X^{(s)}$ effectively in-place, and to efficiently implement the cleanup phase.

3.1 Local Partition

To use all parallelism within a GPU thread block, we in principle want to apply the state-of-the-art algorithm for GPUs—a scan-based implementation [15]—on the local subarrays $X^{(s)}$. However, this is not in-place. So instead of running this algorithm on all of $X^{(s)}$, we cut it into chunks of a fixed size which we process one after the other. While this limits the available parallelism, it ensures that the space overhead is independent of the input size, rendering our algorithm an in-place variant. Since we have limited the physically available parallelism to individual GPU thread blocks, the limited parallelism does not impede on the overall performance.

We illustrate this algorithm in Fig. 3. The key idea is to maintain read and write pointers for the left and right side of the array, r_l, w_l, w_r, r_r. At any time, we maintain the following invariants:

- we have $\text{pred}(X^{(s)}[0, w_l))$,
- we have $\neg \text{pred}(X^{(s)}[w_r, n))$,
- we buffer $X^{(s)}[w_l, r_l)$ and $X^{(s)}[r_r, w_r)$, and
- the data in $X^{(s)}[r_l, r_r)$ is not partitioned yet.

At the start of the algorithm, we initialise w_l, r_l to the first index of $X^{(s)}$, w_r, r_r to one past the last index of $X^{(s)}$ and then establish the invariant by buffering b elements at r_l, r_r and advancing these pointers. We then repeatedly read in b elements either starting at r_l or ending at r_r, partition it using the scan-based algorithm, write it back to w_l, w_r, and update the pointers. The invariants are maintained if we read at r_l when $|X^{(s)}[w_l, r_l)| \geq |X^{(s)}[r_r, w_r)|$.

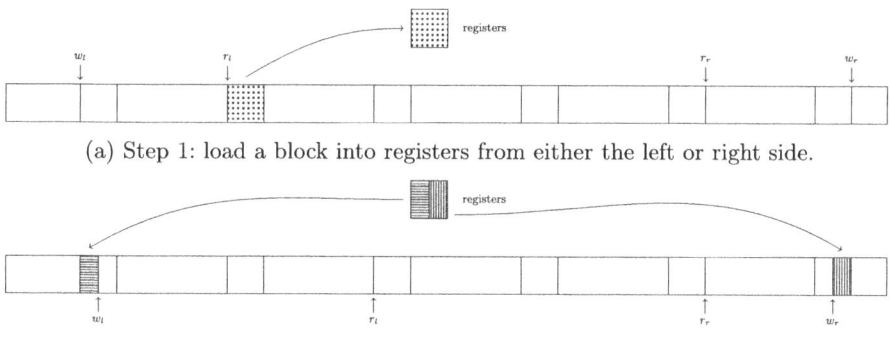

(a) Step 1: load a block into registers from either the left or right side.

(b) Step 2: partition, write elements to w_l, w_r, and update pointers.

Fig. 3. An iteration of the local partition algorithm where we read from the left

3.2 Cleanup

The most straightforward way of swapping L and R is to split each into p chunks of roughly equal size and then make each processor swap one of these chunks. The usual way of partitioning a set Y into p chunks is to take chunksize $C = \lceil |Y|/p \rceil$, and then give indices $[sC, \min((s + 1)C, n))$ to processor $P(s)$. Unfortunately, there is no straightforward way to index L and R from 0 to $|L|$, so we have to do some work.

We used an index set $J := \{s : m_s > m\}$ to express L and R. We can test whether $s \in J$ by computing $w_s = |X^{(s)}[0, m)| - |X^{(s)}[0, m_s)|$. This is negative if and only if $s \in J$. Furthermore, if $s \in J$, then $w_s = -|X^{(s)}[m, m_s)|$ and if $s \notin J$, then $w_s = |X^{(s)}[m_s, m]|$. We then partition $\{w_s : 0 \leq s < p\}$ into negative and non-negative values, yielding permutation σ and a split α such that $w_{\sigma(s)} < 0$ if and only if $s < \alpha$. This permutation lets us to express L and R as

$$L = \bigcup_{s=0}^{\alpha-1} X^{(\sigma(s))}[m, m_{\sigma(s)}), \quad R = \bigcup_{s=\alpha}^{p-1} X^{(\sigma(s))}[m_{\sigma(s)}, m).$$

We can now define an order on L as follows: let j_s be the jth element in $X^{(\sigma(s))}[m, m_{\sigma(s)})$, and k_t the kth element in $X^{(\sigma(t))}[m, m_{\sigma(t)})$. Then $j_s < k_t$ if $s < t$ or $s = t$ and $j < k$. The case R is analogous, except we take the jth element in $X^{(\sigma(s))}[m_{\sigma(s)}, m)$ instead of $X^{(\sigma(s))}[m, m_{\sigma(s)})$. We illustrate this in Fig. 4.

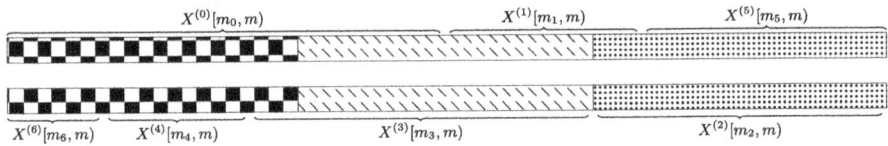

Fig. 4. Example of L and R for $w = [-9, -4, 6, 7, 3, -5, 2]$, and permutation $\sigma = [0, 1, 5, 6, 4, 3, 2]$. The split α is 3. The patterns divide the arrays in three chunks. (The actual algorithm would use $p = 7$ chunks.)

To determine where sth chunk of L starts, we must find the processor index t and local offset j such that the $s \cdot C$th element of L is the jth element of $X^{(t)}[m, m_t)$. As the index of the first element in $X^{(\sigma(t))}[m_{\sigma(t)}, m)$ is $\sum_{i=0}^{t-1} |w_{\sigma(i)}|$, index sC falls in $X^{(\sigma(t))}[m_t, m)$ whenever

$$\sum_{i=0}^{t-1} |w_{\sigma(i)}| \leq sC < \sum_{i=0}^{t} |w_{\sigma(i)}|.$$

This is equivalent to

$$\left\lceil \sum_{i=0}^{t-1} |w_{\sigma(i)}|/C \right\rceil \leq s < \left\lceil \sum_{i=0}^{t} |w_{\sigma(i)}|/C \right\rceil,$$

which can be efficiently computed. The local offset of sC is then $sC - \sum_{i=0}^{t-1} |w_{\sigma(i)}|$. The case R is analogous.

3.3 Data Movement Analysis

The local partition always reads and writes each element, resulting in $2n$ data movement where n is size of X. After the local partition, we have to move only the incorrect elements in the cleanup phase. Therefore, it suffices to consider the number of incorrect elements after the local partition to derive bounds on the total data movement. We derive a worst-case bound in Theorem 1, and a probabilistic bound in Theorem 2.

Worst-Case Input. A GPU has a fixed number of SMs and computational resources per SM, making the choice of p thread blocks and b threads per block independent of the input. For this reason, the following theorem states that the local partition can place at most $n/2 + O(1)$ elements incorrectly.

Theorem 1. *After the local partition, at most $n/2 + pb$ elements are placed incorrectly.*

Proof. The crucial idea behind the proof is that $|L| = |R|$, so we do not have to bound $|L|$ and $|R|$, but only $\min(|L|, |R|)$. We can express upper bounds for $|L|$ and $|R|$ in terms of m and the number of processors that have an excess of elements to the left. If this bound is increasing in either variable for $|L|$, it is decreasing for $|R|$, and the other way around. This means either upper bound can be large, but not both of them at the same time, so the bound on $\min(|L|, |R|)$ is small.

For $s \in J$, the elements in $X^{(s)}[0, m)$ are placed correctly, and for $s \notin J$, the elements in $X^{(s)}[m, n)$ are correct. This gives us a lower bound on the correct elements before m

$$\sum_{s \in J} |X^{(s)}[0, m)| > |J| \cdot \left(\frac{m}{p} - b\right).$$

Hence

$$|R| < m - |J| \cdot \left(\frac{m}{p} - b\right) = \left(1 - \frac{|J|}{p}\right) \cdot m + |J|b.$$

Similarly,

$$\sum_{s \notin J} |X^{(s)}[m, n)| > (p - |J|) \cdot \left(\frac{n - m}{p} - b\right),$$

so

$$|L| < n - m - (p - |J|) \cdot \left(\frac{n-m}{p} - b\right) = \frac{|J|}{p} \cdot (n - m) + (p - |J|)b.$$

As $|L| = |R|$, we have

$$|L| < \min\left(\frac{|J|}{p} \cdot (n - m) + (p - |J|)b, \left(1 - \frac{|J|}{p}\right) \cdot m + |J|b\right)$$

$$\leq \min\left(\frac{|J|}{p} \cdot (n - m), \left(1 - \frac{|J|}{p}\right) \cdot m\right) + \min((p - |J|)b, |J|b).$$

Considering $|J|/p$ a variable, the expression $|J|/p \cdot (n - m)$ is an ascending line, and $(1 - |J|/p) \cdot m$ a descending. So the minimum is the intersection of the two lines, which gives $|J|/p = m/n$. Substituting this value obtains upper bound $m/n \cdot (n - m)$. Using calculus we find this is at most $n/4$ (for $m = n/2$). Analogously, we have $\min((p - |J|)b, |J|b) \leq p/2$. We conclude $|L| < n/4 + pb/2$.

Using $|L| = |R|$ we derive the final upper bound on the number of incorrect elements $|L| + |R| = 2|L| < n/2 + pb$. □

Random Input. The intuition behind the analysis on random inputs is that the expected value of the local splits m_s will be around index μn, where μ is the probability that the predicate is true. This is also the expected value of the global split m. We can then use strong tail bounds on $\mathbb{P}(|Z - \mathbb{E}[Z]| > k)$ for suitable random variables Z. This is responsible for the ϵn and exponentially decaying probability in Theorem 2. We then bound the difference between the expected value of m_s and μn, which costs us the additional summand $2pb$. We will need the following lemma to combine bounds.

Lemma 1. *Let $Z_1, \cdots, Z_l$ be (not necessarily independent) random variables $\Omega \to \mathbb{R}$. Then*

$$\mathbb{P}\left(\left|\sum_{i=1}^{l} Z_i\right| > k\right) \leq \sum_{i=1}^{l} \mathbb{P}\left(|Z_i| > \frac{k}{l}\right).$$

Proof. By triangle inequality

$$\left|\sum_{i=1}^{l} Z_i\right| \leq \sum_{i=1}^{l} |Z_i|,$$

so $k < \left|\sum_{i=1}^{l} Z_i\right|$ implies there must be some $Z_i > k/l$. In other words,

$$\left\{\omega \in \Omega : \left|\sum_{i=1}^{l} Z_i(\omega)\right| > k\right\} \subseteq \bigcup_{i=1}^{l} \left\{\omega \in \Omega : |Z_i(\omega)| > \frac{k}{l}\right\}.$$

The lemma now follows from subadditivity. □

Theorem 2. *For i.i.d. random inputs $X[0], \cdots, X[n-1]$ or a randomly permuted input, we have to accept that $2pb$ elements may be in incorrect position after the local partition. However, it is extremely unlikely that the fraction ϵ of incorrect elements is much larger than $O(\sqrt{p/n})$. To be more precise, for I the set of incorrect points:*

$$\mathbb{P}(|I| > 2pb + \epsilon n) \leq 4p \exp\left(-\frac{\epsilon^2 n}{3p}\right).$$

Example 1. The default values of our algorithm are $p = 4096$, $b = 512$. Suppose we partition an array of 8 GB of doubles, so $n = 10^9$. The bound starts being less than 100% when we look at more than 1.1% of values being incorrect ($\epsilon = 0.011$). The probability that more than 1.1% of values are incorrect is at most 87%. The probability that more than 1.3% are wrong is no more than 1.7%, and the probability that more than 2% of values are wrong is at most $3 \cdot 10^{-10}\%$.

Proof. The number of incorrect elements is

$$|I| = \sum_{s=0}^{p-1} \left| |X^{(s)}[0,m)| - |X^{(s)}[0,m_s)| \right|.$$

We can express these random variables with indicator functions

$$Y_i(\omega) = \begin{cases} 1 & \text{if } \text{pred}(X_i) \\ 0 & \text{if } \neg\,\text{pred}(X_i) \end{cases},$$

which gives

$$m = \sum_{i=0}^{n-1} Y_i, \quad C_s := |X^{(s)}[0,m_s)| = \sum_{i \in I^{(s)}} Y_i$$

$$D_s := |X^{(s)}[0,m)| = b \cdot \left\lfloor \frac{m}{pb} \right\rfloor + m \mod b.$$

For both i.i.d. random input and randomly permuted input, the indicator functions Y_i are i.i.d. Bernoulli random variables.

With this notation, the applications of Lemma 1 give

$$\mathbb{P}\left(|L| + |R| > 2pb + \epsilon n\right) \leq \sum_{s=0}^{p-1} \mathbb{P}(|D_s - C_s| > 2b + \epsilon n/p). \qquad (1)$$

Both C_s and m are binomial distributions, with success rate $\mu = \mathbb{E}[Y_i]$, which means we can apply Hoeffding's inequality on them. To that end, we use $||I^{(s)}| - n/p| \leq b$ and $|D_s - m/p| \leq b$ to obtain upper bound

$$|D_s - C_s| = \left| \left(\frac{m}{p} - \frac{n}{p}\mu\right) + (|I^{(s)}|\mu - C_s) + D_s - \frac{m}{p} + \frac{n}{p}\mu - |I^{(s)}|\mu \right|$$

$$\leq \left| \left(\frac{m}{p} - \frac{n}{p}\mu\right) + (|I^{(s)}|\mu - C_s) \right| + b + \mu b$$

$$\leq \left| \left(\frac{m}{p} - \frac{n}{p}\mu\right) + (|I^{(s)}|\mu - C_s) \right| + 2b.$$

We conclude that $|D_s - C_s| > 2b + \epsilon n/p$ implies

$$\left| \left(\frac{m}{p} - \frac{n}{p\mu}\right) + \left(|I^{(s)}|\mu - C_s\right) \right| > \frac{\epsilon n}{p}.$$

Again by Lemma 1, we have

$$\mathbb{P}(|D_s - C_s| > 2b + \epsilon\frac{n}{p}) \leq \mathbb{P}\left(|\frac{m}{p} - \frac{n}{p}\mu| > \epsilon\frac{n}{2p}\right) + \mathbb{P}\left(||I^{(s)}|\mu - C_s| > \epsilon\frac{n}{2p}\right).$$

Both m and C_s are sums of independent random variables, so by Hoeffding's inequality, we have

$$\mathbb{P}\left(||I^{(s)}|\mu - C_s| > \frac{\epsilon n}{2p}\right) \leq 2\exp\left(-\frac{\epsilon^2 n^2}{2p^2 |I^{(s)}|}\right).$$

As $2p^2|I^{(s)}| \leq 2p^2(n/p + b) = 2pn + p^2 b \leq 2pn + pn = 3pn$, we find upper bound

$$\mathbb{P}\left(\left||I^{(s)}|\mu - C_s\right| > \frac{\epsilon n}{2p}\right) \leq 2\exp\left(-\frac{\epsilon^2 n}{3p}\right). \tag{2}$$

Also by Hoeffding's inequality, we have

$$\mathbb{P}\left(\left|\frac{m}{p} - \frac{n}{p}\mu\right| > \frac{\epsilon n}{2p}\right) = \mathbb{P}\left(|m - n\mu| > \frac{1}{2}\epsilon n\right) \leq 2\exp\left(-\frac{1}{2}\epsilon^2 n\right). \tag{3}$$

The theorem follows by combining inequalities 1, 2, and 3. □

4 Implementation

We implement this algorithm in CUDA, using the CUB library [16]. This library contains implementations of several building blocks, implemented on the level of warps, thread blocks, and the entire device. The code [11] is available on GitLab.

We do the scan-based partition on the level of thread blocks. By default, we use 128 threads per block and 4 items per thread, which gives block parameter $b = 128 \cdot 4 = 512$. These values are C++ template parameters and can be changed by the user. CUB contains a scan and scatter function, which we use to straightforwardly build the local partition.

The value for p is also a template parameter. The optimal choice of p would be the number of SMs multiplied by the number of blocks that can be mapped to each SM concurrently (the *occupancy*) if these would be optimally scheduled. However, our experiments indicated that the scheduling is not always optimal, and this parameter would have to be changed for each architecture. So long as $pb \ll n$, it does not hurt to take p big. For this reason we have chosen default 4096.

The partition in the cleanup phase is small, so we use the out-of-place implementation of CUB to compute σ. We also use CUB's scan function to compute $\sum_{i=0}^{t} |w_{\sigma(i)}|$ for $t = 1, \cdots, p$.

5 Performance Evaluation

As partitioning has a small amount of work per element, the performance will be limited by bandwidth. We can evaluate the performance of our algorithm by comparing the achieved bandwidth with the peak bandwidth the GPU is capable of. We estimate this peak bandwidth by using one of the STREAM [13] benchmarks, a collection of simple computations that stresses the memory subsystem of a computer. To most closely match the structure of a partition, we have chosen for SCALE. This operation multiplies all elements of an array by a fixed constant α (we have chosen $\alpha = 2$).

5.1 Methodology

We use a consumer GPU (3070 Ti) and two server GPUs (A30, H100) for our measurements, with 8 GiB, 24 GiB, 80 GiB of VRAM. We use NVCC versions 12.6.77, 12.6.68, 12.6.20, and CUB versions 1.017.02, 2.005.00, 2.005.00.

The CUDA compiler NVCC generates an intermediate representation which is compiled to machine code by the driver just before execution. After the first execution, the compiled machine code can be fetched from an instruction cache. Furthermore, the clock frequency is not constant. For this reason, we do some untimed warmup runs before our measurements. We call the partition function in a loop until 500 GB of data has been moved.

We repeat each of these experiments ten times and report the mean and standard deviation through error bars.

5.2 Discussion

We investigate two variables for each machine and data type: input size, and input structure. This is graphed in Fig. 5, where we use a logarithmic scale on the x-axis with each point a factor two apart. We investigate data types `float`, `double`, and `struct { int x; int y; }`. We construct an input that gets within pb of the worst case of Theorem 1 by setting $X^{(s)}$ to pred for even s, and to $\neg$ pred for odd s. As we have chosen p even, the local partition will place $n/2$ elements incorrectly. For random input we generate values such that $\mathbb{P}(\text{pred}(X[i])) = 0.5$. We also generate a structured input that is already partitioned, and one that is reversed partitioned, e.g. partitioned according to $\neg$ pred. For CUB the results are within a standard deviation for all input structures, so we only graph one.

We do all our measurements on a range of sizes. Our algorithm uses arrays of f 8 GB, 24 GB, 80 GB respectively, or about 93 % of the available VRAM. CUB can partition arrays half as large. There is also a maximum of $2^{31} - 1$ elements because CUB uses an `int` type internally for offsets.

There are three types of overhead that explain why our algorithm does not attain the performance of STREAM.

First, the local partition and index arithmetic of block-cyclic arrays increase the latency between load and stores. This limits the performance of our algorithm to 89% 99% of STREAM on large, non-adversarial arrays. There is no significant difference between the reverse partitioned and uniform input structures, indicating that the local partition placed most points correctly. This agrees with Theorem 2. CUB also needs to do local partitioning, but does not need index arithmetic, yielding slightly better performance on `float` and `double`: 92% 99% of STREAM. For the `struct` of `int` the performance drops to as little as 76% of our performance. We were unable to pinpoint the exact cause, but believe the more complicated data type inhibits optimising one of the many C++ abstractions CUB uses.

Second, our algorithm has significant constant overhead. We do ten kernel calls as opposed to CUB's one, and the cleanup phase also has large constants.

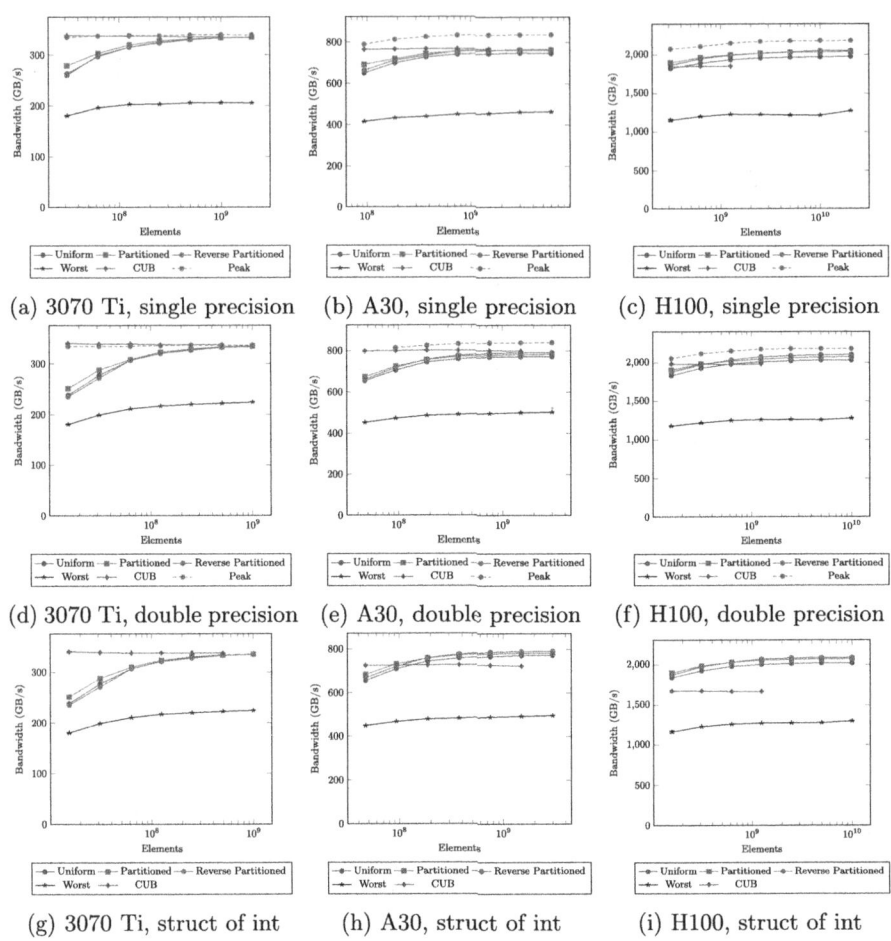

Fig. 5. Bandwidth partition algorithms

This causes a noticeable drop in performance for small arrays, but the performance is still at least 79 % of STREAM's for arrays of non-adversarial input. It is interesting that CUB is slightly faster than STREAM on the 3070 Ti, and that the already partitioned input is slightly faster than the reverse partitioned input. This suggests that writing back identical memory is slightly faster for small arrays.

Third, the cleanup phase moves a significant amount of data for adversarial arrays. We expect the performance for the worst-case input to be roughly linear in data movement, so this bandwidth should be a fraction $2n/(3n) \approx 0.67$ of random input. This is also observed in practice, where the bandwidth of worst-case input is 0.63% 0.67% of the bandwidth of random input.

6 Related and Future Work

The main structure of a local partition and a cleanup phase resembles an algorithm by Francis et al. [8]. The difference is that we use a block-cyclic distribution instead of a cyclic distribution, and have a parallel cleanup phase, instead of partitioning $[\min_s m_s, \max_s m_s]$ sequentially.

The local partition can be seen as the GPU analogue of an AVX-512 partition algorithm [5]. A thread-block replaces the CPU core, and a scan-based partition algorithm [4] within that thread block replaces the AVX-512 partition instruction.

Gu et al. use a more abstract model of parallel in-place algorithms [9] based on the work-span model [17]. This algorithm is work-efficient and makes a trade-off based on a parameter ϵ between $O(n^\epsilon \log(n))$ span and $O(n^{1-\epsilon})$ auxilary space. Their implementation targets multicore machines instead of GPUs.

Partitioning is usually not used on its own, so we will mention some motivating applications. A classification algorithm such as the Support Vector Machine (SVM) [7] finds a hyperplane separating points in $\mathbb{R}^n$. To compute efficiently on these two sets, it can be useful to partition them in memory, where pred is their position relative to the hyperplane. The same predicate is used in computational geometry, where the Quickhull [2] algorithm recursively partitions points based on their orientation to a hyperplanes. Not all algorithms have fixed predicates. The sorting algorithm Quicksort [10] can choose any element as pivot to compare to.

These applications suggest opportunities for future work. The SVM algorithm can be extended to multiclass SVM which partitions data in more than two classes. Similarly, sorting algorithms aim to reduce the number of passes over the input by partitioning in multiple classes as well. One of these algorithms, IPS4o [1], is parallel and in-place. It maps well to CPUs, but to map well to GPUs a SIMD/SIMT approach to filling the bins is needed.

7 Conclusion

We have designed an in-place partition algorithm and implemented it for GPUs. This algorithm can handle cases that are twice as large as that of the state-of-the-art CUB implementation. For the cases we expect users to be most interested in – large, non-adversarial arrays – we obtain 97% 100% of CUB's performance and 89% 99% of the hardware's peak. The limitations of our work are small arrays or arrays with an adversarial structure, where the performance may drop to 53%. We have proven a worst-case bound on data movement, and a probabilistic bound for random input.

We viewed the GPU as a distributed computer by looking at thread blocks as nodes and threads within a block as SIMD lanes. This allows algorithms from the literature to be reinterpreted, serving as starting point for this algorithm. It also simplifies the description and analysis.

Disclosure of Interests. The authors have no competing interests to declare that are relevant to the content of this article.

Artifact Availability. The artifact is available in Zenodo repository [12].

References

1. Axtmann, M., Witt, S., Ferizovic, D., Sanders, P.: In-place parallel super scalar samplesort (IPSSSSo). In: 25th Annual European Symposium on Algorithms (ESA 2017). Leibniz International Proceedings in Informatics (LIPIcs), vol. 87, pp. 9:1–9:14. Schloss Dagstuhl–Leibniz-Zentrum fuer Informatik (2017). https://doi.org/10.4230/LIPIcs.ESA.2017.9
2. Barber, C.B., Dobkin, D.P., Huhdanpaa, H.: The quickhull algorithm for convex hulls. ACM Trans. Math. Softw. **22**(4), 469–483 (1996). https://doi.org/10.1145/235815.235821
3. Bisseling, R.H.: Parallel Scientific Computation: A Structured Approach Using BSP. Oxford University Press (2020). https://doi.org/10.1093/oso/9780198788348.001.0001
4. Blelloch, G.: Scans as primitive parallel operations. IEEE Trans. Comput. **38**(11), 1526–1538 (1989). https://doi.org/10.1109/12.42122
5. Bramas, B.: A novel hybrid quicksort algorithm vectorized using AVX-512 on intel skylake. Int. J. Adv. Comput. Sci. Appl. **8**(10) (2017). https://doi.org/10.14569/IJACSA.2017.081044
6. Cederman, D., Tsigas, P.: GPU-quicksort: a practical quicksort algorithm for graphics processors. ACM J. Exp. Algorithmics **14** (2010). https://doi.org/10.1145/1498698.1564500
7. Cortes, C., Vapnik, V.: Support-vector networks. Mach. Learn. **20**, 273–297 (1995)
8. Francis, R., Pannan, L.: A parallel partition for enhanced parallel quicksort. Parallel Comput. **18**(5), 543–550 (1992). https://doi.org/10.1016/0167-8191(92)90089-P
9. Gu, Y., Obeya, O., Shun, J.: Parallel In-Place Algorithms: Theory and Practice, pp. 114–128 (2021). https://doi.org/10.1137/1.9781611976489.9
10. Hoare, C.A.: Quicksort. Comput. J. **5**(1), 10–16 (1962)
11. Koopman, T.: GPU-partition-inplace (2025). https://gitlab.com/thomas637/gpu-partition-inplace
12. Koopman, T., Scholz, S.B., van Gastel, B.: Artifact of the paper: partitioning in-place on massively parallel systems (2025). https://doi.org/10.5281/zenodo.15576891
13. McCalpin, J.D., et al.: Memory bandwidth and machine balance in current high performance computers. IEEE Comput. Soc. Tech. Comm. Comput. Archit. (TCCA) Newsl. **2**(19-25) (1995)
14. Mei, G.: CudaChain: an alternative algorithm for finding 2D convex hulls on the GPU. Springerplus **5**(1), 1–26 (2016). https://doi.org/10.1186/s40064-016-2284-4
15. Merrill, D., Garland, M.: Single-pass parallel prefix scan with decoupled look-back. Technical report, NVIDIA (2016)
16. NVIDIA Corporation: CUB. https://github.com/nvidia/cccl
17. Shiloach, Y., Vishkin, U.: An o(n2log n) parallel max-flow algorithm. J. Algorithms **3**(2), 128–146 (1982). https://doi.org/10.1016/0196-6774(82)90013-X

Multidisciplinary, Domain-Specific and Applied Parallel and Distributed Computing

Quantum Delta Encoding: Optimizing Data Storage on Quantum Computers with Resource Efficiency

Jiale Zhang, Xilong Che, Yuzhe Fan, and Juncheng Hu(✉)

College of Computer Science and Technology, Jilin University, Changchun, China
jlzhang22@mails.jlu.edu.cn, jchu@jlu.edu.cn

Abstract. In recent years, numerous studies have explored efficient methods for encoding classical data into quantum systems by leveraging Quantum Random Access Memory (QRAM) to facilitate subsequent data processing tasks. However, current state-of-the-art encoding techniques rely on extensive multi-qubit controlled-NOT gates and require complex quantum gate decompositions to ensure compatibility with existing hardware. Other approaches have attempted to employ quantum neural networks for state preparation–either to enable quantum data compression or to perform quantum Fourier transforms for preserving frequency-domain information–but these methods typically involve significant preprocessing and fail to accurately recover the original classical data. In this paper, inspired by classical Delta Encoding, we propose Quantum Delta Encoding (QDE), which stores the majority of data in a benchmark and encodes only the deviations via entanglement, thereby significantly reducing the need for entangled qubits and quantum gates during storage. Moreover, QDE can seamlessly integrate with QRAM to support subsequent quantum data processing tasks–such as image processing and data encryption–thus mitigating the additional errors and losses associated with repeated classical-to-quantum data exchanges. We evaluate the advantages of QDE over state-of-the-art models using real-world datasets and assess its robustness against quantum noise. Experiments conducted on both the IBM Quantum platform's simulator and two real superconducting quantum computers confirm the validity and potential of the QDE approach. All codes and data are available at https://github.com/kennyZhangsky/Quantum-Delta-Encoding.

Keywords: Quantum Data Storage · Quantum Signal Processing · Parallel Processing · Quantum Algorithm

1 Introduction

The explosive growth in data generation driven by advancements in information technology has necessitated the development of efficient data compression techniques. Classical compression algorithms [8], however, struggle to keep pace with this expansion, as they require $O(N)$ bits to store a dataset of N elements. This limitation arises from the representational capacity of a single bit, the smallest unit in classical computing. Since Richard Feynman introduced quantum computing in 1982 [3], quantum computers have leveraged their entanglement and parallelism to revolutionize data storage [20,22] and processing [1,19].

A key challenge for data processing on quantum computers is the need to encode classical data into quantum states. Quantum data encoding schemes can be divided into two categories based on the encoding of amplitude and computational basis states: Amplitude Encoding and Basic Encoding [11]. While Amplitude Encoding requires fewer qubits, it can only probabilistically recover classical data, and the quantum state preparation is significantly more complex compared to the lossless Basic Encoding scheme. Basic Encoding, which is more suited for the Noisy Intermediate-Scale Quantum (NISQ) era [18], has found particular application in quantum image processing, as seen in approaches such as OCQR [9], BRQI [12], QIRC [13], MQIR [25] and NGQR [21]. These encoding schemes use multi-qubit controlled-NOT gates to entangle quantum bit strings that encode pixel and coordinate information, enabling lossless data recovery. Since data is encoded into binary bit strings in the computational basis, this type of encoding is more suitable for Quantum Random Access Memory (QRAM) [4], facilitating parallel quantum data retrieval and avoiding frequent classical-to-quantum data conversions, thus aiding subsequent quantum data processing tasks.

However, as dataset sizes increase, the length of control qubit strings grows, making extensive qubit entanglement increasingly challenging and quantum circuit decomposition more complex [9,12,21,24]. Some approaches attempt to transform data into the frequency domain using Fourier-like transforms [6,17] or leverage trained quantum neural networks for quantum data compression [2,7]. However, these methods require substantial preprocessing and often fail to achieve accurate data recovery, rendering them unsuitable for QRAM and difficult to integrate with subsequent quantum data processing tasks in quantum computers [23–25]. A lossless quantum data encoding scheme that optimizes both qubit consumption and quantum state preparation complexity while remaining compatible with QRAM has yet to be fully explored.

To address these challenges, we propose Quantum Delta Encoding (QDE), a resource-efficient, lossless data encoding model designed for quantum computers. By integrating Basic Encoding with classical Delta Encoding [15], QDE stores the majority of data in a benchmark while encoding only the deviations through entanglement, thereby significantly reducing the requirement for quantum resources. Moreover, the QDE state stored in a quantum computer is directly accessible by QRAM, facilitating subsequent quantum data processing tasks such as quantum image processing and data encryption. We evaluate the performance of QDE on real datasets and assess its resilience to quantum noise in comparison with state-of-the-art models. Detailed theoretical analysis and experimental results obtained from two superconducting quantum computers on the IBM Quantum platform confirm the following advantages of QDE:

Let k denote the number of bits required to represent δ, the maximum binary difference value of all elements relative to a benchmark γ.

1. QDE requires only $\log N + \log k + 1$ entangled qubits to store a set of N elements, which is fewer than that required by any existing quantum data storage model.
2. For storing a set or image of size $2^n \times 2^n$, QDE improves upon the runtime complexity of existing models, reducing it from $O(n \cdot 2^{2n})$ to an optimized upper bound of $O(n)$.
3. Subsequent QDE-based image processing operations are feasible through QRAM. Moreover, compared to state-of-the-art lossless quantum data storage models, QDE exhibits stronger noise resilience.

2 Background and Challenges

In this section, we primarily summarize the current challenges of quantum data storage. Due to space constraints, a detailed introduction to the preliminaries of quantum computing is not provided; for more information, please refer to Reference [16].

Quantum Data Encoding. Quantum data encoding can be broadly classified into two categories [11]. The first category, Basis Encoding, encodes data into the computational basis of a quantum state. For instance, a 3-bit string 110 can be represented as a 3-qubit system $|110\rangle$. The second category, Amplitude Encoding, encodes data into the amplitude of a quantum state. For example, a set $\chi = \{25, 50, 100, 150\}$ can be encoded on a quantum computer as $|\chi\rangle = \frac{1}{\sqrt{25^2+50^2+100^2+150^2}}(25|00\rangle + 50|01\rangle + 100|10\rangle + 150|11\rangle)$.

Basic Encoding stores data in the computational basis states, allowing for lossless data recovery due to the orthogonal state separability theorem [16]. In contrast, Amplitude Encoding represents data in the amplitude of a quantum state. While it requires fewer qubits than Basic Encoding, data recovery is probabilistic and necessitates additional quantum measurements.

Quantum Random Access Memory. Quantum Random Access Memory (QRAM) [4] is the quantum analogue of classical RAM, enabling efficient access and retrieval of large-scale data within quantum systems. Unlike classical storage, QRAM leverages quantum superposition and entanglement to facilitate parallel data access, significantly enhancing data processing speed. The QRAM read operation is mathematically expressed as:

$$\sum \alpha_s |s\rangle |0\rangle \xrightarrow{QRAM} \alpha_s |s\rangle |D_s\rangle, \quad (1)$$

where QRAM queries a superposition state $|s\rangle$ of the address register and returns the corresponding data $|D_s\rangle$ stored in the s-th memory cell. As QRAM outputs a binary information string D_s, it is inherently well-suited for Basic Encoding-based quantum data encoding models.

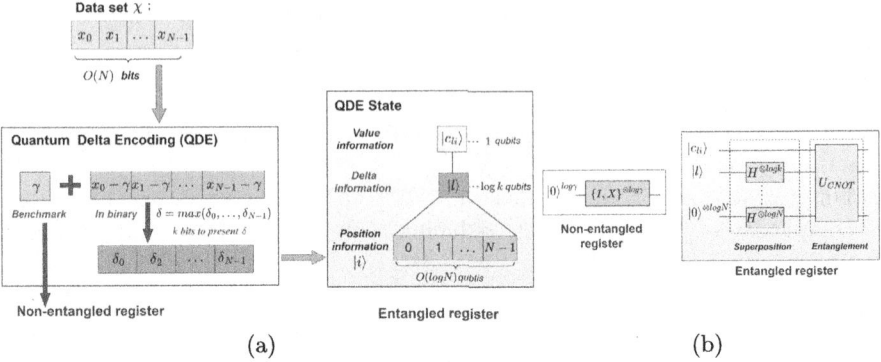

Fig. 1. (a) Workflow of QDE model for storing an N-element set. (b) Quantum circuit construction of QDE model.

Quantum Data Compression. Despite the intrinsic parallelism of quantum computing, research on quantum data compression for optimizing data storage in quantum systems remains limited. Some studies employ Fourier-like transforms to map classical information into the frequency domain for storage [6,17]. However, since these methods encode data in amplitude states, they do not support exact classical data recovery. Another approach leverages quantum neural networks for data compression [2,7], where classical information is retrieved through expectation value measurements. While these techniques reduce qubit requirements and quantum circuit depth, they suffer from several limitations: they do not ensure precise classical data recovery, require extensive pre-training, and pose challenges in integrating with QRAM for subsequent quantum data processing. These challenges arise because quantum neural networks cannot explicitly store data, and measurement-induced wavefunction collapse introduces additional overhead due to repeated classical-to-quantum data exchanges [10].

3 Quantum Delta Encoding

To address the above challenges, we propose Quantum Delta Encoding (QDE), which seamlessly integrates with QRAM while simultaneously optimizing both entangled qubits consumption and state preparation runtime complexity.

3.1 Methodology

As shown in Fig. 1(a), by integrating Basic Encoding with classical delta encoding, our proposed Quantum Delta Encoding (QDE) model comprises two principal components: the benchmark γ and the corresponding δ information.

As depicted in Fig. 1(b), storing the benchmark γ requires only a quantum NOT gate (X), a simple quantum gate that does not generate any entanglement.

The QDE model encodes most of the information of γ via a sequence of non-entangled qubits while utilizing fewer entangled resources for the δ information. In the subsequent discussion, we elaborate on the quantum circuit construction for encoding the δ information, hereafter referred to as the QDE state $|QDE\rangle$.

Consider a set $\chi = \{x_0, \ldots, x_{N-1}\}$ with N elements. After defining a benchmark γ, the set χ can be decomposed as $\gamma + \chi'$, where $\chi' = \{x_0 - \gamma, \ldots, x_{N-1} - \gamma\}$. The maximum difference, denoted by $\delta = \text{Max}(\chi')$, is then determined. Let k represent the number of bits required to encode δ in binary. Consequently, $\log k$ qubits are required to store the δ information for all elements, and $\log N$ qubits are necessary to index the N elements.

Thus, the total number of qubits required for the QDE state $|QDE\rangle$ is $\log N + \log k + 1$, which can be expressed as follows:

$$|QDE\rangle = \frac{1}{\sqrt{2}^{\log(N \cdot k)}} \sum_{l=0}^{k-1} \sum_{i=0}^{N-1} |c_{li}\rangle |l\rangle |i\rangle, \quad (2)$$

where $c_{li} \in \{0, 1\}$ denotes the binary value at the l-th position of the k-bit string for the i-th element. For example, a 2×2 grayscale image within a grayscale range of $\{0, 255\}$ requires 8 bits to represent the binary values of the pixel intensities. To index the positions within this 8-bit binary string, $\log 8 = 3$ qubits are needed. Additionally, $\log 2 \times 2 = 2$ qubits are required to index the specific pixel locations. Moreover, an additional qubit is needed to represent the binary value corresponding to each index of δ and its positional information i. Notably, if the dataset contains negative elements, an additional qubit is required to represent the sign of the data.

The QDE model can be extended to store a color image with R, G, and B channels by employing an additional two qubits, as described by the following:

$$|\psi\rangle = \frac{1}{\sqrt{2}^{\log(N \cdot k)}} \sum_{l=0}^{k-1} \sum_{i=0}^{N-1} |r_{li}\rangle |g_{li}\rangle |b_{li}\rangle |l\rangle |i\rangle, \quad (3)$$

where $|r_{li}\rangle$, $|g_{li}\rangle$, and $|b_{li}\rangle$ denote the binary values of the R, G, and B channels at the l-th position for the i-th pixel, respectively. In this context, three benchmarks, γ_r, γ_g, and γ_b, are defined for the respective channels.

Figure 1(b) illustrates the quantum circuit construction of the QDE model. The benchmark setting operation in the non-entangled register only requires the quantum X gates without incurring any entanglement resource cost [16]. The QDE state setting requires the H gates to produce superposition in the computational basis of $\{|0\rangle, |1\rangle\}$ and the multi-qubit controlled-NOT gates, U_{CNOT}, to entangle the δ and element position information i. The control qubits for the U_{CNOT} gate are represented as a $\log N + \log k$-bit string, determined by both the δ and i information, with the target qubit being $|c_{li}\rangle$. Algorithm 1 provides a summary of the process for storing an N-element set using the QDE model.

3.2 Resource Cost Analysis of QDE

Section 3.1 demonstrates that the entangled qubits required for QDE. Here, we present the following discussion on the cost of runtime complexity:

Algorithm 1. QDE model for storing an N-element set χ

INPUT $\chi = x_0, \ldots, x_{N-1}$
OUTPUT $\gamma, |QDE\rangle$
PROCEDURE
  Find γ, δ and k: $\chi' = \{x_0 - \gamma, \ldots, x_{N-1} - \gamma\}$; $\gamma = min(\chi')$; $\delta = max(\chi')$
  Benchmark setting: γ stored in non-entangled register.
  Initialization: $|0\rangle^{\log(N \cdot k)}$
  Superposition: $\longrightarrow \sum_{l=0}^{k-1} \sum_{i=0}^{N-1} |0\rangle \otimes |l\rangle |i\rangle$
  Entanglement: $\longrightarrow \sum_{l=0}^{k-1} \sum_{i=0}^{N-1} |c_{li}\rangle |l\rangle |i\rangle = |QDE\rangle$
MEASUREMENT
  Measure the non-entangled register;
   Obtain γ
  Measure the entangled register;
   Obtain $|QDE\rangle$
RETURN $\gamma, |QDE\rangle$

Theorem 1. *Consider a data set χ of size $N = 2^n \times 2^n$, with k the number of bits required for the maximum difference value δ. The entangled qubits consumption of QDE is bounded within the interval $[0, 2n + \log k + 1]$.*

Proof. Similar to classical Delta Encoding, QDE performs efficiently when handling data with small variations. The parameter k represents the degree of difference between data points; as k increases, the storage performance of QDE deteriorates. Notably, when $k = 0$, indicating that all data values are identical, QDE does not require any entanglement resources and only utilizes $2n$ qubits in a superposition state. In this case, QDE represents the most resource-efficient encoding method while still leveraging the quantum advantage of parallelism.

For time complexity, we follow the established complexity analysis for quantum image representation methods [20, 22]. In the NISQ era, the runtime complexity of single-qubit gates and two-qubit CNOT gates is considered to be 1 [18]. All multi-qubit controlled-NOT gates, U_{CNOT}, must be decomposed into single-qubit and CNOT gates. The decomposition of a U_{CNOT} gate with $O(n)$ control qubits has a runtime complexity of $O(n)$. We present the following discussion:

Theorem 2. *Consider a data set χ of size $2^n \times 2^n$, with k representing the number of bits required for the maximum difference value δ. The runtime complexity for preparing χ on quantum computers using QDE is bounded as follows:*

1. **Lower Bound:** *The runtime complexity for preparing χ on quantum computers using QDE has a lower bound of $O(3k(2n + \log k)2^{2n}) \approx O(n \cdot 2^{2n})$.*
2. **Optimal Condition:** *Under optimal conditions, where QDE achieves its maximum encoding efficiency, the runtime complexity requirement for a QDE state is $O(n)$.*

Proof. We take the application in color images as an example to illustrate the runtime complexity of QDE model. Following the storage of benchmarks in the non-entangled register, the primary workflow for preparing a QDE state is divided into two steps as shown in Fig. 1(b).

At the beginning, the initial state of the quantum system is initialized as $|\psi_0\rangle = |0\rangle^{\otimes 2n + \log k + 3}$ for a $2^n \times 2^n$ color image.

step1: We use two important single quantum gates I and H to complete the construction of this quantum operation as $U_1 = I^{\otimes 3} \otimes H^{\otimes \log k + 2n}$. Equation (4) illustrates the quantum transformation from the initial state $|\psi_0\rangle$ to the middle state $|\psi_1\rangle$ through the quantum operator U_1.

$$|\psi_1\rangle = U_1 |\psi_0\rangle = \frac{1}{\sqrt{2}^{2n+\log k}} \sum_{l=0}^{k-1} \sum_{i=0}^{2^{2n}-1} |0\rangle^{\otimes 3} \otimes |l\rangle |i\rangle. \quad (4)$$

step2: 2^{2n} sub-operation A_i encodes the δ value for the $i-th$ pixel of one channel. Each A_i is a $2n + \log k$-$CNOT$ gate so the quantum operator of **step2**, U_2 can be expressed as $U_2 = \prod_{i=0}^{2^{2n}-1} A_i$. Then the function of U_2 of step2 is described as follows:

$$U_2 |\psi_1\rangle = \frac{1}{\sqrt{2}^{2n+\log k}} \sum_{l=0}^{k-1} \sum_{i=0}^{2^{2n}-1} |r_{li}\rangle |g_{li}\rangle |b_{li}\rangle |l\rangle |i\rangle = |\psi\rangle. \quad (5)$$

Following the aforementioned steps, a color digital image is encoded and stored in a QDE state on a quantum computer. In non-entangled register, benchmark setting requires no more than $\log \gamma$ single quantum gates X which cost $O(\log \gamma)$. In the entangled register, U_1 in **step1** requires no more than $2n + \log k$ single quantum gates H which cost $O(2n + \log k)$.

U_2 in **step2** has to set the δ value for all pixels in the quantum image. The entire operation consists of $2^n \times 2^n$ sub-operations (A_i). Each sub-operation A_i is a $2n + \log k$-$CNOT$ gate, e.g., U_{CNOT} gate with $\log k + 2n$-bit string. Every U_{CNOT} gate can be divided into $O(2n + \log k)$ single quantum gates, which costs $O(2n + \log k)$ and every channel requires at most k U_{CNOT} gates. For every pixel, at most $3 \times k$ U_{CNOT} gates are required. Then the runtime complexity of **step2** is $O(3k \cdot (2n + \log k) 2^{2n})$.

Therefore, the overall runtime complexity of preparing a $2^n \times 2^n$ color image into a QDE state is at most $O(3k \cdot (2n + \log k) 2^{2n} + (2n + \log k) + \log \gamma) \simeq O(3k \cdot (2n + \log k) 2^{2n}) \approx O(n \cdot 2^{2n})$. As stated in Theorem 1, when all data values are identical, no entanglement resources are required, and the QDE state can be efficiently prepared using only $O(n)$ H gates to generate a superposition over the computational basis of $\{|0\rangle, |1\rangle\}$. In this optimal case, the runtime complexity of preparing the QDE state reduces to $O(n)$.

Table 1 presents a comparison of quantum resource consumption between the QDE model and the most recent quantum models. In summary, our QDE model not only guarantees accurate classical data recovery and seamless integration with QRAM but also achieves substantial optimization in both the number of entangled qubits and runtime complexity.

Table 1. Quantum resource consumption comparison of QDE and recent quantum models for storing a $2^n \times 2^n$ color image, highlighting the advantages of our QDE model in terms of optimization.

Method	Year	Entangled Qubits	Runtime Complexity	Data Recovery
OCQR [9]	2018	$2n + 10$	$O(n \cdot 2^{2n})$	Accuracy
QIRC [13]	2021	$2n + 8$	$O(n \cdot 2^{2n})$	Accuracy
MQIR [25]	2021	$2n + 7$	$O(n \cdot 2^{2n})$	Accuracy
HPBRQI [14]	2023	$2n$	$O(2^{4n})$	Probability
PE-NGQR [21]	2024	$2n + 8$	$O(n \cdot 2^{2n})$	Accuracy
CE-NGQR [21]	2024	$2n + 6$	$O(n \cdot 2^{2n}) \leq O(n^2 \cdot 2^{2n})$	Accuracy
Our QDE	/	$[0, 2n + 6]$	$O(n) \leq O(n \cdot 2^{2n})$	Accuracy

3.3 Subsequent Quantum Data Processing Through QRAM

The quantum data $|QDE\rangle$, as presented in Eq.(2), can be retrieved via QRAM in accordance with Eq.(1). Specifically, the transformation is given by

$$\sum \alpha_s |s\rangle |0\rangle \xrightarrow{QRAM} \alpha_s |s\rangle |\psi_s\rangle, \qquad (6)$$

where $|\psi_s\rangle = |QDE\rangle$ denotes the quantum data stored in the s-th address register. Once retrieved, the data can be directly processed for applications such as quantum image processing and data encryption.

Assuming $|\psi_s\rangle = |\psi\rangle$ (as Eq. 3) represents a QDE quantum image, common quantum image processing operations–ranging from pixel value adjustments (e.g., channel conversion, color complementation) to geometric transformations (e.g., horizontal flipping, Fourier transforms)–can be applied with efficiency similar to that of Basic Encoding-based models [12,21,25].

Furthermore, QDE integrates seamlessly with various quantum data processing algorithms [20,22]. For instance, quantum image encryption [23] based on the Quantum Fourier Transform involves three steps: applying Quantum Fourier Transform U_F, then $R_y(\theta_l)$ with $\theta_l = \frac{2\pi \cdot \mu(p+q)}{2^l}$ (where p and q are large prime numbers, $l = 0, 1, \ldots, 2n - 1$, and μ is a rotation adjustment factor), and finally Inverse Quantum Fourier Transform $U_F^\dagger$. This process transforms the state $|\psi\rangle = \sum_{i=0}^{2^{2n}-1} c_i |i\rangle$ into $|\psi_R\rangle = U_F^\dagger \bigotimes_{l=0}^{2n-1} R_y(\theta_l) U_F |\psi\rangle$, and the decryption process is given by $|\psi\rangle = U_F^\dagger \bigotimes_{l=0}^{2n-1} R_y(-\theta_l) U_F |\psi_R\rangle$.

Successful decryption requires that both communicating parties possess the primes p and q and apply the correct sequence of frequency- and time-domain transformations. As the image size increases, the key space expands, thereby enhancing encryption security. Additionally, encryption methods based on the Feistel structure [5], and the Arnold transform [25] are also compatible with QDE; their detailed discussion is also omitted here.

3.4 Measurement and Data Recovery

It must be acknowledged that although all quantum encoding methods require only $O(n)$ qubits to store 2^n elements, recovering classical information still necessitates $O(2^n)$ measurements [16,20,22], ultimately negating the quantum advantage; our QDE method is no exception. Consequently, we have previously emphasized the direct processing of quantum data via QRAM to avoid repetitive classicalâĂŞquantum data exchanges. Let the quantum measurement operation be defined as: $M = \sum_{l=0}^{k-1} \sum_{i=0}^{2^{2n}-1} I \otimes |li\rangle \langle li|$.

After applying M to the QDE state, the first qubit $|c_{li}\rangle$ returns the binary information at the l and i−th position, yielding either $|0\rangle$ or $|1\rangle$. Therefore, by combining this result with the benchmark γ in a non-entangled register, the classical color digital image can be accurately retrieved from the QDE state.

4 Experiment and Analysis

4.1 Case Study on Simulator and Real Quantum Hardware

In the first case, we demonstrate the storage of a simple $N = 4$ element set $\chi = \{2024, 2025, 2026, 2027\}$ on both a simulator *qasm* and the 127-qubit superconducting quantum computer *ibm_sherbrooke* on the IBM Quantum platform.

In the first step of QDE, a benchmark $\gamma = 2024 = 11111101000$ is selected and stored in a non-entangled register using seven X gates. Then, $\chi' = \{0, 1, 2, 3\} = \{\delta_0 = 00, \delta_1 = 01, \delta_2 = 10, \delta_3 = 11\}$ in binary, yielding $\delta = \max(\chi') = 11$ and $k = 2$. The total qubits required for the QDE state $|\chi\rangle$ is $\log N + \log k + 1 = 4$. Constructing the quantum circuit for this QDE state requires three H gates and four U_{CNOT} gates. The 1's positions in χ' are located at 0 in δ_1 (01), 1 in δ_2 (10) and 0 & 1 in δ_3 (11). Consequently, the control qubit strings for U_{CNOT} gates are 001, 110, 011, and 111, as illustrated in Fig. 2(a). The theoretical QDE state of χ (ignore the equal coefficient) is represented by:

$$|\chi\rangle = |0000\rangle + |0100\rangle + |0010\rangle + |1110\rangle + |1001\rangle + |0101\rangle + |1011\rangle + |1111\rangle. \tag{7}$$

Figure 2(b) presents the simulation results of the quantum circuit depicted in Fig. 2(a) after 20,000 shots using the *qasm* simulator. To validate these findings, we replicated the experiment on the IBM Quantum platform's *ibm_sherbrooke* superconducting quantum computer, which has an Error Per Logical Gate

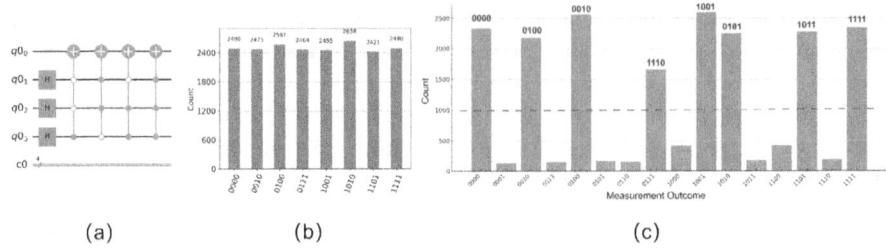

(a)　　　　　　　　(b)　　　　　　　　(c)

Fig. 2. (a) QDE state quantum circuit construction for the 4-element set: 2024, 2025, 2026, 2027. (b) Simulation result of (a) using *qasm* after 20,000 shots. (c) Experimental result of (a) obtained from the 127-qubit superconducting quantum computer *ibm_sherbrooke* after 20,000 shots.

($\gamma = 2020, \delta = 7$)	($\gamma = 100, \delta = 1924$)	($\gamma = 2024, \delta = 0$)	Method	Bits/Entangled Qubits	Runtime complexity
2024 2020 2021 2022	2024 100 200 255	2024 2024 2024 2024	NEQR	15	≈ 708
			MQIR	10	≈ 2056
2020 2025 2022 2021	2000 1555 1888 1234	2024 2024 2024 2024	BRQI	9	≈ 2056
			PE-NGQR	9	≈ 4016
2024 2023 2026 2020	120 560 780 988	2024 2024 2024 2024	CE-NGQR	15	> 2056
			(a), QDE	8	≈ 914
2027 2022 2025 2022	1655 1800 1350 300	2024 2024 2024 2024	(b), QDE	9	≈ 1043
			(c), QDE	0	≈ 15

(a)　　　　　　　　(b)　　　　　　　　(c)

Fig. 3. (a)-(c) Three $N = 4 \times 4$−element sets with different γ and δ values, along with a quantum resource comparison between QDE and recent models for storing (a)-(c).

(EPLG) of 1.9%, a median T_1 relaxation time of 275.91 μs, and a median T_2 dephasing time of 189.21 μs as illustrated in Fig. 2(c). Disregarding the noise below 500 counts, both results from *qasm* and *ibm_sherbrooke* are consistent with the expected theoretical state $|\chi\rangle$.

4.2　Performance Analysis and Test on Real Data Set

Similar to classical Delta Encoding, QDE exhibits excellent performance for storing data with minimal variations. We consider three datasets with different data distributions, as shown in Figs. 2(a)-(c), and the accompanying table summarizes the quantum resource consumption of QDE compared to state-of-the-art models. It is evident that QDE achieves optimal performance in terms of both the number of entangled qubits and runtime complexity. Notably, when all elements are identical($\delta = 0$ as in Fig. 3(c)), QDE incurs no entanglement cost and its runtime complexity decreases exponentially from $O(n \times 2^{2n})$ to $O(n)$, making it the most resource-efficient method in such cases.

We further evaluate the storage performance of QDE across various real-world datasets. Table 2 presents the bit and entangled qubit costs for storing three datasets with similar characteristics: the 1966 New York Stock Exchange opening prices (Stock), real-time electricity consumption in Tetouan, Morocco (Electricity Usage), and the 2010 U.S. Walmart Consumer Price Index (Price).

Each dataset is limited to 128 samples, and our QDE model outperforms both classical Delta Encoding [15] and recent lossless quantum data storage models.

Table 2. Bits/entangled qubits cost comparison of QDE, Delta Encoding and recent quantum data storage models on three real data sets.

Method	Stock	Electricity usage	Price
Delta Encoding	568	1550	180
NEQR [24]	17	23	15
MQIR [25]	13	13	12
BRQI [12]	12	12	11
PE-NEQR [12]	14	14	13
CE-NEQR [12]	12	12	11
Our QDE	**11**	**12**	**10**

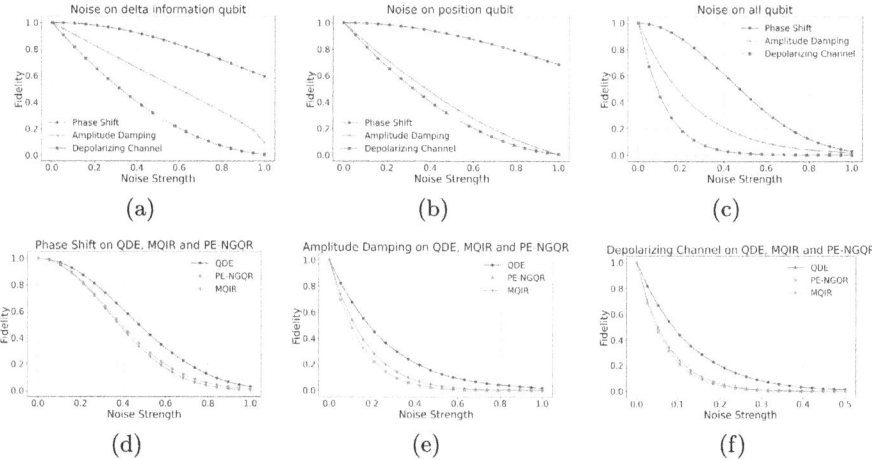

Fig. 4. (a)-(c) The impact of different types of noise on various components of the QDE circuit under increasing noise intensities. (d)-(f) The effect of three types of noise on the QDE state storing χ, as well as on BRQI and PE-NGQR.

4.3 Analysis of Quantum Noise Impact

Like other quantum data representation models based on Basic Encoding, the final computational states of QDE are equally probable. This significantly facilitates the identification and filtering of outliers during data recovery. In this section, we further discuss the impact of three common noise models in quantum computing [16,18]–Phase Shift, Amplitude Damping, and Depolarizing Channel– on the QDe state.

For clarity and ease of understanding, we simulate the impact of noise on various components of the QDE circuit using the 4-qubit QDE state $|\chi\rangle$ from Subsect. 4.1. The intensity ranges for the three noise types are initially set to $[0, 1]$ (Fig. 4(f) with range of $[0, 0.5]$), and we examine their effects on the fidelity of the quantum state at two specific qubit positions: the delta information qubit $|l\rangle$ and the first position qubit of $|i\rangle$. Additionally, we consider a worst-case scenario where all three noise types affect every qubit simultaneously. Detailed results are provided in Fig. 4(a), Fig. 4(b), and Fig. 4(c).

Our findings indicate that, as noise intensity increases, phase shift noise has the least detrimental effect on QDE state fidelity, followed by amplitude damping noise, while depolarizing noise exerts the most severe impact. This behavior is attributable to the fact that QDE, being based on Basic Encoding, is relatively insensitive to phase shifts. In contrast, amplitude damping noise introduces significant deviations in the amplitudes of certain deterministic computational basis states, and depolarizing noise drives the quantum state toward complete randomness, resulting in the greatest degradation in fidelity. Under conditions where noise affects all qubits, both amplitude damping and depolarizing noise cause substantial fidelity degradation, whereas QDE shows a degree of resilience against phase shift noise.

Furthermore, as shown in Fig. 4(d), 4(e), and 4(f), we compare the effects of the three noise types on the QDE state storing χ with their impacts on BRQI and PE-NGQR, where noise is applied to all qubits. Although all three encoding methods, based on Basic Encoding, exhibit similar trends, our QDE degrades at a slower rate and demonstrates stronger noise robustness.

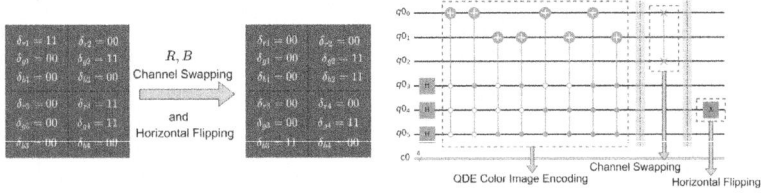

Fig. 5. R, B channel swapping and horizontal operations on a 2×2 color image along with their corresponding quantum circuit construction.

4.4 Subsequent Image Operations

In this case, we perform R, B channel swapping (pixel value adjustment) along with horizontal flipping operations (geometric transformation) on a 2×2 color image using the quantum circuit shown in Fig. 5. The original QDE image prior

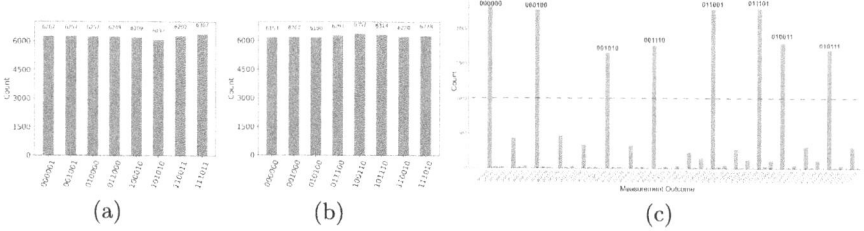

Fig. 6. (a) and (b) the simulation results before and after R, B channel swapping and horizontal flipping. (c) is the result from the 127-qubit superconducting quantum computer *ibm_kyiv* after 20,000 shots.

to these operations is represented as $|\varphi_1\rangle = |100000\rangle + |100100\rangle + |010001\rangle + |010101\rangle + |000010\rangle + |000110\rangle + |110011\rangle + |110111\rangle$. Followed these two operations, the quantum state evolves into $|\varphi_2\rangle$ as $|\varphi_2\rangle = |000000\rangle + |000100\rangle + |011001\rangle + |011101\rangle + |001010\rangle + |001110\rangle + |010011\rangle + |010111\rangle$.

Simulation results obtained using the *qasm_simulator* (50,000 shots) are shown in Figs. 6(a) and 6(b), corresponding to the states $|\varphi_1\rangle$ and $|\varphi_2\rangle$, respectively. These findings validate the effectiveness of our QDE model for image processing. For instance, the initial pixel values (100000, 100100) at position (00) are transformed to (000000, 000000), illustrating the impact of R and B channel swapping combined with a horizontal flip from pixel (10) to (00).

Besides, we also conduct these two image operations on another 127-qubit superconducting quantum computer, *ibm_kyiv* with 1.6% EPLG, T_1=277 μs and T_2=109 μs, as shown in Fig. 6. The results over 500 counts correspond to the expected theoretical state $|\varphi_2\rangle$, further validating the applicability of our QDE technique for subsequent data processing tasks on NISQ devices.

5 Conclusion

In this paper, we present a design for Delta Encoding executed on a quantum computer (QDE), which demonstrates reduced resource consumption compared to existing quantum data storage methods. QDE integrates seamlessly with QRAM, thereby enhancing the efficiency and potential of subsequent quantum data processing algorithms. Experiments conducted using the IBM Quantum platform's simulator and on real superconducting quantum computers have confirmed that QDE exhibits superior resistance to quantum noise and is particularly well suited for NISQ devices. Our future research will focus on exploring the application of QDE in quantum machine learning and quantum communication.

Disclosure of Interests. The authors declare no relevant competing interests.

References

1. Anil, G., Vinod, V., Narayan, A.: Generating universal adversarial perturbations for quantum classifiers. In: Proceedings of the AAAI Conference on Artificial Intelligence, vol. 38, pp. 10891–10899 (2024)
2. Dilip, R., Liu, Y.J., Smith, A., Pollmann, F.: Data compression for quantum machine learning. Phys. Rev. Res. **4**(4), 043007 (2022)
3. Feynman, R.P., et al.: Simulating physics with computers. Int. J. Theor. Phys. **21**(6/7) (2018)
4. Giovannetti, V., Lloyd, S., Maccone, L.: Quantum random access memory. Phys. Rev. Lett. **100**(16), 160501 (2008)
5. Guo, L., Du, H., Huang, D.: A quantum image encryption algorithm based on the Feistel structure. Quantum Inf. Process. **21**, 1–18 (2022)
6. Haque, M.E., Paul, M., Ulhaq, A., Debnath, T.: Advanced quantum image representation and compression using a DCT-EFRQI approach. Sci. Rep. **13**(1), 4129 (2023)
7. Huang, C.J., et al.: Realization of a quantum autoencoder for lossless compression of quantum data. Phys. Rev. A **102**(3), 032412 (2020)
8. Jayasankar, U., Thirumal, V., Ponnurangam, D.: A survey on data compression techniques: from the perspective of data quality, coding schemes, data type and applications. J. King Saud Uni. Comput. Inf. Sci. **33**(2), 119–140 (2021)
9. Liu, K., Zhang, Y., Lu, K., Wang, X., Wang, X.: An optimized quantum representation for color digital images. Int. J. Theor. Phys. **57**(10), 2938–2948 (2018)
10. Kwak, Y., Yun, W.J., Jung, S., Kim, J.: Quantum neural networks: concepts, applications, and challenges. In: 2021 Twelfth International Conference on Ubiquitous and Future Networks (ICUFN), pp. 413–416. IEEE (2021)
11. LaRose, R., Coyle, B.: Robust data encodings for quantum classifiers. Phys. Rev. A **102**(3), 032420 (2020)
12. Li, H.S., Chen, X., Xia, H., Liang, Y., Zhou, Z.: A quantum image representation based on Bitplanes. IEEE Access **6**, 62396–62404 (2018)
13. Mandal, A., Banerjee, S., Panigrahi, P.K.: Quantum image representation on clusters. In: 2021 IEEE International Conference on Quantum Computing and Engineering (QCE), pp. 89–99. IEEE (2021)
14. Mandal, A., Banerjee, S., Panigrahi, P.K.: Hybrid phase-based representation of quantum images. Int. J. Theor. Phys. **62**(6), 115 (2023)
15. Mogul, J.C., Douglis, F., Feldmann, A., Krishnamurthy, B.: Potential benefits of delta encoding and data compression for http. In: Proceedings of the ACM SIGCOMM'97 Conference on Applications, Technologies, Architectures, and Protocols for Computer Communication, pp. 181–194 (1997)
16. Nielsen, M.A., Chuang, I.L.: Quantum Computation and Quantum Information. Cambridge University Press (2010)
17. Pang, C.Y., Zhou, R.G., Hu, B.Q., Hu, W., El-Rafei, A.: Signal and image compression using quantum discrete cosine transform. Inf. Sci. **473**, 121–141 (2019)
18. Preskill, J.: Quantum computing in the NISQ era and beyond. Quantum **2**, 79 (2018)
19. Wang, T., Tseng, H.H., Yoo, S.: Quantum federated learning with quantum networks. In: ICASSP 2024–2024 IEEE International Conference on Acoustics, Speech and Signal Processing (ICASSP), pp. 13401–13405. IEEE (2024)
20. Wang, Z., Xu, M., Zhang, Y.: Review of quantum image processing. Arch. Comput. Methods Eng. **29**(2), 737–761 (2021). https://doi.org/10.1007/s11831-021-09599-2
21. Xing, Z., Yuan, X., Lam, C.T., Machado, P.: NGQR: a novel generalized quantum image representation. IEEE Trans. Emerg. Top. Comput. (2024)

22. Yan, F., Venegas-Andraca, S.E., Hirota, K.: Toward implementing efficient image processing algorithms on quantum computers. Soft. Comput. **27**(18), 13115–13127 (2023)
23. Yang, Y.G., Xia, J., Jia, X., Zhang, H.: Novel image encryption/decryption based on quantum fourier transform and double phase encoding. Quantum Inf. Process. **12**, 3477–3493 (2013)
24. Zhang, Y., Lu, K., Gao, Y., Wang, M.: NEQR: a novel enhanced quantum representation of digital images. Quantum Inf. Process. **12**, 2833–2860 (2013)
25. Zhu, H.-H., Chen, X.-B., Yang, Y.-X.: A multimode quantum image representation and its encryption scheme. Quantum Inf. Process. **20**(9), 1–21 (2021). https://doi.org/10.1007/s11128-021-03255-1

ScaleRunner: A Fast MPI-Based Random Walk Engine for Multi-CPU Systems

Florian Willich[1] and Henning Meyerhenke[1,2](✉)

[1] Humboldt-Universität zu Berlin,
Berlin, Germany
f.willich@hu-berlin.de
[2] Karlsruhe Institute of Technology (KIT),
Karlsruhe, Germany
meyerhenke@kit.edu

Abstract. Random walks (RWs) on graphs have a plethora of applications, both in theory and practice. One of the currently most important applications is representation learning (RL) – finding a suitable embedding of a graph into some low-dimensional geometric space. The demand for fast RW algorithms lead to a variety of RW engines targeting different computing architectures. In this paper, we address multi-CPU systems and aim at improving upon existing random walk engines such as KnightKing when running first- and second-order RW algorithms. To this end, we introduce ScaleRunner, a C++ library with full CMake integration that executes random walks in parallel.

Our main acceleration techniques for ScaleRunner are: (i) each random walk is modeled as a task deployed to a thread-pool, balancing the work load on each CPU separately; (ii) integration of the dynamic graph data structure DHB to speed up graph data caching operations; (iii) collective MPI I/O routines to speed up graph input, path output, and postprocessing operations. Our experiments use a variety of popular benchmark graphs to execute RW algorithms commonly used in RL applications. On average, ScaleRunner speeds up first-order RWs by one order of magnitude and second-order RWs by two orders compared to KnightKing.

Keywords: Distributed Random Walks · Parallel Graph Computations · Rejection Sampling · MPI Collective I/O

1 Introduction

A random walk (RW) on a graph $G = (V, E)$ is a stochastic process for which the random variable X_i denotes the vertex $v \in V$ visited in iteration i. In its simplest form, a random walk chooses the next vertex X_{i+1} uniformly at random from the neighbors of v, but many variations exist. While in first-order RWs the transition probabilities between neighbors are fixed, these probabilities depend in second-order random walks on X_{i-1}, i.e., the vertex that was visited before the current one X_i. RWs on graphs have a plethora of usages and applications, both in theory [13] and in practice [23]. The RW-based measure *commute time*, for example, is closely related to *effective resistances* in electrical networks [13]. Both form a metric on a graph, used for example for graph clustering [26].

One of the currently most popular applications of RWs is representation learning (RL), whose goal (in our context) is to embed a graph into a lower-dimensional geometric space. The resulting embedding shall facilitate a correct data classification while minimizing the amount of data points required for feature representation. Several successful RL techniques for graphs are based on random walks. For example, the algorithms *node2vec* [10] and *deepwalk* [17] use the co-occurrence of graph vertices in short random walks to determine their proximity in the embedding; these two algorithms and follow-up variations have been shown to yield high-quality graph embeddings [3].

To obtain high-quality embeddings, sufficiently many random walks are needed. For graphs of non-trivial size, this becomes compute-intensive. Since each RW is independent, executing them in parallel seems obvious and beneficial. It thus does not come as a surprise that RW engines have been written for a wide range of parallel architectures, with some of the most common ones being multi-core SINGLE-CPU [12,19,21,24], MULTI-CPU [25], and GPU [14,20]. Each architecture has its advantages and disadvantages. While GPUs offer a particularly good speed-energy tradeoff, they are limited in terms of memory. For massive graphs it is thus necessary to employ multi-core machines with large shared memory or, better yet in terms of scalability and therefore parallel performance, MULTI-CPU systems with distributed memory. The conceptual starting point for our work was KNIGHTKING [25], a widely used RW engine and a popular choice for MULTI-CPU systems. While it offers some required functionality, we spotted room for improvement in terms of usability and performance: (i) as KNIGHTKING is built as a standalone application, it cannot be integrated easily into other applications or computational pipelines; (ii) its I/O routines do not rely upon MPI; (iii) the granularity of the thread parallelism employed may often lead to load imbalances.

Contributions. In this paper, we introduce SCALERUNNER, a modular C++ library with full CMake integration that uses hybrid parallelism (MPI+OpenMP) to execute first- and second-order RWs on MULTI-CPU systems. Its open-source code and a demo application showcasing how to use SCALERUNNER can be found on GitHub[1]. Our neighborhood sampling methods provide functionality for both unweighted and weighted graphs. As part of SCALERUNNER, we also contribute the I/O layer GDSB. It reads in graphs in parallel (and does so 2.5× faster on average than highly optimized text-based graph POSIX I/O), stores them in the dynamic graph data structure DHB [9], and writes path data to disk. DHB, in turn, is chosen because it works particularly well for graphs with skewed degree distributions. In our systematic experiments on 17 popular benchmark graphs, we compare SCALERUNNER with the MPI-based RW engine KNIGHTKING. Our results show that SCALERUNNER

---

[1] https://github.com/hu-macsy/ScaleRunner.

is on average significantly faster than KNIGHTKING. When taking the geometric mean of all algorithmic speedups vs KNIGHTKING, SCALERUNNER's throughput is 16.7× higher for first-order RWs and 112.0× to 124.7× higher for different second-order RWs.

2 Preliminaries and Related Work

We consider simple directed graphs $G = (V, E)$ with $n := |V|$ vertices, $m := |E|$ edges, and density $\rho(G) := \frac{m}{n(n-1)}$. A weighted graph $G = (V, E, \omega)$ additionally carries a weight function $\omega : E \to \mathbb{R}$. The outgoing neighborhood of a vertex u is defined as $N^+(u) := \{v \in V \mid (u, v) \in E\}$; its cardinality is called the (outgoing) degree of u: $\deg^+(u) := |N^+(u)|$. We denote the maximum (outgoing) degree of graph G as $\deg^+_{\max}(G)$ and the average as $\overline{\deg^+}(G)$. If a graph is unweighted but a weight is required, we assign the weight function $\omega : E \to \{1\}$.

2.1 Random Walks

A random walk on a graph G begins on some start vertex $v_0 \in V$ and then visits vertices of G iteratively in a random manner, thereby creating a walk $\chi = (v_0, v_1, \ldots, v_L) \in V$ with L steps [13]. When visiting $u \in V$, the next vertex in the walk is chosen based on a probability distribution. In so-called *first-order* random walks, this distribution only depends on u, the current vertex. One often uses a transition probability matrix P to store the distribution: entry $p_{u,v}$ denotes the probability of traversing the edge (u, v) from vertex u to vertex v. In *second-order* random walks, the probability to move from the current vertex u to the next one not only depends on u, but also on its predecessor in the walk.

Random walks are very useful in both theory and in practice. (Mainly) Theoretical works use them for example in spectral graph theory [5], exploit them for provably efficient solvers of certain linear systems [11] and related problems [2], or for the analysis of randomized diffusion processes [7] – to name just a few. On the practical side, a recent survey [23] mentions many machine learning applications such as computer vision, text analysis, recommender systems, network analysis, and representation learning.

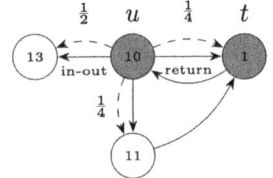

Fig. 1. Single-step example for node2vec ($p = 1$ and $q = \frac{1}{2}$); the walk is located on vertex $u = 10$, coming from $t = 1$. The probabilities for the next vertex are given next to the dashed arrows.

One distinguishes different types of random walks based on their probability distribution. The classic random walk (CRW) defines that the next vertex after u is chosen uniformly at random from $N^+(u)$: $p_{u,v} = \frac{1}{\deg^+(u)}$ [23]. Several variations exist, e.g. lazy random walks that stay on the current vertex with probability > 0 or the classic random walk with restart (RWR), which can always jump back to the start vertex with probability $c > 0$. Other popular first-order algorithms are PageRank and personalized PageRank, see [23].

The node2vec RW algorithm [10] is a prominent example for second-order random walks: in addition to the currently visited vertex u, the walk stores the previously visited vertex t. Moreover, node2vec uses two parameters, p (return) and q (in-out). The transition probability for edge (u,v) in node2vec, which is now extended by one dimension, is then defined as $p_{u,v,t} = \frac{\beta(u,v,t)}{\sum_{i \in N^+(u)} \beta(u,i,t)}$, where $\beta(u,v,t) = \frac{1}{p}$ if $v = t$, $= 1$ if $t \in N^+(v)$, and $= \frac{1}{q}$ if $t \notin N^+(v)$, see Fig. 1 for an example. Walking similarly to a breadth-first manner requires $p \leq 1$ and $q > 1$, whereas mimicking a depth-first manner requires $p \geq 1$ and $q < 1$. The co-occurrence of vertices in fixed-length second-order RWs can be used as a similarity measure, which is employed in representation learning to compute a structure-preserving embedding for further analysis, also see [23].

2.2 Related Random Walk Engines

Given the breadth of applications, there are several requirements for a random walk engine: (i) It should support a variety of RW types, at least first- and second-order RWs. The implementation should be generic, but allow the instantiation of specific RWs by the user via a convenient API. (ii) To integrate the engine into some larger workflow, it is advantageous if the engine is provided as a library. (iii) The computed walks should be provided as output in a single file or in some data structure returned from a library call. (iv) High speed by using parallelism since many applications require a large number of RWs. Table 1 lists the portrayed engines and the respective requirements they fulfill.

Table 1. List of relevant random walk engines and their features.

Name & Reference	RW Type		Library	Path Accessibility	Parallelism		Architecture
	First-Order	Second-Order			Threads	Processes	
GRAPHWALKER [21]	✔	✘	✘	✘	✔	✘	SINGLE-CPU
THUNDERRW [19]	✔	✔	✘	✘	✔	✘	SINGLE-CPU
FLASHMOB [24]	✔	✔	✘	✘	✔	✘	SINGLE-CPU
GRASORW [12]	✔	✔	✘	✘	✔	✘	SINGLE-CPU
SKYWALKER [20]	✔	✔	✘	✘	✔	✘	GPU
FLOWWALKER [14]	✔	✔	✘	✘	✔	✘	GPU
KNIGHTKING [25]	✔	✔	✘	✘	✔	✔	MULTI-CPU
Ours: SCALERUNNER	✔	✔	✔	✔	✔	✔	MULTI-CPU

GRAPHWALKER [21] is a multi-threaded engine for SINGLE-CPU systems, where each thread handles the next unprocessed random walk – and this happens independently from other threads and random walks (*walk-centric perspective*). It addresses several implementation challenges by (i) using a *state-aware I/O model* which dynamically loads subgraphs from disk depending on the current state of a walk, and (ii) buffering and offloading walk states asynchronously to disk to reduce the memory footprint. Like GRAPHWALKER, THUNDERRW [19] is multi-threaded for shared memory. Based on the observation that a walk-centric perspective can lead to memory stalls, THUNDERRW implements a *step-centric model*. In this model, prefetching ensures that a thread processes only vertices whose data required to compute the next step is already in cache.

The third multi-threaded engine FLASHMOB [24] addresses memory latency issues in a different way: it partitions the input graph hierarchically to fit the resulting subgraphs into different cache levels. In their experiments, the FLASH-MOB authors use graphs that fit into L1 to L3 cache and those that must be streamed from DRAM. After analyzing the frequency of vertex visits running a first-order RW for multiple graphs, they emphasize the importance of addressing high-degree vertices for obtaining high speed [24, Sec. 3]. They also implemented an *edge sampling* method to mitigate certain memory locality issues.

GRASORW [12] was written to compute RWs on large graph files that do not fit into the RAM of a SINGLE-CPU system, similar to GRAPHWALKER. To fulfill this requirement, they partition the original graph into blocks and dynamically load these blocks into memory. When holding a subgraph in memory, they make progress for all scheduled RWs currently walking on vertices cached in memory.

SKYWALKER [20] is made for single-GPU systems. Instead of using a sampling method for computing the next step, SKYWALKER queries an alias table, which takes constant time. This remedies caching problems occurring with graphs that have a non-negligible number of high-degree vertices. FLOWWALKER is also a single-GPU engine, but it follows a sampler-centric RW computation model [14]. The program addresses memory space issues of GPU engines such as SKY-WALKER and implements a special sampling technique for GPUs.

The above mentioned engines scale on a single compute node using multi-threading or single-GPU parallelism. In order to reach higher speeds (especially for massive graphs), an additional scaling layer along compute nodes is required.

KNIGHTKING [25] targets MULTI-CPU systems and is composed of C++ programs that employ hybrid parallelism using MPI+OpenMP. The graph is 1D-distributed over the compute nodes, where each compute node owns a disjoint subgraph (plus ghost vertices). Initially, each compute node is responsible for a fair share of random walks. Yet, when a random walk leaves a node's subgraph, it is transferred to the neighboring compute node. Other than SKYWALKER, KNIGHTKING uses acceptance-rejection sampling [4] to compute the next step. Even though this may suffer from a high number of rejections, it can help to avoid a large alias table.

As argued above and visible from Table 1, none of the portrayed engines fulfills all requirements. GPU-based engines cannot handle massive graphs, shared-memory engines do not exploit multi-CPU scalability, while KNIGHTKING is a collection of programs with usability deficiencies (such as not separating file I/O routines from the walk engine), which limits the possible usage areas.

Note that DISTGER-PIPE [6] is a recent MULTI-CPU engine we became aware of too late to include it in detail, e.g. in our experiments. It offers first- and second-order RWs and end-to-end embedding functionality for RL. In their RW experiments, the authors observe an average speedup compared to KNIGHTKING of 3.32. Our average speedup on KNIGHTKING, in turn, is at least 16 (Sect. 4).

3 SCALERUNNER RW Engine: Design and Implementation

3.1 Challenges and Overview

A parallel random walk engine does not only need fast RW computations, it should also be easy to use for implementing application-specific RW algorithms. The challenge here is to find the right balance between (i) a simple and powerful API to implement RW algorithms, and (ii) requirements the user of the engine has to fulfill in order to accelerate the implemented algorithm. For example, the user may need to provide program data in specified ways, such as thread-private or -shared data to support race-free multi-threading. Also, to handle large data sets smoothly, RW engines should provide fast I/O routines.

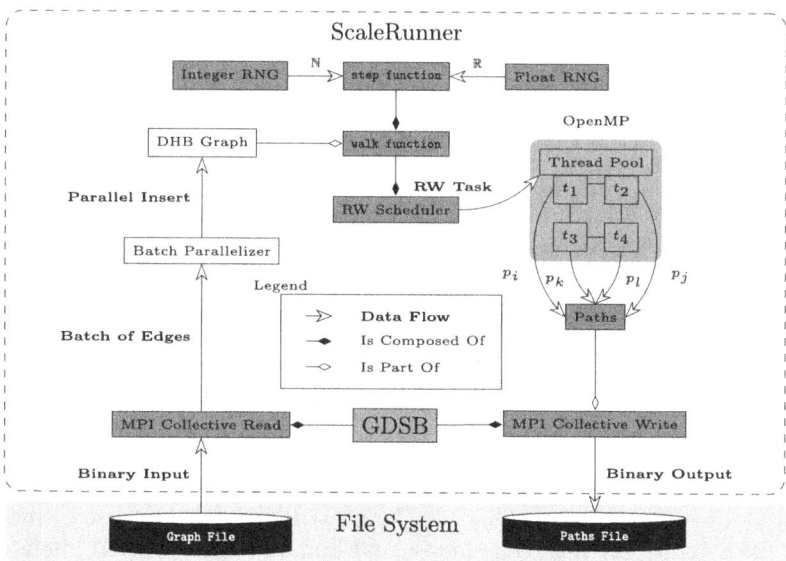

Fig. 2. Overview of our software architecture. SCALERUNNER is designed such that the I/O components can easily be exchanged. By default, file I/O is handled using MPI collective routines provided by our libray GDSB: after inserting all edges into the graph data structure DHB, the *RW Scheduler* deploys tasks to a thread pool executing the specified RW algorithm. An RW algorithm is separated into two functions: (i) the walk function, which calls (ii) the step function to make a step based on random numbers from random number generators (RNG). Every task inserts the generated path data into a pre-allocated path object, which allows for streaming of path data using MPI file output routines. Finally, all paths are written to disk using MPI collective file write routines ready for postprocessing.

Furthermore, when randomly sampling the neighborhood for second-order RW algorithms, the edge transition probabilities depend on the previous step; (re)setting the probabilities accordingly requires careful optimization. Finally, the produced paths have to be stored to memory without fragmentation to (a) stream path data to disk fast, or (b) use in downstream software components.

Figure 2 shows an overview of our software architecture, together with a short explanation of all layers and components in the caption. Details are given in Sect. 3.2, its structure follows the data flow from input over processing to output.

3.2 SCALERUNNER Components

Binary Input Using GDSB. For handling the graph and path I/O for SCALE-RUNNER, we additionally contribute the Graph Data Structures & Benchmark (GDSB) library as separate tool, designed as an open-source C++ library[2]. GDSB provides an ecosystem for experimental graph algorithmics including graph data structures, graph file I/O routines with full MPI functionality, as well as utilities to implement and run experiments.

When reading in graph data, relying on the original text files provided by graph repositories such as NetworkRepository (NR) or SNAP is undesired for two reasons: (i) a non-negligible number of instances does not follow the file format meticulously; (ii) reading in large text files is slow and thus inhibits the overall processing pipeline. To address these issues, we convert all graphs to the binary format of GDSB. This format does not only improve the read performance, but also enables our tool to read edge data using MPI file I/O routines.

Using GDSB, SCALERUNNER reads in batches of edges collectively on all compute nodes. By not reading in all edges at once into the dynamic graph data structure DHB described below, we limit the intermediate buffer size of the edges that are read. Especially for large graph data sets this is an important aspect to limit the amplitude of the memory footprint for graph data input routines.

DHB. The dynamic graph data structure DHB [9], short for *dynamic hashed blocks*, stores vertex neighborhoods both array- and hash table-based. This approach allows constant-time edge access and update routines. DHB allows us to stream data from disk by inserting batches of edges in parallel using multiple threads, which is handled by the new *Batch Parallelizer*.

By collectively reading in the same edge batches on all compute nodes, we replicate the graph data on each node. We do not consider this a severe limitation since most graphs fit into the memory of each compute node of a modern cluster when considering the compute intensity of downstream tasks such as graph machine learning. Using the Batch Parallelizer, DHB's block-based architecture allows to insert edges with different source ID in a multi-threaded context. To this end, the Batch Parallelizer first sorts the edges by their source and then distributes the sorted array over all threads to be inserted.

---

[2] GDSB Release Version 1.0: https://github.com/hu-macsy/graph-ds-benchmark.

DHB is specifically developed for reducing the cache locality issues of random neighborhood accesses in graphs with a skewed degree distribution. Those graphs usually have a small, but non-negligible number of high-degree vertices (HDVs). As observed by Yang et al. [24, Sec. 3], those HDVs are the vertices with the highest visit frequency in RWs. Since the block-based design of DHB efficiently caches these HDVs, RWs are less likely to yield cache misses on such graphs.

Random Number Generation. Each call of the `step function` (representing a single step of a RW) requires random numbers in certain intervals such as $[0, N(u))$ and a sampling algorithm that determines the next vertex accordingly.

When sampling W random walks in total, each of length L, one requires $\Theta(W \cdot L)$ random numbers to be drawn. Hence, the random number engine employed as well as the concrete way to use it has significant impact on its execution time [15]. In our implementation, each thread owns a *Mersenne Twister* engine as well as a single distribution object per random number type T; this object is used to generate random numbers in $[0, \max(T)]$. For each random number within the desired interval, we apply type-safe modulo operations [8].

Sampling Within the Step Function. The sampling function for choosing the next vertex to walk to is called $\Theta(W \cdot L)$ times. For high speed it is thus important to carefully optimize the sampling algorithm used in the `step function`.

An obvious method to sample from $N^+(u)$ (when visiting $u \in V$) is called *inverse transform sampling* [16], whose sequential implementation is visualized in Fig. 3a. First, with $\alpha(v)$ being the edge transition probability of $v \in N^+(u)$ and $\widehat{\alpha} := \sum_{v \in N^+(u)} \alpha(v)$ the corresponding sum, we draw a random number $r := rand[0, \widehat{\alpha}]$. Second, we accumulate $acc := acc + \alpha(v)$ over the neighbors until $acc \geq r$. Hence, in total, for sequential inverse transform sampling, we draw one random number and iterate twice over $N^+(u)$.

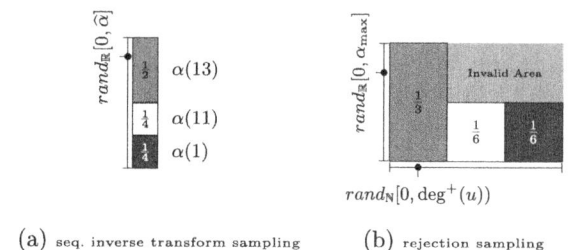

(a) seq. inverse transform sampling (b) rejection sampling

Fig. 3. Sampling algorithm examples based on the node2vec sampling step of Fig. 1. (a) Sequential inverse transform sampling with color reference for the edge transition probabilities $\alpha(13), \alpha(11)$ and $\alpha(1)$. (b) Rejection sampling where a random throw has a chance of $\frac{1}{3}$ to be rejected by hitting the invalid area.

Rejection sampling [25], in turn, is based on the idea of representing the transition probabilities on a rectangle of size $\deg^+(u) \times \alpha_{\max}$, where $\alpha_{\max} := \max_{v \in N^+(u)} \alpha(v)$. To identify the next vertex, rejection sampling first computes $\alpha_{\max}$, followed by a random integer draw $r_i = rand_{\mathbb{N}}[0, \deg^+(u))$ to choose the x-coordinate. Then, the method requires an additional random floating point number $r_f = rand_{\mathbb{R}}[0, \alpha_{\max}]$ to *throw a dart* on the y-coordinate, see Fig. 3b. If the invalid area was hit, we repeat the sampling step. Otherwise, we identify the neighbor v corresponding to the area that was hit. In total, for rejection sampling we draw two random numbers and iterate once over $N^+(u)$, i.e., one additional random number but one less iteration over $N^+(u)$.

A third option would be to optimize for outliers in the rejection sampling algorithm, thereby reducing the total number of rejections [25, p.529]. Yet, in our preliminary experiments, rejection sampling was the by far fastest method. Thus, in the experiments of Sect. 4, SCALERUNNER uses rejection sampling only.

RW Scheduler and Walk Function. The `walk function` takes the `step function` as well as the DHB object as parameters and computes a single walk. Each walk represented by the `walk function` is then dispatched to a thread pool by the *RW Scheduler*. Here, we make use of an OpenMP task-based system where each walk represents a task [18]. A task is scheduled to be executed by any thread available. Each of the $\hat{p}$ compute nodes must compute $\frac{W}{\hat{p}}$ RWs. Setting the granularity of each task to one random walk mitigates inherent problems of load imbalances due to different computational efforts in different RWs.

Binary Output. Finally, SCALERUNNER writes the produced path data to a single file using collective MPI file I/O routines on all compute nodes. Using such collective I/O improves the speed; its disadvantage is the requirement to provide a pointer to a consecutive memory segment containing the path data. We always allocate an array of size $W \cdot L$, even if a walk is shorter than L. When packing data instead, each thread would need its own dynamically allocated memory segment. Such dynamic allocation would introduce two issues: (i) it would be slower than a single allocation before scheduling walks, and (ii) we would need to collect the thread-private data and map the memory segments to the layout required for collective MPI file output, also slowing down the output routine.

The described path output method can easily be exchanged or modified. Postprocessing applications can also use the *Paths* data structure directly.

4 Experiments

4.1 Setup

HW/SW Environment. All experiments[3] were run on a cluster with 16 compute nodes (= # processes), each equipped with 2× 12-Core Intel Xeon X6126

---

[3] SclaeRunner Experiments: https://github.com/hu-macsy/ScaleRunner-Exp.

Table 2. List of graph instances used in our experiments: original names, our introduced synonyms, assigned category and its color, common graph metrics.

Name	Synonym	Origin	Category	Color	n	m	$\deg^\dagger_{\max}$	$\deg^\dagger$	$\rho(G)$
web-NotreDame	NotreDame	SNAP	web		326K	1.47M	3.44K	4.6	1.385e-05
rt-retweet-crawl	retweet	NR	social		1.11M	2.28M	2.54K	2.1	1.841e-06
cage14	cage14	NR	biological		1.51M	2.41M	38	1.7	1.065e-06
europe_osm	europe_osm	NR	road		50.9M	5.44M	13	0.2	2.100e-09
Amazon0601	Amzn0601	SNAP	collaboration		403K	3.39M	10	8.4	2.082e-05
human_gene2	human_gene2	NR	biological		14.3K	8.04M	4.59K	561	3.912e-02
web-Google	Google	SNAP	web		916K	5.11M	456	5.6	6.079e-06
roadNet-CA	roadNet	SNAP	road		1.97M	5.53M	12	2.9	1.424e-06
rec-amazon-ratings	amzn-ratings	NR	collaboration		2.15M	2.15M	1	1	4.660e-07
rec-epinions-user-ratings	epns-user	NR	collaboration		756K	13.7M	162K	18.1	2.393e-05
inf-road-usa	road-usa	NR	road		23.9M	28.9M	8	1.3	5.031e-08
bn-human-Jung2015_M87125334	hmn-Jung-MX5334	NR	biological		1.83M	40.3M	2.31K	22.1	1.206e-05
soc-LiveJournal1	LiveJournal	SNAP	social		4.85M	68.5M	20.3K	14.2	2.914e-06
soc-orkut	orkut	NR	social		3M	106M	3.14K	35.5	1.184e-05
bn-human-Jung2015_M87126525	hmn-Jung-MX6525	NR	biological		1.83M	146M	6.98K	80	4.376e-05
web-uk-2005-all	web-uk-2005-all	NR	web		39.5M	921M	5.21K	23.4	5.917e-07
soc-twitter-mpi-sws	twitter-mpi	NR	social		41.7M	1.47B	3M	35.3	8.464e-07

(HT) CPUs, and 192 GB RAM. The compute nodes are inter-connected by a 100 Gb Infiniband Omnipath network. C++ code was compiled using GCC v12.3 and MPICH v4.2.0. For setting up and running all experiments, we use the framework SIMEXPAL [1]. Our competitor KNIGHTKING could not succeed for some instances due to program crashes during RWs, rendering compute nodes unreachable. An extensive and time-costly search for the issue was unsuccessful. All instances marked as *failed* in the following have failed repeatedly.

In order to run systematic and reliable experiments, we adapted[4] the KNIGHTKINGI/O code to use collective MPI routines. For the comparisons, we report throughput in RWs per millisecond (ms) as well as the algorithmic speedup (throughput of SCALERUNNER divided by throughput of KNIGHTKING) for each graph instance excluding graph or path I/O times.

Data Sets. Information on the origin of all graphs used in our experiments including several basic metrics is shown in Table 2. If a graph data set contains timestamped edges, the edge data with the higher timestamp is used. We preprocess the graph data by converting every graph instance to the open-source binary format of the library GDSB. This process does not modify the data but allows for faster binary read operations. Moreover, if a graph is undirected, we interpret it as bidirected. Weights are represented in single-precision. Parameterized random walk algorithms of second order embed community and centrality measures well when computing $\mu \ll n$ paths [10,17]. Our choice of computing n random walks in each experiment is therefore sufficient.

---

[4] kklib "KnightKing as a library": https://github.com/hu-macsy/kklib.

4.2 Evaluation

First Order: CRW. First, we investigate a a Classic Random Walk (CRW), which is an important fundamental use case for measuring the performance of our tool. We compute n paths of length 80 on 16 compute nodes. A similar setting was proposed by the authors of KNIGHTKING. As can be seen in Fig. 4, for all instances SCALERUNNER produces more than 10 000RWs per ms.

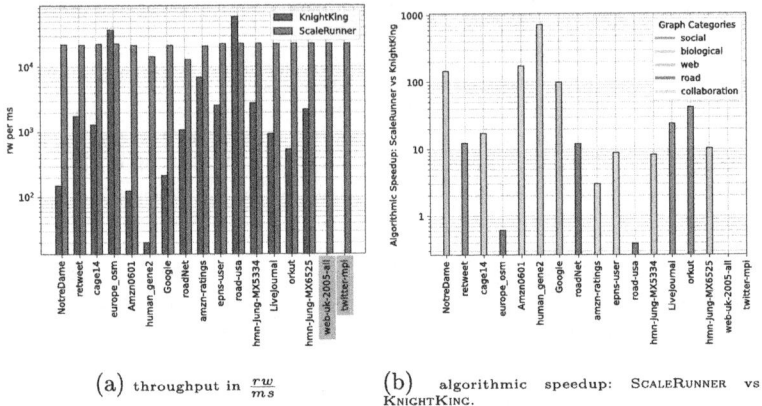

(a) throughput in $\frac{rw}{ms}$

(b) algorithmic speedup: SCALERUNNER vs KNIGHTKING.

Fig. 4. Experiment executing the first-order RW algorithm CRW. (a) Number of RWs per ms: $\frac{rw}{ms}$. Graph names in gray have failed for KNIGHTKING. (b) Algorithmic speedup of SCALERUNNER compared to KNIGHTKING for all graph instances KNIGHTKING could solve. Higher is better.

Our tool SCALERUNNER generally outperforms KNIGHTKING in terms of throughput, with the exception of two *Road Networks* ■: europe_osm and road-usa. In general, we expect that for *Road Networks* ■, the RWs in KNIGHTKING cross compute node frontiers less frequently due to the graphs' high diameter. The graph data structure DHB used in SCALERUNNER, in turn, is optimized for graphs with certain characteristics such as a skewed degree distribution. These characteristics are not prevalent in road networks, which have a low density and degrees closely concentrated around the (rather small) mean.

Second-Order RW: node2vec. Due to the necessary recomputation of the transition probabilities in second-order RWs, the node2vec algorithm is expected to reveal our engine's sensitivities to the different graph categories. We use the same parameters, experiment setup, and evaluation methods as in the first-order RW experiment above. For the node2vec hyperparameters (p, q), we present experiments using setting $(1, \frac{1}{2})$. The other setting $(1, 2)$ shows a similar trend, as can be observed from the aggregated algorithmic speedup plot in Fig. 6a. As can be seen in Fig. 5a, SCALERUNNER is faster than KNIGHTKING on all graphs now. In Fig. 5b we show the corresponding algorithmic speedups: for

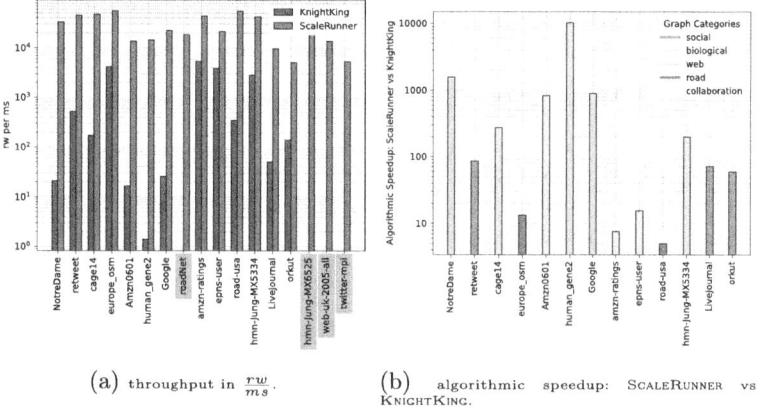

Fig. 5. Results for second-order RW algorithm node2vec with hyperparameter setting $p = 1$, $q = \frac{1}{2}$: (a) throughput (graph names in gray failed for KNIGHTKING), (b) algorithmic speedup of SCALERUNNER per graph. Higher is better.

Webgraphs ■ our tool significantly outperforms KNIGHTKING by two orders of magnitude. For *Biological Networks* ■, SCALERUNNER demonstrates an even higher advantage over KNIGHTKING, achieving performance gains from two to four orders of magnitude. At the other end of the spectrum, we observe a smaller performance advantage for *Road Networks* ■ than for the other categories. Yet, notice that we still outperform KNIGHTKING by a significant factor.

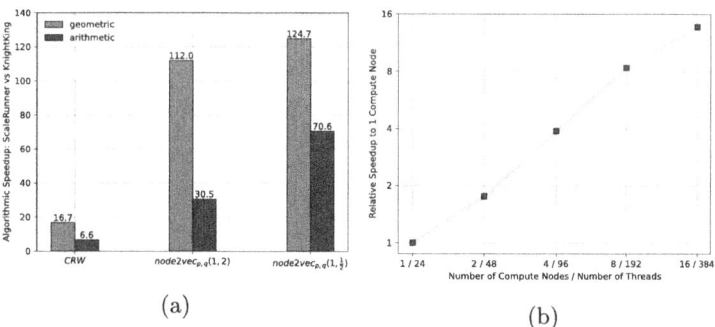

Fig. 6. (a) Cumulative algorithmic speedups comparing our tool SCALERUNNER with KNIGHTKING for all successful experiments. **geometric:** average algorithmic speedup (geometric mean of all graph instances); **arithmetic:** relative running time using the sum of all RW experiment durations. (b) Strong CPU scaling results w.r.t. throughput for SCALERUNNER.

Aggregated Algorithmic Speedups and Strong Scaling. In Fig. 6a we show the average algorithmic speedup compared to KNIGHTKING running first- and second-order RW algorithms. For averaging these ratios, we use the geometric mean; it has the additional advantage of being insensitive to samples at the extremes. Regarding the algorithmic speedup, SCALERUNNER is 16.7× on average faster than KNIGHTKING for the CRW algorithm (first order). The second-order RW algorithm node2vec is accelerated even more: SCALERUNNER is 112.0× ($q = 2$) to 124.7× ($q = \frac{1}{2}$) faster. We think that $node2vec_{p,q}(1,2)$ has a lower algorithmic speedup than $node2vec_{p,q}(1,\frac{1}{2})$ because an RW is more likely to explore distant vertices if $q > p$; hence, this setting is disadvantageous for graph data caching, reducing the throughput at which an RW is computed. Also note that KNIGHTKING fails on the three largest graphs, which leads to a distorted average, likely to our disadvantage given the general trend.

Finally, we showcase CPU strong scaling for SCALERUNNER in Fig. 6b from 1 to 16 compute nodes (24 to 384 threads). The speedups are computed as ratios of the respective average throughput on all graph instances on 2 to 16 compute nodes compared to one – and show a (desirable) nearly-linear scaling behavior.

5 Conclusions and Future Work

The goal of this work was to improve the performance of executing first- and second-order random walk algorithms for MULTI-CPU systems. To this end, we implemented the C++ library SCALERUNNER using MPI+OpenMP parallelism. SCALERUNNER provides a simple, yet powerful API to implement first- and second-order random walks – with a focus on performance-optimized RW functionality for unweighted *and* weighted graphs. Our experimental results show significant throughput improvements over KNIGHTKING. They also indicate that higher gains are possible for more complex RW algorithms.

Other than KNIGHTKING, our tool replicates the full graph on each compute node. If extreme-scale graphs exceed this memory, we would have to distribute different parts of the graph with a graph partitioner. This is left for future work because typical downstream tasks would take extremely long on such large graphs. More importantly, we plan to execute large-scale experiments on a cluster with more than 16 compute nodes. So far, crashing compute nodes when running KNIGHTKING were problematic for executions on clusters not managed by us.

Acknowledgments and Artifact Availability. This work is partially supported by German Research Foundation (DFG) grant GR 5745/1-1 (DyANE).

The artifact is available in the Zenodo repository [22].

Disclosure of Interests. The authors have no competing interests to declare that are relevant to the content of this article.

References

1. Angriman, E., et al.: Guidelines for experimental algorithmics: a case study in network analysis. Algorithms **12**(7) (2019)
2. Angriman, E., Predari, M., van der Grinten, A., Meyerhenke, H.: Approximation of the diagonal of a Laplacian's pseudoinverse for complex network analysis. In: 28th Annual European Symposium on Algorithms, ESA 2020. LIPIcs, vol. 173, pp. 6:1–6:24. Schloss Dagstuhl–Leibniz-Zentrum für Informatik (2020)
3. Cai, H., Zheng, V.W., Chang, K.C.C.: A comprehensive survey of graph embedding: problems, techniques, and applications. IEEE Trans. Knowl. Data Eng. **30**(9), 1616–1637 (2018)
4. Casella, G., Robert, C.P., Wells, M.T.: Generalized accept-reject sampling schemes. Lect. Notes Monogr. Ser. **45**, 342–347 (2004)
5. Chung, F.R.K.: Spectral Graph Theory. American Mathematical Society (1997)
6. Fang, P., et al.: Information-oriented random walks and pipeline optimization for distributed graph embedding. IEEE Trans. Knowl. Data Eng. **37**(1), 408–422 (2025)
7. Giakkoupis, G., Saribekyan, H., Sauerwald, T.: Spread of information and diseases via random walks in sparse graphs. In: 34th International Symposium on Distributed Computing, DISC 2020. LIPIcs, vol. 179, pp. 9:1–9:17. Schloss Dagstuhl - Leibniz-Zentrum für Informatik (2020)
8. Goualard, F.: Drawing random floating-point numbers from an interval. ACM Trans. Model. Comput. Simul. **32**(3) (2022)
9. van der Grinten, A., Predari, M., Willich, F.: A fast data structure for dynamic graphs based on hash-indexed adjacency blocks. In: 20th International Symposium on Experimental Algorithms (SEA 2022). LIPIcs, vol. 233, pp. 11:1–11:18. Schloss Dagstuhl – Leibniz-Zentrum für Informatik (2022)
10. Grover, A., Leskovec, J.: Node2vec: scalable feature learning for networks. In: Proceedings of the 22nd ACM SIGKDD International Conference on Knowledge Discovery and Data Mining, pp. 855–864. KDD '16, ACM, New York, NY, USA (2016)
11. Kyng, R., Meierhans, S., Probst, M.: Derandomizing directed random walks in almost-linear time. In: 63rd IEEE Annual Symposium on Foundations of Computer Science, FOCS 2022, Denver, CO, USA, pp. 407–418. IEEE (2022)
12. Li, H., Shao, Y., Du, J., Cui, B., Chen, L.: An i/o-efficient disk-based graph system for scalable second-order random walk of large graphs. Proc. VLDB Endow. **15**(8), 1619–1631 (2022)
13. Lovász, L.: Random walks on graphs: a survey, Technical report, Yale University, Department of Computer Science (1994)
14. Mei, J., et al.: Flowwalker: a memory-efficient and high-performance GPU-based dynamic graph random walk framework. arXiv preprint arXiv:2404.08364 (2024)
15. Michaels, R.: Fast, high-quality pseudo-random numbers for non-cryptographers in c++ (2022). https://www.youtube.com/watch?v=I5UY3yb0128
16. Pandey, S., Li, L., Hoisie, A., Li, X.S., Liu, H.: C-saw: a framework for graph sampling and random walk on GPUs. In: SC20: International Conference for High Performance Computing, Networking, Storage and Analysis, pp. 1–15 (2020)
17. Perozzi, B., Al-Rfou, R., Skiena, S.: Deepwalk: online learning of social representations. In: Proceedings of the 20th ACM SIGKDD International Conference on Knowledge Discovery and Data Mining, pp. 701–710. KDD '14, ACM, New York, NY, USA (2014)

18. Podobas, A., Karlsson, S.: Towards unifying OpenMP under the task-parallel paradigm. In: Maruyama, N., de Supinski, B.R., Wahib, M. (eds.) OpenMP: Memory, Devices, and Tasks, pp. 116–129. Springer, Cham (2016)
19. Sun, S., Chen, Y., Lu, S., He, B., Li, Y.: ThunderRW: an in-memory graph random walk engine. Proc. VLDB Endow. **14**(11), 1992–2005 (2021)
20. Wang, P., et al.: Skywalker: efficient alias-method-based graph sampling and random walk on GPUs. In: 30th International Conference on Parallel Architectures and Compilation Techniques (PACT), pp. 304–317 (2021)
21. Wang, R., Li, Y., Xie, H., Xu, Y., Lui, J.C.S.: Graphwalker: an i/o-efficient and resource-friendly graph analytic system for fast and scalable random walks. In: USENIX Annual Technical Conference (ATC) 2020. USENIX Association, USA (2020)
22. Willich, F., Meyerhenke, H.: Artifact of the paper: Scalerunner: a fast MPI-based random walk engine for multi-CPU systems (2025). https://doi.org/10.5281/zenodo.15593388
23. Xia, F., Liu, J., Nie, H., Fu, Y., Wan, L., Kong, X.: Random walks: a review of algorithms and applications. IEEE Trans. Emerg. Top. Comput. Intell. **4**(2), 95–107 (2020)
24. Yang, K., Ma, X., Thirumuruganathan, S., Chen, K., Wu, Y.: Random walks on huge graphs at cache efficiency. In: Proceedings of the ACM SIGOPS 28th Symposium on Operating Systems Principles, pp. 311–326. SOSP'21, ACM, New York, NY, USA (2021)
25. Yang, K., Zhang, M., Chen, K., Ma, X., Bai, Y., Jiang, Y.: Knightking: a fast distributed graph random walk engine. In: Proceedings of the 27th ACM Symposium on Operating Systems Principles, pp. 524–537. SOSP '19, ACM, New York, NY, USA (2019)
26. Yen, L., Fouss, F., Decaestecker, C., Francq, P., Saerens, M.: Graph nodes clustering based on the commute-time kernel. In: Advances in Knowledge Discovery and Data Mining, pp. 1037–1045. Springer, Berlin, Heidelberg (2007)

External GPU Biconnected Components

Abhijeet Sahu[1(✉)], Andaluri S. P. V. M. Aditya[1], G. Ramakrishna[1], Malleti Sai Nikhil[1], Kishore Kothapalli[2], and Dip Sankar Banerjee[3]

[1] IIT Tirupati, Tirupati, India
{cs22s501,cs21b002,rama,cs21m009}@iittp.ac.in
[2] IIIT Hyderabad, Hyderabad, India
kkishore@iiith.ac.in
[3] IIT Jodhpur, Jodhpur, India
dipsankarb@iitj.ac.in

Abstract. As the scale of graph analytics continues to grow, many applications require identifying biconnected components (BCCs) and cut vertices in graphs that exceed the memory capacity of a single GPU. This paper presents an out-of-core, GPU-based batch processing algorithm designed to efficiently compute BCCs and cut vertices in massive graphs that do not fit entirely into device memory. We propose a novel batch technique to process the graph incrementally, and maintain a Biconnectivity Compressed Graph to compute BCCs and cut vertices. Experimental results on a range of large-scale benchmark graphs demonstrate that our technique achieves competitive performance compared to state-of-the-art CPU solutions, enabling the handling of graph instances previously considered intractable on GPU platforms.

Keywords: Large-scale graphs · Biconnected components · Articulation points · Cut vertices · Out-of-core processing · GPU · Batch processing

1 Introduction

Processing large-scale graphs is increasingly vital across many fields as both the complexity and size of networked data continue to grow. A recent survey [14] reports that many organizations now manage graphs containing billions of edges and requiring hundreds of gigabytes of storage, highlighting the need for scalable parallel approaches. Although parallel architectures (e.g., multi-core CPUs and GPUs) have driven advancements in graph analytics, the limited on-board memory of GPUs [1] remains a major obstacle for handling large-scale graph data. Indeed, the most pressing challenge in GPU-based graph applications, according to [14] is performing computations on these massive graphs.

Among various graph-theoretic tasks, the identification of *cut vertices* (articulation points) and *biconnected components* (BCCs) is especially important. Cut

---

[1] For example, NVIDIA A100 GPUs typically have only 40 GB of on-board memory.

vertices reveal critical junctions in networks (e.g., for routing or vulnerability analysis), whereas BCCs denote maximal subgraphs that remain connected after removing any single vertex. These properties underpin a range of higher-level algorithms, including partitioning, centrality computations and planarity testing [6]. As large-scale graph processing frequently employs divide-and-conquer strategies, designing efficient GPU-based methods to identify these components remains a key challenge.

Although biconnectivity is a classical problem solved in theory over half a century ago, it continues to attract interest in modern parallel contexts. Wadwekar and Kothapalli proposed the first GPU-based parallel algorithm for BCC [18], constructing a breadth-first search (BFS) tree, then using fundamental cycle traversals of non-tree edges to build an auxiliary graph whose connected components directly yield the BCCs.

Beyond this early GPU-focused effort, various approaches exist across different architectures. In sequential settings, the Hopcroft-Tarjan (HT) algorithm [8] runs in linear time via depth-first search (DFS) to identify BCCs. Tarjan and Vishkin (TV) [17] introduced a classic parallel method that replaces DFS with an arbitrary spanning tree (AST), transforming the input graph G into a skeleton graph G'. Although elegant, this approach expands the vertex set to $O(m)$ (each edge in G becomes a vertex in G'), leading to substantial memory overhead.

To reduce the size of G', Cong and Bader [3] proposed the *TV-filter*. They construct a BFS tree T of G and a spanning forest F of $G - T$. Any edge not in $T \cup F$ is deemed "non-essential" for biconnectivity, thereby reducing $|V(G')|$. Although BFS-based approaches work well in standard parallel or GPU environments, BFS traversals can be challenging to implement efficiently in an external setting. More recently, Dong et al. [5] introduced *FAST-BCC*, now considered the state of the art for multicore implementations. Their algorithm identifies the BCCs of G by finding connected components of a subgraph $G' \subseteq G$, comprised of non-critical edges in a spanning tree T plus cross edges in $G - T$.

All of these methods implicitly assume that the full graph (all edges along with extra auxiliary data structures) fits into GPU memory. In contrast, we consider a scenario in which the GPU can store all vertices (i.e., $\mathcal{O}(n)$ space) but does not have enough memory for the complete set of edges, which may be significantly larger. We refer to this GPU-EXTERNAL-MEMORY (GEM) model, wherein the limited onboard memory in GPU cannot accommodate all edges. In this work, we address the *out-of-memory* setting for GPUs by proposing a new algorithm that efficiently computes BCCs on large graphs whose edge set exceeds GPU memory capacity while retaining the GPU's computational advantages.

We use $G = (V, E)$ to denote a connected and undirected graph with $|V| = n$ vertices and $|E| = m$ edges. A *cut vertex* in G is a vertex whose removal (along with its incident edges) results in a disconnected graph. A maximal subgraph of G without any cut vertex is called a *biconnected* component. Given a graph G, the *Biconnected Components* (BCC) problem seeks to identify all the biconnected components of G.

1.1 Our Contributions

From the preceding discussion, it is evident that designing an BCC algorithm in GEM model to handle massive graphs remains a challenging problem. Our key contributions are:

- We design a novel algorithm to solve BCC in GEM model. Our algorithm maintains a compressed graph H of G in GPU, where multiple vertices of G are merged into a single vertex in H, $size(H) = O(n)$, and BCC(G) can be obtained from H, where $n := |V(G)|$. To the best of our knowledge, this is the first parallel space-efficient out-of-memory BCC algorithm capable of handling massive graphs that exceed GPU memory capacity in practice.
- We introduce *biconnectivity compressed graph* (BCG) of a graph along with necessary properties. These properties help to obtain BCCs of the input graph.
- We provide exhaustive proofs to support the correctness of the proposed algorithm, ensuring both theoretical rigor and practical applicability.
- We evaluate our algorithm on large, real-world datasets, demonstrating that it outperforms state-of-the-art approaches in efficiency and scalability.

1.2 Related Work

Multiple graph management frameworks have evolved to move data back and forth between CPU and GPU [11,13,16] to deal with the out-of-memory issues in GPU. The Subway framework loads all the active graph edges to GPU [13] in every iteration of a graph algorithm. Ascetic and Liberator frameworks only load active graph edges that do not appear in GPU, using unified virtual memory and zero-copy mechanism [11,16]. These frameworks help programmers use existing PRAM-based graph algorithms and implementations and increase productivity. However, there is no bound on the number of times graph data is loaded from CPU to GPU, as PRAM-based algorithms are borrowed to GEM model. Inspired by functional programming, the Graph-Reduce framework uses the Gather-Apply-Scatter (GAS) method to handle graphs that do not fit into GPU [15]. GAS paradigm may not be directly applicable for graph problems such as BCC. Even so, these frameworks do not address the question of the number of passes of the input needed by a given computation. This poses questions on their efficiency. In our work, we design a new algorithm to solve BCC suitable for GEM model, in which we load all the edges of G from CPU to GPU precisely twice in the entire algorithm. In particular, our algorithm uses $O(n)$ space in GPU.

2 Preliminaries and Biconnectivity Compressed Graph

In this section, we describe two ways of representing important details of biconnected components in a graph, namely *implicit-bcc* labels and *labels and component head* (LCH) representations, along with a brief description about the state-of-the-art multicore algorithm for BCC [5]. Later, we define *biconnectivity compressed graph* (BCG) of a graph along with necessary properties.

Implicit-BCC Labels. The labels assigned to vertices of a graph are called *implicit-BCC* labels if they satisfy the following two conditions: 1) Two non-cut vertices are assigned the same label if and only if they belong to the same BCC 2) The label of a cut vertex is distinct from the labels of all other vertices. For a graph G, we use an array $I[\cdot]$ to store the *implicit-BCC* labels of G, and an example is shown in Fig. 1.

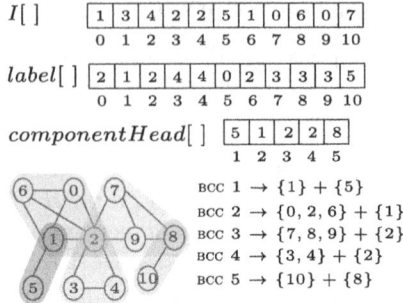

Fig. 1. *Implicit-BCC* array and LCH.

LCH Representation for BCCs. For a connected graph G, the Label and ComponentHead (LCH) representation is defined with respect to a spanning tree of G rooted at r. The $label[\cdot]$ array contains labels for all vertices expect r, representing the BCC to which each vertex belongs. Each distinct label is associated with a component head vertex. It is important to note that all vertices sharing the same label, along with its component head, form a BCC in G. An example of this representation is shown in Fig. 1 where $r = 5$. More details about this representation are discussed in [2,5].

FAST-BCC Algorithm. For a connected graph G as input, this algorithm ([5]) begins by constructing a rooted spanning tree T of G. A tree edge $(parent[u], u)$ is referred to as *fence* edge if no nontree edge from $u's$ subtree escapes from $parent[u]'s$ subtree. Tree edges that are not fence are called *plain* edges. A skeleton graph G' is constructed with plain edges in T and all cross edges of G with respect to T. BCCs information of G is obtained from the connected components of G' in the LCH format.

Biconnectivity Compressed Graph (bcg). Let G and H be two graphs, and let $f : V(G) \rightarrow V(H)$ be an onto function. The graph H is referred to as a *biconnectivity compressed graph* (BCG) of G with mapping f, if f satisfies the following four properties.

Property 1. If u is a cut vertex in G then $f(u) \neq f(v)$ for any $v \in V(G)$ such that $v \neq u$.
Property 2. For any two distinct noncut vertices u, v from different biconnected components of G, $f(u) \neq f(v)$.
Property 3. Let u, v, and w be three distinct vertices in G and u', v', and w' are the vertices in H, where $f(u) = u'$, $f(v) = v'$, and $f(w) = w'$. A cut vertex w separates u and v in G if and only if w' separates u' and v' in H, and w' is a real cut vertex. A cut vertex x in H is referred to as ***real*** if $|f^{-1}(x)| = 1$.
Property 4. For every edge $e(u', v')$ in H there exists an edge between (u, v) in G, where $u \in f^{-1}(u')$ and $v \in f^{-1}(v')$.

We have three types of vertices in a BCG H of G, namely *real cut vertices*, *false cut vertices*, and *block vertices*. A cut vertex that is not real is called a **false cut vertex**, and a noncut vertex is referred to as a **block vertex**. In Fig. 2, for a graph G shown in (a), a BCG H_2 with mapping function M_2 are shown in (e). In H_2, the vertices $\{0, 2, 4, 8\}$ are real cut vertices, 6 is a false cut vertex, and $\{1, 3, 5, 7, 9, 10\}$ are block vertices.

3 GEM-BCC Algorithm

We begin this section with the necessary notation and terminology. Later, we elaborate on the purpose and details of various subroutines that will be used in the main algorithm. Finally, we present our GEM-BCC algorithm.

Notation. The edges of an input graph $G = (V(G), E(G))$ appear as a sequence $(e_1, e_2, \ldots, e_m)$ of edges in the edge stream format, and need not fit into the GPU memory at once. So, $E(G)$ is divided into k consecutive batches $B_1, B_2, \ldots, B_k$, such that each B_i fits in GPU, where each B_i denotes the i-th batch of edges, and $k = \lceil |E|/b \rceil$. We use G_0 to denote a spanning tree of G and H_0 to denote the same spanning tree. For each $1 \leq i \leq k$, we define G_i as $G_{i-1} + B_i$.

For each $1 \leq i \leq k$, we use H_i and M to denote a BCG of G_i and the corresponding mapping function from $V(G)$ to $V(H_i)$, respectively. Suppose G_{i-1} is disconnected, a non-cut vertex in G_{i-1} can become a cut vertex in G_i. To avoid this, we consider G_0 as a spanning tree of G and ensure that for each $0 \leq i \leq k$, G_i is connected.

High-Level Overview of GEM-BCC Algorithm. Our GEM-BCC algorithm runs in two passes. In the first pass, all batches of edges are processed to construct a spanning tree of G and initialize a compressed graph in GPU, with the spanning tree, to ensure that the compressed graph is always connected. In the second pass, we consider each batch of edges at a time, expand the existing compressed graph by including them, and compress it again using an in-memory GPU algorithm for BCC. After the second pass is over, we obtain BCCs of G in LCH representation from the BCCs of the repaired compressed graph.

Later, we prove in Lemma 6 that the compressed graph in GPU is a BCG, and thus Theorem 1 ensures the proof of correctness of our GEM-BCC algorithm.

Challenges. To obtain a concrete algorithm from the high-level overview, we work on the following key challenges.

1. After including a new batch of edges to the existing compressed graph maintained in GPU, what vertices in the current graph need to be merged to compress further?
2. How do we identify certain non-essential edges from the current compressed graph and ensure that the size of the updated compressed graph is bounded by $O(n)$?
3. How do we maintain a mapping function from the vertices in the original graph to the vertices in the compressed graph, so that BCC of G can be obtained back from the compressed graph?

3.1 Subroutines

GEM-spanning-tree(G): This subroutine constructs a spanning tree of the given graph G. The full edge stream $E = (e_1, e_2, \ldots, e_m)$ of edges need not fit into the GPU memory at once. So, we divide E into batches $B_1, B_2, \ldots, B_k$, such that each B_i fits in GPU. This subroutine starts with an empty spanning forest. During i^{th} iteration ($1 \leq i \leq k$), we apply GPU-based parallel incremental algorithm [7], to update the existing spanning forest by processing a batch B_i of edges. The computational depth of this subroutine is $O(k \log^2 n)$, with a total work complexity of $O(kn + m) \log n$.

Transform(B, M): This subroutine takes a batch B of edges and a mapping function M as input. For each edge (u, v) in B, we obtain the transformed edge $(M(u), M(v))$ in parallel and then remove self-loops and duplicate edges by applying parallel compaction [9]. The computational depth of this subroutine is $O(\log |B|)$, with a total work complexity of $O(|B|)$.

Compress-Graph(G): This subroutine is meant for merging all the non-cut vertices in a BCC into a single vertex while retaining cut vertices as it is. To accomplish this, we first run GPU version of FAST-BCC algorithm ([5]) on G to obtain the IMPLICIT-BCC array $I[\cdot]$, and then invoke TRANSFORM($E(G), I$). The depth of this procedure is bounded by $O(\log^2 n)$.

BCC-Repair(H, M): This procedure receives a compressed graph H of G and a mapping array that maps $V(G)$ to $V(H)$. We apply a GPU-based FAST-BCC algorithm ([5]) on H and treat false cut vertices as non-cut vertices to obtain labels for $V(H)$ and component heads for labels. The graph induced on the vertices with the same label and its component head is a maximal subgraph without a real cut vertex. In our GPU version of the FAST-BCC algorithm, we include fence edges $(parent[u], u)$ in the skeleton graph if $parent[u]$ is a false cut vertex, in accordance with the requirements for this subroutine. The depth of this procedure is bounded by $O(\log^2 n)$.

3.2 Algorithm

Now, we shall describe Algorithm 1. Initially, the input graph G appears in CPU in the edge stream format. Our GEM-BCC algorithm proceeds in two passes. In the *first pass*, we construct a spanning tree H_0 of G using GEM-SPANNING-TREE subroutine and store H_0 in GPU.

In the *second pass*, we partition the edge stream $(e_1, \ldots, e_m)$ of G in CPU into k consecutive batches, denoted as $B_1, B_2, \ldots, B_k$, ensuring that each batch individually fits to GPU memory. As we go forward, we merge multiple vertices into a single vertex in GPU. To precisely know which set of vertices are merged into which vertex, we maintain a mapping function represented using an array $M[\cdot]$. At the beginning, for each vertex $v \in V(G)$, we initialize $M(v) = v$ in parallel in Line 2. During the ith-iteration of Algorithm 1, we copy a batch B_i of edges from CPU to GPU and perform the following operations in GPU. We first apply the mapping M to the edges in B_i and include the transformed edges in

Algorithm 1: GEM-BCC Algorithm

Input: A Graph $G(V, E)$ in edge stream format, batch size B
Output: BCC labels for edges and cut vertex status for vertices in G.

1 $H_0 \leftarrow$ GEM-SPANNING-TREE(G)
2 **for** each vertex v **do in parallel** $M[v] = v$
3 **for** $i = 1$ to k **do**
4      $H_{i-1} \leftarrow H_{i-1} +$ TRANSFORM(B_i, M)
5      $(H_i, I) \leftarrow$ COMPRESS-GRAPH(H_{i-1})
6   **for** each vertex $u \in V(G)$ **do in parallel** $M[u] \leftarrow I[M[u]]$
7      $H_i \leftarrow$ TV-FILTER(H_i)
8 $(l[\cdot], ch[\cdot]) \leftarrow$ BCC-REPAIR(H_k, M)
9 **for** each vertex $v \in V(G)$ **do in parallel**
10      $label[v] \leftarrow l[M[v]]$
11 **for** each distinct label j **do in parallel**
12      $componentHead[j] \leftarrow M^{-1}(ch[j])$

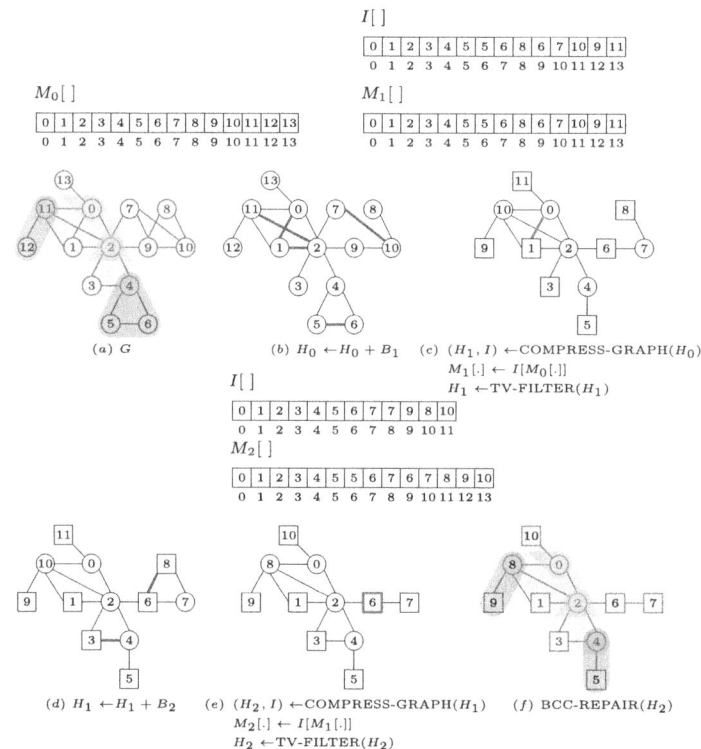

Fig. 2. Illustration of Algorithm 1. (a) An input graph G and BCCs of G. (b) B_1 edges are shown in blue (c) Edges in red color represent the non-essential edges to be removed by TV-FILTER (d) B_2 edges are shown in blue (e) False cut vertex is shown in red color (f) False cut vertices are treated as non-cut vertices and hence vertices 2, 6, and 7 appear in a single set.

the current compressed graph H_{i-1}, using the subroutine TRANSFORM. Due to the inclusion of a new batch of edges, the number of edges in H_{i-1} is increased. We now obtain an IMPLICIT-BCC $I[\cdot]$ of H_{i-1} and compress H_{i-1} to H_i by using the subroutine COMPRESS-GRAPH. It can be observed that M and I are mapping functions from $V(G)$ to $V(H_{i-1})$ and $V(H_{i-1})$ to $V(H_i)$, respectively. We perform function composition $I \circ M$ to update M in Line 6 so that the new function maps from $V(G)$ to $V(H_i)$. At this stage, $|E(H_i)|$ need not be bounded by $O(|V(H_i)|)$. To achieve this, we eliminate non-essential edges in H_i by exposing it to TV-FILTER algorithm.

After processing all k batches, we are ready with the compressed graph H_k. Due to the appearance of fake cut vertices, there is no one-to-one mapping between BCC(G) and BCC(H_k). We now apply BCC-REPAIR on H_k to obtain labels to $V(H_k)$ and a component head to each label, such that $(V_1, \ldots, V_r)$ is a vertex decomposition of $V(H_k)$, where V_i denotes a set of vertices with a same label along with its component head and $H[V_i]$ does not have a real cut vertex.

Finally, we obtain labels of $V(G)$ and their component heads from the labels of H_k and their component heads using the mapping function M in Lines 9–12. For a vertex u in H_k, note that $|M^{-1}(u)| = 1$, when u is a component head, because every component head is a real cut vertex. The correctness of this algorithm is formally proved in Theorem 1. An illustration of this algorithm is shown in Fig. 2. The total depth of Algorithm 1 is bounded by $O(k(diameter(H_1) + \log^2 n))$ and total work is bounded by $O((kn + m)\log n)$. For each $1 \leq i \leq k$, $|E(H_i)| \leq |V(H_i)| \leq n$, and $|B_i|$ is $O(n)$, the space requirement of this GEM-BCC algorithm in GPU is $O(n)$.

Obtaining Cut Vertices. From Property 3 of BCG, there is a one-to-one mapping between cut vertices in G and real cut vertices in H_k. All cut vertices in H_k can be retrieved by applying GPU variant of Fast-BCC algorithm [5], and then identify the real cut vertices using the mapping function M. The inverse maps of these real cut vertices correspond to the cut vertices in G.

4 Correctness of External-BCC Algorithm

There are three main operations performed during every iteration of our algorithm. In this section, we prove that after every operation, the resultant compressed graph is a BCG. Later, we show the proof of correctness of the entire algorithm in Theorem 1. Complete proofs can be found at GitHub.

Lemma 1. *Let G be a connected graph. Let H be a BCG of G with a mapping function $f : V(G) \to V(H)$. Suppose we add a batch B of edges to G, and let B' be the transformed edges of B by applying f. Then, $H + B'$ is a BCG of $G + B$ and f remains the associated mapping function.*

Lemma 2. *Let G be a graph. Let H and $f : V(G) \to V(H)$ be compressed graph and mapping function returned by COMPRESS-GRAPH subroutine applied on G. Then, H is a BCG of G with mapping function f.*

Proof. We know *Implicit-BCC* labels represented by f satisfy following properties:

i. If u is a cut vertex in G then $f(u) \neq f(v)$ for any $v \in V(G)$ such that $v \neq u$. Hence Property 1 is satisfied.
ii Two non cut vertices are given same label if and only if they belong to same biconnected component. Hence Property 2 is satisfied.
iii Due to the way of constructing H, $E(H) = \{(f(u), f(v)) \mid (u,v) \in E(G), f(u) \neq f(v)\}$. Hence Property 4 is satisfied.

We now prove that f satisfies Property 3, to declare that H is a BCG of G. Let u, v, and w be three distinct vertices in G and u', v', and w' are the vertices in H, where $f(u) = u'$, $f(v) = v'$, and $f(w) = w'$.

We first consider the forward case, in which the cut vertex w separates u and v in G. Let m denote the number of connected components in $G - w$. Then u and v reside in two different components. For each $1 \leq i \leq m$, let S_i denote the set of vertices in i^{th} component. We have the following observations:

Obs 1. $\bigcup_{i=1}^{m} S_i = V(G) \setminus \{w\}$
Obs 2. $S_i \cap S_j = \emptyset$ for $i \neq j$
Obs 3. For any two vertices p and q such that $p \in S_i$, $q \in S_j$, and $i \neq j$, $(p,q) \notin E(G)$.

For each $1 \leq i \leq m$, we define $S'_i = \{f(v) \mid v \in S_i\}$. By Property 1 of BCG, only w maps to w', and by Obs 1, we can infer that $\bigcup_{i=1}^{m} S'_i = V(H) \setminus \{w'\}$. Let p and q be vertices in S_i and S_j respectively, where $i \neq j$. Then p and q do not belong to same biconnected component in G, since all paths between them pass through w. By Property P2, $f(p) \neq f(q)$. This fact along with Obs 2 follows that $S'_i \cap S'_j = \emptyset$. From Obs 3, there is no edge connecting any vertex in S_i to any vertex in S_j in G. By Property 4, there is no edge connecting any vertex in S'_i to any vertex in S'_j in H. Therefore, the subgraph $H[S'_1 \cup \ldots \cup S'_m]$ is disconnected while $H[S'_1 \cup \ldots \cup S'_m \cup \{w'\}]$ is connected, because $V(H) = S'_1 \cup \ldots \cup S'_m \cup \{w'\}$. This implies that u' and v' can only reach each other through w' in H. In other words, w' is a cut vertex in H that separates u' and v'. Furthermore, due to Property 1, only one vertex w maps to w', and thus w' is a real cut vertex in H and separates u' and v'.

Now we examine the other direction in which the real cut vertex w' separates u' and v' in H. Let m denote the number of connected components in $H - w'$. Then u' and v' reside in two different components. For each $1 \leq i \leq m$, let S'_i denote the set of vertices of H in i^{th} component. We have the following observations:

Obs 4. $\bigcup_{i=1}^{m} S'_i = V(H) \setminus \{w'\}$
Obs 5. $S'_i \cap S'_j = \emptyset$ for $i \neq j$
Obs 6. For any two vertices p' and q' such that $p' \in S'_i$, $q' \in S'_j$, and $i \neq j$, $(p', q') \notin E(G)$.

For each $1 \leq i \leq m$, we define $S_i = \{f^{-1}(v) \mid v \in S'_i\}$. By the definition of real cut vertex, only w maps to w'. By Obs 4 and the fact that f is well defined for every vertex in G, $\bigcup_{i=1}^{m} S_i = V(G) \setminus \{w\}$. Since f is a function, each vertex in $V(G)$ has unique image in $V(H)$. This fact along with Obs 5 follows that $S_i \cap S_j = \phi$ where $i \neq j$. Let p' and q' be vertices in S'_i and S'_j respectively, where $i \neq j$. From Obs 6, no edge exists between p' and q' in H. Due to construction procedure of H using IMPLICIT-BCC, no edge between p' and q' implies no edge between any vertex $u \in f^{-1}(p')$ and any vertex $v \in f^{-1}(q')$. So there are no edges between vertices in S_i and S_j in G. The subgraph $G[S_1 \cup \ldots \cup S_m]$ is disconnected while $G[S_1 \cup \ldots \cup S_m \cup \{w\}]$ is connected, because $V(G) = S_1 \cup \ldots \cup S_m \cup \{w\}$. Consequently, w is a cut vertex in G and separates u and v, and thus Property 3 is satisfied. Therefore H is the BCG of G.

Lemma 3. *Let G be a connected graph. Let H be a BCG of G with a mapping function $f : V(G) \to V(H)$. Let H' be a graph obtained by TV-FILTER(H). Then, H' is a BCG of G and f remains the associated mapping function.*

Lemma 4. *Let H' be a BCG of G with mapping function $f1 : V(G) \to V(H')$ and H'' be a BCG of H' with mapping function $f2 : V(H') \to V(H'')$. Then, H'' is a BCG of G with mapping function $f3 : V(G) \to V(H'')$ where $f3 = f2 \circ f1$.*

Lemma 5. *Let G be a graph. G is a BCG of itself with mapping function f where $f(i) = i$ for all $i \in V(G)$.*

Lemma 6. *For $i \in \{2, \ldots, l\}$, let H_i be a graph obtained after processing batch B_i of edges on H_{i-1} using Lines 4–8 of Algorithm 1. If H_{i-1} is a BCG of G_{i-1}, then H_i is a BCG of G_i.*

Theorem 1. *Algorithm 1 identifies BCCs of G correctly.*

Proof. Line 1 of the Algorithm 1 correctly constructs a spanning tree of G, which is represented by H_0. We recall that G_0 is same as H_0 before the second pass begins. Line 2 initializes mapping M as an identity function. By Lemma 5, H_0 is a BCG of G_0 with mapping M. After k iterations in the algorithm are over, we are ready with a compressed graph H_k and the updated mapping function M. By Lemma 6, H_k is a BCG of G with mapping function M. BCC-REPAIR subroutine correctly computes the label and component head arrays of graph H_k that satisfy the following property: a subgraph induced on all vertices having the same label along with its component head forms a maximal subgraph of H_k with no real cut vertices. By Property 3 of BCG, subgraph induced on inverse maps of vertices having the same label and inverse map of the component head in graph G form a maximal subgraph with no cut vertices in G. Hence, vertices having the same label along with the component head of the label form BCCs in G.

5 Experimentation

In this section, we introduce the datasets and the configuration of the experimental platform. We then analyse the performance and scalability of the proposed algorithms compared to the baseline algorithms. Finally, we highlight key insights and the influencing factors of the GEM-BCC algorithm.

Table 1. List of graph datasets along with their statistics used in our experiments.

Datasets	|V|	|E|	|BCC|	Baselines			Ours	abv.
				F-BCC$_{cpu}$	WK	F-BCC$_{gpu}$	E-BCC	
Road Networks								
road_usa	23M	57.7M	7.3M	0.9		0.8	0.2	0.2	RU
europe_osm	50M	108.1M	43.4M	1.2		0.94	0.4	0.4	EO
Web Crawls								
Webbase-2001	118M	1.01B	30.4M	4.3	OOM	OOM	1.3	WB
IT-2004	41M	2.05B	4.9M	2.1	OOM	OOM	1.1	IT
SK-2005	50M	3.62B	4M	2.3	OOM	OOM	1.7	SK
Social Networks								
Twitter7	41M	2.41B	1.9M	8.7	OOM	OOM	1.4	TW
com-Friendster	65M	3.61B	14M	12.3	OOM	OOM	2.6	CF
Random Graph								
GAP-URAND	134M	4.29B	1	34.2	OOM	OOM	2.6	GU
Biomedical Hypothesis Generation Systems								
Moliere-2016	30M	6.68B	1.4M	16.8	OOM	OOM	2.7	ML
Agatha-2015	183M	11.6B	18.4M	40	OOM	OOM	2.5	AG

5.1 Experimental Setup

All experiments were conducted on a NVIDIA A100 GPU (40 GB memory, 2.04 TB/s memory bandwidth, 6 MB L2 cache, and 128 KB L1 cache per Streaming Multiprocessor, with 80 SMs total), paired with an AMD EPYC 7742 CPU (64 cores, 4 MB L1 cache, 32 MB L2 cache, and 256 MB L3 cache) supporting hyperthreading for up to 128 simultaneous threads. All codes were implemented in C++ and CUDA, compiled using NVCC version 11.4 with the flags -O3 -arch=sm_80, and GCC version 9.4.0. We used 1024 threads per CUDA block, and enabled CUDA streams to overlap data transfers with kernel execution. The NVIDIA CUB library was used for device-side operations such as scan, sort etc. wherever applicable.

Although TV-FILTER theoretically bounds the number of edges to $O(n)$, its overhead can be significant in practice primarily due to BFS. To avoid this, we only apply TV-filter selectively. We pre-allocate space for up to 2 × batch-size edges on the GPU, and only invoke TV-FILTER if the graph exceeds this capacity after multiple iterations without shrinking. To assess the performance and scalability of our algorithms, we selected ten diverse, publicly available datasets [1,4,10,12]. These graphs range in size from around 50 million to 10 billion edges, as summarized in Table 1. Each experiment was run ten times and the reported results are the averages of these trials. The source code, data, and / or other artifacts have been made available at github.

5.2 Comparison with State-of-the-Art BCC Algorithms

We evaluated our proposed algorithm, GEM-BCC (E-BCC), by comparing it against two publicly available baseline methods: FAST-BCC on CPU (F-BCC$_{cpu}$) and Wadwekar & Kothapalli's GPU-based algorithm (WK), along with a GPU variant of Fast-BCC (F-BCC$_{gpu}$).

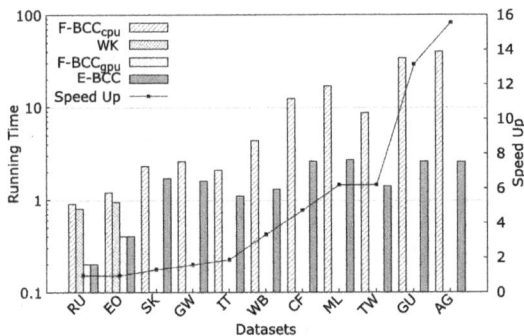

Fig. 3. Speedup comparison of E-BCC, F-BCC$_{cpu}$, WK, and F-BCC$_{gpu}$. Empty plots indicate instances where the respective algorithm failed to execute due to out-of-memory (OOM) errors.

We use the notation OOM (Out of Memory) in Table 1 to indicate instances where the WK algorithm was unable to execute due to insufficient GPU memory. The reason for this is that WK algorithm requires substantial memory not only to store the input graph but also to manage auxiliary data structures resulting in $O(n+m)$ space. A detailed analysis reveals that each vertex generally requires at least 8 bytes, and each edge needs a minimum of 16 bytes for representation. Additionally, WK allocates approximately 810 auxiliary arrays proportional to the vertex count and few to the edge count, significantly exacerbating memory usage. In contrast, due to the higher available CPU memory, the F-BCC algorithm successfully executed across all tested graph instances.

Notably, while the state-of-the-art GPU algorithm (WK) frequently exhausted available memory, our E-BCC algorithm consistently processed all tested graphs without issue. As shown in Fig. 3, E-BCC demonstrates significant performance gains over the multicore F-BCC, achieving a maximum speedup of 15x and an average speedup of about 6x across most datasets. For the RU and EO datasets, however, the speedup remains close to 1; as for speed up, we compare E-BCC's runtime to that of the best-performing baseline. When the data fits into GPU memory, E-BCC effectively matches the best static GPU-based BCC algorithm, as it avoids many of the overheads otherwise involved.

5.3 Impact of Different Batch Sizes

In this section, we examine how the algorithm's running time varies with different amounts of GPU memory. As the GPU memory capacity increases, the number of

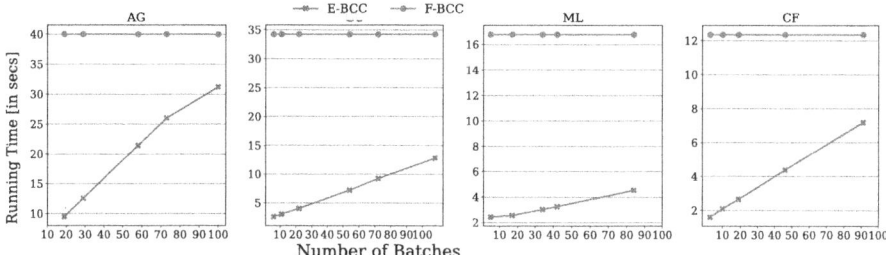

Fig. 4. Running Time vs Number of Batches

batches decreases. Figure 4 illustrates that fewer batches lead to shorter running times, primarily because the algorithm is repeated over fewer batches. This trend aligns with our theoretical expectation as the depth of our algorithm depends on the number of batches. Consequently, in practice, it is most efficient to utilize the maximum available GPU memory to minimize the number of batches. Notably, we were able to process four of our largest datasets using as small as 10 GB of GPU memory.

6 Conclusion

We introduced GEM-BCC, a GPU based out-of-memory algorithm that processes large graphs exceeding the on-board memory by using batch processing. Although its runtime can be comparable to multicore CPU implementations in some scenarios, the primary goal is to enable GPU-based processing of large datasets that traditional in-memory algorithms cannot handle. We provided a comprehensive proof of correctness and demonstrated the scalability across a diverse set of datasets. As future work, this model can be extended to other graph problems, providing a promising direction for scalable graph analytics on massive datasets.

Disclosure of Interests. The authors have no competing interests to declare that are relevant to the content of this article.

Acknowledgements and Artifact Availability. This work is partially supported by a grant from the Department of Science and Technology (DST), India, under the Core Research Grant Scheme vide Ref. No: CRG/2023/005225. The source code, data, and/or other artifacts have been made available at github.

References

1. Ahmed, N., Rossi, R.: The network data repository with interactive graph analytics and visualization. In: Proceedings of the Twenty-Ninth AAAI Conference on Artificial Intelligence (AAAI 2015) (2015). https://networkrepository.com
2. Ben-David, N., et al.: Implicit decomposition for write-efficient connectivity algorithms. In: International Parallel and Distributed Processing Symposium (IPDPS 2018), pp. 711–722. IEEE (2018). https://doi.org/10.1109/IPDPS.2018.00080
3. Cong, G., Bader, D.: An experimental study of parallel biconnected components algorithms on symmetric multiprocessors (SMPS). In: Proceedings of the 19th IEEE International Parallel and Distributed Processing Symposium (IPDPS 2005), pp. 45–54. IEEE (2005). https://doi.org/10.1109/IPDPS.2005.307
4. Davis, T., Hu, Y.: The university of Florida sparse matrix collection. ACM Trans. Math. Softw. **38**(1), 1–25 (2011). https://doi.org/10.1145/2049662.2049663
5. Dong, X., Wang, L., Gu, Y., Sun, Y.: Provably fast and space-efficient parallel biconnectivity. In: Proceedings of the 28th ACM SIGPLAN Annual Symposium on Principles and Practice of Parallel Programming (PPoPP 2023), pp. 52–65. ACM (2023). https://doi.org/10.1145/3572848.3577488
6. Hochbaum, Dorit S..: Why should biconnected components be identified first. Disc. Appl. Math. **42**(2–3), 203–210 (1993). https://doi.org/10.1016/0166-218X(93)90046-Q
7. Hong, C., Dhulipala, L., Shun, J.: Exploring the design space of static and incremental graph connectivity algorithms on GPUs. In: International Conference on Parallel Architectures and Compilation Techniques, pp. 55–69 (2020). https://doi.org/10.1145/3410463.3414658
8. Hopcroft, J., Tarjan, R.: Efficient algorithms for graph manipulation. Commun. ACM **16**(6), 372–378 (1973). https://doi.org/10.1145/362248.362272
9. JáJá, J.: Parallel Algorithms. Addison-Wesley (1992)
10. Leskovec, J., Krevl, A.: SNAP datasets: Stanford large network dataset collection (2014). http://snap.stanford.edu
11. Li, S., et al.: Liberator: a data reuse framework for out-of-memory graph computing on GPUs. IEEE Trans. Parallel Distrib. Syst. **34**(6), 1954–1967 (2023). https://doi.org/10.1109/TPDS.2023.3268662
12. Nguyen, D., Lenharth, A., Pingali, K.: A lightweight infrastructure for graph analytics. In: Proceedings of the 24th ACM Symposium on Operating Systems Principles (SOSP 2013), pp. 456–471. ACM (2013). https://doi.org/10.1145/2517349.2522739
13. Sabet, A.H.N., Zhao, Z., Gupta, R.: Subway: Minimizing data transfer during out-of-GPU-memory graph processing. In: Proceedings of the 15th European Conference on Computer Systems (EuroSys 2020), pp. 12:1–12:16. ACM, New York, NY, USA (2020). https://doi.org/10.1145/3342195.3387537
14. Sahu, S., Mhedhbi, A., Salihoglu, S., Lin, J., Özsu, M.T.: The ubiquity of large graphs and surprising challenges of graph processing: extended survey. VLDB J. **29**, 595–618 (2020)
15. Sengupta, D., Song, S.L., Agarwal, K., Schwan, K.: Graphreduce: processing large-scale graphs on accelerator-based systems. In: International Conference for High Performance Computing, Networking, Storage and Analysis. SC '15, ACM, New York, NY, USA (2015). https://doi.org/10.1145/2807591.2807655
16. Tang, R., et al.: Ascetic: enhancing cross-iterations data efficiency in out-of-memory graph processing on GPUs. In: International Conference on Parallel

Processing (ICPP 2021), pp. 41:1–41:10. ACM (2021). https://doi.org/10.1145/3472456.3472457
17. Tarjan, R., Vishkin, U.: An efficient parallel algorithm for graph biconnectivity. SIAM J. Comput. **14**(4), 862–874 (1985). https://doi.org/10.1137/0214061
18. Wad, C., Kothapalli, K.: A fast GPU algorithm for biconnectivity computation. In: Proceedings of the 10th International Conference on Contemporary Computing (IC3 2017), pp. 1–6. IEEE (2017). https://doi.org/10.1109/IC3.2017.8284293

Disaggregated Design for GPU-Based Volumetric Data Structures

Massimiliano Meneghin[1] and Ahmed H. Mahmoud[2]($^\boxtimes$)

[1] Autodesk Research, 20124 Milan, MI, Italy
massimiliano.meneghin@autodesk.com
[2] MIT CSAIL, 02139 Cambridge, MA, USA
ahdhn@mit.edu

Abstract. Volumetric data structures typically prioritize data locality, focusing on efficient memory access patterns. This singular focus can neglect other critical performance factors, such as occupancy, communication, and kernel fusion. We introduce a novel *disaggregated* design that rebalances trade-offs between locality and these objectives—reducing communication overhead on distributed memory architectures, mitigating register pressure in complex boundary conditions, and enabling kernel fusion. We provide a thorough analysis of its benefits on a single-node multi-GPU Lattice Boltzmann Method (LBM) solver. Our evaluation spans dense, block-sparse, and multi-resolution discretizations, demonstrating our design's flexibility and efficiency. Leveraging this approach, we achieve up to a 3× speedup over state-of-the-art solutions.

Keywords: Data layout · Parallel · Simulation · GPU · LBM

1 Introduction

Since the 2000s, the *memory wall* [1,23] has underscored the critical importance of data locality optimizations in computational tasks. This challenge is especially acute in memory-bound volumetric physics simulations, prompting research into strategies such as blocking [4], time-tiling [22], polyhedral optimizations [2], and cache-oblivious methods [5].

Although GPUs provide high memory bandwidth, achieving peak performance also requires addressing occupancy, load balancing, synchronization overhead, and data movement. Traditionally, volumetric data structures are designed to improve data locality first, with other optimizations (e.g., overlapping computation and communication [16], time skewing [22], kernel fusion [20], tiling [19]) introduced afterward. Because these methods are not considered during data structure design, significant performance opportunities are lost. We argue that additional objectives should be incorporated into volumetric data structure design. While data locality remains essential, selectively compromising it can improve end-to-end performance by addressing other goals.

In this paper, we propose *disaggregated design* for volumetric data structures, which balances multiple performance objectives by:

1. **Grouping voxels based on desired properties:** Rather than relying solely on spatial locality, we cluster voxels according to the traits most relevant for performance.
2. **Applying traditional data locality optimizations within each group:** Within these groups, we still exploit locality as appropriate while addressing other performance targets.

We evaluate our *disaggregated* approach on a LBM fluid solver running on single- and multi-GPU systems, achieving:

- A zero-copy multi-GPU implementation that overlaps computation and communication for dense discretizations, **minimizing transfer overhead** and delivering up to a 3× speedup over state-of-the-art solutions.
- A disaggregated interface and layout for block-sparse data structures that **reduce high register pressure** in complex boundary conditions (e.g., regularized LBM [10]), achieving up to a 2× speedup over naive implementations without extra boundary-data storage.
- A multi-resolution grid representation that **maximizes kernel fusion** in regions unaffected by neighboring cells of different sizes, yielding up to a 26% performance improvement on a single GPU.

In Sect. 2, we formalize the disaggregated design methodology. Sections 3, 4, and 5 apply this approach to dense, sparse, and multi-resolution volumetric grids, respectively. Section 6 presents our evaluation using LBM solvers across multiple GPU architectures. We discuss related work in Sect. 7 and conclude in Sect. 8.

2 Disaggregated Design Method

Voxel-based representations, derived from Cartesian discretization, include **dense** (every voxel in a multidimensional interval is allocated), **sparse** (an irregular subset of the interval), and **multi-resolution** (voxels of different sizes in a single interval). Traditional design efforts have focused on data locality to reduce the growing gap between compute speed and memory latency. However, other performance-critical optimizations—e.g., minimizing communication overhead, reducing register pressure, and maximizing kernel fusion—are equally important. To address these, we introduce *disaggregated design*, a multi-objective method for volumetric data structures defined as follows:

Definition 1. *Given an optimization objective Φ to be considered alongside data locality, a disaggregated design maps data over a voxelized domain into a 1D memory space in four steps:*

1. **Definition:** *Identify properties $\mathcal{P}1, \ldots, \mathcal{P}n$ influencing Φ.*
2. **Classification:** *Group voxels $\mathcal{G}_1, \ldots, \mathcal{G}_n$ based on those properties.*
3. **Mapping:** *Within each group $\mathcal{G}_i$, map voxel data to memory using classical data-locality optimizations.*

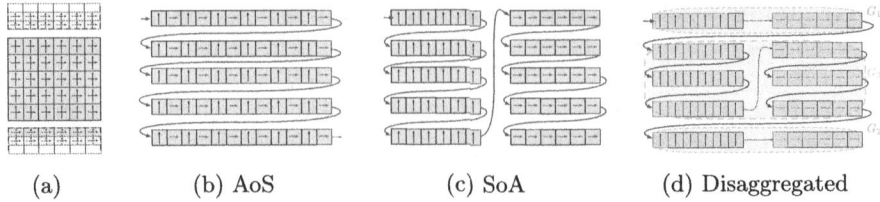

Fig. 1. Illustration of a five-point stencil on a two-component vector field in a 2D domain with partitioning along one axis (a) and three different memory layouts (b,c,d).

4. **Operations:** *Apply group-specific operations to maximize Φ.*

By incorporating objectives beyond locality (**definition**), grouping voxels accordingly (**classification**), and then applying classical optimizations locally (**mapping**), we enable targeted **operations** that yield higher end-to-end performance. Success depends on whether gains from optimizing Φ_i outweigh potential drawbacks, e.g., sub-optimal locality since locality may suffer if inter-group optimizations are underutilized or increased complexity since additional indexing is needed for separate groups.

We study disaggregated design within a **for-each** data-parallel pattern applying a side-effect-free function to each voxel. Under this model, we consider three compute patterns: (1) *Map Pattern* where each voxel depends only on local data, (2) *Uniform Stencil Pattern* where each voxel queries its neighbors (e.g., convolution), and (3) *Multi-resolution Stencil Pattern* where varying voxel sizes require neighbor access at different resolutions.

In the following, we apply disaggregated design to dense (Sect. 3), sparse (Sect. 4), and multi-resolution representations (Sect. 5). We then detail its performance impact on a fluid simulation solver in Sect. 6.

3 Disaggregation on a Dense Domain

In this setup, a dense grid is divided across multiple GPUs, each handling one partition. In stencil computations that require neighbor data, fetching data directly from neighboring GPUs each iteration is highly inefficient due to communication overhead. To mitigate this, each partition maintains a *halo region* (Fig. 1a). Synchronizing these halos (the *halo update* [16]) can significantly add to execution time if performed before every stencil step. *Overlapping Computation and Communication* (OCC) addresses this by dividing the stencil update into two phases. First, **private** voxels (relying only on local data) are processed while the halo is updated in parallel. Then, **shared** voxels (requiring neighbor data) are computed. This hides communication costs and improves scalability on multi-GPU systems.

We adopt a communication model [3] with a constant setup time, t_{setup}, plus a term proportional to message size ($size$(msg)) and the interconnect throughput, b_{com}, such that $t_{send}(\text{msg}) = t_{setup} + \frac{size(\text{msg})}{b_{com}}$. If exchanged data resides in disjoint memory regions, multiple transfers are required.

We consider a 2D stencil on a vector field, where each point stores a 2D vector. Two common layouts are *Array-of-Structures* (AoS) and *Structure-of-Arrays* (SoA). SoA typically yields better coalesced GPU memory access [21]. For a grid of size $d_x \times d_y$, partitioned along one dimension (Fig. 1a), the halo-update time for a generic partition can be approximated as:

$$t_{halo\_update} = \alpha t_{setup} + \beta \frac{size(T)}{b_{com}} \qquad (1)$$

where α is the number of transfer operations, and β the total number of elements sent. With a 1D decomposition, $\alpha \geq 2$ (upper and lower neighbors), and $\beta = 2 \cdot d_y$ for shared boundary elements.

Using AoS (Fig. 1b) keeps shared-voxel data contiguous, minimizing α to 2, but it breaks coalesced GPU access [21]. Conversely, SoA (Fig. 1c) preserves coalesced accesses but splits data, increasing α to 4. This increase occurs because the 2D components are stored non-contiguously in memory, as illustrated by the four distinct regions in Fig. 1c. To reduce the number of communication operations, the data would need to be copied into a contiguous buffer.

Table 1. Comparison of disaggregated, AoS, and SoA layouts for a five-point stencil using the model in Eq. 1. The 2D domain has dimensions $d_x \times d_y$, with a 1D partition along the y-axis.

	α	β	Coalesced
AoS	2	$2 \cdot d_x$	No
SoA	4	$2 \cdot d_x$	Yes
Disag SoA	2	$2 \cdot d_x$	Yes

To reduce α while retaining coalesced accesses, we apply *disaggregated design*. We define $\mathcal{P}_1$ and $\mathcal{P}_2$ to enforce contiguous mapping for voxels shared with the upper ($\mathcal{G}_1$) and lower ($\mathcal{G}_2$) neighbors, while remaining private voxels form $\mathcal{G}_3$ (Fig. 1d). We then map each group in SoA format, preserving $\mathcal{P}_1$ and $\mathcal{P}_2$.

Table 1 compares these layouts, showing that the *disaggregated SoA* merges the benefits of AoS (minimal transfers) with SoA's coalesced memory access.

4 Disaggregation on a Sparse Domain

When the region of interest in a simulation domain is significantly smaller than the full domain, dense representations become inefficient. In these scenarios, *sparse* representations are preferred, allocating data only for actively used voxels and thus conserving memory and compute resources. A common use case in sparse domains involves handling boundary conditions in physics solvers, where computations on each voxel may vary based on its boundary type. For instance, in computational fluid dynamics, no-slip conditions are enforced on boundary voxels at walls, whereas interior (non-boundary) voxels typically follow the Navier–Stokes equations.

The ratio of boundary to total voxels is often small, as boundaries generally scale with surface area rather than volume. Here, we assume a block-sparse

Table 2. Comparison of the disaggregated design vs. a naive approach for a map pattern involving complex boundary conditions in a block-sparse representation. # Kernels is the number of kernels launched; # Blocks is the number of blocks per kernel; # Registers is the register usage; Storage quantifies additional space needed for boundary metadata (s_w is the memory size per boundary voxel, b_size is the number of voxels in a block, and s_i is the size of the indexing type).

	# Kernels	# Blocks	# Registers	Storage	Indexing
Naive	1	$n_b + n_{nb}$	r_b	$s_w n_{nb} b_\text{size}$	Direct
Disag - Bitmask	2	$n_b + n_{nb}$	r_b	$s_i(n_b + n_{nb})b_\text{size}$	Indirect
		$n_b + n_{nb}$	r_{nb}		
Disag - Mem	2	n_b	r_b	0	Direct
		n_{nb}	r_{nb}		

representation (commonly managed by space-filling curves) though other layouts are possible. The computational load on boundary voxels varies based on their type, introducing a few challenges for efficient GPU implementations:

- **Register pressure:** Additional registers may be needed for boundary computations, decreasing kernel occupancy.
- **Memory overhead:** Managing boundary conditions often requires per-voxel metadata, increasing memory requirements.

Let r_nb be the resource needs for non-boundary computations and r_b for boundary computations. We focus on the practical case $r_\text{b} > r_\text{nb}$, which can degrade performance by reducing occupancy and increasing memory usage.

Naive Approach. A naive solution launches a single kernel for all voxels. Because boundary logic is included, the kernel's resource demand is $r = \max(r_\text{nb}, r_\text{b}) = r_\text{b}$. Even though most voxels only need r_nb, the kernel is constrained by r_b. This often leads to suboptimal occupancy and high memory usage, i.e., allocating a full buffer for all voxels, even though only some are boundary voxels.

Disaggregated Approach. Sparse domains typically exhibit heterogeneous workloads, with boundary voxels requiring significantly more resources. The *disaggregated design* alleviates this by separating the domain into two groups:

- **Boundary Group** ($\mathcal{G}_\text{b}$): Blocks containing at least one boundary voxel.
- **Non-Boundary Group** ($\mathcal{G}_\text{nb}$): Blocks with only non-boundary voxels.

This separation allows two specialized kernels, each optimized for its target group. Next, we consider two implementations of this concept:

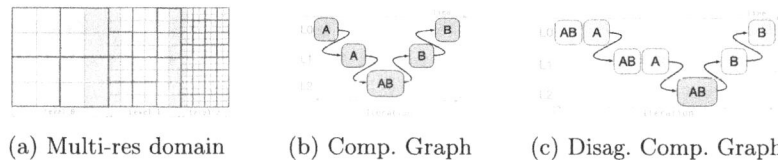

(a) Multi-res domain   (b) Comp. Graph   (c) Disag. Comp. Graph

Fig. 2. A multi-resolution domain with three levels (a) where red blocks lie near resolution transitions, and green blocks are farther away. The computational graph (b) shows dependencies between two kernels: both run on red and green blocks, but kernel B waits for cross-level boundary data. Fusing kernels is traditionally feasible only at the finest resolution level. In the disaggregated approach (c), green blocks fuse computations at any level, while red blocks execute two kernels sequentially once boundary data is available, reducing iteration time. (Color figure online)

Memory-Based Grouping: All boundary blocks are contiguous in memory, followed by non-boundary blocks. Each group is processed by a separate kernel, removing the need for runtime checks on block type and simplifying memory access.

Bitmask-Based Grouping: In this implementation, we use a bitmask at runtime to distinguish block types. Since the spans of the two groups are no longer contiguous, both kernels must execute over the entire domain. Memory for boundary-specific data is allocated using *indirect indexing*, where a unique identifier is assigned to each voxel. This identifier maps boundary voxels to their metadata, which is stored in a contiguous buffer.

Table 2 summarizes these approaches. We examine the performance results and trade-offs of these two implementations in Sect. 6.2.

5 Disaggregation on a Multi-resolution Domain

Multi-resolution data structures handle voxels of varying sizes in one domain (Fig. 2), supporting both *intra-level* stencil operations (within a single resolution) and *cross-level* interactions (between adjacent resolutions).

During each time step in multi-resolution solvers [9], only voxels near resolution boundaries require cross-level communication. Figure 2 distinguishes green (intra-level only) from red (cross-level) voxels. Due to producer/consumer dependencies, iterations are typically split into two steps and can be fused only at the finest level (Fig. 2b).

Using the disaggregated design, we improve memory throughput by maximizing kernel fusion for intra-level computations. Voxels far from resolution jumps do not need cross-level data, so their iterations can fuse at any resolution level. To formalize this, we define a discrete distance property, $\mathcal{P}_d$, measuring how close a voxel is to a resolution jump (distance 0 indicates immediate proximity). Each resolution level is partitioned into: (1) $\mathcal{G}_i$: Blocks where all voxels have distance

≥ 1, allowing fully fused operations, and (2) $\mathcal{G}_c$: Blocks with at least one voxel at distance 0, requiring separate cross-level and intra-level steps.

We apply a standard memory locality layout to each group within each level. Under disaggregation, $\mathcal{G}_i$ blocks use fused kernels across resolution levels, whereas $\mathcal{G}_c$ blocks wait for boundary data (Fig. 2c). This approach minimizes memory pressure for $\mathcal{G}_i$ while preserving accurate cross-level operations for $\mathcal{G}_c$.

6 Evaluation and Discussions

We evaluate the disaggregated design method using a fluid dynamics simulation based on LBM on dense, sparse, and multi-resolution grids. We selected LBM as a representative application since it could benefit from many of the objectives our design method targets. LBM models the time evolution of *velocity distribution functions* (f_i) along discrete lattice directions $e_i = (e_1, \ldots, e_q)$. In 3D, we use lattices with 19 (D3Q19) or 27 (D3Q27) directions. Each f_i value, or *population*, evolves through a *collide-and-stream* process. *Collision* is a nonlinear, local operation that modifies f_i at each lattice point. Here, we employ the BGK single-relaxation-time model for the collision [8]. *Streaming* is a non-local advection of f_i values along each of the Q discrete directions via a stencil.

In optimized GPU LBM implementations, collision, streaming, and boundary conditions are often fused into a single kernel [6]. We use the work of Meneghin et al. [16] as our baseline since they achieve state-of-the-art results on single- and multi-GPU.

6.1 Improving LBM Scalability

We evaluate our disaggregated design on a lid-driven cavity flow problem [12] within a cubic domain, using LBM and a dense voxel representation on single-node multi-GPU systems. We analyze both a theoretical communication model (Sect. 3) and runtime performance.

Reference Implementation. In single-node multi-GPU systems, inter-GPU communication can occur via PCI or faster interconnects like NVLink. Here, we use native `cudaMemcpyPeer` for best performance [7]. Because these systems typically house up to 8–16 GPUs, we use a 1D partitioning scheme [7], giving each partition at most two neighbors (upper and lower) and enabling efficient zero-copy memory transfers.

Figure 3a shows LBM data dependencies with green *private* voxels (computed locally) and red *shared* voxels (requiring data from an adjacent partition). At the lattice granularity, some populations remain local (white or gray), while others must be exchanged (red or blue). Only certain populations of each shared voxel are transferred, which is a defining feature of the LBM streaming operation.

Efficient OCC is critical for achieving fine-grain scalability in LBM [16]. Figure 3c show the computation graph where private-voxel computation is overlapped with halo exchanges for shared voxels, hiding latency and improving performance. This OCC-based implementation is our baseline reference.

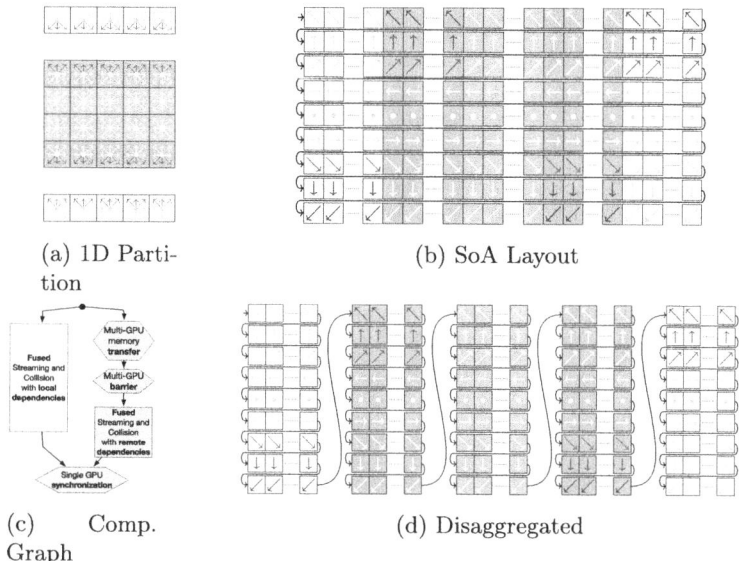

Fig. 3. (a) 1D-partitioned LBM grid: white arrows show local dependencies, and red/blue arrows show dependencies from upper/lower partitions. (c) Computation graph with OCC in the reference implementation. (b,d) SoA and disaggregated SoA layouts for a D2Q9 lattice in 2D, with black arrows indicating memory mapping. (Color figure online)

Modeling Communication Overhead. The parameters α and β from Eq. 1 vary with LBM lattice and data layout (Table 3). Under AoS, all populations in a voxel are contiguous, yielding $\alpha = 2$ transfers (one for each neighbor), but forcing β to include unneeded populations. Conversely, in SoA (Fig. 3b), populations are contiguous *per direction*, increasing α but minimizing β. Table 3 shows that AoS has a smaller α but higher β, while SoA has the opposite trade-off.

Disaggregated Optimization. We now extend the disaggregated layout introduced for stencil operations on a vector-valued field to fully support *zero-copy* communication by including halo regions. These halos enable direct data sharing without additional staging buffers. Concretely, we define distinct properties to ensure contiguous mappings for each critical region: upper halos, upper boundary voxels, lower boundary voxels, and lower halos. As with our original design, each of these groups is mapped using an SoA layout. Figure 3d shows both how the domain is split into groups and how these

Table 3. LBM communication parameters for Eq. 1; s is half the shared voxels: d_x in 2D and $d_x \cdot d_y$ in 3D.

	D2Q9		D3Q19		D3Q27	
	α	β	α	β	α	β
AoS	2	18 s	2	38 s	2	54 s
SoA	6	6 s	10	10 s	18	18 s
Disag SoA	2	6 s	2	10 s	2	18 s

groups are placed in memory. In this arrangement, any data that needs to be transferred or received resides contiguously—the solid-colored (red or blue) populations in Fig. 3d. This means each group's data is placed in a continuous block, allowing for a minimal number of bulk transfers. In the D2Q9 example, this disaggregated SoA configuration results in an α value of 2, so each partition sends just one message per neighbor. Meanwhile, β remains at 6, representing the exact amount of data required by the stencil. Table 3 shows that for D3Q19 and D3Q27, the disaggregated layout delivers similarly optimal α and β values, consistently outperforming basic AoS or SoA alone. Overall, the disaggregated SoA layout combines AoS-like benefits of minimal transfer operations with SoA's advantage of transferring only the necessary populations. By maintaining zero-copy efficiency, it reduces overhead in inter-partition data exchanges, making it theoretically the most communication-efficient layout for multi-GPU LBM.

Benchmarking. We measure runtime on a lid-driven cavity flow with a cubic domain, using boundary conditions from Latt et al. [12]. Table 4 lists three single-node multi-GPU systems tested, spanning high-end (A100), midrange (A10), and previous-generation (V100) GPUs. A100 and V100 use NVLink; A10 relies on PCI. We exclude AoS due to poor coalesced performance in LBM. Figure 4a compares disaggregated and SoA layouts for 3D D3Q19 and D3Q27 lattices, using the Million Lattice Updates per Second (MLUPS) metric.

Table 4. Machines used in benchmarking.

Name	Arch	GPUs	Mem	Interc.
DGX-A100	A100-SXM4	8	40 GB	NVLink-2
AWS p3	V100-SXM2	8	16 GB	NVLink-1
AWS g5	A10	8	24 GB	PCI

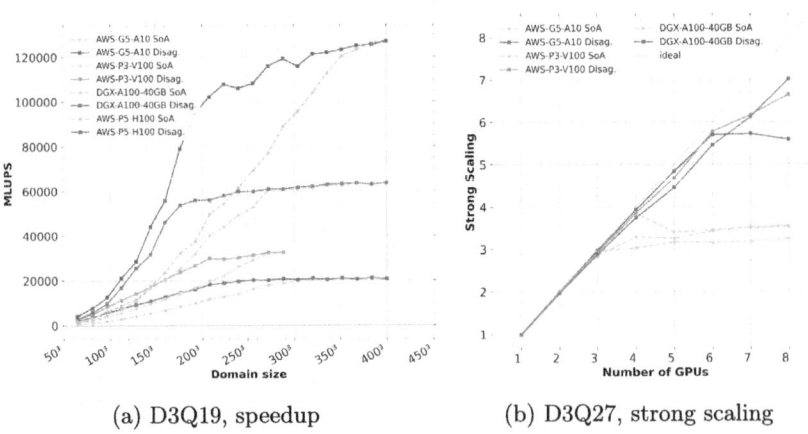

(a) D3Q19, speedup (b) D3Q27, strong scaling

Fig. 4. (a) MLUPS performance of disaggregated vs. SoA on an 8-GPU lid-driven cavity flow (D3Q19). (b) Strong scaling for D3Q27 on a 192^3 domain.

Disaggregated consistently matches or outperforms SoA, especially on smaller domains: up to 4× speedup below 150^3, about 2.5× from 150^3–250^3, and 1.5× for larger volumes. This reduction in performance improvement for larger domains is well explained by Eq. 1: with 1D partitioning, the impact of β (the amount of data transferred) increases with domain size while the number of private voxels grows cubically with the domain edge length L—significantly increasing the amount of computation that can be overlapped with communication. Finally, Fig. 4b shows strong scaling for 192^3 domains. While traditional methods struggle to exceed 3× scaling from a single GPU, the disaggregated layout consistently achieves 6× or more, regardless of GPU architecture.

6.2 Improving LBM Register Allocation

We evaluate the effect of disaggregation on register usage by simulating fluid flow over an obstacle in a cubic domain. The simulation uses a block-sparse grid, with each block containing 4^3 voxels. This setup resembles a typical wind tunnel, where a *bounce-back* boundary condition [13] is applied to obstacle surfaces. Additionally, an *inflow* boundary condition is applied to one face, and an *outflow* boundary condition is applied to the opposite face.

The bounce-back boundary condition is *register-light*, requiring $2Q$ populations. By contrast, the inflow and outflow faces use a *regularized* boundary condition [11], which is *register-heavy*, needing $3Q$ populations. Combining bounce-back and regularized boundaries in one kernel forces resource requirements to accommodate $\max(2Q, 3Q) = 3Q$, potentially over-allocating registers for most voxels. Because the fraction of regularized voxels is $\mathcal{O}(\frac{1}{x})$ relative to domain size x, this wastes registers on the majority of the grid.

Disaggregated Solution. To address this, we classify voxels needing the regularized method as *boundary*, while bounce-back and other voxels are *non-boundary*. Any block containing at least one regularized voxel is marked a *boundary block*; the rest are *non-boundary blocks*. We then assign each category to its own specialized kernel, reducing register pressure for non-boundary blocks. This layout can be implemented by storing boundary blocks contiguously in memory or by using a bitmask to identify them. Both approaches let non-boundary voxels be processed using fewer registers, thus improving occupancy. Table 2 summarizes these advantages, showing how disaggregation avoids register-related bottlenecks.

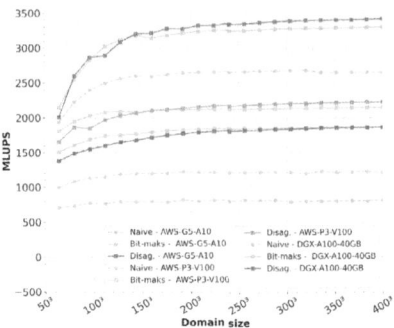

Fig. 5. Performance comparison (single GPU) between the naive implementation and the disaggregated approach (both bitmask and continuous block allocations). The domain uses a D3Q27 lattice on a block-sparse grid, with regularized inflow and outflow boundaries [11].

Benchmarks. We ran this scenario on a single GPU from each system in Table 4, letting CUDA compiler determine register allocation and spilling. Figure 5 shows the performance (MLUPS) for D3Q27 across different domain sizes. In every tested case, the disaggregated solutions (bitmask or memory-based) outperform the naive approach. Gains can reach 2× on V100 and A10 and 1.3× on A100. On V100, the naive kernel needs 55 registers– matching the boundary kernel in the disaggregated case–and suffers spills for the entire domain. Under disaggregation, only the smaller boundary block regions invoke the 55-register kernel, while the majority use a lower-resource kernel. For a domain of size 368, the naive approach has 2.2× more L2-DRAM traffic, explaining the 2× speedup.

On A100, all kernels (naive and disaggregated) also require 55 registers. Spilling occurs only in the naive approach, yet the A100's larger L2 cache reduces its overall penalty, limiting speedup to around 1.3×. Still, data traffic between L2 and DRAM is 1.3× higher for the naive kernel, matching the measured performance improvement. Finally, regarding memory overhead for boundary conditions, the regularized method stores a d-component velocity vector (where $d = 2$ in 2D and $d = 3$ in 3D). Let F be the floating-point type and I the indexing type. Then $s_w = \text{sizeOf}(F) \cdot d$ and $s_i = \text{sizeOf}(I)$. As noted in Table 2, only the disaggregated approach avoids additional storage for boundary voxels; other methods typically allocate boundary-related data throughout the entire domain.

6.3 Improving Multi-resolution LBM Kernel Fusion

We evaluated a single-GPU optimized multi-resolution LBM solver [14] enhanced with the disaggregated design. The data structure comprises multiple uniform block-sparse grids (one per resolution level), along with transition metadata to manage inter-level dependencies.

In multi-resolution LBM, each time step entails two key inter-level operations: (1) *Explosion* where collision results at one resolution feed into lower-resolution levels and (2) *Coalescence* where streaming data from higher resolution levels merges into lower-resolution blocks.

Table 5. Performance comparison of our disaggregated multi-resolution LBM approach vs. a state-of-the-art baseline [14] on a lid-driven cavity flow. *Size* is the length of the virtual finest-level box; *Distribution* lists the fraction of active voxels per level (finest to coarsest); *Baseline* is baseline's MLUPS; *Ours* is our MLUPS; and *Gain* is computed as ($Ours - Baseline$)/$Baseline \times 100\%$.

GPU	Size	Distribution	Ours	Baseline	Gain
A100	512^3	77, 4, 0.4	6072	4824	**25%**
A100	512^3	73, 3, 0.5, 0.003	6018	4769	**26%**
V100	320^3	15, 1, 0.1	4421	3770	**17%**
V100	320^3	15, 1, 0.1, 0.002	4422	3770	**17%**
V100	480^3	53, 4, 0.4	5006	4047	**23%**
V100	480^3	53, 4, 0.3, 0.008	5005	4050	**23%**
A10	320^3	15, 1, 0.1, 0.002	4083	3982	**2%**
A10	480^3	53, 4, 0.3, 0.008	4483	4306	**4%**
A10	512^3	77, 4, 0.4	4093	3901	**4%**
A10	512^3	73, 3, 0.5, 0.003	3890	3719	**4%**

These create dependency edges in a graph similar to Fig. 2b, with operator A for collision and B for streaming. Except at the finest resolution, explosion and coalescence prevent kernel fusion without additional processing.

We classify blocks as: (1) $\mathcal{P}_{\text{uniform}}$ which are blocks that operate uniformly and don't require inter-level synchronization and (2) $\mathcal{P}_{\text{jump}}$ which are blocks containing at least one voxel near a resolution jump, needing explicit explosion/coalescence handling. Using the disaggregated interface, we eliminate unneeded synchronizations at the kernel level. For $\mathcal{P}_{\text{uniform}}$ blocks, we fuse collision and streaming into a single kernel. For $\mathcal{P}_{\text{jump}}$ blocks, the original multi-step execution is preserved to correctly process inter-level data.

Table 5 shows a lid-driven cavity flow benchmark at multiple resolutions on three different GPUs. In all configurations, the disaggregated approach outperforms the baseline. On the A100, a high-end architecture, improvements can reach 26% for domains of size 512^3. The V100 also achieves up to 23% on 480^3 grids. These speedups stem from merging collision and streaming on uniform blocks, thus reducing overhead where inter-level dependencies are not needed.

In contrast, the A10 exhibits smaller gains (2–4%), largely due to register spilling penalizing performance more acutely on midrange GPUs with smaller cache sizes and lower memory bandwidth. Nonetheless, the disaggregated method consistently demonstrates advantages for larger domains and higher active-voxel counts, confirming its suitability for diverse multi-resolution setups.

7 Related Work

While extensive research has been conducted on optimizing stencil computations, most efforts focus on improving data locality. To the best of our knowledge, this work is the first to propose a data structure design methodology aimed at multi-objective optimization, where data locality can be strategically traded off for other performance goals.

Optimizing Communications via Data Layout: Zhao et al. [24] introduced a layout scheme for block representations designed to minimize communication overhead and enable zero-copy communication. Their approach incorporates virtual memory techniques to reduce the impact of indirect indexing which is effective for stencils with a radius that is a multiple of four. However, for stencils with a radius of one, users must resort to time tiling, which can increase message sizes or become infeasible if reductions are involved. While their method demonstrates significant speedups on distributed systems, it does not address the challenges of multi-cardinality fields.

Reducing Register Pressure and Spilling: Managing register pressure and minimizing spilling are critical challenges in GPU computing. Temporal blocking techniques, e.g., register blocking, serialize one domain dimension to improve data reuse [15]. Other strategies leverage GPU shared memory to mitigate the impact of spilling [17]. However, no prior work has explored using data structure design to address register pressure.

Kernel Fusion: Kernel fusion is a well-known optimization for memory-bound problems, as it reduces memory pressure by keeping shared data in registers between consecutive kernels. This technique is widely used in dense LBM implementations [12] and multi-resolution representations [18]. However, existing works do not explore leveraging data layouts to facilitate kernel fusion.

8 Conclusion and Future Work

Past advances in volumetric computation have helped data-structure designers create layouts that emphasize memory access efficiency. In this work, we introduced *disaggregated design*, a unified framework that broadens the optimization focus beyond data locality to include minimizing multi-GPU data transfers, reducing register pressure, and maximizing kernel fusion. Our analytical models and empirical results confirm the benefits of these objectives, while also clarifying the potential drawbacks of more intricate indexing schemes and slightly compromised locality. Ultimately, the overall gains depend on whether the performance improvements outweigh these costs.

This study represents the first in-depth analysis of disaggregated design and its practical scope. Several directions remain for future exploration: (1) extending the applicability of the disaggregated design to other spatial data structures, e.g., unstructured meshes and hash grids, and (2) exploring additional optimization objectives tailored to diverse computational workloads, e.g., load balancing for particle-based simulations.

Acknowledgments. The authors express their gratitude to Hesam Salehipour, Mehdi Ataei, and Oliver Hennigh for their invaluable insights into the intricacies of LBM and their support in providing data on H100 architecture. Ahmed Mahmoud acknowledges the generous support of National Science Foundation grant OAC-2403239.

Disclosure of Interests. The authors have no competing interests to declare that are relevant to the content of this article.

References

1. Asanovic, K., et al.: A view of the parallel computing landscape. Commun. ACM **52**(10), 56–67 (2009). https://doi.org/10.1145/1562764.1562783
2. Bondhugula, U., Hartono, A., Ramanujam, J., Sadayappan, P.: A practical automatic polyhedral parallelizer and locality optimizer. In: Proceedings of the 29th ACM SIGPLAN Conference on Programming Language Design and Implementation, pp. 101–113. PLDI 2008, Association for Computing Machinery, New York, NY, USA (2008). https://doi.org/10.1145/1375581.1375595
3. Culler, D., et al.: LogP: towards a realistic model of parallel computation. SIGPLAN Not. **28**(7), 1–12 (1993). https://doi.org/10.1145/173284.155333
4. Endo, T.: Applying recursive temporal blocking for stencil computations to deeper memory hierarchy. In: 2018 IEEE 7th Non-Volatile Memory Systems and Applications Symposium (NVMSA), pp. 19–24 (2018). https://doi.org/10.1109/NVMSA.2018.00016
5. Frigo, M., Leiserson, C.E., Prokop, H., Ramachandran, S.: Cache-oblivious algorithms. ACM Trans. Algorithms **8**(1) (2012). https://doi.org/10.1145/2071379.2071383
6. Geier, M., Schönherr, M.: Esoteric Twist: an efficient in-place streaming algorithmus for the lattice Boltzmann method on massively parallel hardware. Computation **5**(2), 19 (2017). https://doi.org/10.3390/computation5020019
7. Kraus, J.: Multi-GPU programming models. https://www.nvidia.com/en-us/on-demand/session/gtcfall21-a31140/
8. The Lattice Boltzmann Method. GTP, Springer, Cham (2017). https://doi.org/10.1007/978-3-319-44649-3
9. Lagrava, D., Malaspinas, O., Latt, J., Chopard, B.: Advances in multi-domain lattice Boltzmann grid refinement. J. Comput. Phys. **231**, 4808–4822 (2012). https://doi.org/10.1016/j.jcp.2012.03.015
10. Latt, J., Chopard, B., Malaspinas, O., Deville, M., Michler, A.: Straight velocity boundaries in the lattice Boltzmann method. Phys. Rev. E **77**(5), 056703 (2008)
11. Latt, J., Chopard, B., Malaspinas, O., Deville, M., Michler, A.: Straight velocity boundaries in the lattice Boltzmann method. Phys. Rev. E **77** (2008). https://doi.org/10.1103/PhysRevE.77.056703
12. Latt, J., Coreixas, C., Beny, J.: Cross-platform programming model for many-core lattice Boltzmann simulations. PLOS ONE **16**(4), 1–29 (2021). https://doi.org/10.1371/journal.pone.0250306
13. Lavallée, P., Boon, J.P., Noullez, A.: Boundaries in lattice gas flows. Physica D **47**(1), 233–240 (1991). https://doi.org/10.1016/0167-2789(91)90294-J
14. Mahmoud, A.H., Salehipour, H., Meneghin, M.: Optimized GPU implementation of grid refinement in lattice Boltzmann method. In: Proceedings of the 38th IEEE International Parallel and Distributed Processing Symposium, pp. 398–407 (2024). https://doi.org/10.1109/IPDPS57955.2024.00042

15. Matsumura, K., Zohouri, H.R., Wahib, M., Endo, T., Matsuoka, S.: AN5D: automated stencil framework for high-degree temporal blocking on GPUs. In: Proceedings of the 18th ACM/IEEE International Symposium on Code Generation and Optimization, pp. 199–211. CGO 2020, Association for Computing Machinery, New York, NY, USA (2020). https://doi.org/10.1145/3368826.3377904
16. Meneghin, M., Mahmoud, A.H., Jayaraman, P.K., Morris, N.J.W.: Neon: A multi-GPU programming model for grid-based computations. In: Proceedings of the 36th IEEE International Parallel and Distributed Processing Symposium, pp. 817–827 (2022). https://doi.org/10.1109/IPDPS53621.2022.00084
17. Sakdhnagool, P., Sabne, A., Eigenmann, R.: Optimizing GPU programs by register demotion: poster. In: Proceedings of the 24th Symposium on Principles and Practice of Parallel Programming, pp. 405–406. PPoPP 2019, Association for Computing Machinery, New York, NY, USA (2019). https://doi.org/10.1145/3293883.3297859
18. Schornbaum, F., Rüde, U.: Massively parallel algorithms for the lattice Boltzmann method on nonuniform grids. SIAM J. Sci. Comput. **38**, C96–C126 (2016). https://doi.org/10.1137/15M1035240
19. Tran, N.P., Lee, M., Hong, S.: Performance optimization of 3D lattice Boltzmann flow solver on a GPU. Sci. Programm. **2017**(1) (2017). https://doi.org/10.1155/2017/1205892
20. Wang, X., et al.: A massively parallel and scalable multi-GPU material point method. ACM Trans. Graph. **39**(4) (2020). https://doi.org/10.1145/3386569.3392442
21. Wittmann, M., Zeiser, T., Hager, G., Wellein, G.: Comparison of different propagation steps for lattice Boltzmann methods. Comput. Math. Appl. **65**(6), 924–935 (2013). https://doi.org/10.1016/j.camwa.2012.05.002
22. Wonnacott, D.: Using time skewing to eliminate idle time due to memory bandwidth and network limitations. In: Proceedings 14th International Parallel and Distributed Processing Symposium, pp. 171–180. IPDPS 2000 (2000). https://doi.org/10.1109/IPDPS.2000.845979
23. Wulf, W.A., McKee, S.A.: Hitting the memory wall: implications of the obvious. ACM SIGARCH Comput. Archit. News **23**(1), 20–24 (1995). https://doi.org/10.1145/216585.216588
24. Zhao, T., Hall, M., Johansen, H., Williams, S.: Improving communication by optimizing on-node data movement with data layout. In: Proceedings of the 26th ACM SIGPLAN Symposium on Principles and Practice of Parallel Programming, pp. 304–317. PPoPP 2021, Association for Computing Machinery, New York, NY, USA (2021). https://doi.org/10.1145/3437801.3441598

SQ-DeAR: Sparsified and Quantized Gradient Compression for Distributed Training

Xinrui Yang[iD] and Shaohuai Shi[✉][iD]

Harbin Institute of Technology, Shenzhen, Shenzhen, China
{xinruiy.stu,shaohuais}@hit.edu.cn

Abstract. The data-parallel distributed training technique is a de facto approach in training large-scale deep neural networks (DNNs) using synchronous stochastic gradient descent (S-SGD). However, S-SGD requires iteratively aggregating the distributed gradients through an AllReduce collective, which easily results in significant data communication across distributed GPUs and thus limits the scaling efficiency of the training system. In this paper, we propose an efficient and practical gradient sparsification and quantization algorithm, named SQ-DeAR, which not only significantly reduces the communication traffic through gradient sparsification and quantization, but also allows overlapping communications with both feed-forward and backpropagation computations through decoupling the communication collective operation. In addition, to improve the computation efficiency of gradient sparsification, we design a batched gradient sparsification to reduce the number of GPU launches. Performance evaluation on a 32-GPU cluster shows that SQ-DeAR outperforms state-of-the-art solutions by $1.17\times - 7.0\times$.

Keywords: Distributed Training · Gradient Compression · Collective Communication · Decoupled AllReduce

1 Introduction

The use of distributed synchronous stochastic gradient descent (S-SGD) with data parallelism is prevalent for training large-scale deep neural networks (DNNs) [2,4] in multi-GPU setups. In S-SGD, each worker performs computation to calculate local gradients (say $g_i \in \mathbb{R}^d$, $i = 0, 1, ..., P - 1$ on an P-GPU cluster) with the training data and then aggregate the gradients among all workers to generate an identical gradient (i.e., $g = \sum_{i=0}^{P-1} g_i$) to update the model parameter. The AllReduce operation, a collective communication mechanism, is widely used to do the gradient aggregation in modern distributed training frameworks [4,8]. However, with an increase in the number of workers, the significant data communication overhead resulting from gradient aggregation emerges as a key limitation in distributed training.

There are extensive studies to accelerate training through optimization of gradient aggregation in two main directions [24,33]. First, system optimization strategies have been well integrated in modern distributed training framework like PyTorch-DDP [8] including efficient collective algorithms to reduce the overhead of gradient aggregation (e.g., the ring all-reduce primitive [11], adaptive task scheduling methods to overlap computations and communications (e.g., wait-free back-propagation or WFBP [25], tensor fusion [18,19], tensor partitioning [14], and decoupled AllReduce or DeAR [34]). The second approach involves data compression techniques [31], including strategies like gradient quantization [17,27], sparsification [9,10,13,22], and low-rank decomposition [26,35], to reduce the communication volume while preserving model accuracy. There are some approaches to jointly use sparsification and quantization to achieve more aggressive data compression like AC-SGD [32], JointSQ [30].

Nonetheless, current algorithms that incorporate gradient quantization, sparsification, or a blend of both, encounter multiple challenges. Primarily, the process of gradient quantization frequently introduces considerable precision errors in aggregated gradients, which in turn negatively impacts convergence and accuracy [12]. Additionally, the commonly used top-k gradient sparsification method leads to irregular indices for the communicated gradients, necessitating an All-Gather operation to collect both gradients and their indices [16,21], an approach we refer to as TopKAllGather, which becomes exceedingly inefficient at large P. Moreover, existing methods that combine quantization and sparsification, aside from inheriting these specific limitations, are chiefly designed to minimize communication overhead, lacking optimizations for system-level enhancements like WFBP or DeAR.

To address the above three limitations, we introduce a new algorithm called SQ-DeAR (sparsified and quantized gradient compression with decoupled AllReduce). Specifically, during the backward pass, we apply gradient sparsification akin to TopKA2A [13] and utilize a quantization method to disseminate the aggregated gradients in their quantized form during the forward pass. This approach enhances practicality in density and ensures that performance is not constrained by the AllGather operation in the forward pass. Moreover, aggregating sparsified gradients using TopKA2A demands multiple local sparsification, equal to the number of GPUs, which is generally inefficient on GPUs. To tackle this inefficiency, we introduce an optimized kernel named BatchedMSTopK, which selects the top-k gradients in a single batch, thereby boosting computational efficiency. Our extensive experiments on a 32-GPU cluster reveal that SQ-DeAR markedly surpasses existing top-tier solutions.

2 Background and Preliminaries

2.1 Synchronous SGD or S-SGD

In SGD (or its variants like Adam), given a mini-batch of training data $B = (x_i, y_i)$, the loss function $L_B(\theta)$ is computed as the average of the per-example loss across all samples, which we call feed-forward (FF). The gradient $g = \frac{\partial L_B(\theta)}{\partial \theta}$ is then computed through backpropagation (BP), which is then used to update the model parameters. When SGD is applied to multi-GPU environments, each worker independently computes gradients on its local mini-batch and synchronizes gradients across all workers using AllReduce (i.e., $g_i \in \mathbb{R}^d$, $i = 0, 1, ..., P-1$ on a P-GPU cluster) before updating the model. For a d-dimensional gradient vector, the communication complexity of the popular ring-based AllReduce [13,16] is

$$T_{AR} = 2(P-1)\alpha + 2\frac{(P-1)}{P}d\beta, \quad (1)$$

where α is the startup overhead and β is the communication time for transmitting one element from one worker to another following the Hockney model [5]. It is seen that with the increased model size, T_{AR} would become larger and be a major performance bottleneck.

2.2 DeAR: Decoupled AllReduce in Distributed Training

Due to the layer-wise structure of DNNs, it is a common practice to overlap the gradient communication tasks with gradient calculation during backpropagation (i.e., wait-free backpropagation or WFBP) [25]. Recently, a more fine-grained tasks overlap was proposed in DeAR [34], which decouples the AllReduce primitive to two continuous communication collectives (e.g., ReduceScatter and AllGather). It enables ReduceScatter to be overlapped with BP and AllGather to be overlapped with FF while the overall communication traffic remains unchanged.

2.3 Gradient Compression

Gradient Sparsification. For the d-dimensional gradient, gradient sparsification only selects the top-k gradients according to the magnitude of their values (named top-k sparsification), reducing communication volume by d/k times theoretically, and k is much smaller than d, e.g., $k = 0.01d$ or $k = 0.001d$. However, each worker independently selects its top-k elements would result in irregular indices from its d-dimensional vector, so AllReduce cannot be directly applied. Instead, AllGather is often used to aggregate both gradient values and their corresponding indices, named TopKAllGather, which has a communication complexity of

$$T_{TopKAllGather} = 2(P-1)\alpha + 2(P-1)k\beta. \quad (2)$$

Gradient Quantization. Quantization reduces the number of bits used to represent gradient values. Common quantization schemes include fixed-point representation (8-bit or 16-bit) and stochastic rounding. Compared to the original 32-bit representation, q-bit quantization reduces the communication traffic by $32/q$ times. In this paper, we focus on $q = 8$ for ease of presentation, but our method is eligible for other bit width representation. However, when g_i is represented by lower bits, taking the 8-bit floating point (FP8) as an example, i.e., $\hat{g}_i = \text{FP8}(g_i)$ [12], the aggregation of gradients become

$$\hat{g} = \hat{g}_0 + \hat{g}_1 + ... + \hat{g}_{P-1}. \quad (3)$$

The accumulation of the low-bit gradients would be easily overflow and thus it sacrifices the model convergence.

3 SQ-DeAR: Algorithm Design

Our sparsified and quantized gradient compression together with DeAR aims to 1) reduce the communication complexity that is not linear to the number of GPUs (i.e., enjoying the good property of AllReduce but having less communication volume) using gradient sparsification and quantization, 2) alleviate the low-bit overflow problem during aggregation using gradient quantization, and 3) allow the communication tasks to be overlapped with both FF and BP computation tasks like DeAR. We demonstrate the algorithm in two phrases as follows.

First, we exploit the TopKA2A algorithm [13] for gradient sparsification during BP. Specifically, for a d-dimensional gradient vector g_i on GPU i, we split it into P chunks $[g_i^j], (j = 0, 1, ..., P-1)$, where P is the number of GPUs, and then apply top-k selection for all chunks

$$(\kappa_i^j, \iota_i^j) = \text{MSTopK}(g_i^j, k/P), \tag{4}$$

for $j = 0 \to P - 1$, where MSTopK [13,22] is an efficient approximate top-k operator to select top k/P elements (κ_i^j) and their corresponding indices (ι_i^j) from the input vector g_i^j. We design a more efficient batched version for the above top-k selection, named BatchedMSTopK, with more details in §3.1. The selected top-k elements are then aggregated through two AlltoAll communications (one for values and one for indices). At this phrase, AlltoAll communications are overlapped with gradient computations during BP.

Second, after the sparsified gradients are aggregated through AlltoAll, *they are accumulated using the original 32-bit precision locally*, which recovers the k-dimensional gradient to a d-dimensional gradient vector, say $g_{|i}$, which means GPU i has the ith part of g. We then quantize $g_{|i}$ into a representation of 8 bits (it is configurable to other low-bit representations and we use 8 bits for ease of presentation), i.e.,

$$\begin{aligned}\hat{g}_{|i} &= \text{Quantize}(g_{|i}, scale, zero\_point) \\ &= \text{clamp}(\text{round}\left(\frac{g_{|i}}{scale}\right) + zero\_point, -128, 127),\end{aligned} \tag{5}$$

where $scale$ and $zero\_point$ are set to control the scaling factor and zero offset, respectively. The quantized gradients are then aggregated via AllGather to aggregate all partial gradients across all workers, i.e., $\hat{g} = \text{AllGather}(\hat{g}_{|i})$ for $i = 0, 1, ..., P-1$. Finally, each GPU reconstructs the full-precision 32-bit gradients by dequantizing the aggregated data:

$$\tilde{g} = \text{Dequantize}(\hat{g}, scale, zero\_point) = \frac{(\hat{g} - zero\_point)}{scale}, \tag{6}$$

which is used for updating the model parameters.

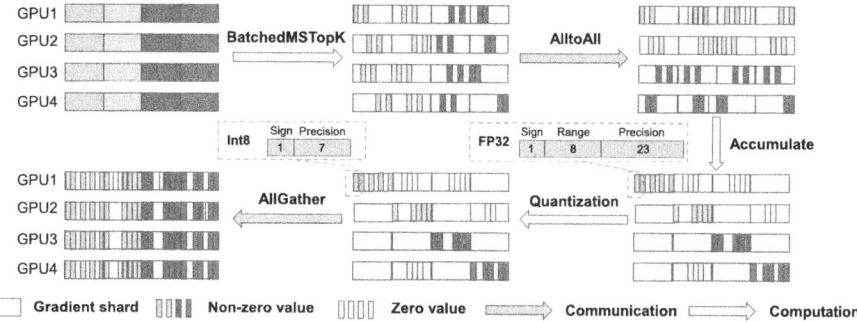

Fig. 1. An example of SQ-DeAR using 4 GPUs. Each GPU splits its local gradient vector to four shards. Then each GPU applies BatchedMSTopK locally to select top-k gradients, which are aggregated through AlltoAll communications, followed by a local accumulation on the aggregated gradients. After that, the 32-bit sparsified gradients are quantized to 8 bits, which are gathered through an AllGather operation to generate the identical gradient.

An example of 4 GPUs to demonstrate the whole process of SQ-DeAR is illustrated in Fig. 1. The pseudocode of SQ-DeAR is shown in Algorithm 1. Lines 1–3 initialize the result tensor and determine the number of selected elements ($k = \rho \times d$). Lines 4–6 apply BatchedMSTopK to extract the top-k elements along with their indices, which are then exchanged using AlltoAll operations. Lines 7–10 reconstruct the sparsified gradient by accumulating the received values at the corresponding positions. Line 11 quantizes the reconstructed gradients to reduce the communication overhead, and Line 12 performs an AllGather operation to collect the quantized gradients from all GPUs. Finally, Line 13 dequantizes the gathered gradients to restore their original precision before returning the final result.

Table 1. Communication complexity of different training algorithms. P is the number of workers, and d is the number of model parameters. $k = \rho \times d$ is the number of selected gradients to be aggregated.

Algorithm	Time Cost
PyTorch-DDP [8]	$2(P-1)\alpha + 2\frac{P-1}{P}d\beta$
TopKAllGather [22]	$2(P-1)\alpha + 2(P-1)k\beta$
DeAR [34]	$2(P-1)\alpha + 2\frac{P-1}{P}d\beta$
TopKA2A [13]	$3(P-1)\alpha + (2k+d)\frac{P-1}{P}\beta$
SQ-DeAR (ours)	$3(P-1)\alpha + (2k+\frac{qd}{32})\frac{P-1}{P}\beta$

Communication Complexity. Compared to TopKA2A, we reduce the All-Gather communication to a lower bit representation such that the communication during FF may not become the performance bottleneck. In contrast to the

Algorithm 1. SQ-DeAR

Input: $g_i \in \mathbb{R}^d, \rho, P, scale, zero\_point$
1: **Initiate** $\tilde{g}_i = [0] \in \mathbb{R}^d$;
2: $[g_i^0, g_i^1, ..., g_i^{P-1}] \leftarrow g_i$; ▷ Partition the gradient to P chunks (virtually)
3: $k = \rho \times d$;
4: $[(\kappa_i^j, \iota_i^j)] = \text{BatchedMSTopK}([g_i^j], k/P)$; ▷ for $j = 0, 1, ..., P-1$
5: $\kappa_{|i} = \text{AlltoAll}([\kappa_i^j])$;
6: $\iota_{|i} = \text{AlltoAll}([\iota_i^j])$;
7: **for** $j \in [P]$ **do**
8:     $\kappa = \kappa_{|i}[j], \iota = \iota_{|i}[j]$;
9:     $\tilde{g}_i[\iota] + = \kappa$;
10: **end for**
11: $\hat{g}_i = \text{Quantize}(\tilde{g}_i, scale, zero\_point)$;
12: $\hat{g} = \text{AllGather}(\hat{g}_i)$;
13: $\tilde{g} = \text{Dequantize}(\hat{g}, scale, zero\_point)$;
14: **Return** $\tilde{g}$;

traditional quantization techniques, our SQ-DeAR approach allows for the accumulation of quantized gradients in 32-bit full precision, thereby mitigating the risk of compromising model convergence. A full comparison of communication complexity can be found in Table 1.

3.1 BatchedMSTopK: A Batched Approximate Top-k Operator

According to Eq. 4, it is seen that the number of MSTopK operations on the local gradient is equivalent to the number of workers, which means the number of GPU kernel launches is linearly increased to P. It would introduce significant launching overheads when P is large. To address this problem, we propose a multi-sampling algorithm capable of batch processing multiple gradient partitions, named BatchedMSTopK. The core idea of BatchedMSTopK is to leverage binary search on each shard while processing all shards in a batch simultaneously, enabling efficient parallel execution.

Formally, assume that we split the gradient, $x \in \mathbb{R}^d$, to a batch of tensors $\{x_1, x_2, \ldots, x_P\}$, where each tensor $x_j \in \mathbb{R}^{d/P}$ and d/P is the dimension of each tensor. Let ρ denote the density of selected elements, i.e., $k = \rho \cdot d$. First, we load all tensors in parallel into contiguous memory. Second, for each tensor x_j, the absolute values $a_j = \text{abs}(x_j)$ are computed in parallel, followed by initial threshold estimation using the mean $\bar{a}_j = \text{mean}(a_j)$ and maximum $u_j = \text{max}(a_j)$. These values are cached in GPU shared memory to minimize redundant global memory accesses. Next, an interleaved binary search is performed across GPU warps for each tensor x_j. During N sampling iterations, the threshold $thres_j$ is dynamically adjusted based on the count of elements nnz_j (the number of non-zero values exceeding $thres_j$): if $nnz_j \leq k$, the threshold is halved to $thres_j/2$; otherwise, it is doubled to $2 \cdot thres_j$. This ensures rapid convergence to an

Table 2. DNN details for experiments. "BS" denotes the mini-batch size per GPU. "# Layers" represents the number of learnable layers. "# Tensors" and "# Param." denote the number of learnable parameter tensors and the number of elements (million) in these tensors, respectively.

Tasks	Models	BS	# Layers	# Tensors	# Param.(M)
Image	VGG16	64	16	32	138.4
Classification	VGG19	64	19	38	143.7
NLP	BERT-Base	64	105	206	110.1
Pre-training	BERT-Large	16	201	398	336.2
LLM Fine-tuning	GPT2	1	12	148	123.7

approximate threshold range $[thres_{j,1}, thres_{j,2}]$, where $thres_{j,1}$ and $thres_{j,2}$ bracket the exact top-k threshold.

This process is performed in parallel with the threshold search for each tensor. Finally, we use the thresholds to obtain the values and indices of the k largest elements. This design enables BatchedMSTopK to achieve scalable and efficient top-k sparsification for a batched input, which is useful under that the AlltoAll implementation of sparse gradient communication. Figure 2 illustrates the process of selecting elements of the gradient tensor for the traditional Top-k and BatchedMSTopK.

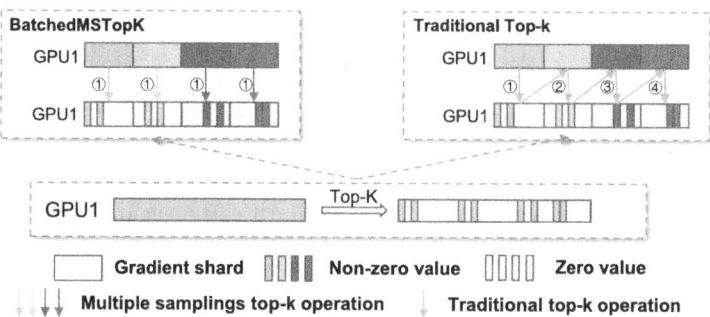

Fig. 2. The traditional sequential Top-k algorithm (four shards of the data should be sequentially executed by the GPU) and our BatchedMSTopK (four shards are executed on the GPU in parallel if there are enough SMs on the GPU.

4 Evaluation

4.1 Experimental Settings

Testbeds. The experiments are conducted on a 32-GPU cluster comprising 8 compute nodes, each equipped with four Nvidia GeForce RTX 2080Ti GPUs (11

GB RAM per GPU). The intra-node GPU communication is PCIe 3.0 x 16 interfaces, while inter-node connectivity is a 10 Gigabit Ethernet (10GbE) backbone. Our software stack includes Ubuntu 20.04 LTS, PyTorch 1.8.1, CUDA 12.0, and NCCL 2.18.5, managed through OpenMPI 5.0 framework. All distributed communication primitives are implemented using NCCL's APIs.

Workloads. We select five representative DNN architectures spanning three application domains including computer vision, NLP, and LLM pretraining. CNNs include VGG16 and VGG19 [23] trained on ImageNet [3], while the BERT [7] variants comprised both base (110M parameters) and large (340M parameters) configurations. For generative modeling evaluation, GPT-2 [15] is used in full-parameter fine-tuning on the tiny-Shakespeare corpus [6]. Detailed architectural specifications and hyperparameter configurations are documented in Fig. 2. The input tensor dimensions are standardized as follows: 224×224×3 images for CNNs, 64-word sequences for BERT models, and 1024-token batches for GPT-2 training iterations.

Baselines. Our proposed new framework was benchmarked against multiple state-of-the-art distributed training systems: PyTorch-DDP and DeAR as conventional baselines, along with compression-enabled implementations including TopKAllGather, TopKA2A and JointSQ. All comparative systems were implemented within the PyTorch ecosystem to ensure consistent evaluation conditions.

4.2 Training Speed

We evaluate the iteration time of our SQ-DeAR against state-of-the-art baselines, including PyTorch-DDP, DeAR, TopKAllGather, TopKA2A, and JointSQ. The speedup results, normalized to PyTorch-DDP (baseline = 1), are presented in Fig. 3. In the experiments, we use a density of 0.02, a setting in real-world training to maintain model accuracy (the convergence of gradient compression has been well studied in existing works [1,30], so we mainly focus on the time performance). Besides, we observe that TopKAllGather leads to memory overflow (OOM) when the batch size is set to 64, so we reduce the batch size to 32. Furthermore, when training the BERT-Large model with batch sizes of 64, 32, 16, or 8, TopKAllGather encounters OOM errors due to its increasing memory demands.

Overall, our SQ-DeAR outperforms all the compared algorithms on the five configured models. PyTorch-DDP only pipelines communication with the backpropagation computation tasks. In contrast, SQ-DeAR allows the communication tasks are pipelined simultaneously with the feed-forward and backpropagation computation tasks to achieve better results, with performance improvements of 65%–184% over PyTorch-DDP.

DeAR improves over PyTorch-DDP by 13%–61%, attributable to its utilization of communication pipelines with both feed-forward and backpropagation computing tasks. However, since it does not compress the gradients, it suffers from performance degradation in the face of a model with a high communication-to-computation ratio such as BERT_Large. On the contrary, TopKAllGather and

SQ-DeAR: Sparsified and Quantized Gradient Compression 177

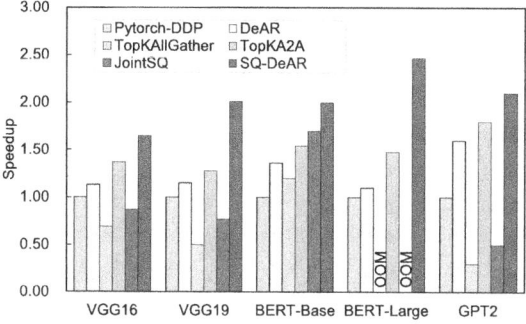

Fig. 3. Speedups over PyTorch-DDP. TopKAllGather and JointSQ run OOM on BERT-Large.

TopKA2A, which have performed gradient sparsification, achieve better results on models with a large number of parameters, with 20% and 54% improvement over PyTorch-DDP, respectively. However, their results are still not as good as our SQ-DeAR, which overcomes the limitations of the other algorithms, has fine-grained schedules and gradient compression during both BP and FF. In summary, SQ-DeAR achieves $1.17\times-7\times$ speedups over PyTorch-DDP, DeAR, TopKAllGather, TopKA2A, and JointSQ.

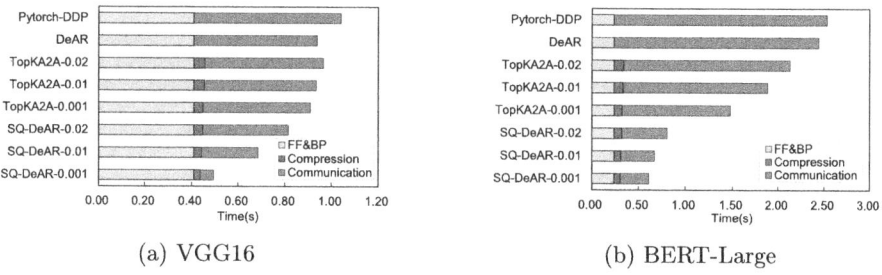

Fig. 4. Time breakdown under different densities. For example, SQ-DeAR-0.01 indicates a density of 0.01 is applied in SQ-DeAR. The communication time includes the non-overlap part only.

4.3 Iteration Time Breakdown

To comprehensively evaluate the efficiency gains of our hybrid gradient communication scheme, we analyze the time breakdown of training iterations across VGG16 and BERT-Large models under varying densities $\rho = 0.02, 0.01, 0.001$

for TopKA2A and SQ-DeAR. The iteration time consists of three parts: feedforward (FF) and backpropagation (BP) computation time, compression computation time, and non-overlapped communication time[1]. The results are shown in Fig. 4. As we use the same PyTorch backend, the FF and BP computation times are the same for the same model. Among all methods, SQ-DeAR has the best performance under different compression ratios. The improvement of SQ-DeAR becomes more significant with higher compression ratios (i.e., lower densities). Moreover, in VGG16, the iteration of TopKA2A becomes almost constant with different densities as it is main limited by the AllGather communication during FF. Our SQ-DeAR effectively tackles the issue through a quantized method.

4.4 Efficiency of BatchedMSTopK

In order to assess the efficiency of BatchedMSTopK in comparison to the baseline MSTopK, we carried out comprehensive experiments using an NVIDIA RTX 2080Ti GPU. These experiments varied the number of chunks between 4 and 64, as well as tensor dimensions ranging from 1 million to 128 million. The count of selected elements is calculated as a hundredth of the vector dimension, specifically $k = 0.01 \times d$. The results, illustrated in Fig. 5, clearly indicate that BatchedMSTopK substantially reduces the computation time under all configurations. In the configured tests, BatchedMSTopK runs $1.55\times - 7.10\times$ faster than MSTopK.

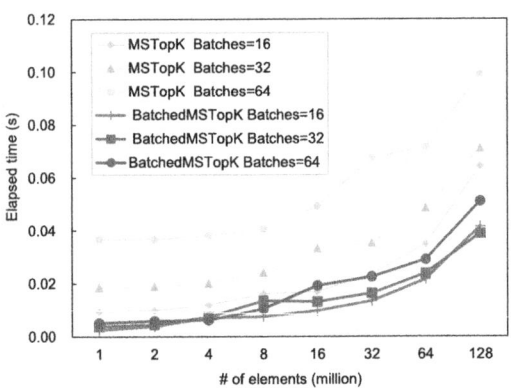

Fig. 5. Time performance of MSTopK and BatchedMSTopK. For each experiment, we run 5 warmup iterations and 100 iterations to measure the average elapsed time.

---

[1] Due to the overlap between computations and communications, we exclude the hidden time.

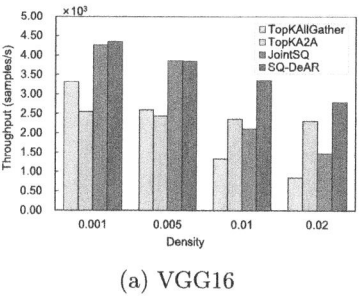
(a) VGG16

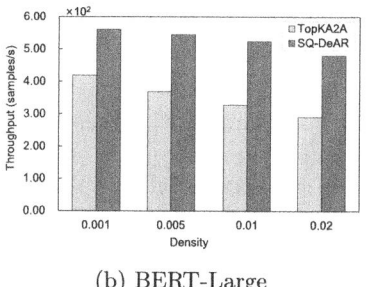
(b) BERT-Large

Fig. 6. Effect of different densities on a 32-GPU cluster. TopKAllGather and JointSQ run OOM in BERT-Large.

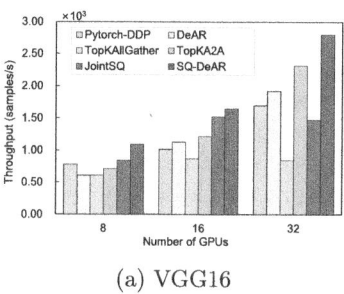
(a) VGG16

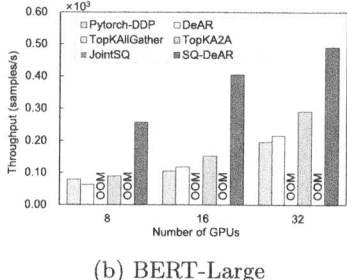
(b) BERT-Large

Fig. 7. Effect of varying # of GPUs. TopKAllGather and JointSQ runs OOM in some cases.

4.5 Studies on the Compression Ratio and # of GPUs

Effects of Compression Ratio. The experimental results reveal notable performance differences among TopKAllGather, TopKA2A, and SQ-DeAR under varying compression ratios ρ. As shown in Fig. 6, SQ-DeAR achieves $1.28\times$–$1.71\times$ higher throughput than TopKAllGather on both models at $\rho = 0.001$, highlighting improved compression efficiency via BatchedMSTopK optimizations. On the BERT-Large model, SQ-DeAR reaches 561.6 tokens/s at $\rho = 0.001$, outperforming TopKA2A's 419.59 tokens/s. At higher density, e.g., $\rho = 0.02$, SQ-DeAR remains superior (481.2 tokens/s vs. 290.7 tokens/s on BERT-Large), demonstrating its effectiveness with low-bit compression.

Effects of # of GPUs. We evaluate the impacts of the number of GPUs with 8, 16, and 32 GPUs and the results are shown in Fig. 7. The scalability evaluation across 8 to 32 GPUs highlights the robust performance of SQ-DeAR in distributed training. Specifically, SQ-DeAR achieves up to 235% improvement on training throughput over existing algorithms. Notably, TopKAllGather and JointSQ fail to complete training on BERT-Large due to out-of-memory (OOM) errors, while our SQ-DeAR maintains stable execution.

5 Related Work

Numerous studies have been proposed to try to address the issue of gradient communication in distributed learning frameworks. A detailed overview is available in the latest survey paper [33]. We mainly introduce some very related research. First, in system-level optimization, effective architectures for AllReduce communication have been developed with varying configurations [28], aiming at enhancing large-scale distributed deep learning via programmable switches. Nonetheless, these architectures necessitate specific hardware, posing challenges for integration across various distributed training scenarios. Second, in algorithm and system co-design perspective, ZeRO++ [27] seeks to improve training efficacy by adopting AlltoAll collective communication for quantized gradients, rather than utilizing AllGather or ReduceScatter in gradient quantization. Despite this, the compression efficacy of ZeRO++ may not match sparsification techniques due to the inherent limitations of quantization. Techniques such as OMGS-SGD [20] and Cupcake [29] attempt to fuse different layers through nearly optimal scheduling of sparsified gradient communication and computation. However, these approaches heavily depend on the performance predictions of computation and communication, which might be inaccurate in practical applications, thereby affecting solution quality. More recently, the gradient sparsification approach has been well optimized through AlltoAll in TopKA2A [13] compared to traditional sparsified communication, but the performance TopKA2A is still limited by the dense communication in AllGather during the feed-forward computation.

6 Conclusion

In this study, we introduce an innovative algorithm, SQ-DeAR, which encompasses a sparsified and quantized gradient compression alongside a decoupled AllReduce, aimed at accelerating the distributed training of deep neural networks (DNNs). During the backpropagation phase, gradients are sparsified and communicated through an AlltoAll communication mechanism, enabling overlap with gradient computation. Conversely, during the feed-forward phase, gradients that have been aggregated via AlltoAll are quantized into low-bit precision values and subsequently aggregated using an AllGather operation, which can concurrently process feed-forward computations. To further enhance the gradient sparsification performance within SQ-DeAR, we developed a batched approximate top-k operator, termed BatchedMSTopK, which selects the top-k elements from multiple data chunks utilizing a single GPU kernel. Comprehensive experiments were executed to evaluate the convergence and time performance of SQ-DeAR on a 32-GPU cluster employing various widely-used DNN architectures. The experimental findings reveal that SQ-DeAR performs $1.17\times-7.0\times$ times faster compared to contemporary leading methods such as PyTorch-DDP, DeAR, TopKAllGather, TopKA2A, and JointSQ.

Acknowledgments. The research was supported in part by the National Natural Science Foundation of China (NSFC) under Grant No. 62302123 and Shenzhen Science and Technology Program under Grant No. KJZD20240903104103005, Grant No. KJZD20230923114213027 and Grant No. KJZD20230923115113026.

Disclosure of Interest. The authors have no competing interests to declear that are relevant to the content of this article.

References

1. Alistarh, D., Grubic, D., Li, J., Tomioka, R., Vojnovic, M.: QSGD: communication-efficient SGD via gradient quantization and encoding. In: NeurIPS, vol. 30 (2017)
2. Dean, J., et al.: Large scale distributed deep networks. In: NIPS, pp. 1223–1231 (2012)
3. Deng, J., Dong, W., Socher, R., Li, L.J., Li, K., Fei-Fei, L.: ImageNet: a large-scale hierarchical image database. In: CVPR, pp. 248–255. IEEE (2009)
4. Goyal, P., et al.: Accurate, large minibatch SGD: training ImageNet in 1 hour. arXiv:1706.02677 (2017)
5. Hockney, R.W.: The communication challenge for MPP: intel paragon and MEIKO CS-2. Parallel Comput. **20**(3), 389–398 (1994)
6. Karpathy, A.: Char-RNN (2015). https://github.com/karpathy/char-rnn
7. Kenton, J.D.M.W.C., Toutanova, L.K.: BERT: pre-training of deep bidirectional transformers for language understanding. In: NAACL-HLT, vol. 1, pp. 4171–4186 (2019)
8. Li, S., et al.: PyTorch distributed: experiences on accelerating data parallel training. arXiv preprint arXiv:2006.15704 (2020)
9. Li, S., Hoefler, T.: Near-optimal sparse allreduce for distributed deep learning. In: PPoPP, pp. 135–149 (2022)
10. Lin, Y., Han, S., Mao, H., Wang, Y., Dally, W.J.: Deep gradient compression: reducing the communication bandwidth for distributed training. In: ICLR (2018)
11. von Luxburg, U., Bengio, S., Wallach, H., Fergus, R., Vishwanathan, S., Garnett, R.: https://github.com/baidu-research/baidu-allreduce
12. Peng, H., et al.: FP8-LM: training FP8 large language models. arXiv preprint arXiv:2310.18313 (2023)
13. Peng, J., Li, Z., Shi, S., Li, B.: Sparse gradient communication with AlltoAll for accelerating distributed deep learning. In: ICPP, pp. 148–157 (2024)
14. Peng, Y., Zhu, Y., Chen, Y., Bao, Y., Yi, B., Lan, C., Wu, C., Guo, C.: A generic communication scheduler for distributed DNN training acceleration. In: SOSP, pp. 16–29 (2019)
15. Radford, A., Wu, J., Child, R., Luan, D., Amodei, D., Sutskever, I., et al.: Language models are unsupervised multitask learners. OpenAI blog **1**(8), 9 (2019)
16. Renggli, C., Ashkboos, S., Aghagolzadeh, M., Alistarh, D., Hoefler, T.: SparCML: high-performance sparse communication for machine learning. In: SC, pp. 1–15 (2019)
17. Seide, F., Fu, H., Droppo, J., Li, G., Yu, D.: 1-bit stochastic gradient descent and its application to data-parallel distributed training of speech DNNS. In: INTERSPEECH, pp. 1058–1602 (2014)
18. Shi, S., Chu, X., Li, B.: MG-WFBP: Efficient data communication for distributed synchronous SGD algorithms. In: INFOCOM, pp. 172–180. IEEE (2019)

19. Shi, S., Chu, X., Li, B.: Exploiting simultaneous communications to accelerate data parallel distributed deep learning. In: INFOCOM, pp. 1–10. IEEE (2021)
20. Shi, S., et al.: Communication-efficient distributed deep learning with merged gradient sparsification on GPUS. In: INFOCOM, pp. 406–415. IEEE (2020)
21. Shi, S., et al.: A distributed synchronous SGD algorithm with global top-k sparsification for low bandwidth networks. In: ICDCS, pp. 2238–2247 (2019)
22. Shi, S., et al.: Towards scalable distributed training of deep learning on public cloud clusters. In: MLSys, vol. 3, pp. 401–412 (2021)
23. Simonyan, K., Zisserman, A.: Very deep convolutional networks for large-scale image recognition. arXiv preprint arXiv:1409.1556 (2014)
24. Tang, Z., Shi, S., Wang, W., Li, B., Chu, X.: Communication-efficient distributed deep learning: a comprehensive survey. arXiv preprint arXiv:2003.06307 (2020)
25. Vogels, T., Karimireddy, S.P., Jaggi, M.: Poseidon: an efficient communication architecture for distributed deep learning on GPU clusters. In: ATC, pp. 181–193 (2017)
26. Vogels, T., Karimireddy, S.P., Jaggi, M.: PowerSGD: practical low-rank gradient compression for distributed optimization. In: NeurIPS, pp. 14269–14278 (2019)
27. Wang, G., et al.: Zero++: Extremely efficient collective communication for giant model training. ICLR (2024)
28. Wang, R., Dong, D., Lei, F., Ma, J., Wu, K., Lu, K.: Roar: a router microarchitecture for in-network allreduce. ICS (2023)
29. Wang, Z., Wu, X., Xu, Z., Ng, T.: Cupcake: a compression scheduler for scalable communication-efficient distributed training. MLSys **5**, 373–386 (2023)
30. Xie, W., et al.: JointSQ: joint sparsification-quantization for distributed learning. In: CVPR, pp. 5778–5787 (2024)
31. Xu, H., et al.: Grace: a compressed communication framework for distributed machine learning. In: ICDCS, pp. 561–572 (2021)
32. Yan, G., Li, T., Huang, S.L., Lan, T., Song, L.: AC-SGD: adaptively compressed SGD for communication-efficient distributed learning. IEEE J. Sel. Areas Commun. **40**(9), 2678–2693 (2022)
33. Yu, E., Dong, D., Liao, X.: Communication optimization algorithms for distributed deep learning systems: a survey. IEEE Trans. Parallel Distrib. Syst. **34**(12), 3294–3308 (2023)
34. Zhang, L., Shi, S., Chu, X., Wang, W., Li, B., Liu, C.: Dear: accelerating distributed deep learning with fine-grained all-reduce pipelining. In: ICDCS, pp. 142–153. IEEE (2023)
35. Zhang, L., Zhang, L., Shi, S., Chu, X., Li, B.: Evaluation and optimization of gradient compression for distributed deep learning. In: ICDCS, pp. 361–371. IEEE (2023)

SWBWA: A Highly Efficient NGS Aligner on the New Sunway Architecture

Lifeng Yan[1], Zekun Yin[1(✉)], Qixin Chang[1], Tong Zhang[1], Zhisong Wang[1], Xiaohui Duan[1], Bertil Schmidt[2], and Weiguo Liu[1(✉)]

[1] School of Software, Shandong University, Jinan, China
{lifeng.yan,cqx,tong.z,wzssdu}@mail.sdu.edu.cn,
{zekun.yin,sunrise.duan,weiguo.liu}@sdu.edu.cn
[2] Institute for Computer Science, Johannes Gutenberg University, Mainz, Germany
bertil.schmidt@uni-mainz.de

Abstract. Sequence alignment is a crucial step in next-generation sequencing data analysis. However, most sequence aligners face performance challenges due to high computational complexity and extensive random memory access patterns, making them a significant bottleneck in the overall analysis pipeline, such as the industry gold standard BWA-MEM. The next-generation Sunway platform, with its high computational power and unique heterogeneous architecture, presents new opportunities for enhancing the efficiency of sequence alignment. In this work, we introduce SWBWA, a high-accuracy and high-performance sequence aligner designed for the new Sunway architecture. By redesigning the parallel framework tailored for Sunway, performing software prefetching optimization, vectorizing the striped Smith-Waterman algorithm, and addressing memory access bottlenecks in bigshare mode, SWBWA achieves a 330× speedup over the single-threaded unoptimized version. Additionally, SWBWA running on a Sunway workstation can achieve 1.2–1.4× speedups compared to BWA-MEM running on a dual-socket 48-core x86 server, while ensuring nearly identical output. The source code is publicly available at https://github.com/RabbitBio/SWBWA.

Keywords: Sequencing read alignment · Bioinformatics · HPC · Sunway architecture

1 Introduction

1.1 Architecture of the New Sunway Platform

The SW26010-Pro, which is the processor of the new Sunway platform, features six Core Groups (CGs), each with a Management Processing Element (MPE) and 64 Compute Processing Elements (CPEs), providing strong support for complex parallel workloads [20]. The Sunway memory hierarchy consists of three segments: *shared*, *private*, and *cross*. The shared segment provides a common memory space within a CG, accessible by both the MPE and CPEs. The private segment is exclusive to each CPE, ensuring localized memory access. The cross segment enables interleaved addressing across all six CGs, allowing synchronized memory access among them. Additionally, each CPE is equipped with 256KB of high-speed Local Data Memory (LDM), which can be manually managed by the user or partially configured as hardware-controlled cache to optimize computational efficiency. Typically, each CG runs a separate process bound to its MPE, with inter-process communication handled via the Message Passing Interface (MPI). Alternatively, we can also employ the bigshare mode, launching a single process only on the MPE of CG0 to manage all 384 CPEs on the chip, eliminating the need for MPI within a single node or workstation.

The SW26010-Pro processor is initially designed for the Sunway supercomputing platform. In recent years, small workstations equipped with a single SW26010-Pro have emerged, facilitating the use of the Sunway architecture beyond large-scale supercomputers. By combining Sunway workstations with bigshare mode, multi-process configurations are no longer needed, simplifying the adaptation and deployment of software originally developed for single-node x86 platforms. This approach promotes the wider adoption of the Sunway platform and contributes to the development of its software ecosystem, enabling more accessible and versatile applications beyond supercomputing environments.

1.2 Sequencing Read Alignment

Recent years have seen a tremendous increase in the volume of data generated in the life sciences, especially propelled by the rapid progress of next-generation sequencing (NGS) technologies with corresponding high-throughput technologies producing hundreds of millions of short DNA fragments (called reads) in a single run. Alignment of sequencing reads to a given reference genome (also called read mapping) is a computationally intensive step within common NGS data analysis pipelines, posing significant challenges in terms of memory consumption and computational burden when processing large-scale datasets [14]. It plays a crucial role in identifying genomic variations, reconstructing genomes, analyzing evolutionary relationships, personalized medicine, and metagenomics [6]. Currently, most alignment tools employ a seed-and-extend strategy to balance efficiency and accuracy. In this approach, the seeding phase rapidly identifies candidate alignment locations by matching short sequence fragments (seeds) typically consisting of k-mers (short DNA substrings of length k), while the extension phase performs a more precise alignment to validate these candidates and compute full alignment scores.

Minimizers [10], as employed in Minimap2 [8], select the smallest hash value within a sliding window to identify seeds in order to reduce storage and computational overhead, thereby improving alignment efficiency. Mashmap [5] combines Minimizers and MinHash to propose a new method for computing Jaccard similarity, further reducing the number of k-mers to enhance efficiency. Strobealign [13] incorporates strobemers [12] and syncmers [3], which construct seeds from multiple spaced k-mers, enhancing robustness in sequence matching. Furthermore, to optimize the extension phase, particularly the computationally expensive Smith-Waterman algorithm [16], various acceleration techniques have been developed, including SIMD vectorization [1] and Hardware-based solutions such as FPGA [11] and GPU [9,15] accelerators, significantly improving computational efficiency.

The powerful computational capabilities of the Sunway platform provide a strong foundation for addressing alignment performance bottlenecks. On Sunway TaihuLight [4], which is based on the previous-generation SW26010 processor, several alignment tools such as S-Aligner [2] and FMapper [18] have been successfully deployed. These tools adopt an "all-mode" alignment strategy, which reports all possible mapping locations that satisfy a given constraint, such as an edit distance threshold. While computationally intensive, this approach aligns well with the architecture of the SW26010 processor. However, due to limitations in main memory, LDM, and cache size, the SW26010 processor struggled to efficiently deploy software based on any-best mode algorithms, such as the industry-standard BWA-MEM [7], which selects only the best or a few top-scoring alignments for each sequencing read to reduce computational overhead. With the architectural advancements of the SW26010-Pro processor, including automatic data caching and increased main memory capacity, the efficient deployment of BWA-MEM on the new Sunway platform has now become feasible.

1.3 Contributions

In this work, we port and optimize BWA-MEM on the new Sunway platform, leveraging several optimization strategies to fully exploit the heterogeneous many-core architecture. Our key contributions include:

- Design of a parallel framework and memory management strategy to maximize the utilization of all CPEs and LDM, achieving a 17× speedup compared to the single-threaded MPE version.
- Optimization of FM-index accesses through software prefetching and redundant computation reduction, combined with the vectorization of the striped Smith-Waterman (SSW) algorithm using Sunway's SIMD instructions, significantly accelerating both the seeding and extension phases.
- Development of an all-CPE-based dynamic task partitioning framework for the bigshare mode to achieve better offloading and enabling overlapping of compute- and memory-intensive tasks, achieving an additional 30% performance improvement.
- Reducing the iCache and CPE private memory access problems in bigshare mode, leading to a 2× performance boost.

Overall, we propose SWBWA, an efficient NGS read alignment tool optimized for the Sunway workstation platform with a single SW26010-Pro processor, fully utilizing all CGs without requiring MPI. Compared to BWA-MEM running on a dual-socket 48-core x86 server, SWBWA achieves an average 1.3× speedup while delivering nearly identical results.

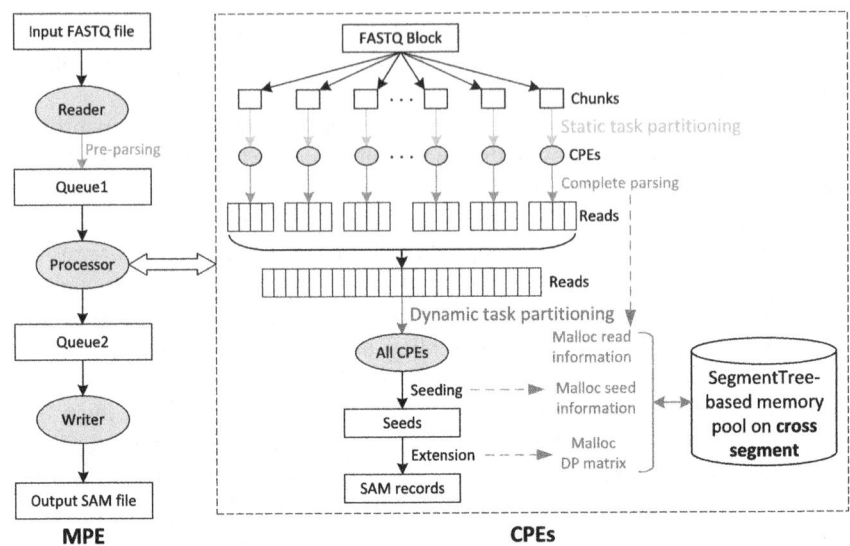

Fig. 1. Workflow of SWBWA. Blue indicates the parsing strategy, yellow and red represent task partitioning strategies, and green shows CPE memory management. (Color figure online)

2 Design of SWBWA

2.1 Parallelization Strategies for the Sunway Architecture

BWA-MEM employs a single-producer, multiple-consumer parallel strategy, where a producer thread parses the raw input file to generate FASTQ records, multiple consumer threads dynamically fetch and process data using an atomic index, and a writer thread outputs data in SAM format. As the number of threads increases, the performance of this strategy is progressively limited by the producer, particularly on the Sunway platform, where the single-core frequency is relatively low. To address this issue, SWBWA adopts the efficient FASTQ parsing method proposed in SWQC [19] for the Sunway platform. The MPE is only responsible for file I/O and simple block partitioning, while the entire parsing task is offloaded to multiple CPEs for parallel execution. We employ a hybrid static-dynamic task allocation strategy to ensure data order while maximizing multi-CPE parallelism. Figure 1 illustrates the workflow and parallelization strategy of SWBWA. The following subsections provides further details including asynchronous I/O and efficient task partitioning.

SWBWA initializes three threads–Reader, Processor, and Writer–on the MPE to handle file reading, CPE launch, and file writing, respectively. These threads exchange data over two shared queues, *Queue*1 and *Queue*2. Additionally, the entire workflow follows a FASTQ block-based streaming approach, allowing memory usage to be controlled by adjusting the block size and queue capacity. When the program starts, the Reader thread continuously reads input data in blocks (default size: 32 MB), performing pre-parsing while ensuring that no FASTQ record spans across two blocks by adjusting the tail pointer (illustrated in blue in Fig. 1). The Processor thread retrieves FASTQ blocks from *Queue*1 and launches multiple CPEs for parallel parsing. In this step, SWBWA applies static task partitioning based on block size, where each CPE handles a designated chunk (default size: $32\,\text{MB}/386 \approx 85\,\text{KB}$) according to its index (illustrated in orange in Fig. 1). Each CPE then fully parses its assigned chunk, formats it into FASTQ records, and merges them into a large array. After formatting, all CPEs utilize a global atomic variable to dynamically fetch FASTQ records from this array, enabling dynamic task allocation (illustrated in red in Fig. 1). Then, each FASTQ record undergoes the seeding and extension phases to generate SAM information. To ensure high accuracy, we directly adopt the corresponding algorithms from BWA-MEM, using the FM-index for seed searching and the SSW algorithm for precise alignment, as detailed in the BWA-MEM paper [7]. Finally, the CPEs organize the SAM records into an ordered data block based on their index and pass it to the Writer thread for file output.

For task partitioning, SWBWA employs a hybrid static-dynamic strategy to ensure both efficiency and sequence order. First, SWBWA applies a static task partitioning strategy based on chunk size and CPE ID during data parsing. This approach is adopted because the complexity of FASTQ parsing is directly proportional to the chunk size, ensuring load balance while avoiding the overhead of maintaining atomic variables. In contrast, the computational complexity of the seeding and extension phases varies significantly across different FASTQ records. For instance, some low-abundance reads may yield zero seeds, while others may generate multiple matching locations (such as those stemming from repetitive genomic regions). Consequently, applying static partitioning would result in severe load imbalance, making dynamic task allocation essential.

Additionally, we enable the bigshare mode on the Sunway workstation, allowing a single process to manage all 384 CPEs. This approach eliminates the need for MPI and avoids synchronization and communication challenges when multiple processes write a single ordered file. However, the native bigshare mode on Sunway encounters certain performance issues, which are particularly pronounced in SWBWA. We provide our optimization details of the bigshare mode in Sect. 2.3.

2.2 Software Prefetching and SIMD Acceleration

Similar to BWA-MEM, in the seeding phase, SWBWA utilizes the FM-index data structure for efficient string matching and subsequent extension, identifying super maximal exact matches (SMEMs) for each read. Identified SMEMs are then processed using a B-tree-based chaining method, generating the final seeds. In this phase, a key performance bottleneck is random accesses to the FM-index. To address this issue, we employ software prefetching strategies. Specifically, during forward extension, match positions computed in one iteration are accessed in the next, enabling effective prefetching. Likewise, it can also be applied to backward extensions by leveraging data dependencies. Additionally, BWA-MEM computes all four possible bases (ACGT) during string extension, but only one is used in the final result, leading to computational redundancy. We optimize the extension process without modifying the index structure, particularly in forward extension, where the computation is reduced to one-fourth of the original amount.

In the extension phase, SWBWA employs the SSW algorithm to accurately extend the seeds, generate CIGAR information, and then produce output in SAM format. Vectorized implementations of the SSW algorithm are a common and effective method for accelerating pairwise alignment computations based on dynamic programming [1]. During the implementation of a SIMD-optimized algorithm on Sunway CPEs, we encounter several challenges. The first challenge is the absence of a critical "compare-select" instruction in the CPE's fixed-point instruction set. To overcome this, we emulate this operation using a combination of comparison, logical operations, and addition instructions. The second challenge is that CPEs only support int32-granularity instructions, lacking native support for int16 and int8 operations. To address this, we convert int8/int16 data into fp16 for computation, doubling the utilization of vector registers. We manually implement non-overflowing addition and subtraction within the 0–255/65535 range to compensate for the lack of native int8/int16 support. Additionally, we store both the dynamic programming matrix and the scoring matrix of the SSW process in the CPE's high-speed LDM, significantly reducing memory access times.

With these optimizations, we mitigate random memory access delays in the seeding phase and accelerate SSW computation for the extension phase. However, fundamental bottlenecks remain unchanged: seeding is still memory-bound, while extension remains compute-bound. In BWA-MEM's block-based processing, all threads first complete seeding, synchronize with a barrier, and then proceed with extensions. Evidently, this leads to underutilized compute resources in the first phase and inefficient memory bandwidth usage in the second. SWBWA eliminates this barrier, allowing both phases to overlap, maximizing hardware resource utilization.

2.3 Optimizing Sunway Bigshare Mode

We avoid using MPI in single-node environments by adopting the bigshare mode. In this mode, the process is bound to CG0, with all code segments and program memory allocated in the main memory of CG0 (Fig. 2). However, this setup introduces performance issues related to iCache misses and CPE private space accesses. The following subsections discuss these challenges and present corresponding solutions.

Mitigating iCache Contention. The SW26010-Pro processor lacks an L2 iCache and is equipped only with a 32KB L1 iCache; thus, once an iCache miss occurs, instructions can only be fetched from main memory. In bigshare mode, processes are bound to CG0, and all CPEs across the six CGs share a single code

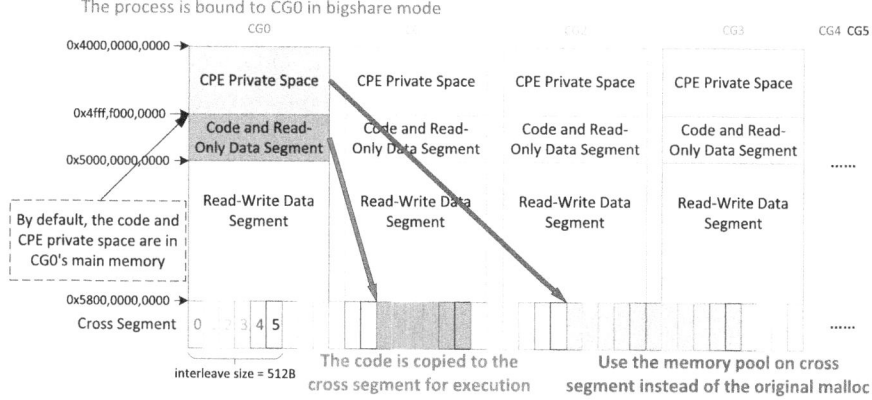

Fig. 2. Addressing performance bottlenecks in bigshare mode.

segment stored in CG0's main memory. This arrangement means that whenever an iCache miss occurs, all CPEs must compete for CG0's memory bandwidth, while the memory resources of the other five CGs remain underutilized, drastically reducing instruction fetch efficiency. To verify this, we have conducted a performance evaluation of iCache behavior using a straightforwardly parallelized version of SWBWA (see Table 1). The results show that when running on a single CG, due to extensive macro expansion and redundant instruction duplication, iCache miss overhead accounts for 16% of the total execution time. In bigshare mode, this issue is further exacerbated, with overall iCache miss overhead increasing to 31%, and some functions such as bwa_gen_cigar2 reaching as high as 85%. As a result, the bigshare mode version (6 CGs) achieves only a 2× speedup compared to the single CG version.

Figure 2 illustrates the memory space organization of the Sunway platform. The address range from 0x4000,0000,0000 to 0x5800,0000,0000 corresponds to the private space within each CG, which is not shared across CGs. This region includes the CPE private space, code segment, and data segment of each CG. Beyond 0x5800,0000,0000 is the cross segment, which employs an interleaved addressing scheme (interleave size is 512B) across six CGs and is shared among CGs. More formally, the range [0B, 512B) in the cross segment is physically mapped to CG0, [512B, 1024B) to CG1, [1024B, 1536B) to CG2, and so on, as illustrated in Fig. 2. Therefore, utilizing the cross segment can effectively alleviate memory access imbalance among CGs.

To address the iCache performance issues under the bigshare mode, SWBWA proposes a cross segment instruction loading strategy: copying the code segment from the main memory of CG0 to the cross segment for execution, as illustrated in green in Fig. 2. Specifically, at the beginning of the program, SWBWA first retrieves the starting address of the code segment (typically beginning with 0x4FFF, denoted as oldTextSegAddr) along with its size. It then allocates an equivalent memory space (beginning with 0x5800, denoted as newTextSegAddr)

Table 1. iCache performance evaluation.

Function	Single CG			Bigshare Mode (6 CGs)		
	Total[a]	iCache[b]	Ratio(%)	Total	iCache	Ratio(%)
run_alignment	936.9G	150.0G	16.01	492.6G	152.6G	30.98
seeding	689.1G	118.1G	17.14	391.8G	94.4G	24.09
collect_intv	284.5G	17.8G	6.26	159.0G	47.8G	30.06
btree_chain	188.8G	16.3G	8.63	116.4G	14.2G	12.20
mem_chain2aln	144.9G	59.4G	40.99	63.4G	11.8G	18.61
mem_sort_dedup	12.4G	4.9G	39.52	4.1G	2.3G	56.10
extension	247.7G	31.3G	12.64	129.3G	73.7G	57.00
mem_matesw2	196.8G	7.5G	3.81	71.1G	11.6G	16.32
mem_sort	34.1G	2.7G	7.92	15.5G	2.3G	14.84
bwa_gen_cigar2	15.4G	3.7G	24.03	12.9G	11.0G	85.27

[a] Total execution cycles counted using penv_slave0_cycle_count
[b] iCache miss penalty cycles counted using penv_slave2_l1ic_misstime_count

in the cross segment and manually assigns executable permissions. Subsequently, we copy the code to the cross segment and start the CPE by redirecting its program counter (PC) to the new CPE function address. Since this strategy changes the storage location of the code and the CPE startup mechanism, the following issues need to be addressed:

1. Some native CPE APIs (such as spawning and joining operations) may become invalid. To address this issue, we reimplement the CPE startup and shutdown functions using __uncached atomic variables, ensuring that the MPE and CPE can perform task scheduling and synchronization properly.
2. Although the CPE code is copied to the cross segment for execution, the function jump addresses in the original global offset table (GOT) still point to the old segment, causing function call failures due to excessive jump offsets. To resolve this, we first extract the instructions requiring relocation and the corresponding GOT items (denoted as badGotItems) from the relocation section (.rela.text1). We then copy a new GOT to the cross segment and update badGotItems by applying an offset (segOffset = newTextSegAddr - oldTextSegAddr) to redirect them to the new code segment. Additionally, the global pointer (GP) must also be adjusted by segOffset to ensure the correct resolution of all global variables and function jump addresses.
3. On the Sunway platform, to enhance performance and avoid thread synchronization overhead, the heap used by the CPE malloc operation and the I/O buffer for fprintf are typically private and stored in the CPE's thread local storage (TLS). However, instructions and function jumps involving TLS are generally addressed through control and status register (CSR) rather than GP, making the above strategy ineffective. To address this, we copy the relevant CPE private spaces to the cross segment and update the respective CSR

to point to the new space. Additionally, we update the corresponding code sections using relocation information from the .rela.slave_tls section.

In summary, by adopting the cross segment instruction loading strategy, SWBWA effectively mitigates iCache contention and reduces the performance loss caused by iCache misses under the bigshare mode. It is important to note that this strategy does not reduce the number of CPE iCache misses but instead balances instruction access requests across all CGs, thereby reducing the cost of each iCache miss and improving performance.

Efficient CPE Memory Access. Similar to the code segment, in bigshare mode, all program memory is allocated in the main memory of CG0, including the reference genome (allocated via the MPE malloc interface) and the intermediate results of the CPEs (allocated via the CPE malloc interface). The random access to the reference genome occurs during the seeding phase and represents the largest performance bottleneck in the entire program. Additionally, SWBWA involves numerous memory allocation requests by CPEs (as shown in green in Fig. 1), most of which are of unknown size and cannot be preallocated by the MPE in advance. The operations on these CPE-allocated memory span the entire alignment process and significantly impact CPE performance. As a result, we face a challenge similar to the previous iCache issue, with memory accesses concentrated in CG0, wasting bandwidth in other CGs. Therefore, redirecting CPE malloc-allocated addresses from private space to the cross segment is essential. To verify this, we compare the read/write performance on these two types of spaces (as shown in Fig. 3). The results indicate that when randomly reading/writing a memory space exceeding 128KB (the data cache size), the cross segment achieves around a 1.6× speedup compared to the CPE private space. When the accessed memory is within the cache size, the cross segment is still faster.

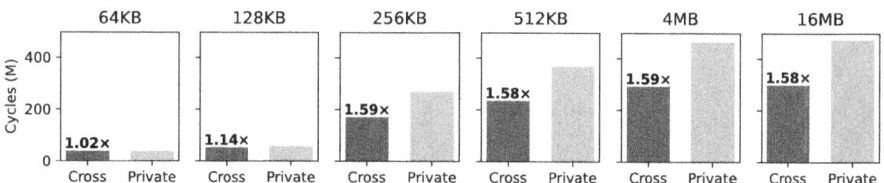

Fig. 3. Performance comparison for accessing different memory types in bigshare mode.

The Sunway platform provides the _sw_xmalloc interface for MPE, enabling direct allocation in the cross segment. By simply passing the -xmalloc parameter to the loader, all MPE malloc calls are automatically replaced with _sw_xmalloc in bigshare mode. Therefore, efficient access to the reference genome is not a major challenge. However, the CPE lacks APIs for allocating cross segment space directly, requiring manual memory management to handle operations in the cross segment. SWBWA implements a memory pool using the cross segment, redirecting CPE malloc-allocated space to the cross segment (as shown in the purple in Fig. 2). To efficiently manage the memory pool while minimizing source code modifications, we redesign the `malloc`, `realloc`, and `free` functions using a non-recursive segment tree. Initially, the MPE preallocates a large block from cross segment (with an average of 8MB per CPE) as the memory pool, which consists of elements with only power-of-two sizes. Accordingly, when a CPE calls `malloc`, the requested size is rounded up to the nearest power-of-two before accessing the memory pool. Then, SWBWA efficiently locates the first available space in the segment tree corresponding to the adjusted size, returns the address, and updates the tree. Similarly, during `free`, it identifies the corresponding segment tree based on the address and updates it accordingly. In this way, the CPE private space, originally allocated by `malloc` and bound to CG0, is redirected to the cross segment, significantly improving memory access efficiency under bigshare mode.

3 Performance Evaluation

We first analyze the performance of different versions of SWBWA, demonstrating the improvements achieved by our proposed optimization techniques. We then compare the performance of SWBWA on the Sunway workstation with the latest version of BWA-MEM (v0.7.18) on a 48-core x86 server using various types of datasets. The Sunway workstation is equipped with a single SW26010-Pro processor, 96 GB of RAM, and runs UnionTech OS with SWGCC 7.1.0 as the compiler. The x86 Intel server features two Intel Platinum 8260 processors, 256 GB of RAM, and operates on Rocky Linux with GCC 9.4.0 for compilation. Both platforms are equipped with high-speed SSDs to reduce the impact of I/O speed on software performance. Table 2 presents the datasets used in the tests, covering different file sizes, sequence lengths, and sequencing technologies, all of which are freely available on the NCBI website.

Table 2. Dataset information.

NCBI Accession	#Reads	Read Length	Sequencing Technology	File Size
SRR2496709[a]	12,607,411	100bp	DNA targeted sequencing	6.6 GB
SRR12131337[b]	20,502,735	141bp	RNA sequencing	16.2 GB
SRR7963242[c]	387,488,829	150bp	Whole genome sequencing	280.0 GB

[a] https://www.ncbi.nlm.nih.gov/sra/?term=SRR2496709
[b] https://www.ncbi.nlm.nih.gov/sra/?term=SRR12131337
[c] https://www.ncbi.nlm.nih.gov/sra/?term=SRR7963242

3.1 Performance Comparison of Different SWBWA Versions

Figure 4 shows the performance of SWBWA across different optimization stages using the SRR2496709 dataset on the Sunway workstation. The single-threaded MPE version takes 25,145 s to complete (2,921 s for the seeding phase and 22,224 s for the extension phase); however, for better readability, this result is not shown in the figure. In Fig. 4, the red line represents the speedup of each optimized version compared to the MPE version, while the bar chart compares the execution times and highlights the speedup achieved by each version over its predecessor. Starting from the "remove barrier" version, the seeding and extension phases are merged, making it impossible to measure their execution time separately; therefore, only the earlier versions display individual timings for these two phases. Additionally, the file I/O time is not shown in the figure because it is executed asynchronously with computation, and the test platform is equipped with high-speed SSDs, which completely hides the I/O overhead. Overall, compared to the MPE version, the optimized SWBWA achieves a 330× speedup, fully leveraging the computational power of the multi-CPE architecture and the high-speed LDM resources of the Sunway platform.

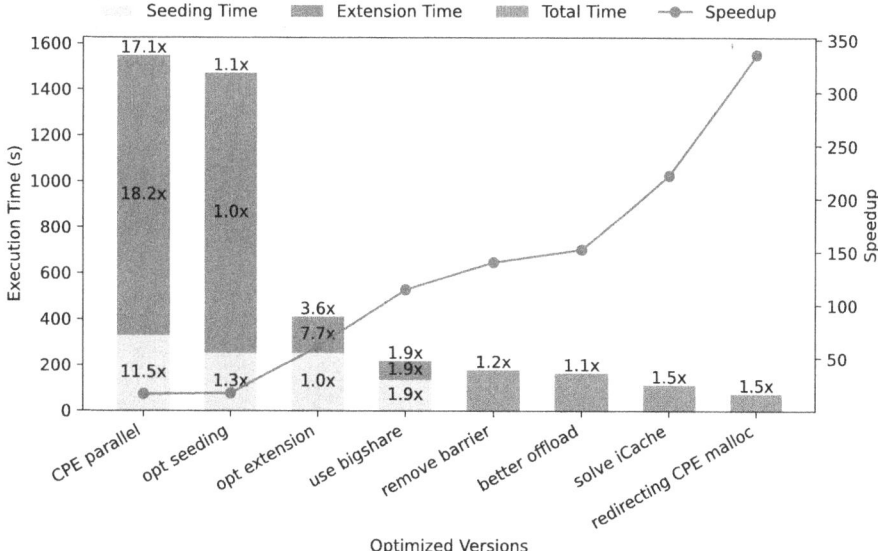

Fig. 4. Comparison of different SWBWA versions. The red line indicates the speedup over the MPE version, and the numbers on the bars show the speedup over the preceding version. (Color figure online)

From Fig. 4, we can observe that the "CPE parallel" version, which utilizes 64 CPEs for parallel acceleration, achieves less than a 20× speedup. This limited parallel efficiency is mainly due to the random memory accesses to the FM-index and the frequently used SSW computation matrix, both stored in main memory. On Sunway platform, the bandwidth for CPEs directly accessing main memory is highly limited, which restricts scalability across multiple CPEs. Therefore, in subsequent versions, we optimize random memory accesses and maximize the utilization of LDM wherever possible. The "opt seeding" version improves FM-index access by employing software prefetching and reducing redundant memory accesses, achieving a 30% performance improvement. The "opt extension" version optimizes LDM utilization and incorporates CPE vectorization for the SSW algorithm, achieving a significant 7.7× speedup. The "use bigshare" version utilizes all six CGs but achieves only around a 2× speedup compared to the previous version. This is mainly due to the amplification of load imbalance when scaling from 64 CPEs to 384 CPEs in bigshare mode, as well as performance constraints related to CPE iCache misses and private memory access (discussed in detail in Sect. 2.3). The following four versions progressively address these issues, reducing the average iCache miss time to around 8%, and ultimately achieving a 5.7× speedup in bigshare mode compared to the single-CG version.

Table 3. Runtime comparison of SWBWA and BWA-MEM on different datasets.

Dataset	Software	Runtime (s)	Speedup	Memory Usage (GB)
SRR2496709	SWBWA	74.83	1.23x	11.24
	BWA-MEM	92.41	-	10.78
SRR12131337	SWBWA	150.49	1.43x	10.80
	BWA-MEM	214.47	-	10.41
SRR7963242	SWBWA	7353.42	1.24x	14.01
	BWA-MEM	9125.60	-	13.89

3.2 Comparison with X86 Platform

We compare the performance of SWBWA with BWA-MEM, the industry gold standard for NGS alignment on an x86 platform, which is widely validated and serves as a reliable benchmark. Our evaluation focuses solely on speed rather than accuracy since SWBWA produces nearly identical results to BWA-MEM. The minor differences arise from the statistical inference of insert size distribution in interleaved alignment regions, which can vary with different block sizes. Even BWA-MEM itself yields slightly different results depending on block size settings. When using the same block size or processing single-end data that does not involve insert size distribution inference, SWBWA generates output identical to BWA-MEM. Additionally, several optimized versions of BWA-MEM exist on the x86 platform, such as BWA-MEM2 [17], which improves performance by adjusting FM-index compression levels. However, BWA-MEM2 has significantly higher memory requirements as it relies on an alternative indexing strategy and requires rebuilding the index which would exceed the main memory capacity of the Sunway architecture. In contrast, SWBWA can directly use the index built by BWA-MEM while maintaining nearly the same memory footprint (see Table 3).

Table 3 presents the performance comparison between SWBWA and BWA-MEM. SWBWA runs on the Sunway workstation, while BWA-MEM runs on a 48-core x86 server. The results demonstrate that SWBWA achieves a notable speedup across various types of sequencing data, with an average speedup of 1.3×.

4 Conclusion

In this paper, we propose SWBWA, the first efficient implementation of BWA-MEM on the Sunway platform. By fully adapting it to the Sunway architecture and leveraging multi-CPE parallelism, LDM, and vector instructions, SWBWA achieves over 300× speedup compared to the unoptimized MPE version and delivers consistent performance improvements over BWA-MEM on an x86 platform. SWBWA further enriches the software ecosystem for sequencing data analysis on the Sunway platform, representing a key milestone in our comprehensive NGS pipeline deployment plan. Furthermore, by addressing two major performance bottlenecks in bigshare mode, we establish an efficient, MPI-free software migration approach on Sunway workstations. This enables porting of software originally designed for single-node x86 environments without requiring MPI adaptations, thereby also contributing to the development of the Sunway software ecosystem. Source code is written in C++ and publicly available at https://github.com/RabbitBio/SWBWA.

For future work, we plan to extend SWBWA to a multi-node version to fully exploit the computational resources of the Sunway supercomputing platform for large-scale biological data analysis. Additionally, we plan to encapsulate our optimizations for bigshare mode into a library or loader, enabling performance improvements without modifying program source code.

Acknowledgments. This work is partially supported by NSFC Grants 62102231; Shandong Provincial Natural Science Foundation (ZR2021QF089); Engineering Research Center of Digital Media Technology, Ministry of Education, China; DFG RMaP project C01.

Disclosure of Interests. The authors have no competing interests to declare that are relevant to the content of this article.

References

1. Daily, J.: Parasail: SIMD C library for global, semi-global, and local pairwise sequence alignments. BMC Bioinform. **17**, 1–11 (2016)

2. Duan, X., et al.: S-aligner: Ultrascalable read mapping on Sunway Taihu light. In: 2017 IEEE International Conference on Cluster Computing (CLUSTER), pp. 36–46. IEEE (2017)
3. Edgar, R.: Syncmers are more sensitive than minimizers for selecting conserved k-mers in biological sequences. PeerJ **9**, e10805 (2021)
4. Fu, H., Liao, J., Yang, J.o.: The Sunway Taihulight supercomputer: system and applications. Sci. China Inf. Sci. **59**, 1–16 (2016)
5. Jain, C., Dilthey, A., Koren, S., Aluru, S., Phillippy, A.M.: A fast approximate algorithm for mapping long reads to large reference databases. J. Comput. Biol. **25**(7), 766–779 (2018)
6. Kosugi, S., Momozawa, Y., Liu, X., Terao, C., Kubo, M., Kamatani, Y.: Comprehensive evaluation of structural variation detection algorithms for whole genome sequencing. Genome Biol. **20**, 1–18 (2019)
7. Li, H.: Aligning sequence reads, clone sequences and assembly contigs with BWA-MEM. arXiv preprint arXiv:1303.3997 (2013)
8. Li, H.: Minimap2: pairwise alignment for nucleotide sequences. Bioinformatics **34**(18), 3094–3100 (2018)
9. Müller, A., Schmidt, B., Membarth, R., Leißa, R., Hack, S.: ANYSEQ/GPU: a novel approach for faster sequence alignment on GPUS. In: Proceedings of the 36th ACM International Conference on Supercomputing, pp. 1–11 (2022)
10. Roberts, M., Hayes, W., Hunt, B.R., Mount, S.M., Yorke, J.A.: Reducing storage requirements for biological sequence comparison. Bioinformatics **20**(18), 3363–3369 (2004)
11. Rucci, E., Garcia, C., Botella, G., De Giusti, A.E., Naiouf, M., Prieto-Matias, M.: OSWALD: OpenCL smith-waterman on Altera's FPGA for large protein databases. Int. J. High Perform. Comput. Appl. **32**(3), 337–350 (2018)
12. Sahlin, K.: Effective sequence similarity detection with strobemers. Genome Res. **31**(11), 2080–2094 (2021)
13. Sahlin, K.: Strobealign: flexible seed size enables ultra-fast and accurate read alignment. Genome Biol. **23**(1), 260 (2022)
14. Schmidt, B., Hildebrandt, A.: Next-generation sequencing: big data meets high performance computing. Drug Discov. Today **22**(4), 712–717 (2017)
15. Schmidt, B., Kallenborn, F., Chacon, A., Hundt, C.: Cudasw++ 4.0: ultra-fast GPU-based smith–Waterman protein sequence database search. BMC Bioinform. **25**(1), 342 (2024)
16. Smith, T.F., Waterman, M.S., et al.: Identification of common molecular subsequences. J. Mol. Biol. **147**(1), 195–197 (1981)
17. Vasimuddin, M., Misra, S., Li, H., Aluru, S.: Efficient architecture-aware acceleration of bwa-mem for multicore systems. In: 2019 IEEE International Parallel and Distributed Processing Symposium (IPDPS), pp. 314–324. IEEE (2019)
18. Xu, K., Duan, X., Müller, A., Kobus, R., Schmidt, B., Liu, W.: FMapper: scalable read mapper based on succinct hash index on Sunway Taihulight. J. Parallel Distrib. Comput. **161**, 72–82 (2022)
19. Yan, L., et al.: SWQC: efficient sequencing data quality control on the next-generation Sunway platform. Futur. Gener. Comput. Syst. **164**, 107577 (2025)
20. Zhu, Q., Luo, H., Yang, C., Ding, M., Yin, W., Yuan, X.: Enabling and scaling the HPCG benchmark on the newest generation sunway supercomputer with 42 million heterogeneous cores. In: Proceedings of the International Conference for High Performance Computing, Networking, Storage and Analysis, pp. 1–13 (2021)

SimPart: A Simple Yet Effective Replication-Aided Partitioning Algorithm for Logic Simulation on GPU

Yi-Hua Chung[1], Shui Jiang[2], Wan-Luan Lee[1], Yanqing Zhang[3], Haoxing Ren[3], Tsung-Yi Ho[2], and Tsung-Wei Huang[1](✉)

[1] University of Wisconsin-Madison, Madison, WI, USA
{yihua.chung,wanluan.lee,tsung-wei.huang}@wisc.edu
[2] The Chinese University of Hong Kong, Hong Kong, China
{sjiang22,tyho}@cse.cuhk.edu.hk
[3] Nvidia Corporation, Santa Clara, CA, USA
{yanqingz,haoxingr}@nvidia.com

Abstract. Replication-aided partitioning (RAP) has recently been introduced to facilitate the design of parallel logic simulation algorithms. By replicating overlapped work, RAP can significantly reduce the cost of inter-thread synchronization. However, the state-of-the-art RAP algorithm, RepCut, relies on time-consuming hypergraph construction and partitioning, where minimizing cut size corresponds to reducing replication. To overcome this runtime challenge, we introduce *SimPart*, a simple yet highly effective and efficient GPU-parallel replication-aided partitioner. SimPart tackles the partitioning problem directly without solving another proxy problem and proposes a hybrid strategy that can maximally utilize GPU threads for simulation atop our partitions. Compared to RepCut, SimPart achieves an average speedup of 23× in partitioning and 1.58× in GPU-parallel simulation, while increasing the original graph size by only 0.3%.

Keywords: RTL simulation · Graph partitioning · Task graph parallelism

1 Introduction

Graph partitioning is an integral component in the design of parallel logic simulation algorithms [1,9,13,18]. Traditional partitioning algorithms focus on partitioning a circuit graph into a top-down *task dependency graph* (TDG) where each task represents a disjoint partition of work and each edge represents a dependency between two tasks. For instance, in Fig. 1(a), the input graph is partitioned to a TDG of three tasks and two dependencies, where each task encapsulates a disjoint set of work from the original graph (e.g., nodes 1, 2, and 4 in task 1). By delegating TDG scheduling to a task graph runtime, such as [6], we can efficiently parallelize logic simulation algorithms without the need

---

Y.-H. Chung and S. Jiang—Contributed equally to this work.

to manage complex scheduling details. As a result, this type of *disjoint set-based partitioning* (DSP) has been widely used in existing logic simulators, such as Verilator [13], RTLFlow [9], TaroRTL [11], and ESSENT [1].

Although DSP can offer promising speedup through TDG parallelism, it incurs non-negligible scheduling overhead related to task synchronization and load balancing [6]. This overhead is further exacerbated when leveraging GPUs to accelerate logic simulation [18]. Specifically, excessive task dependencies can significantly impact both device-level and streaming multiprocessor (SM)-level scheduling performance, primarily due to load balancing and inter-block synchronization [12]. To address this issue, *replication-aided partitioning* (RAP) has been recently introduced to eliminate task dependencies via *replicating overlaps*. Take Fig. 1(b) for example, instead of partitioning the circuit graph to three non-overlapped tasks, RAP divides the circuit into two totally independent tasks with node 5 replicated in both task 1 and task 2. While replication introduces additional work per task, modern GPUs offer thousands of threads that applications can leverage to exchange replication for performance gains. For instance, by adding one more thread to run node 5, we can replace expensive inter-block synchronization (microseconds) with more efficient intra-block synchronization (tens to hundreds of cycles [9,17]).

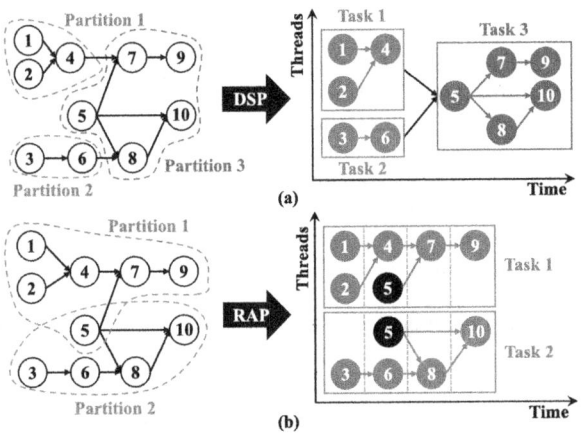

Fig. 1. Two partitioning approaches in parallel logic simulation: (a) disjoint set-based partitioning (b) replication-aided partitioning.

While there is an increasing adoption of RAP by modern logic simulators [2,14,16,18], the process of RAP is time-consuming. As originally introduced in RepCut [15], this process involves first constructing a *proxy hypergraph* from the original graph and then applying a *hypergraph partitioner* to solve this proxy problem, where minimum cut translates to minimum replication under a balance constraint. However, constructing the proxy hypergraph is not cheap since it requires traversing the graph multiple times to identify overlapped cones for hyperedges. For large hypergraphs, even state-of-the-art parallel hypergraph partitioners [4,7] can take several minutes to converge to a reasonable cut size. As a result, this runtime cost makes RepCut challenging to use in a dynamic environment, such as simulation code optimization [9] and hardware fuzzing [10], where the partitioner is iteratively applied to a simulation graph that changes dynamically.

To tackle this problem, we introduce *SimPart*, a GPU-parallel replication-aided partitioner to facilitate the design of parallel logic simulation algorithms. Unlike RepCut, which was originally designed for CPU-parallel logic simulation algorithms, SimPart is specifically designed for GPU-parallel simulation. We summarize our technical contributions below:

- We introduce a simple yet highly effective and efficient algorithm that directly tackles the partitioning problem without solving another time-consuming proxy problem.
- We leverage the property of circuit graphs to propose a DSP-RAP hybrid strategy that effectively constrains the replication region while balancing the parallel efficiency between DSP and RAP.
- We leverage conditional CUDA Graph to design a GPU-parallel simulation framework atop our partition, which can reduce kernel call and control-flow overheads.

We evaluate the performance of SimPart on a set of RTL simulation graphs generated by RTLFlow [9], an open-source RTL simulator we developed with Nvidia Research. Compared to RepCut, SimPart achieves an average of 23× speedup in partitioning and 1.58× speedup in GPU-parallel simulation, while increasing the original graph size by only 0.3%.

2 Background

Logic simulation is essential for verifying design functionality. A circuit is modeled as a directed graph, where nodes represent logic elements (e.g., RTL instructions, gates) and edges capture data dependencies. Simulation evaluates this graph by propagating inputs through logic elements to produce outputs, often iterated over multiple testbenches and configurations for coverage. Large designs can yield graphs with millions of nodes and edges, leading to long simulation times [18].

To mitigate this runtime challenge, existing simulators have introduced various partitioning algorithms to distribute work across CPU or GPU threads. As shown in Table 1, existing partitioning algorithms can be categorized to DSP and RAP, where the former disallows overlapping nodes among tasks while the latter allows them. For instance, Verilator [13] uses a DSP algorithm that iteratively clusters adjacent nodes into macro tasks and formulates dependent macro tasks into a TDG. Parallel execution of a TDG is achieved with a scheduler that manages inter-task dependencies and load balancing across threads. Most DSP-based simulators follow this paradigm but adopt different clustering heuristics [1,9,11,19].

Table 1. Comparison between SimPart and existing parallel logic simulators.

	Verilator [13]	RTLFlow [9]	RepCut [15]	GL0AM [18]	SimPart (**Ours**)
Partitioning algorithm	DSP	DSP	RAP	RAP	**DSP+RAP**
Simulation platform	CPU	GPU	CPU	GPU	**GPU**

On the other hand, RAP focuses on replicating a small portion of the graph to break task dependencies for reduced inter-thread synchronization. Although initially introduced by RepCut [15] for implementing a CPU-parallel RTL simulator, RAP has proven especially useful for designing GPU-parallel simulators [18]. Specifically, by assigning a few additional GPU threads to run replicated logic elements, we can eliminate expensive inter-block synchronization and enable uninterrupted thread execution. Despite these advantages, RepCut requires solving a *proxy hypergraph partitioning* problem, where a hyperedge cut implies its corresponding nodes need to be replicated across different partitions. Unfortunately, hypergraph partitioning is NP-hard. Even with state-of-the-art parallel hypergraph partitioners [4,7], finding a partition with a decent cut size can still take a long time to converge, especially for large graphs (e.g., 3–5 min for a graph of 23M nodes [4]).

3 SimPart

Figure 2 gives an overview of SimPart, which consists of three stages, *majority-based grouping*, *DSP-RAP hybrid partitioning*, and *GPU-parallel simulation*. First, SimPart introduces a majority-based grouping algorithm that assigns group IDs to nodes based on their major connectivity, which is efficiently implemented through a one-pass BFS traversal on the GPU. Second, SimPart employs a DSP-RAP hybrid partitioning strategy with multiple backward traversals to identify partitions that balance synchronization cost and GPU thread utilization. Finally, we present the GPU-parallel simulation framework atop our partition.

3.1 Majority-Based Grouping

Instead of solving another time-consuming proxy hypergraph partitioning problem like RepCut [15], we propose a simple yet effective algorithm called *majority-based grouping*. The goal of majority-based grouping is to determine a partition group for every primary output (PO) that will minimize the number of replications. Specifically, we assign each node in the circuit graph to a group based on a majority count that reflects its predecessors' connectivity. This grouping method can achieve a similar effect to the hypergraph formulation in RepCut but with significantly reduced computation time. Our majority-based grouping algorithm consists of two main steps, *initial grouping* and *group propagation*.

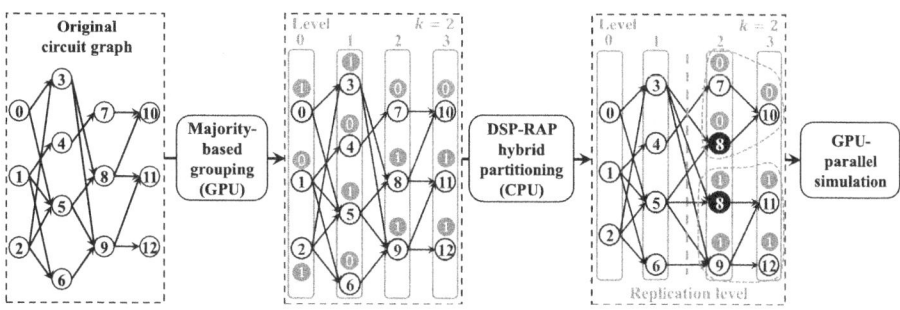

Fig. 2. Overview of SimPart under two partitions ($k = 2$ and $\gamma = 3$). In majority-based grouping, we leverage GPU to quickly assign a partition group to each node through a level-by-level parallel traversal. In DSP-RAP hybrid partitioning, we perform a backward traversal from the POs to the threshold replication level, where parallel cones are identified by replicating their overlaps (node 8 in both cones). Nodes before the replication level are partitioned into disjoint, non-overlapping groups level by level (\{0, 1, 2\} and \{3, 4, 5, 6\}).

The goal of initial grouping is to assign each primary input (PI) an initial group ID for later propagation. In this step, each PI is assigned a group ID based on the majority count of its successors, with the count calculated under modulo k for k partitions. The intuition is to assign group IDs based on primary node connections and encourage the later propagation to place connected nodes in the same group. For example, node 1 in Fig. 2 is assigned a group ID of 0, since the modulo outputs of its three successors are 0, 1, and 0 for nodes 4, 5, and 6 under $k = 2$. After assigning group IDs to the PIs, the goal of group propagation is to propagate these IDs from PIs to POs, keeping connected nodes in the same group as much as possible. To this end, we perform a BFS to traverse the circuit graph level by level. When a node is traversed (once its predecessors' dependencies are resolved), we will assign it a group ID based on the majority count of its predecessors' group IDs. For example, node 5 in Fig. 2 is assigned a group ID of 1, since the group IDs of its three predecessors are 1, 0, and 1 for nodes 0, 1, and 2, respectively.

A key advantage of our majority-based grouping algorithm is its high data parallelism during group propagation, as nodes at the same level can operate independently of each other. To maximally leverage this parallelism, we introduce a GPU-parallel majority-based grouping algorithm. We present a GPU-parallel majority-base grouping algorithm, as shown in Algorithm 1. Algorithm 1 consists of two steps, initial grouping (lines 1–13) and group propagation (lines 14–30). We use the compressed sparse row (CSR) data structure to store the input graph, as commonly done in many GPU-accelerated graph algorithms [8,9].

In step one (lines 1–13), we assign one GPU thread to process each PI. Each thread determines the group ID for its assigned PI (indexed by *PIIdx*) based on the majority count of its successors, stored in the PI's *outputs* array (line 3). For each successor, the thread calculates the modulo of its index under k

Algorithm 1. Majority-based grouping

```
 1: parallel for each thread {   /* Step 1: Initial grouping */
 2:     /* Assign group ID to PIs */
 3:     for each outNodeIdx ∈ outputs of PIIdx
 4:         mod = outNodeIdx % k; accum[mod]++
 5:     /* Assign a group ID based on the majority count */
 6:     Group[PIIdx] = argmax(accum)
 7:     /* Initial BFS queue Q */
 8:     for each outNodeIdx ∈ outputs of PIIdx
 9:         atomicSub(in_degree[outNodeIdx], 1)
10:         /* Enqueue nodes whose parent dependencies are resolved */
11:         if in_degree[outNodeIdx] == 0 then {enqueue outNodeIdx in Q}
12:     level[PIIdx] = 0; totalLevels = 0; accum.clear()
13: }
14: Grp_propagation_kernel {   /* Step 2: Group propagation */
15:     parallel for each thread {
16:         nodeIdx = dequeue Q; level[nodeIdx] = totalLevels
17:         /* Assign group IDs based on majority count */
18:         for each inputIdx ∈ inputs of nodeIdx
19:             groupIdOfInput = Group[inputIdx]; accum[groupIdOfInput]++
20:         /* Maintain BFS queue Q */
21:         for each outNodeIdx ∈ outputs of nodeIdx
22:             atomicSub(in_degree[outNodeIdx], 1)
23:             if in_degree[outNodeIdx] == 0 then {enqueue outNodeIdx in Q_tmp}
24:     }
25: }
26: while Q is not empty do {
27:     Q_tmp ← empty queue
28:     call Grp_propagation_kernel #blocks =⌈Q.size()/1024⌉, #threads =1024
29:     Q ← Q_tmp; totalLevels++; accum.clear()
30: }
```

and increments the corresponding count in an accumulation array, *accum* (lines 3–4). This array stores the counts of modulo results for each group, allowing the thread to assign the PI to the group with the highest count. Each PI's assigned group ID is stored in the *Group* array (line 6). After this, each thread initializes the queue *Q* for group propagation (lines 8–11) by inserting resolved successors (via updating their *in_degree* count with atomicSub). Finally, each thread sets its PI node level to 0 and initializes *totalLevels* to track circuit levels (line 12).

In step two, the function runs a while loop until all nodes receive a group ID (lines 14–30). In each iteration, it launches *Grp_propagation_kernel* to process all nodes in *Q* using ⌈*Q.size()*/1024⌉ blocks each of 1024 threads (the thread count can be configured by applications). Each thread dequeues a node, assigns it a level index in *totalLevels* (line 16), and a group ID based on its predecessors' group majority. It then updates the BFS queue by decrementing each output node's *in_degree* using atomicSub and enqueues nodes with zero *in_degree* (lines

21–23). After processing, the main loop updates Q with Q_tmp, increments *totalLevels*, and repeats until all nodes are grouped (lines 26–30).

3.2 DSP-RAP Hybrid Partitioning

The goal of RAP is to perform multiple backward traversals to construct a fanin cone for each group ID starting from the POs, while replicating nodes with different group IDs. However, as this traversal goes deeper towards level 0, the risk of over-replication significantly increases. For example, applying RAP to the middle graph in Fig. 2 will yield two partitions with many replications, as shown in Fig. 3, where all nodes in level 0 are replicated. While RAP can create two fully independent partitions that can be processed by two separate GPU blocks in parallel, over-replicated nodes may oversubscribe threads during simulation. Additionally, circuit graphs typically exhibit a long-tailed distribution after levelization, with more parallel nodes at earlier levels than the later levels, as shown in Fig. 4.

To understand the impact of this property, we assume that pure DSP yields a level-by-level GPU-parallel simulation and pure RAP yields k independent instances of level-by-level GPU-parallel simulation (see Fig. 1(b)). If we roughly characterize the parallel efficiency to the ratio of GPU thread utilization to synchronization overhead, then pure RAP yields low parallel efficiency at earlier levels due to fixed thread count processing potentially many replicated

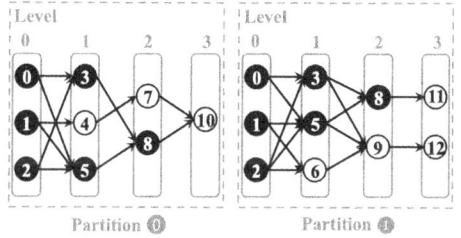

Fig. 3. Unconstrained RAP can result in over-replication (marked in black), which oversubscribes GPU threads during simulation.

nodes with frequent intra-block synchronizations. As we progress with fewer nodes, the number of intra-block synchronizations decreases, thus increasing its parallel efficiency. On the other hand, pure DSP can yield high parallel efficiency at earlier levels due to unrestricted thread counts and less frequent intra-block synchronization. However, as we progress, the cost of inter-block synchronization dominates the performance and reduces its parallel efficiency.

To balance parallel efficiency between synchronization cost and GPU thread utilization, we propose a DSP-RAP hybrid strategy that constrains the replication region to a threshold level during the backward traversal. We define γ as the upper bound on the number of nodes at the level where backward traversal stops. We refer to this level as *replication level*. For example, in Fig. 2, with $\gamma = 3$, the replication level is level 1, as it is the first backward level with more than three parallel nodes. A larger γ favors RAP-based simulation with more intra-block synchronizations, which reduces parallel efficiency and increases simulation time. Conversely, a smaller γ leans towards DSP-based simulation, resulting in more costly inter-block synchronization (microseconds).

By default, SimPart sets γ to the GPU block size since it guarantees each replicated partition to be processed within a thread block with minimal synchronization overhead.

Algorithm 2 presents our DSP-RAP hybrid partitioning strategy. First, we determine the replication level l_γ as the first backward level containing more than γ nodes (line 1). Next, we form RAP partitions by constructing a fanin cone for each group ID starting from POs until l_γ (lines 3–4) and replicating nodes with different group IDs from that of POs (lines 5–6). Finally, we assign each of the remaining levels to a DSP partition (lines 7–12).

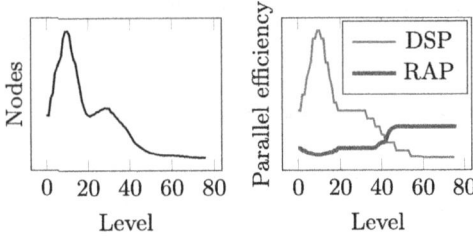

Fig. 4. Node distribution across levels for the real circuit edit_dist [9], and parallel efficiency for two partitioning strategies.

Algorithm 2. DSP-RAP hybrid partitioning

1: $l_\gamma = \mathbf{argmax}_l \{numNodes[l] > \gamma\}$
2: **for each** $v \in \{v \mid level[v] == totalLevels - 1\}$ { /* RAP */
3:    $rap\_part[Group[v]] = \{x \mid x \in \text{fanin\_cone}(v) \text{ and } level[x] > l_\gamma\}$
4:    **for each** $y \in rap\_part[Group[v]]$
5:       **if** $Group[y] \neq Group[v]$ **then** {replicate y}
6: }
7: **for each** $l \in \{l_\gamma, \cdots, 1, 0\}$ { /* DSP */
8:    $new\_part = \{\}$
9:    **for each** $v \in \{v \mid level[v] == l\}$
10:      $new\_part.\text{insert}(node)$
11:   $dsp\_part = dsp\_part \cup new\_part$
12: }

3.3 Conditional CUDA Graph-Based Simulation Framework

A key advantage of SimPart is its simple linear structure for kernel scheduling, starting with DSP-based simulation followed by RAP-based simulation. However, iterative kernel launches can incur non-negligible CPU overhead, especially for large graphs with many levels. Additionally, logic simulators often iterate through multiple inputs, resulting in frequent CPU-GPU interactions for control-flow decisions. Figure 5(a) illustrates these two challenges. To overcome these challenges, we leverage the latest *conditional CUDA Graph* [3] to design a simulation framework that encapsulates both simulation kernels and dynamic control flow within a single GPU-resident graph entity. As shown in Fig. 5(b), we create a conditional CUDA Graph node to represent the while-loop condition, which iteratively invokes our simulation kernels until no more inputs remain.

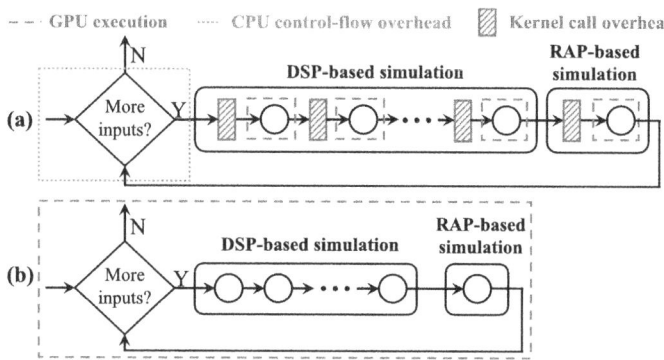

Fig. 5. GPU-parallel simulation framework atop our partition using (a) stream-based and (b) conditional CUDA Graph-based executions.

This strategy not only reduces iterative kernel call overhead but also decreases CPU involvement in decision-making.

The idea of our GPU-parallel simulation kernels is level-by-level parallel propagation, where multiple GPU threads process parallel nodes within each level simultaneously. While this idea is common in GPU-accelerated CAD algorithms [5,18], we outline our kernels in Algorithm 3 and Algorithm 4 for completeness.

Algorithm 3. DSP-based simulation

1: **DSP_sim_kernel** {
2:    **parallel for each thread** tid
3:       $res[tid] = $ run_logic_operation_of($nodes[tid]$)
4: }
5: **DSP_based_sim** {
6:    **for each** $l \in \{0, 1, ..., totalLevels\text{-}1\}$
7:       call **DSP_sim_kernel** $\#blocks = \lceil \#nodesAtLvl\_l/1024 \rceil$; $\#threads = 1024$
8:       **sync_kernel** /* inter-block sync */
9: }

The key difference between Algorithm 3 and Algorithm 4 lies in the scope of level-by-level propagation: DSP operates across partitions with inter-block synchronization, while RAP processes individual partitions within a single kernel launch. Specifically, in RAP-based simulation (Algorithm 4), we assign a GPU block to simulate each partition using just one kernel launch (line 13). Within each block, additional passes are required if the number of parallel nodes at a level exceeds the block size (lines 5–newinlinkFigdalg::RAPsim::l99). Threads are synchronized at the end of each iteration (i.e., intra-block synchronization).

Algorithm 4. RAP-based simulation

```
 1: RAP_sim_kernel {
 2:    parallel for each block {
 3:       for each l ∈ {0, 1, ...,totalLevels-1}
 4:          passes = ⌈#nodesAtLevel_l_in_Partition/1024⌉
 5:          for each pass ∈ {0, 1, ..., passes-1}
 6:             parallel for each thread tid
 7:                res[tid] = run_logic_operation_of(nodes[tid]); tid += 1024
 8:             sync_threads /* intra-block sync */
 9:          sync_threads /* intra-block sync */
10:    }
11: }
12: RAP_based_sim {
13:    call RAP_sim_kernel #blocks = k, #threads = 1024
14: }
```

4 Experimental Results

We implemented SimPart in CUDA/C++ and compiled it with nvcc v12.3 using -O3 and -std=c++20. Experiments were conducted on a 64-bit Linux machine with 32 Intel Core i5-13500 cores (4.8 GHz) and an Nvidia RTX A4000 GPU. We evaluated SimPart on logic graphs generated by the RTLFlow simulator [9]; graph statistics are shown in Table 2, with the "_eval" suffix indicating larger variants with added logic elements. Without loss of generality, we simulate a batch of 12 simulation inputs. Since the inputs are independent, increasing the number of inputs does not affect the results but further amplifies the performance gap between SimPart and the baseline.

We consider the state-of-the-art RepCut [15] as our baseline. We use CPU to construct the proxy hypergraph and use Mt-KaHyPar [4] with 16 threads to derive k partitions, as it delivers the best runtime performance on our machine. For comparison, we simulate on both CPU and GPU using OpenMP and our RAP-based kernel, respectively. On CPU, one OpenMP thread runs one partition, following RepCut's original setting. By default, we set the number of partitions (k) to 16, yielding good performance for both RepCut and SimPart. For SimPart, γ is set to 1024 to match the GPU kernel block size, balancing DSP and RAP performance on our machine. Both k and γ are tunable for platform-specific optimization. All results are averaged over 10 runs.

4.1 Overall Performance Comparison

Table 2 compares the overall performance between RepCut and SimPart. We can observe that RepCut spends a large amount of time on solving the proxy hypergraph problem, including building the hypergraph and partitioning the hypergraph. While Mt-KaHyPar reduces partitioning time by 1.9–3.6× by using 16 threads, it still has an average 23× gap compared to SimPart due to our GPU-powered partitioning algorithm. In terms of partition sizes, SimPart outperforms

Table 2. Overall performance comparison between RepCut [15] and SimPart with $k = 16$. Partition quality is evaluated based on the resulting simulation time on CPU (RepCut only) and GPU. The average ratios of replication, partitioning time, and simulation time are measured relative to the original graph size ($|V|$ and $|E|$), T_{Part} in SimPart, and T_{Sim}^G in SimPart.

Benchmark			RepCut [15]						SimPart				
	$|V|$	$|E|$	T_{Build}^{C1}	T_{Part}^{C1}	T_{Part}^{C16}	T_{Sim}^{C1}	T_{Sim}^{C16}	T_{Sim}^G	$R_{|V|}$	$R_{|E|}$	T_{Part}	T_{Sim}^G	$R_{|V|}$	$R_{|E|}$
edit_dist	164K	164K	590.3	1492	438.6	439.5	281.8	5.1	1.01765	1.01765	72.3	3.2	1.00528	1.00528
matrix_mult	176K	174K	737.4	1024	384.6	895.6	450.2	6.2	1.00235	1.00235	86.6	3.4	1.03148	1.03148
b19	255K	255K	2058	4377	1203	169.1	40.3	7.5	1.00911	1.00911	77.3	4.0	1.00210	1.00210
leon2	1.6M	1.6M	10054	12478	5501	6846	900.2	35.5	1.00166	1.00166	213.3	21.2	1.00000	1.00000
leon3mp	1.2M	1.2M	6893	12542	4513	4648	528.5	27.3	1.00487	1.00487	146.1	16.1	1.00000	1.00000
netcard	1.5M	1.5M	9120	24578	7209	7589	1184	30.7	1.02060	1.02060	155.9	18.4	1.00000	1.00000
edit_dist_eval	1.3M	1.3M	5193	7432	3148	54791	10555	25.6	1.00209	1.00209	160.5	18.1	1.00000	1.00000
matrix_mult_eval	1.4M	1.4M	6531	5545	2886	76191	13465	29.0	1.00004	1.00004	779.2	17.3	1.00002	1.00002
b19_eval	2.0M	2.0M	15976	37299	10872	4157	811.6	39.4	1.00147	1.00147	925.2	24.3	1.00000	1.00000
leon2_eval	12.9M	12.9M	91500	64697	44711	165011	29598	235.5	1.00021	1.00021	2483	169.5	1.00000	1.00000
leon3_eval	20.0M	20.0M	106012	128188	57139	219415	38024	327.5	1.00004	1.00004	2971	259.0	1.00000	1.00000
netcard_eval	24.0M	24.0M	143731	766218	218582	1530950	283890	371.8	1.00000	1.00000	2866	292.4	1.00000	1.00000
Avg. ratio	1.000	1.000	-		68.45	23.13	1344.76	255.04	1.58	1.005	1.005	1.000	1.000	1.003	1.003

$|V|$: Number of nodes T_{Build}: Hypergraph construction time
T_{Sim}^{Cn}: Simulation time on CPU, with n threads T_{Part}: Partitioning time
$|E|$: Number of edges T_{Part}^{Cn}: Partitioning time on CPU, with n threads
T_{Sim}^G: Simulation time on GPU $R_{|V|}$, $R_{|E|}$: Ratio of replicated nodes and edges

RepCut in nearly all graphs except matrix_mult, where hypergraph partitioning achieves a near-optimal solution. On average, SimPart reduces replication by 40% compared to RepCut (0.3% vs. 0.5%). This improvement is due to SimPart's replication constraint, which reduces the risk of over-replication in most cases. Further, the NP-hard nature of hypergraph partitioning makes it challenging for Mt-KaHyPar to find the optimal cut size that minimizes replication for RepCut.

Next, we evaluate the quality of partitions based on the resulting simulation time. Compared to CPU-based simulation on RepCut's partitions, our GPU-based simulation can achieve an average speedup of 1344× over 1 CPU thread (column of T_{Sim}^{C1}) and 255× over 16 CPU threads (column of T_{Sim}^{C16}). When using our GPU simulation kernel to RepCut's partitions, we can still achieve an average speedup of 1.58× (columns of T_{Sim}^G). Again, we attribute this speedup to our DSP-RAP hybrid partitioning strategy, which strikes a balanced trade-off between synchronization costs and GPU thread parallelism.

4.2 Performance Under Different Numbers of Partitions

Figure 6 compares the performance between RepCut and SimPart for different partition counts (k), which directly impact the parallelism available for simulation. We can observe that as k increases, RepCut's runtime to solve the proxy hypergraph problem also increases. Take leon2 for example, when k increases from 16 to 128, RepCut's runtime increases from 14.3 to 20.2 s. This runtime cost makes RepCut challenging to use in a dynamic environment, such as simulation-driven hardware fuzzing [10], where the partitioner is iteratively applied to a

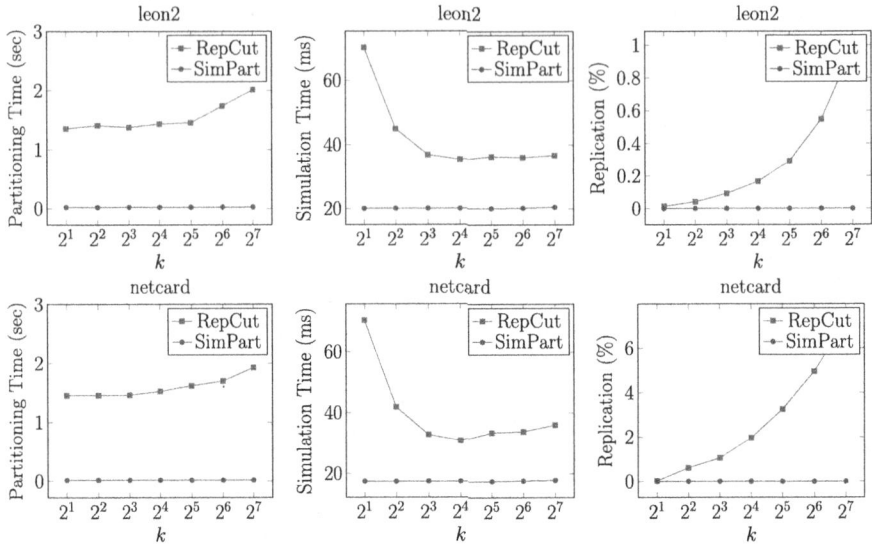

Fig. 6. Comparisons of partitioning time (left), partition quality (middle), and partitioned graph size (right) between RepCut and SimPart at different k.

simulation graph that changes dynamically. On the other hand, SimPart has very low partitioning times regardless of k (all $\leq$ 230 ms). We attribute this efficiency to our GPU-powered partitioning algorithm.

In terms of the partition quality, measured at the resulting simulation time on GPU, SimPart is always faster than RepCut (middle plot). As k increases, RepCut generates more parallel partitions to accelerate the simulation, yet eventually reaching a saturation point at 16 partitions.

Beyond 16 partitions, we begin to see diminishing performance returns in RepCut, primarily due to over-replication, which can be revealed in the bottom plot. On the contrary, the simulation time on our partitions consistently outperforms RepCut across all values of k. We attribute this speedup to SimPart's DSP-RAP hybrid partitioning strategy, which avoids over-replication while maximizing the parallel efficiency across all levels of the circuit graph.

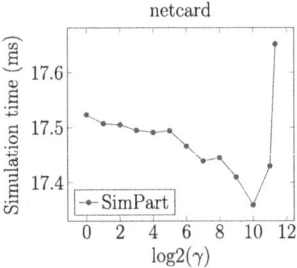

Fig. 7. Partition quality vs. γ.

4.3 Analysis of Replication Threshold

We study the impact of the replication threshold, γ, on the partition quality. As shown in Fig. 7, the curve forms a U-shape as γ increases. As discussed in Sect. 3.2, a larger γ favors RAP-based simulation with more intra-block synchronization, which reduces parallel efficiency and thus increases simulation time. Conversely, a smaller γ leans towards DSP-based simulation, resulting in more costly inter-block synchronizations. At the two extremes of $\gamma = 0$ and $\gamma = \infty$, the simulation reduces to pure level-by-level DSP and pure RAP, neither of which achieves optimal performance. With $\gamma = 1024$, SimPart can balance the parallel efficiency between DSP and RSP to achieve optimal simulation performance.

4.4 Ablation Analysis of Conditional CUDA Graph

To highlight the advantage of our conditional CUDA Graph-based simulation framework, we analyze the simulation time with and without conditional CUDA Graph. As shown in Fig. 8, SimPart with conditional CUDA Graph outperforms RepCut across all circuits. Without CUDA Graph, SimPart still achieves better performance than RepCut in all but two small circuits (edit_dist and b19), which highlights the effectiveness of our partitioning algorithm. For SimPart itself, conditional CUDA Graph achieves an average speedup of 27%, with the highest speedup of 2.23× observed in b19. We attribute this improvement to the integration of simulation kernels and control-flow decisions into a single GPU-resident graph, which reduces kernel call overhead and decreases CPU involvement in decision-making.

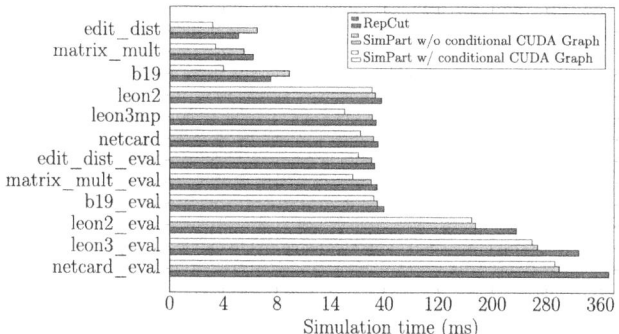

Fig. 8. Simulation time of RepCut vs. SimPart with and without conditional CUDA Graph.

5 Conclusion

In this paper, we have introduced *SimPart*, a simple yet highly effective and efficient GPU-parallel replication-aided partitioner to facilitate the design of parallel RTL simulation algorithms. SimPart addresses the partitioning problem directly, without relying on a proxy problem, and proposes a hybrid strategy that makes the most of GPU parallelism when simulating the circuit on our partition. Compared to RepCut, SimPart achieves an average of 23× speedup in partitioning and 1.58× speedup in GPU-parallel simulation, while increasing the original graph size by only 0.3%.

Acknowledgment. This project is supported by NSF grants 2235276, 2349144, 2349143, 2349582, and 2349141. This research was also conducted by ACCESS – AI Chip Center for Emerging Smart Systems, supported by the InnoHK initiative of the Innovation and Technology Commission of the HKSAR Government.

Disclosure of Interests. The authors have no competing interests to declare that are relevant to the content of this article.

References

1. Beamer, S., et al.: Efficiently exploiting low activity factors to accelerate RTL simulation. In: ACM/IEEE DAC, pp. 1–6 (2020)
2. Emami, S.: Highly Parallel RTL Simulation. Ph.D. thesis, EPFL (2024)
3. Gaiser, J., et al.: Dynamic control flow in cuda graphs with conditional nodes (2024)
4. Gottesbüren, L., et al.: Scalable shared-memory hypergraph partitioning. In: 23rd Workshop on ALENEX 2021, pp. 16–30. SIAM (2021)
5. Huang, T.W., et al.: OpenTimer v2: a new parallel incremental timing analysis engine. IEEE TCAD **40**, 776–789(2021)
6. Huang, T.W., et al.: Taskflow: a lightweight parallel and heterogeneous task graph computing system. IEEE TPDS **33**, 1303–1320 (2022)
7. LaSalle, D., et al.: Multi-threaded graph partitioning. In: IEEE IPDPS, pp. 225–236 (2013)
8. Lee, W.L., et al.: G-kway: multilevel GPU-accelerated k-way graph partitioner. In: ACM/IEEE DAC (2024)
9. Lin, D.L., et al.: From RTL to CUDA: a GPU acceleration flow for RTL simulation with batch stimulus. In: Proceedings of the 51st ICPP, pp. 1–12 (2022)
10. Lin, D.L., et al.: GenFuzz: GPU-accelerated hardware fuzzing using genetic algorithm with multiple inputs. In: ACM/IEEE DAC (2023)
11. Lin, D.L., et al.: TaroRTL: accelerating RTL Simulation using coroutine-based heterogeneous task graph scheduling. In: Euro-Par (2024)
12. Olmedo, I.S., et al.: Dissecting the CUDA scheduling hierarchy: a performance and predictability perspective. In: IEEE RTAS, pp. 213–225 (2020)
13. Snyder, W.: Verilator 4.0: open simulation goes multi- threaded (2018)
14. Tong, J., et al.: BatchSim: parallel RTL simulation using inter-cycle batching and task graph parallelism. In: IEEE ISVLSI (2024)
15. Wang, H., et al.: RepCut: superlinear parallel RTL simulation with replication-aided partitioning. In: ACM ASPLOS, pp. 572–585 (2023)
16. Wang, H., et al.: Don't Repeat Yourself! ACM ASPLOS, Coarse-Grained Circuit Deduplication to Accelerate RTL Simulation. In (2024)
17. Wong, H., et al.: Demystifying GPU microarchitecture through microbenchmarking. In: 2010 IEEE ISPASS, pp. 235–246. IEEE (2010)
18. Zhang, Y., et al.: GL0AM: GPU logic simulation using 0-delay and re-simulation acceleration method. In: IEEE/ACM ICCAD (2024)
19. Zhou, K., et al.: Khronos: fusing memory access for improved hardware RTL simulation. In: IEEE/ACM Micro, pp. 180–193 (2023)

Efficient Task Graph Scheduling for Parallel QR Factorization in SLSQP

Soumyajit Chatterjee[1](✉), Rahul Utkoor[2], Uppu Eshwar[1], Sathya Peri[1], and V. Krishna Nandivada[3]

[1] Indian Institute of Technology,
Hyderabad, India
{ai22mtech02005,
ch21btech11034}@iith.ac.in,
sathya_p@cse.iith.ac.in
[2] QUALCOMM India Private Limited,
Hyderabad, India
[3] Indian Institute of Technology Madras,
Chennai, India
nvk@iitm.ac.in

Abstract. Efficient task scheduling is paramount in parallel programming on multi-core architectures, where tasks are fundamental computational units. QR factorization is a critical sub-routine in Sequential Least Squares Quadratic Programming (SLSQP) for solving non-linear programming (NLP) problems. QR factorization decomposes a matrix into an orthogonal matrix Q and an upper triangular matrix R, which are essential for solving systems of linear equations arising from optimization problems. SLSQP uses an in-place version of QR factorization, which requires storing intermediate results for the next steps of the algorithm. Although DAG-based approaches for QR factorization are prevalent in the literature, they often lack control over the intermediate kernel results, providing only the final output matrices Q and R. This limitation is particularly challenging in SLSQP, where intermediate results of QR factorization are crucial for back-substitution logic at each iteration. Our work introduces novel scheduling techniques using a two-queue approach to execute the QR factorization kernel effectively. This approach, implemented in high-level C++ programming language, facilitates compiler optimizations and allows storing intermediate results required by back-substitution logic. Empirical evaluations demonstrate substantial performance gains, including a 10x improvement over the sequential QR version of the SLSQP algorithm.

Keywords: Non Linear Programming · Parallel Computing · DAG Sch-eduling

1 Introduction

In modern engineering, the demand for efficient optimization techniques is critical across disciplines such as structural engineering, material sciences, and molecular dynamics. Nonlinear programming (NLP) has emerged as a fundamental

---

GitHub Repository: https://github.com/PDCRL/ParSQP

tool for addressing complex design challenges, as these problems involve intricate, nonlinear relationships that govern system performance and reliability. In structural engineering, NLP facilitates the optimization of large-scale structures, while in material sciences, it enables the development of novel materials with tailored properties. Similarly, molecular dynamics relies on nonlinear equations to model particle interactions, requiring advanced optimization techniques to accurately capture complex behaviors. As the complexity and dimensionality of design spaces continue to expand, advanced computational methods are essential for achieving efficient and scalable solutions.

SLSQP: Sequential Least Squares Quadratic Programming [12] is a well established algorithm for solving NLP problems involving constrained, smoo-th, and differentiable functions. At each iteration, SLSQP constructs a quadratic approximation of the nonlinear objective function while employing a linearization of the constraints, resulting in a quadratic programming (QP) subproblem that determines the search direction for updating decision variables. Despite its effectiveness, the sequential execution of core linear algebra operations poses computational challenges, particularly in high-dimensional optimization problems. As problem dimensionality increases, these sequential computations introduce performance bottlenecks, necessitating the exploration of more efficient and scalable approaches [8,14].

QR Factorization: Enhancing algorithm efficiency is key for progress in optimization driven fields. The QR Factorization is a mathematical technique used to decompose a matrix A into an orthogonal matrix Q and an upper triangular matrix R. Methods like Householder transformations achieve this by iteratively applying a sequence of reflection matrices H_k to A. Each H_k is constructed from the current state of the k-th column. The *critical intermediate results* of this process are the components defining these Householder reflectors. The final R matrix resides in the upper triangle, while Q is implicitly represented as the product of the H_k transformations ($Q = H_1 H_2 \ldots H_m$). In algorithms like SLSQP, which iteratively solve systems of equations or least-squares problems arising from Quadratic Programming (QP) subproblems, these stored intermediate results are paramount. They allow for the efficient application of Q or Q^T to various matrices and vectors without explicitly forming the (potentially dense) matrix Q. This repeated application is fundamental to updating solutions and Lagrange multipliers within SLSQP. QR Factorization is a critical sub-routine of SLSQP that is invoked multiple times, making the management and parallel computation of these intermediate results crucial for overall algorithmic performance.

This study presents parallel techniques for QR factorization that harness the advantages of concurrent task execution. By decomposing QR factorization into smaller, independent tasks suitable for parallel processing, an asynchronous Directed Acyclic Task Graph (DATG) scheduling mechanism is employed to optimize execution while preserving task dependencies.

Empirical evaluations demonstrate substantial performance gains in solving large-scale NLP problems using the SLSQP algorithm. The results underscore the transformative impact of parallel computing techniques on QR factorization, reinforcing the necessity for high-performance numerical methods within open-source optimization frameworks.

Our Contributions: The key contributions of this work are as follows.

- Developed a dynamic algorithm that schedules QR factorization into smaller tasks using asynchronous DATG scheduling Alg. 5.
- Integrated the optimized parallel QR factorization method into the SLSQP implementation of the open-source NLOPT library.
- Comprehensive evaluations demonstrated a 10x improvement of the parallel QR technique over the sequential QR version of the SLSQP algorithm.

2 Background

2.1 SLSQP → Descent Direction Computation → QR

The Sequential Least Squares Programming (SLSQP) problem is formulated as a constrained optimization problem, typically expressed in the following mathematical form:

$$\min_x f(x), \tag{1}$$
$$\text{subject to:} \quad h(x) = 0, \quad h : \mathbb{R}^n \to \mathbb{R}^m, \tag{2}$$
$$g(x) \leq 0, \quad g : \mathbb{R}^n \to \mathbb{R}^p. \tag{3}$$

SLSQP is an efficient algorithm for solving NLP problems subject to equality and inequality constraints. It seeks to find the minimum of a non-linear objective function while ensuring the satisfaction of constraints. The core of SLSQP involves iteratively approximating the solution using a line search approach to compute the descent direction.

SLSQP determines the descent direction by solving a QP sub-problem at each iteration. This QP is derived from the first and second derivatives, gradients and Hessians, of the Lagrangian function associated with the objective function and constraints. QR factorization plays a pivotal role in this process by providing an efficient method to solve the system of linear equations arising from the Karush-Kuhn-Tucker (KKT) conditions [16].

Using QR factorization, SLSQP ensures numerical stability and efficiency in solving the KKT system, thereby accelerating the computation of descent directions in constrained optimization problems.

2.2 QR Factorization Using Householder Transformations

Given a matrix A of size $m \times n$, the goal is to compute an orthogonal matrix Q and an upper triangular matrix R such that: $A = QR$. The Householder [9] algorithm achieves this by iteratively constructing and applying reflection vectors to transform A into Q and R, either in-place or out-of-place. Considering the importance of QR Factorization in SLSQP, we next consider efficient ways to parallelize QR Factorization.

Algorithm 1. QR Factorization using Householder Reflections

1: **Initialize:** Set $Q = I$ (identity matrix) and $R = A$.
2: **for** each column index $j = 1$ to $\min(m, n)$ **do**
3:     Extract column vector $x = R[j : m, j]$.
4:     Compute $\alpha = -x_1 \cdot \|x\|$.
5:     Set $u = x + \alpha e_1$, where e_1 is the first standard basis vector.
6:     Normalize $u = u/\|u\|$.
7:     Compute Householder matrix $W = I - 2\frac{uu^T}{\|u\|^2}$.
8:     Apply transformation: $R \leftarrow WR$.
9:     Update $Q \leftarrow QW^T$.
10: **end for**
11: **return** Q, R satisfying $A = QR$.

3 Our Methodology: Efficient Parallel QR Factorization

Algorithm 1 outlines QR decomposition's mathematical logic via Householder reflections. This formulation is further expressed in Algorithm 2, representing the standard computational structure frequently employed in linear algebra kernels such as QR factorization, Cholesky decomposition, and LU decomposition. The SLSQP algorithm from the NLOPT library uses an in-place QR factorization technique based on Householder transformations.

Algorithm 2 represents the in-place transformation of matrix A into the upper triangular matrix R. The algorithm relies on two key computational kernels: 1) update_pivot_row and 2) update_trailing_non_pivot_row. Both kernels operate at the row level, updating individual elements with a linear time complexity, each involving a fixed number of arithmetic operations.

Algorithm 2 Transform matrix A to upper-triangular form.

1: **Input:** A, a $m \times n$ non-singular real matrix.
2: **for** $i = 1$ to m **do**
3:     $(up, b) \leftarrow$ UPDATE_PIVOT_ROW(A, i)
4:     **for** $j = i + 1$ to n **do**
5:         UPDATE_TRAILING_NON_PIVOT_ROW(A, i, j, up)
6:     **end for**
7: **end for**
8: **Output:** Matrix A in upper-triangular form.

In Algorithm 2, for a given value of i, $1 \leq i \leq m$, all tasks $T_{i,*}$ represent computations at the ith iteration of the outer loop. The pivot update calculation of the ith row is performed first (task $T_{i,i}$), representing a call to the kernel update_pivot_row. Then all the rows of the entire trailing sub-matrix, with $j > i$, are updated (task $T_{i,j}$), by a call to update_trailing_non_pivot_row.

To model the dependency constraints between tasks, we construct a directed acyclic graph (DAG) Fig. 1(b), where the vertices represent tasks, and the edges encode dependencies. An edge $e : T \to T'$ indicates that T' can start only after T is completed, regardless of the availability of resources. Each $T_{i,j}$ task in Fig. 1(b) represents a call to the kernel update_trailing_non_pivot_row, which can be executed in parallel once its parent tasks are complete. Therefore, any task $T_{i,j}$ always has two parent nodes $T_{i,i}$ and $T_{i-1,j}$ (except for all tasks $T_{i,j}$ in the first level of Fig. 1(b) where it has only one parent) whose execution must be completed before the execution of task $T_{i,j}$ can begin. The dependency of $T_{i,j}$ on $T_{i,i}$ denotes the dependency within a single iteration according to Algorithm 2 where the pivot row update needs to be completed first before proceeding with the row updates of the non-pivot rows. However, the dependency of $T_{i,j}$ on $T_{i-i,j}$ denotes the dependency across iterations where a row in the given input matrix can only be updated in the current iteration if it had been successfully updated by a call to the kernel update_trailing_non_pivot_row in the previous iteration.

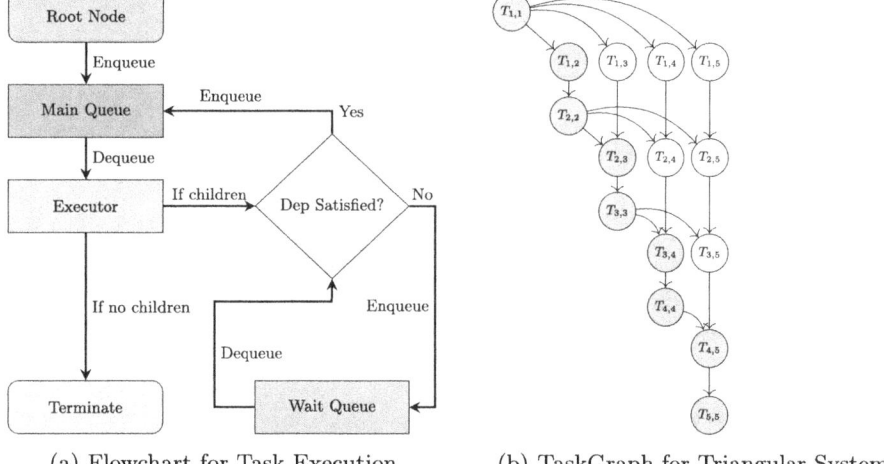

(a) Flowchart for Task Execution (b) TaskGraph for Triangular System

Fig. 1. Task Execution Flowchart and Task Graph

3.1 Optimizing Thread Workload for Parallel Task Execution

Even though all the tasks $T_{i,j}$ describe the availability of parallel tasks for the threads, however, the call to the kernel update_trailing_non_pivot_row only updates a single non-pivot row. We, therefore, want a mechanism to control the amount of work per thread. We introduce two control parameters α and β and design two new kernels Task 1 and Task 2, which allows us to increase/decrease the amount of work available per thread by coalescing smaller tasks into larger chunks. The parameter β determines how many non-pivot rows each thread updates simultaneously using the update_trailing_non_pivot_row kernel, rather than processing one row at a time. The parameter α controls the number of iterations in which these β rows are updated once the pivot computations for the α rows are complete. Accordingly, Task 1 performs α pivot computations, enabling efficient batched updates of non-pivot rows in chunks of β (Task 2) over α iterations.

3.2 DAG Scheduling Using Barriers

Given the task graph $G = (V, E)$ in Fig. 1(b), where V represents the set of nodes and E represents the set of directed edges. A directed edge (i, j) between two task nodes t_i and t_j indicates that t_i must be completed before t_j can commence. A straightforward approach to schedule the DAG in Fig. 1(b) across multiple processors while preserving the dependencies is to use **barriers**–a synchronization mechanism that ensures all threads reach a specific point before proceeding further. In Fig. 1(b), each task $T_{i,j}$ depends on both $T_{i,i}$ and $T_{i-1,j}$, necessitating two synchronization points:

Algorithm 3. Function: Task 1

1: **Input:**
   – Matrix mat of size $m \times n$, *pivot_start*, *row_chunk_start*.
2: **Global:** global_up_array, global_b_array, α, β.
3: *pivot_end* $\leftarrow$ *pivot_start* $+ \alpha$
4: *row_chunk_end* $\leftarrow$ *row_chunk_start* $+ \beta$
5: **for** *lpivot* $=$ *pivot_start* **to** *pivot_end* $- 1$ **do**
6: $\quad (up, b) \leftarrow$ UPDATE_PIVOT_ROW(*mat*, n, *lpivot*)
7: $\quad$ **if** up or b is **undefined then**
8: $\quad\quad$ **continue**
9: $\quad$ **end if**
10: $\quad$ global_up_array[lpivot] $\leftarrow up$
11: $\quad$ global_b_array[lpivot] $\leftarrow b$
12: $\quad$ **for** $j = lpivot + 1$ **to** *row_chunk_end* $- 1$ **do**
13: $\quad\quad$ UPDATE_TRAILING_NON_PIVOT_ROW(*mat*, n, lpivot, j, up, b)
14: $\quad$ **end for**
15: **end for**
16: **Output:** Updated matrix mat.

- A barrier after $T_{i,i}$ ensures that the update_pivot_row kernel completes before executing parallel tasks $T_{i,j}$.
- A second barrier at the end of each iteration ensures that all tasks $T_{i,j}$ complete before proceeding to the next iteration, as $T_{i+1,j}$ depends on $T_{i,j}$.

However, barriers impose a rigid execution order, limiting parallel efficiency. For instance, if $T_{i,j}$ belonging to a critical path completes, the next $T_{i+1,i+1}$ could begin execution immediately, which after completion can unleash more parallel tasks from the next level. Yet, due to barriers, all threads must wait for the slowest task to complete, even when additional work is available.

Algorithm 4. Function: Task 2

1: **Input:**
   – Matrix mat of size $m \times n$, pivot_start, row_chunk_start.
2: **Global:** global_up_array, global_b_array, α, β.
3: $pivot\_end \leftarrow pivot\_start + \alpha$
4: $row\_chunk\_end \leftarrow row\_chunk\_start + \beta$
5: **for** $lpivot = pivot\_start$ **to** $pivot\_end - 1$ **do**
6: $\quad up \leftarrow global\_up\_array[lpivot]$
7: $\quad b \leftarrow global\_b\_array[lpivot]$
8: $\quad$ **for** $j = lpivot + 1$ **to** $row\_chunk\_end - 1$ **do**
9: $\quad\quad$ UPDATE_TRAILING_NON_PIVOT_ROW(mat, n, lpivot, j, up, b)
10: $\quad$ **end for**
11: **end for**
12: **Output:** Updated matrix mat.

3.3 DAG Scheduling Using LockFree Queues

A key observation from Fig. 1(b) is that traversing the critical path (highlighted nodes) allows more tasks $T_{i,j}$ to be executed in parallel across different levels. This approach reduces synchronization overhead by requiring only a single dependency check, specifically in $T_{i-1,j}$. Based on this insight, we propose a dual-queue scheduling mechanism for DAG execution: one queue handles the parallel generation of tasks, while the other ensures that dependencies are satisfied before execution.

As illustrated in Fig. 1(a), our approach leverages two centralized, lock-free global queues–main_queue and wait_queue–which are shared among all threads for task scheduling. The main queue contains tasks that any available thread can immediately execute. When a critical path task $T_{i,i}$ is completed, it loads its child tasks $T_{i,j}$ into the main_queue after verifying the completion of their parent $T_{i-1,j}$. If the parent has already completed the task, the child task is immediately available for execution. Otherwise, the task is placed in the wait queue, allowing threads to continue executing readily available tasks from the main queue instead of waiting for the pending parent task to complete. This strategy, as depicted in Algorithm 5 ensures that threads prioritize active execution over spinning or waiting for dependencies to resolve, thereby improving overall responsiveness. Upon completing a task from the main queue, a thread checks the wait queue for deferred tasks. If a task's parent has completed, it is moved to the main queue for immediate execution. Otherwise, it is enqueued back into the wait queue for re-evaluation in subsequent iterations.

3.4 DAG Scheduling Using Priority Queues

In Baskaran's work [2], each vertex in the DAG is associated with two metrics: top level (topL) and bottom level (bottomL). For any vertex v in DAG G, the topL(v) is defined as the longest length of the path from the root node to the vertex v, excluding v.

Algorithm 5. Thread Work

```
 1: Global: lockfree main_queue, wait_queue; dependency_table tb
 2: while true do
 3:     if main_queue ≠ ∅ then
 4:         curr_task ← main_queue.pop()
 5:         if curr_task.type = 1 then
 6:             Task1(curr_task.params)
 7:             tb[curr_task] = True
 8:             for child ∈ curr_task.children do
 9:                 if ∀p ∈ child.parent, tb[p] = True then
10:                     main_queue.push(child)
11:                 else
12:                     wait_queue.push(child)
13:                 end if
14:             end for
15:         else if curr_task.type = 2 then
16:             Task2(curr_task.params)
17:             tb[curr_task] = True
18:             if curr_task ∈ CriticalPath then
19:                 task1 = curr_task.children[0]
20:                 main_queue.push(task1)
21:             end if
22:         end if
23:     end if
24:     if wait_queue ≠ ∅ then
25:         old_task ← wait_queue.pop()
26:         if ∀p ∈ old_task.parent, tb[p] = True then
27:             main_queue.push(old_task)
28:         else
29:             wait_queue.push(old_task)
30:         end if
31:     end if
32:     if ∃ task ∈ tb, tb[task] = False then
33:         continue
34:     else
35:         break
36:     end if
37: end while
```

Similarly, bottomL(v) is defined as the length of the longest path from v to the leaf node (vertex with no children). The tasks are prioritized based on the sum of topL(v) and bottomL(v) or just the bottomL(v). Nodes that are part of the critical path will have higher priority, and as we move away from the critical path, the priority value of the nodes decreases. We use this technique to assign priority values to each node in the task graph, ensuring that critical-path tasks are executed earlier to accelerate the release of dependent parallel tasks.

Our proposed approach in Sect. 3.3 employs standard lock-free queues that execute DAG nodes without prioritization. Replacing them with global lock-free **priority queues** allows nodes to be ordered based on predefined criteria. This prioritization ensures that critical-path nodes execute earlier, thereby accelerating the release of dependent parallel tasks. However, maintaining priority order introduces overhead from rebalancing the data structure, which can degrade performance for large queues. Our implementation utilizes Intel TBB **concurrent priority queues** and **concurrent queues** to optimize task scheduling.

4 Experimental Results

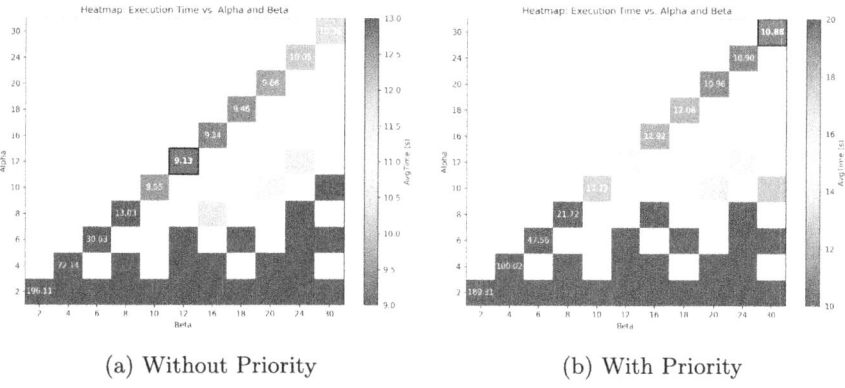

(a) Without Priority (b) With Priority

Fig. 2. Heatmap views for the parameter sweep.

4.1 Parameter Tuning for Parallel QR Factorization

(a) Heatmap Analysis: In this experiment, an exhaustive sweep over the parameters α and β (ranging from 2 to 32) was conducted on a fixed matrix size of 10800×10800 using 26 threads. The primary objective was to minimize execution time. Figure 2 presents heatmap visualizations for two cases: without priority scheduling and with priority scheduling. The results reveal that the optimal configuration occurs when α equals β, with $\alpha = \beta = 12$ in the absence of priority scheduling and $\alpha = \beta = 30$ under priority-based scheduling.

(b) Bar Graph Analysis: Fig. 3 illustrates the evolution of optimal $\alpha = \beta$ settings across various matrix sizes and thread counts (26, 52, and 104 threads), highlighting how computational load influences parameter tuning. The yellow highlighted band indicates the range in which the optimal parameter values consistently fall across different matrix sizes. A key insight from the results is that, as the number of threads increases, the variability in the optimal $\alpha\beta$ values diminishes. This convergence suggests that, under higher parallelism, finer granularity (i.e., lower α and β) is preferred to maximize workload distribution and minimize execution time.

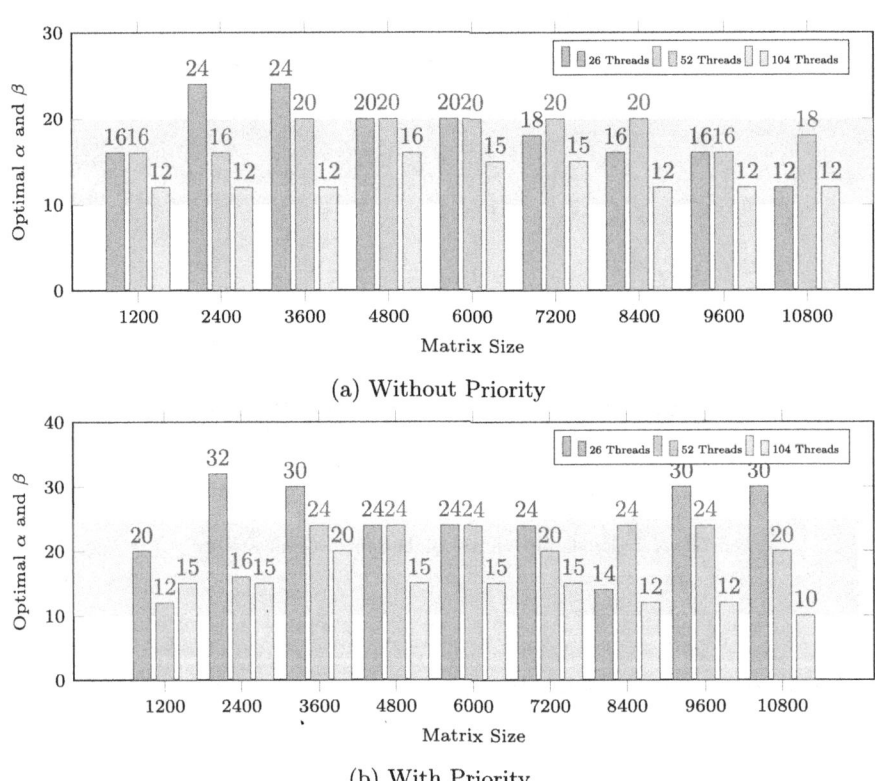

Fig. 3. Bar graphs of best configurations across different matrix sizes.

4.2 Scalability Analysis

In this experiment, we assesses the scalability of our proposed algorithm on dense square matrices with dimensions ranging from 300×300 to 10800×10800. The optimal α and β values determined in Experiment 4.1 were employed consistently. To capture the impact of parallelism, tests were performed using 26 and 52 threads.

To assess the effectiveness of our approach, we compare three different methods: (i) a parallel DAG execution method that employs synchronization barriers and (ii) two variants of our proposed approach–one incorporating a priority-based scheduling mechanism and another without priority. This comparative analysis provides insights into the efficiency and scalability of the proposed methodology under varying computational loads.

Figure 4a (26 threads) and Fig. 4b (52 threads) display the execution time trends as the matrix size increases. The results clearly demonstrate that both variants of our method (with and without priority scheduling) significantly outperform the barrier-based parallel DAG execution. However, the priority-free variant performs slightly better than priority-based due to the overhead introduced by priority queues. The additional overhead stems from the fact that priority queues reorder nodes according to their priority values and require more frequent data structure re-balancing.

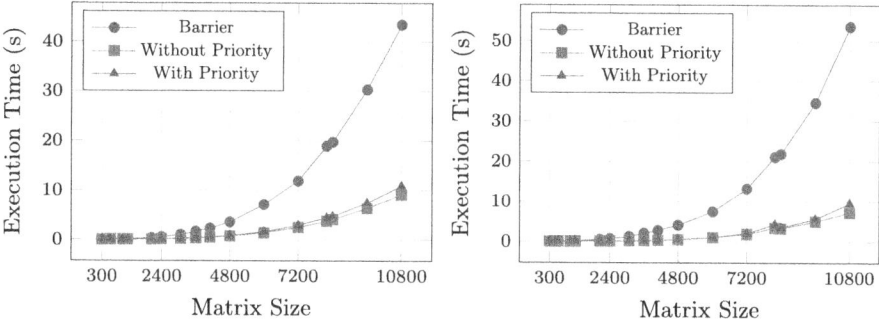

(a) Exec. Time vs Matrix Size (26 Threads) (b) Exec. Time vs Matrix Size (52 Threads)

Fig. 4. Scalability comparison of the proposed algorithm for different matrix sizes.

4.3 Throughput Evaluation

In this experiment, we evaluate the throughput of various algorithms by incrementally increasing the number of threads (in multiples of 4) for a fixed matrix size of 8192×8192, while using the optimal α and β values from Experiment 4.1. Figure 5 plots the execution time (on a logarithmic scale) against thread count for three methods: barrier-based, without priority, and with priority scheduling.

The results align with the previous experiment, confirming that our proposed method (with and without priority) outperforms the parallel DAG execution with barriers. However, the priority-based variant is slightly less efficient due to its additional overhead.

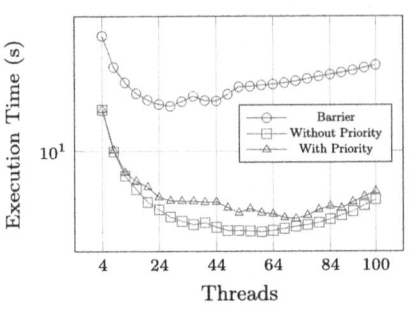
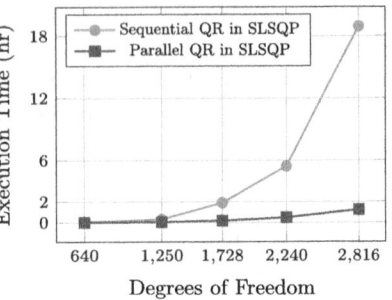

Fig. 5. Throughput Evaluation

Fig. 6. SLSQP Performance

4.4 Impact of Parallel QR Factorization in SLSQP

In this experiment, we examine the influence of integrating our proposed parallel QR approach into the SLSQP framework within the NLOPT library. Our focus is on large-scale boundary value problems involving implicit constitutive relations under both elastic and inelastic responses. [1].

To assess performance, we compare a baseline SLSQP implementation equipped with sequential QR factorization against an SLSQP version that leverages our parallel QR factorization. We evaluated these approaches over a range of problem sizes defined by degrees of freedom (DOF) equal to 640, 1250, 1728, 2240, and 2816. Here, the term "degrees of freedom" denotes the total number of unknowns, such as nodal displacements, stresses, or auxiliary state variables, emerging from the discretizations of the governing partial differential equations and boundary conditions. Consequently, an increase in DOF results in a proportional increase in the dimension of the system matrix factorized by SLSQP.

Figure 6 shows the execution times (in hours) corresponding to each DOF level for both sequential and parallel QR implementations. Notably, when the DOF reaches 2816, the parallel QR variant completes its tasks in approximately 1.21 h, whereas the sequential counterpart requires nearly 18.91 h. This substantial improvement in computational efficiency becomes increasingly pronounced as the DOF grows, reflecting the strong scalability of the parallel approach.

5 Related Works

The NLOPT [10] library's SLSQP [12] algorithm is a recognized open-source, numerically stable solver for nonlinear optimization, valued for its customizability. However, unlike continuously evolving contemporaries such as IPOPT [3] (open-source) and SNOPT [7] (commercial), SLSQP has seen limited recent advancements. To address this, Joshy et al. introduced the PySLSQP [11] package, enhancing SLSQP's utility by bridging Python with the original Fortran code, thereby facilitating easier modification and addressing limitations in current formulations, particularly those in NLOPT. Concurrently, significant progress has been made in parallel QR decomposition. Buttari et al. [4] introduced a Parallel Tiled QR factorization method using a DAG for scheduling. Baskaran et al. [2] contributed with compiler-assisted dynamic scheduling using lock-based priority queues, and building on this, Roshan et al. (Dathathri et al.) [6] developed dynamic scheduling techniques with lock-free priority queues for QR factorization. This research extends existing approaches by enhancing the NLOPT SLSQP solver through the integration of advanced asynchronous parallel algorithms. Departing from traditional synchronous strategies, this method incorporates novel parallel scheduling techniques inspired by the dynamic and lock-free approaches developed for QR factorization, aiming to improve both performance and scalability. For managing the interdependent tasks within QR decomposition, this work employs a variation of DAG scheduling, drawing upon established efficient DAG scheduling methodologies [13, 15].

6 Conclusions and Future Work

This study integrates a highly parallel QR factorization into NLOPT's SLSQP routine by decomposing the factorization into numerous independent micro-tasks and coordinating them with an asynchronous, dependency-aware DAG scheduler. The resulting workflow markedly cuts computational overhead and achieves consistent speed-ups across a broad suite of benchmark problems, underscoring the value of fine-grained parallelism in nonlinear constrained optimization. In future work, we will substitute the classical Householder QR with a tiled implementation [2, 4, 6]. Tiling will expose even finer parallel granularity, facilitate NUMA-aware task placement, and enable closed-form selection of tuning parameters α and β, thereby eliminating costly parameter sweeps. Moreover, tiling naturally reduces queue-transfer contention between wait and execution queues by improving spatial locality and minimizing remote memory traffic. We further intend to generalize this tiling and scheduling strategy to the full suite of linear-algebra kernels invoked by SLSQP–such as rank-update, triangular solve, and Cholesky-related operations–ultimately delivering a solver that scales robustly on diverse multicore and many-core architectures.

Acknowledgments and Artifact Availability. We extend our deepest gratitude to Dr. Saravanan, Professor of Civil Engineering, Indian Institute of Technology, Madras, for providing us with the dataset for the experiment 4.4. We also thank the anonymous reviewers for their useful comments. The artifact for this work is available in the Zenodo repository [5].

Disclosure of Interests. This work is partly funded by CRG 009391 & 001090, GoI (Government of India).

References

1. Ananthapadmanabhan, S., Saravanan, U.: Multi-field formulations for solving plane problems involving viscoelastic constitutive relations. Appl. Eng. Sci. **13**, 100120 (2023)
2. Baskaran, M.M., Vydyanathan, N., Bondhugula, U.K.R., Ramanujam, J., Rountev, A., Sadayappan, P.: Compiler-assisted dynamic scheduling for effective parallelization of loop nests on multicore processors. ACM Sigplan Notices **44**(4), 219–228 (2009)
3. Biegler, L.T., Zavala, V.M.: Large-scale nonlinear programming using IPOPT: an integrating framework for enterprise-wide dynamic optimization. Comput. Chem. Eng. **33**(3), 575–582 (2009)
4. Buttari, A., Langou, J., Kurzak, J., Dongarra, J.: Parallel tiled QR factorization for multicore architectures. Concurr. Comput. Pract. Exp. **20**(13), 1573–1590 (2008)
5. Chatterjee, S., Utkoor, R., Eshwar, U., Peri, S., Nandivada, V.K.: Artifact of the paper: efficient task graph scheduling for parallel QR factorization in SLSQP (2025). https://doi.org/10.5281/zenodo.15602262
6. Dathathri, R., Mullapudi, R.T., Bondhugula, U.: Compiling affine loop nests for a dynamic scheduling runtime on shared and distributed memory. ACM Trans. Parallel Comput. (TOPC) **3**(2), 1–28 (2016)
7. Gill, P.E., Murray, W., Saunders, M.A.: SNOPT: an SQP algorithm for large-scale constrained optimization. SIAM Rev. **47**(1), 99–131 (2005)
8. Gill, P.E., Saunders, M.A., Wong, E.: On the performance of SQP methods for nonlinear optimization. In: Defourny, B., Terlaky, T. (eds.) Modeling and Optimization: Theory and Applications. SPMS, vol. 147, pp. 95–123. Springer, Cham (2015). https://doi.org/10.1007/978-3-319-23699-5_5
9. Householder, A.S.: Unitary triangularization of a nonsymmetric matrix. J. ACM (JACM) **5**(4), 339–342 (1958)
10. Johnson, S.G.: The NLopt nonlinear-optimization package (2007). https://github.com/stevengj/nlopt
11. Joshy, A.J., Hwang, J.T.: PYSLSQP: a transparent python package for the SLSQP optimization algorithm modernized with utilities for visualization and post-processing. arXiv preprint arXiv:2408.13420 (2024)
12. Kraft, D.: Algorithm 733: TOMP-Fortran modules for optimal control calculations. ACM Trans. Math. Softw. **20**, 262–281 (1994). https://doi.org/10.1145/192115.192124
13. Kwok, Y.K., Ahmad, I.: Dynamic critical-path scheduling: an effective technique for allocating task graphs to multiprocessors. IEEE Trans. Parallel Distrib. Syst. **7**(5), 506–521 (1996). https://doi.org/10.1109/71.503776
14. Liu, F., Fredriksson, A., Markidis, S.: A survey of HPC algorithms and frameworks for large-scale gradient-based nonlinear optimization. J. Supercomput. **78**(16), 17513–17542 (2022)
15. McCreary, C., Khan, A.A., Thompson, J.J., McArdle, M.E.: A comparison of heuristics for scheduling DAGS on multiprocessors. In: Proceedings of the 8th International Symposium on Parallel Processing, pp. 446–451. IEEE Computer Society, USA (1994)
16. Nocedal, J., Wright, S.: Numerical optimization. In: Springer Series in Operations Research and Financial Engineering, pp. 1–664. Springer Nature, New York (2006). https://doi.org/10.1007/978-0-387-40065-5_16.pdf

Breaking the I/O Barrier: 1.2 Tb/s Ethernet Packet Processing on a GPU

John W. Romein[(✉)]

ASTRON (Netherlands Institute for Radio Astronomy), Dwingeloo, The Netherlands
romein@astron.nl
https://www.astron.nl/

Abstract. Radio telescopes produce enormous amounts of data. Many of them use GPU clusters to combine the digitized antenna signals, usually in real time. Achieving high data rates is challenging: the PCIe bandwidth of discrete GPUs is limited, and without RDMA, handling 200 or 400 Gb/s Ethernet packets with telescope data is difficult.

The NVIDIA Grace Hopper is a novel, innovative system that eliminates the I/O bottleneck of traditional, discrete GPUs by using NVLink instead of PCIe. This opens the door to higher data rates, but faster hardware alone is not enough. In this paper, we combine hardware and software innovations to process Ethernet packets at no less than 1.2 Tb/s, a huge improvement over what was previously possible. We use the Data Plane Development Kit to minimize the receive overhead, and use a new feature that allows packet processing directly by the GPU. We demonstrate the data handling in a correlator application, analyze the performance, and show how to reduce the energy use.

The presented innovations enable the use of GPUs for more powerful telescopes with much higher data rates. The results are also of interest to (GPU) applications from other application domains with high I/O demands, especially if RDMA is not available.

Keywords: GPU · Ethernet · DPDK · Grace Hopper · Radio Astronomy

1 Introduction

Radio telescopes produce enormous amounts of data, and with the relentless drive to build more powerful instruments, these data rates increase and increase. Most telescopes combine the data from tens or hundreds of receivers, to obtain higher sensitivity and image resolution. This data is transported, typically over Ethernet, to a central location where the data is combined by what is called a *correlator*. Due to the high data rates, these data are usually correlated in real time. In the past, this was done using custom-built electronics, ASICs, or DSPs, but nowadays this task is performed by FPGAs or GPUs.

The choice to use FPGAs or GPUs for a correlator depends on multiple factors. Generally, FPGAs are considered to be better at I/O, but difficult to program, while GPUs are better at compute, and allow much more flexible and complex processing pipelines. Instruments with moderately high data rates, like CHIME [9], LOFAR [7], and the MWA [13], use GPU-based correlators. However, for instruments with the highest data rates, like ALMA [8] and the two SKA sites, new FPGA-based correlators are being developed, as GPU systems were deemed less suitable to handle tens of terabits per second.

During the past decade, the computational performance of successive GPU generations increased by roughly two orders of magnitude, partly because of the introduction of tensor cores, that can be efficiently used for signal-processing tasks like correlations and beam forming [19,22]. In the same period, the PCIe bandwidth increased by less than a single order of magnitude, thus the gap between computational performance and I/O performance widened. To profit from the hundreds of tera-ops/s of computational processing power from present-day GPUs, we would need to stream in data at more than a terabit per second—far beyond the 200 or 400 Gb/s PCIe gen 4 or gen 5 bus speeds of recent, discrete GPUs and network interfaces.

Fig. 1. Schematics of the Grace Hopper Superchip (source: NVIDIA).

The recently introduced *Grace Hopper Superchip* [17] turns out to be a game changer. These innovative systems do not only contain the most powerful GPU to date, the traditional PCIe link between CPU and GPU is replaced by NVLink, that provides seven times more bandwidth than PCIe gen 5 (see Fig. 1). This essentially eliminates the I/O bottleneck of discrete GPUs. The figure also shows four PCIe links (on the left), but in practice, Grace Hopper systems have at most three PCIe slots available for network interfaces (NICs). Each slot can hold one 400 Gb/s Ethernet (GbE) NIC or a dual-port 200 GbE NIC, for a total of 1200 Gb/s of Ethernet connectivity, six times more than a PCIe gen 4 GPU can handle.

However, faster hardware alone is not enough to achieve 1.2 Tb/s at the application level. Such data rates cannot be handled by the Operating System

(OS): the interrupt, context switching, and packet-copying overheads are prohibitive. And as we will show below, even the CPU memory is too slow to act as a packet buffer. We need techniques that bypass the OS, and stream packet data directly from the NICs into GPU memory. Normally, one would use RDMA techniques like RoCE or GPUdirect [15] for this, but as the data comes from FPGAs, RDMA would severely complicate the FPGA firmware. Instead, we use the Data Plane Development Kit (DPDK) [4] to receive and handle network packets without OS overhead, and we use a recent DPDK addition, called *GPUdev* [5], that allows Ethernet packets to be processed directly by the GPU. This proved to be an essential technique to achieve high data rates.

The main contributions of the paper are the following. Through a combination of software and hardware innovations, we demonstrate a GPU correlator that receives and processes 1196 Gb/s of Ethernet packets, a 6–20-fold improvement over previous-generation GPU correlators. This result shows that in general I/O is no longer the GPU's Achilles heel. We explain the techniques and optimizations that are necessary to achieve this data rate. We analyze the network, CPU, and GPU performance, show how to reduce the energy use, and discuss the strengths and weaknesses of the DPDK approach.

Although this study is driven by the challenges from radio astronomy, the results apply to (GPU) applications from any domain that demands high data rates, especially in situations where the use of RDMA is not possible.

This paper is structured as follows. In Sect. 2, we provide some background information on radio telescopes, GPU correlators, and DPDK. Section 3 describes several DPDK-based implementations of a GPU correlator, for which we analyze the performance and energy efficiency in Sect. 4. Section 5 discusses advantages and disadvantages of the DPDK approach, and Sect. 6 describes related and future work. Section 7 concludes.

The software developed for this publication is available online [1,2].

2 Background

In this section, we briefly describe how data flows in a radio telescope system, up to the point that telescope data has been combined by what is called the correlator. A complex post-correlator processing pipeline then takes care of calibration and imaging, but this is outside the scope of this paper. Figure 2 depicts the data flow between the antennas and the correlator. On the left, antenna signals are digitized by Analog-to-Digital Converters (ADCs), controlled by FPGAs. The FPGAs also filter and packetize the data. The filter separates the signals into disjoint frequency bands, that can each be processed independently by the different GPU correlator machines on the right. As discussed in the introduction, correlators can be built from either FPGA or GPUs; in this paper we assume a GPU-based correlator. In contrast, the digitizers on the left are always FPGAs, as GPUs cannot control and read ADCs.

As each digitizer FPGA holds the signals from all frequency bands of one antenna, while a GPU correlator node needs one frequency band of all antennas,

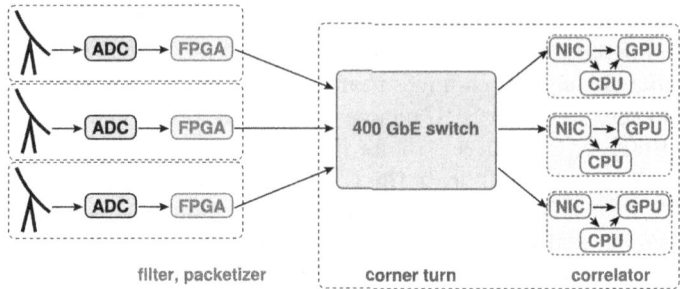

Fig. 2. Data flow from antennas to GPU correlator systems.

the data transport from the FPGAs to the GPU systems forms a left-to-right any-to-any pattern, which is known as the "corner turn". In other words: each FPGA sends packets to all GPU correlator systems, and each GPU correlator system receives packets from all FPGAs. The corner turn is performed on the network switch in the middle of the figure, which is physically close to the GPU correlator systems.

Depending on the telescope, the FPGAs digitizers and the GPU correlator systems may be any distance between a few meters and thousands of kilometers apart (the distance between the two outermost antennas is one of the factors that determines the eventual image resolution). We use Ethernet as the transportation method, because Ethernet is well supported by both the FPGAs and by the GPU systems. Moreover, Ethernet works over any distance. Often, these Ethernet packets are formatted as UDP/IP packets, so that they can be routed. By design, the data transport is unreliable, as a reliable protocol like TCP would severely complicate the FPGA firmware and requires additional buffering, while in a real-time environment there is generally no time for retransmissions anyway. Also, the post-correlator processing pipeline may discard data for other reasons (in particular, due to Radio Frequency Interference), so the pipeline is well capable of handling missing data. Apart from UDP/IP/Ethernet headers, the packets contain an application-specific header with a timestamp of the precise time that the first sample in the packet was taken, the antenna number, and the frequency band number. The packet payload typically contains a few thousand consecutive (filtered) antenna samples, so that the size of the whole packet does not exceed the jumbo frame limit (9000 bytes), while the header size is small compared to the payload size.

A complicating factor of a correlator application is that we cannot assume that the data from all antennas arrive at the same time in a correlator system. Packets from a thousand kilometer distant antenna may arrive tens or even a hundred milliseconds later than from a nearby antenna. To combine the samples, the input streams from the different antennas must be realigned. Therefore, each correlator system maintains a ring buffer in which the input data is buffered, typically for hundreds of milliseconds or a few seconds. For each antenna, a separate ring buffer is used. The ring buffer is selected by the antenna-number value in the packet header, and the location within the ring buffer where samples from the packet payload are stored is determined by the header's timestamp value modulo the ring-buffer size. The ring-buffer data is continuously overwritten by newer data, so there is only a limited amount of time available to process the data. The data also needs to be available in the buffer while it is being transferred to the GPU.

This paper focuses on the receipt and processing of the network packets in the GPU systems, on the right in Fig. 2. Whereas in the 10 and 40 GbE era UDP/IP packets could be received through the operating system, the interrupt, context switching, and packet copying overheads are too large for 100 Gb/s Ethernet and beyond. Hence, we need a mechanism that bypasses the operating system in the critical receive path. As we strive to achieve line speeds from *multiple* network interfaces, we choose the Data Plane Development Kit (DPDK), also because of its recently added support for GPUs.

DPDK is a toolkit that allows an application to take full control over a network interface, bypassing the OS. The main functions are the functions that take care of receiving and sending Ethernet packets, and the ones that manage packet buffers in memory pools. Any network protocol on top of Ethernet also has to be implemented in user space. For simple protocols like UDP/IP, the application will likely implement the protocol stack itself, but for complex protocols like TCP/IP, it is probably more convenient to use an open-source user-level library like F-Stack [3]. As a DPDK application can send and receive any Ethernet packet on a network, which is a severe security threat, DPDK applications run with an elevated privilege level (as superuser, or with some specific capabilities). The toolkit is supported by all major NIC vendors, but the GPUdev extension currently only works with NVIDIA NICs and NVIDIA GPUs. We elaborate on the use of DPDK in the next section.

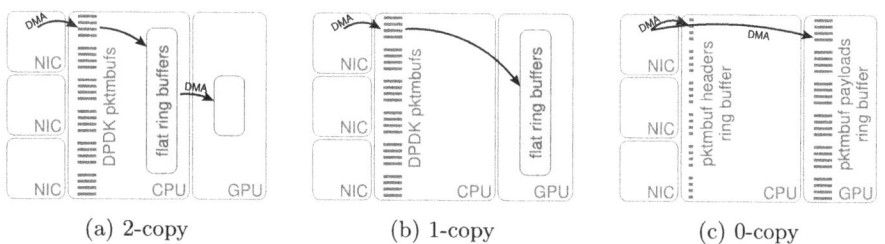

Fig. 3. Copy behavior of the different implementations.

3 Implementation

We implemented three correlator variants. Each of them uses DPDK, but the data paths are different. Figure 3a depicts how the most straightforward implementation of a GPU correlator works: the packets are received in DPDK packet buffers, the packet data is copied into the ring buffers in CPU memory, and after some time, when all data for a particular time interval has arrived (or should have arrived), the section of ring-buffer data for that time interval is copied to GPU memory, for each antenna. Subsequently, the GPU processes the data. We call this the *2-copy* variant, as receiving data from the NIC is generally not counted as a "copy" action.

The second variant does not have the ring buffers in CPU memory, but in GPU memory (see Fig. 3b). Here, the packets are still received in DPDK packet buffers, but their contents are copied into the GPU ring buffers. We call this the *1-copy* variant. Alternatively, we could have stored the ring buffers in CPU memory and let the GPU channel filter kernel read the ring buffer contents through unified memory, but despite the use of NVLink, this makes the channel filter kernel prohibitively slow, so we do not further consider this alternative.

The third variant, the *0-copy* variant, works quite differently (see Fig. 3c). Rather than implementing the ring buffer as a flat memory buffer, we use a giant amount of DPDK packet buffers as "ring buffer", and process the data at a later moment directly from the packet buffers. For this, we use the recently added GPU support in DPDK, *GPUdev* [5], that allows allocating packet buffers in GPU memory. DPDK also allows splitting packets, and receive packet fragments in different memory pools. We allocate one memory pool in CPU memory and another memory pool in GPU memory, and split incoming packets so that each packet header (56 bytes) is received in CPU memory, and the associated packet payload (8192 bytes) is received in GPU memory. Important to note is that 99.3% of the packet data is directly DMAed from the NIC into GPU memory, bypassing CPU memory. The packet headers contain the timestamps and antenna numbers, that determine the location in the ring buffer. The timestamps and antenna numbers are inspected by the CPU, and a pointer to the packet payload (in GPU memory) is placed in the ring buffer. The ring buffers thus contains pointers to packet payload buffers instead of the samples themselves. After all packets from a certain time interval should have arrived, the CPU copies the ring buffer payload pointers to the GPU, and launches the filter and correlator kernels that we describe in Sect. 3.1.

Even though we use almost 74 GB (77%) of the GPU memory for buffering packet payloads, the buffer fills up quickly at high data rates. At the maximum data rate of 1.2 Tb/s, the 9.4-million entry packet buffer is completely filled after only 0.52 s. The GPU processes blocks of 18 GB of data (one quarter of the ring buffer size), which corresponds to 0.13 s at the highest data rates, so that the remainder of the ring buffer is used to receive new packets, while there is also sufficient time to overcome the packet arrival time differences from the different antennas.

At first, using large amounts of GPU memory with GPUdev did not work well. During program initialization, the GPU memory is registered by DPDK to make it accessible to the NICs, but registering a few gigabytes of GPU memory was prohibitively slow (taking hours), and was exponentially slower for even larger sizes. We fixed this in DPDK's mlx5 driver, by sorting a list of segments only once instead of for each added segment. A patch is available [2].

We distribute the packet-handling work over multiple CPU cores, by using multiple receive queues. Each receive queue is associated with one CPU thread that continuously polls the queue for incoming packets. The amount of receive queues (and thus CPU cores) is an adjustable parameter. The antenna streams are divided over the available receive queues; consecutive packets from the same antenna always end up in the same receive queue.

As all cores and CPU memory in the Grace CPU are in the same NUMA domain, there is no need to bind threads to specific cores. Yet we distinguish between threads that poll a NIC receive queue and threads that do not; the polling threads make as few system calls as possible (to not stop receiving packets for an extended period of time), while (blocking) system calls are performed by the latter group of threads.

DPDK's per-core memory pool cache plays a crucial role in obtaining good performance. This is a 512-entry per-core cache where a core can quickly allocate and deallocate packets from, instead of using the much slower shared pool. We found that, regardless of how many cores are used, data rates beyond 800 Gb/s are impossible without effective use of the memory pool cache. This limits the freedom in application design choices. First, one cannot receive a packet by one core, hand it over another core that manages the GPU, and let the GPU-managing core deallocate the packet when the GPU is ready, because the receiving core would always encounter an empty cache and the deallocating core a full cache. Second, one cannot deallocate large amounts of packets in one go (even though a burst deallocation function is available). Instead, after a packet has been processed, we defer packet deallocation, so that every time a new packet is received, another unused packet is deallocated. This keeps the cache usually in a partially filled state.

Fig. 4. Simplified view of the GPU processing pipeline.

3.1 GPU Processing

Although a comprehensive study of the GPU kernels is outside the scope of this paper, we briefly describe the signal-processing operations performed by the GPU. The GPU performs three major tasks: it handles the input packets (this only applies to the 0-copy variant), and subsequently channelizes and correlates the signals (see Fig. 4). The last two tasks are standard signal-processing operations that basically every (GPU) correlator performs.

Even though packet handling and channel filtering are depicted as two operations, they are performed by the same GPU kernel. The channel filter comes from a newly developed GPU library, that combines a PolyPhase Filter Bank (FIR filters and FFT), delay compensation (optional), bandpass correction (optional), and a memory transpose in a single GPU kernel. All these operations are fused in a single kernel, to reduce the number of GPU memory accesses. The library compiles the GPU code at run time, applying specific optimizations that depend on the given number of antennas, frequency channels, etc. We use the runtime compilation property also to provide the library with custom GPU code that reads input data from DPDK packet payloads, rather than a flat memory buffer. This is a nice separation of responsibilities: the filter library itself is oblivious of DPDK, yet the GPU channel filter kernel is heavily involved in processing the DPDK packets.

The second GPU kernel is a correlator kernel that combines the antenna data by pairwise multiplication and integration of the filtered antenna samples. This kernel comes from the *Tensor-Core Correlator* library [22], that performs these operations on tensor cores. It is the fastest (GPU) correlator to date.

Once the data from all antennas should have arrived in the ring buffers (possibly with a time offset), the GPU processes blocks of 18 GB of data; a quarter of the ring buffer size. Consecutive blocks are slightly overlapping, as the FIR filters in the channelizer are in fact convolutions that need some historical data from the previous block. This complicates the implementation. Due to the large data blocks on which the GPU operates, the kernel launch overhead is negligible. Yet, the kernels are launched by a different thread than the CPU threads that receive DPDK packets, as the kernel launches may involve (blocking) system calls.

We considered using a persistent GPU kernel that would poll for new incoming packets, and immediately process (channelize) new packet data. The advantage of that would be that the packet-buffer size could be kept small, decreasing the DPDK overhead. However, it may increase the energy use, as it keeps the GPU busy at all times, even if there is no new data to process. Unfortunately, a persistent kernel is difficult to implement in this case, for several reasons. In particular, the realignment in time of the channelized data prior to correlation (which requires some sort of ring buffer as well), but also the missing support for persistent kernels in the filter library, the internal state that a filter must maintain, the deallocation of processed packets, and CPU–GPU synchronization all add to the complexity. Therefore, we refrained from using a persistent kernel.

3.2 Correlator Output

In this study, we do not specifically optimize for high output data rates, as the output data rate of a correlator is typically (much) lower than the input data rate. If the output is written to file, we use the new cuFile library from the CUDA toolkit to write data directly from GPU memory to file. Alternatively, the data can be sent over a TCP connection to an external system. For simplicity, we do this via the operating system (and another virtual instance of one of the NICs), which works fine for speeds up to about 50 Gb/s. If the output data rate requirements for a specific instrument setup would exceed this, the output data path should also be optimized (either through DPDK, or some RDMA protocol), but at such high output data rates, the biggest challenges would not be in the correlator itself, but in the post-correlator processing pipeline.

4 Performance

We analyze the application and DPDK performance on the CPU and GPU. Although in reality antenna data are digitized and packetized by FPGAs near the individual antennas, in this experimental setup we use a CPU-based packet generator that mimics the FPGA behavior, for practical reasons. We only evaluate the performance of a single GPU correlator system, as multi-GPU correlator systems operate independently of each other, since they each process a different frequency band, so multi-GPU scaling is trivial. The corner turn does *not* scale trivially, and can impose high packet-switching requirements on the switch, but this is outside the scope of this paper.

The measurements were performed on two QCT S74G-2U Grace Hopper systems with 96 GB HBM3 and 480 GB LPDDR5 memory (one for the packet generator, the other one for the GPU correlator), using a patched version of DPDK 24.03 (see Sect. 3) and Linux kernel 6.5.0-1024-nvidia-64k. For availability reasons, we use a mixture of 400 GbE and dual-port 200 GbE ConnectX-7 NICs, for a total of 1200 Gb/s per system (in each direction). To simplify the software, we split the 400 GbE NICs into two virtual 200 GbE NICs, so that the software does not need to distinguish between different link speeds. In practice, we saw that a single 400 GbE link and two bundled 200 GbE links behaved similarly. SSH connections are routed via a separate USB-Ethernet dongle, to not interfere with the high-speed network interfaces. Unless stated otherwise, 12 (out of 72 available) CPU cores are used to poll the NICs and insert the packets in the circular buffer.

We simulate 72 antennas and 8 bits per sample, typical numbers for a radio telescope. For other instruments, the ratio between the amount of I/O and computations may be different. The I/O bandwidth scales proportionally to the number of antennas, but the amount of computations scales quadratically. Fewer bits per sample reduces the amount of I/O, but has no impact on the amount of computations.

We seek for the largest amount of data that a Grace Hopper system could receive and process in real time, without packet loss (the correlator should normally not lose data, even though the remainder of the processing pipeline tolerates it). Figure 5 shows the obtained network bandwidth, for each of the three variants. The 2-copy variant runs up to 309 Gb/s without packet loss. The 1-copy variant works best with 24 cores, and achieves a data rate of 670 Gb/s. The 2-copy and 1-copy variants can actually process higher data rates, but start to drop packets then, something that we wish to avoid. Only the 0-copy variant is able to process packets at 1.2 Tb/s. This means that the application is still limited by network bandwidth, but this bandwidth is six times higher than what was possible with previous-generation GPUs. And as we will see later, the GPU would not be able to handle a much higher data rate, so the GPU compute power and I/O capabilities are fairly balanced.

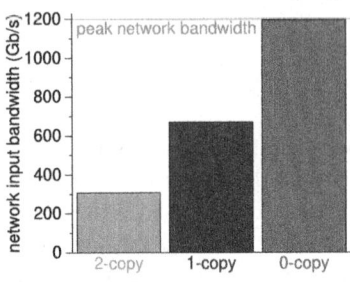

Fig. 5. Achieved input network bandwidth (without packet loss).

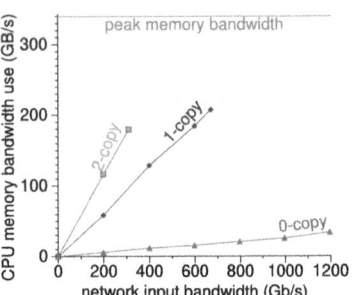

Fig. 6. CPU memory bandwidth use.

Figure 6 shows the actual CPU memory bandwidth use, which is a scarce resource for the 2-copy and 1-copy variants. Unfortunately, there are no performance counters that measure the CPU memory bandwidth use directly, so we measured and added the memory traffic from the local CPU cores, NVLink, and PCIe busses, as described in the *Grace Performance Tuning Guide* [18].

From the figure, we see that the 2-copy and 1-copy variants would never scale to 1.2 Tb/s, as their extrapolated graphs exceed the memory bandwidth that is available. A separate benchmark measured the memory bandwidth at 340 GB/s, which is consistent with what the Tuning Guide [18] reports. Yet, we see that the 2-copy and 1-copy variants do not get close to the 340 GB/s bandwidth use as they start losing packets; this already happens around 200 GB/s. For the 2-copy variant, this is mostly due to the irregular CPU-to-GPU transfers: due to the high NVLink link speed, these transfers can claim all the available CPU memory bandwidth, leaving insufficient memory bandwidth for packet receipt. The 1-copy variant does not suffer from this, still the memory access pattern is not optimal to reach full bandwidth without packet loss.

In fact, the 0-copy variant is the only variant that does not suffer from insufficient CPU memory bandwidth; the figure shows that its actual memory bandwidth use is low. In the remainder of this section, we only consider the 0-copy variant.

Note that, unlike CPU memory bandwidth, GPU memory bandwidth is amply available; the 150 GB/s that is needed to store packet payloads, is only a small fraction of the 3.5 TB/s that is available.

4.1 Energy Efficiency

A well-known technique to improve the energy efficiency of a GPU (and many other processors) is to run the application at a reduced clock frequency [21]. As the GPU idles for 23% of the time at the default (and highest supported) clock frequency, there is room to reduce the clock speed, down to the point that it

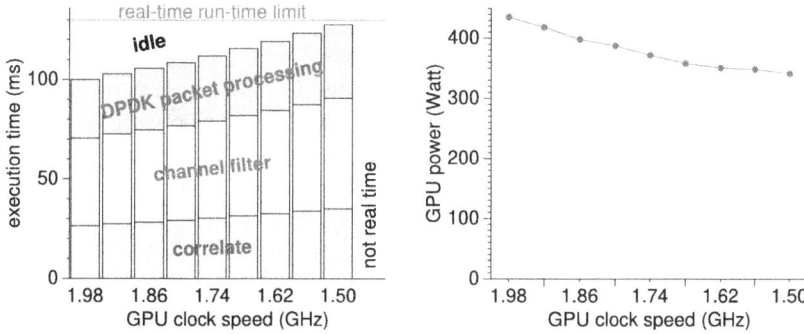

Fig. 7. GPU performance and energy efficiency. On the left: the time spent in the different kernels, as a function of clock frequency (note that the DPDK packet handling is in fact part of the filter kernel, but its execution time is shown separately). On the right: the power use.

just does not lose real-time behavior (see Fig. 7). This way, we can reduce the energy consumption already by 96 W.

Similarly, we can reduce the CPU clock frequency (see Fig. 8). Note that, unlike the GPU kernels, the packet-handling CPU cores never idle but keep on polling the NICs to check if new packets have arrived. When using only 6 CPU cores to handle the incoming packets, there is hardly any room to reduce the clock frequency without packet loss. However, if we increase the number of polling cores to 12, we can decrease the clock frequency all the way down to 1.8 GHz, without observing packet loss. This way, we can decrease the CPU power from 119 W (with 6 fast-running cores) to 69 W (with 12 slow-running cores). We see no additional benefit from increasing the number of polling cores to 18, because the clock speed cannot be reduced any further without packet loss.

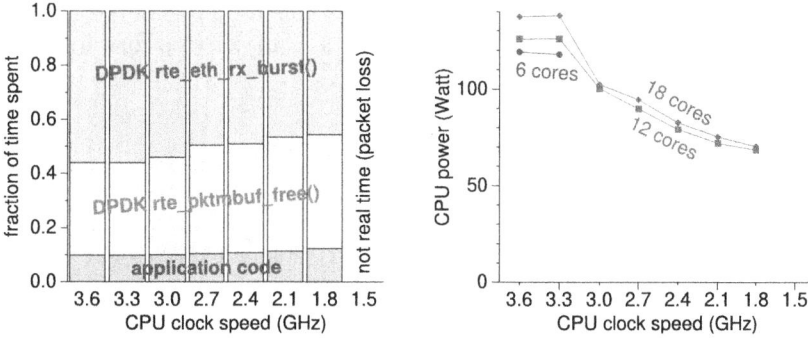

Fig. 8. CPU performance and energy efficiency. On the left: the time spent in DPDK and in the application code, as a function of clock frequency. On the right: the energy use.

5 Discussion

So far, we learned that the DPDK approach, and in particular its recent support to receive packet payloads in GPU memory, yield extremely high data rates on streaming data, and good application performance. However, there are some drawbacks to this approach. First, the DPDK model provides no method to control *where* packet payloads are received in GPU memory. As a result, the GPU spends 22%–27% of the time collecting the input data from the scattered packet payloads: looking up an input sample requires an extra pointer indirection, and GPUs have no huge page support to reduce the amount of TLB misses.

Second, splitting packets increases DPDK's internal CPU overhead, because the header and payload buffers are allocated and deallocated from separately managed memory pools. We tried receiving the full packet (header and payload) in GPU memory. As, in this case, the relevant metadata (timestamp, antenna number) are in GPU memory, either the CPU needs to retrieve this data from GPU memory so that it can place the packet in the circular buffer, or the GPU itself should fully handle the packet and maintain the circular buffer itself. Unfortunately, for the former approach, the DPDK toolkit refused to register unified (managed) memory, so that the memory would have been accessible by the NIC, CPU, and GPU. And the latter approach is difficult to implement. For example, when the GPU finished processing a packet, it cannot return the packet fragments to the mbuf pool and should leave this to the CPU, but then it is difficult to make efficient use of DPDK's mbuf cache, which is crucial for performance.

Finally, the presented 0-copy method is difficult to integrate into existing GPU correlator applications like the LOFAR [7] and AARTFAAC [20] correlators, due to the different way in which input data is stored, the different roles of CPU threads, and the prohibitive costs of thread synchronization for every received packet. The application that we use for this demonstration, was written from scratch (except for the GPU kernels) so that DPDK could be properly integrated.

On the other hand, we have not seen any competing approach that yields such high data rates, and given the enormous increase in achieved data rates, we consider the DPDK and GPUdev solution as a major step forward.

6 Related and Future Work

So far, GPU correlators have only been built for radio telescopes with moderate data rates, like CHIME (for a total of 6.6 Tb/s divided over 1024 GPUs) [9], LOFAR (236 Gb/s) [7], AARTFAAC (120 Gb/s) [20], and MWAX (11 Gb/s) [13], to name a few. It is also worth noting what has *not* been built: so far, GPU and NIC technology were not ready for instruments like ALMA, which is currently being upgraded to 63 Tb/s [8]. This study shows that a 63 Tb/s GPU correlator is feasible. But we also need more efficient packet handling in the AARTFAAC and LOFAR correlators, as their networks are currently being upgraded to 400/100 GbE, allowing much higher data rates.

Others tried ibverbs to bypass the operating system, e.g., in the SPEAD2 packet-handling library [12] or in an experimental setup [10]. The performance that was obtained with it in practice, fell 10–30% short of the used Ethernet line rates (200 and 400 Gb/s, respectively).

NVIDIA Holoscan [16] is a framework that supports implementing applications for real-time sensor processing on GPUs. Holoscan is used in a setup with the Allen Telescope Array, where Holoscan's Advanced Network Operator is used to process 100 GbE data, bypassing the CPU [11]. As Holoscan is built on top of DPDK, it should be able to perform similarly to what we report.

The DOCA toolkit [14] is a collection of SDKs that provide (low-level) access to NVIDIA NICs and DPUs, some of which allowing packet receipt in GPU memory (e.g., DOCA Ethernet and DOCA GPUnetIO). A recent addition to the toolkit, DOCA DPA (and the driver layer DOCA FlexIO) is highly promising, as it allows programming the Data-Path Accelerator with application-specific code. As a next step, we plan to explore DOCA DPA, and try to run code on the NIC that inspects the header of an incoming packet, computes a destination address within a flat ring buffer in GPU memory (based on the header's antenna number, frequency band number, and timestamp), and DMAs the packet payload directly from the NIC into the GPU ring buffer. If we can make this work, it would nearly eliminate the CPU and GPU overhead that we encounter with DPDK.

7 Conclusions

Many radio telescopes use GPU clusters to process antenna data, in real time. The desire to build more powerful radio telescopes results in higher data rates, that must be handled by such GPU systems. However, the I/O bandwidth of successive, discrete GPU generations did not keep pace with the increase in computing power, and, in the absence of RDMA, truly efficient methods to receive and handle network packets with telescope data were missing.

This paper demonstrates an enormous increase in network packet processing rates, through a combination of hardware and software innovations. The Grace Hopper architecture eliminates the PCIe bandwidth limitation, the Data Plane Development Kit (DPDK) removed the operating system overhead of receiving network packets, DPDK's recent support for GPUs allowed receiving packet data directly from the network interface into GPU memory, and the GPU application processes network packet payloads. Without these innovations, handling packets at a few hundred Gb/s was already difficult, but we demonstrate that 1.2 Tb/s per GPU is possible now, with a reasonable balance between GPU compute performance and I/O capabilities. The performance analysis shows that the CPU and GPU overheads from handling the network packets is noticeable but not prohibitive. We also showed that tuning clock frequencies led to a 145 W reduction in energy use, without losing real-time performance. Future work targets methods that further reduce the overhead, but the presented approach already enables the processing of much higher telescope data rates.

Acknowledgments. This work received funding from the European Southern Observatory through the ALMA GPU correlator study; from the European Commission through the RADIOBLOCKS grant (HORIZON-INFRA-2022-TECH-01, Grant Agreement 101093934); from the Netherlands eScience Center/SURF through the RECRUIT and PADRE grants; and from the Netherlands Organization for Scientific Research (NWO) through the DAS-6 [6] grant. We thank Cliff Burdick and Adam Thompson from NVIDIA for their advise.

Disclosure of Interests. The authors have no competing interests to declare that are relevant to the content of this article.

References

1. DPDK correlator. https://gitlab.eso.org/alma/gpu-correlator/dpdk-correlator
2. DPDK mlx5 patch. https://www.astron.nl/~romein/dpdk-mlx5-24.11.patch
3. F-Stack. https://www.f-stack.org/
4. The Data Plane Development Kit. https://www.dpdk.org/
5. Agostini, E.: Boosting Inline Packet Processing Using DPDK and GPUdev with GPUs (2022). https://developer.nvidia.com/blog/optimizing-inline-packet-processing-using-dpdk-and-gpudev-with-gpus/
6. Bal, H., et al.: A medium-scale distributed system for computer science research: infrastructure for the long term. IEEE Comput. **49**(5), 54–63 (2016)
7. Broekema, P.C., et al.: Cobalt: a GPU-based correlator and beamformer for LOFAR. Astron. Comput. **23** (2018)
8. Carpenter, J., Brogan, C., Iono, D., Mroczkowski, T.: The ALMA2030 Wideband Sensitivity Upgrade (2022). https://arxiv.org/abs/2211.00195
9. Denman, N., et al.: A GPU spatial processing system for CHIME. J. Astron. Instrum. **9** (2020)
10. Liu, W., Burnett, M.C., Werthimer, D., Kocz, J.: A 400 Gbit ethernet core enabling high data rate streaming from FPGAs to servers and GPUs in radio astronomy. Astron. Soc. Pac. **136**(12) (2024)
11. Ma, P.X., et al.: A Deployed Real-Time End-to-End Deep Learning Algorithm for Fast Radio Burst Detection (2025, under review)
12. Merry, B.: SPEAD2. https://spead2.readthedocs.io/
13. Morrison, I.S., et al.: MWAX: a new correlator for the Murchison widefield array. Publ. Astron. Soc. Austral. **40**, e019 (2023)
14. NVIDIA: DOCA. https://docs.nvidia.com/doca/sdk/doca+ethernet/
15. NVIDIA: GPU Direct. https://developer.nvidia.com/gpudirect/
16. NVIDIA: Holoscan. https://www.nvidia.com/en-us/clara/holoscan/
17. NVIDIA: GH200 Grace Hopper Superchip Architecture (2024). https://resources.nvidia.com/en-us-grace-cpu/nvidia-grace-hopper/
18. NVIDIA: Grace Performance Tuning Guide (2024). https://docs.nvidia.com/grace-perf-tuning-guide/measuring-performance.html
19. Oostrum, L., et al.: The tensor-core beamformer: a high-speed signal-processing library for multidisciplinary use. In: IEEE IPDPS 2025, Milan, Italy (2025)
20. Prasad, P., et al.: The AARTFAAC all-sky monitor: system design and implementation. J. Astron. Instrum. **5**(4) (2016)
21. Price, D.C., Clark, M.A., Barsdell, B.R., Babich, R., Greenhill, L.J.: Optimizing performance-per-watt on GPUs in high performance computing. Comput. Sci. Res. Dev. **31**(4), 185–193 (2015). https://doi.org/10.1007/s00450-015-0300-5
22. Romein, J.W.: The tensor-core correlator. Astron. Astrophys. **656**(A52), 1–4 (2021)

GECKO: A Write-Optimized Adaptive Radix Tree for Disaggregated Memory

Tianyu Wan, Shijia Gong, Yangyang Hu, and Jianxi Chen[✉]

Wuhan National Laboratory for Optoelectronics, Huazhong University of Science and Technology, Wuhan, Hubei, China
{wanty,gong_shijia,hyy23,chenjx}@hust.edu.cn

Abstract. Disaggregated memory separates compute and storage nodes into two independent pools, connected via RDMA or CXL links. Disaggregated memory improves resource utilization, saves cost overhead, and ensures elastic scalability of memory and compute resources. Tree indexes are essential guarantees in storage systems, such as databases or key-value storage. Existing disaggregated memory systems suffer from poor write performance, mainly due to concurrency conflicts, frequent Structure Modification Operation (SMO) operations, and high lock overhead on tree index.

To solve the problem, we propose GECKO, a write-optimized Adaptive Radix Tree index structure for disaggregated memory. We leverage 1) a write-optimized buffer node to handle concurrent writes, improving write performance, 2) a threshold-based splitting strategy to reduce splits and optimize SMO operations, 3) a post-insertion lock design to reduce lock overhead and reduce insertion tail latency. We compare GECKO with state-of-the-art solutions. Experiments show that GECKO improves throughput by 1.43×–3.21× under write workloads. Additionally, it reduces SMO operation time by 88.5% and decreases lock time by 87.9%.

Keywords: Disaggregated memory · Index structures · Write optimization

1 Introduction

In modern data centers, the cost of memory is notably exorbitant, but memory utilization is very inefficient. Research reports indicate that the total cost of memory accounts for 50% of hardware expenditure [14], but according to Google, Microsoft, and Alibaba, data center memory utilization is only 20% [9,10,16]. The low memory utilization is due to the tight coupling between the CPU and memory, with the CPU only able to use the memory resources on the current physical machine. Data from Azure data centers shows that after 85% of the CPU is rented to virtual machines, there is an average of more than 10% of idle memory, also known as the memory stranding problem [1]. The rapid development of network technology has freed the CPU and memory from the limitations of physical hosts. The disaggregated memory architecture allows the CPU and memory to expand independently, improving resource utilization. In recent years, the academic community has invested a lot of research in the field of disaggregated memory architecture [2,3,15,17,19,20]. The disaggregated memory architecture separates the CPU and DRAM, forming compute nodes (CN) and memory nodes (MN). CN and MN are connected via a fast network (such as RDMA and CXL). CN Clients access MN data through index structure based on disaggregated memory, thereby separating the CPU and memory [5,7,8].

Tree indexing on disaggregated memory can provide higher performance for applications, such as databases and key-value (KV) stores. Existing tree indexes based on disaggregated memory can achieve read performance as low as 1 Round Trip Time (RTT), but performance is poor under write-intensive loads. This is mainly due to inefficiency in writing indexes on disaggregated memory. Index structures based on B+ tree on disaggregated memory use leaf nodes to store a batch of KV pairs and use locks to solve concurrency conflicts. However, coarse-grained locks lead to high tail latency. B+ tree needs to read the entire leaf node before writing to get the address to write, and the entire key and value are stored inside the leaf node. Longer key-value pairs lead to larger read amplification, saturating the bandwidth and affecting insertion performance. Indexes based on Adaptive Radix Tree (ART) use RDMA CAS primitives to achieve lock-free insertion, reducing lock overhead during writes. However, SMOs are more frequent, leading to additional RTT and limiting I/O per second [11,12,18].

Existing state-of-the-art solutions include Sherman [18], CHIME [11], and SMART [12]. SMART is the most advanced ART tree on disaggregated memory. SMART uses RDMA CAS primitives to solve concurrency conflicts, achieving a completely lock-free structure during insertion. SMART greatly reduces lock overhead, but the number of SMOs in ART is considerable, requiring additional remote operations to modify internal nodes during insertion, reducing bandwidth during insertion. CHIME uses internal nodes of B+ tree and hopscotch-hash leaf nodes to balance cache occupancy and read amplification. Hopscotch hash is used to solve hash collision problems, using neighborhoods to store conflicting KV pairs. Using hopscotch hash nodes can reduce reads from the node level to the neighborhood level. Although it can effectively reduce read amplification, it needs to lock the entire leaf node during insertion, read the KV in the hopscotch hash neighborhood to determine whether an update operation is needed, and coarse-grained locks and read amplification during insertion lead to low write performance and high tail latency. Sherman is a write-optimized B+ tree on disaggregated memory. Reduce the need to write the entire leaf node during insertion through a two-level versioning mechanism. However, the coarse-grained node lock limits its write performance. In summary, there are three main problems that are difficult to solve for write-intensive workloads:

a. Intensifying Competition in Write and Update: In disaggregated memory architecture, compute nodes are unaware of each other, and write-write concurrency conflicts are a significant issue. Existing solutions typically write KV pairs and use CAS to point to KV pairs to resolve conflicts. This method leads to retrying failed RTTs, introducing an additional RTT. Conflict in update operations is also a problem that needs to be addressed. Existing solutions typically use locks to update data. Although using a version mechanism or checksum to achieve lock-free read and write may read invalid data, leading to retries, conflicts between updates and updates will still block, affecting overall performance.

b. Excessive SMO leads to Poor Performance: Focus on tree structure, existing solutions will cause excessive splitting during insertion, leading to frequent SMO operations. This is costly in a disaggregated memory architecture. On the one hand, excessive splitting will cause frequent concurrency conflicts, affecting performance. On the other hand, SMO will cause the invalidation of the inner node of the compute node cache, requiring frequent updates to the compute node cache, resulting in poor performance.

c. The High Cost of Coarse-grained Lock: Current structures split on the basis of locks, with a large lock granularity, resulting in a high cost of splitting. During splitting, the entire node needs to be locked, making other operations impossible and reducing concurrency performance. Other nodes will frequently attempt to access the locked node during splitting, wasting additional bandwidth and reducing performance.

We propose GECKO, a write-optimized adaptive radix tree index combining ART inner node and array-based buffer nodes. We use buffer nodes to absorb writes, reducing the number of SMOs. Our inspiration comes from ROART [13], an ART structure designed for persistent memory. However, there are still several design challenges that need to be addressed to make it run on a disaggregated memory architecture. This paper makes the following contributions:

- We analyze the writing methods of existing tree indexes on disaggregated memory and identify three main problems: intensifying competition in write and update, excessive SMO operations and high cost of splitting locks.
- We design GECKO, a write-optimized ART index structure that combines ART trees and array-based buffer nodes. GECKO uses SMO-friendly buffer node design, threshold based write optimization strategy, and optimistic post-insertion lock design to achieve excellent performance.
- Experiments show that we improve throughput by $1.43\times$–$3.21\times$ compared to the state-of-the-art tree indexes on disaggregated memory under write workloads while SMO operation time is reduced by 88.5%, and lock time is reduced by 87.9%, respectively.

The remainder of this paper is structured as follows. Section 2 presents the background and motivation of our disaggregated memory index. Section 3 details the design of GECKO. Section 4 presents the results of the evaluation. Finally, Sect. 5 concludes the whole paper.

2 Background and Motivation

2.1 The Disaggregated Memory Architecture

Disaggregated memory separates compute nodes and memory nodes, connected via RDMA or CXL. Compute nodes typically have more CPUs and less memory, while memory nodes have more memory and fewer CPUs. Due to the immaturity of CXL technology, most existing indexes on disaggregated memory are based on one-sided RDMA design, with compute nodes using RDMA READ, WRITE, and atomic operations RDMA CAS and FAA to access memory nodes. One-sided operations ensure that the weak CPU of the memory node is bypassed during data transfer, improving overall performance [5,7,8].

2.2 Index on Diagggregated Memory

Tree indexes are essential guarantees in storage systems, such as databases or KV storage. As more and more storage systems are deployed on disaggregated memory architectures, high-performance tree index designs become particularly important. We focus on write-intensive loads, where the performance of existing tree indexes is poor. CHIME and Sherman are two state-of-the-art B+ tree indexes based on disaggregated memory. CHIME adopts B+ internal nodes and Hash leaf nodes to balance cache occupancy and read amplification. Sherman uses hierarchical on-chip locks and two-level versioning mechanisms to some extent solve concurrency conflicts. Both of them need to lock the entire node during insertion and SMO, and the write performance limit is quickly reached as the number of threads increases. SMART is the most advanced ART index on disaggregated memory. SMART adopts lock-free internal nodes and lock-based leaf nodes, greatly reducing lock overhead. However, the more frequent SMO introduces additional RTT, reducing its write performance.

Table 1. SMART SMO time and total insertion time.

SMO time(ms)			Insert cnt	Insert time(ms)	SMO ratio
Leaf merge	Node split	Node extend			
614880425	58525	96638755	120034	2288870499	31.1%

2.3 Motivation

Tree structures on disaggregated memory, whether B+ or ART, will encounter performance degradation issues during writes. We use experiments to prove our point. As shown in Fig. 1, we show the process of CHIME, the latest solution based on B+ tree, gradually decreasing performance as the Key and Value increase. CHIME stores the entire Key in internal nodes, while CHIME locks the

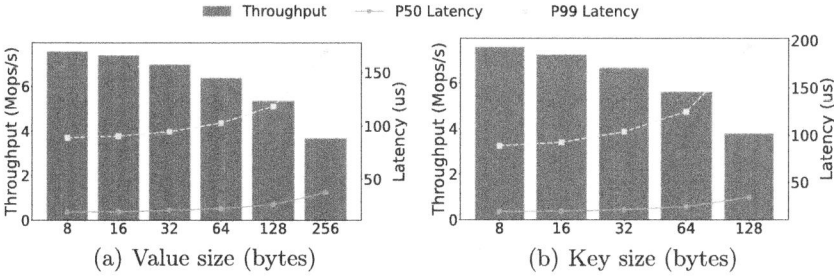

Fig. 1. The performance decreasing as the key and value size of CHIME increase.

node each time it writes and reads the KV in the Hopscotch Hash neighborhood, causing read amplification each time it inserts, leading to performance degradation. For Value, it adopts remote storage, that is, storing part of the Value and pointers in leaf nodes, with the pointers pointing to the address where the other part of the Value is stored, leading to an additional read, causing performance degradation. As shown in the Table 1, the ratio of SMART's SMO time to the total insertion time is shown. SMART is the most advanced ART solution based on disaggregated memory. We statistically calculate its SMO time, including Leaf merge, Node split, and Node extend, and find that it accounts for 31.1% of the total insertion time. Each SMO operation introduces an additional RTT to generate a new internal node, reducing write performance.

In general, existing tree indexes on disaggregated memory will encounter performance degradation issues during writes, mainly due to concurrency conflicts, frequent SMO operations, and high lock overhead on tree index. We hope to solve the problem of inefficient writes. We propose GECKO, a ART index structure for disaggregated memory that combines ART internal nodes and array-based buffer nodes. First, we use a write-friendly buffer node and use RDMA FAA primitives to solve write-write concurrency conflicts, achieving retry-free lock-free insertion. Second, we use a threshold-based splitting strategy to reduce the number of SMOs while reducing the tree height, further improving the insertion and read performance. Finally we use a post-insertion optimistic lock design to reduce the delay caused by other operations being blocked due to the lock overhead caused by the buffer node split.

3 GECKO Design

3.1 Overview

To address the three challenges we encountered under write-intensive loads, we propose three corresponding designs: SMO-friendly buffer node design, threshold-based write optimization strategy, and optimistic post-insertion lock design.

SMO-Friendly Buffer Node Design: GECKO is an index structure designed to enhance performance under write-intensive loads. First, we design a buffer

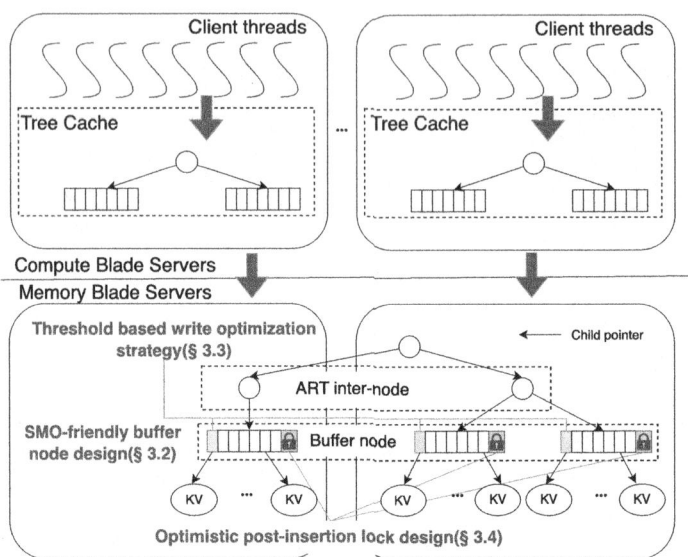

Fig. 2. Framework overview of GECKO.

node that combines the array of leaf nodes and the ART structure of internal nodes. When inserting, buffer nodes are generated first. To absorb writes, the buffer node has no prefix key and only stores a counter that records the number of inserted keys. We treat both insertions and updates as insertions. Specifically, when inserting, we first use FAA to increase the counter, which also indicates the number of slots to insert, then write the KV pair, and finally write the pointer to the KV pair into the slot. Compared to competing for slots with CAS after writing, our solution can reduce the number of failed CAS retries, improving overall parallel insertion performance.

Threshold Based Write Optimization Strategy: Treating updates as insertions can achieve better performance, but it also presents challenges for subsequent splits. Since treating updates as insertions leaves duplicate keys in the buffer node, SMO operations will occur more frequently. To address this issue, we propose a threshold-based write optimization strategy. Specifically, we set a threshold for splitting. First, we merge all duplicate keys with their latest value. Then, if the number of distinct keys does not exceed the threshold, we update the buffer node instead of splitting it. Otherwise, we perform a split operation and generate the next layer of buffer nodes. Through the threshold-based write optimization strategy, we effectively reduce the number of SMOs.

Optimistic Post-insertion Lock Design: Each time we perform an SMO, we need to lock the node and determine whether an SMO is required based on the threshold. The cost of locks is not negligible. Solutions based on B+ tree use coarse-grained locks, locking the entire node each time a write occurs, reducing concurrency performance. We propose an optimistic post-insertion lock design. When inserting, if we find that the counter obtained by FAA is already greater than 256, indicating that the node is in a split state, we optimistically assume that the node split has been completed. We then read the corresponding node again and perform the next operation based on the type of node read. If a buffer node is read, we continue to insert into the current node. If an internal node is read, a split has already been performed, and we read the next level of buffer nodes and perform the insertion operation. We also check the node's counter after optimistic reading to confirm that it is in a completed state. If it is not completed, we issue a read request again. Compared to traditional node split operations, the optimistic read design can reduce an RTT and concurrency issues during splitting.

3.2 SMO-Friendly Buffer Node Design

The GECKO Structure: The GECKO consists of two parts: internal nodes and buffer nodes. The internal nodes are composed of ART internal nodes, and the buffer nodes are an array without prefix keys, only storing a counter that records the number of inserted keys and leaf node pointer. Like other tree indexes on disaggregated memory, GECKO caches upper layers of the index in the compute node. The overall structure of GECKO is shown in Fig. 2. Our structural modifications are mainly on the buffer nodes, which can maximize the absorption of writes and generate as few SMOs as possible.

Internal Node: Internal node consists of ART internal nodes, each internal node contains partial keys and child pointers. Internal nodes are logically connected through pointers, and the partial keys from the root node to the leaf node form a complete key. All internal nodes are cached on the compute node. To verify the validity of the cache, we borrowed the design of reverse pointers from SMART. The reverse pointer is used to point to the parent node. If the reverse pointer of the cache and the memory node are not the same, the cache is invalidated.

Buffer Node: Buffer node is an array without common prefix keys, only recording the number of inserted keys and the prefix sum and pointer of the leaf node. The structure of the buffer node is shown in Fig. 3. The design of the buffer node is to absorb writes and reduce the number of SMOs. Therefore, when inserting, buffer nodes are generated first. To further improve the performance of insertion, we treat update operations as insertions. Updates do not modify the value of the same key but continue to insert data into empty slots. If all intermediate nodes are to be cached in the compute node, remote pointers to all data items need to be cached, requiring a huge cache space. After weighing the options, we choose not to cache buffer nodes to save cache space. If the buffer node already exists, we use FAA to modify the counter. The counter also indicates the number of slots to insert. According to the return value of FAA, we directly use Write to write the address and prefix key to the corresponding slot.

SMO Operation: When the buffer node becomes full, a split operation is triggered. We lock the buffer node to ensure data consistency. Then, we read all the

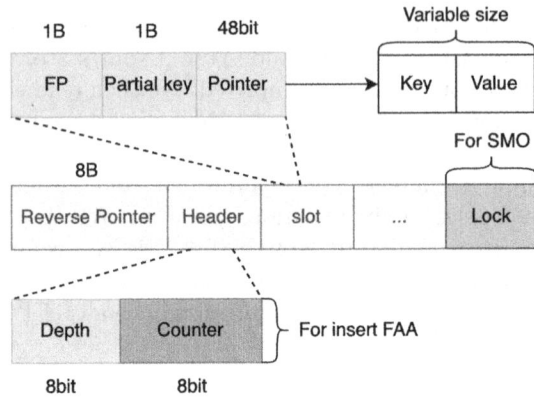

Fig. 3. The buffer node of GECKO.

leaves it contains into the compute node. Next, we compute the common prefix of these leaves and replace the buffer node with a new internal node. Subsequently, we generate new buffer nodes as needed and attach them to the internal node. These buffer nodes continue absorbing subsequent writes, ensuring efficiency and scalability.

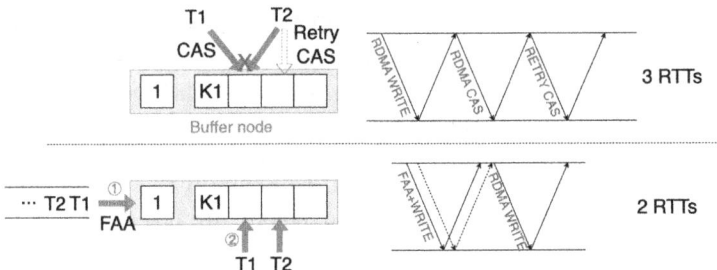

Fig. 4. Insert and update conflicts.

Insert and Update Operation: Insert and update operations are treated as insertions. When inserting, we first use FAA to increase the counter, which also indicates the number of slots to insert, then write the KV pair, and finally write the pointer to the KV pair into the slot. As shown in Fig. 4, compared to competing for slots with CAS after writing, we use doorbell batching to combine FAA and Write KV pairs into one operation, reducing the RTT overhead caused by CAS retries and improving overall parallel insertion performance, like Sherman.

3.3 Threshold Based Write Optimization Strategy

During splitting, treating update operations as insertions will increase the number of insertions. Frequent SMO operations will increase insertion latency and tree height. SMO operations will also cause frequent changes in the intermediate structure, frequent invalidation of the compute node cache, further reducing performance. To address this issue, we propose a threshold-based splitting optimization strategy.

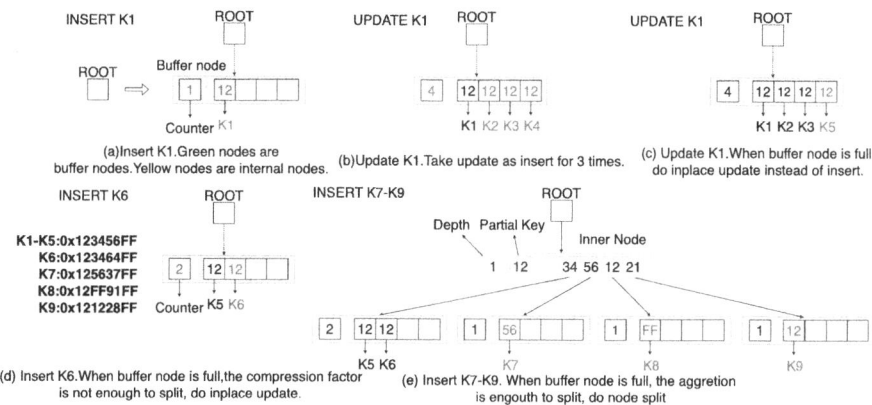

Fig. 5. Basic operations of GECKO.

Threshold Counters: Compression factor is a measure of update operations. We set a threshold in each buffer node. When the FAA operation finds that the counter is 256, the slot is full, and a split operation is triggered. Similar to the SMO process, the compression factor is calculated based on the number of pre-split nodes to determine whether a split is required. As shown in Fig. 5. There are two choices here: one is to split directly, and the other is to merge all updates without splitting. We do not split when the compression factor is high because the number of newly generated nodes is small, and a large number of update operations are merged. Splitting at this time will greatly increase the number of splits. When the compression factor is greater than the threshold, update operations are merged, that is, multiple updates are combined into one, reducing the impact of out of place update; when the compression factor is less than the threshold, an SMO split is performed. At this time, there are fewer update operations, a new buffer node is generated, and the original buffer node is transformed into an internal node. Additionally, Fig. 5c shows the case of inplace update, which will be detailed in the Sect. 3.4 on SMO and write conflicts.

3.4 Optimistic Post-insertion Lock Design

Through the threshold-based SMO split strategy, we effectively reduce the number of SMO operations. However, the lock overhead during splitting is still not negligible. Each time we perform an SMO, we need to lock the buffer node and determine whether an SMO is required based on the threshold. The impact of locks is mainly in three aspects: 1. reading when locking; 2. writing when locking; 3. lock competition.

SMO and Read Conflicts: When we perform an SMO, we need to lock the buffer node. To address the issue of reading when locking, we adopt cacheline versioning to solve the problem. Since the slot of the buffer node is less than 64 bytes, we add a pair of version numbers to each slot of the buffer node. When reading, we read the version number, and if the version numbers are inconsistent, we read again. Compared to previous work, our lock and version are generated in the buffer node, and our leaf node does not need cacheline versioning to ensure read-write consistency. Our KV is updated out of place and written out of place, so we have better support for variable-length KVs compared to other solutions.

SMO and Write Conflicts: SMO operations and write operations are mutually exclusive. During SMO, writing is blocked. However, in the SMO-friendly buffer node design we propose, we treat update operations as insertions. Updates do not modify the value of the same key but continue to insert data into empty slots. To avoid being blocked as much as possible, we allow updates to be executed after the buffer node is full. Specifically, when we find that the buffer node is full and needs to split, we issue a CAS lock slot and READ read buffer node at the same time. If we find a key with a common prefix that matches, we read the corresponding key, write the latest KV, and then use CAS to modify the slot. If there is no matching key, this is an Insert operation, and we decide whether to perform a split operation based on the compression factor.

SMO Conflicts: When performing an SMO, other threads that want to insert will continue to try to lock the buffer node for SMO operations, leading to a large amount of competition and wasted NIC bandwidth. Our approach is that when the original value of the Counter obtained by FAA is greater than 256, it indicates that the node is full. In this case, a thread has already performed an SMO operation on the node, so the current thread does not issue a CAS operation to obtain the lock but tries to read the node. The result of the read is ensured by cacheline versioning. We use a two-level version design similar to CHIME: one is the Node Version, which is modified during SMO, and the other is the Entry Version, which is modified during Insert operations. When reading, we read the Node Version, and if the Node Version is inconsistent, we read again. This can avoid a large amount of competition and improve concurrency performance.

4 Evaluation

4.1 Experimental Setup

Workloads. We run all experiments using the r650 machines on Cloudlab (4CNs and 1 MN) [6]. Each machine has a 100Gbps Mellanox ConnectX-6 IB RNIC. Each RNIC is connected to a 100Gbps Ethernet switch. We allocate 64GB DRAM and 1 CPU core to each MN for network connections and memory allocation. Each CN has 4GB DRAM and 64 CPU cores, with each core acting as a client. Before starting the experiment, we use large pages to register memory in the MN to reduce RNIC page translation cache misses [5]. We use YCSB [4] benchmark to generate three workloads,(a) write-only, (b) write-intensive(50% Insert and 50% Read), (c) read-only. Skewed workloads follow the Zipfian request distribution ($\theta = 0.99$), which is commonly observed in real-world workloads. To demonstrate our support for variable-length KVs, we use KVs with a length of 128 bytes for experiments.

Comparisons. We compare CHIME with the state-of-the-art tree indexes on disaggregated memory: SMART (radix tree), CHIME (B+ tree), and Sherman (B+ tree).

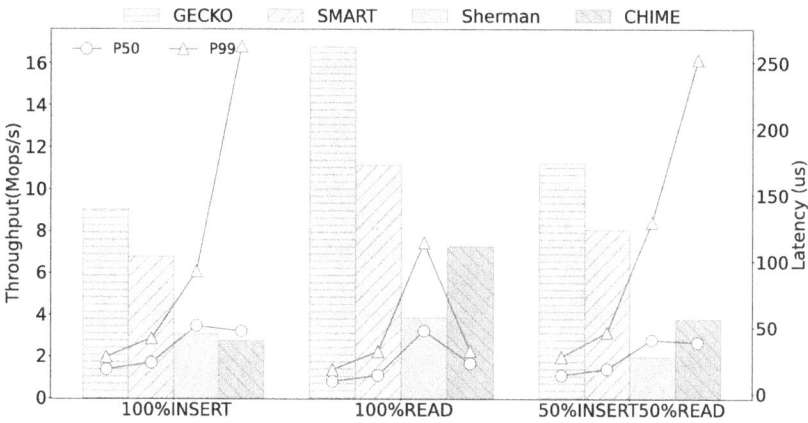

Fig. 6. The performance comparison of tree indexes on disaggregated memory.

4.2 Overall Performance

We first compare the performance of GECKO with existing solutions. As shown in Fig. 6, we conduct three types of load tests based on YCSB: write-only load, read-only load, and read-write mixed load. Our experimental results show that under write-intensive loads, GECKO can improve write performance by 1.43× compared to the state-of-the-art solution, mainly due to the design of the buffer node, which can reduce SMO operations during writes, use RDMA FAA operations, and reduce concurrent write conflicts; under read-intensive loads, GECKO can improve read performance by 1.54× compared to the best solution, mainly due to the buffer node reducing the height of the tree, reducing query overhead; under read-write mixed loads, GECKO can improve performance by 1.41×, fewer SMOs avoid frequent updates to the compute node cache, improving read-write mixed performance. For insert tail latency, GECKO can reduce p99 latency by 35.3%–93.5% compared to other solutions, and reduce p50 latency by 19.1%–67.4%. This is mainly due to our optimization of the number of SMO operations and locks, which effectively reduces SMO operations and write operations blocked by SMO, improving tail latency performance.

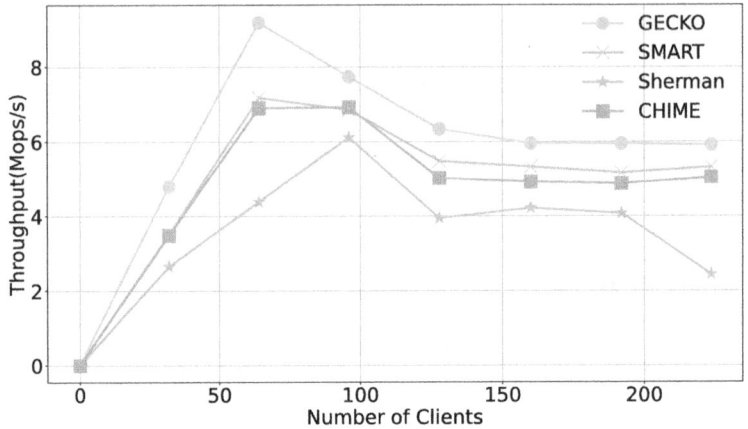

Fig. 7. Scalability of GECKO.

4.3 Scalability

GECKO also ensures good scalability. As shown in Fig. 7, when the number of threads grows to 64, the performance of GECKO reaches to 9.74 Mops, significantly better than other solutions, and then decreases as the number of threads increases and concurrent conflicts increase, and remains stable.

We attribute this improvement to two aspects. On the one hand, based on the reduction of the cache node, the retry caused by concurrent write conflicts is reduced, and the performance of the RDMA NIC is more efficient; on the other hand, our optimistic post-insertion lock design reduces invalid SMO retries and performs well in high-concurrency scenarios. The performance of GECKO is always better than other solutions, which proves that we have good scalability.

4.4 Overhead Analysis

Through the performance comparison of GECKO and existing solutions, we analyze the performance overhead of GECKO. As shown in Table 2, we compare the SMO times, SMO time, read node time, and lock overhead of GECKO and existing solutions, and calculate their proportions of the total operation time. Duo to the RDMA CAS used by SMART for lock-free internal node modification, the lock ratio is not counted. Our experimental results show that compared to SMART, GECKO reduces the number and time of SMOs, accounting for only 0.15% of the total operations and 2.82% of the total operation time, while

Table 2. Compare to SMO times.

	SMO cnt ratio	SMO time ratio	Read node time ratio	Lock ratio
SMART	33.94%	24.50%	23.59%	-
CHIME	4.60%	9.10%	61.95%	13.40%
Sherman	2.71%	8.58%	28.53%	17.30%
GECKO	0.15%	2.82%	8.23%	2.10%

SMART accounts for 33.94% and 24.5%, which is also the performance bottleneck of SMART during insertion. An SMO operation takes 1-2 more RTTs than an insertion, which is time-consuming; compared to CHIME, the read node time of GECKO drops from 61.95% to 8.23%, mainly because CHIME stores KVs in nodes, causing a large read amplification; compared to Sherman, the lock overhead of GECKO drops from 17.3% to 2.1%, reducing the poor performance caused by Sherman's coarse-grained locks. In summary, GECKO optimizes various bottlenecks during writes, with significant results.

4.5 Sensitivity Analysis

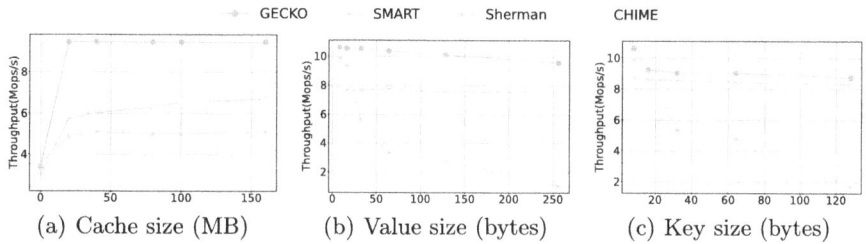

Fig. 8. Sensitivity analysis of GECKO.

Through the change of cache size, key size, and value size, we analyze the performance sensitivity of GECKO compared to other solutions. As shown in Fig. 8, for cache size, at the same cache size, GECKO achieves higher performance, proving the effectiveness of our cache; for key size and value size, when the key and value are larger than 8B, the original key-value pairs that cannot be accommodated need to be stored out of place, which will increase an RTT and make updating key-values more difficult. GECKO has a certain performance decline when the key size grows to 20B, but it still has the highest performance and remains unchanged afterwards; the value size remains unchanged, mainly because our buffer node only stores pointers, not complete key-value pairs.

5 Conclusion

In this paper, we propose and implement GECKO, a RDMA-based ART index on disaggregated memory to improve write performance. GECKO achieves excellent write performance while ensuring balanced read performance by reducing concurrency conflicts, frequent SMO operations, and high lock overhead. By designing a write-friendly buffer node, GECKO improves concurrent insertion performance during writes; through a threshold-based SMO strategy, GECKO reduces the number of SMOs, reduces the tree height, and ensures throughput; GECKO also optimizes concurrency through optimistic post-insertion locks, minimizing the impact of locks on read and write operations. Experiments show that GECKO outperforms existing solutions under write-intensive loads and achieves balanced read performance.

Acknowledgments. The research work is supported by the Key Research and Development Program (No. 2024YFB4505104) and the National Natural Science Foundation of China (No. U22A2027).

Disclosure of Interests. The authors have no competing interests to declare that are relevant to the content of this article.

References

1. Athanassoulis, M., Kester, M.S., et al.: Designing access methods: the rum conjecture. In: EDBT 2016, pp. 461–466 (2016)
2. Calciu, I., Imran, M.T., et al.: Rethinking software runtimes for disaggregated memory. In: ASPLOS, pp. 79–92 (2021)
3. Cao, W., Zhang, Y., et al.: Polardb serverless: a cloud native database for disaggregated data centers. In: Proceedings of the 2021 International Conference on Management of Data, pp. 2477–2489 (2021)
4. Cooper, B.F., Silberstein, A., et al.: Benchmarking cloud serving systems with YCSB. In: ACM Symposium on Cloud Computing, pp. 143–154 (2010)
5. Dragojević, A., Narayanan, D., et al.: {FaRM}: fast remote memory. In: NSDI 2014, pp. 401–414 (2014)
6. Duplyakin, D., Ricci, R., et al.: The design and operation of {CloudLab}. In: 2019 USENIX Annual Technical Conference (USENIX ATC 2019), pp. 1–14 (2019)
7. Gouk, D., Lee, S., Kwon, M., Jung, M.: Direct access, {High-Performance} memory disaggregation with {DirectCXL}. In: USENIX ATC 2022, pp. 287–294 (2022)
8. Guo, C., Wu, H., et al.: RDMA over commodity ethernet at scale. In: Proceedings of the 2016 ACM SIGCOMM Conference, pp. 202–215 (2016)
9. Guo, J., et al.: Who limits the resource efficiency of my datacenter: an analysis of alibaba datacenter traces. In: Proceedings of the International Symposium on Quality of Service, pp. 1–10 (2019)
10. Li, H., Berger, D.S., et al.: Pond: CXL-based memory pooling systems for cloud platforms. In: ASPLOS, pp. 574–587 (2023)
11. Luo, X., Shen, J., et al.: Chime: a cache-efficient and high-performance hybrid index on disaggregated memory. In: SOSP, pp. 110–126 (2024)

12. Luo, X., Zuo, P., et al.: {SMART}: a {High-Performance} adaptive radix tree for disaggregated memory. In: 17th USENIX Symposium on Operating Systems Design and Implementation (OSDI 2023), pp. 553–571 (2023)
13. Ma, S., et al.: {ROART}: range-query optimized persistent {ART}. In: 19th USENIX Conference on File and Storage Technologies (FAST 2021), pp. 1–16 (2021)
14. Morgan, T.P.: CXL and Gen-Z iron out a coherent interconnect strategy. The Next Platform, available online at (2020)
15. Ruan, Z., Schwarzkopf, M., Aguilera, M.K., Belay, A.: {AIFM}: {High-Performance}, {Application-Integrated} far memory. In: 14th USENIX Symposium on Operating Systems Design and Implementation (OSDI 2020), pp. 315–332 (2020)
16. Tirmazi, M., Barker, A., et al.: Borg: the next generation. In: Proceedings of the Fifteenth European Conference on Computer Systems, pp. 1–14 (2020)
17. Tsai, S.Y., Shan, Y., Zhang, Y.: Disaggregating persistent memory and controlling them remotely: an exploration of passive disaggregated {Key-Value} stores. In: 2020 USENIX Annual Technical Conference (USENIX ATC 2020), pp. 33–48 (2020)
18. Wang, Q., Lu, Y., Shu, J.: Sherman: a write-optimized distributed B+ tree index on disaggregated memory. In: Proceedings of the 2022 International Conference on Management of Data, pp. 1033–1048 (2022)
19. Zhang, M., Hua, Y., Zuo, P., Liu, L.: {FORD}: fast one-sided {RDMA-based} distributed transactions for disaggregated persistent memory. In: 20th USENIX Conference on File and Storage Technologies (FAST 2022), pp. 51–68 (2022)
20. Ziegler, T., Nelson-Slivon, J., Leis, V., Binnig, C.: Design guidelines for correct, efficient, and scalable synchronization using one-sided RDMA. Proc. ACM Manag. Data $\mathbf{1}(2)$, 1–26 (2023)

Scalable OpenMP Remote Offloading via Asynchronous MPI and Coroutine-Driven Communication

Jhonatan Cléto®, Guilherme Valarini®, Marcio M. Pereira®,
Guido Araujo®, and Hervé Yviquel$^{(\boxtimes)}$®

Universidade Estadual de Campinas (UNICAMP), Campinas, Brazil
j256444@dac.unicamp.br, hyviquel@unicamp.br

Abstract. Heterogeneous multi-node clusters with accelerators, such as GPUs, are increasingly the standard for HPC, where the MPI+OpenMP approach is commonly used for application development. However, this approach poses significant challenges for developers, especially in managing communication, synchronization, and load balancing across distributed nodes and accelerators. To address these challenges, this paper proposes the MPI Proxy Plugin (MPP), an extension of the LLVM OpenMP Offloading runtime that transparently offloads OpenMP target regions to remote accelerators via MPI. By abstracting communication and using the asynchronous mechanisms of MPI with C++20 coroutines, MPP provides a scalable alternative to MPI+OpenMP, enabling simpler development of heterogeneous HPC applications through the familiar OpenMP programming model. Experimental results show that MPP achieves excellent scalability. For compute-intensive proxy applications, it scales nearly linearly, reaching 63× speedup from 1 to 64 GPUs. While naive data transfers can degrade performance, this research reveals that extending OpenMP Target with collective operations (e.g., multi-device broadcast) simplifies development and improves performance, achieving up to 10× speedup in communication-bound benchmarks.

Keywords: HPC · OpenMP · MPI · Remote Offloading · GPUs

1 Introduction

Modern scientific applications increasingly rely on heterogeneous computing systems to meet the growing computational demands of simulation, data analytics, and machine learning workloads. To achieve performance under such demanding workloads, larger clusters of computing nodes containing multi-core CPUs, GPUs, and FPGA accelerators became the workhorse of modern HPC [4]. However, the complexity of programming these heterogeneous systems has become a significant barrier to portability and efficiency due to the need for diverse programming models [6].

OpenMP provides a convenient shared-memory parallelism model for multi-core processors and accelerators, with target offloading directives (since version

4.0) enabling compute-intensive task offloading to local devices like GPUs [9], while MPI serves as the standard for distributed memory message-passing across HPC clusters [8]. However, combining these models introduces significant challenges in communication, synchronization, and load balancing, particularly in multi-node environments where OpenMP lacks remote offloading capabilities, forcing programmers to rely on explicit MPI code for inter-node communication at the cost of increased complexity and reduced portability [6]. Addressing these issues requires an integrated approach that bridges OpenMP's accelerator model with seamless remote device offloading in heterogeneous systems.

This paper introduces the **MPI Proxy Plugin** (MPP), an extension to LLVM's OpenMP Target runtime that transparently offloads OpenMP target regions to remote accelerators across HPC clusters via MPI, eliminating the need for extensive code modifications. Integrated with LLVM's liboffload infrastructure, MPP acts as a proxy layer between the host runtime and remote nodes, abstracting MPI communication complexities. To expand MPP's access, its implementation will be fully open-sourced and submitted to the LLVM repository[1], thus ensuring accessibility and collaboration within the community. The main contributions of this paper include:

- A **liboffload plugin** that transparently extends OpenMP target offloading to remote accelerators in HPC clusters without requiring modifications to existing OpenMP code.
- An **event-driven communication system** combining parallel communication channels, asynchronous MPI operations, and C++20 coroutines to minimize latency, improve throughput, and overlap computation with communication.
- A **scaling analysis** demonstrating MPP's efficiency in strong/weak scaling scenarios with proxy and real-world applications.
- An initial proposal of a **multi-device collective operation extension** to the OpenMP Target model (`ompx_target_bcast`).

The remainder of this paper is structured as follows: Sect. 2 covers task-based parallelism and offloading concepts, Sect. 3 details the MPI Proxy Plugin's design, Sect. 4 reviews related work, Sect. 5 evaluates MPP's performance, Sect. 6 discusses limitations and proposes extensions to OpenMP target model, and Sect. 7 summarizes contributions and future directions.

2 Background

Task-based parallel models like OpenMP, enable scalable parallelism by allowing the programmer to define tasks, which are then managed by a runtime library for parallel execution. OpenMP's `task` directive enables non-blocking execution of code regions, with dependencies managed via the `depend` clause. The version 4.0 of the standard introduced the accelerator model, which allows OpenMP target

---

[1] available on https://github.com/llvm/llvm-project.

regions to be offloaded to accelerators like GPUs [2,5], through the `target` directive. That directive uses `map` clauses (`to`, `from`, `tofrom`) to manage host-device data transfers and `nowait` for asynchronous execution. Multi-device offloading is supported via the `device` clause, enabling workload distribution across accelerators while the host manages dependencies and data coherence. The liboffload (formerly libomptarget) [1], part of the LLVM ecosystem, enables OpenMP target task offloading to accelerators through a layered architecture. It comprises three layers: an agnostic layer managing host-side structures and operations for device offloading, a plugin-independent layer providing standardized interfaces for device operations, and vendor-specific plugins implementing hardware support. Currently, LLVM supports plugins for AMD GPUs, NVIDIA GPUs, and ELF64 CPUs. Integrated into LLVM's framework, liboffload simplifies developer workflows while optimizing cross-platform execution.

Although OpenMP provides a convenient, portable model for parallel and heterogeneous applications, its use is limited by the memory and processing power of a single node, making it unsuitable for scaling across multiple nodes. In contrast, MPI supports distributed-memory parallelism by enabling nodes in a cluster to communicate via explicit message passing. Combining OpenMP for intra-node parallelism with MPI for inter-node communication allows HPC applications to efficiently distribute workloads across thousands of nodes while still leveraging fine-grained parallelism within each node. However, this hybrid approach poses challenges for developers, who must explicitly manage communication, synchronization, and workload distribution. In heterogeneous environments, these challenges intensify as programmers must also navigate a complex memory hierarchy to offload computations to various accelerators. Thus, this paper examines how to extend the OpenMP target model to support scalable, transparent offloading of computations to remote accelerators—eliminating the need for explicit MPI communication management.

3 The MPI Proxy Plugin

The MPI Proxy Plugin (MPP) proposed in this paper, is a new communication layer built on the LLVM liboffload architecture, enabling transparent offloading of target tasks to remote accelerators over an HPC network. This section describes the plugin's architecture, core features, and its extension of OpenMP target offloading capabilities to support remote devices.

3.1 Architecture Overview

The MPP acts as a proxy layer between the host machine's liboffload and the remote device plugins, facilitating communication through MPI. The architecture abstracts the nodes in the cluster into two main roles:

– **Host Node:** The node responsible for running the OpenMP application and managing liboffload. It generates tasks and offloads them to both local and remote devices, managing communication and synchronization.

– **Worker Node:** Each Worker Node manages the remote devices on its respective machine. It runs a lightweight version of liboffload, providing access to available accelerators. Multiple Worker Nodes can exist in a cluster, allowing the Host Node to utilize a distributed pool of remote devices.

Unlike other liboffload plugins, MPP uses a different binary for Worker Nodes than for the application. This design choice promotes a clear separation of concerns, enabling improvements to the Worker Node without being constrained by the liboffload plugin interface. MPP architecture, depicted in Fig. 1, illustrates the interaction between the MPI communication layer, the MPI Proxy Layer, and the device plugins. Both Host and Worker Nodes use the MPI Proxy Layer to manage tasks and communication across local or remote devices, enabling seamless integration of remote devices into the OpenMP offloading model. The decentralized design allows devices on the same or different nodes to communicate directly without involving the Host Node. When a data transfer is initiated, the MPP checks device locations. If both devices are on the same Worker Node, internal Plugin X (a placeholder for any liboffload plugin - e.g., AMD, CUDA) handles the transfer. If on different Worker Nodes, the plugin coordinates direct transfers between them, bypassing data staging on the Host Node. This optimizes network resources and reduces the Host Node's load.

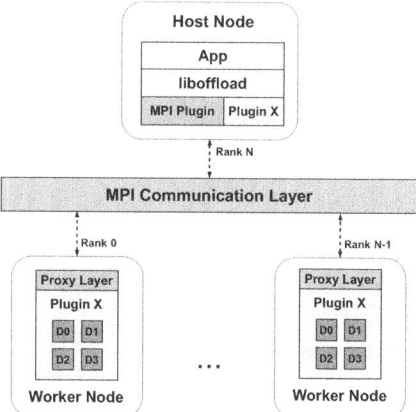

Fig. 1. MPI Proxy Plugin Architecture: The Host Node runs liboffload and its plugins, while Worker Nodes use a proxy for remote access. MPI ranks coordinate communication, enabling both local and remote offloading.

One of MPP's main features is hiding MPI communication from the OpenMP application. Remote devices appear as generic MPI devices, with OpenMP semantics masking any differences from local ones. The plugin integrates with liboffload, adding remote devices to the standard OpenMP device list so that applications can reference devices by ID regardless of their location. To support separate binaries for Host and Worker Nodes, the plugin uses the Multiple Program Multiple Data (MPMD) model. As shown in Listing 1, Worker Nodes are launched first, followed by the main application binary for proper rank assignment. MPI assigns Worker Nodes ranks 0 to $N-2$ and the Host Node rank $N-1$ (with N being the total process count), simplifying device management by clearly mapping Host identifiers to remote devices.

```
mpirun -np 2 worker-node : -np 1 ./app
```

Listing 1. Launching an OpenMP target applications with MPP.

3.2 Distributed Event System

OpenMP target offloading requires efficient communication and execution management due to its dynamic, concurrent nature. To address this, MPP's **Event System** enables dynamic MPI communication, allowing multiple threads to make concurrent MPI calls using C++20 coroutines for non-blocking operations. MPI is initialized in MPI_THREAD_MULTIPLE mode to support multi-threaded access, with a pool of MPI communicators and round-robin tag scheduling enabling parallel message exchanges over independent channels. Leveraging MPI's internal mechanisms, such as Virtual Communication Interfaces [18], which provide dedicated transmit, receive, and completion queues, the Event System enhances efficiency and performance in multi-threaded environments. The Event System defines several key components:

- **Event:** OpenMP target tasks are represented as events, implemented as coroutines. These events abstract key operations such as memory allocation, data transfers, and task execution on remote devices. Each event manages the communication between nodes, with origin and destination sides allowing matching MPI Send/Receive operations for efficient task execution.
- **Event Queue:** Events can be suspended and resumed, allowing the plugin to queue them for execution. This queue ensures that events are processed in order, and it allows events to be paused while waiting for non-blocking MPI operations without blocking the threads.
- **Offload Thread:** The Offload Thread runs on the Host Node and is responsible for dispatching tasks to remote devices. It creates and manages events, ensuring synchronization at the end of target regions. If the application performs synchronous offloading, the Offload Threads will be standard OpenMP threads. For asynchronous offloading with the `nowait` clause, they become hidden helper threads [14].

- **Gate Thread:** Running on each Worker Node, the Gate Thread listens for event notifications from other nodes. It gathers task information and enqueues the corresponding events for execution on the local accelerators.
- **Event Handler:** A set of threads on Worker Nodes responsible for executing events in the Event Queue. There are two types of Event Handlers: execution handlers, which manage task execution, and communication handlers, which handle communication and data transfers. This separation enables the overlap of communication and computation, preventing blocking during task execution.

3.3 Task Offloading and Execution Flow

As shown in Fig. 2, when offloading a target region, the Host's Offload Thread generates task events and queues them (**1**). Once ready (**2**), it notifies the corresponding Worker Node (**3**), where the Gate Thread enqueues the event locally (**4**). The Event Handler retrieves it (**5**), manages data exchanges, and prepares execution. If a non-blocking MPI operation is needed (**5.a**), the event is suspended and re-queued (**5.b**) until data is available. Execution is then triggered via Plugin X (**6**), which enqueues it in a queue-like structure (e.g., CUDA Stream), allowing asynchronous processing. For asynchronous offloading with nowait, the Host skips target task synchronization, using MPI queries to track background task progress without delays.

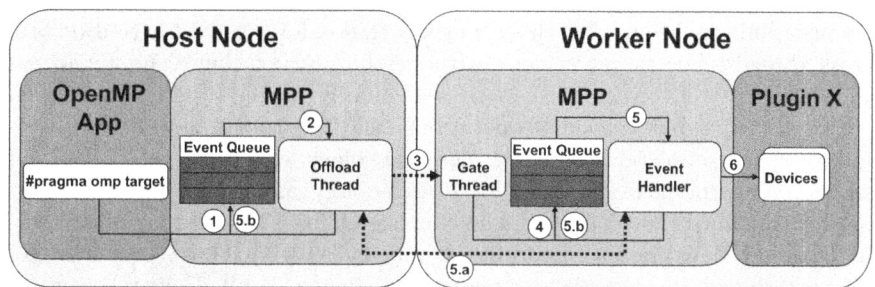

Fig. 2. Event System Overview: Depicts how the Host sends offload events to Worker Nodes, which asynchronously manage tasks using event queues and MPI communication for efficient distributed processing.

Listing 2 demonstrates an event using a coroutine to launch a target kernel during task offloading. The coroutine suspends execution (line 11) while waiting for non-blocking MPI communication to complete (line 8). Once the data is received and all requests are finalized, the kernel is launched on the target device (line 15), followed by sending a completion notification to the Host Node (line 17). This approach combines multithreading, coroutines, and asynchronous MPI communication to enable fully asynchronous and scalable execution.

```
 1  EventTy launchKernel(...) {
 2    ...
 3    // Receive data to the launchKernel Event
 4    MPI_Irecv(...);
 5    ...
 6    // Wait until all pending requests finish.
 7    while (!Completed) {
 8      if (int MPIErr = MPI_Testall(...); MPIErr)
 9        co_return createError(MPIErr);
10      // Suspension point
11      co_await std::suspend_always{};
12    }
13    ...
14    // Launch the target kernel on the specified device
15    RemotePluginManager.launch_kernel(...);
16    // Event completion notification
17    MPI_Isend(...);
18    ...
19  }
```

Listing 2. Coroutine for launching a kernel in MPP's Event System. It manages MPI communication and suspends execution while waiting for non-blocking operations to complete.

3.4 Synchronization Mechanisms

The MPI Proxy Plugin manages asynchronous offloading and remote task execution using an event system that queues events, allowing them to be paused, resumed, and synchronized with *sync* events that enforce correct execution order across threads. For target regions without the `nowait` clause, liboffload calls the plugin's `synchronize` method to sequentially process events—each event, composed of non-blocking MPI operations (via `MPI_Isend` and `MPI_Irecv`), is monitored for completion using `MPI_Testall`, blocking the Offload Thread until finished. With the `nowait` clause, MPP uses `query_async` to resume coroutine-based events until they complete, allowing the Offload Thread to continue without blocking. This design integrates seamlessly with OpenMP's asynchronous behavior, though its reliance on repeated `MPI_Testall` calls leads to busy waiting due to MPI's lack of background progress tracking [19]. Proposed solutions like MPIX Stream [20] could enhance efficiency in future implementations.

4 Related Work

Extending the OpenMP target model to offloading computation to remote devices across an HPC cluster, as an alternative to the hybrid MPI+OpenMP approach, was studied for some previous work. Patel and Doerfert [10] introduced Remote OpenMP Offloading by extending the OpenMP target model to distributed systems using RPC via gRPC or UCX for target task offloading without source code changes. Despite optimizations by Lu et al. [7], as they mentioned, this approach faced performance issues at scale. Shan et al. [12] improved it by integrating MPI, reducing latency and overhead in multi-GPU environments, especially with Nvidia GPUs. However, their model lacked support for asynchronous operations and struggled in communication-heavy tasks, as noted in their paper. The Remote Offloading plugin, introduced in LLVM 12, was deprecated by version 17, and the MPI-based version is no longer publicly available. Yviquel et al. [17] introduced the OpenMP Cluster (OMPC) model, which provided a unified framework for offloading tasks to remote nodes. OMPC employs MPI for inter-node communication, eliminating the need for developers to write MPI code manually. Despite its advancements, OMPC primarily focuses on CPU utilization and does not natively support accelerator computation using pure OpenMP, requiring additional vendor-specific APIs such as CUDA or OpenCL for GPU support. Despite prior research, a unified and scalable offloading solution remains needed. The MPI Proxy Plugin integrates MPI into the OpenMP runtime, it differs from previous work by enabling scalable and asynchronous offloading to remote accelerators without code changes.

5 Experiments

To evaluate the performance of the MPI Proxy Plugin (MPP), a series of experiments was conducted, including micro-benchmarks, proxy applications, and real-world scientific simulations. An overview of the experimental setup is provided in this section, followed by a discussion of the key findings and performance analysis across these scenarios.

Experiments were conducted on the OGBON Cluster at SENAI/CIMATEC. OGBON nodes feature Intel Xeon Gold 6240 CPUs, 384 GB RAM, four Tesla V100 GPUs, and two Mellanox ConnectX-5 100 Gb/s network cards. The primary software stack included Clang 20.0, CUDA 12.8, and MPICH 4.3 integrated with UCX 1.18.0 and CUDA-Aware support. Each experiment involved conducting 5 trials for each data point represented on the graphs. The error for each measurement was estimated using the bootstrapping[2] method, and translucent error bands were added to the graphs to visualize this uncertainty. Spinner [3], an open-source tool for parameter sweeping in HPC benchmarks was used to speed up experiment execution and ensure reproducibility.

5.1 Proxy Applications

XSBench [16] and RSBench [15] are proxy apps modeling Monte Carlo neutron transport: XSBench handles macroscopic cross-section lookups, while RSBench employs the memory-efficient multipole method. Both aid HPC performance analysis of tools like OpenMC [11]. Their OpenMP target implementations were extended from single- to multi-device offloading. Workload and memory usage scales with problem size: RSBench requires 4.9 MB (small) and 25.5 MB (large), whereas XSBench uses 240 MB and 5.6 GB, respectively.

---

[2] See https://en.wikipedia.org/wiki/Bootstrapping_(statistics).

In strong scaling experiments with 10^{10} fixed lookups across 1 to 64 GPUs (1 to 16 Worker Nodes), RSBench's compute-intensive kernel with high computation-to-communicationratio (CCR) achieved near-linear scalability with MPP, reaching 62.5× speedup on 64 GPUs for the large size, as seen in Fig. 3a. In the small size, the communication cost is more significant and the speedup increases slowly as more GPUs are used. Figure 3b shows XSBench results. For small size, MPP achieved up to a 6× speedup, though this benefit diminished with more GPUs. For large size, increased transfers negated parallel gains, yielding near-constant execution times and even slowdowns as GPUs increased. XSBench's kernel performs far less computation than RSBench and incurs a high initial communication cost that scales with the number of GPUs. Consequently, distributing its minimal workload across GPUs yields little performance gain, as computation time is much shorter than data transfer time.

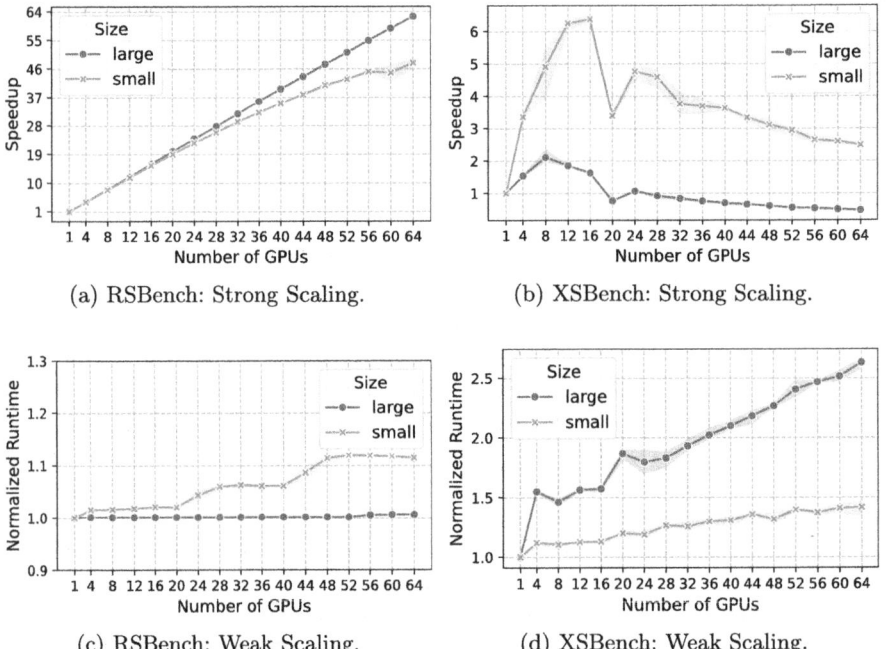

Fig. 3. Proxy-apps results measured relative to execution time on a single GPU.

For weak scaling experiment, the workload per GPU was kept constant, 10^{10} lookups per device, while the total number of GPUs was increased from 1 to 64. RSBench exhibited consistent weak scaling, as shown in Fig. 3c, maintaining near-constant execution times as GPUs increased, especially for the large size. The weak scalability of XSBench is not as good as that of RSBench, as shown in Fig. 3d. As the GPU count increases, the execution time rises, especially for the large size, due to higher data transfer per GPU. The Host Node becomes a bottleneck, unable to sustain the throughput required to scale XSBench.

5.2 Simwave

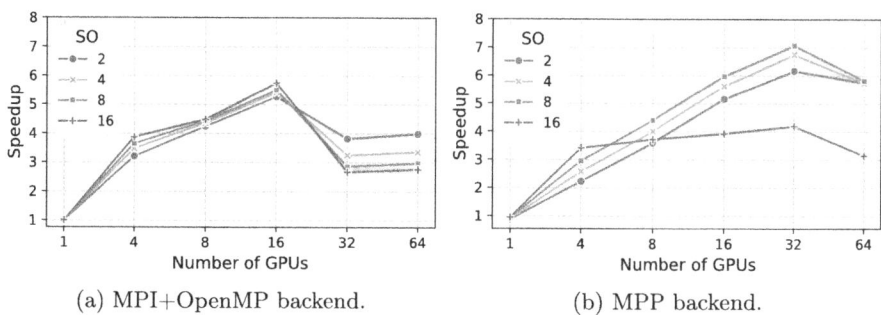

Fig. 4. Simwave results measured against execution time on a single GPU for a set of spatial orders (SO).

Simwave [13] is a Python library for simulating acoustic wave propagation in variable-density media, pairing a user-friendly Python interface with a high-performance C backend for CPU/GPU computation. Critical parameters include grid size, which dictates memory and runtime demands, spatial order that trades accuracy for larger halo regions and communication overhead, and iteration count, which escalates communication costs due to repeated halo exchanges. Simwave has been implemented with OpenMP for multi-device execution on a single node and MPI+OpenMP for multi-node execution. In this experiment, the OpenMP version was executed with MPP to enable multi-node scalability by offloading to remote devices. The performance of the MPI+OpenMP and MPP versions was then compared under identical GPU and network configurations.

In Fig. 4, Simwave's strong scaling is shown for a 1024^3 grid over 400 iterations, tested on 1–64 GPUs (1–16 nodes). As presented in Fig. 4a, the MPI+OpenMP backend scales up to 16 GPUs, achieving nearly 5.5× speedup across spatial orders. However, beyond 16 GPUs, performance is impacted by communication overhead, resulting in reduced speedup at 32 and 64 GPUs. Figure 4b shows the results for the MPP backend, from 1 to 4 GPUs the speedup is fewer than in the MPI+OpenMP version, but in the 8 to 64 range, the speedup is comparable or higher than that version reaching up to a 7× speedup. Nevertheless, for higher spatial orders (16), communication cost significantly affects the speedup. Better scalability is observed with the MPP backend at higher GPU counts due to its transparent management of data transfers. The runtime efficiently handles transfers across local and remote devices, abstracting data movement and synchronization behind the omp_target_memcpy routine. In contrast, in the MPI+OpenMP version, data transfers must be explicitly managed using MPI routines (e.g. MPI_Send, MPI_Recv), requiring careful coordination to achieve efficient overlap between computation and communication. As more remote GPUs are utilized, communication efficiency becomes increasingly difficult to maintain, leading to performance challenges for Simwave.

6 Extending the OpenMP Target Model

The results in Sect. 5, show that the MPI Proxy Plugin (MPP) extends the OpenMP target model, enabling task offloading to remote devices and good scalability across HPC cluster nodes. However, in data-transfer heavy applications such as XSBench, communication overhead between Host Node and devices can bottleneck scalability, particularly in internode communication.

XSBench suffers from high data transfer overhead because, as shown in Listing 3, during initialization the Host Node sends large amounts of data to every device. The app naively transfers all the data to each GPU in parallel using OpenMP threads, but the bandwidth of the Host Node cannot keep up as the number of devices increases. Essentially, that transfer is a *broadcast*. To reduce this overhead, a smarter broadcast routine (ompx_target_bcast), that leverages device locality, was implemented. Initially, the Host Node sends data to one GPU per Worker Node; then, each Worker Node distributes those data to its other GPUs using p2p communication, speeding up transfers. Listing 4 shows the signature of the proposed ompx_target_bcast routine, it receives the source device information (src_ptr, size, and src_device) and the addresses of the targets (previously allocated with omp_target_alloc) in the devices. In this paper the broadcast operation was implemented as a routine, but in an integration in the OpenMP standard, it can be replaced by a new directive like target bcast.

```
1 #pragma omp parallel for num_threads(num_devices)
2 for (int K = 0; K < num_devices; K++)
3   ...
4   #pragma omp target teams distribute parallel for \
5       map(to: data[:size]) \
6       device(K)
7   xsbench_kernel(data, ...);
```

Listing 3. XSBench original implementation.

As shown in Fig. 5, replacing the naive transfer with the broadcast routine improved both strong and weak scalability. For the small size, strong scalability achieved up to 10× speedup, while in the large size, the MPP accelerated execution by up to 4×. In the weak scaling experiment, in both problem sizes, the execution time grows much slowly than the original version. This experiment illustrates the potential of extending the OpenMP target model beyond simple computation offloading to accelerators. Introducing remote device support in the model, adding knowledge about the topology of the devices in the cluster, and providing syntax for collective operations across devices can boost performance of applications in these distributed environments.

```
1  // Bcast routine signature
2  void ompx_target_bcast(void *src_ptr, void **dst_ptrs, unsigned long size, int src_device);
3  ...
4  ompx_target_bcast(host_data_ptr, devices_data_ptrs, ..., host_device);
5  ...
6  #pragma omp parallel for num_threads(num_devices)
7  for (int K = 0; K < num_devices; K++)
8  ...
9    #pragma omp target teams distribute parallel for \
10        is_device_ptr(devices_data_ptrs[K]) \
11        device(K)
12    xsbench_kernel(devices_data_ptrs[K], ...);
```

Listing 4. XSBench implementation using `ompx_target_bcast`.

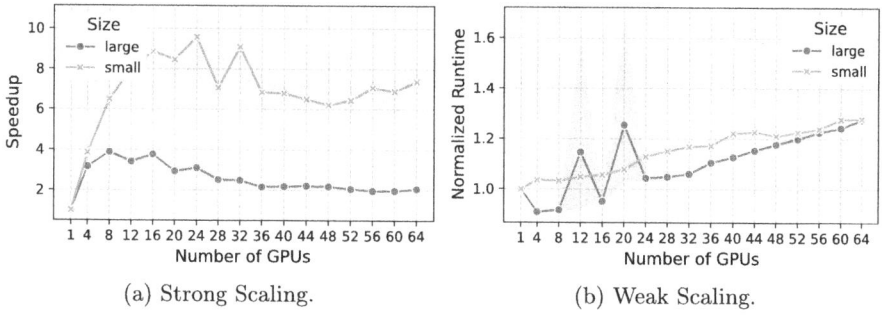

(a) Strong Scaling.   (b) Weak Scaling.

Fig. 5. XSBench results using the `ompx_target_bcast` routine.

7 Conclusions and Future Work

This paper introduces the **MPI Proxy Plugin** (MPP), enabling OpenMP target offloading to remote accelerators in distributed systems via asynchronous MPI and coroutine-driven communication. MPP integrates transparently with LLVM's liboffload, requiring no code modifications while scaling applications across cluster nodes. Evaluations on RSBench, XSBench, and Simwave demonstrate MPP's efficacy, achieving significant speedups despite data-transfer bottlenecks in communication-heavy workloads like XSBench. Future work includes optimizing data transfers through locality-aware strategies and advanced MPI techniques such as collective operations. These enhancements aim to mitigate bottlenecks and further improve scalability. MPP establishes a foundation for extending OpenMP offloading to distributed heterogeneous systems, advancing HPC application portability and performance in multi-node environments.

Acknowledgments. This work is supported by Petrobras under grants 2018/00347-4 and 2022/00096-7, by the São Paulo Research Foundation (FAPESP) under grants 2019/26702-8 and 2024/04232-8, by the Coordenação de Aperfeiçoamento de Pessoal de Nível Superior – Brasil (CAPES) - Finance Code 88887.947685/2024-00, and FAEPEX/UNICAMP through the Programa de Incentivo a Novos Docentes (PIND) under grant 2553/23. We also thank SENAI/CIMATEC for computational resources.

Disclosure of Interests. The authors have no competing interests to declare that are relevant to the content of this article.

References

1. Antao, S.F., et al.: Offloading support for OpenMP in clang and LLVM. In: 2016 Third Workshop on the LLVM Compiler Infrastructure in HPC (LLVM-HPC), pp. 1–11 (2016). https://doi.org/10.1109/LLVM-HPC.2016.006
2. Bertolli, C., et al.: Integrating GPU support for OpenMP offloading directives into Clang. In: Proceedings of the Second Workshop on the LLVM Compiler Infrastructure in HPC (2015). https://doi.org/10.1145/2833157.2833161
3. Ceccato, R., Cléto, J., Leite, G., Rigo, S., Diaz, J.M.M., Yviquel, H.: Spinner: enhancing HPC experimentation with a streamlined parameter sweep tool. In: 2024 International Symposium on Computer Architecture and High Performance Computing Workshops (SBAC-PADW), pp. 1–11 (2024). https://doi.org/10.1109/SBAC-PADW64858.2024.00013
4. Chatterjee, S., et al.: Integrating asynchronous task parallelism with MPI. In: Proceedings - IEEE 27th International Parallel and Distributed Processing Symposium, IPDPS 2013, pp. 712–725 (2013). https://doi.org/10.1109/IPDPS.2013.78
5. Huber, J., et al.: Efficient execution of OpenMP on GPUs. In: 2022 IEEE/ACM International Symposium on Code Generation and Optimization (CGO), pp. 41–52 (2022). https://doi.org/10.1109/CGO53902.2022.9741290
6. Laguna, I., Marshall, R., Mohror, K., Ruefenacht, M., Skjellum, A., Sultana, N.: A large-scale study of MPI usage in open-source HPC applications. In: International Conference for High Performance Computing, Networking, Storage and Analysis, SC (2019). https://doi.org/10.1145/3295500.3356176
7. Lu, W., et al.: Towards efficient remote OpenMP offloading. In: Klemm, M., de Supinski, B.R., Klinkenberg, J., Neth, B. (eds.) IWOMP 2022. LNCS, vol. 13527. p. 17–31. Springer, Heidelberg (2022). https://doi.org/10.1007/978-3-031-15922-0_2
8. MPI Forum: MPI: A Message-Passing Interface Standard Version 4.1. Technical report, MPI Forum (2023)

9. OpenMP Architecture Review Board: OpenMP application programming interface version 6.0. Technical report, OpenMP Architecture Review Board (2024)
10. Patel, A., Doerfert, J.: Remote OpenMP offloading. In: Proceedings of the 27th ACM SIGPLAN Symposium on Principles and Practice of Parallel Programming, PPoPP 2022, pp. 441–442. Association for Computing Machinery, New York (2022). https://doi.org/10.1145/3503221.3508416
11. Romano, P.K., Horelik, N.E., Herman, B.R., Nelson, A.G., Forget, B., Smith, K.: OpenMC: a state-of-the-art Monte Carlo code for research and development. Ann. Nucl. Energy **82**, 90–97 (2015). https://doi.org/10.1016/j.anucene.2014.07.048
12. Shan, B., Araya-Polo, M., Malik, A.M., Chapman, B.: MPI-based remote OpenMP offloading: a more efficient and easy-to-use implementation. In: Proceedings of the 14th International Workshop on Programming Models and Applications for Multicores and Manycores, pp. 50–59 (2023). https://doi.org/10.1145/3582514.3582519
13. de Souza, J.F., et al.: Simwave - A Finite Difference Simulator for Acoustic Waves Propagation. CoRR abs/2201.05278 (2022). https://arxiv.org/abs/2201.05278
14. Tian, S., Doerfert, J., Chapman, B.: Concurrent execution of deferred OpenMP target tasks with hidden helper threads. In: Chapman, B., Moreira, J. (eds.) LCPC 2020. LNCS, vol. 13149. pp. 41–56. Springer, Cham (2020). https://doi.org/10.1007/978-3-030-95953-1_4
15. Tramm, J.R., Siegel, A.R., Forget, B., Josey, C.: Performance analysis of a reduced data movement algorithm for neutron cross section data in Monte Carlo simulations. In: Markidis, S., Laure, E. (eds.) EASC 2014. LNCS, vol. 8759, pp. 39–56. Springer, Cham (2015). https://doi.org/10.1007/978-3-319-15976-8_3
16. Tramm, J.R., Siegel, A.R., Islam, T.Z., Schulz, M.: XSBench - the development and verification of a performance abstraction for monte carlo reactor analysis. In: PHYSOR 2014 - The Role of Reactor Physics toward a Sustainable Future. Kyoto (2014). https://www.mcs.anl.gov/papers/P5064-0114.pdf
17. Yviquel, H., et al.: The OpenMP cluster programming model. In: Workshop Proceedings of the 51st International Conference on Parallel Processing, New York, NY, USA (2023). https://doi.org/10.1145/3547276.3548444
18. Zambre, R., Sahasrabudhe, D., Zhou, H., Berzins, M., Chandramowlishwaran, A., Balaji, P.: Logically parallel communication for fast MPI+threads applications. IEEE Trans. Parallel Distrib. Syst. **32**(12), 3038–3052 (2021). https://doi.org/10.1109/TPDS.2021.3075157
19. Zhou, H., Latham, R., Raffenetti, K., Guo, Y., Thakur, R.: MPI progress for all. In: SC24-W: Workshops of the International Conference for High Performance Computing, Networking, Storage and Analysis, pp. 425–435 (2024). https://doi.org/10.1109/SCW63240.2024.00063
20. Zhou, H., Raffenetti, K., Guo, Y., Thakur, R.: MPIX stream: an explicit solution to hybrid MPI+X programming. In: Proceedings of the 29th European MPI Users' Group Meeting, pp. 1–10 (2022). https://doi.org/10.1145/3555819.3555820

SProBench: Stream Processing Benchmark for High Performance Computing Infrastructure

Apurv Deepak Kulkarni[✉] and Siavash Ghiasvand[✉]

Center for Scalable Data Analytics and Artificial Intelligence (ScaDS.AI), Center for Interdisciplinary Digital Sciences (CIDS), TUD Dresden University of Technology, Dresden, Germany
{apurv.kulkarni,siavash.ghiasvand}@tu-dresden.de

Abstract. Recent advancements in data stream processing frameworks have improved real-time data handling, however, scalability remains a significant challenge affecting throughput and latency. While studies have explored this issue on local machines and cloud clusters, research on modern high-performance computing (HPC) infrastructures is yet limited due to the lack of scalable measurement tools. This work presents SProBench, a novel benchmark suite designed to evaluate the performance of data stream processing frameworks in large-scale computing systems. Building on best practices, SProBench incorporates a modular architecture, offers native support for SLURM-based clusters, and seamlessly integrates with popular stream processing frameworks such as Apache Flink, Apache Spark Streaming, and Apache Kafka Streams. Experiments conducted on HPC clusters demonstrate its exceptional scalability, delivering throughput that surpasses existing benchmarks by more than tenfold. The distinctive features of SProBench, including complete customization options, built-in automated experiment management tools, seamless interoperability, and an open-source license, distinguish it as an innovative benchmark suite tailored to meet the needs of modern data stream processing frameworks.

Keywords: Stream Processing · Benchmark suite · HPC cluster · Slurm

1 Introduction

Modern big data processing is built around two main paradigms: batch processing and stream processing. Batch processing involves collecting, storing, and processing data in scheduled intervals, while stream processing processes data as it arrives, enabling real-time analysis. This real-time capability supports timely decision-making and ensures seamless operations. With data being generated, processed, and shared at unprecedented rates, often exceeding gigabytes per second [6], raw data typically undergoes significant processing and filtering to reduce its size, making analysis more efficient and manageable. Data Stream Processing (DSP) focuses on processing data immediately upon acquisition, eliminating the need for intermediate storage.

In recent years, DSP frameworks have advanced significantly, mostly driven by hardware innovations. Frameworks like Apache Flink [15], Apache Spark Streaming [2], and Apache Kafka Stream [1] have improved in areas such as memory management [4,5], support for diverse databases, edge computing compatibility [16], and efficient state management. Each framework specializes in specific aspects of stream processing. Given the diversity of DSP tasks, the setup of these frameworks and the underlying hardware are critical for ensuring the functionality of the entire stream processing pipeline. Benchmarking these frameworks against modern stream processing demands provides valuable insights into their performance across various metrics. It highlights strengths, identifies limitations and bottlenecks, and helps select the most suitable framework for specific tasks. Additionally, benchmarking reveals how effectively the underlying hardware is utilized.

Although stream processing frameworks are increasingly relied upon, there are notable gaps in existing comparative studies of these frameworks. One major limitation is the lack of evaluations conducted under real-world conditions, where the complexities of hardware configurations and scalability are challenging to replicate in controlled environments. Furthermore, the inherent variability of real-world data streams makes accurate simulation and benchmarking difficult. Most studies to date are restricted to small-scale experiments, with limited exploration of how DSP frameworks perform on large-scale systems and High-Performance Computing (HPC) environments. HPC systems utilize parallel processing and distributed computing on large-scale clusters to efficiently manage complex computational tasks, making them essential for real-time stream and batch processing of massive datasets across various domains. It is therefore essential to evaluate DSP frameworks also on large-scale and HPC systems. However, to the best of our knowledge, no suitable benchmarking tools currently exist for this purpose. This highlights the need for developing more robust and scalable benchmarking suite to effectively bridge these gaps.

This work introduces *SProBench*, a highly scalable and high-throughput stream processing benchmark specifically designed to seamlessly support large-scale HPC systems. SProBench is open source[1] and provides native support for the Slurm batch management system. SProBench is designed to generate high-velocity data streams, capable of producing millions of events per second. It offers configurable parameters, including event size, data distribution, and frequency, enabling the simulation of realistic workloads to accurately assess the performance and scalability of any stream processing framework.

This work is organized as follows: Sect. 2 reviews the current literature and explains how the proposed benchmark bridges the gaps. Section 3 provides a comprehensive explanation of the design of the benchmark, including its architecture, workloads, metrics. Section 4 demonstrates the functionality of the benchmark

---

[1] Available from https://github.com/apurvkulkarni7/SProBench.

in a scalability experiments, and Sect. 5 concludes this work providing future directions.

2 Related Works

Over the past decade, DSP benchmarking tools have undergone substantial advancements to address increasing data complexity and evolving computational requirements. Most benchmarks focus on latency and throughput as the main metrics, often complementing them with another metric such as memory or CPU usage. For effective benchmarking of DSP frameworks, the frequency, distribution and size of the generated workload should represent the real-world scenarios.

Earliest works like Linear Road Benchmark [7] measured the performance of the streaming frameworks, such as AURORA and STREAM, with the focus on latency. The data consisted of simulated traffic and sensor data for toll systems, with a workload consisting of aggregation and joining queries on a database. Yahoo streaming benchmark (YSB) [9] is another popular benchmark that focuses on metrics like throughput and latency to asses scalability of the streaming frameworks such as Apache Storm, Flink and Spark Streaming. In YSB, the data consisted of synthetically generated advertisement campaign, on which, workloads such as mapping, filtering, transformation, joining and windowing were performed. DSPBench [8] which is a benchmark suite for distributed DSP systems, covers a wider range of application domains including finance, telecommunications, and sensor networks. This benchmark employs metrics such as throughput, latency, memory, network, and CPU usage to measure the performance of Apache Storm and Spark Streaming frameworks. Theodolite [11,12] is a benchmarking method for evaluating the scalability of cloud-native applications, particularly stream processing within micro-services. The benchmark consists of different processing pipelines providing the capability to test different operations of the framework and uses non-traditional approaches to measure the performance, namely using metrics such as required number of processing instances per workload. Among enterprise benchmark suites, ESPBench [13] is designed to evaluate DSPs using business and sensor data from manufacturing scenarios. Its workload includes queries that cover core stream processing functionalities, and it provides a toolkit for data ingestion, result validation, and objective latency measurements. The benchmark is used to compare systems like Apache Spark Streaming, Flink, and Hazelcast Jet, highlighting the importance of result validation. OSPBench [17] benchmark evaluates the scalability of stream processing jobs in Flink, Kafka Streams, Spark Streaming, and Structured Streaming using national traffic data and two distinct pipelines, namely memory intensive and CPU intensive. It analyses both horizontal and vertical scaling using metrics such as latency, throughput, scaling efficiency, CPU, garbage collection (GC), network IO, file-system and disk IO. There are also more specific benchmark tools such as SPBench [10], which only supports C++ based frameworks like FastFlow. To gauge the performance it relies on metrics like latency, throughput, CPU and memory usage, and consists of various workloads ranging from computer vision application like lane detection and person recognition to compression-decompression workloads. While most benchmark suites support Linux based systems, to the best of our knowledge, none of them supports SLURM integration. Theodolite, built for cloud-native apps, may work with Kubernetes and integrate with SLURM via plugins or configurations. However, this potential integration is not reported in the literature. Table 1 shows a comparative overview of different DSP benchmark suites.

Table 1. Comparison of data steam processing benchmarks

Benchmarks	Native Metrics					Ext. Metrics					DSP Framework							Support			
	Latency	Throughput	CPU usage	Memory usage	Garbage collection	CPU mem. bandwidth	Network usage	filesystem read/write	I/O	Energy	Aurora/Stream	Apache Storm	Apache Flink	Apache Spark	Apache Kafka	Hazelcast Jet	Fastflow/Windflow	Experiment Automation	SLURM	Message Broker	Max Doc. Throughput
Linear Road	•										•										0.1 M/s
YSB	•	•										•	•	•							0.2 M/s
DSPBench	•	•	•	•		•						•		•						•	0.8 M/s
Theodolite	•												•	•	•	•				•	1.0 M/s
ESPBench	•	•	•				•	•					•	•						•	0.1 M/s
SPBench	•	•	•	•													•				0.5 K/s
OSPBench	•	•	•	•		•	•						•	•	•					•	0.8 M/s
SProBench	•	•	•	•		•	•	•	•	•		○	•	•	○	○		•	•	•	40 M/s

● - full support, ○ - partial support

Empirical results from running existing benchmark suites in our test environment revealed two key challenges: first, many benchmark suites demonstrate inefficient execution and cannot fully utilize available resources; second, a considerable number of benchmarks are built on outdated frameworks, which have undergone significant updates and major version changes, making the original benchmarks less relevant and less effective for evaluating modern computing systems. Additionally, we found that most benchmark suites struggle to scale beyond a certain throughput threshold. While the scalability of benchmark suites is influenced by various parameters, our experiments observed a maximum throughput ranging from 1 to 4 million events, consistent with findings reported in the existing literature [11,12]. Although some benchmarks specified the size of each event [17], explicit evidence of throughput in terms of event size was absent in the majority of benchmarks. The benchmarks reviewed in this work showed limited flexibility for testing individual components, such as the message broker and stream processor, and offered minimal support for custom message sizing. Furthermore, they were not fully optimized to seamlessly support multiple experiments on HPC systems, particularly those utilizing SLURM. These aspects introduced challenges in pinpointing bottlenecks within the pipeline and addressing inefficiencies during benchmark execution. The SProBench benchmark suite introduced in this work addresses the previously mentioned limitations through several key improvements. These include seamless integration with SLURM, customizable event sizing, automated support for running multiple concurrent experiments on SLURM, and enhanced flexibility for evaluating various components such as message queues and stream processing frameworks. Additionally, SProBench's workload generator exhibits remarkable scalability, exceeding 20 million events per second and achieving a throughput of approximately 0.5 GB/second on a single node, demonstrating its ability to handle high-volume data generation effectively.

3 SProBench

Stream processing benchmark suites often consist of 3 common components: *workload generator* to simulate the data stream, *monitoring unit* to collect relevant metrics, and *post-processing unit* which aggregates and validates the monitoring data. The flexibility and comprehensiveness of each of these components are crucial factors that significantly influence the overall performance, accuracy, and usability of each benchmark suite. Additionally, the design of a practical benchmark suite demands several key factors, including user-friendly interface, centralized and flexible configurations, interoperable framework interface, high scalability, and automation. The benchmark suite proposed in this work is designed based on a flexible modular architecture comprising independent components, which makes SProBench adaptable to virtually any cluster topology and DSP framework. Figure 1 provides a schematic representation of SProBench's architecture, highlighting its key components. The workload generator simulates various real-world workloads as well as custom workloads per user settings. Message broker decouples the workload generator and stream processing layer. The stream processing layer performs computation on the stream generated by workload generator, and consists of different stream processing application logic for different frameworks. In the current implementation, Apache Flink, Apache Spark Streaming, and Apache Kafka Stream are fully integrated. SProBench's well-defined interface and modular architecture enable seamless integration of any other DSP framework with minimal modifications.

All components are monitored using different metric collector tools such as throughput and latency collector, as well as java management extension (JMX) tool which collects metrics related to the java virtual machine. Other system metrics like network and memory bandwidth are collected using external monitoring tools such as Pika [19] and MetricQ [14]. The monitoring layer transmits all metrics to a central storage. The stored metrics are then aggregated and validated by the post-processing unit and are utilized for further offline analysis.

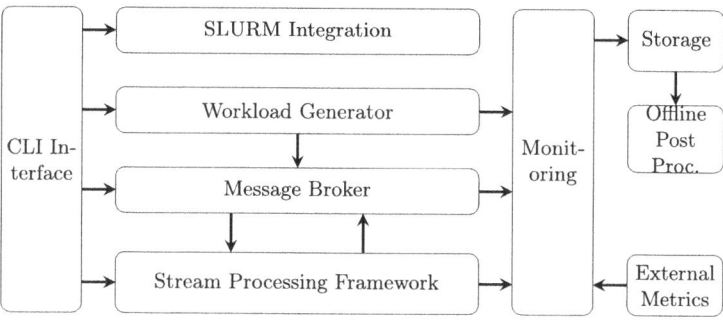

Fig. 1. Benchmark architecture

In addition, SProBench provides a command-line interface (CLI) for the orchestration of all components, setting up frameworks, compiling the resources and performing the benchmarks. The CLI enables out-of-the-box execution of benchmark suite on local machines as well as on SLURM-based clusters, supporting both interactive and batch executions. CLI's internal workflow management utility provides fully automatic, reproducible, and scalable benchmarking experiments. This interface also facilitates the allocation of resources in a SLURM-based environment. By referencing the memory and CPU requirements specified in the configuration file, the interface automatically determines the appropriate SLURM job parameters. Once the resources are allocated, the interface defines all the environment variables necessary for the benchmark processes. A single configuration file serves as a master control point for setting up various options across all components in the benchmark. This streamlined approach enables the execution of multiple experiments with ease, allowing for efficient testing of different scenarios. For instance, by maintaining a consistent parallelism in the processing pipeline, it is possible to test multiple workloads without modifying or need of creating multiple configuration files. This flexibility is achieved through a well-defined configuration file along with the powerful CLI interface, which can be tailored to accommodate diverse testing requirements and scenarios.

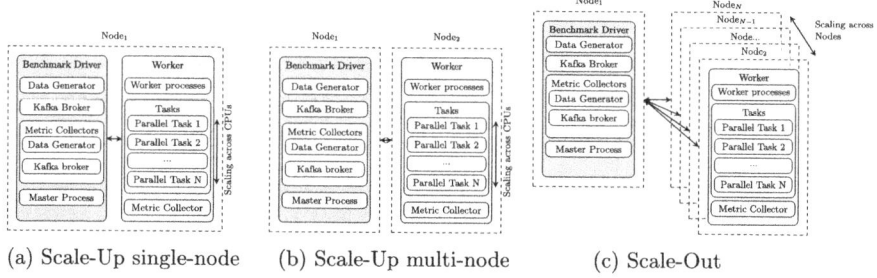

(a) Scale-Up single-node (b) Scale-Up multi-node (c) Scale-Out

Fig. 2. Benchmark process setup for scale-up and scale-out experimentation

SProBench provides flexibility in grouping and organizing its components across various setups. These setups enable different levels of isolation between the benchmark driver and worker components. Figure 2 illustrate several example scenarios of scale-up and scale-out experiments, respectively.

3.1 Benchmarking Workflow

Workflow management in large-scale benchmarking is challenging due to the complexity of coordinating processes, datasets, and resources. Scaling workflows becomes harder as benchmarks grow, requiring efficient task management and resource utilization. Inconsistent workflows and poor documentation of setups, such as missing details on software versions or configurations, hinder reproducibility. To address these issues, the SProBench workflow management system logs every step of an experiment for traceability. It automates most benchmarking tasks, reduces human error, and ensures consistency across experiments.

The benchmarking workflow via SProBench begins with obtaining the code repository and compiling the benchmark suite for the target environment. Afterwards, the benchmark parameters need to be adjusted in the central configuration file; which is the only manual step of the benchmarking workflow. In this configuration file, parameters such as workload, number of nodes and CPUs, degree of parallelism, memory, and so forth are defined. Upon setting the configuration, the benchmark can be executed using the provided entrypoint script and relevant flags. The script then identifies the target environment and whether it operates in interactive or batch mode. In case of an interactive job, the script verifies that sufficient resources are allocated according to the configuration file and then initiates the benchmark. Conversely, for batch jobs the script calculates the required resources and submits a batch job request, which runs in the background and executes the benchmark within it. Once the benchmarking process commences, the required directory structure is created, followed by the initiation of necessary processes and the processing pipeline. Figure 3 illustrates an abstract overview of the benchmarking workflow.

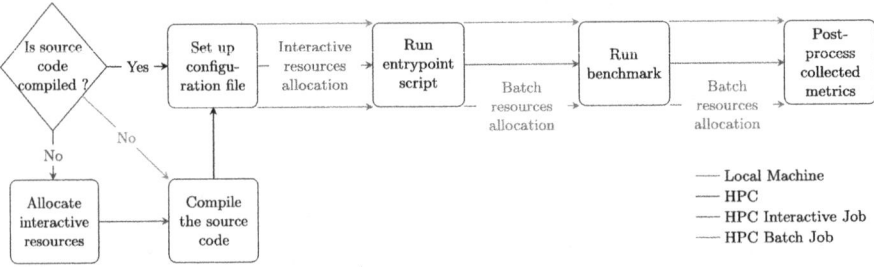

Fig. 3. Benchmark Workflow

Once the benchmarking process is complete, the post-processing scripts are executed to process the collected metrics. The benchmark suite allows multiple experiments to be run from a single configuration file, either with different configurations or the same configuration. This enables simultaneous benchmarking e.g., with various workloads of 5M and 10M events, or multiple runs by the same workload. In addition, the transparent handling of parallel batch job execution and job dependencies is ensured.

3.2 Workload Generation

SProBench's workload generator produces synthetic data streams similar to real-world scenarios. This multi-threaded Java application can produce up to 500,000 events per second per instance. For increased throughput, multiple workload generators can operate in parallel. The workload generator automatically adjusts the number of generators based on the requested total load specified in the configuration, thereby eliminating the need for users to manually manage this aspect.

The workload generator offers extensive customization options, allowing users to tailor characteristics such as frequency, throughput, and record size to create any desired workload. By default, SProBench's workload generator produces synthetic streams of sensor data. Each generated event follows a JSON format, containing a timestamp, sensor ID, and temperature value. The workload generator supports *constant*, *random*, and *burst* generation patterns. In constant mode, it produces events at a fixed frequency, whereas in random mode it generates events at a variable rate. The random workload generation rate is subject to constraints such as minimum and maximum pauses between data generation and minimum and maximum frequencies of data generation. In contrast, the burst mode produces data in bursts at a specified interval, with a desired workload frequency. Notably, the burst mode can be considered a special case of the random interval generation, where the minimum and maximum pauses between data generation are the same, and the data generation frequency is constant. The configuration file allows users to further fine-tune the workload generation by specifying parameters such as memory and CPU usage. Additionally, the workload generator has the capability to set the size of each generated event, with the minimum event size being 27 bytes.

3.3 Processing Pipeline

Based on insights from the literature and empirical analysis, this work covers three distinct classes of processing pipelines namely: *pass-through*, *CPU-intensive*, and *memory-intensive* [12,17]. Figure 4 depicts an overview of different processing pipelines. Message brokers are positioned at both ends of the processing pipelines, serving as data queues for the incoming and outgoing data streams. As shown in Fig. 4, before pushing the data into any of the processing pipelines, the workload generator sends the data to the message broker; in this example Apache Kafka. The left-hand message broker serves as the ingestion source, where raw data streams originate. Message broker on the right-hand serves as the egestion target, where processed data streams are received. The central section of the pipeline consists of stream processing engines to process the incoming data streams using frameworks like Apache Flink, Apache Spark Streaming or Kafka Stream. SProBench defines three processing pipelines for each framework: pass-through, CPU-intensive, and memory-intensive. These pipelines allow users to thoroughly compare how the same processing logic is executed across different SDP frameworks. It is worth noting that these predefined pipelines are designed based on extensive experimentation, but users can also define custom processing logic tailored to their specific benchmarking objectives with minimal modifications.

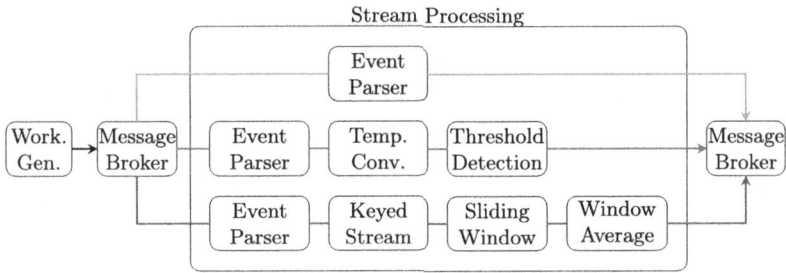

Fig. 4. Processing Pipline

The pass-through pipeline, depicted by the green line in Fig. 4, is defined as baseline for evaluating the performance of the benchmark suite and the target system. In this configuration, the generated data is transmitted through the message broker, ingested by the streaming engines, and then forwarded to the message broker without undergoing any processing. CPU-Intensive pipeline, shown by the red line in the Fig. 4, is designed to perform computationally intensive tasks, resulting in elevated CPU utilization. As explained in previous section, the default workload in SProBench consists of synthesized sensor data. In agreement with the default workload, the CPU-Intensive pipeline consists of various transformation operations. These operations are utilized to perform a range of tasks, including parsing incoming sensor data into a tuple and converting the incoming sensor temperature data to degrees Fahrenheit, which then is checked against a certain threshold. Memory-intensive pipeline is designed to assess the capability of stream processing frameworks in handling stateful operations. This pipeline includes transformation processes that parse incoming sensor data. The data stream generated by default workload generator in this work is keyed by the sensor ID. As illustrated by the blue line in Fig. 4, a sliding window is applied to calculate the average temperature for each sensor ID over the runtime period. The calculated mean temperature for each sensor ID is then maintained as part of the operation's state.

3.4 Metric Collection

There are numerous metrics that can be considered to evaluate DSP framework's performance in conjunction with system performance. As discussed in Sect. 2, many benchmark suites consider throughput and latency for their evaluations, along with CPU and memory usage. In addition, metrics and properties such as resource efficiency, scalability, fault tolerance and time (runtime/startup) have been utilized in stream processing benchmarks [18].

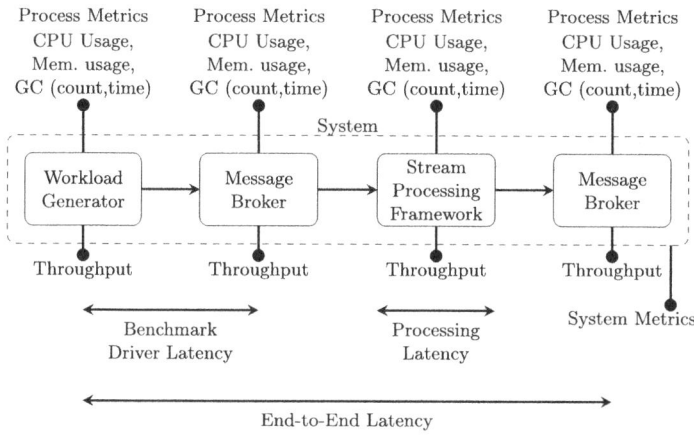

Fig. 5. Metrics Monitoring and Collection

Inspired by previous works, SProBench utilizes throughput, latency, CPU usage, memory usage, garbage collection (count and time), network usage, I/O, and energy consumption to evaluate the performance of stream processing frameworks and the underlying systems. Metrics such as throughput are collected in terms of processed events per second, as well as in terms of size, i.e., processed size in Megabytes per second. Throughput and latency are measured at several locations, as shown in Fig. 5. Latencies measured at different locations help in gathering information on different scales such as message benchmark driver latency, processing latency, and end-to-end latency, which in turn facilitates the identification of bottlenecks in each pipeline.

In addition to metrics related to data processing, SProBench also monitors and collects process metrics including memory usage and garbage collection (time and count). As described earlier, to collect metrics from JVM-based processes, a Java based application is designed that relies on the JMX API [3] to gather all process metrics. Furthermore, SProBench also monitors the target system's performance using external monitoring facilities. Metrics collected in this step are highly dependent on the target system and its available monitoring mechanisms. In the experiment described in Sect. 4, MetricQ [14] was used to collect energy consumption data of the underlying system, and other system metrics including

CPU usage, system usage (memory bandwidth, FLOP, instructions per cycle, filesystem read/write), and network usage were collected using Pika [19].

4 Experiment

This section presents the performance of SProBench via experimental results. Initially, experiments focus on scaling the benchmark with the Workload generator and Message Broker (Apache Kafka), demonstrating extreme scaling as presented in Table 1. Subsequently, scale-up experiment is conducted using the full processing pipeline, which involves the Workload generator, Message Broker (Apache Kafka), and Stream processing framework (Apache Flink). For the proposed experiments Barnard HPC cluster powered by Red Hat Enterprise Linux is used. Barnard features 630 nodes, each equipped with dual Intel Xeon Platinum 8470 CPUs, delivering 104 cores per node. Additionally, each node has 512 GB of RAM, implemented as 16 DDR5 memory modules operating at 4800 MT/s. This configuration yields a total of 65,520 computational cores, making it suitable for large-scale parallel computing tasks and data-intensive research applications. For the following experiments, a maximum of 200 GB of main memory is allocated for workers, with approximately 2 GB of heap memory allocated for each workload generator and 5 GB for Kafka, with 20 threads for I/O and 10 threads for network operations. Each event has a size of 27 bytes.

First experiment investigates the workload scaling behavior in a simplified setup consisting solely of a workload generator and a Kafka message broker. The configuration follows the setup described earlier, with the addition of 4 Kafka topic partitions and input workloads generated at rates of up to 0.5 million events per second. The goal is to evaluate the scalability of both the workload generator and the Kafka broker, focusing on determining the maximum achievable throughput using multiple parallel generators in this streamlined configuration.

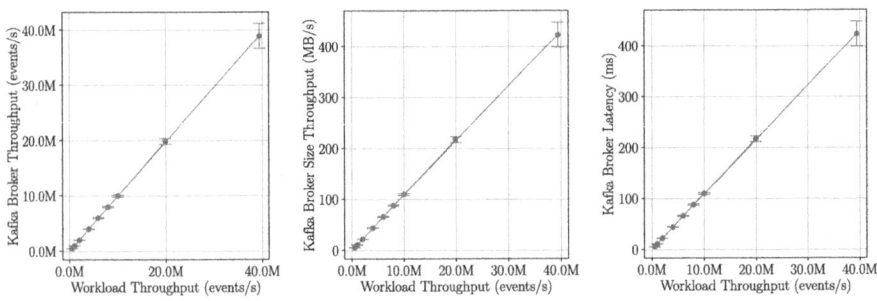

Fig. 6. Scaling performance of Workload generator - Message Broker setup

Figure 6 illustrates the linear scaling behavior of a Kafka broker system as workload throughput increases. The results show a consistent 1:1 relationship between the broker system's throughput and the workload generator output.

The broker latency exhibits a similar linear scaling pattern as the workload intensifies.

Second experiment showcases the benchmark's ability to manage workloads with full process utilization, employing resources at varying levels of parallelism (1, 2, 4, 8, and 16 cores). A CPU-intensive pipeline is used to showcase the benchmark's workings, with a constant workload frequency ranging from 0.5 million to 8 million events per second. Figure 7 illustrates the benchmark's performance with varying number of cores (Parallelism). The framework demonstrates near-linear scalability initially, with performance plateauing at higher parallelism levels. This pattern is mirrored in latency metrics. As parallelism increases, throughput improves but latency rises, indicating diminishing returns. This tradeoff underscores the importance of careful framework optimization and configuration to achieve optimal performance on the given hardware according to the usecase.

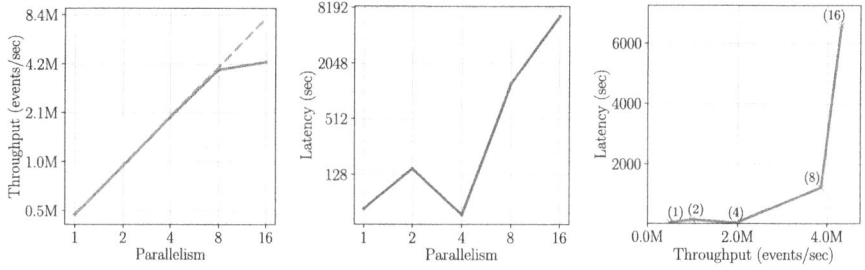

(a) Parallel. Vs Throughput   (b) Parallelism Vs Latency   (c) Throughput Vs Latency

Fig. 7. Parallelism Vs Throughput and Latency

Figure 8 illustrates the benchmark's performance metrics at various levels of parallelism (1, 2, 4, 8, and 16 threads, represented by different colored lines)

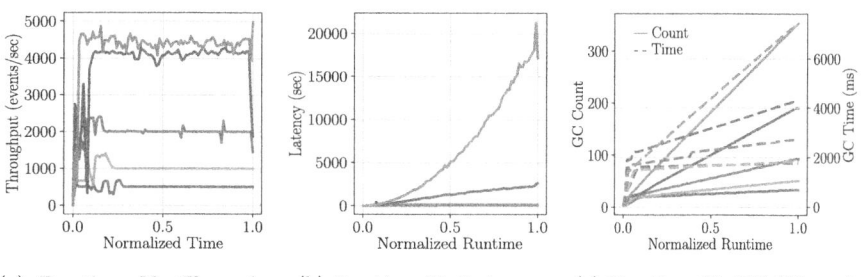

(a) Runtime Vs Throughput   (b) Runtime Vs Latency   (c) Runtime Vs GC (Young)

Parallelism: — 1, — 2, — 4, — 8, — 16

Fig. 8. Metrics across normalized runtime

throughout the runtime. Figure 8a and 8b display how throughput and latency change over normalized runtime. It can be observed that, higher parallelism (purple line, 16 CPUs) achieves the highest throughput but also causes increasing latency compared to lower thread counts. Figure 8c presents garbage collection (GC) metrics, demonstrating the rise in both GC count and duration over time, indicating that higher levels of parallelism typically necessitate increased garbage collection activity. These figures highlight the tradeoffs in the stream processing: while higher parallelism counts can improve throughput, they also introduce higher latency penalties and increased resource consumption.

5 Conclusion and Future Works

This work introduces SProBench, a novel, modular, and highly scalable data stream processing benchmark suite. It is designed to align with the latest advancements in stream processing frameworks and leverage the capabilities of modern HPC systems. Effective assessment of DSP frameworks, which benefit from the vast resources and high computational capacity of modern computing systems, requires benchmarking tools capable of fully utilizing available resources and pushing both hardware and software to their limits. As summarized in Table 1, existing benchmark suites face certain challenges in execution efficiency and may introduce performance constraints. These factors can impact the precise assessment of DSP framework capabilities. Addressing this gap, SProBench emerges as a highly efficient and scalable solution. SProBench demonstrates exceptional performance, with a single instance of its workload generator outperforming most existing benchmark suites. When utilizing parallel instances, SProBench's throughput exceeds that of all other benchmark suites by more than tenfold, showcasing its remarkable efficiency and scalability. In addition, fully configurable workloads and pipelines, native support of Slurm and popular DSP frameworks, automatic experiment workflow management, feature-rich post-processing capabilities, and an open-source software stack make SProBench stand out among the DSP benchmarking suites.

Future plans include the comprehensive integration of other widely-used DSP frameworks and conducting large-scale benchmarking on real-world clusters. Additionally, more pre-defined pipelines and workloads will be developed to further enhance the benchmarking capabilities.

Acknowledgements. The authors acknowledge the financial support by the Federal Ministry of Education and Research of Germany and by Sächsische Staatsministerium für Wissenschaft, Kultur und Tourismus in the programme Center of Excellence for AI-research "Center for Scalable Data Analytics and Artificial Intelligence Dresden/Leipzig", project identification number: ScaDS.AI.

Disclosure of Interests. The authors have no competing interests to declare that are relevant to the content of this article.

References

1. Apache Kafka. https://kafka.apache.org/documentation/streams/. Accessed 17 Mar 2025
2. Apache spark - unified engine for large-scale data analytics. https://spark.apache.org/. Accessed 17 Mar 2025
3. Java Management Extensions Guide. https://docs.oracle.com/en/java/javase/23/jmx/introduction-jmx-technology.html. Accessed 10 Mar 2025
4. Memory Management improvements for Flink's JobManager in Apache Flink 1.11 — flink.apache.org. https://flink.apache.org/2020/09/01/memory-management-improvements-for-flinks-jobmanager-in-apache-flink-1.11/. Accessed 17 Mar 2025
5. What is the Spark Tungsten Project? — databricks.com. https://www.databricks.com/glossary/tungsten. Accessed 17 Mar 2025
6. Amount of Data Created Daily (2024). https://explodingtopics.com/blog/data-generated-per-day. Accessed 10 Mar 2025
7. Arasu, A., et al.: Linear RoadA stream data management benchmark. In: Proceedings 2004 VLDB Conference, pp. 480–491. Elsevier (2004). https://doi.org/10.1016/B978-012088469-8/50044-9
8. Bordin, M.V., Griebler, D., Mencagli, G., Geyer, C.F.R., Fernandes, L.G.L.: DSPBench: a suite of benchmark applications for distributed data stream processing systems. IEEE Access **8**, 222900–222917 (2020). https://doi.org/10.1109/ACCESS.2020.3043948
9. Chintapalli, S., et al.: Benchmarking streaming computation engines: storm, flink and spark streaming. In: 2016 IEEE International Parallel and Distributed Processing Symposium Workshops (IPDPSW), pp. 1789–1792 (2016). https://doi.org/10.1109/IPDPSW.2016.138
10. Garcia, A.M., Griebler, D., Schepke, C., Fernandes, L.G.: SPBench: a framework for creating benchmarks of stream processing applications. Computing **105**(5), 1077–1099 (2023). https://doi.org/10.1007/s00607-021-01025-6
11. Henning, S., Hasselbring, W.: Benchmarking scalability of stream processing frameworks deployed as microservices in the cloud. J. Syst. Softw. **208**, 111879 (2024). https://doi.org/10.1016/j.jss.2023.111879
12. Henning, S., Hasselbring, W.: Theodolite: scalability benchmarking of distributed stream processing engines in microservice architectures. Big Data Res. **25**, 100209 (2021). https://doi.org/10.1016/j.bdr.2021.100209
13. Hesse, G., Matthies, C., Perscheid, M., Uflacker, M., Plattner, H.: ESPBench: the enterprise stream processing benchmark. In: Proceedings of the ACM/SPEC International Conference on Performance Engineering, pp. 201–212. ACM (2021). https://doi.org/10.1145/3427921.3450242
14. Ilsche, T., Hackenberg, D., Schone, R., Bielert, M., Hopfner, F., Nagel, W.E.: MetricQ: a scalable infrastructure for processing high-resolution time series data. In: 2019 IEEE/ACM Industry/University Joint International Workshop on Data-Center Automation, Analytics, and Control (DAAC), pp. 7–12. IEEE (2019). https://doi.org/10.1109/DAAC49578.2019.00007
15. Katsifodimos, A., Schelter, S.: Apache flink: stream analytics at scale. In: 2016 IEEE International Conference on Cloud Engineering Workshop (IC2EW), p. 193 (2016). https://doi.org/10.1109/IC2EW.2016.56
16. Markl, V.: Nebulastream - data stream processing in massively distributed, heterogeneous, volatile environments. In: Proceedings of the 18th ACM International Conference on Distributed and Event-Based Systems, DEBS 2024, pp. 1–3.

Association for Computing Machinery, New York (2024). https://doi.org/10.1145/3629104.3672505
17. Van Dongen, G., Van Den Poel, D.: Influencing factors in the scalability of distributed stream processing jobs. IEEE Access **9**, 109413–109431 (2021). https://doi.org/10.1109/ACCESS.2021.3102645
18. Vogel, A., Henning, S., Ertl, O., Rabiser, R.: A systematic mapping of performance in distributed stream processing systems. In: 2023 49th Euromicro Conference on Software Engineering and Advanced Applications (SEAA), pp. 293–300 (2023). https://doi.org/10.1109/SEAA60479.2023.00052
19. Winkler, F., Knüpfer, A.: Automatic detection of HPC job inefficiencies at TU Dresden's HPC center with PIKA. In: Bienz, A., Weiland, M., Baboulin, M., Kruse, C. (eds.) High Performance Computing, pp. 295–306. Springer, Cham (2023). https://doi.org/10.1007/978-3-031-40843-4_22

NetSenseML: Network-Adaptive Compression for Efficient Distributed Machine Learning

Yisu Wang, Xinjiao Li, Ruilong Wu, Huangxun Chen, and Dirk Kutscher[✉]

The Hong Kong University of Science and Technology (Guangzhou),
Guangzhou, China
{ywang418,xli886,rwu408}@connect.hkust-gz.edu.cn,
{huangxunchen,dku}@hkust-gz.edu.cn

Abstract. Training large-scale distributed machine learning models imposes considerable demands on network infrastructure, often resulting in sudden traffic spikes that lead to congestion, increased latency, and reduced throughput, which would ultimately affect convergence times and overall training performance. While gradient compression techniques are commonly employed to alleviate network load, they frequently compromise model accuracy due to the loss of gradient information. This paper introduces NetSenseML, a novel network adaptive distributed deep learning framework that dynamically adjusts quantization, pruning, and compression strategies in response to real-time network conditions. By actively monitoring network conditions, NetSenseML applies gradient compression only when network congestion negatively impacts convergence speed, thus effectively balancing data payload reduction and model accuracy preservation.

Our approach ensures efficient resource usage by adapting reduction techniques based on current network conditions, leading to shorter convergence times and improved training efficiency. We present the design of the NetSenseML adaptive data reduction function and experimental evaluations show that NetSenseML can improve training throughput by a factor of 1.55 to 9.84× compared to state-of-the-art compression-enabled systems for representative DDL training jobs in bandwidth-constrained conditions.

Keywords: Distributed Systems · Systems for Machine Learning · DNN Training · Gradient Compression

1 Introduction

Training large-scale distributed machine learning models, such as large language models [5,22], imposes considerable demands on the network infrastructure, often resulting in sudden traffic spikes that lead to congestion, increased latency, and reduced throughput, ultimately affecting convergence times and overall training performance.

As distributed machine learning is becoming more widely used, deployments are moving away from proprietary network technologies and isolated workloads toward shared infrastructure and multi-tenant deployments [6]. Distributed Data-Parallel (DDP) training is currently the dominant paradigm for large-scale distributed machine learning [17]. In DDP, gradient communication poses a significant challenge, particularly due to its bursty nature: Periods of computation are followed by sudden bursts of transmission and exchange of the gradient tensor. In such shared environments, unmitigated overload can result in substantial communication volume, potential overload, and packet loss, which can significantly impact the overall training process. Applying traditional congestion control algorithms, such as CUBIC [9] and BBR [7] in protocols such as TCP [3] and QUIC [14], can ensure reliable transmission without overload by adapting sending rates and thus throughput, but it would also decrease training throughput and thus increase convergence times, since machine learning application layers can only adapt their behavior indirectly, as a response to observed transport layer throughput, if at all.

Gradient compression has emerged as a promising solution for mitigating this communication bottleneck by reducing the volume of gradient data exchanged [12]. Techniques such as quantization [16], pruning [10] and sparsification [18] compress gradients to reduce the amount of data transmitted. However, existing gradient compression schemes often fail to accelerate the training process without compromising model accuracy, thereby introducing a trade-off between communication efficiency and training performance.

To address these challenges, we introduce NetSenseML, an adaptive gradient compression framework for distributed machine learning that dynamically monitors network conditions and actively responds to congestion by adjusting compression ratios. NetSenseML aims to reduce Time to Accuracy (TTA), defined as the time required to reach a target model accuracy, effectively balancing transmission efficiency, convergence speed, and overall training performance through techniques such as quantization, pruning [11,15] and sparsification.

In the network sensing phase, NetSenseML begins by carefully monitoring gradient transmission times and estimating the available bandwidth to gauge the current state of the network, thereby adjusting the gradient compression ratio in real time based on these assessments. This adaptive approach allows NetSenseML to tailor gradient compression, in the adaptive compression phase, by appropriately applying quantization, pruning, and sparsification, aligned with the measured compression ratio and density of the gradients. This strategy ensures the optimal adjustment of the compressed gradient size to fit the prevailing network conditions and maximize bandwidth efficiency.

Our experiments demonstrate that in constrained bandwidth environments with multiple workers, NetSenseML significantly enhances the efficiency of data transmission and model training performance. Furthermore, the algorithm maintains robust data transmission and model training speeds, in multitask scenarios and under challenging bandwidth conditions, effectively balancing network utilization and training efficiency.

The main contributions of our research are as follows.

1. To the best of our knowledge, NetSenseML is among the first systems to use transmission times and bandwidth estimates to detect network conditions, thereby driving the dynamic tuning of gradient compression ratios based on perceived network conditions, improving network utilization and training efficiency.
2. NetSenseML ensures the retention of essential gradient information, even in extreme network scenarios by adjusting compression strategies based on the compression ratio and gradient density characteristics, thus minimizing the impacts of compression on model accuracy.
3. Rigorous testing in environments with limited bandwidth and diverse tasks shows that NetSenseML can guarantee efficient gradient transmission, stable and fast model convergence, and maintain high model accuracy, effectively minimizing the trade-offs between key performance metrics.

2 Scenarios for Network-Adaptive DL Training

NetSenseML is designed for use in arbitrary network scenarios within Wide Area Network (WAN) environments. Training a deep neural network (DNN) involves three steps: forward propagation (FP), backward propagation (BP), and the parameter update. Distributed training addresses GPU memory constraints by dividing data across multiple GPUs, each holding a complete model copy. However, this approach requires frequent gradient synchronization across GPUs, leading to intensive communication. As models grow larger, requiring partitioning across GPUs, communication demands increase further. In such cases, the network bandwidth becomes a critical bottleneck.

We consider two WAN training scenarios:

Scenario 1: Multi-cluster communication through a wide area network. When computational resources are insufficient, training tasks often use wide area network connections across data centers to accelerate the process and improve resource efficiency. A typical example of this model is CloudLab [8], which consists of multiple clusters distributed across various locations, providing researchers with full control over computing, networking, and storage resources.

Scenario 2: Offloading to Public Cloud Platforms. Multi-clusters do not always guarantee sufficient resources. For example, CloudLab [8] offers limited allocations per user, often requiring researchers to wait in a queue based on the usage of others. In such cases, public cloud resources serve as ideal complements to local resources. Although public cloud services are often costly, the combined use of lab resources and cloud services proves to be significantly more economical than relying solely on public cloud rentals.

A key challenge in these environments is that the interconnection bandwidth over WANs is significantly lower than the bandwidth available within laboratory clusters or between nodes in public cloud environments. As a result, during the

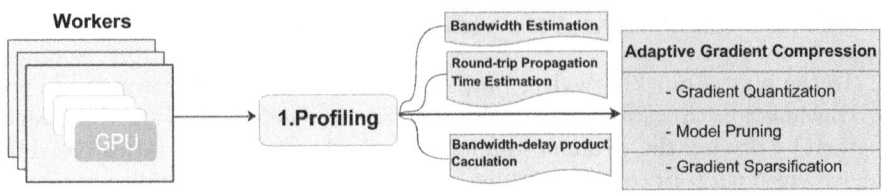

Fig. 1. NetSenseML Overview

BP process, the computed gradients must remain in the GPU/CPU memory of the nodes, waiting until the buffered data are successfully transmitted. This delay can substantially increase the overall training time and reduce GPU utilization.

3 Related Work

Modern distributed machine learning frameworks, such as PyTorch DDP [4], generate a substantial volume of data packets that accumulate in communication queues, slowing down iteration speed. To address this challenge, DC2 [1] leverages a delay monitoring component to track communication latency for each training iteration, enabling dynamic adjustment of gradient compression. Crux [6] infers network congestion by analyzing GPU utilization, allowing it to optimize the data transmission volume. Espresso [24] emphasizes the coordination between different hardware components and communication links during the compression process, aiming to optimize communication time.

Despite existing work that estimates network conditions based on latency, GPU utilization, and bandwidth, there is a lack of effective estimation of actual network capacity.

4 NetSenseML: Network-Aware Gradient Compression for Efficient Distributed Machine Learning

Our goal is to transmit as much gradient information as possible under limited bandwidth, unpredictable network connectivity, and constantly changing network conditions, thereby maintaining model accuracy and convergence speed. As shown in Fig. 1, the architecture includes a profiling module, which continuously monitors network status through bandwidth estimation, round-trip propagation time estimation, and bandwidth-delay product calculation, and an adaptive gradient compression module that dynamically adjusts gradient quantization and model pruning to select the optimal feasible data rate.

4.1 Network Status Sensing and Adaptive Compression Ratio Adjustment

We accurately modeled the available network capacity prior to each gradient aggregation. To do this, we monitor the bottleneck bandwidth (BtlBw) and the

Algorithm 1: Network Status Sensing and Adaptive Compression Ratio Adjustment

Data: Transmission intervals, Data size, RTprop, Compression ratio
Result: *ratio*: Ratio used for gradient compression

1 **Step 1: start-up:**
2   Set ratio ← 0.01;
3   **foreach** *step in start-up phase* **do**
4   Quickly increase the compression ratio ;
5   ratio ← min(1, ratio + β_1);
6 **Step 2: NetSense:**
7   **foreach** *gradient transmission interval i* **do**
8   Measure EBB and RTT for interval $i-1$;
9        $EBB_{i-1} \leftarrow \frac{\text{data\_size}_{i-1}}{RTT_{i-1}}$;
10   Update BtlBw and RTprop;
11   BtlBw ← EBB_{Max};
12   RTprop ← RTT_{Min};
13   Measure BDP;
14   BDP ← BtlBw × RTprop ;
15   Adjust compression ratio ;
16   **if** $data\_size > 0.9 \times BDP$ **then**
17   ratio ← max(0.005, ratio × α) ;
18   **else**
19   ratio ← min(1, ratio + β_2)

round-trip propagation time (`RTprop`) during each gradient transmission interval to sense and analyze the state of the network as shown in Fig. 2, and adjust the compression ratio based on the bandwidth delay product (BDP). When the transmitted data size is less than the BDP, the round-trip time (`RTT`) remains relatively constant at its minimum value, i.e., `RTprop`.

In this phase, the network bandwidth is underutilized. However, as the size of the transmitted data exceeds the BDP, the `RTT` increases significantly, indicating a state of network congestion where the data sent surpass the network's transmission capacity, i.e., `BtlBw`. Our goal is to adjust the compression ratio so that the size of the compressed gradients approximates the BDP as closely as possible. This approach maximizes bandwidth utilization, enabling higher data throughput, which in turn enhances model accuracy and accelerates convergence speed.

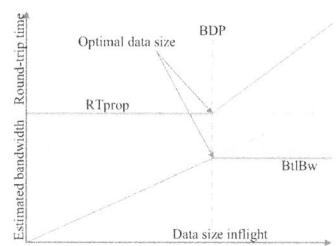

Fig. 2. Network status sensing based on `BtlBw` and `RTprop`.

In BBR [7], the packet sending rate during the startup phase increases rapidly until packet loss or excessive RTT occurs, at which point BBR detects the network's capacity limit. In NetSenseML, we initially set the gradient compression ratio to a lower value and rapidly increase this ratio during the first few steps of training until excessive RTT is detected.

Existing RTT-dependent congestion control mechanisms such as MLT [23] employ reactive strategies that activate only after substantial queue accumulation, typically when RTT exceeds twice the propagation delay. This delayed response allows severe congestion to develop, risking packet loss that critically degrades distributed training performance.

NetSenseML introduces proactive congestion prevention through real-time bandwidth-delay product monitoring. As BDP defines the network's maximum in-flight data capacity, approaching gradient volumes trigger immediate compression before measurable RTT increases. By maintaining transmitted data below the BDP threshold during parameter synchronization phases, our method eliminates queue buildup at intermediate nodes, sustaining optimal throughput and accelerating model convergence.

Our algorithm is comprised of two specific steps, as shown in Algorithm 1:

Step 1. During the initial start-up phase, we set the compression ratio to 0.01. This ratio is then progressively increased over a limited number of stepsuntil the detection of packet loss or excessive RTT.

Step 2. In the *NetSense* phase, we continuously monitor and evaluate the estimated bandwidth (EBB) and the RTT for each interval. These metrics are crucial for updating the values of BtlBw and RTprop. The compression ratio is subsequently adjusted based on the BDP, which is calculated as the product of BtlBw and RTprop according Eq. (1) to (3). We determine the EBB of the last interval by analyzing the size of the transmitted data and its corresponding RTT, using the maximum observed value as the network's BtlBw, BtlBw = max(EBB), and the minimum recorded RTT as the RTprop, RTprop = min(RTT), under conditions free from network congestion. For data size data_size$_i$ and transmission time RTT$_i$ of interval i, the EBB is calculated by Eq. (1),

$$\text{EBB}_i(\text{data\_size}_i, \text{RTT}_i) = \frac{\text{data\_size}_i}{\text{RTT}_i}. \tag{1}$$

After updating the value of BtlBw and RTprop, BDP is then estimated using Eq. (2), based on RTprop and BtlBw prior to each data transmission,

$$\text{BDP} = \text{BtlBw} \times \text{RTprop}. \tag{2}$$

Consequently, the compression ratio is adjusted in accordance with BDP, as defined in Eq. (3),

$$\text{ratio} = \begin{cases} \max(0.005, \text{ratio} \times \alpha), & \text{data\_size} > 0.9 \times \text{BDP} \\ \min(1, \text{ratio} + \beta_2), & \text{data\_size} \leq 0.9 \times \text{BDP} \end{cases} \tag{3}$$

In our experiment, α is 0.5, β_2 is 0.01.

Algorithm 2: NetSenseCompression: quantization, pruning, and sparsification

Data: Pre-trained model: The initial neural network model,
$grads$: Gradients for compression,
ratio: Ratio used for gradient compression,
tr_q: Quantization check threshold,
tr_d: Gradient density threshold,
Result: Com_grads: Compressed gradients

1 **Step 1: Adaptive Quantization**:
2   **if** $ratio < tr_q$ **then**
3     $L_2 \leftarrow$ calculate_L2_norm($grads$);
4   **if** $L_2 > tr_d$ **then**
5       $grads \leftarrow$ quantize($grads$);
6   ratio $\leftarrow 2 \times$ ratio;
7 **Step 2: Model Pruning**:
8   Get pruning rate;
9   pruning_rate $\leftarrow 0.5 \times (1 - \text{ratio})$;
10   pruned_grads $\leftarrow$ prune_weights(pruning_rate);
11   Set pruned weights' gradients to zero;
12     $grads$[pruned_grads] $\leftarrow 0$;
13 **Step 3: Gradient Sparsification**:
14   $Com\_grads \leftarrow$ top_k($grads$, ratio);
15   Transmit the sparsified gradient over the network;

4.2 Adaptive Compression Based on Quantization, Pruning, and Sparsification

To enhance the precision and accelerate the convergence of the model, we have developed an adaptive compression method that incorporates quantization, pruning, and sparsification, as shown in Algorithm 2. This method optimizes gradient transmission under challenging network conditions

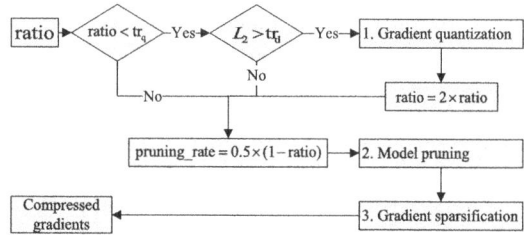

Fig. 3. Adaptive quantization based on L_2 norm.

through quantization, boosts model generalizability via pruning, and maintains critical gradient information through sparsification. Our method consists of the following steps:

Step 1. Adaptive quantization. Adaptive quantization is initiated when the compression ratio falls below a pre-defined threshold, tr_q, as shown in Fig. 3. The gradient's L_2 norm is computed as follows:

- If $L_2 > \text{tr}_d$, indicating substantial informational content, quantization is applied to preserve non-zero gradient transmission. This is essential for maintaining the gradient's integrity under stringent network conditions.
- To accommodate the halved data size resulting from the reduction of gradient representation from 32-bit to 16-bit floating points, the compression ratio is adjusted to ratio = 2 × ratio. This efficient compression aids in optimizing bandwidth use while ensuring data integrity and model performance.

Step 2: Model Pruning. The pruning rate is set using $\text{ratio}_p = 0.5 \times (1 - \text{ratio})$, which targets parameters with smaller weights for pruning:

This process involves setting the gradients of the selected parameters to zero, which not only reduces the load during network transmission by eliminating these gradients from the next sparsification step but also minimizes the disproportionate influence of small weights with large gradients on model training. Such selective pruning is crucial for enhancing the model's generalizability and overall performance.

The parameters affected by pruning are not permanently removed but are only excluded from gradient transmission. This allows these pruned parameters the potential to be gradually reactivated in subsequent training iterations based on new data, thereby maintaining the adaptability and depth of the model's learning capability.

Step 3. Gradient sparsification. We employ the compression ratio as the basis for the sparsification ratio, performing TopK sparsification [2] to eliminate gradients with minimal absolute values, and accumulate the local filtered gradients for further aggregation and transmission. This process is calibrated to ensure that the decision to filter gradients is influenced equally by the model's pruning strategy and the inherent magnitude of the gradients.

This structured approach not only streamlines the handling of data in constrained network environments but also strategically manipulates the model parameters to promote faster convergence and enhance the general robustness of the model.

5 Implementation and Evalution

5.1 Setup and Workloads

We built our testbed using the ESXi virtualization platform with a server equipped with 8 A40 GPUs and an Intel Xeon Platinum 8358P processor with 64 CPU cores.

We developed the NetSenseML prototype on top of the PyTorch distributed framework [4], implementing communication using NCCL [19] over TCP for gradient aggregation. In our implementation, we utilized PyTorch's Distributed Data Parallel communication hook to override the default `allreduce` operation, allowing fine-grained control over how gradients are communicated across workers.

Workloads: We evaluated our NetSenseML prototype by training popular computer vision models on an eight-worker testbed. The models and datasets used in our evaluation included ResNet18 [13] and VGG16 [20], both trained on the CIFAR-100 dataset. We set the per-GPU batch size to 32.

Metrics: We define time-to-accuracy (TTA) as the training time required to reach a target validation accuracy. Additionally, we present the training throughput (measured as images per second, referred to as samples per second) across all training tasks under different scenarios and varying bandwidth conditions. We define convergence time as the time required for the model's accuracy to stabilize at a target threshold, indicating the model has fully converged.

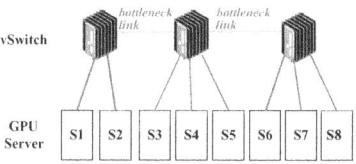

Fig. 4. Evaluation topology.

5.2 Evaluation Scenarios

We conducted experiments under three different scenarios using the topology shown in Fig. 4, creating network performance bottlenecks by adjusting the link bandwidth of two connections to the switch.

Scenario 1: Bandwidth constrained but stable network. We ran several tests using different static bottleneck bandwidths, ranging from 200 Mbps to 10 Gbps, by adjusting the link bandwidth between the switch and other nodes. The bandwidth selection was based on the proportion of the maximum bandwidth required by a training model to avoid latency. These tests, which measured time-to-accuracy, convergence time, and training throughput, showed that NetSenseML can fully utilize the available bandwidth (when TopK and AllReduce cannot), leading to faster convergence.

Scenario 2: Degrading Network Conditions. We gradually reduced all communication bandwidths during the experiment to demonstrate the adaptability of our approach. Training throughput was compared to show that as network conditions deteriorate, NetSenseML can achieve higher throughput by reducing gradient transmission, whereas TopK and AllReduce maintain a constant data volume, leading to network congestion and reduced training throughput.

Scenario 3: Fluctuating Bandwidth with Competing Network Traffic. We simulated a cloud service environment where multiple virtual machines share the same physical host's network resources. Specifically, we ran multiple iperf3 [21] processes in parallel between nodes, periodically sending traffic to test the available bandwidth of the current network links. This generated network interference that competed for bandwidth with the training task. By dynamically adjusting the link bandwidth between switches and nodes, we evaluated the robustness of our approach.

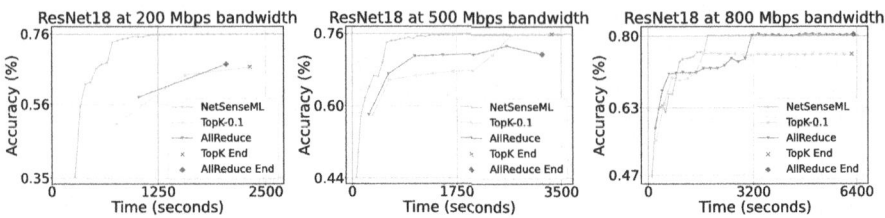

Fig. 5. Time to accuracy (TTA) comparison under different bottleneck bandwidth conditions with ResNet18

5.3 End-to-End Performance

For assessing end-to-end performance, we measured 1) *time-to-accuracy*, 2) *training throughput and communication efficiency*, 3) *dynamic training throughput in degrading network conditions*, and 4) *dynamic training throughput in fluctuating network conditions*.

Time-to-Accuracy. We evaluated NetSenseML against TopK compression (0.1 rate) and AllReduce for ResNet18 and VGG16 models in bandwidth constrained environments (200 Mbps, 500 Mbps, and 800 Mbps). The ResNet18 model size is 46.2MB, making AllReduce impractical without at least 500 Mbps to prevent congestion. Therefore, we tested under bandwidths of 200 Mbps, 500 Mbps, and 800 Mbps.

Under extremely low bandwidth conditions, NetSenseML demonstrates superior convergence speed compared to both AllReduce and TopK. We use the point at which NetSenseML achieves its best test accuracy as the benchmark and terminate the training of AllReduce and TopK at that point.

Figure 5 shows that NetSenseML consistently finds an appropriate compression ratio to maintain stable training and converge effectively, even under bandwidth bottlenecks. At 200 Mbps, NetSenseML significantly improves convergence time and stability compared to TopK and AllReduce, which exhibit both slower convergence and reduced stability. NetSenseML maintains a consistent accuracy curve without major fluctuations, while TopK-0.1 suffers from instability. At 500 Mbps, NetSenseML achieves the target accuracy 5× faster than TopK-0.1. NetSenseML surpasses AllReduce in both convergence speed and stability. Under 800 Mbps, NetSenseML retains its advantage, converging more quickly and steadily to a higher accuracy.

Training Throughput and Communication Efficiency. Table 2 presents a comparison of training throughput and convergence times for NetSenseML, AllReduce, and TopK-0.1 under different bandwidth conditions (Table 1).

The results demonstrate the robustness of NetSenseML in achieving optimal accuracy with significantly reduced convergence time, particularly in challenging low-bandwidth environments.

NetSenseML consistently maintains a specific training throughput across different bandwidth conditions. Taking ResNet18 as an example, when network

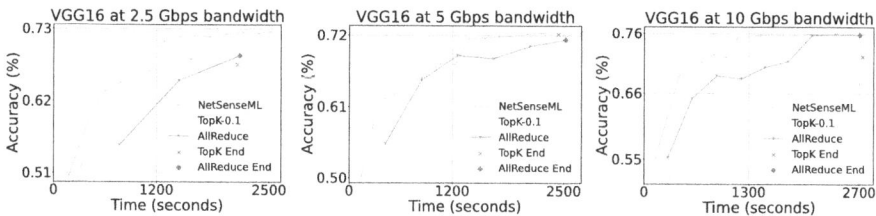

Fig. 6. Time to accuracy (TTA) comparison under different bottleneck bandwidth conditions with VGG16

Table 1. Performance Comparison of ResNet18 under NetSenseML and Other Methods: Training Throughput (samples/second), Convergence Time (seconds), and Best Test Accuracy (%)

Method	Bottleneck Bandwidth	Test Accuracy	Training Throughput	Convergence Time
NetSenseML	200 Mbps	75.79%	642.90	1575
AllReduce	200 Mbps	67.34%	42.20	N/A
TopK-0.1	200 Mbps	66.52%	65.31	N/A
NetSenseML	500 Mbps	76.02%	744.24	1090
AllReduce	500 Mbps	73.24%	179.85	N/A
TopK-0.1	500 Mbps	75.62%	144.27	3252
NetSenseML	800 Mbps	80.18%	824.56	1808
AllReduce	800 Mbps	80.35%	283.60	3150
TopK-0.1	800 Mbps	75.68%	234.77	1920

conditions match the communication scale, avoiding network congestion and preventing increased RTT or packet loss and retransmission, NetSenseML identifies a higher compression rate to avoid compression, optimizing the overall performance. When network limitations become the performance bottleneck for the entire training cluster, such as in cases of network congestion in cloud environments or operational issues in data centers, traditional methods like AllReduce and static compression algorithms like TopK struggle. These methods often slow down the gradient synchronization process, subsequently hindering the entire training process. In contrast, NetSenseML effectively mitigates this issue, adapting dynamically to maintain efficient training.

An interesting observation is that when training ResNet18 under a network bottleneck bandwidth of 200 Mbps, the training throughput of the TopK compression algorithm was higher than that of AllReduce, which aligns with our intuition since TopK has a smaller overall communication volume. However, when the bottleneck bandwidth was increased to 500 Mbps and 800 Mbps, AllReduce achieved higher training throughput compared to TopK-0.1. This can be attributed to the use of the AllGather communication pattern by TopK for gradient synchronization, whereas the NCCL AllReduce operation exhibits a high degree of parallelism, allowing it to efficiently utilize the network link bandwidth.

Table 2. Performance Comparison of VGG16 under NetSenseML and Other Methods

Method	Bottleneck Bandwidth	Test Accuracy	Training Throughput	Convergence Time
NetSenseML	2.5 Gbps	72.04%	172.80	2520
AllReduce	2.5 Gbps	66.52%	43.20	N/A
TopK-0.1	2.5 Gbps	65.12%	96.32	N/A
NetSenseML	5 Gbps	72.55%	199.46	2040
AllReduce	5 Gbps	71.31%	91.58	N/A
TopK-0.1	5 Gbps	72.12%	128.61	2436
NetSenseML	10 Gbps	75.90%	340.35	1808
AllReduce	10 Gbps	75.84%	129.87	2454
TopK-0.1	10 Gbps	72.30%	148.61	2736

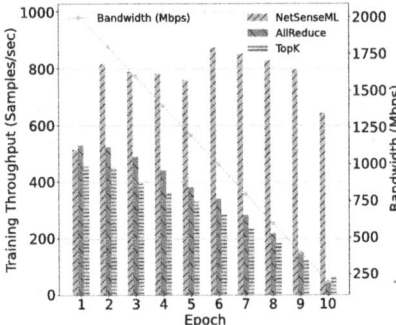

Fig. 7. Impact of Bandwidth Fluctuation on Training Throughput of ResNet18

Dynamic Training Throughput in Degrading Network Conditions. The adaptability of NetSenseML to changing bandwidth conditions is illustrated in Scenario 2, where dynamic training performance is compared between different levels of bandwidth. Using the ResNet18 model, we gradually decreased the bottleneck bandwidth - from 2000 to 200 Mbps in steps of 200 Mbps - and measured training performance at each level. This approach highlights the advantage of NetSenseML over TopK and AllReduce. As network conditions deteriorate, NetSenseML is able to maintain higher throughput by reducing gradient transmission, while TopK and AllReduce maintain constant data volumes, leading to network congestion and reduced throughput.

Figure 7 presents the training throughput of different methods as the initial bottleneck bandwidth of 2000 Mbps gradually decreases to 200 Mbps. In the first epoch, NetSenseML needed time to determine an appropriate compression ratio for the available bandwidth, initially leading to suboptimal throughput. However, as training progressed, NetSenseML adapted effectively, adjusting the compression ratio to accommodate increasingly constrained and adverse network conditions. This adaptability allowed it to maintain consistent training

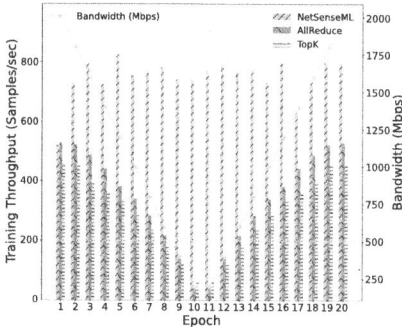

Fig. 8. Impact of Bandwidth Fluctuation on Training Throughput of ResNet18

throughput, which is highly valuable for cloud scenarios where programmers need to quickly observe the final convergence of the model. In contrast, TopK and AllReduce were unable to adapt to the decreasing bandwidth, resulting in lower training throughput as network constraints intensified.

Dynamic Training Throughput in Fluctuating Network Conditions. In Scenario 3, we used the ResNet18 model, and other configurations were kept the same as in Scenario 2. To illustrate the coexistence of our training task with other network applications, we ran iperf3 [21] in a multiprocess setup to compete for the network link, thereby preempting the link between switches and imposing constraints on network traffic during training. Figure 8 shows that regardless of how dynamically competing trafficies, NetSenseML is consistently able to proceed with stable training throughput, demonstrating a significantly higher level of stability compared to static collective communication methods such as AllReduce and TopK.

6 Conclusions

Network fluctuations in bandwidth and latency often degrade resource efficiency, slow model convergence, and reduce accuracy, especially in heterogeneous environments. To address this, we propose NetSenseML, which is an adaptive compression algorithm that dynamically adjusts gradient compression ratios based on real-time network performance.

By monitoring network conditions and estimating bandwidth, NetSenseML applies quantization, pruning, and sparsification to optimize both critical gradient retention and model generalizability. NetSenseML performs well in adapting to a variety of network conditions, ensuring robust and efficient gradient transmission. This adaptability significantly improves the performance of model training and convergence rates in various scenarios, effectively mitigating the typical trade-offs between transmission efficiency, convergence speed, and accuracy.

Acknowledgements. Guangdong provincial project 2023QN10X048, Guangzhou Municipal Key Laboratory on Future Networked Systems (2024A03J0623), the Guangzhou Municipal Science and Technology Project 2023A03J0011, the Guangdong provincial project 2023ZT10X009, and the Natural Science Foundation of China (U23A20339).

Disclosure of Interests. The authors have no competing interests to declare that are relevant to the content of this article.

References

1. Abdelmoniem, A.M., Canini, M.: DC2: delay-aware compression control for distributed machine learning. In: IEEE INFOCOM 2021 - IEEE Conference on Computer Communications, pp. 1–10 (2021)
2. Aji, A.F., Heafield, K.: Sparse communication for distributed gradient descent. In: Palmer, M., Hwa, R., Riedel, S. (eds.) Proceedings of the 2017 Conference on Empirical Methods in Natural Language Processing, Copenhagen, Denmark, pp. 440–445. Association for Computational Linguistics (2017)
3. Alizadeh, M., et al.: Data center TCP (DCTCP). SIGCOMM Comput. Commun. Rev. **40**(4), 63–74 (2010)
4. Ansel, J., Yang, E., , et al.: Pytorch 2: faster machine learning through dynamic python bytecode transformation and graph compilation. In: ASPLOS 2024, pp. 929–947. Association for Computing Machinery, New York (2024)
5. Brown, T.B., Mann, B., Ryder, N., et al.: Language models are few-shot learners. CoRR abs/2005.14165 (2020)
6. Cao, J., et al.: Crux: GPU-efficient communication scheduling for deep learning training. In: ACM SIGCOMM 2024, pp. 1–15. Association for Computing Machinery, New York (2024)
7. Cardwell, N., Cheng, Y., Gunn, C.S., Yeganeh, S.H., Jacobson, V.: BBR: congestion-based congestion control: measuring bottleneck bandwidth and round-trip propagation time. Queue **14**(5), 20–53 (2016)
8. Duplyakin, D., et al.: The design and operation of {CloudLab}. In: 2019 USENIX Annual Technical Conference (USENIX ATC 2019), pp. 1–14 (2019)
9. Ha, S., Rhee, I., Xu, L.: Cubic: a new TCP-friendly high-speed TCP variant. ACM SIGOPS Oper. Syst. Rev. **42**(5), 64–74 (2008)
10. Han, S., Pool, J., Tran, J., Dally, W.: Learning both weights and connections for efficient neural network. In: Advances in Neural Information Processing Systems (NeurIPS), pp. 1135–1143 (2015)
11. Han, S., Pool, J., Tran, J., Dally, W.J.: Learning both weights and connections for efficient neural networks (2015)
12. Han, W., Vargaftik, S., Mitzenmacher, M., Karp, B., Basat, R.B.: Beyond throughput and compression ratios: towards high end-to-end utility of gradient compression (2024)
13. He, K., Zhang, X., Ren, S., Sun, J.: Deep residual learning for image recognition (2015). https://arxiv.org/abs/1512.03385
14. Langley, A., et al.: The quic transport protocol: design and internet-scale deployment. In: Proceedings of the Conference of the ACM Special Interest Group on Data Communication. In: SIGCOMM 2017, pp. 183–196. Association for Computing Machinery, New York (2017)

15. Li, H., Kadav, A., Durdanovic, I., Samet, H., Graf, H.P.: Pruning filters for efficient convnets. In: International Conference on Learning Representations (ICLR) (2016)
16. Li, M., et al.: THC: accelerating distributed deep learning using tensor homomorphic compression (2024)
17. Li, M., et al.: Scaling distributed machine learning with the parameter server. In: 11th USENIX Symposium on Operating Systems Design and Implementation (OSDI 2014), Broomfield, CO, pp. 583–598. USENIX Association (2014)
18. Lin, Y., Han, S., Mao, H., Wang, Y., Dally, W.J.: Deep gradient compression: reducing the communication bandwidth for distributed training. CoRR (2017)
19. NVIDIA: Nvidia collective communications library (NCCL) (2024). https://developer.nvidia.com
20. Simonyan, K., Zisserman, A.: Very deep convolutional networks for large-scale image recognition (2015). https://arxiv.org/abs/1409.1556
21. iPerf Team: iPerf - the ultimate speed test tool for TCP, UDP and SCTP (2024). https://github.com/esnet/iperf
22. Touvron, H., et al.: Llama: open and efficient foundation language models (2023)
23. Wang, H., Tian, H., Chen, J., Wan, X., Xia, J., et al.: Towards domain-specific network transport for distributed DNN training. In: 21st USENIX Symposium on Networked Systems Design and Implementation (NSDI 2024), Santa Clara, CA, pp. 1421–1443. USENIX Association (2024)
24. Wang, Z., Lin, H., Zhu, Y., Ng, T.E.: Hi-speed DNN training with espresso: unleashing the full potential of gradient compression with near-optimal usage strategies. In: Proceedings of the Eighteenth European Conference on Computer Systems, pp. 867–882 (2023)

Efficient Pyramidal Analysis of Gigapixel Images on a Decentralized Modest Computer Cluster

Marie Reinbigler[1(✉)], Rishi Sharma[2], Rafael Pires[2], Elisabeth Brunet[1], Anne-Marie Kermarrec[2], and Catalin Fetita[3]

[1] SAMOVAR, Inria Saclay, Télécom SudParis, IP Paris, 91120 Palaiseau, France
marie.reinbigler@telecom-sudparis.eu
[2] EPFL, Lausanne, Switzerland
[3] SAMOVAR, Télécom SudParis, IP Paris, 91120 Palaiseau, France

Abstract. Analyzing gigapixel images is recognized as computationally demanding. In this paper, we introduce PYRAMIDAI, a technique for analyzing gigapixel images with reduced computational cost. The proposed approach adopts a gradual analysis of the image, beginning with lower resolutions and progressively concentrating on regions of interest for detailed examination at higher resolutions. We evaluated two strategies for balancing accuracy and computational cost in adaptive-resolution selection and validated them on the Camelyon 16 biomedical image dataset. Our results demonstrate that PYRAMIDAI substantially decreases the amount of processed data required for analysis by up to 2.65×, while preserving the accuracy in identifying relevant sections on a single computer. To advance democratization of gigapixel image analysis, we evaluated whether mainstream computers can perform the computation by exploiting the inherent parallelism in the approach. Using a simulator, we estimated the best data distribution and load balancing algorithm according to the number of workers. We implemented the selected algorithms and confirmed that they led to the same conclusions when applied in a real-world setting. Analysis time is reduced from more than an hour to a few minutes using 12 modest workers, offering a practical solution for efficient large-scale image analysis.

Keywords: Gigapixel Images · Pyramidal Analysis · Load Balancing · Decentralized Systems · Heterogeneous Density Problem

1 Introduction

Gigapixel images are omnipresent in various fields like biomedicine and satellite imagery. Featuring a pyramidal multi-resolution structure, they reach sizes of up to $10^5 \times 10^5$ pixels at the highest resolution, equivalent to 40BG of uncompressed data [38]. Among their benefits, they hold immense potential for advancing biomedical research [9,14,17] by providing unprecedented detail and clarity.

The counterpart is a significant computational cost, raising challenges for traditional image analysis methods, especially in processing large datasets efficiently. Deep learning techniques, including convolutional neural networks (CNNs) [24] and vision transformers [21], have shown remarkable results in image analysis [4]. These methods ensure a thorough examination that minimizes the chance of missing essential details as it analyzes the entire image. While effective, they are resource-intensive and not always computable on local facilities.

Typical gigapixel image analysis is initiated with a preliminary coarse detection, which identifies the analysis area, and a tiling process for processing. These tiles can be analyzed either at their highest resolution alone [3,16,19,22] or in conjunction with their contextual lower-resolution counterparts [1,28,31,32,36,37]. Our proposal aims at further enhancing computational efficiency, leveraging the inherent multiresolution structure of these images. By filtering tiles requiring in-depth analysis, PYRAMIDAI preserves computational resources and, thanks to its potential for load distribution, enables optimization of computational load while maintaining analytical rigor. Thus, our contributions are:

- the design of PYRAMIDAI, a pyramidal analysis approach tailored for gigapixel images. This iterative process ensures that only areas of interest are examined at the highest resolution;
- two strategies to determine the threshold of the binary decision to proceed with analysis to a higher resolution level for a specific tile;
- an experimental evaluation using the Camelyon 16 dataset [6], comprising biomedical images. The analysis focuses on detecting metastatic cells. The results demonstrate that PYRAMIDAI significantly optimizes efficiency by reducing the average number of tiles analyzed by up to 2.65× while successfully identifying 90% of the true positive tiles detected through the conventional highest resolution analysis across the entire test set.
- a proposition of load balancing in a distributed setting was simulated for a frugal and democratized access to gigapixel image analysis.

Following contextualization in Sect. 2, PYRAMIDAI's design is presented in Sect. 3. Its application to the Camelyon 16 dataset and evaluation are in Sect. 4. Computations distribution is explored in Sect. 5, before concluding in Sect. 6.

2 Related Work

Due to input size constraints, large multiresolution images are typically divided into tiles that are fed to models for analysis. This approach is commonly utilized for the analysis of biomedical images [3,16,19], or for satellite imaging [18,25]. To better integrate contextual information, prior works have explored the use of lower resolutions by either analyzing multiple resolutions and aggregating the outcomes or selecting an optimal compromise resolution [1,28,32,36,37] with the goal of maximizing the accuracy. Yet those approaches become prohibitively computationally expensive with the increasing size of images.

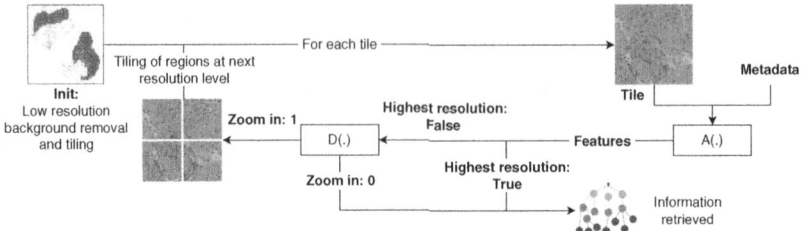

Fig. 1. The analysis starts at a low resolution, for each tile, an analysis block $A(.)$ extracts features. Based on them, a decision block $D(.)$ decides to either stop the analysis at that level for that tile or to zoom-in and process the corresponding tiles at a higher resolution. Extracted features can be further exploited for downstream tasks such as whole slide prediction or segmentation

In this paper, we take an orthogonal approach and focus on computation efficiency. With the advent of Transformer neural network architecture [34] and its adaptation to vision tasks [21], new categories of analysis emerged in both domains [2,4], which strengthen the trend toward increasingly more computation-intensive analysis [20]. Thus, limiting the computation to areas of interest is more important than ever. For example, the Viola-Jones detector [35] processes tiles at one resolution, but applies a cascade of classifiers only on retained tiles from previous tests. Similarly, background removal detects tiles candidates prone to information, such as tissues [5,15], by leveraging one low-resolution level, which sketches a coarse pyramidal approach. The effectiveness of exploiting several resolution levels has been explored in previous work, to progressively refine segmentation [13] with selective zooms, or to progressively increase confidence until a selected threshold [23]. Here, we expand on the pyramidal approach, applying it to a broader range of tasks, including AI-driven analysis, and propose generic methods for zoom-in decisions.

The heavy compute load of an exhaustive execution is handled by parallelizing the known tile analysis load among distributed workers with a central controller [8]. Kumar et al. propose to dynamically balance load among workers using existing schedulers in a grid setting, a more advanced infrastructure than our frugal setting [23]. As the pyramidal execution tree is discovered at runtime, a dynamic load balancing strategy is needed to minimize execution time and adapt to load characteristic changes, like work stealing [7,11,12].

3 Pyramidal Analysis Design

Pyramidal analysis aims to reduce the total amount of processed data by leveraging the different resolution levels of gigapixel images. By selectively analyzing portions of the image, the algorithm trades accuracy for computation performance. This section first presents the pyramidal analysis algorithm (Sect. 3.1), illustrated in Fig. 1, and describes two strategies to select per-level zoom-in decision thresholds (Sect. 3.2), each offering distinct accuracy-performance trade-off.

3.1 The Pyramidal Analysis Algorithm

Once the input tile size is determined, the analysis begins at a low, pre-selected image resolution. Tiles of interest are progressively filtered from one resolution level to the next, up to the highest resolution. Indeed, at each resolution level, an analysis block denoted by $A(.)$ is applied to each remaining tile, potentially supplemented with metadata information tailored to the specific use case, *i.e.*, tile position in the image. The output features are fed into a decision block $D(.)$, whose binary outcome determines whether the pyramidal analysis continues at the next resolution level. Tiles identified as areas of interest are subdivided into higher resolution and start a new iteration of the algorithm. The *scale factor f* of the input multiresolution image indicates that a tile at level R_n corresponds to f^2 new tiles of the same dimension at level R_{n-1}, with R_0 being the highest and R_N the lowest resolution. The analysis and decision blocks are tailored to the specific use case and adapted for each resolution to optimize accuracy.

The efficiency of the pyramidal analysis depends on the density of relevant information in the image at low resolution. Lower densities imply greater speedup as more tiles will be discarded. If most of the tiles are of interest, intermediate pyramid levels filter only a few tiles, *i.e.*, most of the intermediate resolution tiles as well as the highest resolution ones are analyzed. This will lead to poorer performance than the reference analysis at the highest resolution only. In practice, this issue is limited as the maximum slowdown S is bounded by Eq. (1) for a pyramid with an infinite number of levels, and remains relatively small. Our evaluation (Sect. 4) demonstrates that the speedup is greater than 1 on the Camelyon 16 dataset for a wide range of decision thresholds.

$$S(f) = \sum_{R_n=0}^{\infty} \frac{1}{f^{2R_n}} = \frac{f^2}{f^2-1} \qquad S(2) = \frac{4}{3} \approx 1.33; \quad S(3) = \frac{9}{8} = 1.125 \quad (1)$$

Given the size of gigapixel images, the number of tiles to analyze can be considerable, especially in the case of a single-worker execution. The tile-based approach has great potential for load distribution as the analysis can be performed in parallel independently from the tile location or resolution level. However, by design, the total computational load is unknown in advance and increases exponentially when a zoom-in is performed. Thus, a dynamic load balancing policy is needed to distribute the workload among workers at runtime, which is studied in Sect. 5.

3.2 Decision Block Threshold Selection Strategies

The decision block $D(.)$ determines if a zoom-in is required for a particular tile based on the analysis output. $D(.)$ acts as a classifier whose decision threshold needs to be tuned to achieve the desired accuracy-performance trade-off. As for the analysis block, $D(.)$ requires per-resolution parameters, *i.e.*, one threshold per resolution level. The proper tuning of each threshold is crucial to the overall performance and accuracy of PYRAMIDAI, as false negatives can miss areas of interest while false positives can degrade performance.

To ease the tuning of each decision threshold, we propose two strategies for threshold selection. The first maximizes computation performance given an objective user-defined metric expressed as a retention rate of a reference value; here, it denotes the proportion of true areas of interest retained with our pyramidal approach compared to the ones detected by the highest resolution only analysis. The second allows the user to choose a suitable accuracy-performance trade-off through a single graph. Both strategies rely on the F_β score (Eq. 2), the weighted harmonic mean between precision and recall: a higher β favors recall over precision, improving the true positives at the expense of false positives. To tune the thresholds, we first compute the F_β score for all resolution levels on the train set. This requires collecting the predictions for all tiles of all resolution levels. Then, for a given β we select the threshold for resolution level R_n such that it maximizes F_β, i.e. $argmax_{t \in [0,1]}(F_\beta(t))$. This can be approximated by maximizing F_β over a finite set of sampled thresholds.

Metric-Based Threshold Selection. This strategy aims to maximize the speedup under the constraint of an objective minimal retaining rate for a user-defined metric. Starting from a user-provided minimal retention rate r, the strategy consists of maximizing the speedup on a per-resolution level basis such that the isolated impact on the retention rate for each of the n levels is at least the n-th root of r. The isolated impact is computed by considering a pyramidal execution where all resolution levels except the one of interest are pass-through, and results in decision tables similar to Fig. 3 in Sect. 4.4. Using this strategy, β values are selected independently for each resolution level as the smallest β, ensuring an objective retention rate. This ensures that the global retention rate, which is bounded by the product of the n-th individual retention rates, is at least r.

Empirical Threshold Selection. This strategy offers greater flexibility, allowing the user to empirically determine the trade-off between performance and the retention of the user-defined metric. Based on retrieved predictions, for each β value, the pyramidal execution is computed on each gigapixel image of the train set using the thresholds corresponding to the same β at all resolution levels. Based on those executions, the reduction in the number of tiles analyzed, indicative of the speedup, and the retention rate for the final metric compared to the analysis at the highest resolution only can be estimated for each β value. Based on those figures, an empirical selection of β can be made based on a single graph, similar to Fig. 5 (a) presented in Sect. 4.

$$F_\beta = (1+\beta^2) \frac{Precision * Recall}{(\beta^2 * Precision) + Recall} = \frac{(1+\beta^2) * TP}{(1+\beta^2) * TP + \beta^2 * FN + FP} \quad (2)$$

4 PYRAMIDAI Experiments

We evaluate PYRAMIDAI on the Camelyon 16 challenge dataset [6], using the metric-based (Sect. 4.4) or the empirical (Sect. 4.5) thresholds, by comparing against the reference scenario, which analyzes all tiles at the highest resolution after background detection. Section 4.1 introduces the Camelyon 16 use-case, followed by the description of analysis blocks at each resolution level in Sect. 4.2, the computation time measurement strategy in Sect. 4.3 and the impact of these thresholds on the whole image classification accuracy in Sect. 4.6.

4.1 Camelyon Use-Case and Data Preprocessing

The Camelyon [6] dataset is composed of Hematoxylin-Eosin(HE)-stained sentinel lymph node histological images coming from breast cancer patients' biopsies. The training set contains 160 healthy slides and 110 with nodal metastases. 129 additional whole-slide images (49 with and 80 without metastases) are available for test purposes. Those images can reach sizes of about $10^5 \times 2.10^5$ pixels, *i.e.*, up to 80GB of uncompressed data, and include up to 10 resolution levels.

In our experiments, tiles of 224×224 pixels are extracted after a background removal using the Otsu thresholding technique [30] performed with CLAM [26]. Stain normalization was applied using the Macenko method [27] and stainlib [29].

The analysis block $A(.)$ detects the probability of the presence of metastasis in the tile and uses deep learning image classification models detailed in Sect. 4.2. The decision block $D(.)$ is a threshold function with a threshold to be determined according to Sect. 3.2 strategies. The final metric to preserve is the ratio of true positive tiles retained at the highest resolution by our pyramidal approach versus the ones detected by the reference execution, further denoted by *positive retention rate*. Our pyramidal analysis is based on a 3-level pyramid, the highest resolution being level 0 and the lowest being level 2, with a scale factor of 2.

4.2 Analysis Blocks Models

A model was trained for each resolution level in a supervised manner. Each resolution-specific dataset contains up to 192000 tiles extracted from Camelyon 16 whole-slide images, split with 80/20 for training and validation, and pre-processed (see Sect. 4.1). The training set is balanced by keeping all tumoral tiles and randomly selecting the same number of normal tiles. The test set is a random subset of pre-processed tiles extracted from Camelyon 16 test slides. Dataset sizes are summarized in Table 1. Online data augmentation (random flips and rotations) was used. The model architecture is based on the InceptionV3 model [33] with a GlobalAverage2D pooling layer, a dense layer with a depth of 224, and a final sigmoid layer. The weights were randomly initialized for resolutions 0 and 1. Resolution 2 uses initialized Imagenet weights, and the model was obtained via a transfer learning process. Training was based on accuracy, on the Adam optimizer with a learning rate of 10^{-4}. 100 epochs were set up with 1000 steps per epoch. The final model accuracies are summarized in Table 2. The model performance can be qualitatively assessed in Fig. 2.

4.3 Computation Time Measurement

Image pre-processing, dataset creation, and inferences were executed on the supercomputer Jean-Zay. Model training ran on a server with 2 AMD EPYC 7502 with 32 cores, 512 GB of RAM, and a Nvidia Quadro RTX 5000 GPU. Time measurements were performed on a mainstream computer embedding an Intel Core i5-9500 with 6 cores and 16GB of RAM.

Table 1. Train, validation, and test set sizes for each resolution

	Train set size	Validation set size	Test set size
Level 0	26576	38400	92000
Level 1	26134	38400	92000
Level 2	25504	38400	72568

Table 2. Train, validation, and test accuracies for each resolution model

	Train accuracy	Validation accuracy	Test accuracy
Level 0	0.9328	0.9498	0.9480
Level 1	0.9439	0.9590	0.9584
Level 2	0.8982	0.9110	0.9166

 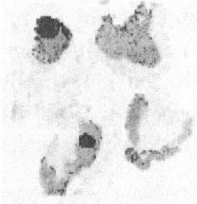 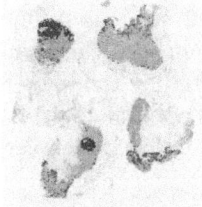 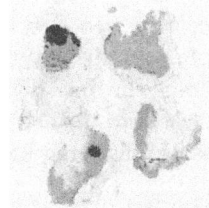

(a) Ground truth. (b) Lowest pyramid resolution. (c) Intermediate pyramid resolution. (d) Highest pyramid resolution.

Fig. 2. Model tumor probability heatmap compared to ground truth. The darker the red, the higher the probability (Color figure online)

Due to the large computation time in an isolation environment induced by the large number of tiles in the test set, which will be analyzed by our method and the reference, we estimated computation time based on the following measurements. The pyramidal analysis has three phases. The first one is the initialization, the retrieval of all tiles at the lowest resolution after background removal. Then, tiles are analyzed by the resolution-specific analysis block, and the decision block is applied. Finally, new tasks are created and added to the working queue if a zoom-in decision is positive. For the reference analysis, only initialization time and analysis block computation time at the highest resolution are considered. For the initialization phase, we measured computation time 1000 times per slide, and for the other phases, 1000 times on one slide, as it is tile-dependent. Results are gathered in Table 3.

Based on the data and the models' prediction probabilities on the test set tiles, we can simulate "post-mortem" computation for reference and pyramidal analysis, knowing the total number of tiles per resolution level that have been analyzed. Task creation time and initialization are not considered in the simulation, as the analysis blocks computation time is dominant.

Table 3. Computation time per phase

	Initialization	Level 0 analysis block	Level 1 analysis block	Level 2 analysis block	Task creation
Time (s)	0.02 ± 0.01	0.33 ± 0.04	0.33 ± 0.03	0.31 ± 0.03	$2.77 \pm 0.89 \cdot 10^{-5}$

4.4 Decision Blocks Tuned with Metric-Based Thresholds

We followed the first methodology from Sect. 3.2 for applications where a minimum value for a metric needs to be guaranteed.

Thirty slides from the training set are tiled at each resolution level, starting with the lowest resolution. Then, the corresponding trained model is applied to each tile of each resolution level, and the inference result, $i.e.$, the probability that the tile contains a tumor, is collected. These probabilities are used to measure precision and recall values for several thresholds. For β values ranging from 1 to 14, we select the threshold maximizing the F_β score. Then, on each slide, we isolate each resolution level, meaning we apply the threshold corresponding to each β score for this resolution and zoom in everywhere in all other resolution levels, to measure its impact on the positive retention rate at the highest resolution. We average this positive retention rate between all thirty slides. Results are summarized in Fig. 3.

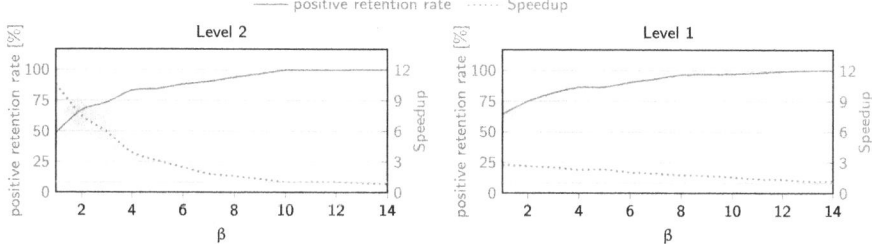

Fig. 3. Impact of each isolated resolution on positive retention rate and speedup

Given an objective positive retention rate for our application, as we have two intermediate resolution levels, we take the square root of the objective value, which will be the objective positive retention rate to be reached for each isolated resolution level. We select the lowest β value that achieves the objective positive retention rate at the highest resolution.

As noticed in Fig. 4, the technique enables to reach the objective value expected on the test set too. For instance, given an objective positive retention rate of 0.90, it results in an intermediate level positive retention rate to be reached of 0.9487, which is achieved at resolution 1 for $\beta = 8$ and by $\beta = 9$ at resolution 2 (Fig. 3). 92% of true positive tiles of the reference analysis are retained with our approach with 2.34 times fewer tiles analyzed, i.e., a speedup of 2.34. These values also highlight the benefit of using multiple-level pyramidal analysis. Indeed, the global objective of positive retention rate of 0.90 considering isolated resolution 1 is reached for $\beta = 6$ with only 2.02 times fewer tiles analyzed; considering resolution 2 only, the objective is reached with $\beta = 7$ with 1.80 times fewer tiles analyzed. Combining resolution levels helps to reduce tiles analyzed while ensuring the same positive retention rate. Using a global objective equal to 0.90, following Sect. 4.3 methodology, we estimated average computation time per slide on the test set to about 1 h 19 min ± 1 h 09 min, compared to 2 h 29 min ± 1 h 34 min for reference execution. The huge standard deviation is explained by the significant variation in the number of tiles per slide by up to a factor of 30.

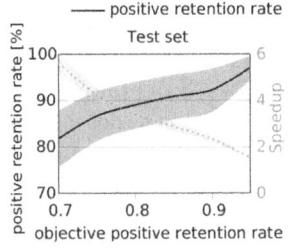

Fig. 4. Trade-off according to an objective positive retention rate (cf. Sect. 4.4)

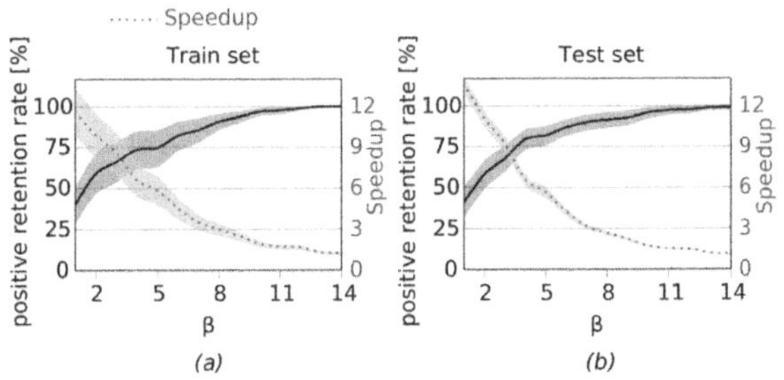

Fig. 5. Trade-off between positive retention rate and speedup in a pyramidal execution according to empirical thresholds of β (cf. Sect. 4.5)

4.5 Decision Blocks Tuned with Empirical Thresholds

As in Sect. 4.4, we measure the precision and recall values for several thresholds, and, for β values ranging from 1 to 14, we select the threshold maximizing the F_β score. The pyramidal analysis is performed using thresholds corresponding to the same β value for each resolution level in the decision blocks. For each β, the positive retention rate and the speedup were measured.

Figures 5 (a) and (b) summarize the results for our use-case, allowing the user to easily decide which trade-off between accuracy and performance to choose by selecting only one β value. This is very useful in applications where losing some accuracy is acceptable or can be compensated for by a post-processing step. Figure 5 outlines the potential of the pyramidal approach to drastically speed up the analysis. For example, given a β value of 5, retaining 80% of positive tiles on the train set, more than 80% of positive tiles of the test set are retained with 5.63× fewer tiles analyzed. For applications sensitive to accuracy reduction as ours, we select the β value retaining 90% of positive tiles on the train set, naming $\beta = 8$, which retains 90% of the test set positive tiles, with a speedup of 2.65. Following the methodology in Sect. 4.3, the average computation time per slide on the whole test set is estimated to be about 1 h 11 min ± 1 h 06 min.

4.6 Whole Slide Image Classification

We assessed the impact of positive tile loss using PYRAMIDAI on the whole-slide image (WSI) classification. We trained a bagging decision tree classifier to predict tumoral images from the distribution of tile prediction probabilities. When stopping predictions at a lower resolution level with PYRAMIDAI, we projected the predicted probability onto all corresponding tiles at the highest resolution. The baseline, without PYRAMIDAI, achieves an accuracy of 0.84. We obtain the same accuracy of 0.84 with a 2.65x speedup when using PYRAMIDAI with an empirical threshold. The metric-based strategy achieves a lower accuracy of 0.77, due to the strategy optimized for true positives retention, and detects tumor presence on 35 WSI slides versus 29 for the baseline, but at the cost of a higher false positive rate.

5 Distributed PYRAMIDAI Experiments

We assess the data distribution and load balancing policies adapted to our pyramidal approach execution for a decentralized cluster of mainstream computers. Section 5.1 presents the implementation of a simulator to estimate the most promising combination of a data distribution strategy and a load-balancing policy. Section 5.2 explores synchronization-based load-balancing policy while Sect. 5.3 assesses the potential of removing synchronization and using a work-stealing-based balancing policy. Section 5.4 describes the implementation of the chosen policy deployed on a real cluster of mainstream computers.

5.1 Simulation Implementation

As stated in Sect. 4.3, most of the time is spent in the analysis blocks execution. Thus, to estimate the load per worker, we consider the maximum number of tiles computed per worker to evaluate the load balancing. Based on the pyramidal execution tree retrieved using thresholds from Sect. 4.5, we simulate an execution offline based on the number of workers, the initial tile distribution on a low-resolution level, and the load balancing policy. The considered initial tile distributions on the lowest resolution are: the **Round-Robin distribution** consisting in iterating over low-resolution tiles and dispatching cyclically one tile per worker until it is exhausted; the **Random distribution** where we shuffle low-resolution tile list and dispatch data by block of balanced size to each worker;

and the **Block distribution** with a sorted low-resolution tile list by location in the image which is dispatched by block of balanced size among workers.

We compared data distribution combined with load balancing policies to the ideal scenario where the oracle knows in advance which tiles and how many will be analyzed at each resolution level and thus dispatches them in a balanced way independently of the resolution level. This is the lowest execution time achievable. We also compare to the previous references: the execution time at the highest resolution only, and the pyramidal approach on a single worker. The results correspond to an average maximum number of tiles analyzed per worker for the entire test set.

5.2 Load Balancing via Synchronizations

As a first naive approach, we balance the load after each resolution level before jumping to the next analysis level, meaning after all low-resolution tiles are analyzed and after all intermediate-resolution tiles pass. We combine this policy with each data distribution strategy. Figure 6a presents the results. From this graph, we can deduce that Round-Robin and Random data distribution strategies provide similar results, with a higher stability for the Round-Robin one. The distribution by blocks of tiles localized in the same region appears to be inefficient, which is explained by the heterogeneity of the distribution of tumoral tissues in the image.

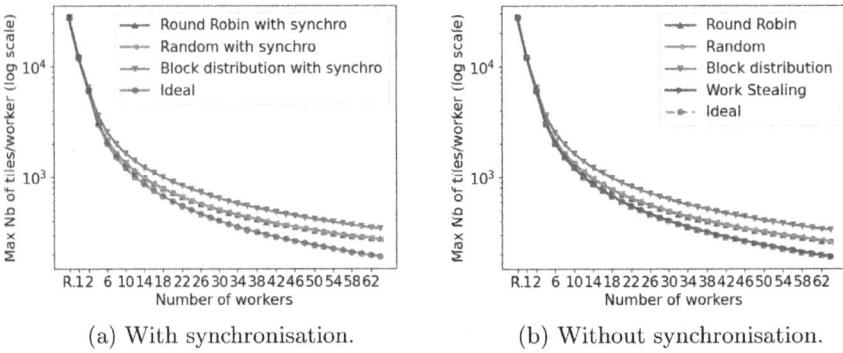

(a) With synchronisation. (b) Without synchronisation.

Fig. 6. Maximum number of tiles analyzed by the busiest worker depending on data distribution strategies and load balancing policies (work stealing or synchronization). R. refers to the number of tiles analyzed for the reference execution on one worker, *i.e.*, the highest resolution only analysis

5.3 Dynamic Scheduling Approach Without Synchronization

Because the tiles' analysis is independent of each other and of the resolution level, we explored the potential of synchronization-free approaches. We tested all data distribution strategies without load rebalancing at runtime, and the Round-Robin approach combined with the dynamic work-stealing policy. The work-stealing strategy consists of randomly choosing a neighbor to be the victim of the work-stealing once the working queue is empty. If it has more than one task remaining, it dequeues one task corresponding to a leaf of the current pyramidal execution graph state and transmits it to the sender. Otherwise, it returns no task, and the thief chooses another victim. In the simulation, message transfer time is neglected as compute time is the dominant factor.

Figure 6b confirms that the Round-Robin technique is the most stable one and that even without dynamic load balancing policies, the maximum load of the busiest worker is close to the one with synchronization and should be favored for its simplicity. With an increasing number of workers, the considered work-stealing method is the most efficient, especially starting with 4 workers, and is equivalent to the ideal case as message passing latency is neglected.

5.4 Deployment on a Cluster of Modest Computers

Simulation results demonstrated that Round-Robin is the most efficient low-resolution tile distribution strategy. For the dynamic load balancing policy, work-stealing is increasingly beneficial with the number of workers, even if close to Round-Robin only with less than 4 workers. We validate these conclusions with a cluster of 12 fully-connected mainstream computers equipped with an Intel Core i5-9500 and 16GB of RAM. Data is replicated among workers without shared memory, allowing compatibility with any topology and extension to subimage replication. The implementation uses the DecentralizePy [10] framework for TCP connections among workers, compatible with decentralized settings and any topology. Each worker has its own queue and uses work-stealing previously described when it is empty. Indeed, it requests a task by message-passing to a neighbor. If the victim has remaining tasks, it sends one back. Otherwise, it sends an empty message. The victim updates its list of potential victims as the sender worker runs out of tasks already. Finally, all workers send their subtrees, including stolen subtrees, back to node 0 for full tree reconstruc-

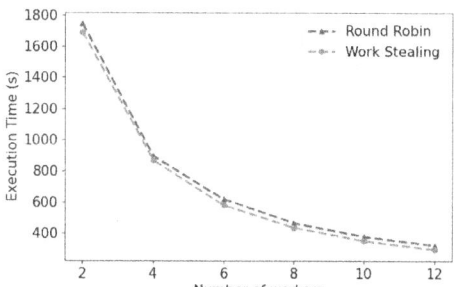

Fig. 7. Average execution time per image for real data using a Round-Robin data distribution according to the number of workers, with and without work-stealing

tion and further processing. The conclusions are verified on three images: one with large tumors, one with several small ones, and one negative image, each measure being computed 3 times. Figure 7 confirms that using the work-stealing technique is adequate for this workload, especially with a growing number of workers.

6 Conclusion and Perspectives

In this paper, we propose a pyramidal approach for gigapixel image analysis, reducing computation compared to the highest resolution-only analysis, suitable for constrained environments. It leverages the multiresolution feature of gigapixel images by starting analysis at a low resolution, tiling tissue regions, and applying an analysis block to each tile. The extracted features feed a decision block that classifies tiles as of interest and proceeds the analysis at the next higher resolution level when required. The decision criterion is a key element to ensure a good trade-off between the global accuracy of the pyramidal analysis and its computational performance compared to the reference. Thus, we propose two strategies to tune decision block thresholds per resolution level. Our methods, evaluated on the Camelyon 16 dataset, demonstrated we could divide by up to 2.65 the number of tiles to be analyzed while detecting 90% of positive tiles among those detected by reference execution. Computation time decreased from over 2 h to 1 h per image on average. PYRAMIDAI's potential to adapt to a modest computing environment is highlighted, especially when combined with a dynamic work-stealing policy. It provides results for an image in about 15 min instead of in more than an hour using 12 mainstream computers. It democratizes access to such analysis for scientists with limited computational resources. Though illustrated on a gigapixel biomedical use case, the approach is generalizable to any gigapixel images, such as satellite or spatial images.

Acknowledgments. The authors acknowledge the financial support of https://www.hi-paris.fr. and the use of HPC resources from GENCI-IDRIS (Grant 2023-AD010614264).

Disclosure of Interests. The authors have no competing interests to declare that are relevant to the content of this article.

References

1. Abdeltawab, H., et al.: A pyramidal deep learning pipeline for kidney whole-slide histology images classification. Sci. Rep. (2021)
2. Adegun, A., Viriri, S., Tapamo, J.R.: Review of deep learning methods for remote sensing satellite images classification: experimental survey and comparative analysis. J. Big Data (2023)
3. Amin-Naji, M., Aghagolzadeh, A., Ezoji, M.: Ensemble of CNN for multi-focus image fusion. Inf. Fusion (2019)

4. Atabansi, C., et al.: A survey of transformer applications for histopathological image analysis: new developments and future directions. BioMedical Eng. OnLine (2023)
5. Babbar, J., Rathee, N.: Satellite image analysis: a review. In: IEEE International Conference on Electrical, Computer and Communication Technologies (2019)
6. Bejnordi, B., et al.: Diagnostic assessment of deep learning algorithms for detection of lymph node metastases in women with breast cancer. JAMA (2017)
7. Blumofe, R.D., Leiserson, C.E.: Scheduling multithreaded computations by work stealing. J. ACM (1999)
8. Bueno, G., et al.: A parallel solution for high resolution histological image analysis. Comput. Methods Programs Biomed. (2012)
9. Childers, M., et al.: Gene therapy prolongs survival and restores function in murine and canine models of myotubular myopathy. Sci. Transl. Med. (2014)
10. Dhasade, A., et al.: Decentralized learning made easy with decentralizepy. In: EuroMLSys 2023. ACM (2023)
11. Fernandes, J.B., et al.: Adaptive asynchronous work-stealing for distributed load-balancing in heterogeneous systems. arXiv:2401.04494 (2024)
12. Freitas, V., et al.: Packsteallb: a scalable distributed load balancer based on work stealing and workload discretization. J. Parallel Distrib. Comput. (2021)
13. Goffe, R., Damiand, G., Brun, L.: A causal extraction scheme in top-down pyramids for large images segmentation. In: SSPR (2010)
14. Gurcan, M.N., et al.: Histopathological image analysis: a review. IEEE Rev. Biomed. Eng. (2009)
15. Huang, P.W., et al.: Deep-learning based breast cancer detection for cross-staining histopathology images. Heliyon (2023)
16. Iizuka, O., et al.: Deep learning models for histopathological classification of gastric and colonic epithelial tumours. Sci. Rep. (2020)
17. Israeli, D., et al.: An AAV-SGCG Dose-response study in a γ-sarcoglycanopathy mouse model in the context of mechanical stress. Mol. Ther. Methods Clin. Dev. (2019)
18. de Jong, K.L., Sergeevna Bosman, A.: Unsupervised change detection in satellite images using convolutional neural networks. In: IJCNN (2019)
19. Kassani, S., et al.: Classification of histopathological biopsy images using ensemble of deep learning networks. In: Computer Science and Software Engineering (2019)
20. Khan, S., et al.: Transformers in vision: a survey. ACM Comput. Surv. (2022)
21. Kolesnikov, A., et al.: An image is worth 16x16 words: transformers for image recognition at scale (2021)
22. Komura, D., Ishikawa, S.: Machine learning methods for histopathological image analysis. Comput. Struct. Biotechnol. J. (2018)
23. Kumar, V., et al.: Parameterized specification, configuration and execution of data-intensive scientific workflows. Cluster Comput. (2010). https://doi.org/10.1007/s10586-010-0133-8
24. LeCun, Y., et al.: Backpropagation applied to handwritten zip code recognition. Neural Comput. (1989)
25. Li, Y., et al.: Deep learning for remote sensing image classification: a survey. WIREs Data Mining Knowl. Discov. (2018)
26. Lu, M.Y., et al.: Data-efficient and weakly supervised computational pathology on whole-slide images. Nat. Biomed. Eng. (2021)
27. Macenko, M., et al.: A method for normalizing histology slides for quantitative analysis. In: IEEE Symposium on Biomedical Imaging: From Nano to Macro (2009)

28. Muhammad, N., et al.: A Multi-resolution Deep Learning Framework for Lung Adenocarcinoma Growth Pattern Classification (2018)
29. Otálora, S., et al.: stainlib: a python library for augmentation and normalization of histopathology H&E images. bioRxiv (2022)
30. Otsu, N.: A threshold selection method from gray-level histograms. IEEE Trans. Syst. Man Cybern. (1979)
31. Rijthoven, M., et al.: HookNet: multi-resolution convolutional neural networks for semantic segmentation in histopathology whole-slide images. Med. Image Anal. (2021)
32. Schmitz, R., et al.: Multi-scale fully convolutional neural networks for histopathology image segmentation: from nuclear aberrations to the global tissue architecture. Med. Image Anal. (2021)
33. Szegedy, C., et al.: Rethinking the inception architecture for computer vision. In: IEEE Conference on Computer Vision and Pattern Recognition (2016)
34. Vaswani, A., et al.: Attention is all you need. In: Advances in Neural Information Processing Systems (2017)
35. Viola, P., Jones, M.: Rapid object detection using a boosted cascade of simple features. In: IEEE Conference on Computer Vision and Pattern Recognition (2001)
36. Wetteland, R., et al.: A multiscale approach for whole-slide image segmentation of five tissue classes in urothelial carcinoma slides. Technol. Cancer Res. Treat. (2020)
37. Xiang, T., et al.: Dsnet: a dual-stream framework for weakly-supervised gigapixel pathology image analysis. IEEE Trans. Med. Imaging (2022)
38. Xu, Y., et al.: Large scale tissue histopathology image classification, segmentation, and visualization via deep convolutional activation features. BMC Bioinform. (2017)

Accelerating Independent Multi-Agent Reinforcement Learning on Multi-GPU Platforms

Samuel Wiggins[1](✉), Nikunj Gupta[1], Grace Zgheib[2], Mahesh A. Iyer[2], and Viktor Prasanna[1]

[1] University of Southern California, Los Angeles, CA, USA
{wigginss,nikunj,prasanna}@usc.edu
[2] Altera Corporation, San Jose, CA, USA
{grace.zgheib,mahesh.iyer}@altera.com

Abstract. Multi-Agent Reinforcement Learning (MARL) enables multiple autonomous agents to simultaneously learn and make decisions in complex, interactive environments. Among various MARL paradigms, Independent Learning (IL) remains a dominant approach due to its simplicity and scalability, where each agent optimizes its policy independently, treating others as part of the environment. While IL eliminates the need for explicit inter-agent communication, existing MARL implementations fail to exploit its inherent parallelism. Current implementations train agents sequentially on a single accelerator, leading to severe underutilization of modern compute resources, particularly on multi-GPU platforms. In this work, we propose a multi-GPU training scheme that efficiently distributes independent agent policies across compute devices without altering the original IL semantics. To further enhance scalability, we design a dynamic load-balancing strategy that adaptively assigns training workloads based on computational demands and the varying capabilities of different GPUs, ensuring efficient utilization of hardware resources. Our approach achieves up to $15.5\times$ higher throughput than state-of-the-art MARL implementations, demonstrating that fully leveraging the parallelism of IL can significantly accelerate MARL training, opening new possibilities for large-scale multi-agent learning in high-dimensional environments. We open-source our work with optimized implementations of widely used independent learning algorithms, enabling scalable MARL training on diverse accelerator platforms.

Keywords: Multi-Agent Reinforcement Learning · Independent Learning · Multi-GPU Training

1 Introduction

Multi-Agent Reinforcement Learning (MARL) extends single-agent reinforcement learning to environments where multiple agents interact dynamically. Agents may exhibit cooperative, competitive, or mixed behaviors, making MARL applicable to a wide range of real-world domains, such as robotics, autonomous driving, and financial trading [19]. A widely adopted approach in MARL is Independent Learning (IL), where each agent learns independently, treating others as part of the environment. IL has shown strong performance in complex environments [3,8,9], and serves as a benchmark for MARL methods. However, scaling to larger problems significantly increases training time [30].

Training independent MARL systems introduces unique computational challenges. Unlike centralized or communication-based MARL approaches [32], IL avoids complex inter-agent modeling, resulting in smaller neural networks with lower computational overhead per agent. Although this makes IL more lightweight, it also leads to the misconception that CPU-based training is sufficient. Larger batch sizes are crucial for stable and efficient learning in deep reinforcement learning, but CPUs struggle with the high-volume parallel computation required for large-scale MARL training [11]. GPUs, with their high-throughput parallel processing capabilities, provide a natural solution, enabling efficient data-parallel policy updates across agents. Yet, most existing MARL implementations fail to fully exploit multi-GPU scalability, significantly limiting training efficiency as the number of agents and environment complexity grow. Despite the potential of GPU acceleration, existing IL frameworks underutilize multiple devices. State-of-the-art libraries [6,11,13] rely on a single GPU, serializing policy optimization and causing inefficiencies as agent count grows. By not exploiting parallel policy update execution, most of these frameworks face limited scalability and resource utilization in large-scale MARL scenarios. Scaling MARL to multiple GPUs requires efficient workload distribution, synchronization, and memory management. Agent-to-GPU assignment must consider compute power, memory bandwidth, and per-algorithm requirements to prevent load imbalance. IL algorithms impose varying computational demands, making static assignment strategies suboptimal across different hardware configurations. Additionally, synchronization is critical to coordinate multiple processes accessing shared structures like the replay buffer and model parameters, ensuring efficient data exchange and preventing contention.

In this work, we propose a training scheme designed to distribute the training of IL systems across multi-GPU platforms. Our main contributions are:

- We conduct a detailed analysis of the state-of-the-art training scheme used for training independent MARL systems using a GPU, identifying limitations and inefficiencies.
- We propose an Independent Multi-GPU training scheme that efficiently distributes agent policy training across multiple GPU devices.
- We propose an adaptive Agent Load Balancer that dynamically distributes and balances the training workload among GPU devices in the system.
- Our multi-GPU implementations achieve up to 15.5× higher system throughput compared to state-of-the-art independent learning implementations.
- We open source[1] our work with three popular independent learning algorithms on the large-scale Pogema [25] environment.

---

[1] https://github.com/SamWiggz/MultiGPU_IL

2 Background

2.1 Multi-Agent Reinforcement Learning

Formally, MARL can be modeled as an N-agent partially observable Markov game [15], defined by the tuple $\langle \mathcal{S}, \{\mathcal{A}^i\}_{i\in N}, \{\mathcal{O}^i\}_{i\in N}, P, \{\mathcal{R}^i\}_{i\in N}, \gamma \rangle$, where $\mathcal{S}$ represents the global state space, $\mathcal{O}_i$ denotes the set of partial observations of agent i, $\mathcal{A}_i$ denotes the action space of agent i, $P: \mathcal{S} \times \mathcal{A}_1 \times \cdots \times \mathcal{A}_N \rightarrow \Delta(\mathcal{S})$ is the transition function, $R_i : \mathcal{S} \times \mathcal{A}_i \rightarrow \mathbb{R}$ is the reward function for agent i, and $\gamma \in [0, 1)$ is the discount factor. Each agent aims to learn an optimal policy $\pi^i(a_i|o_i)$, where $a_i \in A^i$ and $o_i \in O^i$, that maximizes its expected cumulative reward. In independent MARL, each agent treats other agents as part of the environment and learns its policy using standard single-agent reinforcement learning techniques. The goal is to learn an optimal joint policy $\{\pi^i\}_{i\in N}$.

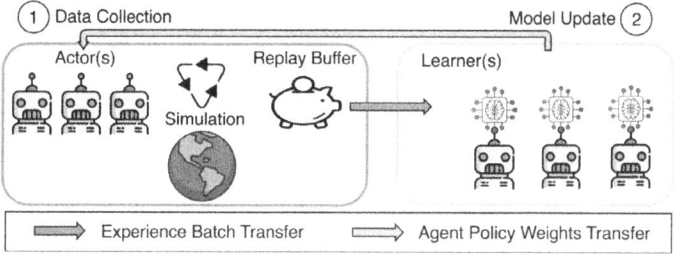

Fig. 1. MARL Training Process

Each MARL training iteration consists of two main phases: (1) Data Collection and (2) Model Update (see Fig. 1). (1) Data Collection: Multiple actors, each running an independent agent policy, interact with parallel environment simulations to generate training experiences. These experiences, typically consisting of observations, actions, rewards, and next states, are stored in a centralized replay buffer for later use. (2) Model Update: One or more learners update the agent policy networks by training on mini-batches of experiences sampled from the replay buffer. Optimization is performed using gradient-based methods, such as stochastic gradient descent (SGD) [22] and Adam [10], which iteratively refine the policy parameters. Once updated, the new policy models are distributed back to the actors for the next training iteration.

2.2 Single-GPU Training Scheme

State-of-the-art MARL libraries [6,11,13,16] support various IL algorithms, but predominantly use a Single-GPU training scheme (Fig. 2), which relies on a single process for both Data Collection and Model Update. In the Data Collection phase, multiple environment simulations run in parallel on general-purpose CPU platforms to maximize experience throughput, ensuring portability across various system configurations. During the Model Update phase, a learner sequentially updates each agent's policy on a GPU using batches of experiences. Policy

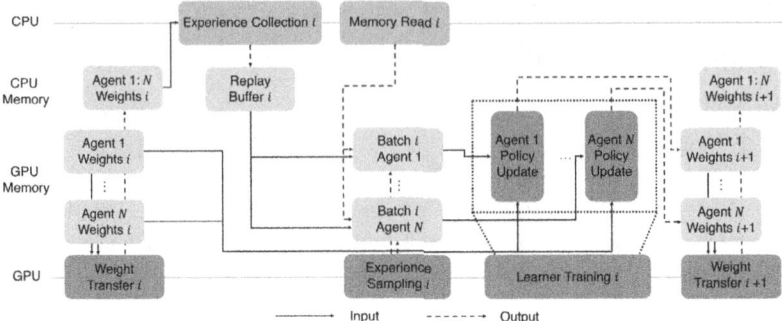

Fig. 2. Single-GPU training scheme used in the many state-of-the-art libraries and implementations. A single GPU learner sequentially trains each agent's policy model.

weights are sent back to the CPU for the next iteration of Data Collection. Agent DNNs in IL are often smaller and less computationally demanding, as they do not model complex inter-agent communication and coordination, making CPU platforms a practical choice for training IL systems. However, large-batch training [11] increases the need for data-parallel processing to enhance throughput.

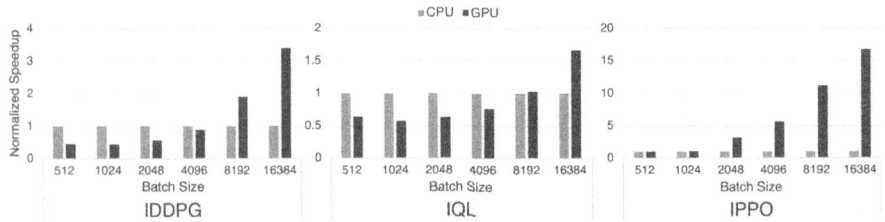

Fig. 3. Normalized speedup comparison between CPU and GPU training across three state-of-the-art independent learning algorithms. We normalized the CPU training time to 1 for each bar plot comparison across varying batch sizes.

We compare the speedup of three IL algorithms, normalized to CPU performance, when the learner is mapped to a 64-core Intel Xeon 6530 CPU or an NVIDIA RTX 6000 Ada GPU (Fig. 3). CPU training is more efficient for smaller batch sizes, as GPU training incurs additional latency overheads, including PCIe transfer costs for experience batches and updated policy weights, as well as kernel launch inefficiencies. These inefficiencies are particularly pronounced for off-policy algorithms such as Independent Deep Deterministic Policy Gradient (IDDPG) [14] and Independent Q-Learning (IQL) [27], which reuse prior experiences from previous training iterations. In contrast, on-policy Independent Proximal Policy Optimization (IPPO) [23] trains exclusively with experiences from the current iteration, while requiring additional operations such as advantage normalization, Kullback-Leibler divergence calculations, and probability ratio clipping before updating the policy models. These computationally intensive operations increase the benefits of data-parallel processing on GPUs. The significantly more data-parallel resources of the RTX 6000 Ada GPU (18,176 CUDA cores) compared to the 64-core CPU enable substantial speedup as batch sizes increase, effectively amortizing the data transfer and kernel launch overheads. Consequently, the results demonstrate that leveraging GPU platforms for IL training is more effective for large batch scenarios.

Despite the advantages of GPUs, most libraries still follow a serialized training approach for IL MARL. A single learner updates all agent policies sequentially, even when agents do not interact or share information. While necessary for communicative MARL, this design unnecessarily constrains IL. Since each policy update is performed one at a time, training time scales linearly with the number of agents, making this approach inefficient for large-scale MARL scenarios. Moreover, sequential execution underutilizes GPU resources, as modern GPUs can efficiently process multiple model updates in parallel. A more effective strategy would be to parallelize policy updates across multiple learners and GPUs, allowing IL agents to train simultaneously, significantly improving training speed and scalability. However, no such solution currently exists, leaving MARL researchers limited to CPU or single-GPU policy training.

3 Related Works

Accelerating Single-Agent RL Scenarios: Numerous prior works have focused on accelerating single-agent reinforcement learning (RL), the basis for independent learning in multi-agent settings. `CleanRL` [7], `Stable Baselines3` [21], and `Dopamine` [2], built on frameworks like `PyTorch` [20], `Ray` [18], and `JAX` [4], implement popular RL algorithms, allowing policy training to be offloaded to a single GPU. `RLLib` [13] and `Tianshou` [28] provide multi-GPU training for single-agent RL algorithms using a distributed data parallel (DDP) training approach [12]. Each GPU hosts a dedicated learner, maintaining a replica of the agent's DNNs. Experience batches are partitioned into micro-batches, each assigned to a specific GPU for training. Gradients are aggregated using a Ring-AllReduce mechanism, followed by updating weights using synchronous optimization methods [10,22]. `Pearl` [17] maps off-policy single-agent RL onto heterogeneous platforms (CPUs, GPUs, and FPGAs), supporting execution of the learner on a single device, using DDP-based multi-GPU training, or distributing models across multiple devices. However, most of these works provide little or no support for MARL, including independent learning. While they focus on optimizing single-agent RL for various hardware platforms, they lack the necessary adaptations for multi-agent scenarios, where multiple policies must be trained and updated.

Accelerating MARL: Many MARL libraries focus on accelerating MARL training on a single GPU using the Single-GPU training scheme (`MARLlib` [6], `PyMARL2` [5], `Warpdrive` [11]). `RLLib`, built on a newer version of Ray compared to `MARLlib`, includes a few IL algorithms but only supports multi-GPU DDP for their single-agent RL algorithms. These libraries adopt the Single-GPU training scheme to provide a unified approach across various classes of MARL algorithms, including IL, ensuring broad compatibility without the need for multiple training schemes optimized for each algorithm class [30]. Several algorithm-specific accelerated implementations have emerged that employ optimizations beyond these general-purpose libraries. Wiggins et al. [31] accelerates MADDPG [16], a multi-agent extension of IDDPG that adds inter-agent communication, on a multi-GPU platform using the DDP approach. Speedup is observed for larger batch sizes, as gradient synchronization and weight update overheads become less significant relative to total training time, whereas for smaller batch sizes, these overheads dominate, making single GPU training more efficient. Cardarilli et al. [1] implements Q-Learning Real-Time Swarm (Q-RTS) on FPGA, where centralized decisions are transmitted to low-power microcontroller-based agents for real-world action execution. Both of these acceleration systems rely on centralized training [24], which contrasts with IL's fully decentralized nature.

4 Independent Multi-GPU Training Scheme

To address the limitations of the Single-GPU training scheme, we propose an Independent Multi-GPU training scheme, which launches multiple learners to distribute the training workload while carefully managing synchronization, memory access, and workload balancing across processes. Consider a system with N agents and M learners, denoted as $G_1, G_2, ..., G_M$. To formally define the agent assignment, we introduce $\mathcal{I}_m$, the set of agents assigned to learner G_m, where $\mathcal{I}$ is the set of all independent agents. Each agent is assigned to exactly one learner, and the partitioning of agents is formulated as follows:

$$\bigcup_{m=1}^{M} \mathcal{I}_m = \mathcal{I}, \quad \mathcal{I}_m \cap \mathcal{I}_n = \emptyset, \quad \forall m \neq n.$$

This enforces disjoint and collectively exhaustive agent assignments, with the total number of agents conserved as $\sum_{m=1}^{M} |\mathcal{I}_m| = N$, where $|\mathcal{I}_m| \neq |\mathcal{I}_n|$. Note that the number of agents assigned to each learner may vary due to differences in the GPU capabilities, such as in data parallel resources, memory bandwidth, or memory capacity. Additionally, GPUs may experience contention for resources during runtime, particularly in multi-user environments such as cloud computing platforms, high-performance computing clusters, or virtualized infrastructures.

Figure 4 illustrates our scheme, which consists of two types of CPU processes: the host process and the actor process, along with the GPU processes referred to as learners. The host process is responsible for instantiating shared resources, initializing agent models, and managing a global shared memory space, which facilitates efficient inter-process communication. Both the agent models and the replay buffer, which stores collected experience data, reside in this shared memory, directly accessible by the actor and learner processes. The actor process is

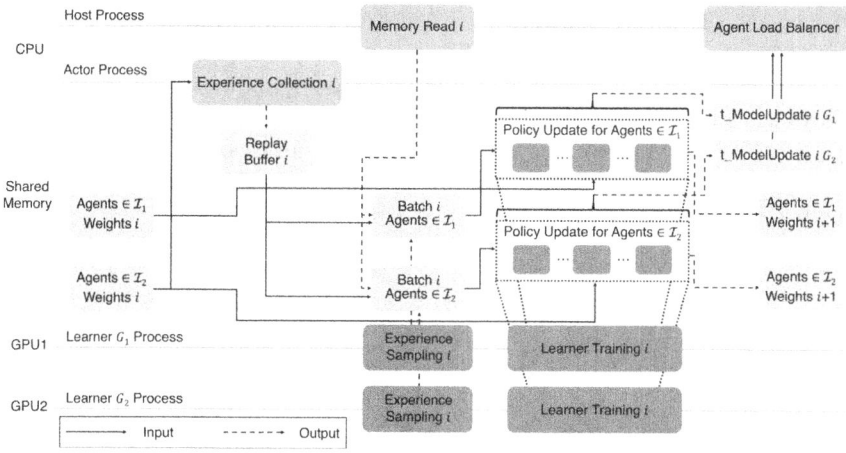

Fig. 4. The Independent Multi-GPU training scheme enables multiple learners to train agent models in parallel. For simplicity, this example shows two GPU learners (denoted as G_1 and G_2), each mapped to a different GPU device. Each learner is responsible for training a different subset of agents, $\mathcal{I}_1$ and $\mathcal{I}_2$, respectively.

responsible for the Data Collection phase, wherein it interacts with the environment by generating experiences. These experiences are appended to the shared replay buffer, from which learners subsequently sample data for training during the Model Update phase. The learners independently sample the experiences from the shared replay buffer and execute the policy optimization process, each being assigned a subset of agents based on the partitioning scheme introduced earlier. Multiple learners can be assigned to the same GPU device, processing agents in parallel to increase resource utilization. Training semantics remain unchanged, as policy updates are performed identically but in parallel. Given the diversity in GPU hardware, where compute power and memory bandwidth can vary significantly across devices, our training scheme incorporates a dynamic workload adaptation mechanism discussed in Sect. 5. The host process continuously monitors the Model Update execution times across learners and dynamically adjusts agent assignments each training iteration.

5 Agent Load Balancer

Since the Single-GPU training scheme only uses a single process, there is no need to balance the load. However, when training with our Independent Multi-GPU training scheme, which launches multiple learners across potentially different GPU devices, determining the optimal partitioning of agents across learners becomes highly non-trivial. Each GPU in the system may have different compute capabilities and memory bandwidth, making it difficult to predict the performance of a given IL algorithm on any specific device. These disparities introduce inefficiencies when using a static allocation scheme, where agents are assigned to

GPUs based solely on pre-determined heuristics. To illustrate this, we conduct an experiment using an NVIDIA RTX A6000 and an NVIDIA RTX 3060, two GPUs with significantly different computational capabilities. The RTX A6000 achieves a peak performance of 38.71 TFLOPS, whereas the RTX 3060 reaches only 12.74 TFLOPS, approximately a 3× difference in theoretical throughput. A naive static allocation strategy would distribute agents based on peak TFLOPS, assigning 75% to the RTX A6000 and 25% to the RTX 3060.

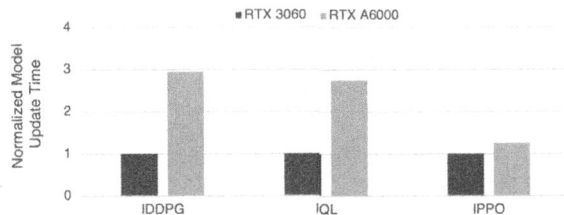

Fig. 5. Model Update time of one learner on an RTX 3060 (normalized to one) and another on an RTX A6000. Agents are distributed based on peak TFLOPS: 25% (256 agents) on the RTX 3060 and 75% (768 agents) on the RTX A6000.

Figure 5 shows a Model Update time comparison using the above agent distribution on a 1024 agent, 8192 batch size experiment (768 agents for the RTX A6000 and 256 agents for the RTX 3060). We normalize the Model Update time of the RTX 3060 to one for each bar comparison. We observe that this agent allocation is suboptimal across all independent learning algorithms. For IDDPG and IQL, utilization is quite low because of the small-scale nature of updating agent DNN models, meaning that the A6000 is not fully leveraged, leading to inefficiencies in resource utilization and diminishing the advantages of using high-performance hardware. In contrast, IPPO achieves higher GPU utilization, as its large-scale batch processing operations better exploit the A6000's parallelism, memory bandwidth, and computational throughput, making it more effective at utilizing more capable hardware. These findings suggest that less powerful GPUs, often overlooked in favor of high-performance accelerators, can play a crucial role in distributed IL training using our Independent Multi-GPU training scheme.

In order to address the difficulty in choosing an agent subset assignment per learner, we introduce an Agent Load Balancer that dynamically distributes subsets of agents to each learner process. During each training iteration, the Agent Load Balancer monitors the Model Update execution time of each learner, denoted as $T_{MU,m}$. Given M learners, the average iteration time across all learners is given by $T_{\text{avg}} = \frac{1}{M} \sum_{m=1}^{M} T_{MU,m}$. Each learner is assigned a proportion of agents to train, denoted as agent ratio R_m, where the total allocation satisfies $\sum_{m=1}^{M} R_m = 1$. We define an adjustment factor for learner G_m as δ_m given by:

$$\delta_m = \frac{T_{\text{avg}} - T_{MU,m}}{\sum_{j=1}^{M} T_{MU,j}}$$

The updated agent ratio, R'_m, for each learner is computed every iteration as:

$$R'_m = \frac{R_m + \delta_m}{\sum_{j=1}^{M}(R_j + \delta_j)}$$

Updating each learner's agent ratio prevents high-performing learners from remaining underutilized while also mitigating bottlenecks caused by excessive agent assignments to lower-performing learners. By iteratively refining agent distribution, the system converges towards a balanced workload that accounts for different GPU performance characteristics, leading to reduced training time.

6 Experiments

6.1 Environments and MARL Algorithms

For evaluation, we use Pogema [25], a multi-agent environment for pathfinding and coordination challenges in dynamic and obstructed spaces. Each agent must navigate from a starting position to a goal while avoiding collisions with static obstacles and other agents. It is highly configurable, allowing adjustments to agent count and obstacle density, making it a scalable testbed for MARL research. It naturally emphasizes decentralized decision-making, making it ideal for evaluating the parallelization of IL training. We evaluate the performance of three IL algorithms in this environment: IDDPG [14], IQL [26], and IPPO [23], spanning both the on-policy and off-policy learning paradigms and serving as strong baselines for independent MARL. We retain the original hyperparameter settings from their respective implementations to ensure fair and reproducible comparisons across algorithms. These defaults have been extensively tuned in prior work to achieve stable convergence and optimal performance, making them well-suited baselines for evaluating multi-GPU efficiency. We systematically vary batch sizes, a critical factor in GPU utilization and system throughput, to evaluate the scalability of our multi-GPU training scheme. Large-batch training is widely popular in MARL [11,13], making this analysis especially relevant.

6.2 Experimental Setup

We conduct experiments on two multi-GPU platforms. The first platform consists of different GPUs, an NVIDIA RTX A6000 and an NVIDIA RTX 3060, connected to an Intel Xeon Gold 6326, allowing us to assess the load balancer's ability to adaptively distribute workloads across GPUs with differing compute capabilities. The second platform consists of four NVIDIA RTX 6000 Ada GPUs connected to an Intel Xeon Gold 6530 via PCIe, which can showcase our training scheme's performance when scaling to platforms with additional GPUs. Table 1 summarizes the specifications of each platform. Our implementations are built using PyTorch v2.4.1 [20], Python v3.10.16, and CUDA v12.4.

Table 1. Platform Specifications

Platform	Device	Process	Hardware Parallelism	External Memory	Frequency	Peak Performance
Server1	CPU Intel Xeon Gold 6326	10 nm	2 sockets, 32 cores	256 GB, DDR4	2.9 GHz	537 GFLOPS
	GPU NVIDIA RTX A6000	8 nm	10752 CUDA cores	48 GB, GDDR6	1.8 GHz	38.71 TFLOPS
	GPU NVIDIA RTX 3060	8 nm	3584 CUDA cores	12 GB, GDDR6	1.8 GHz	12.74 TFLOPS
Server2	CPU Intel Xeon Gold 6530	Intel 7	2 sockets, 64 cores	1 TB, DDR5	2.1 GHz	1.08 TFLOPS
	GPU NVIDIA RTX 6000 Ada (**x4**)	5 nm	18176 CUDA cores	48 GB, GDDR6	2.5 GHz	91.06 TFLOPS

6.3 Metrics

The main metric [31] optimized by an acceleration system for MARL is system throughput in terms of the number of agent-gradient-updates per second (APS): $\frac{\text{number of agents} \times \text{batch size}}{T_{DC}+T_{MU}}$, where T_{DC} and T_{MU} are the execution times of the Data Collection and Model Update phases, respectively. T_{MU} is the metric measured for each learner by the Agent Load Balancer, reflecting how the training load is distributed and adjusted across learners over successive iterations. When using multiple learners, T_{MU} in the APS calculation corresponds to the execution time of the slowest learner.

6.4 Agent Load Balancer Evaluation

We evaluate the performance (Fig. 6) of our Agent Load Balancer by measuring T_{MU} over several iterations on *Server1*, which features GPUs with differing compute capabilities. We launch one learner per device in an experiment with 1024 agents and a batch size of 8192, spanning all three IL algorithms. We use three different initial agent distributions (90%–10%, 50%–50%, and 10%–90% splits) between the two GPUs. As training progresses, we observe that across all algorithms and initial distributions, the Agent Load Balancer quickly converges to a balanced agent assignment. Its overhead is independent of the underlying algorithm and scales only with the number of learners. It introduces an additional latency of at most 11.7–14.1 milliseconds per training iteration and incurs a memory overhead of 4–138 KB for experiments with 2–32 learners. This overhead is negligible, accounting for at most 0.5% of the Model Update training time in the least computationally demanding IQL algorithm. Moreover, the peak memory usage of training IQL reaches 680 MB, which is orders of magnitude higher than the memory footprint of the load balancer. Additionally, the balancer can be toggled off if the training balance is achieved for a set number of

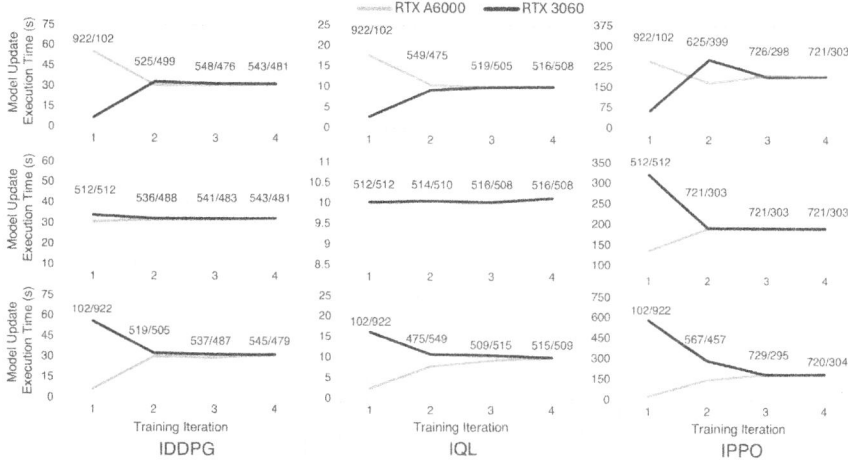

Fig. 6. Model Update execution time (T_{MU}) across all three independent learning algorithms for the first four training iterations. Each row has a different initial agent distribution. The values above each training iteration data point represent the agent distribution between learners, formatted as RTX A6000 agents/RTX 3060 agents.

iterations, completely amortizing the overhead of the balancer after it finds a balanced agent distribution during the first few training iterations.

6.5 Independent Multi-GPU Training Scheme Evaluation

We evaluate our Independent Multi-GPU training scheme against two baselines, Single-GPU and Distributed Data Parallel (DDP), on both *Server1* and *Server2*.

Single-GPU: Uses a single learner to train all agents. This is the training scheme used in most MARL libraries since it is generalizable and supports all MARL algorithms, including those that involve inter-agent communication.

Distributed Data Parallel (DDP): Launches learners up to the number of GPUs in each system. Each learner replicates all agent models, but only processes a subset of the batch. We distributed the batch evenly among these learners. Gradients are synchronized using a Ring-AllReduce mechanism.

Figure 7 compares APS between our Independent Multi-GPU training scheme and the two baselines on a large-scale 1024-agent experiment. We vary the batch size for the off-policy IDDPG and IQL, starting at 4096, and set IPPO at 512, as the latter efficiently utilizes GPU resources and outperforms CPU-based training even for smaller batch sizes (Fig. 3). Empirically, deploying 8 learners per GPU device in our scheme achieves the best balance between policy update parallelization and resource contention in most cases. In contrast, NVIDIA Collective Communication Library (NCCL)-based DDP in PyTorch restricts training to one learner per GPU, limiting the total number of deployable learners in order to prevent potential deadlocks [12]. Our approach overcomes this limitation, allowing for finer-grain parallelism and more efficient GPU utilization. We observe

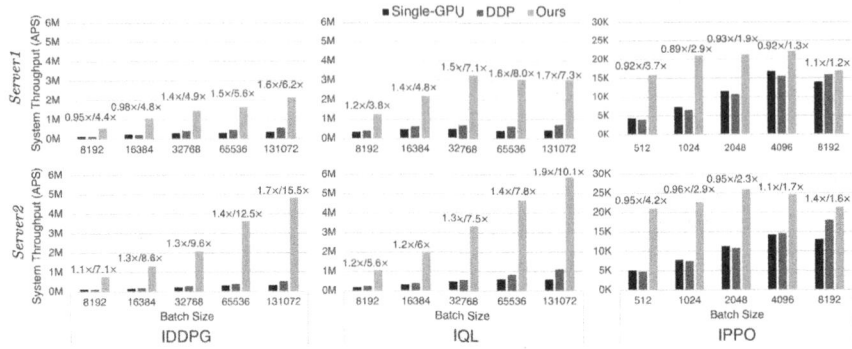

Fig. 7. APS comparison between our Independent Multi-GPU training scheme, Single-GPU, and DDP. Values above each bar show APS normalized to Single-GPU, formatted as normalized DDP/normalized Multi-GPU speedup relative to Single-GPU.

up to 7.3× and 15.5× system throughput for off-policy algorithms IDDPG and IQL on *Server*1 and *Server*2, respectively, consistently outperforming state-of-the-art and DDP-based training across all batch sizes. An increase in speedup is observed on *Server*2 due to additional GPU devices, which enable more parallel learners to fully utilize the expanded GPU resources. Throughput gains are more limited (up to 3.7× and 4.2× on *Server*1 and *Server*2, respectively) for on-policy IPPO, as the Model Update speedup is increasingly constrained by the Data Collection Phase. Unlike off-policy methods that reuse replay buffer data, on-policy methods require a full batch of fresh experiences sampled from the current iteration. As batch sizes scale up, the data collection phase becomes progressively longer, further bounding overall speedup. Regardless, we see increased system throughput across all IL algorithms on both multi-GPU platforms.

7 Conclusion

In this work, we proposed an Independent Multi-GPU training scheme that efficiently scales independent MARL by enabling multiple learners to distribute agent policy network training across multiple GPUs. We also introduced an Agent Load Balancer that dynamically assigns agents to learners during runtime on available and potentially different GPUs, optimizing resource utilization. Our results demonstrated up to 15.5× increased system throughput across multiple independent learning algorithms. We have open-sourced three IL algorithm implementations using the large-scale Pogema environment. While we focused on multi-GPU platforms, our training scheme is also generalizable to CPUs and other accelerators such as FPGAs, and our Agent Load Balancer can also be extended in future work to account for these heterogeneous devices.

Acknowledgments and Artifact Availability. This work was supported by Intel Corporation, the U.S. National Science Foundation (NSF) under grant

OAC-2411446, and the DEVCOM Army Research Lab (ARL) under grant W911NF2220159. **Distribution Statement A:** Approved for public release. Distribution is unlimited. The artifact is available in the Zenodo repository [29].
Disclosure of Interests. The authors have no competing interests to declare that are relevant to the content of this article.

References

1. Cardarilli, G.C., et al.: FPGA implementation of Q-RTS for real-time swarm intelligence systems. In: 2020 54th Asilomar Conference on Signals, Systems, and Computers, pp. 116–120. IEEE (2020)
2. Castro, P.S., Moitra, S., Gelada, C., Kumar, S., Bellemare, M.G.: Dopamine: a research framework for deep reinforcement learning (2018). http://arxiv.org/abs/1812.06110
3. De Witt, C.S., et al.: Is independent learning all you need in the starcraft multi-agent challenge? arXiv preprint arXiv:2011.09533 (2020)
4. Frostig, R., Johnson, M.J., Leary, C.: Compiling machine learning programs via high-level tracing. Syst. Mach. Learn. 4(9) (2018)
5. Hu, J., Jiang, S., Harding, S.A., Wu, H., Wei Liao, S.: Rethinking the Implementation Tricks and Monotonicity Constraint in Cooperative Multi-Agent Reinforcement Learning (2021)
6. Hu, S., et al.: MARLlib: a scalable and efficient multi-agent reinforcement learning library. J. Mach. Learn. Res. 24(315), 1–23 (2023)
7. Huang, S., et al.: CleanRL: high-quality single-file implementations of deep reinforcement learning algorithms. J. Mach. Learn. Res. 23(274), 1–18 (2022). http://jmlr.org/papers/v23/21-1342.html
8. Jiang, J., Lu, Z.: I2Q: a fully decentralized Q-learning algorithm. Adv. Neural. Inf. Process. Syst. 35, 20469–20481 (2022)
9. Jiang, J., Su, K., Lu, Z.: Fully decentralized cooperative multi-agent reinforcement learning: a survey. arXiv preprint arXiv:2401.04934 (2024)
10. Kingma, D.P.: Adam: a method for stochastic optimization. arXiv preprint arXiv:1412.6980 (2014)
11. Lan, T., Srinivasa, S., Wang, H., Zheng, S.: WarpDrive: fast end-to-end deep multi-agent reinforcement learning on a GPU. J. Mach. Learn. Res. 23(316), 1–6 (2022)
12. Li, S., et al.: PyTorch distributed: experiences on accelerating data parallel training. Proc. VLDB Endow. 13(12)
13. Liang, E., et al.: RLlib: abstractions for distributed reinforcement learning. In: International Conference on Machine Learning, pp. 3053–3062. PMLR (2018)
14. Lillicrap, T.: Continuous control with deep reinforcement learning. arXiv preprint arXiv:1509.02971 (2015)
15. Littman, M.L.: Markov games as a framework for multi-agent reinforcement learning. In: Machine Learning Proceedings 1994, pp. 157–163. Elsevier (1994)
16. Lowe, R., Wu, Y.I., Tamar, A., Harb, J., Pieter Abbeel, O., Mordatch, I.: Multi-agent actor-critic for mixed cooperative-competitive environments. Adv. Neural Inf. Process. Syst. 30 (2017)
17. Meng, Y., Kinsner, M., Singh, D., Iyer, M., Prasanna, V.: PEARL: enabling portable, productive, and high-performance deep reinforcement learning using heterogeneous platforms. In: Proceedings of the 21st ACM International Conference on Computing Frontiers, pp. 41–50 (2024)

18. Moritz, P., et al.: Ray: a distributed framework for emerging {AI} applications. In: 13th USENIX Symposium on Operating Systems Design and Implementation (OSDI 2018), pp. 561–577 (2018)
19. Nguyen, T.T., Nguyen, N.D., Nahavandi, S.: Deep reinforcement learning for multiagent systems: a review of challenges, solutions, and applications. IEEE Trans. Cybernet. **50**(9), 3826–3839 (2020)
20. Paszke, A., et al.: PyTorch: an imperative style, high-performance deep learning library. Adv. Neural Inf. Process. Syst. **32** (2019)
21. Raffin, A., Hill, A., Gleave, A., Kanervisto, A., Ernestus, M., Dormann, N.: Stable-baselines3: reliable reinforcement learning implementations. J. Mach. Learn. Res. **22**(268), 1–8 (2021). http://jmlr.org/papers/v22/20-1364.html
22. Ruder, S.: An overview of gradient descent optimization algorithms. arXiv preprint arXiv:1609.04747 (2016)
23. Schulman, J., Wolski, F., Dhariwal, P., Radford, A., Klimov, O.: Proximal policy optimization algorithms. arXiv preprint arXiv:1707.06347 (2017)
24. Sharma, P.K., Fernandez, R., Zaroukian, E., Dorothy, M., Basak, A., Asher, D.E.: Survey of recent multi-agent reinforcement learning algorithms utilizing centralized training. In: Artificial Intelligence and Machine Learning for Multi-Domain Operations Applications III, vol. 11746, pp. 665–676. SPIE (2021)
25. Skrynnik, A., Andreychuk, A., Borzilov, A., Chernyavskiy, A., Yakovlev, K., Panov, A.: POGEMA: a benchmark platform for cooperative multi-agent navigation (2024). https://arxiv.org/abs/2407.14931
26. Tan, M.: Multi-agent reinforcement learning: independent vs. cooperative agents. In: Proceedings of the Tenth International Conference on Machine Learning, pp. 330–337 (1993)
27. Watkins, C.J., Dayan, P.: Q-learning. Mach. Learn. **8**, 279–292 (1992)
28. Weng, J., et al.: Tianshou: a highly modularized deep reinforcement learning library. J. Mach. Learn. Res. **23**(267), 1–6 (2022). http://jmlr.org/papers/v23/21-1127.html
29. Wiggins, S., Gupta, N., Zgheib, G., Iyer, M., Prasanna, V.: Accelerating Independent Multi-Agent Reinforcement Learning on Multi-GPU Platforms (2025). https://doi.org/10.5281/zenodo.15579913
30. Wiggins, S., Meng, Y., Kannan, R., Prasanna, V.: Characterizing speed performance of multi-agent reinforcement learning. In: Proceedings of the 12th International Conference on Data Science, Technology and Applications - DATA, pp. 327–334. INSTICC, SciTePress (2023). https://doi.org/10.5220/0012082200003541
31. Wiggins, S., Prasanna, V.: Accelerating multi-agent DDPG training on multi-GPU platforms. In: 2024 IEEE High Performance Extreme Computing Conference (HPEC), pp. 1–5. IEEE (2024)
32. Zhang, K., Yang, Z., Başar, T.: Multi-agent reinforcement learning: a selective overview of theories and algorithms. In: Handbook of Reinforcement Learning and Control, pp. 321–384 (2021)

ScheInfer: Efficient Inference of Large Language Models with Task Scheduling on Moderate GPUs

Wenxiang Lin[1], Xinglin Pan[2], Shaohuai Shi[1(✉)], Xuan Wang[1], and Xiaowen Chu[2]

[1] School of Computer Science and Technology, Harbin Institute of Technology, Shenzhen, Shenzhen, China
wenxianglin@stu.hit.edu.cn, shaohuais@hit.edu.cn,
wangxuan@cs.hitsz.edu.cn
[2] Data Science and Analytics Thrust, The Hong Kong University of Science and Technology, Guangzhou, Guangzhou, China
xpan413@connect.hkust-gz.edu.cn, xwchu@ust.hk

Abstract. Large language models (LLMs) are known for their high demand on computing resources and memory due to their substantial model size, which leads to inefficient inference on moderate GPU systems. Techniques like quantization or pruning can shrink model sizes but often impair accuracy, making them unsuitable for practical applications. In this work, we introduce ScheInfer, a high-performance inference engine designed to speed up LLM inference without compromising model accuracy. ScheInfer incorporates three innovative methods to increase inference efficiency: 1) model partitioning to allow asynchronous processing of tasks across CPU computation, GPU computation, and CPU-GPU communication, 2) an adaptive partition algorithm to optimize the use of CPU, GPU, and PCIe communication capabilities, and 3) a token assignment strategy to handle diverse prompt and generation tasks during LLM inference. Comprehensive experiments were conducted with various LLMs such as Mixtral, LLaMA-2, Qwen, and PhiMoE across three test environments featuring different CPUs and GPUs. The experimental findings demonstrate that ScheInfer achieves speeds between $1.11\times$ to $1.80\times$ faster in generation phase and $1.69\times$ to $6.33\times$ faster in prompt phase, leading to an overall speedup ranging from $1.25\times$ to $2.04\times$ compared to state-of-the-art solutions, llama.cpp and Fiddler.

Keywords: Large Language Models · Efficient Inference · Model Partitioning · Scheduling

1 Introduction

Large language models (LLMs) are renowned for their exceptional abilities in many AI applications [3,15,17]. These models are very compute- and memory-hungry due to their large model sizes, so they are mainly deployed in data centers equipped with high-end GPUs (e.g., Nvidia Tesla H100) to provide low-latency and high-throughput services [2]. Recently, it is a burgeoning trend towards running LLMs on more accessible local platforms, such as edge devices and personal computers (PCs) with moderate GPUs (e.g., Nvidia RTX 3090) [8,14]. This shift is driven by the need for improved data privacy, model customization [11], and lower inference expenses [15]. Deploying LLMs on moderate GPUs poses a challenge because it requires making the model compatible with these memory limited moderate GPU systems. Current strategies for addressing memory challenges involve model compression and offloading [5,12,18]. Yet, even significantly compressed models may still exceed the memory capacity of moderate GPUs, especially on sparse Mixtures of Experts (MoE) models [7,10]. Leading systems like llama.cpp [6] allocate layers between CPU and GPU memory, easing the demand on GPU resources. For MoE models, Fiddler [9] shifts experts to CPU memory to decrease GPU memory needs. Nevertheless, these approaches use either CPU resources or GPU resources to optimize the inference speed.

To this end, this paper presents ScheInfer, an efficient LLM inference system (Sect. 3.1) designed for local computer systems with one moderate GPU. The main design concept of ScheInfer is to fully utilize the available computing, memory and communication resources of the system. To achieve this goal, ScheInfer partitions the weight tensors of multi-layer perceptions (MLPs) in dense Transformers or experts in sparse MoE Transformers, which occupy most parameters of the model, into three components, 1) CC: parameters stored and executed on the CPU, 2) CG: parameters stored on the CPU and executed on the GPU, and 3) GG: parameters stored and executed on the GPU. By doing this, CC, CG, and GG tasks are possible to be executed simultaneously to fully utilize the available resources of the computer system (Sect. 3.2 and Sect. 3.3).

However, the design of ScheInfer still faces notable challenges in achieving optimal performance. *First, how to determine the sizes of CC, CG, and GG is non-trivial to achieve the minimal inference time due to variations in model size and computer systems.* To address this, ScheInfer builds an optimization model (Sect. 4.1) to determine the optimal slicing rates which indicate how many parameters should be placed on CC, CG, and GG. *Second, due to the different compute characteristics of the prompt phase and the generation phase during inference, the slicing rates may differ between the two phases. An optimal slicing rate for the generation phase can result in suboptimal performance during the prompt phase.* We find that the delay arises from matrix-multiplication (GEMM) of the prompt token by the CC matrix taking significantly longer than other operations in the prompt phase with the optimized slicing rate from the generation phase. Therefore, we split the CPU computation task by dividing its input tokens into two parts: 1) remained to do the computation on the CPU, and 2) transferred together with the weight to the GPU for computation (specially denote the weight transferred as CG$'$). The weights are viewed as CC, CG and GG (for tokens processed on the CPU) and as CG$'$, CG, and GG (for tokens processed on the GPU) in the prompt phase, respectively. Then, we propose a token assignment strategy (Sect. 4.2) that determines the number of tokens run on GPU with CG' and on CPU with CC. We conduct extensive experiments (Sect. 5) with four popular LLMs and three representative testbeds and the experimental results demonstrate that ScheInfer runs 1.25× to 2.04× faster than state-of-the-art inference solutions including llama.cpp and Fiddler.

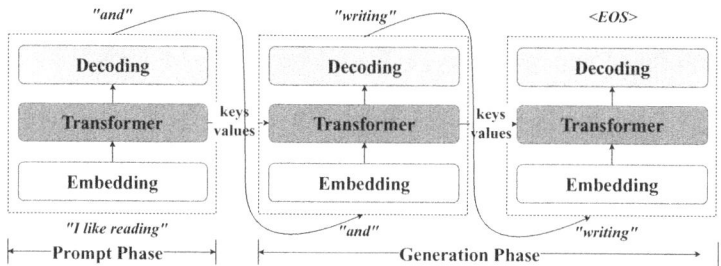

Fig. 1. The generative inference procedure of an LLM

2 Background and Motivations

2.1 LLM Architecture and LLM Inference

Modern LLM architectures are primarily composed of several Transformer layers, each containing a self-attention layer and either an MLP block (for dense LLMs) or an MoE block (for sparse MoE LLMs). Specifically, the MLP block processes input through two fully connected layers (FC1 and FC2) with an activation function [16]. The MoE block utilizes a gating function to allocate tokens to their respective experts, processes them, and then aggregates the results [10].

A typical generative inference process in large language models involves two stages: 1) the prompt phase and the generation phase. The prompt phase creates a KV cache for each layer and generates the first token. The input of this phase is a prompt, such as a lengthy instruction sentence. 2) The generation phase is iterative, updating KV caches and generating tokens step-by-step. The key difference between these phases is that the generation phase is executed multiple times although the input sequence for each iteration is one as shown in Fig. 1.

2.2 Motivations

Insufficient Utilization of Limited Resources. Consumer-grade computers often have limited GPU memory and CPU computational resources. Maximizing these available resources to enhance inference performance presents a significant challenge. Our approach aims to support parallel execution of CPU and GPU tasks, along with efficient communication between CPU and GPU, to maximize resource usage. Inspired by tensor parallelism [4], we propose to partition weight tensors into multiple parts to be executed on CPU and GPU simultaneously.

Determining the Slicing Rate of Each Part. Though we enable the simultaneous execution on both CPU and GPU, how to determine how many parameters (i.e., the optimal slicing rate) should be placed on CPU or GPU is challenging due to varied model sizes and different computing capability of CPU and GPU. Our experimental results demonstrate that the optimal slicing rate can be up to 2.1× faster on average than a manually configured slicing rate (Sect. 5.5). Notably, the optimal slicing rate varies significantly due to its heavy reliance on the computational and storage capacities of consumer-grade devices. There is a large variation in computational and memory capacities among different CPUs, GPUs and the interconnect between the CPU and GPU. Thus, determining the best slicing rate needs to be tailored to each specific consumer-grade computer.

Different Workloads Between Prompt and Generation Phases. The workloads in the prompt and generation phases vary greatly, thus the optimal slicing rate for achieving peak inference performance also varies. *That means we need to consistently combine CC, CG, and GG tensors from both CPU and GPU memory, arrange them into contiguous executable weights, and then allocate them accurately to leverage optimal slicing rates.* Normally, the generation phase takes much more time than the prompt phase. Thus, we fix the slicing rates to those optimized in the generation phase. However, this will result in poor performance in the prompt phase. To alleviate the issue, with the finding that CPU computation takes much longer than other operations, we propose to optimize the number of tokens executed on CPU (i.e. executed with CC tensors).

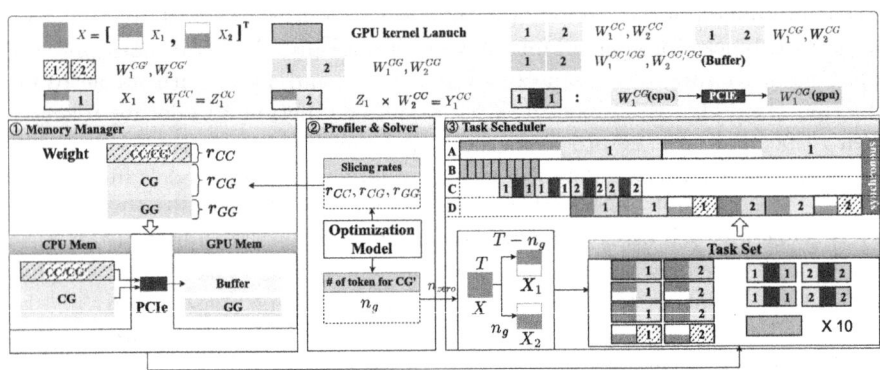

Fig. 2. The system overview of ScheInfer for an MLP block

3 System Design of ScheInfer

3.1 System Overview

To better utilize different resources, we propose our ScheInfer that slices the weight tensors of MLP or MoE layers into three parts to enable the parallel

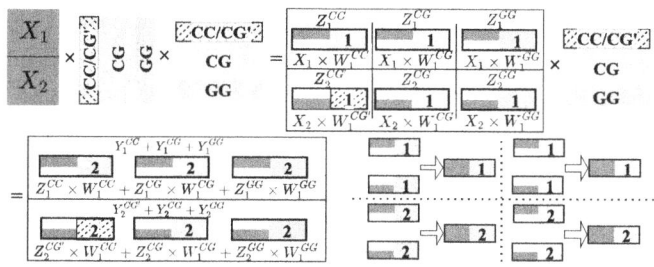

Fig. 3. The illustration of constructing the task set in Fig. 2 with sliced input tokens and weights

execution of different resources (CPU, GPU, and PCIe interconnect between CPU and GPU). To support the parallel execution, the design of our ScheInfer consists of three components, including Memory Manager, Profiler & Solver, and Task Scheduler as shown in Fig. 2. First, Memory Manager slices the weight tensors and supervises the allocation of their storage so as to handle the memory addresses required for transferring weight tensors from the CPU to the GPU. Second, Profiler & Solver involve solving the optimal slicing rates and number of tokens for CG' by profiling running-time information for any given models and hardware. Third, Task Scheduler organizes the execution of the MLP or MoE layers and ensures maximum parallelism by coordinating CPU calculations, GPU computations, GPU kernel launches, and GPU-CPU communications.

3.2 Memory Manager: Slicing Weight Tensors

In Memory Manager, the weight tensors of an MLP or MoE layer are divided into three parts including 1) CC: parameters are stored and executed on the CPU side, 2) CG: parameters are stored on the CPU side while executed on the GPU side, and 3) GG: parameters are stored and executed on the GPU side as shown in Fig. 2 (Memory Manager). Additionally, Memory Manager will maintain the CG' parameters for the prompt phase which share the same memory addresses with CC but will be executed on the GPU side. With these three tensor types, we can simultaneously leverage CPU, GPU, and PCIe resources.

Figure 3 shows an example of our weight slicing in an MLP layer with two linear layers, where we ignore the activation computation for better presentation. Formally, let $X \to [X_1 \ X_2]^\top$ represent the input tensor stored on GPU of the MLP layer with T tokens. Notably, X_1 will be additionally transferred into CPU (negligible cost) to simultaneously calculate with tensors on CPU and GPU. And X_2 is divided by n_g to reduce CPU computation in the prompt phase (detailed in Sect. 4.2). W_1, W_2 represent the weight tensors of FC1 and FC2 in the MLP layer, respectively. W_1 and W_2 are sliced into CC, CG, and GG, that is $W_1 \to [W_1^{CC} \ W_1^{CG} \ W_1^{GG}]$ and $W_2 \to [W_2^{CC} \ W_2^{CG} \ W_2^{GG}]^\top$. The computation of the MLP layer can be divided as:

$$\begin{bmatrix} Z_1^{CC} & Z_1^{CG} & Z_1^{GG} \\ Z_2^{CG'} & Z_2^{CG} & Z_2^{GG} \end{bmatrix} = A(\begin{bmatrix} X_1 \\ X_2 \end{bmatrix} \begin{bmatrix} W_1^{CC} & W_1^{CG} & W_1^{GG} \end{bmatrix}), \quad (1)$$

$$\begin{bmatrix} Y_1^{CC} + Y_1^{CG} + Y_1^{GG} \\ Y_2^{CG'} + Y_2^{CG} + Y_2^{GG} \end{bmatrix} = \begin{bmatrix} Z_1^{CC} & Z_1^{CG} & Z_1^{GG} \\ Z_2^{CG'} & Z_2^{CG} & Z_2^{GG} \end{bmatrix} \begin{bmatrix} W_2^{CC} \\ W_2^{CG} \\ W_2^{GG} \end{bmatrix}, \quad (2)$$

Here, $A(\cdot)$ denotes the activation function applied element-wise. Notably, X_2 will be executed with CG' instead of CC. The CPU handles calculations for Z_1^{CC} and Y_1^{CC}, while the GPU processes the remaining computations (weight tensors stored on the CPU will be transferred to the GPU).

In comparison to the unpartitioned original $Y_1 = W_2(A(W_1 \times X_1))$ and $Y_2 = W_2(A(W_1 \times X_2))$, the output remains identical after concatenating $Y_1^{CC} + Y_1^{CG} + Y_1^{GG}$ and $Y_2^{CG'} + Y_2^{CG} + Y_2^{GG}$ into a final result, akin to Tensor Parallel.

3.3 Task Scheduler: Scheduling Tasks with Different Streams

Task Scheduler provides the capability for executing different types of tasks in parallel and enhances the performance by arranging the CPU computation tasks, GPU computation tasks, and the communication tasks between the CPU and GPU to maximize their overlaps. Be aware that the GPU computation task includes a GPU kernel launch time, which might be similar in duration to the GPU's computational time when only a few tokens are processed during the generation phase. Figure 2 (Task Scheduler) provides an example of our scheduler managing an MLP block (the MoE block functions similarly, as the key difference between MLP and MoE lies in the number of matrix-multiplication or GEMM operations) during the prompt phase with two linear layers. We organize CPU computation tasks, GPU computation tasks, and CPU-GPU communication tasks into a task set for efficient scheduling. Figure 3 illustrates the outcomes of tasks from the sets depicted in Fig. 2. Notably, X_2 allocated n_g tokens from X with T tokens is only to reduce CPU computation during the prompt phase. To reduce the number of kernel lanuching operations, as shown in Fig. 3 (right down), We merge the GPU computation tasks for X_1 with those for X_2. The same applies to Z_1 and Z_2. During the generation phase, n_g is set to zero, and tasks associated with X_2 will be omitted.

With so many tasks, we set up four asynchronous execution streams in the pipelining (independent operations from different streams can be carried out simultaneously), including CPU computation (Stream-A), GPU kernel launch (Stream-B), communication between CPU and GPU (Stream-C) and GPU computation (Stream-D). Additionally, launching a GPU kernel demands minimal computational power, allowing it to proceed concurrently with CPU operations. The CC part is executed in Stream-A, the GG part requires both Stream-B and Stream-D, and the CG and CG' parts require Stream-B, C and D.

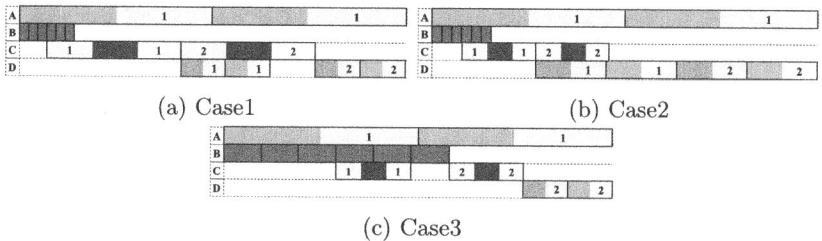

Fig. 4. Three schedule cases (The caption is the same as Fig. 2)

3.4 Profiler and Solver: Optimizing Slicing Rates

For a given model and a testbed, Profiler & Solver first profiles some important parameters to build performance models, and then solves the best rates for CC, CG, and GG (Sect. 4.1 will introduce a general optimization model to determine slicing rates with an intact input tensor without splitting). This module also solves the number of tokens to run with CG' (n_g) in the prompt phases (Sect. 4.2 will present a modification to the optimization model to address n_g.).

4 Optimizing Algorithms in Profiler and Solver

4.1 Algorithm of Optimizing Slicing Rates

To efficiently optimize slicing rates (i.e., r_{CC}, r_{CG}, and r_{GG}) for partitioning weight tensors, we develop a two-stage optimization algorithm. In the first stage, we solve r_{CC} and r_{CG} by fixing r_{GG} which is mainly related to GPU memory. In the second stage, we restrict the search space of r_{GG} into integers and calculate the time cost bonus for each integer using the model from the first stage, which solves the best schedule to assign GPU memory with a greedy algorithm. Notably, optimizing slicing rates will be operated only once.

Performance Models. Let t_G, t_C, t_{C2G}, and t_{Launch} denote the time taken for a GPU GEMM operation, a CPU GEMM operation, data transfer from CPU to GPU, and a GPU kernel launch, respectively. To simply the problem, we model t_{Launch} as a constant and t_G, t_C, t_{C2G} as linear models [13], i.e.,

$$\begin{cases} t_G &= \alpha_G + n_G \cdot \beta_G, \\ t_C &= \alpha_C + n_C \cdot \beta_C, \\ t_{C2G} &= \alpha_{C2G} + n_{C2G} \cdot \beta_{C2G}, \\ t_{Launch} &= \text{constant}, \end{cases} \quad (3)$$

where n_* represents the volume of the communication message or the workload of GEMM (i.e., dimensions of two input matrices), α_* denotes the startup time and β_* represents the time per byte transmitted or per unit of workload processed.

Problem Formulation. During the model inference, $n_{GEMM} = T \cdot M \cdot H$ where T, M, and H denote the number of tokens, the model dimension, the hidden dimension, respectively. The shapes of the input tensor and the weight tensor are $[T, M]$ and $[M, H]$, respectively. Let n_W denote the total bytes of the weight tensor, then we have $n_{G,GG} = r_{GG} \cdot n_{GEMM}$, $n_{C,CC} = r_{CC} \cdot n_{GEMM}$, $n_{G,CG} = r_{CG} \cdot n_{GEMM}$ and $n_{C2G,CG} = r_{CG} \cdot n_W$. According to Eq. 3, we obtain

$$\begin{cases} t_G &= \alpha_G \cdot [sgn(r_{CG}) + sgn(r_{GG})] \\ & + (r_{CG} + r_{GG}) \cdot n_{GEMM} \cdot \beta_G, \\ t_C &= \alpha_C \cdot sgn(r_{CC}) + r_{CC} \cdot n_{GEMM} \cdot \beta_C, \\ t_{C2G} &= \alpha_{C2G} \cdot sgn(r_{CG}) + r_{CG} \cdot n_W \cdot \beta_{C2G}, \\ t_L &= [2 \cdot sgn(r_{CG}) + sgn(r_{GG})] \cdot t_{Lanuch}, \end{cases} \quad (4)$$

where $sgn(\cdot)$ denotes the sign function. Notably, a CG operation requires a launch to transfer data from CPU to GPU and a launch to execute GPU computation, so its coefficient is 2.

Let τ_G^i, τ_C^i, τ_{C2G}^i and τ_L^i denote the completion timestamp of CPU GEMM computation, communication from CPU to GPU and the GPU kernel launch for the i_{th} GEMM computation in an MLP or MoE layer. Thus, the dependency of these tasks can be formally described as

$$\begin{cases} \tau_L^i &= \tau_L^{i-1} + t_L, \\ \tau_{C2G}^i &= \max(\tau_L^i, \tau_{C2G}^{i-1}) + t_{C2G}, \ 0 \leq i \leq n_l, \\ \tau_G^i &= \max(\tau_{C2G}^i, \tau_G^{i-1}) + t_G, \\ \tau_C^i &= \tau_C^{i-1} + t_C, \end{cases} \quad (5)$$

where n_l denotes the number of GEMMs in an MLP or MoE layer. And the time cost of the MLP or MoE layer is represented as $t_{fin} = max(\tau_G^{n_l}, \tau_C^{n_l})$. Thus, our goal is to minimize t_{fin} by changing the slicing rates. In the first stage, we only optimize $r_{CG}, 0 \leq r_{CG} \leq (1 - r_{GG})$ since r_{GG} is related to the GPU memory bound (discussed in Sect. 4.1 GPU Memory Assignment), and $r_{CC} = 1 - r_{CG} - r_{GG}$.

Optimal Solution. It is obvious that $\tau_C^{n_l} = n_l \cdot t_C$. Our main focus lies on $\tau_G^{n_l}$. According to Eq. 5, we eliminate the max functions by the following conditions.

$$Q1: t_L < t_{C2G}; Q2: t_G < t_{C2G}; Q3: t_L < t_G. \quad (6)$$

Under these conditions, we can categorize all scenarios into three distinct cases.

Case1 (Q1 is true and Q2 is true): It indicates the communication time between CPU and GPU is larger than the computation time of GPU GEMM and the launch time of GPU kernels. Thus, the communication between CPU and GPU dominates the overall time cost as shown in Fig. 4a. So we obtain

$$\tau_L^i \leq \tau_{C2G}^{i-1} \text{ and } \tau_G^{i-1} \leq \tau_{C2G}^i, \quad (7)$$

to eliminate the max function in Eq. 5, resulting in

$$\tau_G^{n_l} = t_L + n_l \cdot t_{C2G} + t_G. \tag{8}$$

Case2 (Q1 is true and Q2 is false) or (Q1 is false and Q3 is true): It indicates that the GPU computation dominates the overall time cost as shown in Fig. 4b. So we have $\tau_{C2G}^i \le \tau_G^{i-1}$. Then we can obtain

$$\tau_G^{n_l} = t_L + t_{C2G} + n_l \cdot t_G. \tag{9}$$

Case3 (Q1 is false and Q3 is False): It indicates that the launch time of GPU kernels dominates the overall time cost as shown in Fig. 4c. So we have $\tau_{C2G}^{i-1} \le \tau_L^i, \tau_G^{i-1} \le \tau_{C2G}^i$. Then we can obtain

$$\tau_G^{n_l} = n_l \cdot t_L + t_{C2G} + t_G. \tag{10}$$

As the problem has only one unknown variable, and the highest power is 1. The optimal r_{CG} must lie on the edge points of each cases, including points that $t_L = t_{C2G}$, $t_G = t_{C2G}$, $t_L = t_G$, $\tau_G^{n_l} = \tau_C^{n_l}$, $r_{CG} = 0$ and $r_{CG} = 1 - r_{GG}$. So the time complexity is O(1). Denote an array of these points as X and a corresponding array of t_{fin} as Y. Then, we can obtain the optimal r_{CG}^* and corresponding t_{fin}^* as follows:

$$\begin{aligned} t_{fin}^* &= \min Y, \\ r_{CG}^* &= X[\arg\min Y]. \end{aligned} \tag{11}$$

GPU Memory Assignment. Slicing weight tensors of every MLP or MoE layer by r_{GG}, rather than transferring an entire layer's weight tensors to the GPU, allows us to effectively hide the GPU computation overhead. Importantly, variations in r_{GG} lead to different inference speeds, and higher values do not necessarily yield better performance. Consequently, we introduce a simple yet efficient algorithm to determine the value of r_{GG} for each layer.

Optimizing both r_{GG} and r_{CG} to achieve the best inference speed while keeping GPU memory in check is possible, though it introduces numerous variables and constraints, complicating the optimization challenge. Therefore, we choose to define a set $v_i = \{i/n_G, 1 \le i \le n_G\}$ of r_{GG} (i is integer) and calculate its time cost by Eq. 11. Then, we define the importance $s^{j,t}(v_i)$ of i_{th} value in the set for the j_{th} layer at the t_{th} iteration as

$$s^{j,t}(v_i) = \frac{t_{fin}^*(r_{GG} = v^{j,t-1}) - t_{fin}^*(r_{GG} = v_i)}{(v_i - v^{j,t-1}) \cdot n_m}, \tag{12}$$

where $v^{j,t-1}$ represents r_{GG} in the j_{th} layer at the previous $t-1$ iteration, and $v_i \cdot n_m$ represents the GPU memory cost when $r_{GG} = v_i$. We will calculate the importance of each value and each layer at each iteration. By adhering to a greedy strategy, we choose the most important $s^{j,t}(v_i)$ and update $v^{j,t}$ and continue iterating until the GPU memory is exhausted.

4.2 Token Assignment for the Prompt Phase

To manage varying workloads in the prompt and generation phases, we maintain slicing rates optimized for the generation phase and create a token assignment schedule in Profiler & Solver to regulate CPU token execution during the prompt phase. We initially create CG′, which shares CPU memory addresses with CC but operates on the GPU. Next, we allocate n_g tokens, originally processed by CC, to run with CG′, thereby reducing CPU computation. By modifying n_g, we can reduce the CPU computation time, thereby increasing the overlap.

Tokens run with CG′ will be processed on the GPU, requiring the transfer of CG′ tensors from CPU to GPU. Here, we need to change the unknown variable from r_{CG} to n_g ($0 \leq n_g \leq T$ where T denotes the number of tokens for the input) which affects the value of t_L, t_{C2G}, t_G and t_C by

$$\begin{aligned}
t'_L &= [2 \cdot sgn(r_{CG}) + 2 \cdot sgn(r_{CC}) + sgn(r_{GG})] \cdot t_{Lanuch}, \\
t'_{C2G} &= \alpha_{C2G} \cdot [sgn(r_{CG}) + sgn(r_{CC})] + n_W \cdot \beta_{C2G}, \\
t'_G &= \alpha_G \cdot [sgn(r_{CG}) + sgn(r_{GG}) + sgn(r_{CC} \cdot n_g)] \\
&\quad + [T \cdot (r_{CG} + r_{GG}) + n_g \cdot r_{CC}] MH\beta_G, \\
t'_C &= \alpha_C \cdot sgn(r_{CC} \cdot (T - n_g)) + (T - n_g) \cdot r_{CC} MH\beta_C.
\end{aligned} \quad (13)$$

We can use the same method to compare the time cost at edge points to determine the optimal n_g^*; hence, the introduction will not be reiterated. The pipelining in the prompt phase is shown in Fig. 2.

Table 1. α and β of CPU GEMM, GPU GEMM and PCIe communication for Eq. 3

		GPU GEMM		CPU GEMM		PCIe	Lanuch
		FP16	INT4	FP16	INT4		
α	A	1.0E-7	4.7E-6	7.4E-7	1.1E-5	3.0E-6	4.4E-5
β		3.2E-12	8.1E-13	1.6E-11	5.4E-12	2.6E-11	-
r^2/σ		0.997	0.999	0.988	0.998	0.985	3.4E-6
α	B	1.9E-7	4.6E-6	3.4E-6	1.3E-5	5.8E-6	5.7E-5
β		2.6E-12	6.5E-13	1.5E-11	6.5E-12	2.5E-11	-
r^2/σ		0.997	0.996	0.995	0.998	0.994	5.9E-6
α	C	1.4E-7	6.4E-6	1.8E-6	5.6E-7	3.7E-6	5.2E-5
β		3.6E-12	9.2E-13	2.5E-11	8.4E-12	4.1E-11	-
r^2/σ		0.988	0.989	0.993	0.992	0.999	6.0E-6

5 Evaluation

5.1 Experimental Settings

Testbeds. Experiments are carried out on three testbeds: *Testbed-A*, Nvidia RTX A6000 GPU, Intel(R) Xeon(R) Platinum 8358 CPU and PCIe-4.0x16.

Testbed-B, Nvidia RTX 3090 GPU, AMD EPYC 7742 and PCIe-4.0x16. *Testbed-C*, Nvidia RTX 2080Ti GPU, Intel(R) Xeon(R) Gold 6230 CPU and PCIe-3.0x16. Software environments are Ubuntu-22.04 and CUDA-12.1.

Models. We use both dense and sparse models including LLaMA [15], Qwen [17], Mixtral [7] and PhiMoE [1]. All models in our experiments use quantized parameters of FP16 or INT4.

Baseline Systems. We use Fiddler and llama.cpp as our baselines. Fiddler is particularly optimized for MoE models and llama.cpp is a well-known inference system that utilizes both CPU and GPU resources to accelerate inference.

Workloads. The workloads are derived from the ChatGPT prompts[1].

5.2 Performance Models

We measure the launch time of GPU kernels and the elapsed time with a range of sizes for CPU and GPU GEMM operations and the communication between GPU and CPU to fit the performance models in Eq. 3. As we denote the workload of a GEMM as $n_{GEMM} = T \cdot M \cdot H$, we need to measure two sets of $\alpha_C, \beta_C, \alpha_G, \beta_G$ for each testbed. We also provide r-square r^2 and variance σ to check the accuracy of the performance model. The results are shown in Table 1, which indicates that our linear models can well fit the measured performance.

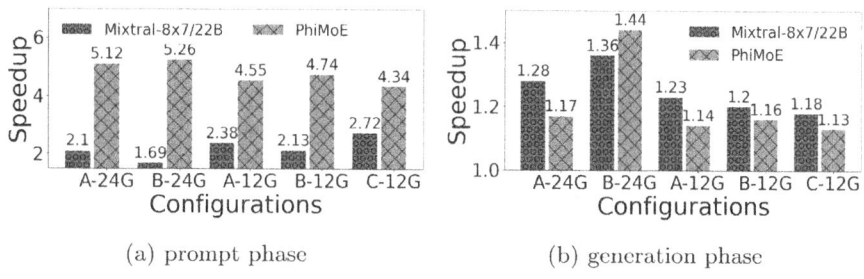

Fig. 5. The speedups of ScheInfer over Fiddler with different configurations

5.3 Performance on the Prompt Phase

We evaluate the speedup of our ScheInfer over Fiddler and llama.cpp with 4bit quantized LLaMA-2-70B, Qwen2-57B-A14B, Mixtral-7B and Mixtral-22B and FP16 PhiMoE, LLaMA-2-13B and Qwen2-14B. The input length is set to 1024 by default. Notably, Mixtral-22B is used only when the GPU memory is 24GB. The results are shown in Fig. 5a and Fig. 6a, which show that ScheInfer achieves speedups ranging from 1.69× to 6.33× over Fiddler and llama.cpp.

---

[1] https://huggingface.co/datasets/MohamedRashad/ChatGPT-prompts.

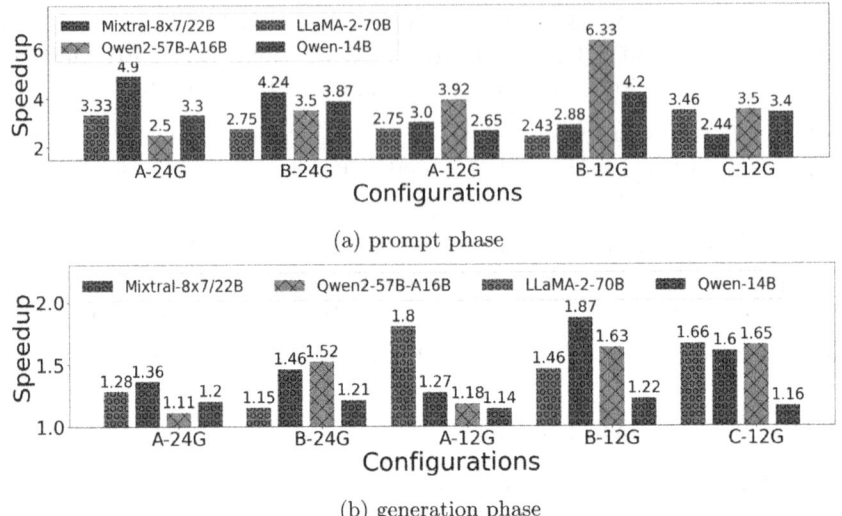

Fig. 6. The speedups of ScheInfer over llama.cpp with different configurations

5.4 Performance on the Generation Phase

Performance comparison in the generation phase is shown in Fig. 5b and Fig. 6b. The results show that ScheInfer achieves speedups ranging from 1.11× to 1.87× over Fiddler and llama.cpp. The time cost of the communication between CPU to GPU is much larger than other operations on our testbeds in the generation phase. Consequently, the improvement is not as pronounced as that observed during the prompt phase.

Putting prompt and generation phases together, ScheInfer achieves end-to-end improvements by 1.25× to 2.04× over llama.cpp and Fiddler.

5.5 Ablation Study

Impacts of the CPU GEMM Speed. To understand the impacts of the CPU GEMM speed, we configure the number of threads in the range of [16, 8, 4, 2] in executing CPU GEMM in the generation phase. The results shows that our ScheInfer achieves average speedups of 1.23×, 1.29×, 1.43×, and 2.4× over Fiddler while 1.45×, 1.48×, 1.63×, and 2.09× over llama.cpp. It shows that ScheInfer is more effective on lower-performance CPUs.

Importance of Slicing Rates. To assess the significance of r_{CG}, we measure the performance in the generation phase using the optimal slicing rates r_{CG} against fixed slicing rates of 0, 0.25, 0.5, and 0.75 on 4-bit quantized Mixtral-7B and LLaMA-2-70B for Testbed A, considering the memory constraints of 12GB and 24GB, respectively. Note that we set $r_{GG} = 0$ to disable the GPU memory assignment schedule and exclude its impact. Furthermore, we conduct experiments using a varying number of CPU threads from 16 down to 2. The experimental results show that our optimal slicing rates result in average speedups of 1.7×, 1.4×, 1.6×, and 2.1× compared to four fixed slicing rates.

Effect of the GPU Memory Assignment. To evaluate how the GPU memory assignment schedule affects ScheInfer, we conduct a performance comparison of our ScheInfer w/ and w/o the GPU memory assignment. Specifically, when the GPU memory assignment is disabled, we set r_{GG} to 0 or 1 and adjust the number of layers with $r_{GG} = 1$ to maximize GPU memory utilization. Testing was conducted on a 4-bit quantized Mixtral-7B, adhering to memory constraints of 12, 16, and 20GB, as well as a 4-bit quantized LLaMA-2-70B with memory constraints of 24, 28, and 32GB for Testbed A. Our findings reveal that GPU memory assignment can result in speed improvements of 1.07×, 1.10×, and 1.15× for Mixtral-7B, and 1.08×, 1.09×, and 1.12× for LLaMA-2-70B.

Necessity of the Token Assignment in the Prompt Phase. To verify the importance of our token assignment schedule during the prompt phase, we perform a performance comparison of our ScheInfer both w/ and w/o token assignment. We conduct experiments using sequence lengths of 64, 256, and 1024 on a 4-bit quantized Mixtral-7B, maintaining a memory limit of 12GB, as well as on a 4-bit quantized LLaMA-2-70B with a 24GB memory limit for Testbed A. The findings indicate that token assignment leads to speed boosts of 1.9×, 5.6×, and 19.1× for Mixtral-7B, and 6.9×, 27.6×, and 45.6× for LLaMA-2-70B.

6 Conclusion

In this work, we proposed ScheInfer, which is an efficient LLM inference system on computer systems with a single moderate GPU. ScheInfer coordinates CPU, GPU, and PCIe communication tasks to utilize available computing resources efficiently to improve the inference speed. Experimental results indicate that ScheInfer surpasses Fiddler and llama.cpp, delivering speedups of 1.11× to 1.80× during generation and 1.69× to 6.33× during prompting, using Mixtral, LLaMA-2, Qwen, and PhiMoE models across three testbeds.

Acknowledgments. The research was supported in part by the National Natural Science Foundation of China (NSFC) under Grant No. 62302123, Grant No. 62272122, and Grant No. 62376073, Guangdong Provincial Key Laboratory of Novel Security Intelligence Technologies under Grant 2022B1212010005, the Guangzhou Municipal Joint Funding Project with Universities and Enterprises under Grant No. 2024A03J0616, Guangzhou Municipality Big Data Intelligence Key Lab (2023A03J0012), Shenzhen Science and Technology Program under Grant No. KJZD20240903104103005, Grant No. KJZD20230923114213027 and Grant No. KJZD20230923115113026, the Colleges and Universities Stable Support Project of Shenzhen, China (No. GXWD20220817164856008 and No. GXW- D20220811173149002), Hong Kong RGC CRF grants under contracts C7004-22G and C6015-23G.

Disclosure of Interest. The authors have no competing interests to declare that are relevant to the content of this article.

References

1. Abdin, M.I., Jacobs, S.A., Awan, A.A., et al.: Phi-3 technical report: a highly capable language model locally on your phone. CoRR abs/2404.14219 (2024)
2. Aminabadi, R.Y., Rajbhandari, et al.: Deepspeed-inference: enabling efficient inference of transformer models at unprecedented scale. In: SC22: International Conference for High Performance Computing, Networking, Storage and Analysis, pp. 1–15. IEEE (2022)
3. Brown, T.B., Mann, B., Ryder, N., et al.: Language models are few-shot learners. In: Advances in Neural Information Processing Systems 33: Annual Conference on Neural Information Processing Systems 2020, NeurIPS 2020, 6–12 December 2020, virtual (2020)
4. Dean, J., Corrado, G., Monga, R., et al.: Large scale distributed deep networks. In: Advances in Neural Information Processing Systems, vol. 25 (2012)
5. Geng, X., Liu, S., Liu, L., Han, J., Jiang, H.: QUQ: quadruplet uniform quantization for efficient vision transformer inference. In: Proceedings of the 61st ACM/IEEE Design Automation Conference, pp. 1–6 (2024)
6. Gerganov, G.: ggerganov/llama.cpp: Port of Facebook's llama model in C/C++. https://github.com/ggerganov/llama.cpp
7. Jiang, A.Q., Sablayrolles, A., Roux, A., et al.: Mixtral of experts. arXiv preprint arXiv:2401.04088 (2024)
8. JosefAlbers, Rémi: Josefalbers/phi-3-vision-mlx: Phi-3.5-mlx (2024). https://doi.org/10.5281/zenodo.13352415
9. Kamahori, K., Gu, Y., Zhu, K., Kasikci, B.: Fiddler: CPU-GPU orchestration for fast inference of mixture-of-experts models. CoRR abs/2402.07033 (2024)
10. Lepikhin, D., et al.: Gshard: scaling giant models with conditional computation and automatic sharding. In: International Conference on Learning Representations (2021)
11. Lyu, H., Jiang, S., Zeng, H., et al.: LLM-rec: personalized recommendation via prompting large language models. In: Findings of the Association for Computational Linguistics: NAACL 2024, Mexico City, Mexico, 16–21 June 2024, pp. 583–612. Association for Computational Linguistics (2024)
12. Ma, X., Fang, G., Wang, X.: LLM-pruner: on the structural pruning of large language models. In: Advances in Neural Information Processing Systems, vol. 36, pp. 21702–21720 (2023)
13. Shi, S., Pan, X., Chu, X., Li, B.: PipeMoE: accelerating mixture-of-experts through adaptive pipelining. In: IEEE INFOCOM 2023-IEEE Conference on Computer Communications (2023)
14. MLC team: MLC-LLM (2023). https://github.com/mlc-ai/mlc-llm
15. Touvron, H., Lavril, T., Izacard, G., et al.: Llama: open and efficient foundation language models. CoRR abs/2302.13971 (2023)
16. Vaswani, A.: Attention is all you need. In: Advances in Neural Information Processing Systems (2017)
17. Yang, A., Yang, B., Hui, B., et al.: Qwen2 technical report. CoRR abs/2407.10671 (2024)
18. Yuan, S., Chen, J., Fu, Z., et al.: Distilling script knowledge from large language models for constrained language planning. arXiv preprint arXiv:2305.05252 (2023)

Uniform Dense Blocking for Efficient Sparse LU Factorization in First-Principles Materials Simulation

Chao Wang[1], Junshi Chen[1](✉), Longsheng Song[1], Haijie Hou[2], Dongdong Tan[1], Yueqiang He[1], Wentiao Wu[1], Sihan Lu[1], and Hong An[1]

[1] School of Computer Science and Technology, University of Science and Technology of China, Hefei, China
{wangc2023,sls_ustc,tandongdong,yueqiang_he,wtwu,lvsh}@mail.ustc.edu.cn,
{cjuns,han}@ustc.edu.cn
[2] Institute of Advanced Technology, University of Science and Technology of China, Hefei, China
haijiehou@mail.ustc.edu.cn

Abstract. Sparse matrix LU factorization is a critical method in direct solvers, playing a significant role in the field of first-principles materials simulation. Matrices in quantum chemistry problems often exhibit locally dense properties, yet their spatial structural characteristics have been overlooked in previous efforts. This paper proposes a novel LU factorization algorithm that leverages application-specific locally dense structures by partitioning sparse matrices into uniform dense blocks. Through systematic integration of level-3 BLAS kernels, the method transforms traditionally memory-bound LU operations into compute-intensive tasks, achieving significant improvements in both computational efficiency and CPU utilization. We conducted performance tests on CPUs from three different vendors, including the x86-based Intel Xeon Platinum 8375C and AMD EPYC 7543, as well as the ARM-based Kunpeng 920. Experimental results demonstrate significant performance improvements compared to the state-of-the-art sparse direct solvers.

Keywords: Sparse LU factorization · First-principles material simulation · Uniform dense block format

1 Introduction

LU factorization is a foundational numerical technique that factorizes a square matrix A into the product of a lower triangular matrix L and an upper triangular matrix U, such that $A = LU$. This decomposition simplifies solving linear systems $Ax = b$ by breaking it into two triangular solves: $Ly = b$ (forward substitution) and $Ux = y$ (backward substitution). LU solvers are particularly advantageous for problems requiring repeated solutions with the same matrix

A but different right-hand sides b, as the factorization is performed only once. The method generalizes Gaussian elimination but preserves the matrix structure, making it computationally efficient for large-scale systems.

In first-principles calculations, a direct LU solver is essential for solving the Kohn-Sham equation, the core equation in density functional theory (DFT). Sparse LU factorization enables efficient handling of the block-sparse Hamiltonian matrix generated from discretization with adaptive local basis functions (ALB), which is crucial in first-principles calculations like DGDFT [14,15] and PEXSI [20]. For example, a conventional DFT calculation for an N-atom system performs $O(N^3)$ floating-point operations, making the solution of Kohn-Sham equations highly time consuming.

State-of-the-art sparse linear solvers (e.g., SuperLU [8,9], UMFPACK [3,4], PARDISO [11,12,21]) accelerate computations by constructing supernode-based dense blocks through column aggregation–grouping columns with similar non-zero patterns into supernodes with zero padding. These supernodes store nonzeros in contiguous memory blocks to exploit spatial data locality, while invoking level-3 BLAS kernels to maximize arithmetic intensity through batched matrix operations. However, their reliance on supernode merging inherently limits the exploitation of fully dense blocking formats.

In first-principles materials simulation, we observe that matrix nonzeros predominantly cluster near the diagonal, forming localized dense regions. The Reverse Cuthill-McKee (RCM) [13] reordering algorithm further enhances this clustering effect, significantly increasing block density. Capitalizing on this property, we propose **BTLU**, a novel solver that integrates RCM reordering with a **Block-Tile** two-level hierarchical structure for both storage and computation. Unlike conventional supernode-based approaches, BTLU explicitly operates on fully dense blocks, eliminating indirect addressing and redundant data movement to construct supernodes. By directly applying level-3 BLAS kernels to these dense blocks, BTLU achieves superior cache utilization and computational efficiency.

Our experimental results highlight the significant performance advantages of BTLU across diverse CPU architectures, including Intel, AMD, and Huawei Kunpeng. We evaluated BTLU against state-of-the-art solvers–SuperLU_MT, PARDISO, and UMFPACK–using a total of 12 Hamiltonian matrices drawn from DGDFT and the SuiteSparse Matrix Collection [7]. BTLU achieves average speedups of 1.78–10.63× in single-threaded mode compared to other solvers. In multi-threaded mode, it delivers average speedups of 4.37–16.84× over SuperLU_MT, demonstrating exceptional scalability across both x86 (Intel/AMD) and ARM (Kunpeng) platforms. These performance gains are driven by BTLU's block-tile hierarchy and RCM-driven locality optimization, which systematically transform sparse LU factorization into compute-intensive, cache-resonant operations.

2 Background

2.1 Sparse LU Factorization

In general, sparse LU factorization can be divided into three steps.

1. Preprocessing: Reordering the matrix improves numerical stability and minimizes fill-in–the introduction of nonzeros in L and U that were zeros in A, ensuring that the subsequent factorization is both memory-efficient and numerically robust.

2. Symbolic factorization: Symbolic factorization determines the nonzero structure of L and U and pre-allocates memory for the LU factors. It also identifies dependencies between matrix entries, facilitating efficient task scheduling.

3. Numerical factorization: Numerical factorization computes the actual entries of L and U using the preprocessed matrix and symbolic structure. Common algorithms include the left-looking and right-looking methods, which differ in how they traverse the matrix.

Our approach is based on the right-looking algorithm. By partitioning the matrix and performing computations accordingly, we adopt a blocked right-looking algorithm, as shown in Algorithm 1.

Algorithm 1. Blocked Right-Looking Algorithm of LU Factorization

1: **Input:** Sparse matrix A in tile form
2: **Output:** Lower triangular matrix L and upper triangular matrix U
3: **for** $k = 0$ to $n - 1$ **do**
4:     // Diagonal tile factorization
5:     $L_{k,k}, U_{k,k} = \text{getrf}(A_{k,k})$
6:     // Panel factorization
7:     **for** $i = k$ to $n - 1$ **do**
8:         $L_{i,k} = \text{solve lower triangular}(A_{i,k}, U_{k,k})$
9:         $U_{k,i} = \text{solve upper triangular}(A_{k,i}, L_{k,k})$
10:     **end for**
11:     // Schur complement update
12:     **for** $i = k + 1$ to $n - 1$ **do**
13:         **for** $j = k + 1$ to $n - 1$ **do**
14:             **if** $i \neq k$ and $j \neq k$ **then**
15:                 $A_{i,j} = A_{i,j} - L_{i,k}U_{k,j}$
16:             **end if**
17:         **end for**
18:     **end for**
19: **end for**

2.2 Reordering Methods

LU factorization generates numerous nonzero fill-ins, which reduces factorization performance. Reordering is crucial for performance improvement, as it can significantly reduce fill-ins during the LU factorization phase. The minimum degree algorithm and the recursive bisection algorithm are the two most widely used reordering algorithms, with AMD(Approximate Minimum Degree) [1,2,5,6] and METIS [16] as their representative implementations, respectively. Almost all mainstream solvers adopt these two algorithms, with METIS being widely used in recent years due to its excellent performance on large-scale matrices.

Unlike the mainstream approach, BTLU uses the RCM algorithm for reordering to reduce the bandwidth of the sparse matrix. It starts by using a breadth-first search (BFS) to assign numbers to nodes. Nearby nodes get similar numbers, keeping them close in the matrix. Finally, it reverses the order of the numbering to further shrink the bandwidth. Given a sparse matrix $A = (a_{ij})$, its bandwidth is defined as the maximum distance between a nonzero element and the diagonal: $\beta = \max_{i,j}\{|i - j| \mid a_{ij} \neq 0\}$.

By compressing the bandwidth, the RCM algorithm clusters nonzero elements near the diagonal, forming an envelope structure, as shown in Fig. 1. During numerical factorization, nonzero fill-ins are confined within the envelope, reducing fill-in while enhancing data locality.

Although RCM introduces more fill-ins than AMD and METIS, its excellent data locality allows it to fully utilize the high peak floating-point performance of modern processors, compensating for the additional computational cost.

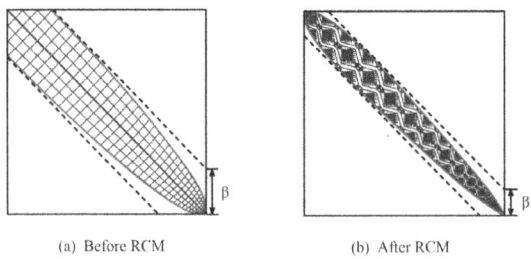

(a) Before RCM   (b) After RCM

Fig. 1. *H2O* matrix. Comparison of bandwidth and envelope structure before and after RCM reordering. The orange outline in the figure represents the envelope of matrix, and β denotes the bandwidth.

2.3 Related Work

The nonzero structure is generally analyzed in the symbolic factorization to transform the appropriate data layout and allocate storage space. Currently, the two most prominent data structures are supernodal [8] and multifrontal [10]. The supernodal method aggregates nonzeros with a similar structure as supernodes. It also reduces indirect addressing overhead through block operations, which makes the algorithm more suitable for the CPU cache architecture, a representative of which is SuperLU [8,9,18,19]. SuperLU aggregates columns with similar structures into column supernodes and then computes them based on left-looking LU factorization using level-2 BLAS. Furthermore, it achieves faster computation speed by reusing supernodes, called BLAS 2.5 [8]. The multifrontal method reorganizes the sparse matrix into a sequence of dense matrices called frontal matrices, and every frontal matrix performs partial decomposition independently to make the algorithm easy to parallelize, a representative of which is UMFPACK [3]. UMFPACK employs a multifrontal method based on right-looking LU factorization, with computations performed using level-3 BLAS. In addition, a widely used method known as PARDISO [11,12,21]. PARDISO uses a combination of left and right-looking level-3 BLAS supernode techniques to improve sequential and parallel sparse numerical factorization performance.

3 BTLU: Block-Tile Format LU Factorization

3.1 Overview

We introduce a novel two-level block-tile storage format specifically designed to exploit the inherent structured dense block patterns in first-principles simulation matrices. Building upon this innovative format, we develop a block-oriented numerical factorization algorithm that naturally benefits from level-3 BLAS kernels, achieving efficient floating-point operation performance. Our proposed solver, **BTLU** (**B**lock-**T**ile format **LU** factorization), implements a three-phase computational workflow:

Phase 1: Static Pivoting and Reordering - BTLU initiates with the MC64 algorithm for numerical stability through static pivot selection, followed by the RCM reordering to optimize matrix bandwidth and local density.

Phase 2: Hierarchical Structure Construction - The sparse matrix undergoes transformation into our proposed block-tile hierarchy, effectively exposing computational regularity while maintaining structural sparsity patterns.

Phase 3: Parallel Numerical Factorization - The core computation phase executes block-based LU decomposition through a hybrid parallelization scheme combining OpenMP multithreading with level-3 BLAS kernel operations, ensuring thread-level parallelism and instruction-level efficiency.

3.2 Locality-Enhanced Reorder Method

Further enhancing the matrix locality and amplifying this characteristic, we employ the RCM reordering algorithm, uniquely tailored for block-tile sparse matrix formats. In contrast to conventional fill-in minimization strategies, RCM explicitly optimizes two critical properties:

Bandwidth Compression – Aggregates nonzeros into a narrow diagonal band, constraining LU factorization fill-ins within this bounded envelope. This clustering effect amplifies block-tile density, enabling full exploitation of level-3 BLAS kernels (e.g., `GEMM`, `TRSM`).

Cache-Friendly Memory Access – The compressed bandwidth inherently limits fill-in spread, reducing both arithmetic complexity and memory footprint by eliminating extraneous computations. Simultaneously, it enforces contiguous data access patterns, minimizing cache misses and indirect addressing overheads.

In the Fig. 2, the raw matrix exhibits extremely dense diagonal blocks with a high concentration of nonzeros, while the off-diagonal regions contain sparsely distributed nonzeros. After RCM reordering, the nonzeros from the diagonal blocks are more evenly spread across the surrounding areas, making the overall distribution more uniform. Additionally, the outer-regions nonzeros shift closer to the center, effectively reducing matrix bandwidth, which decreases computational cost while ensuring a more balanced distribution of nonzeros within each tile. This improves load balancing and increases the proportion of efficient computations. Dense blocking and dense computations naturally excel on matrices with such localized dense structures.

In contrast, METIS reordering disperses nonzeros from the diagonal envelope to other regions, creating numerous sparse sub-blocks. This structure is not well-suited for dense block computation, as it increases zero storage within blocks and requires excessive partitioning, reducing memory efficiency and making it less favorable for our approach. A similar issue arises with AMD reordering, which is why we did not adopt these reordering methods.

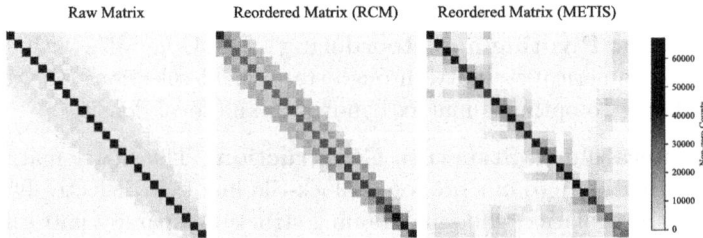

Fig. 2. Non-zeros distribution comparison. The uniformity of the color reflects the distribution of nonzeros: a more even color indicates a balanced distribution, while uneven colors suggest an imbalanced distribution. (Color figure online)

3.3 Block-Tile Format

Leveraging the optimized bandwidth reduction achieved through RCM reordering, we employ a two-level dense-blocking strategy in a block-tile format to enhance the computational intensity of numerical factorization. In this scheme, a **tile** serves as the fundamental computational unit for BLAS operations, enabling efficient utilization of high-performance level-3 BLAS routines. A **block** consists of multiple tiles and is scheduled by OpenMP threads. The block structure influences the execution order of tiles, improving data locality among them and enhancing memory access efficiency in a multi-threaded parallel environment.

Figure 3 illustrates our four-stage matrix transformation pipeline: (1) the original sparse matrix representation, (2) RCM-reordered matrix with optimized bandwidth, (3) tile construction through nonzero pattern analysis, and (4) final block-tile storage format. Our approach begins with a traversal of matrix to identify nonzero elements and determine tile allocation. These tiles are then systematically organized into memory blocks, establishing an efficient management structure. During computation, each thread exclusively processes one block, leveraging the tile-based storage organization to exploit inherent spatial locality. This design significantly improves cache utilization while maintaining data access coherence.

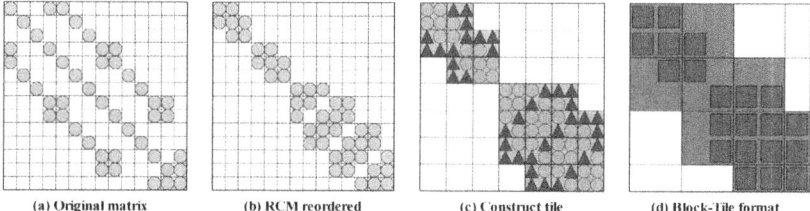

Fig. 3. The progress of constructing block-tile format. (a) is the original matrix. (b) is the matrix structure after RCM reordering. (c) illustrates the first-level tile division. ($\bigcirc$) represents nonzeros in the sparse matrix, ($\triangle$) represents zero fill-ins. (d) illustrates a hierarchical block-tile structure, where finer-grained tiles organize nonzeros at the storage level, and coarser-grained blocks manage tiles at the execution level.

3.4 Multithreading Parallelization of Numerical Factorizaion

BTLU is based on the right-looking LU factorization algorithm and computed using a uniformly sized dense kernel. Numerical factorization progresses layer-wise along block rows and columns, comprising three operations per layer: (1) diagonal block factorization, (2) L/U triangular component computation (TRSM), (3) Schur complement updating (GEMM). BTLU employs a block-based execution model with OpenMP-dynamic scheduling, where each parallel thread operates on assigned blocks using single-threaded level-3 BLAS kernels for tile computations. During computation, the tile inside the block can be saved in the cache and reused to improve the factorization performance.

We propose a dynamic tile allocation strategy that eliminates the need for symbolic factorization. Unlike traditional approaches that pre-allocate memory space based on symbolic analysis, our method performs on-the-fly allocation of fill-in tiles during numerical factorization. This design offers two key advantages: (1) it enables direct cache-level placement of computed blocks by worker threads, optimizing NUMA locality; and (2) it significantly reduces memory access latency. Compared to symbolic factorization, which pre-allocates tiles and incurs substantial overhead due to frequent main memory accesses to retrieve

3.5 Block-Tile Parameter Tuning

The performance of our block-tile numerical decomposition critically depends on the careful selection of block and tile sizes, which involves a three-way trade-off between data locality, zero fill-in, and parallelism. Through extensive experimentation guided by the RCM-derived bandwidth parameter(B), we establish an empirical relationship:

$$\text{TileSize} \approx 0.02B, \quad \text{BlockSize} \approx 0.08B$$

This proportional scaling maintains stable parallelism while controlling fill-in effects, as larger bandwidth values indicate greater inherent parallelism potential. Our parameter selection strategy automatically adapts to matrix characteristics, though users may manually fine-tune these parameters for specific matrix patterns to achieve peak performance.

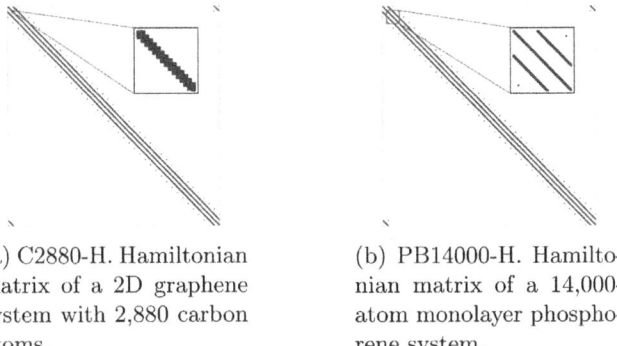

(a) C2880-H. Hamiltonian matrix of a 2D graphene system with 2,880 carbon atoms.

(b) PB14000-H. Hamiltonian matrix of a 14,000-atom monolayer phosphorene system.

Fig. 4. The structured dense blocks in matrices from first-principles materials simulations.

4 Experiment

4.1 Experimental Setup

The experiments were conducted on three CPU computing clusters, including Intel Xeon Platinum 8375C, AMD EPYC 7543, and Kunpeng 920. Details of the hardware configurations are shown in Table 1. The best BLAS library on each platform has been linked to perform the dense kernel operations. For the Kunpeng 920 platform, we use the Kunpeng Math Library (KML) developed by Huawei, whereas OpenBLAS [22] is employed on the AMD platform, and oneMKL [17] is used on the Intel platform. BTLU is evaluated against state-of-the-art solvers, including SuperLU_MT-v4.0.1, Panua-PARDISO-v8.2, and UMFPACK-v6.3.5. UMFPACK is a highly efficient solver optimized for single-threaded execution. PARDISO, a commercial and closed-source solver, is renowned for its exceptional performance. SuperLU_MT is the most popular open-sourced solver.

Table 1. The hardware and software configuration of the tested platforms.

CPU	#Cores	Freq. (GHz)	LLC (MB)	Compiler	Libraries
Intel Xeon Platinum 8375C	32	2.9	54	gcc-11.4	oneMKL-2025.1 openmp-4.1.2
AMD EPYC 7543	32	2.8	256	gcc-11.4	openblas-0.3.20 openmp-4.1.2
Kunpeng 920	40	N/A	32	gcc-14.2 armclang-24.10.1	KML-2.5.0 openmp-4.1.2

Table 2. Matrix detailed information and peak memory usage in each solver.

Matrix	$n(10^4)$	nnz/n	BTLU (MB)	UMFPACK (MB)	SuperLU_MT (MB)
PB14000-H	12.80	720.0	12774.0	13967.7	11882.0
C2880-H	6.91	1080.0	6103.6	5873.7	7461.1
SiO2	15.55	36.8	35859.4	42278.8	53983.0
GaAsH6	6.13	28.1	7102.0	8822.9	10230.2
H20	6.70	33.1	5660.6	5873.7	9093.9
SiO	3.34	39.4	2569.2	2911.2	3484.4
Si10H16	1.70	51.3	934.0	920.3	1043.2
Ga19As19H42	13.3	66.7	30831.9	31821.4	39731.4
Si5H12	1.98	37.1	972.3	1277.6	1572.8
Ga3As3H12	6.13	97.3	7801.3	9043.5	11259.6
Ge87H76	11.29	69.8	22685.8	23995.7	30002.1
Ga10As10H30	11.30	54.0	20070.0	23259.3	29497.1

For the test matrices, two Hamiltonian matrices derived from DGDFT [15] are presented in Fig. 4, along with ten additional matrices selected from the SuiteSparse Matrix Collection, all of which are related to theoretical or quantum chemistry problems. In our experiments, we evaluated the performance of the numerical factorization step—the most time-consuming component—against other solvers under various thread configurations. To evaluate the parallel scalability, we compared BTLU against SuperLU_MT. PARDISO (academic version) supports only one or two threads, and UMFPACK is a single-threaded solver. Therefore, SuperLU_MT was chosen as the representative multithreaded solver for comparison.

4.2 Overall Performance

We tested the BTLU's serial numerical factorization performance and compared it with SuperLU_MT, UMFPACK and PARDISO. The information on the tested matrices is listed on Table 2. Due to the absence of additional buffer allocation for supernode construction, combined with the effects of RCM-based bandwidth reduction and direct operations on dense blocks, BTLU achieves even lower memory consumption compared to other methods. Since PARDISO is available only in its academic version, it does not provide memory usage information.

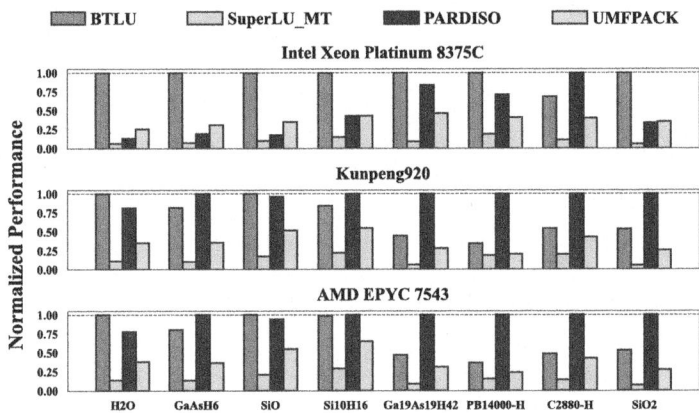

Fig. 5. Normalized numerical factorization performance comparison in single-threaded mode across three test platforms.

The numerical performance, measured as the normalized speedup relative to the best factorization time, is depicted in Fig. 5. BTLU demonstrates the most significant performance on the Intel platform, achieving mean speedups of 10.63× over SuperLU_MT, 2.66× over UMFPACK, and 3.36× over PARDISO. This stems from AVX-512's 512-bit vector processing capability, which fully exploits BTLU's direct and efficient computation characteristics.

While BTLU consistently outperforms open-source solvers, its advantage over the proprietary PARDISO diminishes on AMD and Kunpeng platforms. For structured matrices like *PB14000-H* and *C2880-H*, PARDISO forms large supernodes (9,440 and 8,640 in size), optimizing cache usage—particularly on AMD EPYC 7543 with 256 MB shared L3 cache. In contrast, BTLU uses a fixed 192 × 192 tile with a 2 × 2 block layout, favoring regularity and vectorization. For irregular matrices such as *SiO* and *H2O*, where supernodes are smaller and more fragmented, BTLU's adaptability and hardware acceleration yield clear advantages, highlighting its balance between architectural efficiency and matrix-structure awareness.

Matrices in quantum chemistry typically exhibit a banded structure, implying direct dependencies between consecutive columns. This characteristic poses challenges for UMFPACK's multifrontal method, as increased dependencies make it harder to identify independent columns for parallel computation. In contrast, BTLU is well-suited for handling such structures because its numerical factorization proceeds layer by layer, naturally aligning with the matrix's inherent dependency order. Moreover, the strong local density of these matrices allows BTLU to fully leverage the advantages of dense blocking and dense computations.

SuperLU_MT, on the other hand, employs dynamic pivoting, requiring pivot exchanges during numerical factorization, which introduces significant memory access overhead. On the other hand, BTLU adopts a static pivoting strategy, focusing exclusively on matrix computations during the factorization phase, thereby improving efficiency.

4.3 Parallel Performance

Figure 6 presents the comparative speedup distribution of BTLU versus SuperLU_MT across three platforms using varying thread configurations. The experimental results demonstrate significant performance improvements, with average speedups of 11.60–16.84× on Intel Xeon, 4.52–8.04× on AMD EPYC, and 4.37–12.84× on Kunpeng. The speedup is most pronounced when using 32 threads across all three platforms. This is because, during the Schur complement computation phase, 32 threads are optimally distributed among all blocks, preventing issues caused by insufficient threads or excessive thread switching and idle time.

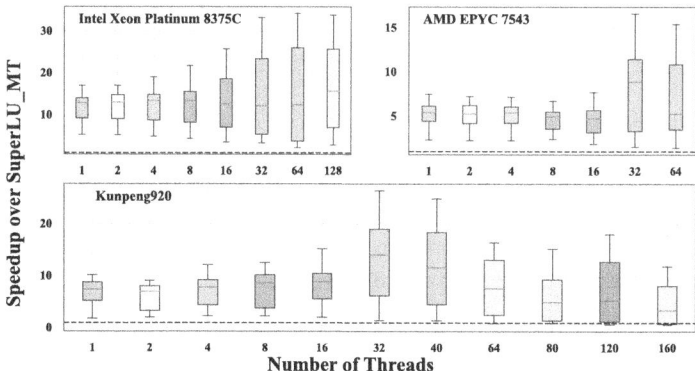

Fig. 6. Comprehensive speedup distribution of BTLU vs. SuperLU_MT across thread counts on three platforms.

The scalability of numerical factorization is illustrated in Fig. 7, demonstrating BTLU's strong performance in multi-threaded parallelism. For instance, BTLU exhibits significant performance improvements on the $Ga19As19H42$ matrix as the number of threads increases. Compared to BTLU's single-threaded execution, BTLU achieves speedups of 26.92× on Kunpeng (40 threads), 23.70×

on AMD (64 threads), and 18.32× on Intel (64 threads). To further enhance performance with higher thread counts, adopting a finer-grained block-tile partitioning strategy and more precise parameter tuning could be explored.

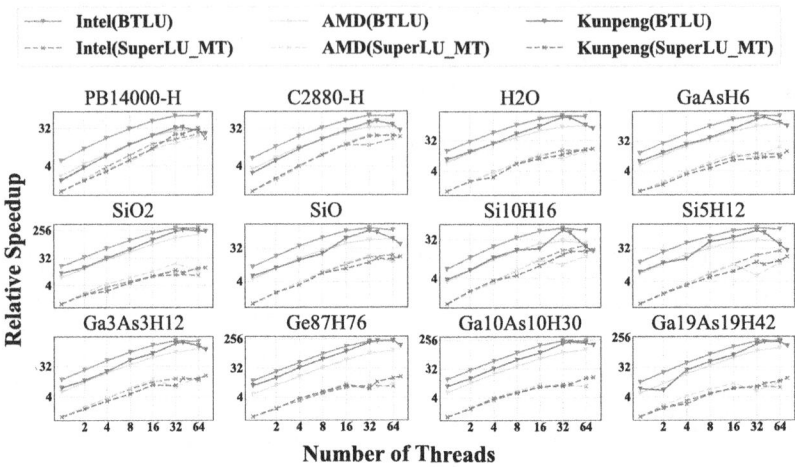

Fig. 7. Speedup of numerical factorization on three platforms relative to the single-threaded performance of SuperLU_MT.

5 Conclusion

First-principles materials simulations generate sparse matrices with distinct local dense patterns along the diagonal, a structural feature leveraged by our proposed BTLU solver. Yet previous studies mainly focused on supernodes for dense computations but did not directly employ dense blocking, overlooking the local dense structures inherent in these matrices. By integrating Reverse Cuthill-McKee (RCM) reordering to concentrate nonzeros and reduce matrix bandwidth, combined with a two-level block-tile partitioning strategy, BTLU adaptively aligns dense block structures with matrix bandwidth. This approach replaces conventional indirect memory accesses with direct operations on contiguous memory blocks through level-3 BLAS high-performance dense matrix operations, thereby transforming memory-bound LU factorization into compute-intensive tasks while maintaining sparsity awareness.

Experimental results show significant performance gains across x86 (Intel/AMD) and ARM (Kunpeng) platforms. Compared to state-of-the-art solvers (SuperLU_MT, UMFPACK, PARDISO), BTLU achieves single-threaded speedups ranging from 1.78× to 10.63×. With multi-threading compared to SuperLU_MT, performance scales significantly, achieving peak average speedups of 16.84× on Intel, 12.84× on Kunpeng, and 8.04× on AMD. Additionally, BTLU reduces memory usage for certain matrices compared to SuperLU_MT and UMF-PACK.

Acknowledgements. This work was supported by the Strategic Priority Research Program of Chinese Academy of Sciences (Grant No. XDB0500102). And this work was partially supported by USTC Kunpeng&Ascend Center of Excellence.

Disclosure of Interests. The authors have no competing interests to declare that are relevant to the content of this article.

References

1. Amestoy, P.R., Davis, T.A., Duff, I.S.: An approximate minimum degree ordering algorithm. SIAM J. Matrix Anal. Appl. **17**(4), 886–905 (1996). https://doi.org/10.1137/S0895479894278952
2. Amestoy, P.R., Davis, T.A., Duff, I.S.: Algorithm 837: AMD, an approximate minimum degree ordering algorithm. ACM Trans. Math. Softw. **30**(3), 381–388 (2004). https://doi.org/10.1145/1024074.1024081
3. Davis, T.A.: Algorithm 832: UMFPACK V4.3—an unsymmetric-pattern multifrontal method. ACM Trans. Math. Softw. **30**(2), 196–199 (2004). https://doi.org/10.1145/992200.992206
4. Davis, T.A.: A column pre-ordering strategy for the unsymmetric-pattern multifrontal method. ACM Trans. Math. Softw. **30**(2), 165–195 (2004). https://doi.org/10.1145/992200.992205
5. Davis, T.A., Gilbert, J.R., Larimore, S.I., Ng, E.G.: Algorithm 836: COLAMD, a column approximate minimum degree ordering algorithm. ACM Trans. Math. Softw. **30**(3), 377–380 (2004). https://doi.org/10.1145/1024074.1024080
6. Davis, T.A., Gilbert, J.R., Larimore, S.I., Ng, E.G.: A column approximate minimum degree ordering algorithm. ACM Trans. Math. Softw. **30**(3), 353–376 (2004). https://doi.org/10.1145/1024074.1024079
7. Davis, T.A., Hu, Y.: The university of Florida sparse matrix collection. ACM Trans. Math. Softw. **38**(1) (2011). https://doi.org/10.1145/2049662.2049663
8. Demmel, J.W., Eisenstat, S.C., Gilbert, J.R., Li, X.S., Liu, J.W.H.: A supernodal approach to sparse partial pivoting. SIAM J. Matrix Anal. Appl. **20**(3), 720–755 (1999). https://doi.org/10.1137/S0895479895291765
9. Demmel, J.W., Gilbert, J.R., Li, X.S.: An asynchronous parallel supernodal algorithm for sparse gaussian elimination. SIAM J. Matrix Anal. Appl. **20**(4), 915–952 (1999). https://doi.org/10.1137/S0895479897317685
10. Duff, I.S., Reid, J.K.: The multifrontal solution of indefinite sparse symmetric linear. ACM Trans. Math. Softw. **9**(3), 302–325 (1983). https://doi.org/10.1145/356044.356047
11. Eftekhari, A., Pasadakis, D., Bollhöfer, M., Scheidegger, S., Schenk, O.: Block-enhanced precision matrix estimation for large-scale datasets. J. Comput. Sci. **53** (2021). https://doi.org/10.1016/j.jocs.2021.101389
12. Gaedke-Merzhäuser, L., van Niekerk, J., Schenk, O., Rue, H.: Parallelized integrated nested Laplace approximations for fast Bayesian inference. Stat. Comput. **33**(1), 25 (2023)
13. George, J.A.: Computer implementation of the finite element method. Ph.D. thesis, Stanford, CA, USA (1971). aAI7205916

14. Hu, W., et al.: 2.5 million-atom AB initio electronic-structure simulation of complex metallic heterostructures with DGDFT. In: SC22: International Conference for High Performance Computing, Networking, Storage and Analysis, pp. 1–13 (2022). https://doi.org/10.1109/SC41404.2022.00010
15. Hu, W., Lin, L., Yang, C.: DGDFT: a massively parallel method for large scale density functional theory calculations. J. Chem. Phys. **143**(12) (2015). https://doi.org/10.1063/1.4931732. http://dx.doi.org/10.1063/1.4931732
16. Karypis, G., Kumar, V.: A parallel algorithm for multilevel graph partitioning and sparse matrix ordering. J. Parallel Distrib. Comput. **48**(1), 71–95 (1998). https://doi.org/10.1006/jpdc.1997.1403
17. Krainiuk, M., Goli, M., Pascuzzi, V.R.: oneAPI open-source math library interface. In: 2021 International Workshop on Performance, Portability and Productivity in HPC (P3HPC), pp. 22–32 (2021). https://doi.org/10.1109/P3HPC54578.2021.00006
18. Li, X.S., Demmel, J.W.: Superlu_dist: a scalable distributed-memory sparse direct solver for unsymmetric linear systems. ACM Trans. Math. Softw. **29**(2), 110–140 (2003). https://doi.org/10.1145/779359.779361
19. Li, X.S., Lin, P., Liu, Y., Sao, P.: Newly released capabilities in the distributed-memory superlu sparse direct solver. ACM Trans. Math. Softw. **49**(1) (2023). https://doi.org/10.1145/3577197
20. Lin, L., Chen, M., Yang, C., He, L.: Accelerating atomic orbital-based electronic structure calculation via pole expansion and selected inversion. J. Phys. Condensed Matter **25**(29), 295501 (2013). https://doi.org/10.1088/0953-8984/25/29/295501. https://dx.doi.org/10.1088/0953-8984/25/29/295501
21. Pasadakis, D., Bollhöfer, M., Schenk, O.: Sparse quadratic approximation for graph learning. IEEE Trans. Pattern Anal. Mach. Intell. **45**(9), 11256–11269 (2023). https://doi.org/10.1109/TPAMI.2023.3263969
22. Xianyi, Z., Qian, W., Yunquan, Z.: Model-driven level 3 BLAS performance optimization on Loongson 3A processor. In: Proceedings of the 2012 IEEE 18th International Conference on Parallel and Distributed Systems, ICPADS 2012, pp. 684–691. IEEE Computer Society, USA (2012). https://doi.org/10.1109/ICPADS.2012.97

Author Index

A

A. Chien, Andrew I-380
Aditya, Andaluri S. P. V. M. III-139
Ahmad Nasif, Kazi Fahim I-366
Ahmad, Sabtain II-365
Allen, Bryce I-54
Almeida, Francisco II-278
An, Hong III-341
An, Xuejun I-337, II-75
Angelopoulos, Spyros III-18
Anton, Semakin I-395
Applencourt, Thomas I-54
Araujo, Guido III-254
Asifuzzaman, Kazi II-175
Augustine, John III-48

B

Bader, David A. III-3
Bai, Zhuoxin II-161
Banerjee, Dip Sankar III-139
Banerjee, Roopkatha I-264
Beaumont, Olivier I-145
Bekele, Solomon I-54
Belcastro, Loris II-321
Benoit, Anne I-380, III-78
Bhattarai, Rajat I-307
Blanco, Vicente II-278
Bourgouin, Raphaël I-145
Brabec, Matyáš II-250
Brandic, Ivona II-365
Brandt, Jim I-205
Brunet, Elisabeth III-298

C

Canon, Louis-Claude I-131
Cao, Huawei I-337
Cavalheiro, Gerson I-100
Cendrier, Joachim I-380
Chakradhar, Srimat I-279
Chandrashekar, Tejus I-264
Chang, Qixin III-183

Chao, Lingwei II-3
Chatterjee, Soumyajit III-211
Che, Xilong III-109
Chen, Ao II-292
Chen, Gang II-89
Chen, Huangxun III-283
Chen, Jianxi III-239
Chen, Jingyi I-395
Chen, Junshi III-341
Chen, Kuan-Hsun III-3
Chen, Xun II-221
Chen, Yunling I-292
Chen, Zhiguang I-292
Chen, Zhitao I-292
Cheng, Jian II-349
Choi, Jinhyeok II-48
Chu, Xiaowen III-327
Chung, Yi-Hua III-197
Ciorba, Florina M. I-205
Cléto, Jhonatan III-254
Coulaud, Olivier III-63
Coviello, Giuseppe I-279
Cui, Huimin II-292
Culver, Christopher II-306

D

Darrin, Maxime I-145
Date, Prasanna II-175
David Núñez Araya, Isaac I-159
de Oliveira Castro, Pablo I-3
de Wolff, Ivo Gabe I-38
Delval, Aurélien I-3
Deng, Bobin I-366
Dhar, Nobel I-366
Dmitry, Tovmachenko I-395
Dominikowski, Przemysław III-63
Dong, Hande II-335
Dong, Jiale II-60
Du Bois, André Rauber I-100
Duan, Xiaohui III-183
Dugois, Anthony I-131

E

Eshwar, Uppu III-211
Eswar, Ananth I-264
Fan, Yuzhe III-109
Fan, Zhihua II-75
Fang, Haining I-114
Feng, Dan II-221
Feng, Xiaobing II-292
Feng, Zhichen II-207
Ferragina, Paolo II-321
Fetita, Catalin III-298
Frisch, Dustin I-71

G

Gainaru, Ana I-219
Ganesh, Vijay II-306
Garby, Jacob II-236
Gentile, Ann I-205
Georgiou, Chryssis III-33
Gerndt, Michael I-159
Ghafoor, Sheikh I-307
Ghiasvand, Siavash III-268
Gokhale, Maya II-33
Gómez, María E. I-233
Gong, Lei II-60
Gong, Shijia III-239
Gu, Cheng II-349
Gu, Jianfeng I-159
Gu, Jianhua I-322, I-410
Guan, Haibing I-395
Guo, Hui II-89
Guo, Kaicheng I-395
Guo, Tianyu II-335
Gupta, Nikunj III-313

H

Ha, Soonhoi I-85
Hao, Qinfen II-132
He, Jingyi II-118
He, Yueqiang III-341
Héam, Pierre-Cyrille I-131
Herault, Thomas III-78
Hernández, Nicolás II-278
Hernandez, Oscar II-306
Ho, Tsung-Yi III-197
Hou, Haijie III-341
Hou, Zhengxiong I-322
Hu, Juncheng III-109
Hu, Yangyang III-239

Hu, Yuchong II-221
Huang, Jun II-18
Huang, Kai I-159
Huang, Libo II-89
Huang, Linpeng II-146
Huang, Tsung-Wei I-24, III-197

I

Iyer, Mahesh A. III-313

J

Jakobsche, Thomas I-205
Jalby, William I-3
James, David I-71
Jecker, Ismaël I-131
Jiang, Shui III-197

K

Kaya, Oguz III-63
Keller, Gabriele K. I-38
Kermarrec, Anne-Marie III-298
Khojastepour, Mohammad A. I-279
Klasky, Scott I-219
Klepl, Jiří II-250
Koopman, Thomas III-93
Kothapalli, Kishore III-139
Kruliš, Martin II-250
Kuhn, Michael I-71
Kulkarni, Apurv Deepak III-268
Kulkarni, Shruti R. II-175
Kumar, Sunil I-351
Kumar, Vivek I-351
Kutscher, Dirk III-283
Kwon, Joonyup II-48

L

Lan, Hao II-132
Lan, Qingqiu I-114
Lee, Wan-Luan I-24, III-197
Leite, Leonardo Saud Maia I-175
Leng, Yichong II-335
Li, Gang II-349
Li, Guangli II-292
Li, Jiali II-161
Li, Wei I-114
Li, Wenming II-75
Li, Xinjiao III-283
Liang, Xiaoyao II-349
Liao, Yunming I-190

Lima Pilla, Laércio III-63
Lin, Cheater II-335
Lin, James I-395
Lin, Pei-Hung II-33
Lin, Qingyin I-292
Lin, Wenxiang III-327
Lin, Xiaolong II-349
Ling, Jiayao II-349
Liu, Duo I-114, II-161
Liu, Feng II-335
Liu, Jun II-161
Liu, Mingxuan I-322, I-410
Liu, Weiguo III-183
Liu, Yong II-132
Liu, Yutong I-322
Lou, Wenqi II-60
Lu, Sihan III-341
Luo, Yi II-18

M
Mahmoud, Ahmed H. III-154
Manzini, Giovanni II-321
Marchal, Loris I-145, III-18
Marinella, Matthew II-175
Marozzo, Fabrizio II-321
Medeiros, Daniel I-175
Meneghin, Massimiliano III-154
Meyerhenke, Henning III-124
Miao, Shuo II-193
Ming, Zhangqiang II-221
Miniskar, Narasinga Rao II-175
Mu, Yudong II-75
Muralidharan, Servesh I-54

N
Nandivada, V. Krishna III-211
Navarro, Marta I-233
Nikhil, Malleti Sai III-139

O
Obrecht, Adrien III-18
Ou, Yang I-292

P
Pallardó-Julià, Vicent I-233
Pallez, Guillaume I-219
Pan, Xinglin III-327
Parlavantzas, Nikos I-248
Parol-Guarino, Volodia I-248

Patel, Hiren II-33
Pei, Songwen II-89
Peng, Ivy I-175, II-33
Perarnau, Swann I-54
Pereira, Marcio M. III-254
Peri, Sathya III-33, III-211
Petit, Salvador I-233
Pham, Ngoc-Son II-48
Piantanida, Pablo I-145
Piduguralla, Manaswini III-33
Pires, Rafael III-298
Pointal, Brice III-63
Prasanna, Viktor III-313
Pritchard, Howard I-307
Pu, Jin II-146

Q
Qi, Zhengwei I-395
Qu, Peng II-193

R
Ramakrishna, G. III-139
Ranawaka, Piyumal II-103
Rao, Kunal I-279
Reinbigler, Marie III-298
Ren, Ao I-114, II-161
Ren, Haoxing III-197
Renault, Etienne I-3
Robert, Yves I-380, III-78
Romein, John W. III-225
Romyull Islam, Md I-366
Rongon, Rubayet Rahman II-264
Roth, Anna-Lena I-71

S
Sahu, Abhijeet III-139
Sahuquillo, Julio I-233
Scheideler, Christian III-48
Schieffer, Gabin II-33
Schmidt, Bertil III-183
Schneidergruber, Thomas II-365
Scholz, Johannes II-365
Scholz, Sven-Bodo III-93
Sedova, Ada II-306
Shanmugavelu, Sanjif II-306
Sharma, Rishi III-298
Sheng, Jiajie I-395
Shi, Ruimin II-33
Shi, Shaohuai III-169, III-327

Shin, Sangwon II-48
Simmhan, Yogesh I-264
Simon, Bertrand III-18
Simsek, Osman Seckin I-205
Son, Jaewoo I-85
Song, Longsheng III-341
Song, Yingchen II-18
Song, Zhuoran II-349
Spaan, Jeffrey III-3
Stenstrom, Per II-103
Suh, Taeweon II-48
Sun, Ninghui II-132
Sun, Penghao II-146
Sun, Yiming I-337
Suo, Kun I-366

T

Taillefumier, Mathieu II-306
Talia, Domenico II-321
Tan, Dongdong III-341
Tan, Yujuan I-114, II-161
Toledo, Pedro II-278
Tong, Jie I-24
Töpfer, Michal II-250
Torri, Atte III-63
Tremodeux, Alix III-78
Trunfio, Paolo II-321
Tsigas, Philippas II-236

U

Utkoor, Rahul III-211

V

Valarini, Guilherme III-254
van Balen, David I-38
van Gastel, Bernard III-93
Varbanescu, Ana-Lucia III-3
Vetter, Jeffrey S. II-175
Videau, Brice I-54
Vivas, Aurelio I-54
Vivien, Frédéric I-380

W

Wahlgren, Jacob I-175
Wan, Tianyu III-239
Wang, Chao II-60, III-341
Wang, Guifeng II-146
Wang, Honglie II-75
Wang, Junhui II-89

Wang, Puxuan I-159
Wang, Qi II-18
Wang, Qingfeng II-18
Wang, Rui II-221
Wang, Xuan III-327
Wang, Xuanzheng II-193
Wang, Xueying II-292
Wang, Yaobin II-18
Wang, Yisu III-283
Wang, Yongwen II-89
Wang, Yun I-395
Wang, Yunlan I-322
Wang, Zhenyu I-114
Wang, Zhisong III-183
Wang, Zihao II-60
Wei, Jianwen I-395
Werthmann, Julian III-48
Wiggins, Samuel III-313
Wijayawardana, Rajini I-380
Williams, Jeremy J. I-175
Willich, Florian III-124
Wu, Hao II-60
Wu, Huan II-18
Wu, Ruilong III-283
Wu, Wentiao III-341

X

Xi, Mengyue II-118
Xiao, Nong II-335
Xie, Xin II-146
Xie, Zuan I-190
Xiong, Tianyu II-3
Xiong, Zhenxuan II-89
Xu, Hongli I-190
Xu, Yang I-190
Xue, Jiangying II-3
Xue, Jingling II-292
Xue, Ruini II-3

Y

Yan, Lifeng III-183
Yan, Wei II-132
Yang, Ling II-89
Yang, Xinrui III-169
Yao, Chenxuan II-221
Yao, Xiaoxia II-75
Yao, Zhiwei I-190
Ye, Xiaochun I-337, II-75, II-132
Yin, Zekun III-183

Author Index

Yoon, Youngchul I-85
Yoshii, Kazutomo I-54
Young, Aaron R. II-175
Yu, Feng II-292
Yusuf Ogras, Umit I-24
Yviquel, Hervé III-254

Z

Zeng, Zhaoyang II-161
Zgheib, Grace III-313
Zhang, Jiale III-109
Zhang, Jiaqi I-337
Zhang, Jie I-337
Zhang, Tong III-183
Zhang, Xianwei II-118, II-335
Zhang, Xin II-207
Zhang, Xinyue I-366
Zhang, Xuan II-349
Zhang, Xuechen II-264
Zhang, Yanqing III-197
Zhang, Youhui II-193
Zhang, Zhiyuan II-75
Zhao, Jiacheng II-292
Zhao, Tianhai I-322, I-410
Zheng, Shengan II-146
Zheng, Xinjue II-221
Zheng, Zhendong II-60
Zheng, Zhong II-89
Zhong, Chengwen I-322
Zhong, Kan I-114, II-161
Zhou, Wenxiang II-221
Zhou, Xuehai II-60
Zhou, Ziang II-132
Zhu, Qi II-132
Zhu, Zihan II-193